CRIMINAL LAW CONVERSATIONS

CRIMINAL LAW CONVERSATIONS

EDITED BY   PAUL H. ROBINSON

STEPHEN P. GARVEY

KIMBERLY KESSLER FERZAN

OXFORD
UNIVERSITY PRESS

OXFORD
UNIVERSITY PRESS

Oxford University Press, Inc., publishes works that further Oxford University's objective of excellence in research, scholarship, and education.

Oxford   New York
Auckland   Cape   Dar es Salaam   Hong Kong   Karachi   Kuala Lumpur   Madrid   Melbourne
Mexico City   Nairobi   New Delhi   Shanghai   Taipei   Toronto

With offices in
Argentina   Austria   Brazil   Chile   Czech Republic   France   Greece   Guatemala   Hungary   Italy
Japan   Poland   Portugal   Singapore   South Korea   Switzerland   Thailand   Turkey   Ukraine
Vietnam

Copyright © 2009 by Oxford University Press, Inc.

Published by Oxford University Press, Inc.
198 Madison Avenue, New York, New York 10016

Oxford is a registered trademark of Oxford University Press
Oxford University Press is a registered trademark of Oxford University Press, Inc.

Library of Congress Cataloging-in-Publication Data

Criminal law conversations / edited by Paul H. Robinson, Stephen P. Garvey, Kimberly Kessler Ferzan.
    p. cm.
  Includes bibliographical references and index.
  ISBN 978-0-19-539163-3 (hardback : alk. paper)
 1. Criminal law—Philosophy. I. Robinson, Paul H., 1948- II. Garvey, Stephen P., 1965-
III. Ferzan, Kimberly Kessler, 1971-
    K5018.C753 2009
    345—dc22   2009003990

1 2 3 4 5 6 7 8 9
Printed in the United States of America on acid-free paper

Note to Readers
This publication is designed to provide accurate and authoritative information in regard to the subject matter covered. It is based upon sources believed to be accurate and reliable and is intended to be current as of the time it was written. It is sold with the understanding that the publisher is not engaged in rendering legal, accounting, or other professional services. If legal advice or other expert assistance is required, the services of a competent professional person should be sought. Also, to confirm that the information has not been affected or changed by recent developments, traditional legal research techniques should be used, including checking primary sources where appropriate.

(Based on the Declaration of Principles jointly adopted by a Committee of the American Bar Association and a Committee of Publishers and Associations.)

You may order this or any other Oxford University Press publication by visiting the Oxford University Press website at www.oup.com

For Sarah, my lifetime conversation partner
—PHR

For Carolyn and Liam
—SPG

For Marc, for his love and support
—KKF

CONTENTS

PREFACE

The means of human communication have dramatically improved over the past several decades, but the form of scholarly intercourse has remained the same. Scholars publish articles to which another scholar may, or may not, respond a year or two, or a decade, later. The strength of this traditional discourse is its deliberateness. Its weakness, at least as a means of scholarly interchange, lies in the fact that the long delay and dispersed audience commonly make it unlikely that scholars will genuinely "join issue," or if they do, that other scholars will easily become aware of the exchange. Blogs, in contrast, provide an immediacy and responsiveness that make for true dialogue, but they tend to sacrifice the deliberateness of the traditional form. What we offer here is a process and a format that we hope retains the virtues of the traditional scholarly form but promotes the kind of targeted conversation in which scholars do join issue.

Another virtue of what we offer is the way in which the issues contained in this collection have been selected. A collection traditionally reflects the scholarly interests of its editors, or perhaps its editors' beliefs about the interests of the scholarly community at large. In this project, the community of criminal law scholars itself has determined the issues to be included.

In early 2008, all English-speaking criminal law scholars were invited to post on the project Web site—http://www.law.upenn.edu/cf/faculty/phrobins/conversations/index.cfm—nominations of any article, book, or chapter that they thought contained issues worth public discussion. In all, 112 pieces were nominated, sometimes by the author but more commonly by another scholar. The members of the scholarly community could "vote" in support of a nomination by publicly expressing an interest in writing a comment on the piece. Nearly 350 expressions of interest in commenting were posted.

When a nomination had attracted three or four expressions of interest in commenting, the author of the nominated work was asked to write and post a "core text" succinctly presenting the central ideas of the nominated piece in 5,000 words or less. Because the core texts, often based on seminal articles in the field, were written in an accessible form, many participants have suggested that the core texts themselves are the most valuable contribution of the project, enabling the ideas presented in the original article to reach a broader audience. Once a core text was posted, edited, and finalized, the commentators posted comments of 800 words or less. Almost 190 comments were posted.

Once the comments were edited and finalized, the author of the original core text posted a reply that addressed each of the comments. Again, authors were encouraged to use direct and accessible style and again operated under word limits, typically 250 words times the number of comments, allocated among the comments as the author chose.

By the end of the process, in late 2008, more than 150 different scholars had submitted more than 1,200 postings of one kind or another to the project Web site.

The present volume includes 31 completed conversations, containing 227 contributions from 107 different contributors. As the reader will quickly see, the conversations present a wide range of issues and extremely diverse points of view—a fine portrait of the interests and perspectives of today's criminal law scholarly community.

—The Editors

TABLE OF CONTRIBUTORS

References are to chapters.

ACKNOWLEDGMENTS

Most of the criminal law scholarly community contributed to this volume in one way or another. Many scholars have no written contribution in this final volume to mark their participation in the project, so we are particularly indebted to them for their invaluable contributions to the nomination and selection process that was at the heart of the project.

Particular thanks, as well as congratulations, go to those who nominated the pieces that produced the conversations contained in this final volume. The community's interest in commenting on those pieces would seem to confirm the wisdom of the nominators' judgments.

Number	Title	Nominator
1	Decision Rules and Conduct Rules: On Acoustic Separation in Criminal Law	Huigens, Kyron
2	Empirical Desert	Markel, Dan
3	Defending Preventive Detention	Slobogin, Christopher
4	The Economics of Crime Control	Teichman, Doron
5	The Difficulties of Deterrence as a Distributive Principle	Kahan, Dan
6	Why Only the State May Inflict Criminal Sanctions: The Case Against Privately Inflicted Sanctions	Harel, Alon
7	Results Don't Matter	Robinson, Paul
8	Post-Modern Meditations on Punishment: On the Limits of Reason and the Virtue of Randomization	Harel, Alon
9	Remorse, Apology, and Mercy	Bandes, Susan
10	Interpretive Construction in the Substantive Criminal Law	Huigens, Kyron
11	Criminalization and Sharing Wrongs	Dempsey, Michelle Madden
12	Monstrous Offenders and the Search for Solidarity Through Modern Punishment	Bandes, Susan

Number	Title	Nominator
13	Against Negligence Liability	Garvey, Stephen
14	Rape Law Reform Based on Negotiation: Beyond the No and Yes Models	Anderson, Michelle J.
15	Provocation: Explaining and Justifying the Defense in Partial Excuse, Loss of Self-Control Terms	Garvey, Stephen
16	Objective versus Subjective Justification: A Case Study in Function and Form in Constructing a System of Criminal Law Theory	Fletcher, George
17	Self-Defense and the Psychotic Aggressor	Dressler, Joshua
18	Self-Defense Against Morally Innocent Threats	Tadros, Victor
19	Self-Defense, Imminence, and the Battered Woman	Kaufman, Whitley R.P.
20	Reasonable Provocation and Self-Defense: Recognizing the Distinction Between Act Reasonableness and Emotion Reasonableness	Harris, Angela
21	Against Control Tests for Criminal Responsibility	Kolber, Adam
22	Abolition of the Insanity Defense	Slobogin, Christopher
23	Entrapment and the "Free Market" for Crime	Robinson, Paul
24	The Political Economy of Criminal Law and Procedure: The Pessimists' View	Buell, Samuel W.
25	Against Jury Nullification	McAdams, Richard
26	Race-Based Jury Nullification: Black Power in the Criminal Justice System	Tuerkheimer, Deborah
27	In Support of Restorative Justice	Medwed, Daniel
28	The Virtues of Offense/Offender Distinctions	Garvey, Stephen
29	The Heart Has Its Reasons: Examining the Strange Persistence of the American Death Penalty	Bandes, Susan
30	Mercy's Decline and Administrative Law's Ascendance	Barkow, Rachel
31	Criminal Law Comes Home	Ristroph, Alice

We also owe a special debt to our many friends and colleagues who helped work out the original plan for the project and to the University of Pennsylvania ITS Department, and Christine Droesser in particular, who produced such an excellent website in execution of that plan. Finally, our thanks go to Kelly Farraday for her administrative and secretarial help on so many aspects of the work.

—The Editors

PART I

PRINCIPLES

1. DECISION RULES AND CONDUCT RULES
On Acoustic Separation in Criminal Law

MEIR DAN-COHEN*

It is an old but neglected idea that a distinction can be drawn in the law between rules addressed to the general public and rules addressed to officials. The neglect of this idea may stem in part from a belief that the laws addressed to officials—I call them *decision rules*—necessarily imply the laws addressed to the general public, the *conduct rules*, and vice versa, so that a single set of rules is in principle sufficient to fulfill both the function of guiding official decisions and that of guiding the public's behavior.

Some scholars view the law as consisting primarily of conduct rules, with the corresponding decision rules implied by them, whereas others privilege decision rules and consider conduct rules as implicit. But both approaches maintain that the connection between the two sets of rules is tight enough to license the reduction of the one to the other: whichever side of the coin is up, the reverse side will be deducible from it as well. My main contention in this core text is that this picture is faulty. The relationship between decision rules and conduct rules is not logical or conceptual but normative and contingent. To fulfill their respective functions the two sets of rules may but need not coincide.

I. THE MODEL

The separation between conduct rules and decision rules can be best understood through a simple thought experiment. Imagine a universe consisting of two groups of people—the general public and officials. The general public engages in various kinds of conduct, whereas officials make decisions with respect to members of the general public. Imagine further that each of the two groups occupies a different, acoustically sealed chamber. This condition I shall call *acoustic separation*. Now think of the law as a set of normative messages directed to both groups. One set, the conduct rules, is directed at the general public and is designed to shape people's behavior. This is done both by instructing the public about the required conduct and by issuing threats to secure compliance.

* Milo Reese Robbins Chair in Legal Ethics, School of Law, University of California, Berkeley. This core text draws from Meir Dan-Cohen, *Decision Rules and Conduct Rules: On Acoustic Separation in Criminal Law*, 97 HARV. L. REV. 625 (1984). A slightly revised version of the original article appears in Meir Dan-Cohen, HARMFUL THOUGHTS: ESSAYS ON LAW, SELF, AND MORALITY 37 (2002).

The other set of messages, the decision rules, is directed at the officials and provides guidelines for their decisions. In such a universe, the law must contain two separate sets of messages, even if these were to be identical.

But would they? This is a contingent matter, and at first glance there appear to be reasons for the two sets of rules to differ both in content and in form. In content, since they serve different functions. Conduct rules are concerned with *conduct control*, whereas decision rules, designed to authorize, constrain, or otherwise guide officials in the wielding of the state's power, are primarily concerned with *power control*. As to form, we might expect the two sets of rules to obey different communicative imperatives, so as to best suit their respective audiences' capabilities. Communicating to legally trained officials suggests a different style than communicating to the legally untutored general public.

The lesson taught by the thought experiment is conceptual, and so holds true not just in the imaginary universe. In the real world, too, we may speak of messages addressed to the general public and intended to shape conduct, and distinguish them from those addressed to officials and aimed at guiding decisions. However, since the public and officialdom do not in fact occupy acoustically sealed chambers, each group may "hear" the normative messages the law transmits to the other group. This affects the relationship between the two sets of rules in three ways.

First, a single provision may simultaneously guide both conduct and decisions and may thus function as both a conduct rule and a decision rule. The actual rules of a legal system are, accordingly, of three kinds. Any given rule may be a conduct rule, a decision rule, or both. The mere linguistic form in which a legal rule is cast does not determine the category to which it belongs. In order to classify a rule and identify its intended audience, we must situate the rule in a world of acoustic separation, and then decide, in light of the policies and values underlying the legal system, whether the rule would in that universe be a directive to the general public, to officials, or to both. The second difference between the real world and our imaginary universe is that, in the imaginary universe, acoustic separation ensures that conduct rules cannot, as such, affect decisions; similarly, decision rules cannot, as such, influence conduct.[1] Not so in the real world. Here, officials are aware of the system's conduct rules and may take them into account in making decisions, and individuals may consider decision rules in shaping their conduct. Real-world decision rules are accordingly likely to have conduct side effects, and real-world conduct rules are likely to have decisional side effects. Third, the possibility of these unintended side effects creates the potential for

---

1. It may seem that some seepage is bound to occur over time even in the imaginary universe. I leave it to the reader's imagination to come up with further devices to prevent this from happening and secure long-term acoustic separation. The point of the thought experiment will survive even if at this stage far-out sci-fi devices would have to be introduced.

conflict between decision rules and conduct rules. Such conflict arises whenever the side effects of one type of rule run counter to a rule of the other type.

An example will help clarify these remarks. It concerns a familiar dilemma posed by the defense of duress. Proponents of the defense emphasize the unfairness of punishing a person for succumbing to pressures to which even his judges might have yielded, whereas its opponents argue, to the contrary, that the law ought to be particularly vigilant when external pressures impel an individual toward crime. This conflict between the imperatives of compassion or fairness on the one side and of deterrence or law enforcement on the other dissolves, however, in the imaginary world of acoustic separation. In that world, the concerns of the advocates of the defense would lead to its adoption only as a decision rule—an instruction to the judge to acquit defendants who committed offenses under duress. Because the defense is not designed to guide conduct, no comparable rule need be included among the conduct rules of the system; conduct in circumstances that give rise to the defense would be guided exclusively by the relevant criminal proscriptions. The ability of acoustic separation to resolve the dilemma to which duress gives rise allows us to diagnose that dilemma as a case of conflict between conduct rules (those defining offenses, in this case) and a decision rule (the defense of duress), a conflict that results from the behavioral side effects that the decision rule of duress is likely to have in the absence of acoustic separation.

II. SOME APPLICATIONS

Acoustic separation, however, is not only a heuristic or diagnostic device. Though officials and the public are not in fact hermetically sealed off from each other, they are not completely intermingled either. As soon as a society can be differentiated into "a public" and "officialdom," it has probably reached a condition of *partial acoustic separation*. Partial acoustic separation obtains whenever certain normative messages are more likely to register with one of the two groups than with the other. Societies differ in their degree of acoustic separation. But just as a society displaying complete acoustic separation is unlikely, so is one in which there is none. It is also likely that within any society the degree of acoustic separation varies both with respect to different groups of the population and different issues.

If this empirical hypothesis is correct, actual legal systems may exhibit some features of the legal system of our imaginary universe. More specifically, actual legal systems may in fact avail themselves of the benefits of acoustic separation by engaging in *selective transmission*—that is, the transmission of different normative messages to decision-makers and to the general public. They can do so in two different ways, active or reactive. Reactive selective transmission consists in simply taking account of existing variations in acoustic separation as factors in shaping legal rules and decisions. The law engages in active selective transmission when it attempts to segregate its messages by employing communicative devices that increase the probability that a certain normative message will reach only its intended audience. I will illustrate both.

As mentioned above, excuses such as duress raise a worry that they will weaken people's resolve and increase the incidence of crime. This would lead us to expect an inverse correlation between the willingness of courts to allow these defenses and the degree of acoustic separation. We can distinguish two kinds of factors that determine the degree of acoustic separation, those relating to the legal sophistication and other characteristics of those likely to commit a particular type of offense, and those concerning the circumstances under which the offense is typically committed. When, as is often the case, an excuse involves an actor of no special legal sophistication caught in circumstances of emergency, high pressure, and emotion, the likelihood of a potential offender being aware of the defense or able to act on such awareness is at its lowest. These conditions of high acoustic separation thus create relatively little risk of undesirable behavioral side effects. In some cases, however, special characteristics or special circumstances reduce acoustic separation. The law can be seen to respond to such situations by disallowing or curtailing the applicable defenses.

Special characteristics of the potential offenders may account for the courts' attitude in prison escape cases. Courts have virtually refused to allow even serious threats of homosexual rape or death to serve as a defense to the charge of escape.[2] The concerns underlying the courts' grudging attitude are vividly conveyed by the leading decision of *People v. Lovercamp*: "However, before *Lovercamp* becomes a household word in prison circles and we are exposed to the spectacle of hordes of prisoners leaping over the walls screaming 'rape,' we hasten to add that the defense of necessity to an escape charge is extremely limited in its application."[3] This apocalyptic vision is best explained by the courts' apparent belief that the relevant constituency, of prison inmates, is highly attuned to legal pronouncements affecting it. Low acoustic separation increases in this case the likelihood of undesirable behavioral side effects of allowing the defense, and accounts for the courts' more restrictive approach.

People v. Carradine,[4] which dealt with the duty to testify, illustrates the legal effects of the second group of factors responsible for low acoustic separation, regarding the circumstances under which the offense is typically committed. The defendant refused to testify in a homicide trial out of fear for her life and her children's lives. In rejecting fear as an excuse the court said: "[Fear] is not a valid reason for not testifying. If it's a valid reason then we might as well close the

---

2. *See* Note, *Intolerable Conditions as a Defense to Prison Escapes,* 26 UCLA L. Rev. 1126, 1126–28 (1979).

3. 43 Cal. App. 3d 823, 831; 118 Cal. Rptr. 110, 115 (1974).

4. 287 N.E.2d 670 (Ill. 1972).

doors."[5] Once again, the court's catastrophic prediction only makes sense in light of an underlying assessment of low acoustic separation stemming from the fact that the decision whether to testify is likely to be the product of deliberation and legal advice.

As I mentioned, the second form that selective transmission can assume is more active, because it involves the use of communicative devices designed to target different audiences. My example concerns a style employed in the statutory definition of some offenses in which ordinary terms are given technical legal meaning. This combination of ordinary language and technical definition is puzzling. If the law intends to speak ordinary language, why use technical legal definitions that distort it? If, on the other hand, the intended normative message is best expressed through technical definitions, the law may do better to coin a technical vocabulary (as in fact it sometime does) rather than use misleadingly familiar terms. Unless, of course, the law intends not one or the other but both.

Indeed, an interpretation that imputes to the law such a double meaning is in some cases quite plausible: the ordinary language of a law defining an offense forms the conduct rule, whereas the technical legal definitions form the decision rule. The different style in which these rules are formulated promotes selective transmission. By framing its imperatives in familiar language, the law echoes and reinforces the layperson's ordinary moral beliefs, whereas the technical legal definitions can effectively guide professional decision-makers. This dual conception of criminal offenses is supported by its ability to resolve a persistent problem concerning the nature of mens rea.

The problem is best illustrated by the famous English case of *Regina v. Prince*.[6] Prince was charged under a Victorian statute that provided that "[w]hosoever shall unlawfully take or cause to be taken any unmarried girl, being under the age of sixteen years, out of the possession and against the will of her father or mother, . . . shall be guilty of a misdemeanor."[7] Even though Prince had reasonably believed that the girl (who in fact was fourteen) was eighteen years old, the court disallowed the defense of mistake of fact and upheld Prince's conviction. Lord Bramwell's opinion deserves, and has received, greatest attention.

> Let us remember what is the case supposed by the statute. It supposes that there is a *girl*—it does not say a woman, but a girl—something between a child and a woman; it supposes she is in the *possession* of her father or mother, or other person having lawful *care or charge* of her; and it supposes there is a *taking*, and that that taking is *against the will* of the person in whose possession

---

5. *Id.* at 672 (quoting *People v. Carradine*, No. A69-27 (Cook County, Ill. Cir. Ct. Oct. 1, 1969)).

6. 2 L.R. Cr. Cas. Res. 154 (1875).

7. Offences Against the Person Act, 1861, 24 & 25 Vict., c. 100, § 55.

she is. It is, then, a *taking* of a *girl*, in the *possession* of some one, *against his will*. I say that done without lawful cause is wrong, and that the legislature meant it should be at the risk of the taker whether or no she was under sixteen. I do not say that taking a woman of fifty from her brother's or even father's house is wrong . . . [W]hat the statute contemplates, and what I say is wrong, is the taking of a female of such tender years that she is properly called a *girl*, can be said to be in another's *possession*, and in that other's *care or charge* . . . This opinion gives full scope to the doctrine of the mens rea.[8]

How can Lord Bramwell maintain that ignoring Prince's mistake of fact is compatible with the requirement of mens rea? Had not Prince, reasonably and genuinely believing that the girl was eighteen years old, acted innocently and in accordance with the law's requirements?

The key to an answer that makes sense of Lord Bramwell's position is his persistent emphasis on the statute's use of the term *girl*. Now the word *girl* is not a legal term, but a term of ordinary language. Lord Bramwell argues, in effect, that the conduct rule issued by the statute should be understood to conform to the ordinary meaning of the statute's language. In this way, the statute can be seen to point to or incorporate the moral prohibition against the abduction of girls from their guardians. Prince's guilt consists in his violating this prohibition. The statutory definition of *girl*, which diverges from the ordinary usage, is no part of the conduct rule, but only an element of the decision rule issued by the statute. The statutory age limit is accordingly addressed exclusively to the judge, who unlike the ordinary citizen, is required both to know of it and to give it effect in his decisions. Indeed, Lord Bramwell gave effect to this statutory definition by insisting that the defendant be punished only if the girl had in fact been under age.

It should not be difficult to discern the logic behind such a decision rule. Moral principles, as well as the terms of ordinary language in which they are couched, tend to have fuzzy edges. The applicability of the moral prohibition against the abduction of girls may well be indeterminate once a victim has reached a certain age. The legal definition of the age at which the prohibition no longer applies serves as a restriction on judges that ensures both a degree of uniformity and, quite possibly, a degree of leniency in the interpretation of conventional morality. Furthermore, by choosing a relatively low age limit, the legislature may provide for the possibility that defendants make mistakes concerning a girl's age.

Just as the refusal in *Prince* and subsequent statutory rape cases to allow a mistake of fact defense need not signify the abandonment pro tanto of the principle of mens rea, more recent willingness to allow the defense need not be taken, as is commonly done, as a measure of increased commitment to mens

---

8. 2 L.R. Cr. Cas. Res. at 174–75.

rea. Instead, both the refusal and the willingness can be seen as responses, based on essentially identical views of mens rea, to different social and moral circumstances. In the leading case, *People v. Hernandez*,[9] the court, while acquitting of statutory rape a defendant who was mistaken about the victim's age, observed that had the statutory age of consent been considerably lower, say ten or fourteen, than the actual eighteen, the defense of mistake would not have been available. Now if the statutory age limit were to define the relevant conduct rule, this distinction between different age limits would not be tenable: a defendant's belief that his partner is eleven years old when she is in fact just under ten may be as genuine and as reasonable as a similar mistake concerning the age of a seventeen-year-old. If the requirement of mens rea demands exculpation in the latter case, it should, on this supposition, demand the same in the former.

However, the distinction the court draws between the two age limits does make sense when we note (as does the court) that one age limit coincides with a viable moral norm, whereas the other does not. When the statutory age limit is low, the statute can be seen to issue a conduct rule that coincides with an indisputable moral norm against having intercourse with, as the court puts it, "infants." When judged in terms of this norm, a defendant's mistaken belief that, say, a nine-year-old was in fact eleven, would be simply irrelevant. But when the statutory age is set at eighteen, the criminal provision no longer corresponds to a viable moral prohibition. In such circumstances, the statutory age of consent conclusively determines the scope of the relevant conduct rule, so that knowledge by the defendant that the female is below that age is indeed required by the principle of mens rea.

Stated more broadly, the message implicit in the *Hernandez* decision is that statutory interpretation must take account of cultural context and prevailing moral norms. A statutory provision may be the harbinger of a new standard of behavior, the embodiment of an existing one, or the mere ghost of an expired morality. In each of these capacities, the provision relates differently to common perceptions (by shaping, reflecting, or ignoring them) and is accordingly amenable to different legal analysis.

As this discussion illustrates, the bifurcated picture of law that insists on the relative independence of conduct rules from decision rules reveals that law stands to morality in a more complicated relationship than is commonly appreciated. It is often complained that legal technicalities create a gap between legal and moral obligation. The technicalities, it is answered, are necessary to check official power, and the gap they create is the inevitable price. In a world of acoustic separation, however, we could have it both ways by promulgating conduct rules coextensive with moral precepts, and decision rules that are more precisely defined and narrowly drawn. The law would thus avoid the charge that it caters

---

9. 393 P.2d 673 (Cal. 1964).

to the "bad people" in the community without increasing the risk of unjust punishment or giving too much free rein to officials.[10] In actual legal systems, in which complete acoustic separation does not obtain, laws defining criminal offenses serve to convey both conduct rules and decision rules. But even here, partial acoustic separation leaves room for doctrines, such as the strict liability approach in *Prince*, that allow the law to accomplish to some degree the different and sometimes contradictory goals served by the two sets of rules.[11]

III. ISSUES OF LEGITIMACY

Ought the law ever take account and advantage of variations in acoustic separation? The most fundamental rule of law requirements that all law be public and clear would seem to offer a resounding negative answer. A closer look reveals a more complicated picture: selective transmission need not impede and may sometimes advance the values associated with the rule of law. I'll make three points in this regard.

First, by insisting on the specificity and clarity of law, the rule of law is said to limit officials' discretion and thereby to curb their potential arbitrariness. But the ability of decision rules to guide decisions effectively and thus to limit official discretion does not depend on broad dissemination or easy accessibility of those rules to the general public. If anything, the opposite is true: the clarity and specificity of decision rules, and hence their effectiveness as guidelines, may be enhanced by the use of a technical, esoteric terminology that is incomprehensible to the public at large.

Second, the rule of law requirement is said to be based on the "root idea" that "the law must be capable of being obeyed" and that hence "it must be capable of guiding the behaviour of its subjects. It must be such that they can find out what it is and act on it."[12] But this idea applies only to conduct rules: ex hypothesi, conduct rules are all one needs to know in order to obey the law. Decision rules, as such, cannot be obeyed or disobeyed by citizens; therefore, knowing them is not necessary, indeed, is irrelevant, to one's ability to obey the law.

Finally, and perhaps most importantly, the rule of law allegedly promotes liberty or autonomy by increasing predictability.[13] But the need for security of

---

10. On the "bad man" conception of criminal law, *see* Oliver Wendell Holmes, Jr., *The Path of the Law, in* COLLECTED LEGAL PAPERS 167, 169–79 (1920).

11. In the original version of this article I discuss additional instances of selective transmission. Those include the "act at your peril" rule in some justification cases, ignorance of law, and the void-for-vagueness doctrine.

12. Joseph Raz, *The Rule of Law and Its Virtue, in* THE AUTHORITY OF LAW 213–14 (1979).

13. *See, e.g.,* Friedrich A. von Hayek, THE ROAD TO SERFDOM 72–78 (1944); John Rawls, A THEORY OF JUSTICE 235–36 (1972); Raz, *supra* note 12, at 220–22.

individual expectations is not a great obstacle to the use of selective transmission when decision rules are more lenient than conduct rules would lead people to expect. In such cases no one is likely to complain of frustrated expectations. True, some individuals may still complain of an infringement of their autonomy by a reduction in predictability: had they known, for example, of the defense of duress, they would not have resisted a strong pressure to commit a crime. However, this complaint overlooks a peculiar feature of defenses such as duress: they melt away as soon as one relies upon them ex ante. An individual who would not have committed an offense but for his knowledge of the existence of such a defense cannot, in most cases, avail himself of the defense. Failure to alert people to a defense such as duress would thus mislead only those who would act on their awareness of the defense with the intent to eventually deny that reliance when they are brought to trial. It is doubtful that such expectations are worthy of protection.

But the discovery that what has been called "the internal morality of law"[14] is compatible with patterns of selective transmission falls far short of justifying them. The option of selective transmission is unattractive, and the sight of law tainted with duplicity and concealment is not pretty.

The lingering distaste is useful, however, in jolting us out of an overly rosy or self-satisfied image of law. To this end we must place the model of acoustic separation in a broader context. Specifically, we must consider it in relationship to law's coerciveness, where "coercion" is often a euphemism for intimidation, brutality, and violence. When dealing with a dog of such ferocity, there is value in the possibility, enhanced by selective transmission, that its bark be mightier than its bite. The use of force, even when justified, is at best a necessary evil, and so a tension pervades the criminal law between the felt necessity and the perceived evil of the means it employs. As we have seen, selective transmission may help mitigate this tension by allowing the law to attain its goals with a lesser amount of force than may otherwise be deemed necessary. That the option of selective transmission can sometimes be rejected only at the cost of increased human suffering does not settle the legitimacy of acoustic separation. Drawing attention to this state of affairs does, however, serve to highlight an important if unpleasant bit of reality. Law is susceptible to a moral predicament that is generally endemic in political life, the predicament of "dirty hands": the need to choose among evils, and so inescapably perform acts that remain repugnant even when justified.[15]

---

14. Lon L. Fuller, THE MORALITY OF LAW (1964).

15. *See, e.g.*, Michael Walzer, *Political Action: The Problem of Dirty Hands, in* WAR AND MORAL RESPONSIBILITY 62 (Marshall Cohen, Thomas Nagel, and Thomas Scanlon eds., 1974).

COMMENTS

DURESS IS NEVER A CONDUCT RULE

KYRON HUIGENS*

According to Meir Dan-Cohen, acoustic separation is a conceptual feature of criminal law. His argument relies heavily on the example of the duress defense. But duress does not support his argument, and it fails to do so in a way that calls into question his claim to be describing a conceptual feature of criminal law.

Dan-Cohen says that duress ordinarily will be strictly construed as a conduct rule and more leniently construed as a decision rule. Without acoustic separation between conduct guidance and decision-making, the lenient constructions of the latter will detract from the strict constructions of the former, and so from the stringency of law. This illustrates the operation of, and reasons for, acoustic separation.

The problem is that duress, conceptually, is never a conduct rule. Duress is always a decision rule—an ex post, evaluative claim that, in spite of having done wrong, one is not a fair candidate for punishment. The Model Penal Code's formulation authorizes the defense if the threat faced was one "which a person of reasonable firmness in his situation would have been unable to resist."[1] In other words, the defense turns on a character trait: the virtue of firmness or, more commonly, the virtue of fortitude. There is nothing problematic about giving virtue a role in a decision rule. A person can be held responsible for his character because he has rational control over his character in the long run. Fortitude's role in a conduct rule, however, is very problematic.

If the rule Dan-Cohen suggests is "to have fortitude when coerced," then it is not a conduct rule at all, at least in the usual sense of the term. Conduct rules govern actions on the occasion of action. A prescription "to have fortitude" demands that one acquire and maintain a virtue. But virtues are acquired and maintained over the long term. The inculcation of virtue is a process of internalization of norms—something that cannot occur at a discrete moment in time, or at a single point of decision. So "have fortitude" is not a rule that governs on the occasion of action, and it is not a conduct rule.

Perhaps Dan-Cohen is suggesting a different conduct rule, something along the lines of "when coerced, act with fortitude." If this is what he means, then a kind of act is prescribed, and not the possession of a character trait. But if I ask, "what is it that I am to do with fortitude?" the answer, apparently, is that I should refrain from committing a crime. But the criminal law always necessarily obligates me to refrain from committing a crime. Any norm inherently demands

---

* Professor of Law, Benjamin N. Cardozo School of Law.
1. Model Penal Code § 2.09 (1980).

compliance. So what more is it that I am to do, above and beyond obeying the law, in order to obey the law with fortitude? Any conceivable interpretation of "comply with the law, and do so with fortitude"—such as "comply with the law and like it" or "comply with the law with a stiff upper lip"—portrays the law in a false light. Criminal law never rewards praiseworthy actions and attitudes, nor punishes their absence.

Perhaps Dan-Cohen's suggested conduct rule is this command: "comply with the law when you otherwise would not do so." But this is meaningless. The counterfactual is impossible to determine. If I do so, then I would have done so. If I do not do so, then I would not have done so. If we frame it as, "comply with the law when you are tempted not to do so," then, again, we are requiring nothing that the law does not already, necessarily, require.

Perhaps the prescription is that I should not commit a crime, with fortitude as one of my reasons for not doing so; that is, for the sake of acting with fortitude. But the only way I can do that act for this reason is to do it because I am trying to attain, or because I am already in possession of, the virtue of fortitude. We are led back to the first difficulty. If this is what the rule means, then it is not a conduct rule because it does not govern action on the occasion of action.

In short, duress does not operate as a conduct rule, because the putative rule does not guide conduct at all; because it is a kind of rule that criminal law never has; or because it is meaningless in that role. At a minimum, this renders duress a bad example of Dan-Cohen's thesis. But what is true of duress might well be true of other decision rules. This calls into question the idea that acoustic separation is a conceptual feature of criminal law.

DECISION RULES AS NOTICE: THE CASE OF FRAUD

SAMUEL W. BUELL*

In statutory form, the conduct rule for the crime of fraud usually consists of little more than the edict "do not defraud another." Courts have elaborated on this edict to make clear that the offense requires some deception, or at least attempted deception, that causes harm or loss to the property interests of another or threatens to do so. And the defendant must act with the "intent to defraud." But everyday economic relations are full of deception and loss. To "intend" something is, in the Model Penal Code's formulation, to have a particular end as one's "conscious object." What does it mean for someone to intend to deceive me in the marketplace? It seems like the telecommunications providers do this every time they get me to sign up for their services.

---

* Associate Professor, Washington University School of Law.

Fraud's conduct rules are so open-textured because fraud is a residual crime. It consists, in essence, of wrongful appropriations of others' property interests that do not violate the basic prohibition on theft. The offense is designed to catch actors who, with one eye on legal regimes, devise novel schemes for separating others from their property. This has been true at least since Lord Coke stated in 1601, "[B]ecause fraud and deceit abound in these days more than in former times. . . all statutes made against fraud should be liberally and beneficially expounded to suppress fraud."[1]

Fraud's conduct rules put courts in a difficult spot. Under a rule that makes it a crime to "intentionally deceive another in order to cause property loss," a prosecutor can too easily place a sharp commercial actor who is not sufficiently blameworthy, and whose activities may be socially welcome, at jeopardy of imprisonment. The solution that courts and many prosecutors have worked out is to deploy a decision rule according to which novel fraudulent conduct will be punished criminally only if the defendant acted with "consciousness of wrongdoing."[2]

Legal actors conduct an ex post mens rea inquiry that travels deeper than the question of "intent to defraud" to consider whether the actor knew what she was doing was normatively wrongful and nonetheless pressed forward to the disadvantage of others. A common method of conducting this inquiry is to look for the famous "badges of fraud" (falsification or destruction of evidence, use of fictitious identities or accounts, and the like). The purpose of this decision-rule inquiry is to select for punishment truly blameworthy actors from among all those who might do harm though deceptive commercial practices.

I do not see well-functioning acoustic separation in the criminal law of fraud. The statutory conduct rule ("do not defraud") does not send a clear message, unless the intended message is to avoid sales talk, which hardly seems consistent with our economy. The conduct rule with judicial gloss ("do not intentionally deceive others causing or risking economic loss") is not clear either, leaving actors guessing about how the law distinguishes between effective negotiation and crime.

The decision rule ("punish only intentionally deceptive actors who caused harm and knew what they were doing was wrongful") is not complex and would appear quite accessible to the kinds of resourceful actors who tend to be subject to fraud prosecutions. Yet this clear and accessible decision rule seems to create a new and undesirable conduct rule: Don't leave any badges of fraud behind and, even if you knew full well that you were making a killing on the latest scam, you are not likely to be punished.

---

1. *Twyne's Case*, (1601) 76 Eng. Rep. 809, 815–16 (K.B.).
2. *See* Samuel W. Buell, *Novel Criminal Fraud*, 81 N.Y.U. L. Rev. 1971 (2006).

The role of notice in Dan-Cohen's acoustic separation model breaks down in the case of fraud. It isn't just that the conduct rule is meaningless as a notice rule. And it isn't just that the decision rule is easily accessible to the relevant nonlegal actors. It's also that, paradoxically, the decision rule is really about notice even though it appears ex post. Only those who acted with "consciousness of wrongdoing" are punished for fraud because, of all who engaged in deceptive commercial practices, punishment is justified only for those who did so appreciating that what they were doing was normatively wrongful. Here, notice is not just a constraint on state action. It is a principle of fault.

One area of doctrine cannot unsettle Dan-Cohen's brilliant thesis. But I am curious to know what he thinks about the law of fraud.

OF DECISION RULES AND CONDUCT RULES, OR DOING THE POLICE IN DIFFERENT VOICES

ANNE M. COUGHLIN*

Meir Dan-Cohen's aim is to revive the "old but neglected idea" that the criminal law is properly separated into "conduct rules" addressed to the general public and "decision rules" addressed to officials who decide who gets punished and who does not. I suspect that some members of the general public would be dismayed to learn that scholars neglect a distinction with which they are painfully familiar. They also would be astonished to hear that (some) attentive scholars are toying with the notion that acoustic separation is good for them. Criminal offenders may be pleased to learn that law is a dog whose "bark [is] mightier than its bite." But what of crime victims? What, say, of rape victims who are led to believe that law will vindicate their interest in sexual autonomy, only to discover that enforcers apply a "technical, esoteric," even "incomprehensible," definition of consent that was hidden from their view?

This criticism accepts Dan-Cohen's premise that there *are* two sets of rules, which *are* and *should be* separated. But I wonder. First, Dan-Cohen needs to do more work separating conduct rules from decision rules; he needs to identify which is which, and persuade us that they are distinct. Second, and what may be the same thing, he must explain how the public comes to hear about and internalize conduct rules but not decision rules. In Dan-Cohen's account, the mechanism for transmitting conduct rules is obscure; he praises what he calls

---

* O.M. Vicars Professor of Law, University of Virginia School of Law. This comment describes ideas developed at more length in my work-in-progress, *Doing the Police in Different Voices*. As fans of Charles Dickens will know, I borrow my title from a line in *Our Mutual Friend*, one of the greatest detective novels of all time.

"selective transmission," without ever identifying the transmission machinery. Do we learn conduct rules from our parents; from other social sources of legal norms; from reading criminal statutes; from reading broad prohibitions, while ignoring technical provisions that constrain or, for that matter, expand the prohibitions; from reading judicial opinions construing the statutes; from viewing media accounts describing who is arrested, who charged, who goes to trial, the arguments made there, who gets sent to jail and for how long, and who is set free; from all of the above?

It might just be me, but there you have it: I'm not sure which rule is which or how we learn them. Furthermore, if there is a distinction, I'm inclined to think that the public learns about criminal prohibitions from some of the stuff falling more on the decision-rule than the conduct-rule side of the distinction.

When arguing that partial acoustic separation is a good thing, Dan-Cohen treats the general public as an (almost) monolith, when it is not. When (ap)praising the value of acoustic separation, he divides the public into two very rough groups, the group of law-abiders and the group of lawbreakers. With these groups in mind, he concludes that having a decision rule (duress may be an excusing condition) that is more lenient than the conduct rule (don't commit a crime, any crime, no matter what, period, full stop) inflicts no harm on the expectations of either. What does the lawbreaker have to whine about? The fact that she thought she was going to be punished, but lo and behold, duress provides an escape hatch? That would be goofy, to say the very least. Nor can the law-abider—one who was tempted to commit the crime but didn't—identify any legitimate interest that was violated by concealment of the decision rule. The conduct rule was clear, she complied with it, for which we applaud her, and had she committed a violation thinking that she could raise a duress defense, her mental state would negate the elements of the defense, so she's better off not knowing about it at all.

But what of the interests of crime victims in the clarity and transparency of conduct rules? For example, women are told—sometimes explicitly, as is the case when they enter military academies or civilian universities—that a rape occurs when an actor has sex with them against their will. The women interpret this conduct rule to mean that the law at least aims to protect them against nonconsensual sex and that it will take steps to vindicate their interest in the promised protection. Thus, when nonconsensual intercourse occurs, the women report the crime to police. They are questioned and told, nope, sorry, that was not rape, for rape is satisfied only by certain technical, esoteric forms of nonconsent, whose definitions are buried in the fine print of definitional provisions or in the pages of dusty court reporters. It was just bad sex, go home, take a shower, forget about it. For victims and their families, who rely on conduct rules to protect them from offenders and to take vengeance for them when the conduct rules fail, acoustic separation may produce uncertainty, insecurity, a loss of autonomy, and a loss of faith in the rule of law.

SEPARATION, BUT NOT OF RULES

LUÍS DUARTE D'ALMEIDA*

When Meir Dan-Cohen holds that "the relationship between decision rules and conduct rules is not logical or conceptual,"[1] he seems to mean to refute two theses:

(a) Decision rules and conduct rules are not independent: the antecedent of a criminal decision rule necessarily includes the infringement (and therefore the existence) of a conduct rule.

(b) Decision rules are necessarily coextensive with the corresponding conduct rules.

Dan-Cohen is wrong in opposing (a). The main argument for (a) was put forward, among others, by H.L.A. Hart: criminal decision rules always presuppose "an offence or breach of duty" and, thus, the corresponding conduct rule.[2] Hart's point is a conceptual one. It concerns the concept of a penal sanction.[3] And even though Hart aimed to dispute the theory that conduct rules may be "reduced" to sanction rules in a representation of the legal system, the case for or against such "reduction" cannot be decided on conceptual grounds: both hypotheses are compatible with (a).[4] *Pace* Dan-Cohen, dismissing the doctrine of "reduction" does not amount to rejecting (a).

As for (b), Dan-Cohen justly contests it. But no one *really* endorses (b): the complete reconstruction of a decision rule draws from a much larger set of statutory provisions than that of the corresponding conduct rule. The logical relationship between both kinds of laws does not concern their content;[5] it means only that if a decision rule is to be considered a *criminal* rule, it necessarily presupposes the violation of a conduct rule.

It follows that an imaginary universe characterized (as Dan-Cohen proposes) by the strict "separation" of conduct rules and decision rules would have no criminal law. For there to be a criminal system it is necessary that judges employ the concept of an offence, and hence that they "apply" conduct rules. In any

---

* Assistant Lecturer, Faculty of Law/LanCog, University of Lisbon, Portugal.

1. Dan-Cohen core text at 3.

2. H.L.A. Hart, THE CONCEPT OF LAW 39 (2d ed. 1994).

3. I tentatively develop this in Luís Duarte d'Almeida, *Against Prohibitions*, PROCEEDINGS OF THE 4TH LATIN MEETING IN ANALYTIC PHILOSOPHY (Carlo Penco et al. eds.), *available at* http://ftp.informatik.rwth-aachen.de/Publications/CEUR-WS/Vol-278/paper02.pdf.

4. A similar point is made by Joseph Raz, THE CONCEPT OF A LEGAL SYSTEM 91–2 (1980).

5. This has been noted by proponents as well as opponents of "reduction." *See* Hans Kelsen, REINE RECHTSLEHRE 119–20 (2d ed. 1960); Raz, *supra* note 4, at 154.

event, I fail to see the need for *bilateral* acoustic separation in Dan-Cohen's imaginary universe: nothing in his argument seems to rely on how much information judges possess about the "public" chamber. The object of theoretical interest is the possibility of public unawareness of how judges decide—not vice versa. Unilateral separation would suffice to preserve the criminal character of judicial decisions.

Nor is there any reason to suppose that the law would pursue its policies solely by publicly announcing "conduct rules." Effective deterrence depends on various factors, including, e.g., the system's efficacy and severity (or rather the citizens' *beliefs* about it, whether true or false). Taking advantage of total acoustic separation, the legislator might issue threats far harsher than those executed, or divulge false data about a fast and merciless judicature. Except by stipulation, we wouldn't employ the language of "conduct rules" and "decision rules" to refer to this system. We would rather speak of a mismatch between how the law really *was* and how the law was *said*—and more or less widely *believed*—to be.

The same holds for the "real" world: the strategically tailored "message" that legal systems broadcast about themselves is surely not restricted to what the law says it requires or prescribes citizens to do. Which policies are best served by such strategies may also be discussed without any reference to a separation between kinds of rules; and that which Dan-Cohen presents as a "conflict between decision rules and conduct rules"[6] could more fittingly be portrayed as a conflict between potentially diverging behavioural consequences of true and false beliefs about the law.

Moreover, the fecundity of Dan-Cohen's construct is undermined by its association with this theory-laden distinction between decision rules and conduct rules—which he ought to abandon. His model delimits an autonomous field of inquiry and evaluation from which many aspects of criminal law may be assessed: how *are* our criminal systems' legislative and judicial decisions constricted—and how constricted *should* they be—by judgments about the behavioral consequences of their own publicity? Focusing on this pattern of deliberation (rather than on the distinction between kinds of rules) naturally expands the range of topics usefully illuminated by the model. For example, consider sentencing dilemmas regarding the amount of punishment to be decreed. Specific deterrence may suggest or require a lighter sentence, whereas general deterrence and the need for public discouragement may call for an exemplarily severe decision. These are natural candidates for analysis under Dan-Cohen's model. But what matters here is public knowledge about how cases happen to be decided, not about applicable decision rules (whether or not judicial decisions are indeed preconditioned by any rule, and irrespective of their precedent-setting force).

---

6. Dan-Cohen core text at 5.

THE CONSTITUTIVE FUNCTION OF CRIMINAL LAW

ADIL AHMAD HAQUE*

Let me pursue two points: the first having to do with the permissible secrecy of decision rules, and the second with the permissible overbreadth of conduct rules. Perhaps more accurately, let me contrast Meir Dan-Cohen's positions in the essay on which his core text is based with the positions taken in his later essay, *Responsibility and the Boundaries of the Self.*[1] There Dan-Cohen argues that principles of inculpation and exculpation shape the contours of personal identity by determining the circumstances under which various attributes, actions, events, and objects count as part of an individual and as a basis for holding that individual legally liable for their causal consequences.

To fulfill this function, legal principles governing the assumption and ascription of responsibility must be "mediated by the existence of widely shared social conventions and understandings regarding the attribution of responsibility, which are themselves articulations of a shared public conception of the self."[2] If, as Dan-Cohen suggests, these principles are not merely to reflect but also to reinforce and improve upon these conventions and understandings, they must at the very least be publicly known. Only if they are publicly articulated can these principles interact with and modify individual and social perceptions of the constituents of the self. The preventative goals discussed in *Decision Rules and Conduct Rules* may be served by shielding the public from information regarding liability conditions, but the constitutive goals of *Responsibility and the Boundaries of the Self* require full disclosure. More generally, rules assigning criminal liability become part of social practices of praise and blame, setting forth common standards of justification and excuse. These evaluative practices are as central a part of community morality as the conduct rules Dan-Cohen argues must be public to be reflected in and at times altered by legal norms.

Conversely, conduct rules, no less than liability rules, may work constitutive changes in and upon the self. It is only upon violation of a conduct rule that one may appropriately be labeled a criminal, a murderer, a thief, and such like. The social stigma commonly associated with criminal punishment is in fact triggered by community knowledge of an offense rather than conviction of the offender. One is stigmatized for being a *criminal*, not merely for being a *convict*, and one's status as such can have sweeping implications for one's own sense of identity and for its social performance, quite apart from actual conviction. It is breach of a conduct rule, not conviction under applicable decision rules, which works

---

* Assistant Professor of Law, Rutgers School of Law–Newark.

1. Meir Dan-Cohen, HARMFUL THOUGHTS: ESSAYS ON LAW, SELF, AND MORALITY 210 (2002).

2. *Id.*

these constitutive changes in one's identity. It would be perverse, therefore, to consign defenses—whether justifications or excuses—to decision rules alone, and subject blameless actors to social stigma.

Moreover, conduct rules protecting individuals imply corresponding rights of individuals, thereby articulating boundaries of selves as well as boundaries between them. In his essay, *The Value of Ownership*, Dan-Cohen argues at length that ascription of property rights adjusts the boundaries of the self, going so far as to state that one stands in the same moral relation to one's property as to one's body.[3] It would be odd indeed if the rights protected by the criminal law, including those protecting bodily integrity, did not similarly contribute to the construction of the self. The constitutive function of conduct rules calls into question Dan-Cohen's contention that no morally significant cost is accrued by overbroad conduct rules conjoined with narrow decision rules. If one of the functions of conduct rules is to mirror and shape popular morality, then it should reflect and sharpen moral distinctions rather than run them together. To take Dan-Cohen's central example, there is indeed agreement that sexual contact between older and younger individuals is morally blameworthy, but the degree of blameworthiness varies with the age of the parties, and ranges from the merely disfavored to the condemnable to the punishable. Because human development is continuous, the distinctions within popular morality are difficult to draw in any particular case. Law can assist popular morality by drawing lines and creating moral "tipping points" in the gradations of blameworthiness appropriate to various acts, supporting the ability of morality to guide both action and evaluation. But to serve these functions the distinctions drawn in law must be made public and interact with existing social practices of praise and blame. Only then can the stigma triggered by breach of conduct rules be graduated to reflect the relative seriousness of morally offensive acts.

---

3. *Id.* at 265, 272–77, 284–87.

ARE THERE TWO TYPES OF DECISION RULES?

ERIC J. MILLER*

Meir Dan-Cohen's celebrated discussion of decision and conduct rules forces us to reevaluate the claim "that the laws addressed to officials. . . [i.e., decision rules] necessarily imply the laws addressed to the general public [i.e., conduct rules]."[1] Instead, he separates decision rules from conduct rules and treats each as

---

* Assistant Professor of Law, Saint Louis University School of Law.
1. Dan-Cohen core text at 3.

commands directed toward different audiences. Conduct rules are mandatory norms addressed to the world at large, intended to achieve *"conduct control"* by directing citizen behavior. Decision rules are an independent set of mandatory norms addressed to judges, intended to achieve *"power control"* by directing judicial decision-making.

One of Dan-Cohen's central points is that publishing *only* conduct rules and not decision rules need not violate the rule of law's "fundamental . . . requirement[] that all law be public and clear."[2] That rule of law requirement is primarily directed toward enabling citizens to guide their conduct in accordance with the law. Accordingly, legislatures would not violate the rule of law's notice requirement by failing to publish decisions rules.

In fact, two types of decision rules can usefully be distinguished. The first type of decision rule tells judges not to convict if, for example, an agent has made a mistake or if her will is overborne. Call these decision rules *excuse-based* decision rules. An example of such a rule is provided, as Dan-Cohen suggests, by the duress doctrine, which instructs judges not to convict a defendant if she can demonstrate that some third party forced her to engage in the prohibited conduct. The duress rule does not expand judicial power but contracts it, by limiting the range of circumstances in which a citizen could be adjudged guilty of a crime. Because the decision rule does not directly affect the proscribed conduct and narrows the power of the judge to criminalize such conduct, nonpublication does not undermine the rule of law.

It might be worth noting that excuse-based decision rules render the defendant a passive participant or nonparticipant in the moral debate over the significance of her conduct. That is, we might consider it an important feature in attributing moral or legal culpability that agents are permitted to explain the significance of their conduct. Dan-Cohen's excuse-based decision rules, to the extent they are acoustically separated from the public, cannot function in this way. Decision rules are addressed to the judge, not the public, and so empower the judge alone to assess the legal and moral significance of the defendant's conduct.

A second type of decision rule authorizes or guides official decision-making without necessarily constraining it. Call these power-directing decision rules. Dan-Cohen suggests power-directing rules operate to clarify official decision-making by limiting discretion. An example of a power-directing decision rule is the "public welfare" or "regulatory offense" doctrine. Under this doctrine, courts use a series of factors to determine whether the statute imposes strict liability or general intent. The power-directing decision rule controls the court's interpretation of the statute. Without notice of the decision rule, however, the public cannot

---

2. *Id.* at 10.

know that they bear the risk of any mistakes about the nature of their conduct, even if they act reasonably and in good faith.

The act of categorizing a statute as regulatory, though authorized and directed by decision norms, has a profound impact on citizen conduct. For example, the government might regulate buying guns, so that buyers must at least ensure that the gun is not a machine gun if they wish to avoid criminal liability.[3] The power-directing decision rule, if it characterizes the statute as imposing strict liability, shifts the risk of reasonable, good-faith mistakes to the buyer. Were it public, the decision rule could change the nature of citizen conduct. People would be less likely to buy the sorts of guns that could be secretly converted into machine guns, or might avoid buying guns altogether, rather than run the risk of illegal conduct.

Perhaps more central for publicizing power-directing decision rules are those cases concerned with sentencing. The sentencing guidelines, for example, are precisely concerned with removing judicial discretion while authorizing the judge to determine the consequences of engaging in illegal conduct. Without knowing what the sentences are, however, the public cannot know how seriously a society takes violations of the various rules. In particular, three strikes laws render otherwise minor crimes subject to extremely lengthy sentences. Yet these appear to be the very sorts of power-directing decision rules that Dan-Cohen thinks need not be communicated to the general public.

Contrary to what Dan-Cohen suggests, these power-directing decision rules should be no less public than conduct rules. They should be public because citizens need to know the rules that guide the behavior of the officials who govern them. After all, power-controlling decision rules are nothing but conduct rules for officials. Citizens need to know how those who govern, govern themselves.

---

3. See *Staples v. United States*, 511 U.S. 600, 628–32 (1994) (Stevens, J., dissenting).

A LIBERAL CRIMINAL LAW CANNOT BE REDUCED TO THESE TWO TYPES OF RULES

MALCOLM THORBURN*

Meir Dan-Cohen's core text raises both conceptual and normative issues. Its central conceptual claim is that the criminal law in the English-speaking world is best understood as divided into two sets of rules. For any given rule, a proper understanding of its place within the policies and values underlying the legal system will tell us that it is either a rule addressed to citizens to help them guide

---

* Assistant Professor, Faculty of Law, Queen's University, Kingston, Canada.

their conduct or a rule addressed to officials to help them decide how to exercise their power over citizens. He considers a number of examples to illustrate this claim.

Dan-Cohen's central normative claim is that some methods of "selective transmission" (making rules available only to officials but not to ordinary citizens) are acceptable despite an apparent conflict with rule-of-law requirements that the law be knowable to those who are subject to it. This is because (a) official discretion can be curbed by effective decision rules even if they are unknown to the citizenry at large; (b) citizens need only be aware of conduct rules in order to guide their conduct appropriately; and (c) although the predictability of law is undermined somewhat by this strategy of "selective transmission," this is usually a price worth paying to maximize the effectiveness of law with a minimum use of coercive measures such as punishment.

I believe that both of these claims are mistaken. As for the conceptual claim, what are we to make of the justification of arrest with a warrant? It appears that there is a decision rule instructing the justice of the peace on how to decide whether or not to grant a warrant. Once issued, the warrant then provides a conduct rule that instructs the police officer how he may behave. So is "arrest with a warrant" a conduct rule or a decision rule? It seems that it is, instead, a conduct rule that issues from the exercise of a decision rule. But how are we to categorize that? (In case Dan-Cohen is tempted to dismiss such an example as unusual, one need only point out that most of administrative law operates in this way: ex ante official decisions reached in pursuance of a set of decision rules result in new conduct rules.)

Dan-Cohen's normative claim is not mistaken so much as a reflection of an unattractive account of criminal law more generally. He suggests that the criminal law is a set of directives from lawmakers to those who must obey them (whether citizens or officials). But most contemporary liberal accounts of political legitimacy would insist that the law ought to be conceived of as a mode of self-government, a set of norms that the citizenry give themselves to govern their relations with one another. According to this view, it is incorrect to suggest that (say) the defense of duress is a rule that should be hidden from the view of the citizenry. Although it is true that citizens ought to try to avoid wrongdoing as such and not merely to avoid punishment for wrongdoing, it is not the job of lawmakers to ensure that this takes place by misleading citizens as to the content of the law. A citizen who happens to be aware of the law ought not to be denied the benefit of the law. The point is rather that the normative consideration underpinning duress is one about the appropriateness of punishment (which is the province of officials to decide) rather than about wrongdoing (which is what should be the primary concern of citizens).

REPLY

MEIR DAN-COHEN

The comments naturally reveal some disagreements, and my own inclination is to side with the critics as much as with my younger self. The rules of the game require, however, that I show some loyalty to the author of the now some twenty-year-old piece on which the core text is based,[1] and at least try to clarify, if not always fully defend, what he had to say.

Kyron Huigens does not question the separation between conduct rules and decision rules, but doubts that my example of duress actually illustrates it: "Dan-Cohen says that duress ordinarily will be strictly construed as a conduct rule and more leniently construed as a decision rule. . . . The problem is that duress, conceptually, is never a conduct rule."[2] I agree, and say as much myself: In a world of acoustic separation, "the concerns of the advocates of the defense would lead to its adoption only as a decision rule. . . . Since the defense is not designed to guide conduct, no comparable rule need be included among the conduct rules of the system."[3] Although this misunderstanding is easy to correct, it may be worthwhile to identify its likely source: an impression that acoustic separation in regard to any given rule requires two different versions of that rule, one being the conduct rule and the other the decision rule. But acoustic separation is not limited to such pair-wise comparisons of individual rules; it concerns instead the possible disparity between the two *sets* of rules. Such disparity exists when one of the two sets contains a provision that has no counterpart in the other set.

Whereas Huigens disputes one of my examples, Samuel Buell presents an intriguing example of his own. The law of fraud, he maintains, poses a challenge to the acoustic separation model. I find Buell's comment to be an instructive illustration of some of the model's complexities rather than a challenge to it. As depicted by Buell, the law of fraud displays a disparity between a broadly formulated conduct rule that predicates liability on the "intent to defraud," and a narrower decision rule, predicating liability on the more demanding standard of "consciousness of wrongdoing." Buell's main worry is that the conduct rule "is meaningless as a notice rule,"[4] supposedly because it applies to commercial practices that are quite common despite their shadiness. But the law of fraud may actually exhibit a disjunction between two aspects of legal control that we

---

1. Meir Dan-Cohen, *Decision Rules and Conduct Rules: On Acoustic Separation in Criminal Law,* 97 Harv. L. Rev. 625 (1984), *reprinted in* Meir Dan-Cohen, Harmful Thoughts: Essays on Law, Self, and Morality 37 (2002). (All page references to this article are to this book).

2. Huigens comment at 12.

3. Dan-Cohen core text at 5.

4. Buell comment at 15.

ordinarily collapse together: normativity and coerciveness.[5] Within the ethically grey area of commercial transactions, the conduct rule requires people to adopt a broad interpretation of the applicable moral constraints and curb any "intent to defraud," whereas the decision rule imposes punishment on the basis of a more restrictive interpretation of those constraints. At least some people will likely believe (correctly, according to my interpretation) that the law tracks their own moral qualms and prohibits shady dealings, though the "chilling effect" that this belief may have on behavior will be due in part to the misconception that coerciveness is coextensive with normativity and that each of these forbidden actions will perforce be punished.

As Buell observes, the law is less likely to have this chilling effect on professional crooks, for whom the narrowly formulated decision rule may create an undesirable "conduct rule" (or rather have an unintended *side effect*, in my terminology), inducing them to carefully erase all "badges of fraud." However, this does not "unsettle" my thesis. Having legally sophisticated offenders is one type of breach in acoustic separation. My aim in this regard is only to draw attention to the relevance of variations in legal sophistication, and other differences in acoustic separation, to the formulation of legal rules.

Anne Coughlin's main observation, highlighting the victims' perspective, is for the most part a welcome expansion of focus. I have some doubts, though, regarding Coughlin's specific concerns. She complains that when decision rules are more lenient than conduct rules, victims will be cheated of two valuable expectations that the more broadly framed conduct rule may have created: that the law would "protect them from offenders" and that it would "take vengeance for them."[6]

As for the first, criminal law does not in general protect the actual victims of a crime; it's too late for that. The protection is against future criminality. And my examples of possible gains associated with acoustic separation stipulate a situation in which a fixed level of crime control can be attained with a lower level of coercion. Other things being equal, that a particular arrangement allows us to attain the same goal at a lesser cost in human suffering counts in favor of the arrangement. However, other things are seldom equal, countervailing considerations bear, and these may often, perhaps always, council on balance against selective transmission. The victims' second frustrated expectation mentioned by Coughlin, regarding vengeance, might be one such countervailing consideration. I should confess that I myself don't find this particular consideration all that appealing, but this is not a disagreement that bears on the merits of the acoustic separation model.

---

5. For an elaboration of this distinction and some of its implications, *see* Meir Dan-Cohen, *In Defense of Defiance*, 23 PHIL. & PUB. AFF. 24 (1994), *reprinted in* Dan-Cohen, HARMFUL THOUGHTS, *supra* note 1, at 94.

6. Coughlin comment at 16.

Luís Duarte d'Almeida objects to my claim that decision rules and conduct rules are conceptually independent, since "the antecedent of a criminal decision rule necessarily includes the infringement (and therefore the existence) of *a* conduct rule."[7] Duarte d'Almeida supports his objection by H.L.A. Hart's claim that "criminal decision rules always presuppose 'an offence or breach of duty' and, thus, *the* corresponding conduct rule."[8] Note, however, the slide between the italicized indefinite and definite articles in the two quoted statements. Whereas Duarte d'Almeida's objection requires the latter, Hart's claim at most supports the former, and is therefore consistent with the predicate criminal conduct varying as between the two types of rules. This seems to me to provide as much conceptual independence between the two sets of rules as this part of the model (i.e., regarding the definition of offenses) seeks to assert. Duarte d'Almeida treats as a separate thesis this denial that decision rules are necessarily coextensive with the corresponding conduct rules, and seems to hold that it is obvious rather than false. I can live with that, and for the sake of brevity, will.

Adil Haque's comment draws insightful and imaginative connections between the present paper and other essays of mine. This breadth of vision, gratifying though it is, puts me on the spot: I am expected to be consistent throughout! Haque points out that in *Responsibility and the Boundaries of the Self* I claim "that principles of inculpation and exculpation shape the contours of personal identity,"[9] and he comments that whereas "[t]he preventative goals discussed in *Decision Rules and Conduct Rules* may be served by shielding the public from information regarding liability conditions, . . . the constitutive goals of *Responsibility and the Boundaries of the Self* require full disclosure."[10]

As I see it, the issue Haque raises is not an inconsistency between my two articles, but rather a tension within law itself between what he aptly labels *preventative* and *constitutive* concerns. Indeed, the last section of *Responsibility and the Boundaries of the Self* is devoted to this tension. I argue there, inter alia, that although "[t]he law is expected to reinforce people's sense of responsibility,"[11] it may in fact weaken it. For example, "aware of the severity of its coercive measures, the law is frequently reluctant to impose liability even when nonlegal responsibility obtains."[12] This tension in turn reflects a deeper one that permeates the law, and to which I have already alluded, between law's coerciveness and its normativity. These two aspects of law do indeed bear differently, sometimes in contradictory manner, on law's constitutive role in the construction of selves.

---

7. Duarte d'Almeida comment at 17 (emphasis added).

8. *Id.* (emphasis added).

9. Haque comment at 19.

10. *Id.*

11. Meir Dan-Cohen, *Responsibility and the Boundaries of the Self, in* Dan-Cohen, *supra* note 1, at 235.

12. *Id.* at 236.

Eric Miller lists some considerations in light of which decision rules will better serve their purposes when known to the general public. There is not enough room for me here to engage such substantive matters, but my general response is that in terms of the acoustic separation model, Miller puts the cart before the horse. If his considerations are sound, then the putative decision rules he discusses ought to be reclassified as being conduct rules as well. The model is an analytical tool designed to help clarify these kinds of matters. One particular consideration mentioned by Miller is, however, puzzling. Focusing on "excuse-based decision rules," he worries that addressing these rules exclusively to the judge deprives defendants of the opportunity "to explain the significance of their conduct."[13] I don't quite see why. Rather, the decision rules that guide the proceedings at this stage will likely instruct the judge to take full account of the defendant's own explanations.

Observing that "citizens need to know how those who govern, govern themselves,"[14] Miller's final objection is an appeal to democratic values. This is also a central theme of Malcolm Thorburn's comment. In responding to this vital concern, let me first set the record straight. When Thorburn reports that "Dan-Cohen's central normative claim is that some methods of 'selective transmission'. . . are acceptable despite an apparent conflict with rule of law requirements that the law be knowable to those who are subject to it,"[15] he has my position exactly backwards. On the one hand, my conclusion is that "the options opened up by acoustic separation are not ruled out by the rule of law ideal."[16] On the other, I insist that compatibility with the rule of law "falls far short of justifying [selective transmission]," that "the option of selective transmission is not an attractive one,"[17] and that "the question of [its] legitimacy. . . is ultimately a matter of substantive moral judgment that the analysis presented here can help clarify but cannot resolve."[18]

If my paper has a polemic edge, it is not the advocacy of selective transmission. Its target is rather a certain facile, rosy, and I think on the whole naïve picture of both law and politics that animates much writing in these areas. The point comes up quite clearly when Thorburn juxtaposes my "unattractive account of criminal law [as] . . . a set of directives from law-makers to those who must obey them (whether citizens or officials)" with "most contemporary liberal accounts of political legitimacy [which] would insist that the law ought to be

13. Miller comment at 21.
14. *Id.* at 22.
15. Thorburn comment at 23.
16. Dan-Cohen, *supra* note 1, at 73.
17. *Id.*
18. *Id.* at 76.

conceived of as a mode of self-government, a set of norms that the citizenry give themselves to govern their relations with one another."[19]

The contrast is well drawn. An avowed goal of the acoustic separation model is indeed to remind us that "even under the best of circumstances, in the freest of democracies, and under the most enlightened of legal systems we are still being ruled."[20] This reminder has two kinds of relevant aims. First, to deny as mostly wishful thinking the picture of self-government as simply a matter of "a set of norms that the citizenry give themselves." Popular oversight of the intricacies and technicalities of a modern legal system is a mirage. Democratic rule-making and oversight must take a mediated, institutional form. But this state of affairs is not only compatible with acoustic separation but is indeed one of its sources.

Second, to be ruled also means to be subject to various forms of violence and brutality. The distribution of these aspects of governance is, however, uneven. The likely participants in this conversation are not often directly subject to the law's coercion, and so can get easily inured to it. On the other hand, as researchers and scholars we have a particularly strong disposition toward such values as candor and openness. Revealing possible tradeoffs between law's openness and its coerciveness was in part an attempt to use these better honed sensibilities as leverage for inducing a keener appreciation of law's ugly underbelly and darker side, aspects more starkly and indeed painfully apparent to others than to ourselves.

Consequently, acoustic separation is not so much an "unattractive account of criminal law," as it is, by design, an account of criminal law *as unattractive*, or at any rate as less attractive than many seem to envisage. Thorburn's (and others') response confirms the worry I express at the conclusion of *Decision Rules and Conduct Rules* that "the response to the concept of selective transmission is liable . . . to be such as sometimes befalls the bearer of bad tidings. Our irritation with the messenger may be in part a disguised expression of our unhappiness with the message."[21]

---

19. Thorburn comment at 23.
20. Dan-Cohen, *supra* note 1, at 76.
21. *Id.*

2. EMPIRICAL DESERT

PAUL H. ROBINSON*

It has long been assumed that the goals of doing justice and fighting crime necessarily conflict. Retributivists and utilitarian crime-control advocates commonly see their dispute as irreconcilable, and in a sense it is. It is argued here, however, that in another sense these two fundamental aims of criminal justice may not conflict. Doing justice may be the most effective means of fighting crime.

The hitch is that it is not moral philosophy's deontological notion of justice that has crime-control power but rather the community's notion of justice, what has been called "empirical desert." This turns out to be both good and bad for constructing a distributive principle for criminal liability and punishment. On the one hand, unlike moral philosophy's deontological desert, empirical desert can be readily operationalized—its rules and principles can be authoritatively determined through social science research into peoples' shared intuitions of justice. On the other hand, people's shared intuitions about justice are not justice in a transcendent sense. People's shared intuitions can be wrong. In the end, however, the retributivist may find that an instrumentalist distributive principle of empirical desert will produce far more deontological desert than any other workable principle that could or would be adopted.

I. THE UTILITY OF DESERT

The crime-control benefits from distributing punishment according to people's shared intuitions of justice arise from a variety of sources.[1] Deviating from a community's intuitions of justice can inspire resistance and subversion among participants—juries, judges, prosecutors, and offenders—where effective

* Colin S. Diver Professor of Law, University of Pennsylvania. This essay is drawn in large part from Paul H. Robinson, DISTRIBUTIVE PRINCIPLES OF CRIMINAL LAW: WHO SHOULD BE PUNISHED HOW MUCH? chs. 7, 8, and 12 (2008); Paul H. Robinson, *Competing Conceptions of Modern Desert: Vengeful, Deontological, and Empirical*, 67 CAMB. L. J. 145–75 (2008); Paul H. Robinson and John M. Darley, *Intuitions of Justice: Implications for Criminal Law and Justice Policy*, 81 S. CAL. L. REV. 1–67 (2007) [hereinafter Robinson and Darley, *Implications*]; Paul H. Robinson, *Why Does the Criminal Law Care What the Lay Person Thinks Is Just? Coercive vs. Normative Crime Control*, 86 VA. L. REV. 1839–69 (2000); and Paul H. Robinson and John M. Darley, *The Utility of Desert*, 91 Nw. U. L. REV. 453–99 (1997).

1. For authorities relating to the claims within this section, *see* Robinson and Darley, *Implications*, *supra* note *, at 18–31.

criminal justice depends upon acquiescence and cooperation. Relatedly, some of the system's power to control conduct derives from its potential to stigmatize violators. With some persons this is a more powerful, yet essentially cost-free mechanism, than the system's official sanction. But the system's ability to stigmatize depends upon its having moral credibility with the community. For a violation to trigger stigmatization, the law must have earned a reputation for accurately assessing what violations do and do not deserve condemnation. Liability and punishment rules that deviate from a community's shared intuitions of justice undermine that reputation.

A system's intentional and regular deviations from desert also undermine efficient crime control by limiting the law's access to one of the most powerful forces for gaining compliance: social influence and internalized norms. The greatest power to gain compliance with society's rules of proscribed conduct may lie not in the threat of official criminal sanction but rather in the influence of the intertwined forces of social and individual moral control. These forces consist of the networks of interpersonal relationships in which people find themselves, the social norms and prohibitions shared among those relationships and transmitted through those social networks, and the internalization by individuals of those norms and moral precepts.

The law is not irrelevant to these social and personal forces. Criminal law, in particular, plays a central role in creating and maintaining the social consensus necessary for sustaining moral norms. In fact, in a society as diverse as ours, the criminal law may be the only society-wide mechanism that transcends cultural and ethnic differences. Thus, the criminal law's most important real-world effect may be its ability to assist in the building, shaping, and maintaining of these norms and moral principles. However, a criminal justice system that intentionally and regularly does injustice and fails to do justice diminishes its moral credibility with the community and thereby its ability to influence conduct by shaping these powerful norms.

The criminal law also can have effect in gaining compliance with its commands through another mechanism. If it earns a reputation as a reliable statement of what the community perceives as condemnable, people are more likely to defer to its commands as morally authoritative in those borderline cases in which the propriety of certain conduct is unsettled or ambiguous in the mind of the actor. The importance of this role should not be underestimated. In a society with the complex interdependencies characteristic of ours, an apparently harmless action can have destructive consequences. When the action is criminalized by the legal system, one would want the citizen to "respect the law" in such an instance even though he or she does not immediately understand why that action is banned. Such deference will be facilitated if citizens are disposed to believe that the law is an accurate guide to appropriate prudential and moral behavior.

The extent of the criminal law's effectiveness in all these respects—in avoiding resistance to and subversion of an unjust system, in avoiding vigilantism sparked by a system that fails to do justice, in bringing the power of stigmatization to bear, in facilitating, communicating, and maintaining societal consensus on what is and is not condemnable, and in gaining compliance in borderline cases through deference to its moral authority—depends to a great extent on the degree to which the criminal law has earned moral credibility with the citizens governed by it. Thus, the criminal law's moral credibility is essential to effective crime control, and is enhanced if the distribution of criminal liability is perceived as "doing justice," that is, if it assigns liability and punishment in ways that the community perceives as consistent with its shared intuitions of justice, "empirical desert." Conversely, the system's moral credibility, and therefore its crime control effectiveness, is undermined by a distribution of liability that deviates from the community's perceptions of just desert.[2]

II. CRITICISMS OF EMPIRICAL DESERT AS A DISTRIBUTIVE PRINCIPLE

A variety of criticisms have been offered against the suggestion that the most effective crime control approach may be found in distributing criminal liability and punishment according to principles that mirror the community's shared intuitions of justice, "empirical desert."[3]

A. Notions of Desert as Hopelessly Vague

A common objection to empirical desert as a distributive principle is its supposed vagueness. Some writers may be willing to concede that desert is not a hopelessly vague concept, that it has some meaning, but would make a related but slightly different criticism: Desert cannot specify a *particular amount* of punishment that *should* be imposed; it can only identify a *range* of punishments that *should not* be imposed because such punishment would be seriously disproportionate.

These complaints are based in part on a failure to appreciate the specific demands of desert and of people's intuitions about it. The confusion arises in part from the failure to distinguish two distinct judgments: setting the endpoint of the punishment continuum and, once that endpoint has been set, ordinally ranking cases along that continuum. Every society must decide what punishment it will allow for its most egregious case, be it the death penalty or life imprisonment or fifteen years. Once that endpoint is set, the distributive challenge that desert must guide is to determine who should be punished and

---

2. The relevant "community" is that to be governed by the contemplated liability rule. In the United States, where the governing criminal laws are contained primarily in state criminal codes, the relevant community for determining a code's rule will be the residents of the state.

3. For authorities relating to the claims within this section, *see* Robinson and Darley, *Implications, supra* note *, at 31–45.

how much. That process requires only an ordinal ranking of offenders according to their relative blameworthiness. The result is a specific amount of punishment for a particular offense, but that amount of punishment is not the product of some magical connection between that violator's offense and the corresponding amount of punishment. Rather, it is the specific amount of punishment needed to *set the offender's violation at its appropriate ordinal rank* according to blameworthiness, relative to all other offenses. If the endpoint were changed, the appropriate punishment for each offender would change accordingly.

Those who complain that empirical desert is vague seem incorrectly to assume that it must provide a universal, absolute amount of punishment as deserved for a given offense no matter the time or jurisdiction. Instead, the content of empirical desert is to ensure that offenders of different blameworthiness are given different amounts of punishment, each to receive an amount that reflects his blameworthiness relative to that of others. Uncertainty about deserved punishment arises not from vagueness in the ordinal ranking of offenses according to offender blameworthiness but rather from differences in the endpoint that different societies adopt or that different people would want their society to adopt. Once that endpoint is set, the *distribution* of punishment to offenders according to empirical desert suffers no vagueness problem.

But this does not fully settle the vagueness complaints. Some writers argue that even ordinal ranking is something that can be done only in the vaguest terms; establishing specific rankings is impossible. The claim is that ranking offenses according to blameworthiness is beyond the ability of people's intuitions of justice. People can roughly distinguish between "serious" and "not serious" cases but cannot provide the nuance needed to do more.

The claim is empirical and empirically it is false. The evidence from a wide variety of studies is quite clear: Subjects display a good deal of nuance in their judgments of blameworthiness. Small changes in facts produce large and predictable changes in punishment.[4] The empirical evidence suggests that people take account of a wide variety of factors and often give them quite different effect in different situations. Alexis Durham offers this summary: "Virtually without exception, citizens seem able to assign highly specific sentences for highly specific events."[5] People's intuitions of justice are not vague or simplistic, but rather sophisticated and complex.

B. Hopeless Disagreement as to Notions of Desert

Another common objection to using empirical desert as a distributive principle is that, even if individuals may have a clear and specific notion of what desert

---

4. *See,* for example, the impressive nuance repeatedly shown by subjects in the eighteen studies reported in Paul H. Robinson and John M. Darley, JUSTICE, LIABILITY, AND BLAME: COMMUNITY VIEWS AND THE CRIMINAL LAW (1995).

5. Alexis M. Durham III, *Public Opinion Regarding Sentences for Crime: Does it Exist?*, 21 J. CRIM. JUST. 1, 2 (1993).

demands, people disagree among themselves. Again, this common wisdom simply does not match the empirical reality. The studies show broadly shared intuitions that serious wrongdoing should be punished and broadly shared intuitions about the relative blameworthiness of different cases.

One recent study illustrates the striking extent of the agreement.[6] Subjects were asked to rank order twenty-four crime scenario descriptions according to the amount of punishment deserved. Despite the complex and subjective nature of the judgments, the researchers found that the subjects had little difficulty performing the task and displayed an astounding level of agreement in their ordinal ranking. A statistical measure of concordance is found in Kendall's W coefficient of concordance, in which 1.0 indicates perfect agreement and 0.0 indicates no agreement. In the study, the Kendall's W was .95 (with p <.001), an astounding result. (One might expect to get a Kendall's W of this magnitude if subjects were asked to judge an easy and objective task, such as judging the relative brightness of different groupings of spots. When asked to perform more subjective or complex comparisons, such as asking travel magazine readers to rank eight different travel destinations according to their level of safety, one gets a Kendall's W of .52. When asking economists to rank the top twenty economics journals according to quality, one gets a Kendall's W of .095.) Even more compelling, the astounding level of agreement cuts across all demographics. People from very different backgrounds, situations, and perspectives all agreed upon the relative blameworthiness of the twenty-four offenders. Similar conclusions are found in cross-cultural studies.[7] The level of agreement is strongest for those core wrongs with which criminal law primarily concerns itself—physical aggression, taking property, and deception in exchanges—and becomes less pronounced as the nature of the offense moves further from the core of wrongdoing. However, the data overwhelmingly refutes the common perception that there is never agreement as to intuitions of justice.

Disagreements among people's intuitions of justice do exist. People obviously disagree about many things relating to crime and punishment, as the endless public debates make clear. But some appearances of disagreement are simply misleading. Poor testing methods will predictably underestimate the extent of agreement. When a test scenario is written ambiguously so that different test

---

6. *See* Paul H. Robinson and Robert Kurzban, *Concordance & Conflict in Intuitions of Justice*, 91 MINN. L. REV. 1829–1907 (2007).

7. *See* Graeme Newman, COMPARATIVE DEVIANCE: PERCEPTION AND LAW IN SIX CULTURES 141–43 (1976); Julian V. Roberts and Loretta J. Stalans, *Crime, Criminal Justice, and Public Opinion, in* THE HANDBOOK ON CRIME & PUNISHMENT 42–43 (Michael H. Tonry ed., 1998) ("[T]here is a significant degree of agreement across countries in terms of the relative seriousness of crimes. Many studies have replicated the relative ranking of crimes across a number of countries, including Canada, Denmark, Finland, Great Britain, Holland, Kuwait, Norway, Puerto Rico, and the United States.").

participants perceive the facts differently, the existence of shared nuanced intuitions of justice itself will predict different judgments among the participants. So, too, when a case in the headlines has social or political implications, its relevant facts commonly will be perceived differently by different people. What one makes of the police testimony in the O.J. Simpson case or the Rodney King case may depend upon how one has come to view police officers from one's daily life experiences. If people draw different conclusions from the testimony, they are likely to have different views of the relevant facts, which predictably results in different views on the liability and punishment deserved.

One may wonder how the extent of agreement among people about intuitions of justice, sometimes at astonishing high levels, could have been missed for so many years. How could the common wisdom have gotten it so wrong? Part of the answer is the above-mentioned failure to distinguish between issues of absolute severity and ordinal ranking. Disagreement about the proper endpoint for the punishment continuum tends to obscure the existing agreement on the ranking of offenses along that continuum. Also as noted, our frequent disagreement with others about cases in the news creates a false impression that we disagree about principles of justice when in fact we only disagree about the case facts.

Because some disagreement does exist, especially as the issue moves out from the core of criminality, it is inevitable that any rule the criminal law adopts will deviate from some people's views. In these situations, advancing the law's crime-control effectiveness means adopting the rule that will least undermine its moral credibility. That commonly will mean adopting the rule that reflects the majority view, but not always. If advancing the criminal law's overall moral credibility with the community is the goal, one would want to take account of the strength of feeling of each of the opposing views.

One might wonder why core intuitions of justice are so widely shared. Whether due to some evolutionarily developed mechanism or to shared social learning, or some combination of the two,[8] it is clear that the source of these intuitions is beyond even the powerful influences of culture or demographics. Because one does not see such differences with respect to core intuitions, it follows that they must be somehow fixed, and therefore will be resistant to attempts by social engineers to manipulate them, at least using the kinds of intrusions on personal autonomy that a liberal democracy would permit. The point here is not to say that our existing intuitions are good or bad. Rather, they are the reality of what it means to be human, and effective social engineers must deal with the world as it exists, not as they wish it was.

---

8. *See* Paul H. Robinson, Robert Kurzban, and Owen Jones, *The Origins of Shared Intuitions of Justice*, 60 Vand. L. Rev. 1633–88 (2007).

C. People's Natural Judgments about Punishment Are Based on Deterrence or Incapacitation, Not Desert

Another criticism leveled against using empirical desert as the basis for distributing criminal liability and punishment is that people's punishment judgments are not really based on desert but rather on factors relating to effective deterrence or incapacitation. That is, when people ostensibly decide what punishment an offender should get, they are really deciding how much punishment is needed to deter or incapacitate. Again, however, the view does not match the available data. Studies examining the criteria on which people rely when making punishment judgments have found it to be desert, justice; people's punishment judgments typically ignore deterrence or incapacitation concerns.

For example, one such study exploring whether desert or incapacitation was the driving force gave participants ten short descriptions of criminal cases, which were generated by combining five levels of case seriousness (theft of a CD, theft of a valuable object, assault, homicide, and assassination) with two levels of criminal history (no prior history or history of actions consistent with the crime committed). Participants were asked to assign a proper punishment to each case without any indication as to what that decision should be based upon, using a 7-point scale of punishment severity and a 13-point scale of criminal liability grades. Participants were thereafter asked to reconsider the scenarios and assign punishments from a just deserts perspective and from an incapacitation perspective.

Punishment assignments based on just deserts were closely aligned with the original intuitive decisions, while punishments assigned using the incapacitation model were not. "What this suggests is that the default perspective of sentencing is indistinguishable from the just deserts perspective, but that both [default and explicit desert] are significantly different from the incapacitation perspective."[9] Other studies, which also pitted justice against deterrence, reinforce this conclusion. People's intuitive default for assigning criminal liability and punishment is just deserts. While participants explicitly endorse deterrence justifications for punishment, they actually meted out sentences "from a strictly deservingness-based stance."[10]

D. Empirical Desert as Inevitably Draconian

Some resistance to relying on empirical desert as a basis to distribute liability and punishment comes not from a challenge to its empirical foundation but rather to its expected results. The line of reasoning goes something like this: (1) I don't like

---

9. John M. Darley, Kevin M. Carlsmith, and Paul H. Robinson, *Incapacitation and Just Deserts as Motives for Punishment*, 24 L. & HUM. BEHAV. 659, 667 (2000).

10. Kevin M. Carlsmith, John M. Darley, and Paul H. Robinson, *Why Do We Punish? Deterrence and Just Deserts as Motives for Punishment*, 83 J. PERSONALITY & SOC. PSYCHOL. 284, 295 (2002).

many of the modern crime control reforms—such as three strikes statutes, lowering the age of prosecution as an adult, strict liability, high penalties for drug offenses, and criminalizing what had previously been regulatory offenses. (2) These reforms are the product of recent democratic legislative action that reflects the community's views. (3) Therefore, giving explicit deference to empirical desert will only increase the influence of the public's apparent preference for such draconian measures.

Such reasoning both misconceives the nature of empirical desert and mistakenly assumes that modern American crime politics produces results that track people's intuitions of justice. In fact, empirical desert has little to do with, and indeed dramatically conflicts with, the modern crime control programs like those listed.

There is a substantial difference between the principles that people intuitively use in assessing relative blameworthiness and the political crime-control programs that their politicians support. The former can be reliably determined only through social science research that manipulates case scenarios and sees what effects the manipulations have on people's liability assessments. The researchers do not even ask subjects what rules they prefer but rather construct for themselves the liability rules that they see the subjects in fact using as they intuitively assess blameworthiness. The latter, political action on crime legislation, is a product of the standard distortions of the political process generally and the special distortions of American crime politics in particular. Media hype and misleading polling produce a fear of crime that politicians take to require harsher crime legislation on pain of political death. The results have little connection with the community's shared intuitions of justice. Indeed, the available data suggests that the noted reforms, rather than tracking people's shared intuitions of justice, seriously conflict with them.[11]

What the above arguments for the utility of desert suggest is that the criminal law's long-term crime-control effectiveness will be hurt by these kinds of modern reforms than conflict with the community's intuitions of justice. Although people may be happy to see their politicians "get tough on crime," it will nonetheless happen over time that, as the deviations from people's intuitions of justice accumulate, people will come to see criminal conviction and punishment as lacking in moral authority and that will weaken the law's ability to harness the power of social influence and the other mechanisms by which the law's moral credibility can promote compliance.

---

11. *See, e.g.*, Robinson and Darley, *supra* note 4, at 139–47 (Study 13), 189–97 (Study 18); Paul H. Robinson and Geoff Goodwin, *The Disutility of Injustice* (forthcoming 2009) (reporting results of empirical studies testing people's intuitions of justice on cases under modern crime-control programs).

E. Empirical Desert as Potentially Immoral

While empirical desert has an easy answer to most of the criticisms noted above, it is vulnerable to one important criticism: it is potentially unjust. While a community may collectively believe that certain conduct is moral or certain punishment is just, those beliefs may be false. Witness the case of slave holders in the pre–Civil War South. Empirical desert can only tell us what people think is just. It cannot tell us what actually is just. In other words, it cannot tell us what an actor "deontologically deserves."

Of course, the potentially immoral objection applies to the use of *any* instrumentalist crime-control principle for the distribution of liability and punishment, and among such principles, empirical desert may be the least objectionable, for it may best approximate a distribution according to true moral blameworthiness. Nonetheless, empirical desert is conceptually and practically distinct from deontological desert, and as such can fairly be criticized when it deviates from deontological desert. In order to avoid doing deontological injustice, a system must be prepared to look beyond empirical desert. It must turn from social science to moral philosophy.

Unfortunately, a look at the methodology of modern moral philosophy suggests that it commonly relies upon philosophers' shared intuitions of justice. A standard analytic form among many moral philosophers today, if not the standard form, is to test variations in a series of hypotheticals according to the philosophers' own intuitions about the proper resolution of each, as in John Rawls's "reflective equilibrium."[12] The differences in their judgments about the intuitively proper resolution of different hypotheticals are used as "data points" from which to derive a moral principle, which can in turn be tested and refined against philosophers' intuitions in new sets of hypotheticals.

As the basis for empirical desert, this is bad science. Social scientists would cringe at the host of methodological problems in reliably assessing intuitions of justice. As a basis for determining the transcendent truth of justice, the practice is equally bad. It creates a bias in favor of moral principles that are consistent with philosophers' intuitions. Moral principles with principled, reasoned support might nonetheless fail to gain currency among philosophers or might be discarded, simply because philosophers as a group think their results inconsistent with their intuitions of justice—a practical veto by philosophers' shared intuitions.[13] Thus, much of current moral philosophy is particularly unreliable in performing the task that empirical desert most needs: an external check to spot instances in which peoples' shared intuitions of justice are unjust in a transcendent sense.

---

12. John Rawls, A Theory of Justice 48 (1971).

13. *See* Paul H. Robinson, *The Role of Moral Philosophers in the Competition Between Philosophical and Empirical Desert,* 48 Wm. & Mary L. Rev. 1831–43 (2007).

This weakness of modern philosophy makes empirical desert both more and less attractive as a distributive principle. On the one hand, insofar as it means that moral philosophy is unavailable to provide the needed transcendent check on intuitions of justice, empirical desert becomes less attractive as a distributive principle because its weakness cannot be easily corrected. On the other hand, insofar as it means that deontological desert, biased toward shared intuitions, provides little or no advantage over empirical desert, empirical desert becomes more attractive as a distributive principle because it at least has authoritative research methods to operationalize desert, which deontological desert does not.

III. CONCLUSION

Some criticisms of empirical desert as a distributive principle for liability and punishment are unfounded, but not all. Arguments that intuitions of justice are hopelessly vague or the subject of eviscerating disagreement either fail to appreciate the rank-order nature of desert judgments or simply make assumptions that are inconsistent with the empirical evidence. Similarly inconsistent with available empirical evidence is the claim that people's intuitions about justice are based on notions of deterrence or incapacitation or that they would lead to draconian legislation. On the other hand, it is a fair complaint that following empirical desert does not ensure true justice, in a transcendent sense. Still, given the practical problems with trying to construct a criminal justice system based upon deontological desert, empirical desert may be the closest that any distributive principle can come to doing true justice in the real world.

An important final point: It is not suggested here that a system ought to slavishly follow empirical desert no matter where it leads. There might be any number of reasons that justify a deviation from it.[14] A deviation rule might so clearly provide a crime-control bonanza that any crimogenic effect from undermining the system's moral credibility would be outweighed by the deviation's crime-control benefits. This may be a rare situation, but the good instrumentalist ought to always be open to it. A deviation also might be justified if the community's shared intuitions of justice are clearly unjust in the transcendent sense. How we would know this given the current state of moral philosophy is unclear, but the possibility ought not be ruled out. Finally, while doing justice and fighting crime are important, indeed fundamental goals of any organized society, they are not the only goals. A society might put high value on limiting governmental power over individuals, for example, which might logically produce liability

---

14. For a fuller account of justifiable deviations from empirical desert, see Robinson, DISTRIBUTIVE PRINICPLES, *supra* note *, at ch. 12.

rules, such as the legality principle, that would predictably cause failures of justice.

The larger point here is not that shared intuitions of justice must always be followed, but rather that, where they are not followed, there can be a cost to crime control effectiveness that ought to be taken into account. A system ought not distribute liability or punishment in ways inconsistent with empirical desert unless there is a clear justification for doing so. Empirical desert ought to be the distributive default; it ought not be ignored, as it commonly is today.

COMMENTS

THE FALSE PROMISE OF EMPIRICAL DESERT

MARY SIGLER*

Paul Robinson outlines a conception of empirical desert designed to reconcile the tension in criminal punishment between the goals of fighting crime and doing justice. He argues that empirical desert, based on people's shared intuitions of justice, is superior to rival conceptions both because it is susceptible of objective measurement and because it will be more effective at controlling crime. Thus, even "the retributivist may find that an instrumentalist distributive principle of empirical desert will produce far more deontological desert."[1]

Robinson's case for empirical desert is problematic in at least two respects. First, Robinson mischaracterizes the methodology of the leading alternative conception, deontological desert, and overlooks its significance in the development of shared intuitions. In addition, he conflates desert with one method of operationalizing it. Although empirical desert may have a role to play in assigning punishment, it should not be confused for desert itself.

Robinson recognizes that "people's shared intuitions about justice are not justice, in a transcendent sense."[2] Empirical desert thus contrasts with deontological desert, which calls for punishment in proportion to an offender's moral culpability. Conceptually indifferent to people's intuitions about justice, deontological desert purports to transcend the contingencies of mere intuition and provide an external check on desert judgments.

The problem with deontological desert, according to Robinson, is its flawed methodology. Whereas empirical desert may be determined through social science research into people's intuitions of justice, deontological desert relies on a more dubious data set. "A standard analytic form among many moral

---

* Professor of Law, Sandra Day O'Connor College of Law, Arizona State University.
1. Robinson core text at 29.
2. *Id.*

philosophers today . . . is to test variations in a series of hypotheticals according to the philosophers' own intuitions about the proper resolution of each. . . ."[3] Empirical desert is unabashedly empirical, but more legitimate, because it draws on the community's collective sense of justice.

This methodological critique misses the mark. Moral reasoning—particularly the process of trying to reconcile values and judgments—is not the special purview of moral philosophers. The allure of reflective equilibrium is that it does not require philosophical expertise, only a sincere desire to develop a reasonably coherent value system. By the same token, the aspiration of the moral philosopher is not to justify his personal value system but to apprehend the enduring values of his community and trace their implications across cases. The process involves gleaning the shared political morality embedded within our traditions and institutions and bringing these to bear in particular contexts. No respectable philosopher aims simply to justify his own values.

Moreover, Robinson's analysis is inattentive to the context in which desert judgments are made. We are all deontologists—*that* is our political morality. As a result, empirical desert is shot through with deontology; ignoring it does not diminish its significance. Although Robinson worries that deontological desert judgments may stray too far from our intuitions of justice, those intuitions are themselves informed by deontological commitments. By neglecting the deontological dimension, and taking intuitions as he finds them, Robinson discounts the possibility of principled debate in terms of our shared commitments.

Finally, Robinson collapses the distinction between desert and one method of measuring it. In his view, the process for determining how much punishment is deserved "requires only an ordinal ranking of offenders according to their relative blameworthiness."[4] However, relative proportionality is not the primary aim of desert judgments. To be sure, we have powerful intuitions that violent offenses should be punished more severely than minor property crimes. But this is a function of our sense that serious crimes merit serious penalties, not just that they merit relatively more punishment than lesser offenses. The desideratum of sentencing judgments is that offenders should be punished in proportion to their desert. The resulting ordinal ranking is a consequence, not a determinant, of that primary objective. As a practical matter, because we lack a reliable means of quantifying desert, we often rely on a second-best approach of relative proportionality. But this method for approximating desert should not be confused with desert itself; nor does it preclude judgments about the *absolute* (dis)proportionality of punishments.

Robinson's case for empirical desert depends on an unwarranted claim of methodological superiority: Because social science techniques make it possible

---

3. *Id.* at 37.
4. *Id.* at 32.

to determine people's shared intuitions of justice, they provide a workable method for determining desert. But as even Robinson seems to acknowledge, desert is a normative, not an empirical, concept. As a result, settling for empirical desert because we can readily ascertain it is a bit like searching for our lost wallet under a bright street lamp even though we dropped it in a dark alley. It would be a lot more convenient, but what we are truly seeking cannot be found there.

COMPLIANCE-PROMOTING INTUITIONS

ADAM J. KOLBER*

Empirical desert purports to capture our intuitions of justice. At most, however, it captures a subset of our justice-related intuitions. I will highlight a few ways in which empirical desert picks and chooses among our intuitions and why choosing pertinent intuitions can be a difficult task.

As Paul Robinson notes, when laypeople engage in acts of mock sentencing, their responses are better explained by a retributive conception of punishment than a consequentialist one. At the same time, laypeople explicitly endorse consequentialist goals when asked about the broad purposes of punishment. This means that laypeople have hybrid punishment intuitions. They are consequentialist in some respects and retributivist in others.

Nevertheless, when seeking to implement empirical desert, Robinson discounts laypeople's consequentialist intuitions almost entirely. He does so because he believes that intuitions elicited by mock sentencing are more useful for generating future compliance than are our more abstract intuitions about the broader goals of sentencing. In other words, Robinson seeks to capture not our intuitions of justice in general but rather the subset of our justice-related intuitions that can be used to promote empirical desert's consequentialist goals.

The selective nature of empirical desert is reflected in its basic methodology. Empirical desert seeks to capture our calmer, more thoughtful intuitions reflected in social science surveys rather than our more heated, spur-of-the-moment punishment intuitions. This seems like a reasonable approach, but the reasons for it are revealing. If Robinson believes that we must focus on our less biased, more deliberative intuitions because these intuitions are more likely to be just in some transcendent deontological sense, then he has departed from his otherwise purely consequentialist argument for empirical desert. If that were the case, we may as well delve deeper into the justification of the substance of lay intuitions.

---

* Associate Professor of Law, University of San Diego School of Law. This comment is adapted from the author's forthcoming symposium article in the *Brooklyn Law Review*.

More likely, Robinson discounts heated, spur-of-the-moment intuitions because he believes that a criminal justice system based on such intuitions will not maximally promote long-run compliance. But it is far from obvious which of our intuitions, when instantiated in the law, best promote compliance. Laypeople likely have the intuition that the attorney-client privilege should be violated in many instances but that intuition is just one of many factors we should consider when deciding the scope of the privilege. Thus, even after empirical-desert advocates identify a widely shared punishment intuition, they must still engage in traditional cost-benefit analysis to determine if the intuition can be used to promote compliance consistent with other consequentialist goals.

When an individual's intuitions of justice deviate from enacted law, empirical-desert advocates claim that the individual will be more likely to comply with the deviating law if he views the legal system as a whole as having appropriate moral authority. Yet, it is not clear if laypeople who understand empirical desert would find such a system to have appropriate moral authority. Empirical desert advocates could test this very issue by assessing lay intuitions about empirical desert itself. Do laypeople think that offenders deserve the punishments intuited by nonspecialists in social science surveys (i.e., empirical desert)? Or do laypeople believe that offenders should receive the punishments they deserve based on a more timeless conception of desert that is meant to square with considered, reflective judgment (i.e., deontological desert)? If lay intuitions better comport with the deontological approach, then laypeople may find unattractive a criminal justice system that is overtly based on empirical desert.

Once again, Robinson would likely say that such broad intuitions about the purposes of punishment are irrelevant to promoting compliance. But it is hard to make such determinations *a priori*. If people report finding a system of deontological desert more attractive than a system of empirical desert, and if such intuitions affects compliance, empirical desert advocates may find themselves in a bind. It could be that we would better promote compliance with a system of empirical desert by hiding its empirical desert features from the public.[1]

In summary, Robinson seeks to capture just the subset of our justice-related intuitions believed to promote compliance. Although empirical desert advocates have made significant strides in understanding our justice-related intuitions, they cannot automatically translate those intuitions into good public policy. Identifying widely-shared punishment intuitions is a difficult task but a

---

1. To some influential theorists, no successful moral theory can advocate its own secrecy. Such theorists defend a "publicity condition," which requires that a system of morality be based on principles that can be announced publicly without thereby undermining those same principles. *See, e.g.,* Immanuel Kant, PERPETUAL PEACE: A PHILOSOPHICAL ESSAY 185 (M. Campbell Smith trans., Swan Sonnenschein & Co. 1903) (1795); John Rawls, A THEORY OF JUSTICE 130, 133 (1971). *But see* Henry Sidgwick, THE METHODS OF ETHICS 489–90 (7th ed., Hackett 1966) (1893).

comparatively easy one relative to picking out intuitions that can usefully be exploited to promote compliance.

A FERTILE DESERT?

MICHAEL T. CAHILL*

I am largely sympathetic to Paul Robinson's defense of empirical desert; my limited concerns might be characterized as skeptical rather than critical. That is, I would probably not object strongly to a substantive criminal law whose rules tracked empirical desert—subject to side constraints, as I note below—but I am not convinced such a scheme would generate crime-control benefits as extensive as Robinson sometimes suggests. (I do agree, though, that it wouldn't do any *worse* than any other strategy, all things considered, and would probably be cheaper than many.) Like Robinson's account, my skepticism is empirical in nature and therefore is, at least potentially, subject to confirmation or refutation by further research. Robinson points to considerable evidence regarding the existence of widely shared moral norms—as he calls them, "intuitions of justice"—but important aspects of the relation between these shared norms and law-abiding behavior (the ultimate goal here) remain unexplored. As a result, empirical desert currently roams in an empirical desert. Unlike the Sahara, though, this desert may prove quite fertile.

Before offering four possible avenues of future inquiry, I'd note (with Robinson) that the most compelling normative objection to empirical desert is that majoritarian moral norms may generate rules that seem troubling from some nonmajoritarian yet compelling moral perspective. I share the concern, but keep in mind that it extends beyond the criminal law: many majoritarian laws, criminal or otherwise, might threaten deeply (and, in fact, widely) held normative commitments to other values such as equality or liberty (which might be seen as imposing deontological moral obligations). Such independent moral commitments can and should constrain the reach of a criminal law rooted in empirical desert, just as they would constrain the reach of *any* system of criminal law. Whether imposing deserved punishment is seen as an instrumental or intrinsic good, everyone agrees that it is not the only good, and therefore must sometimes give way to other considerations.

But that is not the same as saying that a deontological commitment to *desert itself* is needed to temper the mistakes or excesses of empirical desert. Thus an empirical-desert advocate might support reduced punishment for criminal attempts against objections rooted in a deontological account of desert, yet also oppose some prohibitions or punishments that might follow from empirical

---

* Associate Professor of Law, Brooklyn Law School.

desert—perhaps the death penalty, or a ban on sodomy—as violative of some constraining nondesert principle like liberty, autonomy, or human dignity.

Now the four possible areas for exploration, or tests of the potential of empirical-desert-based criminal law as a crime-control tool. First, though internalization of the relevant norms (including, perhaps, a generalized norm of the importance of obeying the law) is surely one determinant of compliance with law, to what extent is the substantive criminal law itself an especially important or effective means of promoting that norm internalization? Other institutions, whether public (schools) or private (churches), might be more significant factors than the criminal justice system in causing (or, where absent or weak, failing to cause) citizens to internalize the relevant norms.

Second, and related to the first point, although it seems almost obvious that compliance will be highest if criminal law prohibits what people already view as wrong, and permits what they don't, how much power does law have to influence or shape what people view as wrong: to *change*, not just reflect, their views about morally appropriate behavior? The extent of criminal law's power to do this—generally, or for some types of norms or rules more than others, or relative to other norm-shaping social or cultural influences—is a fundamentally important, yet largely uninvestigated, consideration in determining the law's role and potential as an instrument of behavior modification.

Third, more work must be done to explore the relation between substantive outcomes and procedural fairness in affecting public perceptions of the system's "justness" and, in turn, its moral authority.[1] Some fine-grained research is needed here, both because substance and process are interrelated and because their relative significance may vary for different rules, or situations, or groups of people.

Finally, norms, like politics, may be local. Different communities or subgroups within a population may have very different attitudes toward the criminal justice system—sometimes due, perhaps, to the criminal justice system's attitude (or perceived attitude) toward those groups. Specific substantive prohibitions (drug laws), punishments (mandatory minimums or three strikes laws), or enforcement practices (profiling) are experienced differently by different segments of the populace. The criminal justice system would do well to examine, or attend to, the ways in which its moral authority (and corresponding power to induce obedience) within specific groups is compromised, perhaps in part by its own doing.

---

1. *See* Paul H. Robinson and Michael T. Cahill, LAW WITHOUT JUSTICE 183–85 (2006).

THE NEW DESERT

ALICE RISTROPH*

The claim that wrongdoers should get their just deserts is hardly novel. But two distinctive discourses of desert have recently become prominent in the theory and practice of criminal sentencing. In one discourse, desert is advocated as a limiting principle that will reverse a long trend of increasingly severe sentences[1]. A second discourse invokes "empirical desert," promising that attention to social science research on desert judgments will lead to sentences that are more democratically legitimate, or more effective as crime control measures.[2]

But there are good reasons to avoid either version of desert rhetoric. First, desert claims have proven elastic: judgments of what is deserved change over time and with changes in sentencing policy, making desert poorly suited to serve as an independent check on policy choices. And although it is true that many people speak in terms of desert—it is a capacious concept that accommodates many different values—the concept also accommodates many factors that should have no role in sentencing decisions. Desert claims are opaque: they can disguise bias, fear, or other arbitrary factors on which they may be based. Desert is too easily invoked, too often biased, and too rarely scrutinized to be an attractive vehicle of sentencing reform.

A critical first question is: what does it means to deserve? Many proponents of desert-based sentencing have sought to free desert from the language of retribution and associated notions of retaliation and vengeance. But once desert is untethered from the retributive principle of an eye for an eye, what does it mean to say that someone deserves a particular punishment?

Not much—or rather, almost anything you like. As the term is used in ordinary language, the claim that *she deserves X* reveals little more than a belief that *she should get X*. The reasons that one might believe that *she should get X* are many, and sometimes contradictory, but most if not all of these reasons can be

---

* Associate Professor, Seton Hall University School of Law. Some of the arguments presented here first appeared in Alice Ristroph, *Desert, Democracy, and Sentencing Reform*, 96 J. CRIM. L. & CRIMINOLOGY 1293 (2006).

1. *See* Norval Morris, *Desert as a Limiting Principle*, in PRINCIPLED SENTENCING 201, 201–06 (Andrew von Hirsch and Andrew Ashworth eds., 1992).

2. Robinson defends empirical desert, but has expressed doubt that desert can serve as a limiting principle. *See, e.g.,* Paul H. Robinson, *The A.L.I. Proposed Distributive Principle of "Limiting Retributivism": Does It Mean Anything in Practice Other than Pure Desert?*, 7 BUFF. CRIM. L. REV. 3, 12 (2003). The American Law Institute endorses both desert as a limiting principle and empirical desert in its proposed revisions to the Model Penal Code's Sentencing Provisions.

captured by the term desert. Like democracy, justice,[3] or the rule of law, desert is an "essentially contested concept."[4] Desert requires external values to give it content.[5] If those external values change and produce revised sentencing policies—if we decide to emphasize incapacitation over rehabilitation, for example—the assessment of how much punishment is deserved is likely to change as well. Similarly, beliefs about desert can be deliberately manipulated with respect to specific offenses. It is widely recognized that date rape and drunk driving came to be viewed as more blameworthy, and thus deserving of more severe punishment, thanks to reform efforts that increased the penalties for these crimes. Notably, empirical research purporting to demonstrate the stability of desert judgments relies on cross-sectional studies (measures of desert assessments in different persons at the same time) rather than longitudinal studies (measures of desert assessments over time). In short, desert is elastic: beliefs about the scope of deserved punishments adjust to accommodate changes in sentencing policy.

For example, the sentences imposed on repeat offenders, offenders with diminished mental ability, and juvenile offenders have increased over the past twenty-five to thirty years. In each of these contexts, proponents of desert as a limiting principle have attributed the sentence increases to the misguided pursuit of other sentencing purposes—usually, incapacitation. In each context, sentencing reformers have urged renewed attention to desert in order to scale back the severe sentences. But even as critics depict the sentences as abandonments of desert, the proponents of the harsher sentences defend them as the offenders' just deserts. If desert is to serve as a limiting principle in criminal sentencing, whose determination of desert is to govern? Desert-based retributivism has been embraced by many legal elites, including the American Law Institute (ALI), precisely because those elites view desert as rigid and *inelastic* at its outer margins. Sentencing schemes in several jurisdictions have been praised as the successful implementation of limiting retributivism. But those jurisdictions did not reduce sentence lengths by appealing to populist conceptions of desert. Instead, elites restricted sentence lengths based on their own determinations of desert, and in many cases, legislatures and the public responded with active resistance to the elite assessments.[6]

---

3. Notwithstanding Paul Robinson's assumption that "doing justice" has been viewed as antithetical to fighting crime, consequentialist theorists have often depicted crime control approaches as a form of justice. Justice, like desert, is a very big tent under which many disagreeing thinkers have staked claims.

4. W.B. Gallie, *Essentially Contested Concepts*, 56 PROC. ARISTOTELIAN SOC'Y. 167 (1956).

5. *See* Julian Lamont, *The Concept of Desert in Distributive Justice*, 44 PHIL. Q. 45, 45 (1994) (arguing that desert is an indeterminate concept that "requires external values. . . to make it determinate").

6. *See* Ristroph, *supra* note *, at 1324.

To create checks on the majoritarian power to punish is not necessarily a bad idea.[7] But desert seems a poor mechanism to accomplish that goal. First, it is unclear that judges or sentencing commissions have any special competence in the assessment of desert. Desert is widely recognized as a subjective moral notion, and desert assessments by elites are likely to be perceived as legitimate only to the extent that they coincide with popular desert assessments. When such coincidence arises, it defeats the function of desert as a limiting principle. Second, because desert has no independent anchor and is dependent on external values, whether nonmajoritarian desert will serve to limit harsh punishments will depend on the particular values of the decision-making elite. Today, most academics and judges seem to view sentences as too harsh—harsher than "deserved"—but a vocal minority argues for still more severe sentences. Under a politically conservative judiciary, there are reasons to doubt that elite assessments of desert will actually produce significant reductions in the severity of sentences.

A separate reason to avoid desert rhetoric is the opacity of desert claims. A desert claim is opaque in that it does not reveal what factors were used to assess desert. Unfortunately, the available evidence suggests that the factors used to determine "deserved" punishments are often ones that have no legitimate place in the legal process. For example, extensive research on capital sentencing indicates that, all else being equal, jurors are more likely to find a defendant deserving of death if he is a Black man who killed a White victim. The social status of the victim, as measured by factors other than race, also seems to influence sentencing decisions, as does the perception that the defendant is an "outsider" to the community in which his crime occurred.[8] Thus, desert may serve as a "placeholder" for prejudice and bias.[9]

Worse, the rhetoric of desert may protect race and class disparities from efforts to eliminate them. The color and poverty of our prison population and death rows are not products of discrimination, the argument goes, but the unfortunate results of the fact that racial minorities and poor people are disproportionately involved in criminal behavior and thus more deserving of punishment. Such reasoning seems to underlie *McCleskey v. Kemp*, the Supreme Court decision acknowledging, then dismissing, racial disparities in capital sentencing.[10] We can decline to scrutinize unexplained and seemingly invidious patterns only

---

7. *See* Alice Ristroph, *Proportionality as a Principle of Limited Government*, 55 DUKE L.J. 263 (2005).

8. *See* Ristroph, *supra* note *, at 1327–31.

9. For a more salutary view of desert as a placeholder, *see* Dan Markel, *Against Mercy*, 88 MINN. L. REV. 1421, 1445 (2004) (describing "desert as a placeholder for three other principles . . . moral accountability for unlawful actions, equal liberty under law, and democratic self-defense").

10. 481 U.S. 279, 313 (1987).

if we are fairly confident in the overall justice of what we do, and the notion of desert provides that confidence.

Similarly, the moral warranty offered by desert may insulate sentencing practices from charges of disutility. Sentencing policies originally motivated by consequentialist concerns, such as long prison terms for recidivists, may become immune to claims of disutility once we have convinced ourselves that the sentences are deserved.

Now, almost everything I have said about desert here seems belied by the "empirical desert" described by Robinson. In part, we are speaking of different things. I am concerned with the desert judgments made by legislators, other public officials, jurors, and ordinary citizens as they select or endorse specific sentences. Robinson's "empirical desert" might be better described as *laboratory desert*: a set of judgments made by research subjects about fictitious crime scenarios, scenarios carefully designed by researchers to avoid any "ambiguity" that will allow "different test participants to perceive the facts differently."[11] In the real world, as Robinson acknowledges, criminal cases will bear "social or political implications" and the "relevant facts . . . will be perceived differently by different people."[12] In the real world, as Robinson acknowledges, prejudice and caprice can shape judgments of desert.[13] And in the real world, as Robinson acknowledges, changes in sentencing policy alter perceptions of what is deserved.[14]

The question, then, is how and whether the laboratory desert judgments collected by Robinson and others should inform real-world sentencing policy. The answer to this question could turn on whether we believe there is a truth of the matter about desert. If there is a right answer to the question how much punishment an offender deserves, then desert intuitions as measured in the laboratory may be attractive if they lead us to that right answer. At one point, Robinson suggests this is the case.[15] Elsewhere, he says that community intuitions of desert may not coincide with "true" desert, and at times he seems to equivocate on whether humans can ascertain right answers to desert questions at all.[16]

---

11. *See* Robinson core text at 33–34.

12. *Id.*

13. Paul H. Robinson and John M. Darley, *The Role of Deterrence in Criminal Law Rules: At Its Worst when Doing Its Best*, 91 GEO. L.J. 949, 984–85 (2003).

14. Paul H. Robinson and John M. Darley, *The Utility of Desert*, 91 Nw. U.L. REV. 453, 473–74 (1997).

15. Robinson core text at 37 ("[E]mpirical desert. . . may best approximate a distribution according to true moral blameworthiness.").

16. *Id.* ("Empirical desert . . . cannot tell us what actually is just."); *id.* at 37–38 (expressing skepticism that philosophical reasoning can identify "transcendental" standards of justice).

Alternatively, one could argue (as Robinson does) that whatever the metaphysical status of desert, the criminal justice system will control crime more effectively if it corresponds to popular beliefs about desert. That seems plausible. But remember: beliefs about desert are not fixed independently of sentencing policy. When community intuitions fail to correspond to policy, it is not obvious which should or will change to match the other. Moreover, the most stable desert intuitions reported by Robinson are judgments about how to rank punishments for various offenses in relation to one another. It seems harmless enough to take the researchers' findings into account when deciding whether to punish carjackers or burglars more severely, though it also seems doubtful that sentencing policies based on the laboratory findings of social scientists will be perceived as *more* legitimate than policies chosen by the ordinary democratic process. What is potentially harmful is an expanded invitation for sentencing decision-makers in the real world to frame their judgments in terms of desert without making explicit, and subjecting to scrutiny, the considerations that underlie those desert judgments. It is unclear whether Robinson would extend such an invitation.

Although I have suggested that desert cannot independently anchor sentencing reform, I do not think that the rhetoric of desert will necessarily foreclose such reform. As a sentencing principle, desert is dangerous, because it is opaque and because it provides a cloak of moral authority that can obscure prejudice or disutility. But desert rhetoric need not be fatal to reform, because desert conceptions are elastic. If we do scale back criminal sentences, and if we can generate popular support for such sentencing reforms, desert conceptions will adjust to view the new sentences as appropriate. To shrink desert conceptions is probably harder than to stretch them, but it does not seem to be impossible. The greatest obstacle to sentencing reform is not that we think in terms of desert, but rather that we have so little inclination to think critically about desert.

KEEPING DESERT HONEST

YOUNGJAE LEE*

Alice Ristroph criticizes desert, claiming that desert claims are "elastic" (they change over time) and "opaque" (they hide ugly illegitimate biases) and that these are reasons to resist desert as a sentencing principle. I agree that desert is elastic and that desert can sometimes be opaque. But its elasticity is not a problem, and its opacity is a reason to scrutinize desert, not to toss it.

First, we should be clear about the sense in which desert is elastic. In support of her claim, Ristroph observes that "[d]esert requires external values to give

---

* Associate Professor of Law, Fordham University School of Law.

it content."[1] This is true. When people say that teachers deserve to be paid more, they mean that what teachers get paid should be proportionate to the valuable work that they do. Without an independent valuation of teachers as performing an important service, such statements would be nonsensical. However, it does not follow that "the claim that *she deserves X* reveals little more than a belief that *she should get X*."[2] An insane person who is a danger to others *should* be committed, but he does not *deserve* to be committed. An ailing eighty-year-old who murdered civil rights workers forty years ago certainly *deserves* to be punished, but whether we *should in fact punish him* is a more difficult question. Desert is one consideration among many in running a criminal justice system, and desert judgments *can* be separated out from judgments as to what ought to be done, all things considered.

Ristroph is correct, however, in noting that desert judgments are "elastic" in the narrower sense that specific beliefs about desert can change over time. She mentions examples of date rape and drunk driving, the perceived blameworthiness of which has gone in one direction. To that list we can also add homosexual conduct, adultery, and miscegenation, the perceived blameworthiness of which has gone in the opposite direction. This kind of elasticity, however, is not a problem. Desert judgments need not remain static over time for them to help us think about state punishment. Levels of public condemnation change as social norms change, and it is simplistic—not to mention fantastic—to dismiss such changes, as Ristroph does, as having been brought about only because sentencing policy-makers "deliberately manipulated" people's moral sentiments.[3]

Ristroph also worries that desert judgments cannot be trusted because they are "opaque." I am sympathetic to her concerns. The difficulty is that desert judgments in the punishment context indicate not just disapproval but also an emotive state. Emotions associated with the practice of blaming are, for example, anger, resentment, indignation, and hatred. It is not that these emotions should be discouraged; in fact, I would consider an inability to get angry or indignant or even hateful at appropriate moments to be a moral defect. Rather, the problem is that such emotions can be excessive and can be driven by sentiments such as cruelty, sadism, inhumanity, and racial prejudice. Such corrupting influences can seep in unannounced and infect our desert judgments in ways that are difficult to police, and Ristroph is right to worry about this.

This, however, does not mean that we should walk away from desert, which seems to be the conclusion that Ristroph wants us to draw. Rather, the problematic nature of desert means that we must be suspicious of our retaliatory impulses and constantly test our specific desert judgments against broad principles of desert and political morality. That desert judgments are, as Ristroph says, "subjective" does

---

1. *See* Ristroph comment at 46.
2. *Id.* at 45.
3. *Id.* at 46.

not mean that such critical scrutiny is impossible. Desert judgments and their accompanying emotions have a cognitive content that can be evaluated as correct or incorrect.[4] How to undertake such self-scrutiny at the institutional level is a question that cannot be answered here, although I have made some suggestions elsewhere.[5]

Is desert worth all this trouble? The answer is yes, both because thinking about criminal law without placing desert at its core is an interpretive mistake and because other sentencing goals—such as incapacitation and deterrence—need to be constrained with principles of desert. I will concede that the final picture is not going to be tidy, but there is no way around the mess. Doing away with desert will be a cure worse than the disease; we must instead pour our efforts into keeping it honest.

---

4. *Cf.* Martha C. Nussbaum, UPHEAVALS OF THOUGHT: THE INTELLIGENCE OF EMOTIONS 19–88 (2001).

5. *See* Youngjae Lee, *Desert and the Eighth Amendment*, 11 U. PENN. J. CON. L. 101 (2009); Youngjae Lee, *Judicial Regulation of Excessive Punishments Through the Eighth Amendment*, 18 FED. SENT'G REP. 234 (2006); Youngjae Lee, *The Constitutional Right Against Excessive Punishment*, 91 VA. L. REV. 677 (2005).

DESERT: EMPIRICAL, NOT METAPHYSICAL

MATTHEW LISTER[*]

Perhaps the most serious objection that can be raised to a theory of punishment is that it gives unjust results. Paul Robinson considers the objection that "empirical desert" may be unjust insofar as it deviates from "transcendental" notions of justice. In a different but related vein, Alice Ristroph claims that any desert-based theory of punishment, including Robinson's "empirical desert" theory, will in practice lead to injustice by providing unwarranted protection to unjustly applied punishment due to racial and class bias. I suggest that embedding Robinson's notion of "empirical desert" within the approach to political philosophy known as "political liberalism" shows the way to meet these challenges and provides indirect support for political liberalism as well.

Political liberalism doesn't attempt to derive moral principles from basic notions or to discover timeless truths. Instead, it starts with the question of what social arrangements are best for people who see themselves as free and equal, reasonable and rational, that is, for a democratic, liberal society that takes itself to be a cooperative venture for mutual advantage over time.

---

* Law clerk to Judge Donald Pogue, U.S. Court of International Trade.

In such a society, the criminal law provides an answer to an assurance problem that people face in forming a just society. Even if people are willing to cooperate (they are reasonable), they will actually do so only if they have good reason to think that others will also cooperate and won't seek to take advantage of them (they are rational). The criminal law is one way to meet this worry. By reducing crime it helps people cooperate more readily. But given the values of a just society, not just any approach to crime reduction will do. Any approach must have the following virtues. First, it must both respect our basic rights and recognize each of us as free and equal, reasonable and rational members. Secondly, it must contribute to its own stability by inculcating norms of cooperation and compliance with just laws. If we have these goals, Robinson's idea of empirical desert turns out to be the best distributive principle for punishment.

Why is this? A system that distributes punishment on grounds other than desert risks treating us unfairly, as examples to others, perhaps; or punishing us more than we deserve, by the lights of our society, thereby making means of us. The empirical desert approach also has the best chance of building internal support for society. If people generally believe that the criminal law is just, because it punishes no more than is deserved, then a willingness to support the rules of society and to cooperate on fair terms is likely to arise. Given this, there's strong reason for political liberals to favor empirical desert as a distributive principle.

How does this help with the question of whether empirical desert promotes injustice? Consider Robinson's worry that empirical desert may be unjust insofar as it departs from "transcendental" notions of desert. Such concerns have little place in political liberalism. As noted, we're developing a notion of desert for our society, one that accepts liberal values. Furthermore, in political liberalism we don't make direct reference to our individual comprehensive moral views or to "transcendental" notions of morality, but rather look to reasons we can all share, and aim at an "overlapping consensus" on these reasons and values.

This is all the objectivity one ought to hope for in the political realm—outcomes are objective when they're the result of objective procedures, not because of an independent moral order. Insofar as we're able to use objective procedures that conform to liberal political values in shaping our notion of punishment, the outcome is just in the only sense that matters for political life. Robinson's notion of empirical desert provides such an objective procedure, and insofar as this is so his worry that empirical desert may depart from "transcendental" notions is misplaced.

This doesn't mean that we're guaranteed substantial justice. No account of punishment could guarantee this, and it's foolish to hold such a standard. But the marriage of political liberalism and empirical desert helps show how injustice can arise, namely, when objective procedures are improperly applied. Nearly all the cases of injustice noted by Ristroph can be seen, not as features of desert as a distributive principle, but as failures of application of objective principles. Racial disparity in sentencing, for example, shows a failure to apply objective procedures and would usually be seen as a mistake by those making it if they realized they were doing so. Unless it can be shown that such failures are bound to be more common under an empirical desert approach, this is no objection at all to it, and to see it as such is to show confusion about the project and the correct level of analysis.

Given political liberalism's natural complement to empirical desert, is Robinson is willing to marry the two together?

RESPONSE TO LEE AND LISTER

ALICE RISTROPH[*]

Youngjae Lee and Matthew Lister reassert the traditional equation of just punishment with just deserts. I want to return the conversation to what I referred to as the *new* desert—to the specific arguments concerning either "empirical desert" or "desert as a limiting principle" (or both). I argued that the elastic and opaque character of desert judgments gave us reasons to question desert's appeal as a principle of sentencing reform, and neither Lee nor Lister has shown otherwise.

On the elasticity of desert, Lee writes, "[I]t is simplistic—not to mention fantastic—to dismiss" changed social norms or changed levels of condemnation "as having been brought about only because sentencing policymakers 'deliberately manipulated' people's moral sentiments."[1] I am not sure where Lee finds the claim of exclusive causation that he attributes to me, but it matters little. Whether sentencing reformers and policy-makers were exclusively, primarily, or only partially responsible for changed attitudes about deserved punishments for date rape and drunk driving, the key point is that attitudes *did* change after penalties for those offenses were increased. If we stay focused on the notion of desert as a limiting principle, the history of these reform efforts suggests a problem. Desert judgments are not independent of actual sentencing policies, and so are unlikely to serve as the "side constraints" on those policies that Lee and others hope they will be.

On the opacity of desert, both Lee and Lister suggest that we can avoid racial bias by doing desert right—by scrutinizing our desert judgments, or by applying "objective principles."[2] The solution to discrimination, on this account, is to stop discriminating. If only it were so easy. There is, of course, a considerable literature on unconscious bias and the psychology of discrimination. Suffice it to say that admonitions to be objective have hardly solved the problem, and there is no reason to believe that these new admonitions will fare any better. Lister suggests

---

[*] Associate Professor, Seton Hall University School of Law.
1. Lee comment at 50.
2. Lister comment at 52.

that at the very least discrimination is no more likely under an approach that relies on "empirical desert" than on any other conception of desert. We cannot assess such a claim until we know more about what an "empirical desert" approach would be. As I noted previously, desert judgments collected by social scientists in the laboratory are different in important ways from those made by actual sentencers. It is still unclear how the laboratory studies could guide real-world sentencing decisions in *individual* cases. And those real-world decisions are the places where we see evidence that bias shapes desert judgments.

EMPIRICAL DESERT AND THE ENDPOINTS OF PUNISHMENT

JOSEPH E. KENNEDY*

Any philosophical theory that describes itself as empirical is bound to occasion controversy among philosophers, and any policy argument that describes itself in terms of desert is bound to occasion controversy among those who study the politics of crime. The aspirational nature of philosophy makes it hostile to limits based on empirical claims about the public's beliefs. The central role that the rhetoric of vengeful desert has played in the advent of mass incarceration in the United States raises questions about whether less draconian visions of desert can ever take hold in the public's mind. Empirical desert's vice and virtue, however, is that it does not operate as either a pure philosophical theory or as policy argument. This neither-fish-nor-fowl quality makes empirical desert difficult to evaluate, but it also allows it to be aspirational in a bounded and useful way.

Although empirical desert operates as both a social science finding and as a theory, it is important to distinguish the two. As a social science finding, one might raise the usual questions about methodology, validity, and robustness. As a philosophy, one might subject it to the usual range of objections to desert-based theories. Empirical desert is perhaps best understood as a social science finding with certain philosophical implications rather than as simply either a finding or a free-standing philosophical theory.

As a social science finding, empirical desert maintains that given an endpoint of maximal permissible punishment, people's ordinal ranking of the blameworthiness of an offense is relatively determinate and culturally universal. This finding has limited utility, of course. Maximum punishments differ greatly between societies. More specifically, everyone recognizes great disparities in the severity of punishment between the United States and Western European societies. The death penalty aside, fewer than 5 percent of sentences in Europe are for a year

---

* Associate Professor of Law, University of North Carolina School of Law.

or longer. In the nineties in the U.S., the average state prison sentence was between five and six years, and more than half of those in prison were serving prison terms in excess of ten years.[1] From a policy perspective, endpoints matter a lot.

Still, empirical desert's findings about ordinal rankings of desert matter a great deal in two related ways. First, they strongly suggest that notions of desert cannot be entirely excluded from any philosophy of punishment that expects to exercise influence over a democratic society in the foreseeable future. Second, it suggests that notions of desert are not infinitely elastic. Although the severity of the punishments attached to various crimes matters a great deal, the fact that very different cultures give similar ordinal rankings to the seriousness of crimes suggests that a basic human understanding of relative desert may exist.

These two philosophical implications matter a great deal for those interested in reforming penal policy. First, empirical desert suggests that the current consensus behind mixed theories of punishment that operates in most jurisdictions is the right approach. Consequentialism will never vanquish deontology. Second, and I think much more importantly, empirical desert may alleviate fears that modern punishment will founder in a sea of cultural relativism.

Much of the energy that has been driving the draconian form of desert that has dominated the crime politics of the United States during the last few decades comes from concerns about moral order in our rapidly changing and very diverse society.[2] To the degree that empirical desert as a finding asserts that ordinal rankings between offenses enjoy a stable consensus, and to the degree that empirical desert as a theory succeeds in justifying a corresponding ordinal ranking of punishments, the argument that punishment must be severe in order to maintain the stability of the moral order is weakened somewhat. This is no small accomplishment for any theory or finding. By itself empirical desert cannot move the endpoints of contemporary punishment back to a more rational place, but it may help in important ways.

These two philosophical implications aside, however, how much further can empirical desert take us as a theory? Empirical desert justifies punishment and tells us which offenses ought to be sentenced more severely than others. Other theories of punishment, however, provide guidance not just for sentencing but for the definition of offenses, excuses, and defenses. What is the scope of empirical desert as a theory of punishment? Does it provide a justification for punishment but not a sufficiently clear purpose?

---

1. Michael Tonry, THINKING ABOUT CRIME: SENSE AND SENSIBILITY IN AMERICAN PENAL CULTURE 22 (2006).

2. Joseph E. Kennedy, *Monstrous Offenders and the Search for Solidarity Through Modern Punishment*, 51 HASTINGS L.J. 829 (2000).

EMPIRICAL DESERT: THE YIN AND YANG OF CRIMINAL JUSTICE

ANDREW E. TASLITZ*

Several of the comments on Paul Robinson's defense of empirical desert—the idea that the criminal law should reflect ordinary people's judgments about desert as reflected in turn in empirical studies—challenge the wisdom of relying primarily on desert as a criminal law guide. But all these critiques share this in common: the authors, all well-respected scholars who are unquestionably among an intellectual elite, each have their own theories to replace Robinson's. But Robinson is not so much applying his own ideas as he is those of ordinary people. His approach is, therefore, more democratic—a way in which social science brings the voice of everyday people into rule-creation—and is more inductive, relying on many specific instances (the results of repeated experiments) to craft broader rules, than that of his critics.

To me, this is no small virtue. Of course, Robinson's position is not wholly divorced from elite theory, for he argues that empirical desert should only be the default choice, free to be overridden, but only for very good reason. This default override by elites is necessary, for example, to avoid endorsing ordinary persons' instincts that may be racist or sexist or reflect some other bias inconsistent with the Nation's constitutional aspirations, if not necessarily its letter.

Nevertheless, Robinson's *presumption* is in favor of ordinary folks. Robinson justifies this presumption as a way to improve compliance with the criminal law. Yet any approach that at least allows ordinary people to have a voice (but not a veto) in the rules that govern them also seems to me to be an inherent good in a democracy. It places a check on the instincts of elites and shows concern for hearing from the governed who, in theory, are also, in our system, the true sovereign. By not slavishly following ordinary folks' will, and permitting departure from that will for good reason, empirical desert also promotes deliberation, and that is an inherent good in a republic as well.

Note too that empirical desert does not poll individuals to ask what they think the criminal law should be. Rather, individuals are faced with concrete scenarios and asked to react to them. The consistency in their reaction reveals a rule at work—a perhaps unconscious rule that they could not otherwise articulate. But tapping into the unconscious is also a virtue, for much of our thinking and feeling takes place at that level and feeds our conscious responses. The moral emotions that motivate people to do right by others originate in the unconscious, perhaps reflecting biological imperatives, perhaps cultural ones, more likely

---

* Welsh S. White Distinguished Visiting Professor of Law, University of Pittsburgh School of Law, 2008–09; Professor of Law, Howard University School of Law.

both. Drawing on the unconscious thus helps to craft rules that reflect either consistent human notions of justice or, at the very least, American ones.

Confronting subjects with concrete, realistic scenarios reflects other important insights as well. It is easy to speak in broad generalities, harder to choose when faced with a specific situation. Some research shows, for example, that individual Whites opposed in theory to affirmative action may in practice follow its dictates when working with another individual of a minority race whose work they get to know and respect. Jurors may reach very different conclusions after hearing all the evidence in a high-profile case than does a public fed media-slanted excerpts plugging into social stereotypes. Justice sometimes lies more in wrestling with the concrete situations of individual lives than in the abstract theorizing of the philosophers.

Empirical desert recognizes this observation's truth, crafting general rules primarily from the outcomes of the many concrete wrestling matches, seeking to balance abstraction with specifics, logic with feeling, deliberation with intuition. In short, empirical desert marries the yin and the yang of justice. My criticism, therefore, is that Robinson justifies his approach too narrowly, namely by the aim of deterrence, when at least one other justification—promoting deliberative, populist democracy—would strengthen his position still more.

LEGITIMACY AS STRATEGY

ADIL AHMAD HAQUE[*]

The legitimacy and stability of a legal system require that the vast majority of citizens voluntarily comply with most of the laws and voluntarily cooperate with law enforcement most of the time, either out of agreement with the substantive justice of the laws or out of respect for the legitimate authority of the government. Both legitimacy and stability suffer if more than a small minority of citizens must be coerced into obeying the law. Yet most criminal law scholars believe that the goal of punishment is not to promote and sustain the support of the many who voluntarily obey the law, but to deter, incapacitate, rehabilitate, or deliver just deserts to the few who do not.

I want to suggest that combining a distributive principle based on what Paul Robinson calls empirical desert with a general justifying aim of what German legal scholars call Positive Generalprävention (Positive General Prevention, or PGP) yields a new and interesting theory of criminal punishment that Robinson, among others, should find appealing. PGP refers to the goal of preventing crime

[*] Assistant Professor of Law, Rutgers School of Law–Newark.

by promoting the voluntary compliance and cooperation of the general population. PGP is

"general" to distinguish itself from special prevention, which uses punishment to prevent crime by the particular offender subject to punishment, rather than by others. It's also "positive" because it seeks to prevent crime not by scaring potential lawbreakers into compliance, but by bolstering the lawabidingness of the rest of the population. Finally, and relatedly, it's about "prevention" generally speaking, rather than "deterrence" as a particular means of prevention. There could be no such thing as positive deterrence, after all.[1]

PGP is achieved by establishing the moral credibility of every aspect of the criminal justice system: policing, prosecution, criminalization, and punishment. Moral credibility is established first by providing security to the general population, so that ordinary people trust the government to provide effective justice and are assured that their voluntary compliance generally will be reciprocated by others. Second, to secure the active cooperation of the community in which they operate, police and prosecutors must use procedures that will be viewed as fair and not as abusive, invasive, or discriminatory. As Robinson has shown, credibility also requires that criminalization and the gradation of punishment closely track public perceptions of the relative seriousness of moral wrongdoing. Finally, to the extent that social, cultural, and economic injustice can undermine the perceived legitimacy of the state as a whole, serious commitment to PGP may require an equally serious commitment to distributive justice.

Robinson identifies a number of crime-control benefits that flow from establishing the moral credibility of the criminal law, but he is wrong to suggest that deviations from empirical desert can be justified simply by offsetting any resulting decrease in voluntary compliance with an increase in coerced compliance. The two forms of compliance are not fungible: states based on consent are intrinsically superior to states based on coercion. It is intrinsically better for officials to seek their population's cooperation, rather than its subjugation, and for citizens to obey the law out of respect for its content or source rather than out of fear of reprisal. PGP should not be viewed merely as a technology of crime prevention, in principle fungible with deterrence and other methods.

PGP addresses citizens as moral agents rather than as egoists or animals and grounds its commitment to substantive and procedural justice on enduring features of moral psychology rather than the highly contingent determinants of instrumental behavior. I hope that Robinson, having embraced empirical desert and rejected general deterrence as a distributive principle, will similarly embrace PGP and reject general deterrence as a general justifying aim of punishment.

---

1. Markus D. Dubber, *Theories of Crime and Punishment in German Criminal Law*, 53 AM. J. COMP. L. 679 (2006).

Conversely, retributivists may provide a morally plausible distributive principle of punishment but struggle to provide a political justification for diverting scarce resources from vital social programs toward a lumbering criminal justice system simply to give offenders their just deserts. PGP appears to provide a viable political justification of punishment while giving distributive effect to widely shared retributive intuitions.

The primary objection to PGP is that, like all consequentialist justifications of punishment including Robinson's, PGP seems to regard the punishment of individual offenders as a mere means to the end of crime prevention. This objection could be overcome by adopting a distributive principle of moral desert, because we do not treat offenders as mere means when we treat them as they deserve to be treated. However, because action is justified not by beliefs but by facts, empirical desert (what people believe offenders deserve), as distinct from moral desert (what offenders actually deserve), does not similarly preclude treatment as a mere means. On the other hand, if empirical desert is the most appropriate method by which to calculate moral desert, particularly in a democratic society, then any divergence between empirical and moral desert may be excused though not justified. As a consequentialist, Robinson must also respond to the "mere means" objection, and I hope he finds the response suggested above worth pursuing.

SENTENCING, EMPIRICAL DESERT, AND RESTORATIVE JUSTICE

LAURA I APPLEMAN*

The Court's recent line of sentencing opinions have shown a new and powerful allegiance to the criminal jury trial right in sentencing.[1] Underlying this sentencing reform is a jurisprudence grounded both in the historical jury right to decide all punishments and in community decisions about blameworthiness. *Blakely* and its predecessors rely on an unspoken theory of community-based retribution that should inform our future understanding of criminal punishment.

Retributive theory, however, does not provide much guidance about how best to translate it into modern sentencing. This is where Robinson's theory of empirical desert enters the picture. Robinson defines empirical retribution as a distributive principle focusing on the blameworthiness of the offender, but assessing punishment based on community intuitions of justice. The primary source of this principle is derived from empirical research into what drives

---

* Assistant Professor of Law, Willamette University.
1. *See, e.g., Blakely v. Washington*, 542 U.S. 296 (2004).

people's intuitions of blameworthiness. Empirical desert does not seek to explore "true" moral blameworthiness, but instead relies on the community's shared intuitions about assigning blameworthiness.

Robinson's conception of empirical desert can be usefully applied to the Court's recent sentencing reforms. The benefit of an empirical desert theory in sentencing is most apparent when you look to its practical consequences. If the criminal law can only truly shape norms if it commands moral respect, then using empirical desert as a framework for modern sentencing simultaneously pays tribute to the Court's understanding of historical jury rights and the practical implications of locating the arbiters of moral blameworthiness within the offender's community.

Criminal law plays a key role in creating and sustaining the moral consensus needed for maintaining social norms in our diverse society. Thus the jury, as representative of the community, must play a part in all sentencing punishments. This is true not only because *Blakely* held that juries must find all facts that increase punishment, but also because this community determination of social norms, via imposition of punishment, might be the only society-wide mechanism that transcends differences.

But empirical desert alone, as applied to sentencing, is not enough. For community justice to work in practical manner—to really reduce and control crime—there should also be a measure of restorative justice incorporated within empirical desert.

The restorative theory of punishment conceptualizes justice as a process that incorporates both the community and the offender in an attempt to repair and reconcile the harm done. In other words, part of restorative justice is the community's willingness to forgive wrongdoers and eventually restore their rights. This is an aspect of modern sentencing that we have entirely ignored, to our detriment.

To ensure our system of criminal sentencing and punishment is both powerful and humane, our underlying philosophy should have two sides to it. The first is Robinson's: empirical desert ensures that the offender feels the moral approbation of the community by having the determination of her punishment handed down by a fair cross-section of that community. The other side is restorative: after punishment is imposed, the critical next step is to restore the offender back into her place within the community. Otherwise, we end up with a perpetual underclass of felons, who once marked can never return to the fold.

How would this work? One important way is to provide for community sanctions, and community involvement in and support for any sort of punishment occurring after incarceration. If these post-prison punishments were grounded in the community—if released offenders had to serve their parole or post-release supervision in the very community they had harmed—it is possible that they would feel more culpability for their transgressions. Moreover, the community itself would be able to feel restored to its original state through the visible imposition of punishment on wrongdoers who had injured it. Finally, community sanctions provide a measure of restorative justice for both the victims and the community. In this way, post-prison punishments such as parole, probation, and post-release supervision can all be seen as critical parts of both empirical desert and restorative justice, translated into the real world.

Combining the lessons of empirical desert and restorative justice to sentencing has tremendous potential. If we accept that our system of incarceration and punishment is deeply flawed when it comes to preventing recidivism, then we should be willing to extend the philosophy of empirical desert and restorative justice from these pages to the streets. Whether empirical, restorative, or some combination of the two, the community's role in imposing punishment cannot end at the courthouse steps.

REPLY

PAUL H. ROBINSON

Mary Sigler mistakenly assumes that empirical desert's purpose is to provide deontological desert—it is the latter that we "are truly seeking"[1]—then criticizes it for not doing so accurately enough. Sigler may be seeking deontological desert, but empirical desert isn't. It is offered as a distributive principle not because it has transcendent justice value, but because it has instrumentalist crime-control value. The best that can be said about it deontologically is that it may produce something less in conflict with deontological desert than would the more traditional instrumentalist distributive principles, such as general deterrence, incapacitation of the dangerous, or rehabilitation. And given the difficulties with operationalizing deontological desert in the face of so much disagreement about its content, the deontologists might find that empirical desert provides a practical way of moving criminal law in that direction. However, if it does so, it is a collateral benefit of empirical desert, not its *raison d'etre*.

For much of her comment, Alice Ristroph seems to make the same false assumption. She attacks "The New Desert," as she calls empirical desert,[2] but with arguments against deontological desert, as if the former is meant to be a stand-in for the latter. But empirical desert is not deontological desert, as the

---

1. Sigler comment at 41.

2. Within what she calls "The New Desert," Ristroph includes "desert as a limiting principle." This labeling is somewhat confusing given that desert as a limiting principle is neither new, having blossomed most recently with Norval Morris several decades ago, nor compatible with empirical desert. The latter provides a specific punishment amount, while the former claims that desert can only identify the extremes that mark the outer boundaries of a broad range of punishment.

core text makes clear: "People's shared intuitions about justice are not justice in a transcendent sense."[3] I defer to Youngjae Lee and Matt Lister to respond to her general antidesert attack and just note again that the rationale for empirical desert is instrumental, not deontological.

Other commentators criticize empirical desert on instrumentalist grounds. Adam Kolber imagines that lay persons have intuitions about all sorts of things other than deserved punishment, such as the societal goals of punishment (or even whether the "attorney-client privilege should be violated").[4] He then imagines that these intuitions might conflict with people's intuitions about deserved punishment, undermining the system's moral authority in people's eyes. He speculates that people might want the punishment imposed by the criminal justice system to be justice in truth, in a transcendent sense, not just justice that tracks people's intuitions because there are crime-control benefits to doing so. In other words, they may want punishment to have a deontological-desert motivation rather than an empirical-desert crime-control motivation.

What he misses is that, from the layperson's point of view, empirical desert *is* deontological desert, both in its distribution and its motivation. They will see no difference between the two. An empirical desert distribution of punishment to them is exactly what true justice requires. Even if you showed people the empirical studies, their reaction is likely to be a so-what shrug. It's all very nice that these psychology studies show that criminal law is doing justice as the community sees it, they might say, but what matters to me is that the system really is doing justice. If you tell me that this also creates crime-control benefits, well all the better.

This lay attitude arises in part from the fact that lay judgments about core wrongdoing are intuitional. As such, they are held with a great confidence and are seen as more like facts than opinions. Intuitions are importantly different from reasoned judgments. People understand that reasoned judgments depend on argument and analysis, and therefore that those judgments could change as new arguments are presented. (Judgments about what a society's goals or motivation for punishment should be, or judgments about the proper scope of the attorney-client privilege are, as far as we can tell, reasoned judgments, not intuitions). Of course, as the liability and the punishment issue moves out from the core of wrongdoing, people's beliefs become less purely intuition and more a mix of intuition and reasoned judgment. The blameworthiness of downloading music from the Internet without a license, for example, is probably a product of people's intuitions about taking property without consent, and of their reasoning

---

3. Robinson core text at 29. I am comforted by Matt Lister's arguments that my "worry that empirical desert may depart from 'transcendental' notions is misplaced" as long as it is situated within political liberalism. Lister comment at 52. As he concedes, however, "This doesn't mean we're guaranteed substantial justice." *Id.*

4. Kolber comment at 42.

about the strength of the analogy between the core wrong and unlicensed music downloading. To laypersons, their intuitions are the truth about justice.

Although Michael Cahill does not object to empirical desert in principle, he's skeptical about the extent of its crime-control benefits and believes that additional research is needed before the issue can be resolved. I agree that our current knowledge regarding its effects is limited and that more research would be extremely valuable, but I do not believe that we need wait for it before preferring empirical desert as the distributive for criminal liability and punishment. As I have tried to demonstrate at length elsewhere, empirical desert may win by default because all alternative distributive principles are so seriously flawed.[5]

In the cartoonish oversimplification that this limited space requires: Deontological desert can't realistically be operationalized. The prerequisites for general deterrence rarely exist. (And even where they do exist, a general-deterrence distribution could be preferred only if it provided greater deterrent effect than that already inherent in an empirical-desert distribution, and only if that greater effect was not outweighed by whatever crime-control costs there are to conflicting with the community's intuitions of justice.) Rehabilitation may make a useful, even essential, correctional policy but can't realistically function as a principle for determining who should be punished how much. Although a distributive principle focusing on incapacitating the dangerous no doubt does have crime-control effectiveness, the same preventive-detention function could be achieved more effectively and with fewer crime-control costs if segregated from the criminal justice system. Cahill may well agree with the general conclusion here when he notes as an aside that empirical desert "won't do any worse than any other strategy all things considered, and would probably be cheaper than many."[6]

One final set of instrumentalist criticisms comes in the last few paragraphs of Ristroph's comment and her reply to Lee and Lister. While perhaps implicitly conceding the crime-control costs that arise for conflicting with the community's intuitions of justice, Ristroph nonetheless discounts the need for empirical desert. To avoid conflict between sentencing polices and the community's intuitions of justice, she suggests, we need simply change people's intuitions. "Beliefs about desert are not fixed independently of sentencing policy."[7] She cites the core-text examples that law has helped change norms for date rape and drunken driving. But norm changes on these kinds of issues are possible because they are not the core of wrongdoing. They are rather seen as analogies to it, and the strength of the analogy, and thereby the condemnable nature of the conduct, is something that can indeed be manipulated. For core wrongdoing, in contrast,

---

5. *See* Paul H. Robinson, Distributive Principles of Criminal Law: Who Should Be Punished How Much? (2008).

6. Cahill comment at 43.

7. Ristroph comment at 49.

intuitions of justice are in fact commonly "fixed independently of sentencing policy," and where this is so, sentencing policy must give way if a conflict is to be avoided.

Perhaps more importantly, the law's power to help in norm changing depends upon its having a reputation as a credible moral authority. That is, it must earn its moral-credibility chips by embodying people's norms before it can selectively spend the chips in trying to change norms.

Ristroph also feels comfortable discounting shared intuitions of justice that conflict with sentencing policy because she thinks it "doubtful that sentencing policies based on the laboratory findings of social scientists will be perceived as *more* legitimate than policies chosen by the ordinary democratic process."[8] The point seems to be: Who is more credible here, some "laboratory" scientist or your democratically elected government? But empirical desert does not derive its legitimacy from its character as "laboratory findings of social scientists," but rather from the fact that its results match people's intuitions of justice, by definition. The real question is: What is more credible here, the community's shared intuitions of justice or the results of the notoriously dysfunctional American crime politics? In fact, American crime politics have generated a host of doctrines that laypeople find to seriously conflict with their intuitions of justice.[9]

In her closing paragraph, Ristroph worries that desert will "provide a cloak of moral authority that can obscure prejudice or disutility."[10] Although this might be a concern with difficult-to-define deontological desert, empirical desert, with its empirical basis, has no such problem.[11] Indeed, empirical desert provides a unique opportunity for developing color-blind principles of justice. If the empirical study subjects are not told the race of the offender during testing, even subconscious biases can have no effect. Thus, sentencing guidelines based upon such principles, for example, can be color-blind. Ristroph properly worries that prejudice may creep back in through the bias of individual sentencers, but of course, this is a problem for any and every distributive principle, not a special problem for empirical desert.

Some commentators offer support of sorts for empirical desert, but for reasons that sometimes give me pause. In some instances, I worry that empirical desert is being asked to do more than can reasonably be expected of it.

---

8. *Id.*

9. For a detailed empirical study of the issue, *see* Paul H. Robinson, and Geoff Goodwin, *The Disutility of Injustice* (forthcoming 2009) (reporting results of empirical studies testing people's intuitions of justice on case under modern crime-control programs).

10. Ristroph comment at 49.

11. She seems to concede this when, after her general anti-desert attack, she writes: "Now, most everything I've said about desert here seems belied by the 'empirical desert' described by Robinson." *Id.* at 48.

Joseph Kennedy would like empirical desert to help "move the endpoints of contemporary punishment back to a more rational place."[12] Unlike people's intuitions on ordinal ranking, judgments about the punishment continuum's endpoints may be culturally dependent. (The good news, on the other hand, is that such judgments are likely more subject to manipulation through social engineering). I don't think we should assume that a jurisdiction that adopts empirical desert as its distributive principle will automatically reduce its maximum penalty.

On the other hand, I do think that adopting empirical desert as a distributive principle may well have the longer-term tendency to reduce punishments generally, for two reasons. First, a distributive principle of empirical desert requires different punishments for cases of different blameworthiness. Many cases today are packed together at the top of the punishment continuum, at life imprisonment, for example, even though many such cases have distinguishably greater blameworthiness than other such cases. Thus, the effect of introducing empirical desert would be to force many of these cases further down the continuum in order to create the differences in punishment that proper ordinal ranking requires.

Another reason to expect lower punishment across the continuum of cases is the reason for the current high sentences. It is not desert that has driven the high sentences in American crime politics. Although politicians may commonly use the rhetoric of desert, an analysis of the rationales driving most modern crime-control programs shows them to be based primarily on theories of general deterrence and incapacitation, as is apparent in such legislation as three strikes statutes, reducing the age for adult prosecution, the felony murder rule, high penalties for drug offenses, and narrowing the insanity defense. To explicitly shift the criminal justice system away from its present coercive crime-control mechanisms is to eliminate the reason for many of the current high sentences. As noted, available data suggests that these modern crime-control programs seriously conflict with people's shared intuitions of justice.[13]

Both Andrew Taslitz and Adil Haque see special value in empirical desert as a distributive principle for reasons beyond its crime-control benefits. Taslitz concludes that "Robinson justifies his approach too narrowly . . . when at least one other justification—promoting deliberative, populist democracy—would strengthen his position still more."[14] Haque offers a criticism similar in kind: Robinson "[i]s wrong to suggest that deviations from empirical desert can be justified simply by offsetting any resulting decrease in voluntary compliance with the increase in coercive compliance." To his mind, even if a deviation from empirical desert produces greater crime-control benefits, it ought to be resisted

---

12. Kennedy comment at 55.

13. *See* Robinson and Goodwin *supra* note 9.

14. Taslitz comment at 57.

because an empirical-desert distribution as a compliance mechanism is "intrinsically superior" to a coercive compliance mechanisms (such as, presumably, the traditional mechanisms of deterrence, incapacitation, and rehabilitation).[15]

I can appreciate the sentiment, but as an instrumentalist (in this context) I'm unsure how much weight to give to this special intrinsic value. Is it so great as to justify a society suffering substantial additional crime that could be avoided if a crime-control calculation suggested that a deviation from empirical desert might be justified in a special case?[16]

Laura Appleman also sees some special value in empirical desert apart from its crime-control potential: its natural consistency with recent Supreme Court sentencing decisions embodying an emerging "jurisprudence grounded in . . . community decisions about blameworthiness" and "an unspoken theory of community-based retribution."[17] It seems possible that the gist of the recent decisions might go only to ensuring jury fact-finding, not lay judgments about blameworthiness. The event-reconstruction role and the normative-judgment role of juries are distinct. The Court's opinions might be read to demand the first but not the second. But more informed interpreters may see a broader jurisprudence in the cases than I do.

I take it as a positive sign that some people think I go too far with empirical desert and others that I do not go far enough.

---

15. Haque comment at 58.

16. For a full account of when deviations from empirical desert might be justified, *see* Robinson, *supra* note 5, at ch. 12.A.

17. Appleman comment at 59.

3. DEFENDING PREVENTIVE DETENTION

CHRISTOPHER SLOBOGIN*

The jurisprudential basis for preventive detention—defined as state intervention against an individual for the purpose of preventing him or her from harming others—is not well developed, especially when contrasted to the robust theoretical literature relating to punishment based on retribution and general deterrence. This relative lack of theorizing is unfortunate, because determinations of dangerousness permeate the government's implementation of its police power. To name a few examples, death penalty determinations, noncapital sentencing, detention of enemy combatants, sexual predator commitment, civil commitment, pretrial detention, and investigative stops by the police often or always depend upon assessments of dangerousness.

In an effort to devise a more coherent jurisprudence of dangerousness, I examine the legitimacy of all of these interventions. I do so by examining and responding to the standard objections to preventive detention: the unreliability objection; the legality objection; the punishment-in-disguise objection; and the dehumanization objection. I conclude that none of these objections, alone or combined, require a prohibition on preventive detention. However, each does impose limitations on its implementation, which are summarized at the end.

I. THE UNRELIABILITY OBJECTION

Probably the most common objection to preventive detention is that it is too error-prone. Even with recent advances in actuarial prediction and structured professional judgment instruments, we are not particularly good at identifying who will recidivate or when. In light of our incompetence at assessing violence risk, the argument goes, preventive detention is unconscionable.

There are several responses to this objection. First, when the goal is prevention of violence rather than its punishment, some relaxation in the required standard of proof is justifiable, a principle the Supreme Court has recognized.[1] The adage that ten murderers should go free before one innocent person is convicted,

---

* Milton Underwood Professor of Law, Vanderbilt University Law School. This core text is drawn from Christopher Slobogin, *A Jurisprudence of Dangerousness*, 98 Nw. U. L. Rev. 1 (2003), which also appears in a revised version in Christopher Slobogin, MINDING JUSTICE: LAWS THAT DEPRIVE PEOPLE WITH MENTAL DISABILITY OF LIFE AND LIBERTY ch. 4 (2006).

1. *See, e.g., Terry v. Ohio*, 392 U.S. 1, 22 (1967).

although perhaps acceptable as an illustration of our commitment to justice, is much harder to swallow when we know that a sizeable proportion of the ten guilty persons will commit another murder if all of them are let go.

Second, although predictive judgments will always be suspect, the retrospective judgments necessary to implement the primary alternative to prevention—waiting until a criminal act has occurred and punishing it based on its relative culpability—are at least as flawed. Mens rea concepts—the primary means of grading responsibility for crime—are notoriously difficult to define and apply in a consistent fashion, and legislatures and courts have yet to develop an objectively neutral and coherent metric for measuring blameworthiness; as a result, offenders with the same level of blameworthiness can easily receive wildly divergent sentences.

Third, again comparing the two systems, mistakes about dangerousness are, at least in theory, much easier to correct than mistakes about culpability. For reasons described below, preventive detention must continually be justified through periodic review. In contrast, periodic review is inconsistent with the notion of punishing a person for his or her past conduct. An offender's culpability for a completed act does not change. Furthermore, once culpability is determined at trial and affirmed on appeal, it is considered res judicata; the issue will never be revisited.

The conclusion that difficulties in measuring dangerousness do not preclude preventive detention does not mean, of course, that preventive detention is permissible upon any showing of risk. There should be both qualitative and quantitative restrictions on the government's efforts to prove the requisite level of dangerousness. I have elsewhere argued that in trying to meet its proof burden regarding dangerousness, the government may rely only on previous criminal acts and expert testimony based on empirically derived and appropriately normed probability estimates, unless the subject of the prediction opens the door to nonstatistical, "clinical" prediction testimony by relying on it to prove he or she is not dangerous. This "subject-first" regime "allows the government to prove dangerousness in the most accurate, least confounding manner, while permitting the offender-respondent to attack the state's attempt at preventive detention on the ground that the numbers do not accurately reflect his or her violence potential."[2]

In addition to this evidentiary restriction, I propose two substantive, "quantitative" restrictions. The *consistency principle* would require that the prediction criterion applied in the preventive detention context be consistent with analogous manifestations of the government's police power, in particular

---

2. Christopher Slobogin, *Dangerousness and Expertise Redux*, 56 EMORY L.J. 275, 317–19 (2006). *See also* Christopher Slobogin, PROVING THE UNPROVABLE: THE ROLE OF LAW, SCIENCE, AND SPECULATION IN ADJUDICATING CULPABILITY AND DANGEROUSNESS chs. 5 and 6 (2006).

the implementation of criminal justice. Thus, for instance, the degree of danger-ousness required for incarcerative preventive detention ought to be roughly equivalent to the degree of dangerousness that permits conviction for inchoate crimes such as conspiracy, reckless endangerment, and driving while intoxi-cated, because both preventive detention and these provisions of criminal law authorize significant deprivations of liberty to protect third parties.

The second substantive limitation on preventive detention, the *proportionality principle*, requires that the degree of danger be roughly proportionate to the proposed government intervention. For instance, greater proof of dangerous-ness would be required for imprisonment than for a stop-and-frisk designed to prevent street crime. Similarly, if incarceration occurs, the likelihood of harm should increase with its duration. And if a death sentence is under consideration (and dangerousness is an aggravating factor), proof of future antisocial conduct should be virtually unassailable. Our current system, which requires increasingly greater proof of risk for street stops (reasonable suspicion), civil commitment (clear and convincing evidence), and capital punishment (proof beyond a reasonable doubt) implicitly recognizes this principle.

Together, the consistency and proportionality principles significantly reduce the impact of unreliable predictions. The consistency principle provides a base-line for the prediction criterion, through assessment of the proof required to sanction other government interventions based on dangerousness. The propor-tionality principle provides a method of graduating the prediction criterion above this baseline, based on the nature and length of the preventive intervention.

II. THE LEGALITY OBJECTION

Even if the standard of proof for preventive detention is established pursuant to the consistency and proportionality principles, dangerousness remains a vague term. In particular, clarification is necessary with respect to both the type of pre-dicted harm that authorizes preventive detention (only physical violence, or theft and minor assaults as well?), and the type of act, if any, that triggers it (only seri-ous crime, any antisocial act, or the presence of biological or environmental "static" risk factors as well?). Statutes that fail to provide such clarification can give rise to an objection based on the principle of legality: they give neither citi-zens nor government officials sufficient notice of the circumstances under which preventive detention can occur, and thus both chill innocent behavior by citizens and increase the potential for abuse by officials.

This objection might lead to two further limitations on preventive detention, one having to do with its goal and the second having to do with its threshold. First, preventive detention should be aimed only at preventing harms that are defined as such by the substantive criminal law. Second, it should occur only after an individual has committed a criminal act or engaged in obviously risky behavior.[3] The legality rationale for these two limitations is that preventive detention that is aimed at preventing vaguely defined or minor antisocial acts, or that is based on a person's static characteristics or on acts that are not obviously risky, would give government officials carte blanche to round up undesirables who are only trivially risky or who, even if they pose a significant threat, have not demonstrated any tendency to carry out it out.

The proposition that preventive detention requires precipitating conduct warrants further explication. Assume the basis of the proposed government intervention consists solely of risk-predictive "characteristics," such as a "violent gene," an inability to empathize, or a biological addiction (all of which might be measurable physiologically, without any reference to behavior). If such traits are associated with the degree of risk required by the consistency and proportionality principles, why shouldn't detention be permitted? The answer has to do with the rule of law. As Herbert Packer asserted, "[i]t is important, especially in a society that likes to describe itself as 'free' and 'open,' that a government should be empowered to coerce people only for what they do and not for what they are." Accordingly, the law should require proof of an act, "a point of no return beyond which external constraints may be imposed but before which the individual is free—not free of whatever compulsions determinists tells us he labors under but free of the very specific social compulsions of the law."[4] If the state's preventive detention power is not limited by the requirement that it prove some affirmative act that is predictive of a legislatively defined danger, then the government, not the individual, controls if and when the government intervenes. Conditions, dispositions, and thoughts, even if highly predictive of danger and identified as such, cannot be the "point of no return" because there is no identifiable "point" at which they can be avoided.

Note that this interpretation of the legality principle also identifies a distinction between the person with an infectious disease and the predator known to be dangerous, a distinction that has eluded commentators who want to maintain quarantine, but who are not sure about open-ended preventive detention.[5] As soon as the infected person goes into the community, he has engaged in obviously risky conduct that is an imminent threat to others. The same cannot be said for the predator. The latter individual must engage in some further, risky or harmful conduct before the state may intervene.

---

3. *Cf. Lambert v. California*, 355 U.S. 225 (1957), which "stands for the unacceptability in principle of imposing criminal liability where the prototypically law-abiding individual in the actor's situation would have had no reason to act otherwise." John Calvin Jeffries, Jr., *Legality, Vagueness, and the Construction of Penal Statues*, 71 VA. L. REV. 189, 211–12 (1985).

4. Herbert Packer, THE LIMITS OF THE CRIMINAL SANCTION 74 (1968).

5. *See, e.g.,* Ferdinand D. Schoeman, *On Incapacitating the Dangerous*, 16 AM. PHIL. Q. 27, 34 (1979).

Does this conduct have to amount to a crime? If, as I suggested above, the danger to be prevented is to be defined with reference to the criminal law, one might reasonably assume that the triggering criteria should be as well. Yet some obviously risky conduct is not criminal. Numerous examples of this fact come from emergency civil commitment cases involving persons alleged to be dangerous to others. Moreover, the Supreme Court has approved investigative stops based on suspicious activity that does not amount to a crime. In the well-known case of *Terry v. Ohio*, for example, the Supreme Court approved an investigative frisk of individuals who appeared to be "casing" a storefront and mumbled responses to a police officer's questions about their conduct, activity that was concededly not criminal.

Note, however, that both of these situations involve conduct that, like the conduct associated with the crime of reckless endangerment or driving while intoxicated, suggests antisocial behavior is imminent. What if the conduct is more attenuated from the potential harm? In answering this question, it is important to remember that the principle of legality is meant to implement two important objectives. In addition to assuring functional notice, the legality principle is meant to control government discretion. Thus, if the triggering act for preventive detention is not an immediate precursor to the predicted harm (as with emergency commitment and investigative stops), it must be linked to a statutorily defined crime such as conspiracy or attempt. Otherwise, the potential for government abuse becomes enormous.

This conclusion could also be seen as an application of the consistency principle discussed earlier. The criminal law's requirement of either significant, imminent risk (as with reckless endangerment) or an anticipatory "dangerous" act (such as in conspiracy and attempt crimes) ought to apply in the preventive context as well. Also consistent with this conclusion are the Supreme Court's recent decisions requiring the government to prove to a neutral tribunal that individuals it has detained as "enemy combatants" are in fact such.[6]

III. THE PUNISHMENT-IN-DISGUISE OBJECTION

Long-term preventive detention based on perceived dangerousness has traditionally been confined to people with serious mental illness. A number of commentators, Justice Stevens among them, have expressed concern that allowing the government to engage in preventive detention beyond this limited sphere would lead to the "evisceration of the criminal law and its accompanying protections."[7] Stevens conjectured that a shadow criminal code would develop to

---

6. See *Hamdi v. Rumsfeld*, 542 U.S. 507 (2004).
7. *Allen v. Illinois*, 478 U.S. 364, 380 (1986) (Stevens, J., dissenting).

deal with individuals thought to be prone to sexual offending, domestic violence, drunken assaults, and the like. Furthermore, because such a shadow system would not constitute a "criminal prosecution" of the type referred to in the Sixth Amendment, the constitutional rules associated with criminal trial need not be followed, thus possibly increasing the potential for malfeasance by state actors.

This objection is rightly concerned with the risk that a robust system of preventive detention could become the preferred method of liberty deprivation because of the perception that it places fewer obstacles in the government's way. But preventive detention need not be prohibited on this ground, or even reserved solely for those with serious mental illness, if it adheres to the admonition in the Supreme Court's decision in *Jackson v. Indiana* that "the nature and duration of commitment bear some reasonable relation to the purpose for which the individual is committed."[8] If this due process principle is carefully followed, preventive detention of people who are not mentally ill could be permissible.

More specifically, preventive detention is constitutional under *Jackson* if three limitations are observed. First, the nature of the government's intervention must bear a reasonable relation to the harm contemplated. For instance, not all individuals who pose a risk require long-term institutionalization, especially if the harm posed is toward the less serious end of the spectrum; thus, preventive *intervention* more accurately describes the subject of this discussion (although I will continue to speak of preventive detention because that is the usual focus of analysis). Second, the duration of the intervention must be reasonably related to the harm predicted. Discharge is required when the individual no longer poses a danger, and treatment is required if it will shorten the duration of confinement. Third, to ensure these requirements are met, the individual is entitled to periodic review, at which the state must show the individual continues to pose the requisite risk (which, under the proportionality principle, should become increasingly difficult over time).

The concern that such review proceedings will be too informal to act as a brake on abuses of discretion can also be answered. It is true that Sixth Amendment rights do not attach at such "civil" review proceedings. But any and all of these rights might still be required under the Due Process Clause, a constitutional provision that, the Supreme Court's juvenile justice jurisprudence makes clear, is triggered whenever significant deprivations of liberty are contemplated.

IV. THE DEHUMANIZATION OBJECTION

The dehumanization objection is that, even if all of the other objections are met, preventive detention shows insufficient respect for the individual because it

---

8. 406 U.S. 715, 738 (1972).

signals either that the person detained does not possess the capacity to choose the good or that, having such capacity, the person will not do so. In the terms moral philosophers have used, the dehumanization objection posits that people who have committed a crime (which the principle of legality usually requires for preventive detention) have a right to be punished for that act, as a method of honoring their autonomous personhood. Subjecting them instead to preventive detention insults their humanity because it ignores the fact that they have made a choice to do harm and, as G.W.F. Hegel put it, regards them not as "rational actor[s]" but "simply as . . . harmful animal[s] which must be rendered harmless."[9]

These types of concerns are difficult to evaluate because they are so abstract. They are most potent when the government creates two systems of liberty deprivation for those who commit antisocial conduct—one designed to punish and the second designed to preventively detain individuals—and then chooses the latter option. In this "two-track" situation, preventive detention palpably signals that the person is different, a "harmful animal" rather than a rational actor who has chosen to commit culpable harm.[10] A good example of this de-humanizing two-track regime is found in states that have adopted the so-called "sexual predator" scheme—note the use of the animalistic word "predator"—which shunts the individual into a separate system either at the charging stage or after sentence is completed.

The dehumanization objection is less powerful, however, when preventive detention is incorporated into the criminal justice system, as occurs with indeterminate sentencing. In such a setting, all offenders are evaluated along a continuum of dangerousness, thereby avoiding the explicit and stigmatizing "dangerous being" label that characterizes the separate sexual predator regime. Moreover, in contrast to the latter regime, detention based on dangerousness in a single-track criminal justice system occurs immediately after a conviction representing that the individual autonomously chose to cause harm, and thus is closely associated with punishment based on desert. At the least, a "weak" version of the right to punishment is maintained in this latter scenario.

Even a two-track system does not violate the right to punishment envisioned by Hegel and others when it is applied to an individual who should not be considered a "rational actor." This exception explains why people with serious mental illness can be subject to long-term preventive detention, either through civil commitment or after an acquittal by reason of insanity. More controversially, I believe the irrational-actor exception also justifies detention of enemy combatants under

---

9. G.W.F. Hegel, Elements of the Philosophy of Right 126 (Allen W. Wood ed., 1991).

10. In fact, research suggests that designation as a sexual predator has both demoralizing and crimogenic effects. See, e.g., Vernon L. Quinsey, Review of the Washington State Special Commitment Center Program for Sexually Violent Predators, 15 U. Puget Sound L. Rev. 704, 705–07 (1992).

orders to kill, terrorists willing to die for their cause, and extremely impulsive individuals such as those sex offenders who are willing to commit their crimes even with a policeman at their elbow. Unlike people with serious mental illness, these latter individuals can be considered autonomous. But they do not deserve the right to punishment because they exercise their autonomy in the wrong direction even when faced with death or a significant punishment.

The dehumanization objection, then, might lead to a prohibition on preventive detention as an alternative or addition to, rather than a component of, punishment, except when it is directed at individuals who are unaware they are engaging in criminal conduct (e.g., the seriously mentally ill) or who are extremely reckless with respect to the prospect of serious loss of liberty or death resulting from the criminal conduct (e.g., terrorists). Those in the first group are irrational in the classic sense captured by the typical insanity defense formulation. Those in the second group are irrational in the sense that they choose to disregard society's most significant prohibitions. Another way to characterize these two groups is that they comprise the universe of individuals who are "undeterrable," i.e., those who are unaffected by the prospect of criminal punishment or significant harm. An alternative regime of liberty deprivation is justifiable for these individuals because the dictates of the criminal justice system have little or no impact on them. At the same time, when government is entitled to exercise either the punishment or the preventive detention option, the punishment route must be taken initially. Given the right to punishment, this presumption fits better with our legal system's preference for autonomy, and prevents unnecessarily unleashing the repugnant labeling effects associated with the preventive detention option.

V. CONCLUSION

Liberty deprivation based on dangerousness is permissible under five conditions, organized here somewhat differently than in the discussion above. The state must show:

> (1) that the individual has engaged in obviously risky conduct—either a crime or behavior that indicates harm is imminent; (2) that the liberty deprivation contemplated is proportionate to the likelihood and magnitude of the predicted harm; (3) that the predicted harm is a crime; and (4) when the preventive intervention is in lieu of conviction or appended to the end of a criminal sentence, that the individual is undeterrable, either due to serious mental illness or to a preference for serious crime over freedom. If preventive intervention occurs, the government must also show periodically: (5) that the nature of the liberty deprivation is no more restrictive than necessary to prevent the harm contemplated and that its duration is proportionately justified by the likelihood and magnitude of the predicted harm.

COMMENTS

SLOBOGIN ON DEHUMANIZATION

MICHAEL LOUIS CORRADO*

To my knowledge, no one has done as much work, and as good, to rein in the state's power to detain as Christopher Slobogin. I have a question, however, about his response to one of the objections he deals with, the dehumanization objection.

The dehumanization objection is, in Slobogin's words, that "preventive detention shows insufficient respect for the individual because it signals either that the person detained does not possess the capacity to choose the good or that, having such capacity, the person will not do so."[1] This is the proposition that criminals are entitled to be punished, which as we know, sounds odd only until we understand the alternative: indefinite detention and treatment. Slobogin's solution to the impediment presented by the objection—an impediment to the imposition of preventive detention—is to make deterrability the criterion for application of the objection: No one is to be preventively detained unless he can't or won't respond to the threat of punishment.

That solution was built into Slobogin's wording of the objection, which would protect only those who are both capable of choosing the good and willing, given the right incentives, to do so. Another way to have worded the objection, one that would have led to a different solution, would have been this:

No one may be preventively detained who is *capable* of responding to the threat of punishment.

Putting it that way, punishment is reserved for those who *can* respond to punishment, whether they will respond or not in the particular case. Preventive detention is reserved for those who cannot. Those who can but will not respond to punishment are punished nevertheless. Depending on the danger they present, their sentence may be long; but we respect their humanity even in the face of the danger they present by giving them the punishment the crime deserves that will, at the same time, deter others. It is *incapacity* that removes an offender from the reach of punishment.

---

* Arch Allen Distinguished Professor of Law and Professor of Philosophy, University of North Carolina Law School. Parts of this comment are adapted from Michael Louis Corrado, *Responsibility and Control*, 34 HOFSTRA L. REV. 59, 73–76 (2005), and *The Entering Wedge: From Salerno to Padilla* (Aug. 22, 2004) (unpublished manuscript, on file with author).

1. Slobogin core text at 72–73.

It is hard to defend this second formulation in the face of the dangers presented by pedophiles and terrorists. Why not just put these scary people away? And that's what Slobogin's modification does: it enables us to lock up, preventively, people who can but won't obey the law—those committed to breaking it; those who are undeterrable. But I don't think those who argue for the second formulation do so because they believe that it would be easy to defend. If we welcome preventive detention for terrorists, will we feel the same "lively repugnance" when it is extended to drug kingpins who are impervious to the threat of punishment? To the producers of child pornography? To hardened criminals of other sorts? How far down this road are we willing to go?

Beyond raising this general question of the appropriateness of what Slobogin is suggesting, I have two more specific questions about his way of formulating it.

The first problem is this: Why does the determined criminal, the one who risks even death to accomplish her goal, lose her humanity? Whatever the metaphor of losing one's humanity may mean, it would hardly seem to apply to those who act out of motives we admire, those who act out of a sense of honor and with great bravery. And yet Slobogin's principle would seem to mean that some such people are less than human, are not entitled to punishment, and may be preventively detained to keep them from causing harm in the future. Think of the civilly disobedient. Think, for example, of the young protestor who broke Israeli law by trying to obstruct a bulldozer and who was run over and killed for her trouble. Perhaps she did not intend to suffer death; perhaps it was all an accident. But would we have thought less of her if we found out that in fact she had known that death was likely and confronted it willingly to make her point? I suggest that the opposite is true. Whatever our political beliefs, we would have been forced to admire her. Yet I believe that, on Slobogin's view, she has lost her humanity, and had she survived, would be properly consigned to indefinite detention rather than punishment.

And how would you distinguish the terrorist, whom we now claim is not protected by the rules of war, from the extraordinary prisoner of war who is actually willing to fight and die for the sake of his country? I suggest that, far from losing their humanity, some of the people we most admire fall into these groups; they represent the highest sort of humanity. And if humanity means that indefinite preventive detention is inappropriate, as Slobogin suggests, then it would be inappropriate at least in the most admirable of these cases.

But there is no morally neutral way, I would suggest, to distinguish between those resisters we admire and those terrorists we abhor. Here, indeed, "when precedent is once established in the case of bad men, who, like pioneers, go before to smooth the way, good men tremble for their safety. . . ."[2] If one loses her humanity on the single ground that she is undeterrable, so does the other.

---

2. 9 ANNALS OF CONG. 538 (1807) (statement of Rep. Randolph).

I would argue that neither does, neither the good nor the evil. We might be willing to say in this metaphorical language that one who, like the sex predator, lacks the human capacity to control her behavior, lacks an essential ingredient of humanity. But one who, in the face of great danger, simply refuses to obey, is doing something human and perhaps more than human. If it honors humanity to punish their behavior, then they should be punished.

The second problem has to do with the definition of undeterrability. To avoid using language that involves the capacity to control behavior, Slobogin formulates the undeterrability criterion like this: The "universe of individuals who are 'undeterrable'" is limited to "individuals who are unaware they are engaging in criminal conduct (e.g., the seriously mentally ill) or who are extremely reckless with respect to the prospect of serious loss of liberty or death resulting from the criminal conduct (e.g., terrorists)."[3] The problem is that the second category draws no clear line between the ordinary criminal and the sort of person that I believe Slobogin would like this category to include.

Every criminal takes a chance that he will be apprehended and punished. How great must the chance be before he moves from the category of the punishable into the category of the detainable? Slobogin says that he must be willing to run a significant risk of a substantial punishment. But how much is significant, and how much is substantial? The punishments that are risked by criminals are sometimes very substantial indeed. In those cases, how great must the risk be before it is significant? Do we determine the amount of risk based upon the criminal's calculations, or by using more objective measures? Using the standards of the criminal law, we would have to say that causing a twenty percent chance of death or of life imprisonment would be more than reckless; it would be something close to depravedheart indifference. Should every criminal who believes that the chance of death or of life in prison for his crime is twenty percent or more be subject to indefinite detention?

The problem is not so much coming up with the right figures as it is in explaining why those a bit on one side of the line should be subject to punishment only, while those a bit on the other side should be subject to indefinite detention. The difference between punishment and detention is not a difference in degree; it is a difference in kind. If Slobogin is right, it depends upon the humanity of the offender. But whatever it is in us that "humanity" stands for, it can't be something that disappears as the actor's tolerance for risk edges up a bit.

---

3. Slobogin core text at 74.

DON'T ABANDON SENTENCING REFORM
TO DEFEND PREVENTIVE DETENTION

MICHAEL MARCUS*

Christopher Slobogin's promotion of "preventive detention" may undermine sentencing reform. Rational sentencing should serve most needs for public safety he would apparently address outside the criminal law. Without reform, mainstream sentencing ignores dangerousness.

Slobogin rightly demands an act amounting to a crime, even if merely "linked to a... crime such as conspiracy or attempt" or "reckless endangerment."[1] He would address only harms defined by the substantive criminal law. His "consistency" and "proportionality" principles require proof of dangerousness sufficient to permit conviction. Although proof of *dangerousness* cannot itself support a conviction, these contentions suggest that the criminal justice system adequately identifies all or nearly all of those persons for whom Slobogin would advocate "preventive detention." He notes that stops, arrests, and mental commitments have increasingly stringent burdens of justification. Convictions do not—shoplifting and murder defendants alike are entitled to proof beyond a reasonable doubt. Nothing in Slobogin's analysis argues for a lower standard for establishing that we have the right person or that the person committed the act prerequisite to preventive detention. Nor does anything in his analysis explain why sentencing after a conviction should not be the mechanism by which to address dangerousness, at least outside the realms of psychosis or infectious disease.

Slobogin cites noncapital sentencing as permeated by dangerousness determinations. In fact, death penalty, dangerous offender, and sexual predator sentencings are exceptions to mainstream sentencing's refusal to devote any responsible attention to dangerousness. Most sentencing is driven by notions of blameworthiness that are so imprecise as to permit an enormous range of sanctions for crimes—notions that protect judges and prosecutors from any responsibility for social outcomes. Yet Slobogin responds to unreliability and vagueness objections as if they came from quarters with standing. Whatever the reliability of determinations of *guilt*, it is absurd to prefer just-desert *sentencing* to preventive detention on either ground. Slobogin's defenses are correct but overlook the irony that those who argue that sentencing for risk reduction is unreliable, unfair, and vague defend a desert-based allocation of detention that is

---

* Circuit Court Judge, Multnomah County, Oregon. This comment is based in part on Michael Marcus, *Responding to the Model Penal Code Sentencing Revisions: Tips for Early Adopters and Power Users*, 17 S. CAL. INTERDISC. L.J. 68 (2007).

1. Slobogin core text at 71.

far worse on all scores. Desert-based sentencing, after all, does not even purport to address risk, let alone punish accurately, predictably, or equitably.

Accurate risk assessment has nothing to do with false positives. Assume two assaults alike in terms of seriousness by offenders alike by prior convictions. If other variables accurately indicate one at a 30 percent likelihood of future violent crime and the other at 1 percent, there are no false positives, no punishments for future crimes, and no inequity when we consider the 30-fold disparity in risk and incapacitate one but treat the other. We surely should not increase severity due to such "static" factors as protected class membership, but it hardly follows that all "static" factors must be disregarded. It is not fair to offenders or their potential victims to ignore the disparity in risk between the psychotic and the merely reckless in allocating incapacitative and rehabilitative responses to the otherwise identical crime.

Vagueness concerns more properly focus on providing fair notice of what is proscribed than on *sentencing*. Few if any potential offenders plan behavior in light of the severity of a potential sanction. Dangerous offenders do not behave less dangerously because we have provided for extended sentences for dangerous offenders.

Slobogin's suggestion that the "alternative regime of liberty deprivation" is necessary for those "who are 'undeterrable'" is an unfortunate nod to retributive theory.[2] The vast majority of offenders are not psychopaths, but neither are they deterred by threatened sanctions. Values, impulse control, peer approval, and tribalism determine the bulk of behavior. Modifying the criminal behavior of those we convict and sentence is a far more responsible objective than maintaining the fallacy that mere retribution serves any social purpose.

The proponents of a "right to be punished" dismiss social causes of crime *because they favor punishment*. They abhor defenses based upon abuse, diminished capacity, or mental defect. The right to be punished needs no vindication, or else we'd allow it to be waived along with counsel, self-incrimination, and even trial. The only content of just deserts worthy of response is that which serves pro-social functions: deterrence (on rare occasion); promoting public values by denunciation or example, and enhancing respect for the persons, property, and rights of others; obviating vigilantism and private retribution; serving actual needs of specific victims; and fostering respect for law and its institutions.

Before we attempt to construct a supplanting mechanism for managing offender risk, we should demand that all sentencing demonstrably serve risk management purposes within the limits of proportionality, and address only the pro-social content of just deserts—which rarely conflicts with best efforts at risk management.

---

2. Slobogin core text at 74.

THE PRESUMPTION OF INNOCENCE VERSUS PREVENTIVE DETENTION

RINAT KITAI-SANGERO*

Christopher Slobogin is correct that most arguments against preventive detention do not negate its legitimacy, but lead instead to greater care in its implementation. The main problem with the concept of preventive detention, however, is the harm caused to the presumption of innocence.

Preventive detention reflects an assumption of guilt and a negative assessment of the detainee's character. An assessment of future dangerousness necessarily violates the presumption of innocence because it assumes a person is not generally disposed to obey the law. The presumption of innocence not only assumes that a person is innocent of a specific offense charged against him. It also assumes that a person is generally law-abiding (which holds true even if he has been convicted in the past). Detention of a person based only on the fear that he will commit a crime assumes guilt. The presumption of innocence serves to protect the individual not only from being punished prior to conviction, but also from restrictions that treat him as an offender before being convicted. Preventive detention cannot be reconciled with the presumption of innocence.

Slobogin believes that the possibility of periodic review concerning the question of dangerousness distinguishes between punishment and prevention. This distinction will give little comfort to the detainee. When a person finds himself in the position of being a defendant, the assumption is that his innocence or guilt will be determined at the conclusion of the criminal process. If the defendant is acquitted, he will be released from detention, although it is hard to say that he is less dangerous on the day of his acquittal than on the prior day.

However, when a person is indefinitely detained, as in the case of the commitment of a sexual predator, his guilt regarding future offenses is in effect conclusively presumed, and he therefore has no way to prove innocence. The passage of time will not necessarily help the detainee to prove he is not dangerous. Unless circumstances change significantly, claims that have not been convincing in the past will probably not be convincing in the present. Since the commitment is linked to dangerousness, indefinite duration of confinement is not ruled out ab initio.

The conflict with the presumption of innocence does not completely rule out preventive detention, since the presumption of innocence may be balanced against other competitive values. Nevertheless, given the presumption's importance, preventive detention should be limited to the most exceptional cases and for defined periods of time. Here, as a practical matter, are still grounds

---

* Senior Lecturer, Academic Center of Law and Business, Ramat Gan, Israel.

for concern. If the notion of preventive detention is accepted in principle, perhaps not many would insist that its practical implementation must be attended with the significant restrictions Slobogin proposes. But without those restrictions, the result could be a boundless expansion of the opportunities to deprive a person of his freedom without the procedural safeguards the criminal law provides.

UNRELIABILITY, INNOCENCE, AND PREVENTIVE DETENTION

MATT MATRAVERS*

Perhaps the most obvious objection to the use of preventive detention is that the predictive technologies we possess are poor, so the rate of false positives is high. One argument Christopher Slobogin offers in reply to this objection is that there is just as much, if not more, unreliability in our measures of blameworthiness and culpability, so a just deserts sentencing regime will be at least as flawed.

The argument seems straightforward: justice demands that offenders get what is appropriate (however defined; that is, "appropriate" could include a dangerousness tariff). In the just deserts model, many offenders will get either more or less than they deserve. In the preventive detention model, some persons will get a greater burden than is appropriate. Yet the claim that these are equivalent is deeply counterintuitive.

The asymmetry between these cases can be explained in one of two ways. First, one might say that the false positive is equivalent to an innocent, and what is objectionable about punishing the innocent is not just that they do not deserve it, but that punishment does not follow from any act or choice of the person. An innocent could not have avoided punishment by acting differently (in the relevant sense), whereas the offender who is punished too severely has somehow put himself at risk. However, another of Slobogin's arguments (considered below) dictates that those preventatively detained have acted in ways that make them liable to this risk.

Second, in the just deserts model rightly convicted offenders deserve *something* and then many receive either more or less of that thing than they deserve. In contrast, in the case of preventive detention, false positives should justly have no burden to carry, yet a burden is applied. Intuitively, these are not equivalent. It is a deeper violation of justice to hold someone in prison for five years when it is inappropriate that he should be burdened at all, than it is to punish a rightfully

---

* Professor of Political Philosophy, Department of Politics, University of York, United Kingdom.

convicted offender with a sentence that is five years shorter or longer than his culpability requires.

It might be thought that this intuition has its origins in an unsavory view that "offenders" are different from the law-abiding, and we should care less about them. I do not think this is right. Rather, the origins lie in our beliefs about desert and justice.

Consider two people who each deserve an equal benefit (praise or reward). One receives more than she is due, the other less. We have the opportunity to correct only one situation. It seems clear to me that we should raise the position of the person with less than she deserves.[1] The converse holds for burdens; a situation in which someone is overburdened is worse from the point of view of justice than one in which someone carries a burden that is too light. It is worse, still, for someone for whom no burden is appropriate and yet a burden is applied. Thus, the unreliability objection cannot be met by alleging equivalent unreliability in the case of blameworthiness even when issues of the "false positive as innocent" are put to one side.

The argument on which Slobogin relies to avoid the "false positive as innocent" is that coercion should only be used in response to what people *do* and not what they *are*. This, he argues, provides a threshold for the use of preventive detention. The potential target of such detention must have engaged in "a crime or behavior that indicates harm is imminent."[2] This threshold is surely both right and necessary, but it is hard to understand how it relates to the fundamental injunction to coerce only on the basis of acts and not assessments of personality. When an offender is refused release at the end of his sentence—or a dangerousness tariff is appended to the end of his sentence—the state is judging that he is a risk; he is likely to give in to the temptation to commit serious harm. *That* is an assessment of who he is, not of what he has done. And that, of course, is why we should worry—as Slobogin does—about the use of preventive detention and the restrictions that should be imposed upon it. My point is that those worries are not dissipated by stipulating that those who are subject to detention must have acted in some risky way in the past.

---

1. This idea is explored in part in Shelly Kagan, *Equality and Desert, in* WHAT DO WE DESERVE? A READER ON JUSTICE AND DESERT 298–314 (Louis P. Pojman and Owen McLeod eds., 1999).

2. Slobogin core text at 74.

THE DANGER OF DANGEROUSNESS AS A BASIS FOR INCARCERATION

JOSEPH E. KENNEDY*

Christopher Slobogin has made what is perhaps the most thoughtful and persuasive arguments possible for permitting preventive incarceration solely on the grounds of future dangerousness. (Note that I object at the outset to the use of the more benign sounding word "detention" to refer to deprivations of liberty that may last for years). Yet I still find myself alarmed at the prospect of such a practice. Simply put, future dangerousness is too dangerous as a sole basis for incarceration because it appeals too directly to our deepest, strongest, and potentially most violent instinct—self preservation.

Slobogin recognizes these "dangers" and tackles them head on. Indeed, one argument in support of his approach might be "if you can't beat them, join them." Because irrational fears of danger drive much of contemporary hyperpunitiveness, we should accept preventive detention and then bring to bear our best efforts to make our assessments of dangerousness rational and reliable. Because Slobogin clearly recognizes the perils of irrational notions of dangerousness, a more precise statement of the argument might be "if you can't beat them, co-opt their concerns while subjecting them to rigorous analysis." Not quite as catchy, but I think it captures the essence.

I am not convinced. Dangerousness is simply too emotionally and rhetorically powerful a category to cabin effectively once acknowledged as a sufficient basis for incarceration. It is our collective heart of darkness, the place where our passions and prejudices rule supreme. Indeed, one might interpret the mass incarceration of recent years as in part the product of seeing punishment as being primarily about self-protection. Why take a chance that a property or drug offender might someday turn violent when we can lock him away for life under a three strikes provision? Why risk putting a violent offender on probation or parole when incarceration eliminates any possibility that he will prey on an unsuspecting member of the public? A preoccupation with dangerousness has brought us to the point where two million people in prison—a roughly 500 percent increase in per capita incarceration over three decades—seems normal.

Can we tame or manage dangerousness as a principle through reason or science? History is not encouraging on this point. We have always looked to science for "silver bullets" to resolve in an overly simple way what are morally and psychologically complex questions about offender conduct. Just as we once readily believed that we could identify criminals by feeling the bumps on their skulls, I fear that what will pass for science in the area of dangerousness will be

---

* Associate Professor of Law, University of North Carolina Law School.

poorly supported hypotheses that will be accepted because they appeal to our thirst for certainty and to our preexisting prejudices about human behavior.

Even relatively "hard" scientific methodologies such as DNA testing have often been administered poorly in our underfinanced and badly regulated system of criminal justice. The softer psychological sciences that would be employed under Slobogin's approach would be infinitely more susceptible to mishandling. Because science is itself produced by people subject to the limitations of their own cultural and social contexts, one cannot imagine it to operate free of the passions and prejudices that notions of dangerousness have historically stirred up.

Assessing future dangerousness is not "rocket science." When you get your rocket calculations wrong, the rocket crashes to the ground and you are confronted with the wreckage of your own mistakes. When society overestimates the dangerousness of certain feared individuals or groups—as it recently has been doing—the damage is rendered invisible by incarceration. We will never know how many people we have incarcerated unnecessarily because the years spent inside a prison tell little or nothing about what their behavior in society might have been.

We cannot and should not exclude concerns about future dangerousness from the decision to incarcerate, but we should reduce—not expand—the role such concerns play. Dangerousness will always appeal to our basest instincts. Incarceration should never be based solely on our worst fears.

REPLY

CHRISTOPHER SLOBOGIN

Michael Corrado suggests that I believe the "determined criminal. . . loses her humanity."[1] He then provides several examples of why he disagrees with that proposition and why the "undeterrability" concept I use is problematic as a definitional matter. First, I am not sure I believe the determined or undeterrable criminal does lose her humanity, whatever that may mean, or that the prevention detention creates that effect. As I noted, the dehumanization objection is an abstract one that is hard to evaluate.

But assuming that objection is viable, Corrado's discussion of undeterrability overlooks two aspects of the "recklessness" component of that concept, which is defined as a readiness to commit *significant* crime even if a *police officer were present*. Thus the Israeli protester he mentions would not qualify as undeterrable, as her crime was simple trespass, and ordinary reckless offenders would not qualify as they are not oblivious to detection in the way some highly impulsive (and very rare) sex offenders and psychopaths are. Admittedly, even under this narrow

---

1. Corrado comment at 76.

definition, some "terrorists" who intentionally kill innocent noncombatants would qualify as undeterrable. But if there is a category of people who are less than human, these people would fit it.

Corrado also mentions prisoners of war, who may be undeterrable, given their orders, yet are deserving of full respect as human. As I noted, to the extent the dehumanization objection to preventive detention is viable, it has strength only when punishment and preventive detention are both options and the latter is chosen over the former (as when sex offenders are treated as predators rather than convicts). In the war setting, preventive detention of enemy combatants is the only option (unless a war crime is committed), and thus the dehumanization objection does not arise.

Despite these rejoinders, Corrado's concern about the ambiguity and potential abuse of the notion of undeterrability is justified. That is why I stated that, if punishment *is* an option, government should be required to pursue that avenue first. Only if punishment is not possible (as with insanity acquittees or enemy combatants, or a sentence has expired) should *pure* preventive detention—that is, a detention based on a risk assessment in a system separate from criminal punishment—be permitted (and only then of people who are undeterrable).

Because I conclude that pure preventive detention should be used sparingly, I doubt that my defense of preventive detention will prove distracting to sentencing reform of the type Michael Marcus advocates. Indeed, because I conclude that dangerousness may legitimately be considered at sentencing, my project is entirely consistent with Marcus's position that the focus of sentencing should be the reduction of recidivism based on risk assessments. Presumably, Marcus would agree that those assessments should be structured so that they accurately reflect differential risk and do not infringe unduly on liberty, which is what the proportionality, consistency, and least drastic means principles are designed to do.

These limitations on preventive detention should also assuage the concerns of Rinat Kitai-Sangero, who argues that preventive detention undermines the procedural protections associated with determinations of guilt. Kitai-Sangero is particularly worried about the effect of preventive detention on the presumption of innocence. In *Bell v. Wolfish*,[2] the U.S. Supreme Court held that the presumption is merely an evidentiary doctrine designed to counteract the fact finder's likely preconceptions about criminal defendants at trial and does not preclude the government from preventively detaining dangerous individuals not convicted of crime. In any event, under my proposal intervention would not occur unless a crime or obviously risky conduct is proven, so even the insult to the presumption that Professor Kitai-Sangero imagines would disappear.

Matt Matravers focuses on a more traditional criticism of preventive detention—that it is based on inaccurate predictions. He responds to my suggestion

---

2. 441 U.S. 520 (1979).

that risk assessment is no less accurate than culpability assessment by stating that "false positives should justly have no burden to carry."[3] If that were true, then sentences that are enhanced because of risk (of the type Marcus favors) are illegitimate. Perhaps Matravers accepts that conclusion. He would still have to explain why it is "just" to preventively detain people with mental illness and not others. Perhaps he doesn't think preventive detention is just even in that situation. Or he does, but based on something akin to the undeterrability rationale that I develop, in which case we are not that far apart, at least when it comes to pure preventive detention (unlimited by retributive considerations).

But a more fundamental answer to Matravers can begin with a question: why is it any less "just" to confine someone because of an erroneous assessment of risk than because of an erroneous assessment of culpability? Matravers states that, in a backward-looking regime, a guilty person clearly deserves *some* punishment, so that a sentence that is five years longer than the person deserves is not as "unjust" as a five-year preventive confinement of someone who would not have committed crime during that period. But the first person is being inappropriately confined just as long as the second person. Moreover, with the protections that I advocate, such confinement is much less likely in a preventive regime.

Joseph Kennedy's appeal against preventive "incarceration" is that detentions based on dangerousness could become the dark maw of government, swallowing offenders forever despite the limitations I would impose. In a worst case scenario, his vision could be correct, at least with respect to the most serious offenders. But of course, as he himself has recognized, three strikes laws, life without parole provisions, truth-in-sentencing statutes, and the abolition of parole in serious cases have already given us that result. Preventive detention is *selective* incapacitation, not general incapacitation of the type we have now, and thus may well be the lesser evil even if we assume government actors will ignore legal constraints.

---

3. Matravers comment at 81.

4. THE ECONOMICS OF CRIME CONTROL

DORON TEICHMAN*

I. INTRODUCTION

According to Gary Becker, it was while searching for parking in New York City—as he calculated the probability of being ticketed and the size of penalty that will be assessed to him if his violation will detected—that he started to think about the economics of crime and punishment. Thus, it would seem like we should all thank New York City, and its enforcement of its local parking laws, for one of the most important contributions to economic and legal scholarship in recent decades. This brief core text begins with a description of Becker's principal conclusions, as set forth in his seminal paper, *Crime and Punishment: An Economic Approach*,[1] and then turns to explore some of the developments in the literature since the publication of the paper.

II. THE ECONOMIC MODEL OF CRIMINAL BEHAVIOR

The economic approach toward criminal behavior focuses on the choices made by criminals. Criminals are not seen as "ill" or drawn to crime in an uncontrollable pathological fashion. Rather, they are seen as rational beings that choose to commit crimes if the utility they expect to derive from crimes exceed the costs associated with them, and no alternative economic activities exist that offer these individuals a higher payoff.

The costs of committing a crime are rich and diverse. For example, peoples' internal moral inclinations might have a large influence on the willingness to commit crimes. The focus of Becker's paper, however, is on the cost that the legal system imposes on crimes. More specifically, the "price" that the legal system imposes on criminals is a result of two policy tools. The first is the sanction imposed on criminals who are caught and convicted by the courts. The second is the probability that a criminal will actually be sanctioned (keeping in mind that this probability is a result of a series of sequential events ranging from the probability that the police will catch the criminal, through the probability that the prosecution will choose to charge him, and ending with the probability that

* The Joseph H. and Belle R. Braun Senior Lectureship in Law, Faculty of Law, Hebrew University of Jerusalem.

1. Gary S. Becker, *Crime and Punishment: An Economic Approach*, 76 J. POL. ECON. 169 (1968).

the courts will convict). The combined effect of these tools renders the expected sanction. At the core of the economic analysis of crime and punishment lies the claim that as the expected sanction rises the attractiveness of committing crimes diminishes, and less people are expected to choose to commit crimes.[2] In other words, much like the demand for beef decreases as the price of beef rises, so the demand for committing crime diminishes as the cost of committing crime rises.

It is often argued that an increase in the probability of detection reduces crime to a greater extent than an equivalent increase in the size of the sanction. This claim can be incorporated into the model by taking into account the risk preferences of potential criminals. Risk-averse individuals are expected to be more deterred by a sanctioning regime based on high and relatively rare sanctions. Risk-seeking individuals, on the other hand, are expected to be more deterred by a sanctioning regime based on low and relatively certain sanctions. Thus, criminals might be risk-seeking, at least in the relevant region of punishments.

III. POLICY IMPLICATIONS

I now turn to the normative implications of the Becker model. The two issues I address here are the optimal *size* of criminal sanctions the state should impose, and the optimal *type* of sanctions it should imposed.

A. The Economics of Expected Sanctions

There is a long-standing debate in the crime-control policy literature over the desirable size of criminal sanctions. According to many scholars the punishment must "fit" the crime and should presumably be "proportional." Although one might find it difficult to disagree with such phrases (after all, who would think that a policy-maker should choose a sanction that does *not* "fit" the crime), we are still left with the question of what such phrases actually mean. From an economic perspective the goal of a crime-control regime is to minimize the social costs of crime. These costs include both the harms created by offenses, and the cost of deterring criminals by apprehending and sanctioning them.

The variables subject to social choice are the resources invested in increasing the probability of detection, and the size and type of sanction inflicted on those criminals who are caught and convicted. As Becker points out, the costs of raising the probability of detection are generally greater than the costs of raising sanctions since public resources need to be spent on policemen, judges, juries,

---

2. The nonlegal aspects of the model can also affect criminal behavior. For example, a rise in the income available from legal actives is expected to lower criminal activity. Similarly, a change in preferences toward greater law-abidingness may reduce crime rates.

and so forth. On the other hand, raising sanctions is relatively cheap, especially if we are dealing with fines. Hence, an optimal crime-control regime should use relatively low apprehension rates and couple them with high sanctions in order to sustain the expected sanction that minimizes social costs. Nonetheless, to the extent that external moral constraints cause actors in the legal system to resist imposing what they see as excessively harsh sanctions (e.g., prosecutors circumventing sanctions by plea bargains, juries refusing to convict guilty offenders), then these constraints should be accounted for in order to prevent a situation in which optimal but harsh sanctions are not actually imposed and inflicted.

Another implication of the model is that expected sanctions should be calibrated to the social harm caused by offenses. Generally, as the harm caused by an offense increases, the optimal level of apprehension and the level of sanction increase as well. As Becker points out, many anecdotal examples demonstrate the tendency to raise both the probability of detection and the level of sanctions with respect to more harmful offenses.

The model also suggests that an efficient crime-control system should employ price discrimination between different types of potential criminals. Experience suggests that potential criminals differ in their sensitivity to legal prices. For instance, the insane or the young are probably less affected by the potential consequences of their choices when compared to other types of potential criminals. Thus, an optimal sanctioning regime should employ lower probabilities of detection and sanctions with respect to groups who are not sensitive to legal prices, and resources should be allocated to deter those who are deterable.

Finally, one should note that while the Becker model focuses on deterring criminals through the calibration of the legal price system, the goal of punishment according to the model is *optimal* deterrence and not deterrence per se. Thus, the Becker model should not be read as a call for endless expenditures on crime control. On the contrary, the model demonstrates that some offenses should not be prevented since the cost of preventing them is prohibitively high.

B. The Economics of Fines and Incarceration
In order to analyze what makes a criminal sanction optimal we should first analyze the benchmark case in which the cost of sanctioning is assumed to be zero. In other words, the costs of detecting, prosecuting, and ultimately punishing criminals are all assumed away. Under such conditions it can be shown that the optimal probability of detection is one, and that sanctions should equal the marginal harm caused by the crime. To the extent that the harm caused by crime exceeds the benefits incurred by criminals, such a regime will reduce crime to zero. Such a system resembles a tort system in which in many cases the probability of detection is unity, and in which the cost of sanctioning tortfeasors is relatively low.

This result—that the legal price should equal the marginal harm—is typical of market models. An implicit assumption in such models is that the price system functions at no cost, and therefore optimality is usually achieved when marginal costs equal marginal benefits. Yet the legal pricing system is different since the application of legal prices may be costly. This cost in turn affects the conditions of optimality. More specifically, if apprehending and convicting criminals is costly, then fines ought to be adjusted upward so that they will cause criminals to internalize the full social costs of their acts.

An additional policy dimension over which decision-makers have control is the type of punishment imposed. I will focus on the use of fines and incarceration as sanctions, ignoring for now other forms of punishment such as probation or corporal punishment. From an economic perspective, fines have several advantages over imprisonment. First, fines are transfer payments from one pocket to the other and therefore represent a small social loss.[3] In contrast, incarceration uses resources in order to build and operate prisons.[4] One should not underestimate the importance of these costs: At the time Becker published his paper the estimated cost of incarceration in the United States was one billion dollars; recent estimates put it at around sixty billion dollars.[5] Second, aside from its transparent budgetary costs, incarceration causes a hidden cost in the shape of offenders' opportunity costs. The current situation in which one out of every one hundred American adults is behind bars represents a significant cost in lost GDP terms. Finally, unlike incarceration, fines can be used in order to compensate victims and restore the status quo ante. Although compensation through the legal system is not necessary from an economic perspective, compensation might alleviate some of the fear and anger toward criminals and help reintegrate them into society without the formal and informal restrictions existing today.

The use of fines is often criticized as immoral since they may be interpreted as a price that criminals pay for the right to commit a crime much like any other commodity is bought in the marketplace. The economic approach toward crime and punishment does not dispute this point: a fine can be seen as a price. Similarly, any other form of sanction (including incarceration) can also be seen as a price. Thus, those who oppose the use of fines as a form of punishment are left with the question: Why should we use an inefficient pricing system and not an efficient one?

Another criticism levied against fines relates to the fact that they ignore differences between the wealth of offenders. Yet if the goal of the crime control system is to minimize the social loss created by crime, and not some type of retributive

---

3. A complete analysis of the social cost of fines should take into account the positive costs associated with collecting fines.

4. A complete analysis in this regard should take account of the fact that some of the costs of operating the prison system are transfers as well since inmates receive basic needs such as food and shelter.

5. *See, e.g.,* Adam M. Gershowitz, *An Informational Approach to the Mass Imprisonment Problem,* 40 ARIZ. ST. L.J. 47, 81 (2008).

goal, then sanctions should only take account of harms and costs and should not take account of offenders' wealth. In any event, fines can be adjusted to take account of an offender's income if a society wishes to promote other values through its criminal-sanctioning system, keeping in mind that doing so produces inefficiencies. For example, it has recently been reported that a wealthy Nokia executive was assessed a $103,000 ticket for driving above the speed limit since fines in Finland are adjusted to wealth.[6] The economic approach toward punishment focuses on treating individuals who created identical risks or harms equally, and not as a way to redistribute wealth.

The analysis thus far does not suggest that fines should be the only way criminals are punished. Whenever the optimal sanction required exceeds the resources of criminals, a sanctioning regime must employ alternatives to fines. This principle seems to describe many of the sanctioning regimes observed in which heinous crimes that create tremendous harm are punished with imprisonment. Finally, given the relative desirability of employing fines, policy-makers ought to develop a flexible system of fines based on an installment plan, since doing so will permit greater reliance on fines and less on imprisonment.

IV. REFINEMENTS

I was once taught that there are two types of "great papers." The first are those that end a long-standing debate by presenting a conclusive argument dispatching all competing claims. The second are those that open a new debate, highlighting a question theretofore overlooked. Becker's paper fits nicely into the latter category. Although the paper did not offer a final and definitive answer to the many questions associated with crime control, it did introduce a new paradigm through which to analyze these questions: that of economic reasoning.

The most important contribution of the Becker model—as I read it—is the insight that crime control (and more generally, law) is yet another service provided by the government to its subjects, and should be evaluated based on cost-benefit analysis. Before Becker, powerful legal terms such as "justice" and "fairness" crowded out the economic perspective from ongoing policy debates. Becker demonstrated that policy decisions relating to law are no different from those relating to health care, education, and markets. The positive tools of economic theory can be employed to model the effects of legal rules on the behavior of decision-makers, and the normative tools of welfare economics can be used to compare the desirability of different policy options.

Following Becker's initial contribution, the concept of expected sanctions as prices has been further developed. George Stigler offered an important refinement

---

6. See $103,000 Speed Trap, NEWSDAY, Jan. 16, 2002, at A8.

to the theory when he pointed out the importance of marginal deterrence.[7] Stigler focused his analysis on the decision of the criminal to engage in additional—marginal—harmful activity. As he suggested, if the law offers a singular severe punishment (taking all of the offender's wealth, for example), then the offender might as well commit the more severe and harmful crime. Thus, optimal sanctions should aim to achieve optimal deterrence at the margin. Additionally, it was shown that the use of low-probability severe sanctions might be undesirable once the incentives of offenders to invest resources in defending against prosecution are accounted for. If, for example, we would supplement our current rather modest traffic fines with fines that equal a substantial amount of drivers' personal wealth, the result would be a sharp increase in the cost of administering the system as the amount of drivers choosing to contest their fine would rise significantly.

Legal scholars have also studied the connection between potential substitution effects and the pricing system created by criminal law. Economists are accustomed to modeling how changes in relative prices bring about substitutions in the decisions of individuals. For example, if the price of beef rises, then some consumers are expected to substitute their consumption of beef with a similar product (say, chicken). Similarly, criminals might shift from one criminal activity to the other as a result of sanction arbitrages created between different types of crimes. For instance, if the sanction applied to dealers of crack cocaine is enhanced, drug dealers might choose to substitute offenses and distribute other drugs. A related phenomenon might occur in a decentralized crime control system in which sanction arbitrages between regions might cause criminals to shift their activity to the more lenient areas. For example, if the expected sanction for auto theft is higher in Michigan than in neighboring states, then auto thieves from Michigan might choose to move their activity to Ohio where their expected profits are higher.

Two other lines of argument stemming directly from the Becker model are worth mentioning. The first deals with shame sanctions. As we have seen, Becker's analysis focused on fines as the most efficient method to punish offenders. Yet the political reality suggests that substituting fines for incarceration is difficult. Thus, it has been suggested that publicly shaming criminals might be desirable. On one hand, shaming is relativity cheap compared to incarceration and can therefore deter criminals at a lower cost. On the other hand, shaming does carry a social symbolic value that fines do not, and therefore may be a viable political option.

Second, legal scholars have recently attempted to enrich the Becker model by incorporating insights from cognitive psychology. For example, Ehud Guttel and Alon Harel have examined the legal implications of the different way in which

---

7. George J. Stigler, *The Optimum Enforcement of Laws*, 78 J. Pol. Econ. 526 (1970).

people perceive uncertainty relating to the past and uncertainty relating to the future.[8] A robust psychological literature demonstrates that people tend to prefer to take risks with respect to events that will take place in the future and not in the past (e.g., they prefer to bet on the result of a die toss that will take place in the future and not one that already took place despite the equal probability to guess the result correctly). This finding may affect the design of an optimal crime-control system. For instance, deterrence may be enhanced by a simple move like determining who the tax authority will audit at the beginning of the tax year rather than at its end. Economic reasoning does not oppose such attempts to adjust the Becker model of crime control. At the end of the day, the question is one of costs and benefits: Does complicating the baseline model create a benefit (in the form of more accurate predictions of the behavior of potential criminals and more efficient policy recommendations) that justifies the cost of the complications?

---

8. *See* Ehud Guttel and Alon Harel, *Uncertainty Revisited: Legal Prediction and Legal Postdiction*, 107 MICH. L. REV. 467 (2008).

COMMENTS

THE LIMITS OF THE ECONOMIC MODEL: BECKER'S *CRIME AND PUNISHMENT*

RUSSELL D. COVEY*

Economic analysis, which is founded on the assumption that people respond to incentives, wisely prompts us to frame questions in terms of the incentives that drive conduct. Gary Becker's landmark essay brilliantly brings that analysis to bear on the problem of crime control, as Doron Teichman ably describes. But Becker's project, which updates the utilitarian theory of Jeremy Bentham and Cesare Beccaria, shares flaws with those earlier theories.[1] Here, I briefly address a few such problems that Teichman fails to mention.

First, the economic approach, like utilitarian theory in general, is hobbled by the daunting problem of calculating social utility. Although the utilitarian maxim that social policy should aim to maximize social utility is perfectly sensible in the abstract, determining which social policies accomplish that goal turns on how utility is defined (and hence on who is doing the defining). The law and economics school tries to simplify matters by replacing the vague utilitarian concept of

---

* Associate Professor, Georgia State University College of Law.

1. *See* Gary S. Becker, *Crime and Punishment: An Economic Approach*, 76 J. POL. ECON. 169, 209 (1968).

utility with the purportedly crisper concept of social income. Wise social planners, Becker argued, will design criminal justice policies with the aim of minimizing the social loss of income caused by criminal activities.

But substituting "income" for "utility" does not make the problem disappear. Should one person's moral disapproval of another's consensual conduct count as a "diseconomy"? Is there a measurable social gain in vengeance? Even setting such ambiguities aside, comparing the costs and benefits of crime control remains difficult. For instance, how should an economist account for "malevolent income"? Should an assessment of social income include the monetarized value of the pleasure derived by the assailant in striking his victim? Certainly, the scope of the crime problem diminishes if we counterbalance the losses suffered by crime victims with the criminals' gains. In assuming social consensus about such questions, Becker assumed away some of the most critical issues of criminal law.

The approach to crime control lauded in Teichman's core text is also susceptible to the familiar accusation that its consequentialist accounting leads to the pursuit of immoral policies because the "end justifies the means." For instance, criminal law doctrines that excuse or mitigate punishment and that are readily understandable in terms of culpability and desert are only awkwardly accommodated by wealth-maximization theory. Although Becker asserted that punishing nondeterrables is socially costly (thus justifying affirmative defenses like insanity and duress), the argument is based on the uncertain empirical claim that culpability-based excuses do not diminish the overall deterrent effect of law. Given widespread popular beliefs that excuses like insanity are easily abused, abolition of affirmative defenses may increase marginal deterrence with little cost. (After all, the institutionalized insane would continue to be a drain on resources). If so, the economic approach to crime control counsels against retaining such defenses. The economic approach also fails to provide reasons to refrain from imposing draconian punishments—torture or life imprisonment—as long as doing so leads to an aggregate social gain in wealth. Yet, there are of course valuable reasons for retaining culpability-based defenses and for barring draconian punishments that have little to do with maximizing society's wealth.

Viewed strictly through the lens of wealth maximization, it is also hard to explain the enforcement of criminal laws against many criminal enterprises (e.g., prostitution or marijuana cultivation) that, but for their illicit nature, would otherwise count toward an increase in social wealth. In an economic sense, the main distinction between crime and noncrime may have more to do with means (the terms of transfer) than ends (the net effect on social wealth). Wealth effects do not distinguish the masseuse from the prostitute, the tomato grower from the pot grower, or perhaps even the husband performing his marital duties from the rapist. Instead, what makes one category legal and the other criminal depends on transactional rules and the distribution of entitlements. The nature of these rules and the consequences for contravening them are essentially political questions that cannot be answered without recourse to theories of rights and distributional justice, and as such, occupy precisely that normative space that economics is ill-suited to address.

I do not for a moment contend that Becker was unaware of these issues. His nuanced and sophisticated essay is quite rightly celebrated as a great achievement, as Teichman argues. But it is all too easy to forget, and hence too often forgotten, that the projects of maximizing social wealth and constructing a just society—of which a just, fair, and morally-defensible criminal law is an essential part—are fundamentally distinct enterprises.

THE ECONOMIC ANALYSIS OF CRIME CONTROL: A FRIENDLY CRITIQUE

ALON HAREL*

Doron Teichman aptly captures the insights of Gary Becker's seminal essay, *Crime and Punishment: An Economic Approach*. Becker's analysis is premised on the conviction that criminal law is a method for crime control; it is a service provided by the government to its citizens, and its provision, like the provision of any other service, ought to be efficient. Criminal law and criminal-law enforcement policy ought to minimize the social costs of crime. These costs include both the harms resulting from crime and the resources invested in crime prevention. To provide this service, one ought to understand the behavior of criminals and evaluate the effectiveness of incentives. Criminals are understood by Becker to be "rational beings that choose to commit crimes if the utility they expect to derive from crimes exceed the costs associated with them, and no alternative economic activities exist that offer these individuals a higher payoff."[1] Although Jeremy Bentham's classical *Introduction to the Principles of Morals and Legislation* developed in a masterful way a similar paradigm, Becker injected into this paradigm greater precision and sophistication by using the mathematical tools of neoclassical economics.

The economic paradigm has proven to be highly fertile for criminal law theory. Economists use it toward a variety of ends: to determine what behavior ought to be regulated by criminal law (rather than, for instance, tort law), the size of the expected sanctions, the optimal composition of the probability and the size of sanctions, the choice between different sanctions (e.g., fines or incarceration),

---

* Phillip P. Mizock and Estelle Mizock Chair in Administrative and Criminal Law, Hebrew University Law Faculty.

1. Teichman core text at 87.

and the details of legal doctrines such as the requirement of intent, the defense of necessity, the treatment of attempts, etc.

A critical examination of Becker's contribution could be based on a global rejection of the efficiency-based paradigm as a tool in the design of law, or at least, rejection of its relevance for criminal law. Alternatively, such a critical examination could share the methodological assumptions of Becker and yet establish that some of his conclusions are either wrong or ought to be revised. Most of this comment adopts the latter approach.

Becker's analysis is a purely deterrence-based analysis. But other traditional goals of punishment such as incapacitation also have an impact on efficiency. Unlike retributive goals, incapacitation can, at least in principle, be analyzed in economic terms. Yet neither Becker nor the tradition following him has provided any new insights concerning incapacitation.

Becker considered two costs that the legal system imposes on criminals: the size of the sanction and the probability of detection. Yet the rich literature on uncertainty and ambiguity indicates the importance of additional factors. The size of the sanction itself is probabilistic and a probabilistic sanction, e.g., a sanction the size of which depends on the outcome of a lottery, may operate differently than a sanction whose size is fixed (nonprobablistic). Similarly, the probability of detection could shift and change in unpredictable ways. Recent behavioral literature indicates that uncertainty with respect to the size of the sanction and the probability of detection may affect the incentives to commit crimes.[2]

Becker believed that punishment should be imposed in order to *internalize* the social harm of criminal conduct. Hence, the size of the expected sanction should equal the marginal harm resulting from the crime. Becker-type sanctions are therefore "internalizing sanctions." They are prices designed to guarantee that the criminal considers the costs resulting from the crime and decides on the basis of the costs and benefits whether to commit the crime or not. In contrast, Richard Posner argues that criminal sanctions should be "gain-annulling": they should be set to completely deter crime by eliminating the prospect of gains on the part of the offender.[3]

Arguably, by extracting the entire gain of the criminal, gain-annulling sanctions would deter "efficient" crimes. Thus, for instance, gain-annulling sanctions would deter a polluter from polluting even when the gains from pollution are larger than its costs. Posner argues that by inflicting gain-annulling sanctions, criminals would use the market to acquire the goods. Gain-annulling

---

2. *See* Alon Harel and Uzi Segal, *Criminal Law and Behavioral Law and Economics: Observations on the Neglected Role of Uncertainty in Deterring Crime,* 1 AM. L. & ECON. REV. 276 (1999).

3. Richard Posner, *An Economic Theory of Criminal Law,* 85 COLUM. L. REV. 1193–1291 (1985).

sanctions are therefore superior to internalizing sanctions because they channel criminals into the market.[4]

There are two interesting and perhaps related issues that pose a great challenge to the law and economics tradition. Becker's analysis blurs the strict dichotomy between criminal law and criminal-law enforcement policy. The size and nature of sanctions as well as the resources invested in police and courts are subjected to the same considerations and are interrelated to each other. In this respect Becker's analysis differs radically from the traditional analysis under which these two issues are regarded as belonging to radically different spheres. Furthermore, although Becker's paradigm was highly influential among theorists, it has barely influenced legal doctrine. It is the dominant conviction among criminal lawyers that criminal law doctrine is grounded in nonutilitarian moral considerations. The question is whether the law and economics tradition can accommodate these intuitions and explain their dominance on efficiency-based grounds or whether it ought to regard these intuitions as simply irrational or incomprehensible.

---

4. For an attempt to design a system which combines both types of sanctions, see Keith Hylton, *The Theory of Penalties and the Economics of Criminal Law*, 1 REV. L. & ECON. 176 (2005).

EFFICIENT DETERRENCE AND CRIME CONTROL

KEITH N. HYLTON*

Gary Becker's famous article on crime generates some controversial reform recommendations for both the substantive and procedural areas of criminal law.[1] In addition to criminal law, Becker's model has implications for tort law and remedies generally. The reaction to Becker's article produced important and long-lasting contributions to legal theory.[2]

---

* Honorable Paul J. Liacos, Professor of Law, Boston University.

1. Gary S. Becker, *Crime and Punishment: An Economic Approach*, 76 J. POL. ECON. 169 (1968). For a discussion of Becker's model and its application to criminal and tort law, see Keith N. Hylton, *The Theory of Penalties and the Economics of Criminal Law*, 1 REV. L. & ECON. 1 (2005).

2. The most important of those reactive articles was Calabresi and Melamed's piece on property rules and liability rules. *See* Guido Calabresi and A. Douglas Melamed, *Property Rules, Liability Rules, and Inalienability: One View of the Cathedral*, 85 HARV. L. REV. 1089 (1972). Calabresi and Melamed noticed that the Becker model would permit "efficient" trespasses, when the gain to the offender exceeded the victim's loss. They developed the theory of property rules, based in part on Ronald Coase's analysis of transaction costs, to correct this troubling feature of the Becker model.

With respect to substantive criminal law, Becker proposes a shift, as Doron Teichman's excellent discussion explains, from a focus on "complete deterrence" to "optimal deterrence." The criminal law is based on what an economist would call a *complete-deterrence approach*. The law seeks to stop serious criminal activity completely rather than regulate it to some socially desirable level. In contrast, an *optimal deterrence approach* would seek to find the optimal level of criminal activity.

An optimal deterrence scheme would not necessarily lead to serious criminals running free. Such a regime probably would involve some use of imprisonment. For example, imprisonment would be among the most efficient punishments available for judgment-proof criminals. For criminals who would be highly productive in the workforce, an optimal deterrence scheme might reduce their sentences or substitute monetary penalties.

The easiest way to see the implications of Becker's analysis is to consider the case of monetary penalties, which are efficient in the sense that they do not impose costs on society in the punishment phase. In a system of primarily monetary penalties, optimal deterrence would be consistent with a wide array of outcomes. First, judgment-proof defendants would have to be punished with some alternative sanction, perhaps incarceration. Second, optimal deterrence may require "complete deterrence" in some cases.

Suppose we can identify offensive activities according the statistical distribution of offender gains and victim losses. For one group of activities, some offender gains exceed victim losses. For example, some people double park because they need to deliver life-saving medicine. Consider now a different group of activities in which the gain to the offender is always (or almost always) less than the loss to the victim. For example, the offenders steal jewelry and sell it for half its value.

Under a system of optimal deterrence, monetary penalties should be based on the harm to the victim when activities are of the first type. For this set of activities, monetary penalties would not completely deter offenders. Monetary penalties would result in optimal deterrence, in the sense that the offending activities are pursued only as long as the gain exceeds the losses imposed on society.

For the second set of activities, where the offender gains are always less than the victim losses, the optimal scheme is one of complete deterrence. Monetary penalties would aim to eliminate any gain on the part of the offender. Moreover, optimal penalties in the complete deterrence case might be based on the offender's wealth.

This brief discussion of theory reveals my main point of departure from Teichman's discussion. Whereas Teichman emphasizes the social-cost internalization role of punishment under Becker's model, I think that feature has to be recognized as simply a part of a far richer model. Becker's model recognizes that social-cost internalization is in general optimal, but in some circumstances complete deterrence is the optimal goal. And although Becker barely explored this point in his original article, when complete deterrence is the goal, wealth may be relevant in determining the optimal punishment.[3]

It happens that in the Becker model complete deterrence can be achieved, when it is socially desirable, by internalizing social costs. But the fact that the social-cost internalizing penalty happens to be optimal across the board within the Becker model does not imply that the *goal* of punishment is always to internalize social costs.

The point that optimal deterrence sometimes requires complete deterrence has implications for tort law. The Becker model implies that an optimal tort system will employ both compensatory and punitive damages. Moreover, punitive damages will serve varying purposes. When the gain to the offender is likely to exceed the loss to the victim, they will reflect a multiplier that accounts for the possibility that the defendant would go unpunished. When the gain to the offender is unlikely to exceed the loss to the victim, the damage award will aim to eliminate any gain to the offender; and because there is no need to avoid over-deterrence in this case, a portion might be added to signal social disapproval.

With respect to criminal procedure law, the Becker model implies, as Teichman notes, a preference for efficient procedures. For example, it would appear to be efficient to reduce expenditures on police and simply increase the penalties for offenses. This would lower the likelihood of being punished but increase its severity. If the severity is increased sufficiently, a given level of deterrence could be maintained while substantially reducing expenditures on enforcement.

This is where Becker's model really does not have much to say for the real world, another point where Teichman and I apparently disagree. Criminal procedure seems to reject the efficient enforcement model, and there is a sound economic justification for this. The reason efficiency plays such a limited role in the law of criminal procedure is explained by public choice theory.[4] The fundamental reason for seemingly inefficient pro-defendant criminal procedures is to discourage and obstruct attempts to use the criminal-law enforcement process as a method of transferring wealth.

---

3. *See* Keith N. Hylton, *Punitive Damages and the Economic Theory of Penalties*, 8 GEO. L.J. 421 (1998).

4. *See* Keith N. Hylton and Vic Khanna, *A Public Choice Theory of Criminal Procedure*, 15 SUP. CT. ECON. REV. 61 (2007); Keith N. Hylton and Vic Khanna, *Political Economy of Criminal Procedure*, Boston Univ. School of Law Working Paper No. 08-16, *available at* http://ssrn.com/abstract=1121441.

LAW, ECONOMICS, AND NEUROETHICAL REALISM

MORRIS B. HOFFMAN*

The very fact that Gary Becker's 1968 essay on economics and the criminal law was the springboard for Doron Teichman's core text speaks volumes about Becker's profound contribution to the law and economics insight and to modern jurisprudence in general.[1] The essential truths that remarkable essay uncovered, and its limitations, still reverberate across almost half a century.

The explanatory power of economics has always lain, paradoxically, in its ability to finesse the intractable problem of human choice. By short-circuiting the most tantalizing question—why do we make the choices we do?—economists have given us impressive tools of prediction and even in some cases prescription. But I suggest these insights all come at the cost of a significant loss of descriptive power, a loss attributable precisely to the economists' traditional unwillingness to open the hood and look inside the engine of human decision-making.

In the real world, human preferences are not the arbitrary choices economists assume. The behaviors most of us engage in to maximize our happiness are bounded (one might even argue they are defined) by underlying principles that label some behaviors socially acceptable and others socially unacceptable. Freedom of contract and principles of supply and demand are insufficient to explain why most psychiatrically unimpaired people derive no happiness from torturing or being tortured, to use Richard Posner's famous example.[2] The law discourages some behaviors (and occasionally encourages others) not simply in order to produce some deterrent equilibrium, but because those behaviors violate, or further, our deeply shared moral intuitions. Almost everyone recognizes the moral core of law,[3] but economists have traditionally had special trouble formalizing it.

They shouldn't. After all, the economists' utility function is a neurological echo of the very forces that drive evolution: traits (including behaviors) will be selected if they give their owner a net selective advantage. The incredible power of human brains is that they allow a kind of warp speed natural selection,

---

* District Judge, Second Judicial District (Denver), State of Colorado; Member, MacArthur Foundation's Law and Neuroscience Project; Research Fellow, Gruter Institute for Law and Behavioral Research; Adjunct Professor of Law, University of Colorado.

1. Gary S. Becker, *Crime and Punishment: An Economic Approach*, 76 J. POL. ECON. 169 (1968).

2. Richard A. Posner, THE ECONOMICS OF JUSTICE 82 (1983).

3. Becker himself recognized this moral core by distinguishing between ordinary torts and what he called "social torts" (or crimes), the latter involving, in his words, "uncompensated harm to others." Becker, *supra* note 1, at 198.

enabling their owners to make present calculations about net selective advantage instead of waiting for their descendents to vote on the choice by either flourishing or dying out. So the economists' assumption that brains do something akin to a utility calculation is quite plausible.

But it is also clear that the brain is not a perfect utility calculator. The evidence, from the realms of experimental economics, cognitive psychology, and neuroscience, is unmistakable—humans not only do not act in ways to maximize utility, they so regularly depart from predicted choices that the departure itself is sometimes predictable.

This "irrationality" flows from the most salient fact about our evolution as an intensely social species. Our brains have been built to navigate the most original of original sins: When do I defect from the group and forego long-term group-based benefits for the short-term gain of the free rider? The answer may be a complex set of neuro-ethical tendencies that I have argued elsewhere coalesce around three principles: exchanges must be voluntary, promises must be kept, and serious violations of the first two principles must be punished.[4] These are not aspirational axioms assumed by some *a priori* theory. Instead, they have arguably been embedded in our brains by natural selection because they were, when we emerged some 100,000 years ago, an efficient solution to the self versus group problem. In a kind of neuro-Aristotelian way, I suggest that what makes most of us most happy, and is therefore the real invisible hand, is hewing closely to those embedded principles.

Teichman is right that Becker's economic insights into the criminal law remain as powerful as ever. But does he agree that the economic analysis of law, or of any human activity for that matter, will always be descriptively incomplete, and ontologically unsatisfactory, without the missing piece of cognitive science?

---

4. Morris B. Hoffman, *The Neuroeconomic Path of the Law, in* LAW AND THE BRAIN (Semir Zeki and Oliver Goodenough eds., 2006).

REPLY

DORON TEICHMAN

The comments do not for the most part contest the core of the Becker model. Rather, they offer new insights and refinements with respect to it. I will continue with this line and extend the arguments presented in my core text and in the comments.

A central implication of Becker's analysis that drew the commentators' attention is his recommendation to adopt a sanctioning regime based on low probabilities of detection coupled with harsh sanctions. As Russell Covey notes in this regard, "[t]he economic approach also fails to provide reasons to refrain from imposing draconian punishments."[1] Yet refraining from draconian sanctions does indeed have a sound economic justification.

First, I argued in my core text that draconian sanctions may raise the incentives of defendants to invest in their defense and could undermine the efficiency of the sanctioning regime. Second, draconian sanctions might create corruption since they allow relatively low-level enforcement agents to inflict tremendous harm on people (assume, for example, a world in which a highway patrol officer can write you a speeding ticket for your entire wealth). Finally, if we add to the Becker model the routine economic assumption of discounting future payments, then the disutility created by adding time at the end of a sentence clearly does not enhance deterrence by much. Thus, an array of secondary considerations (only part of which were presented here) justify forgoing the draconian sanctions Becker suggested.

Covey also claims that economic analysis would advise against the criminalization of some long-recognized crimes, such as prostitution. True, but the Becker model can simply take prohibitions as exogenous and continue to make useful contributions as to *how* those prohibitions should be enforced. In this regard, the economist may view the political system as a tool that reflects the preferences of the public and attempt to help the public achieve its goals in the most efficient way. That said, economic reasoning can provide (and in fact has provided) insights to debates on the content of criminal prohibitions, especially in issues relating to illicit transactions such as drugs, sex, and negative information.[2]

Alon Harel and Keith Hylton both emphasize that, contra Becker, the criminal law aims to achieve *total* deterrence, not optimal deterrence. They fail to take full account, however, of the need to sustain marginal deterrence in a system of total deterrence. Assume Xavier wishes to steal a vehicle in order to get from point A to point B, and doesn't really care which type of vehicle he steals. His personal benefit from stealing a fancy brand name mountain bike and a simple generic bike are almost identical (for concreteness, assume a utility of 10 for the mountain bike and 9 for the generic bike). Nonetheless, the harm caused by stealing the mountain bike will be significantly larger than the harm caused by stealing the generic bike (for concreteness assume a harm of 100 compared to a harm of 50).

Focusing on annulling the benefit derived by Xavier (and thereby achieving total deterrence) suggests that the difference between the sanctions for stealing the two different types of bicycles should be modest. Yet assuming (as some of the commentators would have us assume) that Xavier is not perfectly sensitive to

---

1. Covey comment at 94.

2. *See, e.g.,* Richard A. Posner, Sex and Reason (1992); Richard A. Posner, *Blackmail, Privacy, and Freedom of Contracts,* 141 U. Pa. L. Rev. 1817 (1993); Richard Epstein, *The Moral and Practical Dilemmas of an Underground Economy,* 103 Yale L.J. 2157 (1994).

a small difference in sanctions, the sanction applied should reflect the large difference in harm between the two offenses in order to encourage Xavier to chose the lesser crime in case the criminal justice system fails to deter him.

Morris Hoffman (and to some degree Harel) draws the attention to the emerging fields of law and cognitive psychology, and law and genetics. With respect to the former, economic analysts are perfectly happy to make use of empirical findings that can help create a more accurate model of human behavior. With respect to the later, Hoffman is obviously correct that the study of evolution and genetics can lead to a better understanding of human behavior in general and criminal activity specifically. Nonetheless, the importance of such studies should not be overstated. Economists are reluctant to "open the hood and look inside the engine of human decision-making," and the reason for this reluctance is simple. If one can predict with reasonable certainty the condition of a car without opening its hood (by, say, looking at its exterior and listening to its engine), then one has no reason to open the hood.

Understanding our genetic predispositions can, however, assist crime control efforts in specific areas. Take, for example, infanticide. Genetic theory suggests that stepparents, because they lack a genetic connection to their stepchildren, are far more likely to kill them than are biological parents. This prediction has been confirmed empirically. Studies demonstrate that children are about 100 times more likely to be killed by stepparents than by genetic parents.[3] This information is obviously of great value when designing crime control policies, as it could assist authorities to allocate their limited resources toward suspects (i.e., the stepparents) who are more likely to commit the crime.

I would like to conclude with a point of agreement between Harel, Hylton, and myself. As both Harel and Hylton point out, Becker's ideas had a profound influence on legal theorists, but only limited effect on criminal law and procedure in the "real world." As one of those theorists influenced by Becker, I must agree with this descriptive point. In a quick search covering all U.S. cases reported on Westlaw, I could find only nine opinions citing Becker's classic article (four of which were written by Judge Easterbrook). Alas, those of us who believe that our system of crime control should be rational and efficient have much more work ahead of us.

---

3. Owen D. Jones, *Evolutionary Analysis in Law: An Introduction and Application to Child Abuse*, 75 N.C. L. Rev. 1117, 1207 (1997).

5. THE DIFFICULTIES OF DETERRENCE AS A DISTRIBUTIVE PRINCIPLE

PAUL H. ROBINSON*

Would optimizing deterrence make a good principle to govern the distribution of criminal liability and punishment? Its attractiveness lies in part in what seems like the enormous potential of general deterrence to deter future crime. By punishing the offender at hand, the system can dissuade many others. Still, there is reason to be skeptical about whether distributing criminal liability and punishment to optimize deterrence would in fact have such influence on potential offenders. And even if it did, there are other reasons to be skeptical about its use as a distributive principle.

I. HURDLES IN THE PATH FROM RULE MANIPULATION TO DETERRENT EFFECT

Having a criminal justice system that imposes liability and punishment for violations does deter. Allocation of police resources or the use of enforcement methods that dramatically increase the capture rate can deter. However, it seems likely that manipulating *criminal law*—the substantive rules governing the distribution of criminal liability and punishment—commonly does not materially affect deterrence, contrary to what law and policy-makers have assumed for decades.[1] The claim here is not that criminal law formulation can never influence behavior, but rather, that the conditions under which it can do so are not typical. By contrast, criminal-law-makers routinely formulate criminal law rules on an assumption that the formulation will always have the intended deterrent effect. It is that working assumption that is so disturbing and so dangerous.

---

* Colin S. Diver Professor of Law, University of Pennsylvania. This core text is derived in large part from Paul H. Robinson, DISTRIBUTIVE PRINCIPLES OF CRIMINAL LAW: WHO SHOULD BE PUNISHED HOW MUCH? chs. 3 and 4 (2008) [hereinafter Robinson, DISTRIBUTIVE PRINCIPLES]; Paul H. Robinson and John M. Darley, *Does Criminal Law Deter? A Behavioural Science Investigation*, 24 OXFORD J. LEGAL STUD. 173 (2004) [hereinafter Robinson and Darley, *Does Law Deter?*]; Paul H. Robinson and John M. Darley, *The Role of Deterrence in the Formulation of Criminal Law Rules: At Its Worst When Doing Its Best*, 91 GEO. L.J. 949 (2003) [hereinafter Robinson and Darley, *Deterrence's Role*].

1. For documentation of the point, *see* Robinson and Darley, *Deterrence's Role*, *supra* note *, at 956–71.

For the formulation of a criminal law to have a deterrent effect, three conditions must be present. The target must:

1. know, directly or indirectly, of the rule that is designed to influence him;
2. be capable of and willing to bring such knowledge to bear on his conduct; and
3. perceive the threatened cost of punishment as exceeding the promised gain of the crime.[2]

A. The Target Must Know, Directly or Indirectly, of the Rule that is Designed to Influence Him

In fact, studies show a general ignorance of criminal law rules. People assume the law is as they think it should be. That is, they substitute their own intuitions of justice, or at least those that they believe are shared by others, for the actual legal rules. Consider, for example, a study of people in four states, where each state took a minority view on one doctrine but a majority view on others. The rules at issue were rules that everyone needs to know, not just people in special roles—rules governing the duty to assist a stranger, the use of deadly force and retreat, the duty to report a known felony, and the prohibition against the use of deadly force in defense of property. Yet, there was no measurable difference between states as to what people thought the law was. That is, none of the people in the minority view states knew of their state's special rule formulation. Interestingly, the common view was not always the majority rule, but rather the rule that the people as a group intuitively thought was the right rule.

One could argue, however, that the target of deterrence is not the typical citizen, most of whom abide by law because of internalized norms or social influence. The real target is a subgroup of "potential criminals," unaffected or less affected by such social forces for compliance, and these people have a special incentive to know the law. Researchers who have done work with inmates report very low knowledge of the law among them. But one could argue that a target need not know law in an intellectual sense. Even a rat can be deterred, as shown by the classic behavioral studies where rats trained to press a bar for food will stop pressing the bar if it causes a high enough electric shock. Such "indirect" communication of punishment rules only requires a target to pay attention to his environment and to respond in a way that furthers his best interests.

But learning legal rules is not like pushing the food bar. An enormous number of variables determine the outcome in any given case: variations in investigation, in prosecution, in judging, in procedures, and in the exercise of discretion. For example, when scholars debate using a partially individualized versus a purely objective standard for negligence on deterrence grounds, is it realistic to think that people are really going to alter their conduct according to which formulation

---

2. *See* Robinson and Darley, *Does Law Deter?, supra* note *, at 175–97.

their jurisdiction adopts? A rat can quickly sort out why he is being shocked, but those who hear of the result in a negligent homicide case are not likely to have a clue as to the existence of the deterrence-based doctrinal manipulation.

B. The Target Must Be Capable of and Willing to Bring Such Knowledge to Bear on His Conduct

Even if one assumes the target knows the law, there still can be no deterrent effect unless the target is *capable of and willing to bring such knowledge to bear* on his conduct. The problem is that potential offenders as a group are particularly bad at making rational decisions in their own best interest. Most use drugs and/ or alcohol, which distort their decision-making processes. As a group they are more inclined than the general population to be risk-seekers, rather than risk-avoiders. As a group they are more impulsive and less thoughtful about their actions, often with little concern for the consequences of their conduct.

At the same time, they are commonly acting under states of mind that inter-fere with decisional processes, such as rage or fear. And, among gang members in particular, their conduct is subject to the distorting pressures of *arousal effect* and of *social identity effect* (where a person in a group experiences an identity shift so as to think in terms of group interests rather than personal interests).

C. The Target Must Perceive the Threatened Cost of Punishment as Exceeding the Promised Gain of the Crime

Even if one assumes the target knows the law and is fully capable of calculating his best interests, there will be a deterrent effect only if the target *perceives the threatened cost of punishment as exceeding the promised gain* of the crime. Jeremy Bentham famously talks of deterrent effect as a function of probability, intensity (amount or punitive bite), and delay.

1. Probability The conditioning literature gives us reason to be concerned with regard to probability. For example, in animal studies, if test subjects are not punished each time they press the food bar, but only 50 percent of the time, for example, their responses decrease by 30 percent. Some deterrence is happening. But if they are punished only 10 percent of the time, almost no suppression is observed. Obviously there are limits to how much one can learn from nonhuman studies, but they do suggest that effective deterrence may be quite sensitive to punishment rate. In practice, punishment rates within the typical criminal justice system are quite low, typically less than 50:1 or 100:1 for most kinds of offenses. Luckily, people tend to exaggerate the likelihood of rare events, so the perception of the punishment rate may not be this bad. But here the special incentive of potential offenders to get the true facts may hurt deterrence, for they may learn the truth of the low rates. Another problem for effective deterrence is that many offenders tend to overestimate their ability to avoid punishment—"Others may get caught, but I'm more clever so I won't." Ultimately, it is not the actual punish-ment rate that matters but only the perceived rate among potential offenders.

The net effect of all this is that, as one study found, 76 percent of active criminals and 89 percent of the most violent, don't see the potential for punishment as a factor of which they need to take serious account.

2. Amount (Punitive Bite) Regarding punishment amount, the criminal justice system can certainly impose a punishment bite. There is no question about that. But a program of effective deterrence requires more than this. It must be able to modulate the amount according to the situation. It needs a continuum of punitive bite along which it can move as needed—imposing, for example, more bite for a more serious offense, more bite to compensate for a low detection rate, etc. But there are serious questions about whether the system can reliably modulate punishment as deterrence advocates assume it can. There is dramatically more complexity here than one might realize.

For example, traditional efficient deterrence policy suggests giving a lower penalty to start—perhaps for first-time offenders—then increasing it upon a repeat offense in order to reach the point of effective deterrence (where the cost will exceed the benefit). That is, there is no reason to waste punishment resources by imposing more punishment than may be required. But consider some of the animal studies. In one, pigeons pecking the food bar are deterred by a shock of 80 volts or more. But if one starts with a shock of 60 volts, which will not deter, then gradually increases the shock for each repeated act, the pigeon will continue to take the shock, even above the normally deterring 80 volts, as if learning from each shock that "I can take that," and thus is inclined to try it again. In fact, the pecking continues until the shock is 300 volts! One may wonder whether it is always a good idea in the long run to treat first-time offenders particularly lightly as efficient deterrence might suggest.

A more serious problem is found in the standard mechanism for altering the amount of deterrent threat by altering the *duration* of a prison term. Not all units of imprisonment have the same "bite." Compare Bar 1 with Bar 2, below. The current punishment system assumes that each unit of punishment gives the same punitive bite, as in Bar 1. But the studies suggest that inmates adjust, as in Bar 2. As the prison term progresses, each unit provides less of a bite, although the cost of that bite to the system remains constant, increasing inefficiency. This same kind of dynamic is seen in the "hedonic treadmill" and "subjective well-being" studies: new paraplegics (and lottery winners) have a dramatic change in their affect, but typically adjust back to their prior baseline view of life.

A more serious problem is found in the "duration neglect" studies. In one study, for example, subjects were given a "procedure" that involved a certain amount of pain for a certain period of time and then another procedure giving the same amount of pain for the same duration *plus an additional amount* during which the amount was gradually decreased. When told they had to repeat one or the other of the procedures, most elected the second, although it clearly involved more pain. Such studies reveal that bite is not felt as a function of duration so much as it is a function of two other variables: maximum intensity and end intensity.

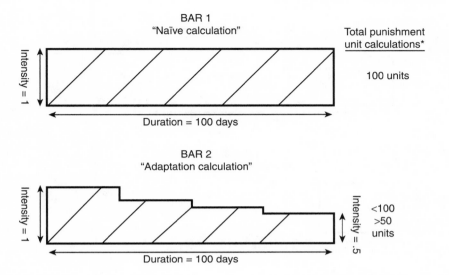

BAR 1
"Naïve calculation"

Total punishment
unit calculations*

Intensity = 1

Duration = 100 days

100 units

BAR 2
"Adaptation calculation"

Intensity = 1

Duration = 100 days

Intensity = .5

<100
>50
units

*Punishment unit calculation = Intensity x Duration = total area within the bar

Consider the implications for the current practice of manipulating the amount of deterrent threat by manipulating the duration of a prison term. Bar 2 below (similar to that above) shows a long term with intensity reduced over time. Bar 3 below, in contrast, shows a shorter term but, because the important endpoint intensity has not had time to dissipate, the perceived punitive bite of the shorter term is actually higher! (The studies suggest that the greatest deterrent effect may be found in short duration and high intensity—what we normally call "torture").

One would want further empirical confirmation of the effect, but the studies are at least unsettling in suggesting how little our current practice seems to take account of the enormous complexity in the process of accurately modulating punishment amount. Other odd dynamics—that conviction may be a stigma to one but a badge of achievement to another, that prison conditions may be harsh to one but an improvement to another, and so forth—add to the unease about whether a deterrence-based system can modulate punishment amount with the accuracy that it needs.

3. **Delay** Of obvious relevance to the matter of delay are studies showing the common dramatic discount given to future harms and benefits. For example, even if a person is certain to get a payment in a year, the person is more likely to take less now than much more in the future—such as $100 now rather than $156 in a year, even though no one can get 56 percent annual interest. Potential offenders similarly discount the effect of distant punishment, even if it is certain, which it hardly is.

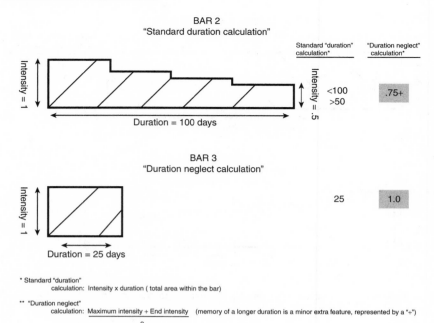

BAR 2
"Standard duration calculation"

BAR 3
"Duration neglect calculation"

	Standard "duration" calculation*	"Duration neglect" calculation*
	<100 >50	.75+
	25	1.0

* Standard "duration"
    calculation: Intensity x duration (total area within the bar)

** "Duration neglect"
    calculation: Maximum intensity + End intensity (memory of a longer duration is a minor extra feature, represented by a "+")

2

Another set of studies showing a dramatic decrease in deterrent effect with only a slight increase in the delay of the punishment are also instructive. In one animal study, dogs were given two dishes with different foods, one preferred and one unpreferred. Dogs eating from the "preferred" food dish were punished for doing so either: (1) after fifteen seconds or (2) after five seconds or (3) immediately. When introduced to the two dishes again in the absence of a punisher, (1) the fifteen-second delay dogs returned to the preferred dish after three minutes, (2) the five-second delay dogs didn't return for eight days, and (3) the no-delay group didn't return for two weeks. Obviously one can't apply the results directly to humans, but it is nonetheless unsettling to see that delay can so seriously erode deterrence, especially given the substantial delays in the typical criminal justice system, where punishment after a guilty plea typically follows seven months after the offense and punishment after a trial follows thirteen months after the offense.

To conclude, contrast these characteristics of the threatened costs of a crime to the perceived benefits of the crime. Although the probability of punishment is perceived to be low, especially given the low punishment rates, the probability of the benefits of the crime are commonly high, and the offender will get the financial or emotional benefit immediately, rather than after the substantial delay perceived for the threatened punishment.

D. Missing a Single Hurdle Is Lethal, But Clearing Them All May Still End in Dissipated Deterrent Effect

Tripping over any one of these three hurdles is fatal to a deterrent effect of any sort. And entire groups of potential offenders may be eliminated by one hurdle or another—some offenders simply will not know of the deterrence-based rule that is intended to influence their conduct, others will not be able to rationally calculate whether it is in their interest to follow the rule, and still others will conclude that the perceived benefits of the offense exceed the perceived costs.

Even if there is a group of potential offenders who are not tripped up by any of the three hurdles, a struggle at each may nonetheless seriously dissipate the ultimate deterrent effect. Imagine the ultimate deterrent effect of a rule manipulation on a dedicated gang member (under the influence of a "social identity" effect) who sees a 50:1 chance of getting caught, and if caught, a good chance of getting off without a conviction, and whose future discounting gives reduced effect to the threat of the distant punishment, and for whom any threat of punishment balances against the prestige the conviction and the immediate gain of money for drugs to feed his addiction, where due to his drug-addled brain and the emotional rush of the gang's planned robbery, he isn't thinking too much about consequences.

The larger point here is that even if the criminal justice system can have an effect in controlling this person's conduct, it can have that effect only in its broadest strokes—through having a general threat from the existence of a punishment system and having a meaningful police presence. The kind of details regarding criminal law formulation that lawmakers and criminal law scholars currently resolve using deterrence analysis are not likely to have an effect.[3]

E. Natural Experiments of Deterrent Effect

But some might argue that although a behavioral science analysis of criminal law's action path says doctrinal formulation can rarely influence conduct, the latter might in fact do so in some mysterious way presently beyond the understanding of human knowledge. We can test this argument by looking at the effect of specific doctrinal formulations on the crime rates they are intended to lower.

The available studies of what one might call *aggregated effects*—that is, studies that do not concern themselves with how a deterrent effect might come about but look strictly to whether an effect of doctrine on the crime rate can be found— are consistent with the conclusions above. A majority of these studies find no discernible deterrent effect from the manipulation of criminal law doctrine. Others claim to find such an effect and these results require explanation. Even if

---

3. *See* Robinson and Darley, *Does Law Deter?*, *supra* note *, at 196–97.

the mechanism of transmission from doctrinal formulation to behavioral influence is unknown, finding such a connection may be inconsistent with some of the claims made here and must be dealt with, especially since many deterrence advocates will speculate that the causal mechanism in the "black box" is deterrence.

To summarize the findings,[4] some of the aggregated-effect studies are simply poorly done and cannot reliably support a conclusion that doctrinal manipulation affects deterrence rates. Others seem undeniably to have found an effect on crime rate, but one may suspect that much, if not most, of this is the result not of deterrence, but of incapacitation. Increasing prison terms, for example, could be taken as a means of providing a greater deterrent threat, but a resulting reduction in crime may be the result of the isolating effect of longer incarcerations rather than their greater deterrent effect. But even if one concludes that some of these studies show a deterrent effect from doctrinal formulation, the specific circumstances of those studies serve generally to affirm the points about the prerequisites of deterrence. That is, these studies involve rules and target audiences that do what is rarely done: they satisfy the prerequisites to deterrence. The circumstances of these studies only serve to illustrate that the existence of such prerequisites is not typical.

F. Conclusion

The conclusion from the above analysis is not that deterrence never works, but rather that it is improper to assume that the manipulation of liability rules to optimize deterrence always works, as is the current general assumption. In fact, rule manipulation can, under the right circumstances—where the prerequisites for deterrence exists—have an effect on conduct "on the street." One can imagine a set of circumstances where there was: good communication of the legal rule manipulation, meaningful punishment rates, a perceived substantial punishment threat against only a moderate benefit from crime, an improved ability to reliably gauge how to calibrate punishment amount, and calculating potential offenders. Unfortunately, the existence of these conditions is the exception rather than the rule.

It is possible that one could change conditions to increase the situations in which the deterrence prerequisites exist. For example, drug treatment programs could have the generally overlooked benefit of making potential offenders more coherent and able to calculate their best interests, making them more susceptible to the deterrent threat of criminal liability and punishment where it does exist. But there are serious limits on what can be done, because improvement commonly requires serious trade-offs against other interests that we think are important. There would be much resistance to the dramatic increase in expenditures,

---

4. For a full account, see *id.* at 197–204.

as well as intrusions into private lives by the government, that would be required to significantly increase deterrence prerequisites, such as higher capture and punishment rates and improved rationality of potential offenders. Even more problematic, reforms that would increase the deterrence prerequisites, such as allowing greater government intrusiveness for crime prevention and investigation or allowing reduced procedural safeguards or standards of proof to increase conviction rates, would violate constitutional mandates.[5]

II. THE PROBLEMS OF COMPLEXITY AND LIMITED INFORMATION

Even if one concludes that the analysis above is unpersuasive—that is, even if one believes that the prerequisites for a deterrent effect commonly are met—there remain good reasons for serious concern about using deterrence as a distributive principle.

One disabling problem for deterrence as a distributive principle is its need for information that is not available, and not likely to be available any time in the foreseeable future. Formulating criminal law rules according to a deterrence analysis can produce erroneous results if based upon missing or unreliable data. Indeed, inadequately informed rules can reduce rather than increase deterrence.

Further, even if full and perfect information were available, the dynamics of deterrence are dramatically more complex than has been supposed. The deterrence process involves complex interactions, like substitution effects, that make deterrence predictions enormously difficult. As others have pointed out, for example, an increased penalty or increased capture rate for a lesser offense may have the effect of encouraging commission of a greater offense. And the deterrence process is dynamic rather than static. Even if a criminal law rule manipulation increases the deterrent effect as hoped, that effect itself can change the existing conditions and thereby change the deterrence calculations.[6]

III. DETERRENCE AT ITS WORSE WHEN TRYING TO DO ITS BEST

Even if one still believes, for whatever reason, that criminal law rule manipulation can produce a deterrent effect and that humans presently can overcome the complexity and insufficient data problems to know how to do such manipulation reliably, there is still reason to be skeptical that deterrence would make a desirable distributive principle for criminal liability and punishment. The problem is this.

---

5. *See* Robinson and Darley, *Deterrence's Role, supra* note *, at 989–1001.
6. *See id.* at 977–80.

Any distributive principle for criminal liability and punishment will produce some deterrent effect (if any is to be had). A deterrence-based distribution makes sense only if it can provide a *meaningfully greater* efficient deterrent effect than that which is already inherent in competing distributions that advance other useful goals, such as doing justice. Thus, deterrence can do better than another distribution—such as a desert distribution—only if it *deviates from* that distribution. That is, a deterrence-based distribution can deter better than a justice-based distribution only by adopting a rule that deviates from desert—that is, a rule that does injustice.[7]

Unfortunately for deterrence, instances of deviation from desert are just those instances in which obtaining a deterrent effect is most difficult. People assume the law is as they think it should be, which is according to their own collective notions of justice—empirical desert. Thus, the deterrence prerequisite of making the deterrence-based rule known becomes a difficult task: Deterrence can only do better than desert by deviating from it, but when it does deviate, the deterrence-based rule is not likely to be known.

Further, these deviation-from-desert cases are also the cases in which the system's deterrence-based rules are least likely to be followed. Because people intuitively assess criminal liability and punishment in terms of justice, rather than deterrence, the exercise of police, prosecutorial, and judicial discretion, as well as jury nullification, can subvert application of deterrence-based deviation rules, thus subverting the deterrence program and confusing the deterrence message.[8]

IV. DETERRENCE'S NEED TO OUTWEIGH ITS CRIMINOGENIC EFFECT IN DEVIATING FROM JUSTICE

Finally, even if one assumes for the sake of argument that a deterrence-based distribution can produce a greater deterrent effect than a desert-based distribution despite its special deviation problems, there is reason to be concerned that the deterrence-based distribution will simultaneously produce crime. Why? Because its deviation from the community's shared intuitions of justice can undermine the criminal law's moral credibility, thereby lessening its crime-control power as a moral authority, and this dynamic may have a significant criminogenic effect.

Deviating from a community's intuitions of justice can inspire resistance and subversion among participants—juries, judges, prosecutors, and offenders— where effective criminal justice depends upon acquiescence and cooperation.

---

7. *See* Robinson, DISTRIBUTIVE PRINCIPLES, *supra* note *, at chs. 7 and 8.

8. *See* Robinson and Darley, *Deterrence's Role*, *supra* note *, at 980–89.

Relatedly, some of the system's power to control conduct derives from its potential to stigmatize violators. With some persons this is more powerful than the threat of official sanction but without its costs. Yet the system's ability to stigmatize depends upon its having moral credibility with the community; for a violation to trigger stigmatization, the law must have earned a reputation for accurately assessing what violations do and do not deserve condemnation. Liability and punishment rules that deviate from a community's shared intuitions of justice undermine that reputation.

The system's intentional and regular deviations from desert also undermine efficient crime control because they limit law's access to one of the most powerful forces for gaining compliance: social influence and internalized norms. The greatest power to gain compliance with society's rules of prescribed conduct may lie not in the threat of official criminal sanction, but rather in the influence of the intertwined forces of social and individual moral control: the networks of interpersonal relationships in which people find themselves, the social norms and prohibitions shared among those relationships and transmitted through those social networks, and the internalization by individuals of those norms and moral precepts.

The law is not irrelevant to these social and personal forces. Criminal law, in particular, plays a central role in creating and maintaining the social consensus necessary for sustaining moral norms. In fact, in a society as diverse as ours, the criminal law may be the only society-wide mechanism that transcends cultural and ethnic differences. Thus, the criminal law's most important real-world effect may be its ability to assist in building, shaping, and maintaining these norms and moral principles. It can contribute to and harness the compliance-producing power of interpersonal relationships and personal morality. However, a criminal justice system that intentionally and regularly does injustice and fails to do justice diminishes its moral credibility with the community and thereby its ability to influence conduct by shaping these powerful norms.

The criminal law also can have an effect in gaining compliance with its commands through another mechanism. If it earns a reputation as a reliable statement of what the community perceives as condemnable, people are more likely to defer to its commands as morally authoritative in those borderline cases in which the propriety of certain conduct is unsettled or ambiguous in the mind of the actor. The importance of this role should not be underestimated. In a society with the complex interdependencies characteristic of ours, an apparently harmless action can have destructive consequences. When the action is criminalized by the legal system, one would want the citizen to "respect the law" in such an instance even though he or she does not immediately understand why that action is banned. Such deference will be facilitated if citizens are disposed to believe that the law is an accurate guide to appropriate prudential and moral behavior.

The extent of the criminal law's effectiveness in all these respects—in avoiding resistance and subversion of an unjust system, in bringing the power of stigmatization to bear, in facilitating, communicating, and maintaining societal consensus on what is and is not condemnable, and in gaining compliance in borderline cases through deference to its moral authority—is to a great extent dependent on the degree to which the criminal law has earned moral credibility with the citizens it governs. Thus, the criminal law's moral credibility is essential to effective crime control, and is enhanced if the distribution of criminal liability is perceived as "doing justice," that is, if it assigns liability and punishment in ways that the community perceives as consistent with their shared intuitions of justice. Conversely, the system's moral credibility, and therefore its crime-control effectiveness, is undermined by a distribution of liability that deviates from community perceptions of just desert.[9]

To summarize, a deterrence-based distribution potentially can forfeit any crime-control gains it might have when its distribution undermines the system's moral credibility with the community it governs. That is, even if one assumes for the sake of argument that there would be some greater deterrent effect of a deterrence-based distribution of punishment over a desert-based distribution of punishment, one would still question whether this marginal benefit exceeds the crime control losses that a deterrence-based system would incur. When combined with the above-discussed problems of unavailable information and complexity, one might conclude that there is too much danger and too little payoff in adopting a deterrence distributive principle.

At the very least, deterrence ought to be taken into account in formulating criminal law rules only in situations where there is some reason to think that the prerequisites for deterrent effect exist and that the rule manipulation will produce a deterrent effect so great as to outweigh the criminogenic effect of the deviation from justice that it will require.

---

9. *See* Robinson, DISTRIBUTIVE PRINCIPLES, *supra* note *, at ch. 8; Paul H. Robinson, *Empirical Desert*, *in* CRIMINAL LAW CONVERSATIONS 29–39 (Paul H. Robinson, Stephen P. Garvey, and Kimberly Kessler Ferzan, eds., 2009).

COMMENTS

DETERRENCE'S COMPLEXITY

RUSSELL D. COVEY[*]

Deterrence theory, simply put, holds that crime can be reduced by ensuring that the expected costs of crime exceed its expected benefits. Thus, a system of punishment that uses deterrence as its primary distributive principle must

---

* Associate Professor of Law, Georgia State University College of Law.

accurately assess the expected costs and benefits of criminal conduct. As Paul Robinson convincingly argues, calibrating expected costs and benefits in a way that is likely to maximize the deterrent function of criminal law is extremely difficult.

Indeed, to state the problem more strongly, deterrence's complexity may render it practically impossible to operationalize. For instance, assume that enhanced deterrent policies are successful in reducing the supply of illegal drugs. Economics 101 tells us that what follows is an increase in the price of illegal drugs. Higher drug prices mean higher profits for suppliers who remain in the market. At some point, sufficiently high profits attract new suppliers, which then increases supply until a new equilibrium is reached. The new, higher price of illegal drugs reduces marginal demand, so in that sense deterrence "works."

But by how much? The answer, of course, depends on the respective slopes of the supply and demand curves. If drug markets are characterized by gradual supply and demand curves—i.e., relative inelasticity—then deterrent penalties might be very costly to pursue while having only minimal impact on criminal activity—which, in fact, seems to be an accurate description of the so-called "war on drugs."[1] Even if deterrent policies succeed in significantly raising supply costs and reducing demand, the reduction in demand must be weighed against the higher profit rate of remaining suppliers. Meanwhile, high illegal drug prices mean that drug consumers transfer a larger share of their income to sellers, which in turn forces some consumers to turn to crime to supplement incomes. This market dynamic is likely typical of many criminal activities—e.g., prostitution, human trafficking, and illegal arms dealing—not just illegal drugs.

Then there is the law of unintended consequences. As with any market, increased costs spur innovation. High criminal penalties provide a competitive advantage to criminals who successfully minimize their likelihood of detection and may shift a greater market share of the surplus from criminal activity to individuals or groups, such as prison-based gangs, juveniles, or criminal enterprises operating across international borders, that are hardest to prosecute or punish. In addition, as Robinson notes, the extent to which deterrent penalties succeed depends on available substitutes. Increasing penalties for burglary will not reduce overall crime if those penalties simply cause would-be burglars to rob or deal crack instead. High inner-city unemployment rates, high drop-out rates, low wages, and high barriers to entry into the legal job market for individuals with criminal records all decrease the likelihood that deterrent penalties alone will actually cause even rational criminals to substitute lawful employment for crime.

---

1. *See, e.g.,* Jefferson M. Fish, *Rethinking Our Drug Policy,* 28 FORDHAM URB. L.J. 9, 54 (2000) (noting that despite extended interdiction campaign, street prices for cocaine and heroin in 1998 were far lower than in 1981 while purity of drugs was far higher).

The efficacy of deterrence, moreover, depends on the degree to which antici-pated criminal penalties make up the costs of criminal conduct. For example, street-level crack dealers might be concerned with getting punished for selling crack, but given that one study reported a one-in-four chance that a dealer in Chicago would be killed during his first four years on the street,[2] many are likely more concerned with getting shot or stabbed by competing dealers. Where a 25 percent chance of death fails to deter new entrants into the crack market, even substantial increases in sentences will probably not have much deterrent effect.

Elasticity in the supply of offenders is also often overlooked. If every crack dealer and burglar thrown in jail for an extended term of incarceration is replaced by another waiting in the wings, punitive sentencing policies will only negligibly impact drug-dealing and burglary rates. It is even possible that, over the long haul, an incapacitation policy might compound the problem of crime and crimi-nal violence where ex-convicts compete with their substitutes for market share upon their release.

In short, crime "markets" are so complex and dynamic that reliable regula-tion through the manipulation of substantive criminal rules may be improbably difficult even if criminals were perfectly rational actors—which they are not. Given this complexity, serious thought should be given not only to deterrence as a distributive principle of punishment, but to the substantive goals of criminal law itself where those goals are dominated by deterrent strategies.

---

2. *See* Steven Levitt and Sudhir A. Venkatesh, *An Economic Analysis of a Drug-Selling Gang's Finances*, 115 Q. J. ECON. 755, 784 (2000).

MAKING DETERRENCE WORK BETTER

DOUGLAS A. BERMAN*

Paul Robinson effectively identifies social and psychological reasons to be skeptical about the efficacy of "distributing criminal liability and punishment to optimize deterrence."[1] But his valuable discussion should not prevent theorists or lawmak-ers from recognizing (1) settings in which the criminal law can play a vital role in shaping behaviors, and (2) statistical evidence suggesting education levels may be an important influence on the efficacy of deterrence. Though Robinson usefully spotlights some of the "difficulties of deterrence as a distributive principle,"[2] a proper response is not a wholesale rejection of deterrence as a justification for

---

* William B. Saxbe Designated Professor of Law, Moritz College of Law, Ohio State University.
1. Robinson core text at 105.
2. *Id.*

criminal liability and punishment. Rather, theorists and lawmakers should respond to Robinson's insights by trying to make deterrence work better.

Deterrence is obviously effective in some settings. When I am late and traffic is light, I would *really* like to drive 100 miles per hour on the super-highways that connect where I live and where I work. Similarly, when I cannot find a parking space near my building, I would *really* like to park in the handicap spots that never seem occupied. But I don't, nor do many other persons who believe they could safely drive 100 m.p.h. and prefer to park close to their destination. The reason: deterrence generally works to secure compliance with traffic laws, and does so even though the probability of punishment is relatively low and the immediacy of the benefit is relatively high. Moreover, one reason deterrence works here is because of the severity of the sanction—I do not want to run the relatively low risk of having to pay the relatively large fines used to punish driving 100 m.p.h. and parking illegally in a handicap spot. Indeed, if fines were only a few dollars for violating these laws, I suspect that many persons (myself included) would drive 100 m.p.h and park in handicap spots more frequently.

The efficacy of deterrence in the traffic context should remind us that some behaviors can be effectively deterred through criminal liability and punishment. Consequently, Robinson's insights do not require rejecting entirely deterrence rationales for crime and punishment, but rather demand that we better assess the types of behaviors people are most likely to forego when the criminal law increases their costs. Indeed, we may need a better psychological study for assessing deterrence: individuals should be asked what crimes they would be more likely to commit if they knew they would barely be punished (e.g., subject to only a small fine or an afternoon in a jail). I suspect many would admit to a greater willingness to commit "victimless" crimes—ranging from illegal parking to drug use to tax evasion—if certain that the personal costs of such behavior would be minor. I also suspect that few would admit to a greater willingness to commit very serious crimes like murder or rape even if assured that they would barely be punished for such behavior.

The relationship between education and crime, as recently summarized in a Justice Policy Institute report, bears emphasis here:

> Overall, individuals incarcerated in U.S. prisons and jails report significantly lower levels of educational attainment than do those in the general population. Research has shown a relationship between high school graduation rates and crime rates, and a relationship between educational attainment and the likelihood of incarceration.[3]

These data alone obviously do not establish a direct connection between education and the efficacy of deterrence. Still, because deterrence depends on

---

3. JUST. POL'Y INST., EDUCATION AND PUBLIC SAFETY 1 (2007).

awareness of the distribution of criminal punishment and an ability to engage in cost/benefit analysis, the theory of deterrence demands some intellectual sophistication, which in turn suggests that more educated populations may respond more cogently to increased punishment.

These insights may support Robinson's suggestion that lawmakers should not expect *marginal increases in punishment* to readily produce a marginal increase in deterrence; the data may actually suggest that policy-makers interested in reducing crime should invest in *marginal increases in educational attainment*. Increasing punishment levels for a crime may only increase deterrence for that one crime and only for more educated populations; increasing educational attainment may increase deterrence for all crimes and do so for populations now failing to fully respond to the deterrent effect of the criminal law.

One closing thought. All of Robinson's points and my responses may converge around an important policy conclusion: marginal increases in *prison sentences* may be the least likely (and most costly) means to increase the deterrent impact of the criminal law. Theorists and lawmakers perhaps must consider much more fully whether alternative punishment schemes and alternative means to enhance personal cost/benefit analysis are essential to making deterrence work better.

IN DEFENSE OF DETERRENCE

DORON TEICHMAN*

Paul Robinson comprehensively criticizes deterrence as a principle for formulating criminal law and designing sanctioning polices. In this brief comment I argue that criminal law affects the behavior of potential criminals and that deterrence should play a role in the distribution of criminal sanctions.

Beginning with the positive aspects of Robinson's argument, it would seem that a large portion of potential criminals *do* fulfill all three of the prerequisites for deterrence. The local and international drug trade, for example, functions like a well-organized for-profit corporation. Drug traders and producers have demonstrated knowledge of legal rules and an ability to rationally adapt to them. For instance, they have exhibited substitution effects both between types of drugs and between geographic areas as a result of legal arbitrages. Obviously, the drug market is only one example. The entire domain of economic crimes in areas such as antitrust, securities, tax, and so forth are also characterized by knowledgeable rational actors that react to legal incentives. Thus, although the structure of a criminal code's self-defense provision might have no effect on people's behavior, it is not clear that *every* aspect of the criminal justice system has no

---

* The Joseph H. and Belle R Braun Senior Lectureship in Law, Faculty of Law, Hebrew University of Jerusalem.

effect on *all* potential criminals. Rather, it would seem that the truth lies somewhere between the claim that the law has (nearly) no deterrent value and the claim that the law has (nearly) perfect deterrent value. Criminal law has some deterrent value, though just how much depends to a great degree on the characteristics of the situations it regulates and the type of people subject to it.

In addition, the empirical studies reviewed by Robinson raise several problems. First, many of them use animals rather than humans as their subjects. Although one cannot ignore such studies, their implications should not be overstated when modeling human decision-making. Second, some of the studies cited deal with specific rather than general deterrence. For example, the study exploring the effect of the delay of sanctions on dogs examined this question with respect to the dogs to which the sanctions were applied. Finally, studies not reviewed by Robison *do* document the deterrent value of criminal sanctions. For instance, in a recent study that measured the deterrent (as opposed to incapacitating) effect of California's three strikes law, the author concluded that "[d]uring the first 2 years after the legislation's enactment, approximately eight murders, 3,952 aggravated assaults, 10,672 robberies, and 384,488 burglaries were deterred in California by the two- and three-strikes legislation."[1]

Robinson's normative argument rests on the assumption that adopting policies supported by deterrence might undermine the credibility of criminal law, which will in turn diminish its crime-control power as a moral authority. Since the ultimate goal of deterrence is to accomplish desirable outcomes, clearly its application must be subject to this concern. Nonetheless, one should be careful not to overstate the scope of this argument for several reasons. First, it is not clear that the empirical evidence for the existence of this effect is any stronger than the evidence with respect to deterrence. Second, people might not have strong moral convictions about many of the issues governed by criminal law. Does most of the public really care what the precise sanction for monopolizing a market is? Policy-makers can design sanctions based on deterrence considerations in areas about which the public is indifferent. Finally, even if the public does hold a strong opinion as to the just outcome, this does not imply that deterrence should be ignored. In many cases just outcomes reflect a "zone of justice," and not a single result. As such, deterrence could still determine the precise size of the sanction within this zone.

An additional problem with Robinson's argument is its focus on incarceration as the sole form of sanctioning. This is clearly an inaccurate description of current sanctioning regimes, given the large role of alternative sanctions such as fines. Fines overcome the problems associated with the reduced deterrent value of prolonged prison terms since each additional dollar added to the fine creates

---

1. *See* Joanna M. Shepherd, *Fear of the First Strike, The Full Deterrent Effect of California's Two and Three Strike Legislation*, 31 J. LEGAL STUD. 159, 200 (2002).

more deterrence. As a result, fines offer a policy tool that can be designed in a precise manner in order to achieve optimal deterrence. Thus, it would seem that Robinson again overstates the scope of his argument.

Finally, although many of the points Robinson presents are an excellent critique of current *practices*, they do not offer a theoretical critique of deterrence. Take for example the issue of the negative value of prolonged sentences. The only way to overcome this problem does not have to be "torture." Rather, one can think of an array of incarceration regimes in which prisoners suffer from increasingly harsher conditions (e.g., food quality, visitation rights, etc.). Alternatively, one can deny prisoners the possibility to get accustomed to their conditions and gain social capital in prison by constantly shifting them between different facilities after relatively short periods of time. My point is not that these suggestions should be adopted immediately; it is merely that one could respond to Robinson's critique of existing practices with proposals to design better ones, i.e., practices that come closer to delivering optimal deterrence.

FOR GENERAL DETERRENCE

JONATHAN S. MASUR*, RICHARD H. MCADAMS,** AND THOMAS J. MILES***

The theory of general deterrence claims that punishing an individual for a crime today will raise the expected costs for anyone contemplating the commission of the offense tomorrow. Robinson's critique of general deterrence misses the mark in several significant respects.

First, much of Robinson's critique focuses on the crimes committed by *undeterred* individuals—e.g., prisoners and gang members. But a fair test of deterrence theory does not look only at those who are undeterred; the success of deterrence comes in those who do not offend because of threatened sanctions. Economists do not claim that everyone can be deterred. Among other reasons, not all people are fully rational, informed, and capable of self-control. Because individuals vary along these dimensions, deterrence theory predicts that those who are relatively rational, informed, and capable of self-control are more likely to be deterred by the threat of punishment, whereas those possessing fewer of these qualities are less likely to be deterred. If most offenders are irrational, uninformed, and impulsive, as Robinson suggests, that outcome is fully consistent with deterrent *success*—because those capable of being deterred are not

* Assistant Professor of Law, University of Chicago Law School.

** Bernard D. Meltzer Professor of Law, University of Chicago Law School.

*** Assistant Professor of Law, University of Chicago Law School.

offending. For example, if most murders are committed by individuals in a fit of rage or under the influence of alcohol, then we are plausibly deterring more calculated murders. That we cannot deter every crime is hardly a reason not to seek to deter those we can. Moreover, instead of thinking of incapacitation theory as a competitor to deterrence theory, it should be thought of as a supplement—precisely when individuals prove themselves undeterrable is when we may think it worthwhile to incarcerate them in order to incapacitate them.

Second, Robinson does not fully confront the empirical evidence on deterrence. A growing empirical literature, primarily by economists, establishes that policing and incarceration have crime-reducing effects.[1] The most compelling of these studies distinguish deterrence from incapacitation, and they do so by examining sentencing enhancements, which depend upon the substantive content of sentencing rules.[2] True, social scientists have not yet empirically investigated all of the criminal law's subtle doctrinal nuances. But the existing studies thoroughly demonstrate that the content of criminal law has the capacity to achieve deterrent effects.

Robinson seeks to avoid much of this empirical literature by conceding that the *existence* of the criminal justice system can deter, as do policing methods that "dramatically increase the capture rate."[3] He offers to distinguish the deterrent effect of the system overall and of policing from the deterrent effect of particular criminal law rules. But this distinction is unexplained and untenable given how broadly Robinson's critique of criminal-law deterrence sweeps. The arguments he advances against the deterrent potential of criminal-law rules are just as readily deployed against the deterrent potential of the system as a whole. If people generally lack information about what is criminalized, lack the capacity or willingness to conform, and inevitably perceive the benefits of offending as exceeding the costs, then they will not respond to the existence of the criminal justice system nor to changes in policing that dramatically increase the probability of detection. Because Robinson's critique cuts so wide a swath, it implies that *all* deterrence claims are false. If so, then *all* of the empirical evidence supporting deterrence, not just that focused on the content of criminal law, cuts against Robinson's claim.

Finally, Robinson argues that prisoners' ability to adapt to the conditions of their confinements will inhibit the power of criminal law to deter by diminishing imprisonment's punitive force. But this criticism misunderstands how—and when—deterrence operates. Deterrence is an ex ante phenomenon: the

---

1. Steven D. Levitt and Thomas J. Miles, *The Empirical Study of Criminal Punishment*, in THE HANDBOOK OF LAW AND ECONOMICS 453–95 (A. Mitchell Polinsky and Steven Shavell eds., 2007).

2. Thomas J. Miles and Jens Ludwig, *Silence of the Lambdas: Deterring Incapacitation Research*, 22 J. QUANTITATIVE CRIMINOLOGY 287 (2007).

3. Robinson core text at 105.

important question is what punishment the prospective criminal *believes* she will suffer if she is caught and convicted, not the punishment she eventually receives. The convicted criminal's experience while in prison is irrelevant; adaptation would interfere with deterrence only if criminals anticipated it, which they don't. Indeed, not only do people typically fail to anticipate adaptation, they usually overestimate the negative impact of an event before they experience it. This is not coincidental; individuals adapt during negative events by relegating unpleasant conditions to the backs of their minds, and focusing upon an upcoming event (while trying to imagine its impact) naturally counteracts this effect.

If prisoners remembered their adaptation, this fact might reduce the specific-deterrent effect of punishment on former inmates, or even impede general deterrence if inmates were able to inform others of their experiences. But the behavioral literature that Robinson employs demonstrates that prisoners will *not* remember their adaptation. Those who succeed in adapting do not learn from their experiences in a way that would interfere with even specific deterrence. Instead, people remember negative experiences (such as prison) as having been worse than they actually were (based on contemporaneous reporting), and they are incapable of drawing upon past memories to make more accurate predictions regarding future events.[4] Absent any sort of learning, adaptation will not diminish the law's power to deter recidivists, and former prisoners will be unable to pass information about the benefits of adaptation to other putative criminals.

Deterrence hardly operates perfectly or ideally in all situations. But many of the criticisms Robinson levels against it find no support in the best available evidence and theory.

---

4. Peter Ayton *et al.*, *Affective Forecasting: Why Can't People Predict Their Emotions?*, 13 THINKING & REASONING 62 (2007).

REPLY

PAUL H. ROBINSON

The prize for the biggest strawman goes to Jonathan Masur, Richard McAdams, and Thomas Miles, who spend the first third of their joint comment defending against an attack on the theory of general deterrence that doesn't exist.[1] As its title advertises, the core text addresses a different issue: whether deterrence makes a good principle for distributing criminal liability and punishment.[2] "Having a criminal justice system that imposes liability and punishment for

---

1. Masur, McAdams, and Miles comment at 122–23.
2. Robinson core text at 105 (emphasis in original).

violations does deter. . . . However, it seems likely that manipulating *criminal law*—the substantive rules governing the distribution of criminal liability and punishment—commonly does not materially affect deterrence. [T]he claim here is not that criminal law formulation can never influence behavior but rather that the conditions under which it can do so are not typical."[3]

Masur, McAdams, and Miles, still in the strawman business, refuse to take "yes" for an answer and, despite the text quoted above, conclude that the text must really be claiming that "*all* deterrence claims are false."[4] Their magical reasoning follows this line of argument: The core text concedes that having a criminal justice system does deter. "The arguments [Robinson] advances against the deterrent potential of criminal-law rules are just as readily deployed against the deterrent potential of the system as a whole."[5] Thus, Robinson's critique implies "that *all* deterrence claims are false."[6]

Of course, the arguments against the deterrent effectiveness of manipulating criminal law rules are *not* "just as readily deployed against the system as a whole."[7] Clearly, the world would be a different place without a criminal justice system. However, trying to influence conduct by manipulating the legal rules within that system is a quite different matter. Most obviously, although targets of deterrence commonly do know that there is a criminal justice system that imposes punishment, they do not know its legal rules. Further, attempts to construct those rules to produce the desired choices requires a level of information about the real world and its dynamics far beyond what we currently know. As Russell Covey makes clear in his comment, the complexity of the dynamics are such that a miscalculation can as easily increase crime, as through substitution effects, as decrease crime. The background deterrent effect of having a criminal justice system has no such complexity, because it attempts no specific manipulation of conduct decisions. (Perhaps distracted by their strawman, Masur, McAdams, and Miles never address the complexity problem.) The fact is we can get the general deterrent benefit of having a criminal justice system *without ever using deterrence as a distributive principle within that system.*

Doron Teichman offers a more coherent challenge, arguing that "a large portion of potential criminals *do* fulfill all three of the prerequisites for deterrence."[8] This is an empirical question, of course, and I am happy to follow wherever the research takes us. However, the presently available evidence gives good reason to be skeptical. Many people will obey the law without any deterrent threat, simply because they have internalized the relevant societal norm. But for those

---

3. *Id.*
4. Masur, McAdams, and Miles comment at 123.
5. *Id.*
6. *Id.*
7. *Id.*
8. Teichman comment at 120.

who have not, we know that most don't know the legal rules, that a large portion have impaired abilities to make rational calculations of future self-interest, and that capture and punishment rates for most offenses are so low as to be of minimal significance. Teichman offers nothing to make one more optimistic.

Could there be instances in which the three prerequisites for deterrent effect do exist? Yes.[9] However, even if the prerequisites do exist and even if the complexity problem did not, it does not follow that general deterrence would make a good distributive principle. Such a distribution of liability and punishment clearly would conflict with the community's judgments about justice and undermine the criminal law's moral credibility, and there is good reason to believe that a criminal law perceived as intentionally and regularly doing injustice and failing to do justice would suffer crime-control costs as its power of social influence is diminished. (Several commentators have challenged the importance of just punishment for crime control purposes, and I refer readers to the conversation on "Empirical Desert," in which I respond to similar comments).

Further, even a distribution of punishment based on desert has some deterrent effect. To be preferred, a deterrence distribution would have to deter more, and that increase in deterrence would have to be so great as to outweigh the crime-control cost of a criminal law with reduced moral credibility. Still further, a deterrence distribution can do better than a desert distribution only where it deviates from desert. Yet it is just those instances of deviation in which deterrence is at its most problematic. The deviations not only undermine the law's moral credibility but also make it difficult to satisfy the first prerequisite for effective deterrence. People assume the law is as they believe it should be (i.e., "empirical desert"). Where law deviates from people's notions of desert, it creates the serious burden of having to educate people to the fact that the law is not as they assume it is.

I agree with Doug Berman's final conclusion, shared by Teichman, that "theorists and lawmakers should respond to Robinson's insights by trying to make deterrence work better."[10] These reforms may, as Berman notes, have little or nothing to do with reforming criminal law. He suggests investing in education, to produce more rational calculators. On the other hand, drug treatment centers, mental health services, and gang intervention might be better investments for this purpose.[11] In a similar vein, I'm skeptical of Teichman's proposed shift to

---

9. I'm not sure that the drug market example that Teichman gives is one of those instances. As Covey points out, "Where a 25 percent chance of death fails to deter new entrance into the crack market, even substantial increases in sentences will probably not have much deterrent effect." Covey comment at 118.

10. Berman comment at 119. *See also* Teichman comment at 122.

11. And no program producing more rational calculation will help if it serves only to make the target realize the weakness of any deterrent threat in the absence of a meaningful punishment rate.

fines. Most of the persons most in need of deterrence are poor, for whom the threat of fine is essentially irrelevant.

Yes, let's try to "make deterrence work better." But even if this happens, there is reason to doubt that a system of improved deterrence will make an attractive distributive principle. It can provide greater deterrence than a desert distribution only be deviating from desert, yet such deviations make deterrence more difficult to achieve and undermine law's moral credibility, and thereby its normative crime control power.

6. WHY ONLY THE STATE MAY INFLICT CRIMINAL SANCTIONS
The Case Against Privately Inflicted Sanctions

ALON HAREL*

I. INTRODUCTION

Criminal sanctions are typically administered by the state. Via its public officials, the state determines the severity of criminal sanctions and carries out the actual infliction of these sanctions. Recent developments are designed to shift some of these powers from the state to individual citizens or other private entities. Shaming penalties are one paradigmatic example of such a shift in powers. In the case of shaming penalties, both the power to determine the severity of sanctions and the power to inflict sanctions are shifted from the state to private citizens. Privately run, for-profit prisons are another example, but here only the power to inflict criminal sanctions is transferred from the state to corporate bodies. A less well-known example of privately inflicted sanctions is the recent initiative to privatize the probationary system in Britain. Here I provide a philosophical perspective on the legitimacy of privately inflicted sanctions.

Many observers have raised concerns with respect to the recent initiatives to privatize the criminal law system. This core text exposes the rationale underlying these concerns. I argue that there is a link between the state's judgments concerning the wrongfulness of the act and the infliction of sanctions. This link is indispensable to the legitimacy of the infliction of criminal sanctions triggered by violating state-issued prohibitions. Insofar as the state is the source of criminal prohibitions, it should also determine the nature and the severity of the sanctions that follow their violation and should inflict these sanctions. Delegating the power to determine the nature and severity of the criminal sanctions (e.g., by using shaming penalties) or delegating the power to inflict criminal sanctions to private entities (e.g., by establishing private prisons) severs the link between the state's judgments concerning the wrongfulness of the act and the determination of the severity of the sanction or the infliction of the sanction. It is impermissible for the state to authorize, encourage, or initiate the infliction of sanctions in the absence of such a link.

* Phillip P. Mizock and Estelle Mizock Chair in Administrative and Criminal Law, Hebrew University Law Faculty. This core text is based on Alon Harel, *Why Only the State May Inflict Criminal Sanctions: The Case Against Privately Inflicted Sanctions*, 14 LEGAL THEORY 113 (2008).

II. JUSTIFICATIONS FOR STATE-INFLICTED SANCTIONS

The distinction between state-inflicted sanctions and privately inflicted sanctions requires some clarification. The privately inflicted sanctions that are the target of my critique are those sanctions inflicted by individuals (or other private entities) at the encouragement or initiative of the state. Thus, it is not claimed here that it is impermissible for individuals to criticize or ostracize convicted offenders on the basis of a judgment that criminals are evil, that they ought to suffer, etc. Instead, what is impermissible is for the state to hand over the determination of the severity of criminal sanctions or the actual infliction of criminal sanctions to private individuals.

I now describe three types of justification for state-inflicted criminal sanctions. Under the first type of justification—the *instrumental justification*—the state is the appropriate agent to inflict criminal sanctions simply because it is impartial or effective. In this view, the infliction of criminal sanctions could in principle be performed by other, nonstate agents. Under the second type of justification—the *normative precondition justification*—the infliction of criminal sanctions by the state achieves goals that could in principle be fully realized through the infliction of sanctions by private agents. Yet, in contrast to the instrumental justification, there are normative constraints that preclude the infliction of sanctions by agents other than the state. Finally, under the third type of justification—the *state-centered justification*—the power to inflict criminal sanctions is an agent-dependent power: a power that can be successfully exercised only by the state. State-inflicted sanctions are designed to realize goals or perform tasks that cannot in principle be performed successfully by private institutions or individuals acting on their own.

Instrumental justifications are premised on the idea that punishment serves important societal goals that could in principle be realized by other nonstate agents. However, the state is seen as more capable or better placed to create the institutions and/or sustain the practices that guarantee that punishment is imposed in accordance with the gravity of the offence.

A well-known instrumental justification of punishment was provided by John Locke. According to Locke, the state should be empowered to inflict sanctions on those who transgress the laws of nature, because the state is less partial than alternative agents in its treatment of offenders, and consequently, less likely to inflict inappropriate sanctions. Interestingly, law and economics scholars often endorse a similar view. In their view, punishment should be supplied by the state because the infliction of sanctions involves a collective action problem. The individual who inflicts a sanction has to bear the costs of inflicting the sanction himself whereas the benefits resulting from the infliction of sanctions (e.g., crime prevention) are enjoyed by everybody. Consequently, individuals have suboptimal incentives to inflict sanctions.

This brief discussion is sufficient to illustrate that two of the most influential views concerning punishment—namely, certain versions of retributivism and

deterrence theories—are instrumental theories. Some (although not all) retributivists argue that punishment is justified in order "to ensure that wrong-doers
receive the suffering which they deserve."[1] Under this view, "necessarily acts of
certain kinds have an intrinsic property that it is fit, appropriate or 'called for'
that the perpetrator suffers for it."[2] But there is no principled reason why the
infliction of deserved suffering must be performed by the state. In fact: "if a
wrong-doer suffers some natural calamity—especially if it is a consequence of
her wrong-doing, or resembles the harm she had done to others—this may be
seen . . . as 'just what she deserves. . . .'"[3] To the extent that desert-based retributivists insist that it is the state rather than other agents that should inflict the
deserved sufferings, it is simply because the state is well placed to determine
what a person deserves and to inflict the sanction.

Deterrence theorists believe that deterrence depends on the probability of
detection and the severity of the sanction. The agency of the state plays no essential
role in the justification of punishment and consequently there is no principled
reason to believe that nonstate agents cannot inflict sanctions that will deter
wrongdoers.

The instrumental justification of *state-inflicted* punishments requires two
steps. First, one must establish that inflicting sanctions for wrongdoing is
appropriate or desirable. The infliction of sanctions of an appropriate magnitude
fulfills an important role, e.g., the infliction of suffering on those who deserve it,
or deterring or preventing crime. Second, one must establish that *state-inflicted*
punishments are in fact the most effective means of inflicting the appropriate
sanctions for transgressions. Punishment under this view can be described as a
task in search of the agent most capable of performing it.

The normative preconditions argument also maintains that punishment can
be imposed by nonstate agents. Punishments inflicted by nonstate agents can in
principle function in the same ways and be valuable for the same reasons as
state-inflicted sanctions. Nevertheless, advocates of normative preconditions justifications maintain that punishment inflicted by nonstate agents is unjust for
principled, noncontingent reasons. A familiar argument along these lines maintains that punishment is designed to deter crimes, but that procedural considerations require that the severity of punishment be determined on the basis of a
democratic deliberative process. It is thus unjust to inflict sanctions (even if these
sanctions are "deserved" or produce efficient incentives) unless certain procedural preconditions are satisfied. Another version of this type of justification
asserts that punishment is inherently a prerogative of the victim. State-inflicted

---

1. R. A. Duff, TRIALS AND PUNISHMENTS 198 (1986).

2. Thomas E. Hill, *Kant on Wrongdoing, Desert, and Punishment*, 18 L. & PHIL. 407, 425
(1999).

3. Duff, *supra* note 1, at 198.

sanctions are thus just because the power to inflict sanctions was voluntarily transferred to the state by its citizens.

The third type of justification, the state-centered justification, takes a more radical route and maintains that state-inflicted sanctions are fundamentally different from sanctions imposed by other agents. Although privately inflicted sanctions may be desirable for various reasons, they are desirable for different reasons than state-inflicted sanctions are. A useful analogy illustrating the nature of state-centered justifications is the blood feud. In a blood feud it is not the mere act of killing that counts; it is rather the performance of the killing by the appropriate agent, i.e., by a (male) member of the victim's family, that counts. It is clear that in the Bible it is only a specific member of the victim's family who had the right and responsibility to kill the slayer with impunity.[4] The agent killing the murderer in a blood feud is not perceived as a means to perform the (allegedly just) act of killing; instead it is the act of killing that provides an opportunity for the appropriate agent to act in order redress the injustice. A killing not performed by the appropriate agent does not therefore constitute a blood feud and cannot redress the injustice.

One influential example of a state-centered justification for state-inflicted sanctions can be traced back to Immanuel Kant's discussion of punishment in the *Metaphysics of Morals*:

> Even if a civil society were to be dissolved by the consent of all its members (e.g., if a people inhabiting an island decided to separate and disperse throughout the world), the last murderer remaining in prison would first have to be executed, so that each has done to him what his deeds deserve and blood guilt does not cling to the people for not having insisted upon this punishment; for otherwise the people can be regarded as collaborators in this public violation of justice.[5]

Under one plausible interpretation, Kant believes that the last murderer has to be executed *before* the dispersion of the society. An attempt to remedy the great injustice of not executing the murderer *before* the dispersion of the society could not be remedied by killing him *after* the dispersion of the society. For this would constitute a private act of killing rather than a public act of execution, and unlike a public execution, a private killing could not be done in the name of the people as a collectivity.

III. IN DEFENSE OF A STATE-CENTERED JUSTIFICATION OF CRIMINAL PUNISHMENT

I will now develop and defend a version of the state-centered justification for state-inflicted criminal sanctions.

---

4. *See, e.g.,* Pamela Barmash, HOMICIDE IN THE BIBLICAL WORLD 24 (2005).

5. Immanuel Kant, THE METAPHYSICS OF MORALS 106 (Mary Gregor ed. and trans., 1996).

At least one intuitive observation supports the state-centered justification of punishment. A criminal conviction may often give rise to (justified or unjustified) infliction of privately inflicted sanctions such as social stigmatization and isolation. Nevertheless, privately inflicted sanctions cannot substitute wholly or in part for state-inflicted sanctions following a criminal conviction. If criminal punishment could successfully be inflicted by nonstate agents, state-inflicted criminal sanctions should arguably, as a matter of justice, be calculated in a way that takes into consideration the sufferings of the criminal that result from privately inflicted sanctions. The private sufferings of the guilty (including private sufferings resulting from the infliction of privately inflicted sanctions) may lead courts to inflict a more lenient sentence out of compassion, but such leniency is discretionary and many theorists have opposed it. This indicates that state-inflicted sanctions are not typically viewed as commensurate with private sanctions. The nonsubstitutability of privately inflicted sanctions for state-inflicted sanctions points to the fundamental role that the state as the agent in charge of inflicting sanctions plays in justifying the infliction of these sanctions. This leaves open, however, the question of whether such a justification can be provided.

Under the state-centered justification developed here, the power to inflict criminal sanctions as well as the power to determine their severity is inextricably linked with the power to issue prohibitions whose violations call for punitive measures. The power to inflict sanctions has to be a state power because of the interdependence between the state's power to issue prohibitions and the power to determine the severity of these sanctions and inflict sanctions triggered by violating these prohibitions. Under this justification, criminal punishment is not merely an important task in search of the agent most capable of performing it; it is interrelated with other powers and duties of the state such that stripping the state of this power disrupts its proper functioning. In the account of criminal sanctions that I will offer, the same agent who is the originator of the criminal prohibitions must also administer the sanctions for the violation of these prohibitions. Given that the state is assigned with the power to issue prohibitions, it alone ought to make determinations concerning the severity of the sanctions (triggered by violating state-issued prohibitions); and then it also ought to inflict these sanctions.

Criminal sanctions are triggered by the violation of state-issued prohibitions. These prohibitions are grounded in the state's judgments concerning the wrongfulness of violating these prohibitions and the appropriateness of inflicting sanctions for violating them. Privately inflicted sanctions are grounded in the private judgments of those who inflict them. They sever the link between the state's judgments concerning the wrongfulness of the act or the appropriateness of the sanctions and the infliction of the sanction. It is therefore impermissible on the part of the state to authorize, initiate, or encourage individuals to inflict suffering on the guilty.

To establish the impermissibility of privately inflicted sanctions, assume that a law-abiding citizen A is asked (or hired) by the state to inflict sanctions on convicted offenders. The state asks A to ostracize persons convicted of a particular offense. Upon being notified about the conviction of person B for this offense, A considers whether she ought to participate in the state-initiated sentencing scheme by ostracizing B or limiting her social interaction with B.

It seems that A's decision to ostracize B could be based on three possible reasons. Ostracizing B could be based on: 1) A's judgment that ostracizing B is a way of fulfilling A's civic obligations, 2) A's judgment that B committed an offence and deserves to be punished, or 3) A's trust that the state made an accurate determination concerning the wrongfulness of B's behavior and the appropriateness of the sanction, without forming any independent judgment with respect to either issue.

Ostracizing B as a way of fulfilling one's civic duties is of course harmful to B, but it is not properly classified as a criminal punishment since it does not presuppose a judgment on the part of A that B has committed a wrong. Inflicting suffering as a means of fulfilling one's civic duty does not presuppose a judgment by A concerning the prior commission of a wrong on the part of the criminal.

Is it permissible for A to inflict suffering on B in order to fulfill his or her civic duty and to do it under circumstances in which A has not formed an opinion concerning the wrongfulness of B's behavior? To establish the impermissibility of such an act, think of the grievance which B can raise against A. Most convincingly, B can argue that it is unjust for A to inflict a suffering without forming a judgment that B committed a wrong. A's assertion that he merely fulfills a civic duty implies that A is willing to inflict this suffering irrespective of whether B has committed a wrong. It seems evident that there can be no civic duty to inflict suffering under these conditions.

Assume now that A ostracizes B because she formed the opinion that B has committed a wrong and deserves to be punished. This is indeed a punishment for wrongdoing, but A's judgment concerning the wrongfulness of B's behavior and the appropriateness of the sanction is a private judgment. The sanction does not reflect a judgment *on the part of the state* concerning the severity of the offence or the appropriateness of the sanction. The person inflicting the sanction may of course happen to form an opinion on these matters identical to that of the state. But this would be a happy coincidence and would not transform the private infliction of suffering into a state punishment.

But is A's infliction of suffering in this case impermissible? As long as A's judgment is a private one made by A on the basis of her own judgment, it may be permissible. Yet it is wrong for the state to approve of the infliction of the sanction under these circumstances. It would be wrong on the part of the state to give A's private judgment greater weight than B's private judgment concerning the wrongfulness of B's behavior. Instead, the state ought to make its own public judgment concerning the wrongfulness of B's action and its ramifications. B has a legitimate grievance if she is subjected to A's state-initiated private sanction (based on A's private judgment), and this grievance is distinct from any grievance she may have in being subjected to an (unjust) public judgment.

Assume finally that A ostracizes B not because she believes it is her civic duty or because she forms an independent judgment concerning the wrongfulness of the act and the appropriateness of the sanction. Instead, A inflicts the sanction because she trusts the state's judgment on these matters. It seems that sanctions inflicted on the basis of such trust are grounded in the state's own judgments and can thus be regarded as criminal sanctions proper. The trustworthy citizen simply functions as an instrument for realizing the state's own judgments.

But it is doubtful whether such trust could be ever justified. If such trust could be justified, the citizen would be exempted from responsibility for the infliction of an inappropriate sanction. The moral responsibility for inflicting such a sanction would rest with the state. Such an exemption from moral responsibility is sometimes justified with respect to state officials such as judges, prison guards, or perhaps even executioners. Citizens are different. They cannot abdicate their responsibility for the infliction of suffering. It is only by becoming an official of the state that such an abdication of responsibility is justifiable.

A citizen who is asked by the state to inflict suffering on a criminal should not rely on the state's judgments when the consequences are so grave. The citizen is required in this situation to form a judgment concerning the appropriateness of the sanction she is to inflict. Inflicting the sanction in these circumstances should therefore to be regarded as a private act on the part of the citizen founded on the citizen's own judgment that the sufferings inflicted are appropriate. Failing to form an independent opinion concerning the appropriateness of the sanction does not transform the act from a private into a public act and does not turn it into a state sanction.

The status of a citizen who is called upon by the state to inflict sanctions thus differs from the status of an official. A judge, a prison guard, or an executioner is often entitled or obligated to faithfully execute the state's sentencing decisions. Such a duty to execute the state's sentencing decisions is not boundless, but it is much broader than the duties borne by a citizen. Demarcating the boundary between citizens and officials is not always easy, but it is this line that explains the difference in the moral responsibility of a judge or a prison guard on the one hand and of a citizen who is asked by the state to participate in the infliction of privately inflicted sanctions on the other. The former is an official who is typically entitled or even required to perform this task irrespective of his private convictions concerning the appropriateness of the sanction; the latter bears moral responsibility for what she does irrespective of whether she follows the state's sentencing guidelines.

IV. CONCLUSION

The power to issue prohibitions and the powers to make determinations concerning the severity of the sanctions and to inflict them are inextricably inter-related. It is impermissible for individuals to inflict sanctions (for violating state-issued prohibitions) without forming an independent judgment with respect to the wrongfulness of the action and the appropriateness of the sanctions. If they form such a judgment, it is impermissible for the state to endorse that judgment. Thus, to the extent that criminal sanctions for violating state-issued prohibitions are justified, they must be inflicted by the same agent who issues the prohibitions.

The suffering inflicted by privately inflicted sanctions is grounded in a private judgment concerning the wrongfulness of the act or the appropriateness of the sanction. By delegating the power to punish to private individuals, the state in effect severs the link between the prohibitions it issues and the suffering inflicted on the offender. The individual who inflicts punishment on the basis of reasons he has acquired from the state acts on what he has come to believe and has judged to be a sufficient basis for action. The contribution to the genesis of his action made by the state's invitation to participate in the infliction of sanctions is, so to speak, superseded by the agent's own judgment.[6] The suffering of the criminal is therefore a "private" suffering—a suffering founded on a citizen's judgments concerning the wrongfulness of the act and the appropriateness of the sanction.

Two recent initiatives to privatize the infliction of sanctions, shaming penalties and private prisons, illustrate the relevance of this conclusion to contemporary controversies. These two initiatives involve two different forms of privatization, both of which are impermissible for that reason. Shaming penalties privatize both the determination of the severity of the sanction and the infliction of the sanction. The agents who shame select the sanctions they wish to inflict (within the boundaries of the law). They are also in charge of inflicting these sanctions. In contrast, the corporations operating private prisons inflict sanctions whose severity is determined by the state.

The examples of shaming penalties and private prisons demonstrate that the debates concerning the justification of state-inflicted sanctions are not merely theoretical. Even if a system in which all criminal sanctions are privately determined and inflicted is not a realistic option, current reforms or reform proposals nonetheless grant private individuals the power to inflict sanctions for wrongdoing. These proposals have often been initiated and discussed by economists, sociologists, and lawyers. I hope to have shown that philosophical considerations provide strong reasons to oppose such schemes.

---

6. This way of articulating my claim is borrowed from the discussion of Scanlon's defense of freedom of speech. *See* Thomas Scanlon, *A Theory of Freedom of Expression*, 1 PHIL. & PUB. AFF. 204, 212 (1972).

COMMENTS
ELIMINATING THE DIVIDE BETWEEN THE STATE
AND ITS CITIZENS

MIRIAM BAER*

Alon Harel's argument in defense of state-centered criminal sanctions is effectively an answer to the age-old question of what is a crime. For Harel, both the determination and implementation of criminal sanctions must be carried out by the "state," or else the "state's" judgment as to what is a crime loses its legitimacy.

Harel's argument, however tightly constructed and internally consistent, is premised on a notion of the "state" that is inconsistent with reality. Consider Harel's view of public officials. According to Harel, public officials are the only people who can determine and inflict criminal sanctions because they act solely as "agents" of the state. That is, they do not exercise their own independent judgment. The "state" exercises judgment and its "judgment" as to what is criminally wrong is impaired when it delegates to private parties its "judgment" as to the determination or infliction of sanctions. In everyday terms, prison guards who collect a public paycheck are state agents because they exercise no independent judgment; independent contractors, however, are not state agents because they do exercise independent judgment.

The cracks in Harel's argument quickly appear when one tries to demarcate the boundary between the moral judgments of private citizens and those of public officials. As any casual observer of criminal law recognizes, not a single area of criminal law exists in which public officials do *not* exercise their own independent moral judgment in executing the criminal laws. A traffic officer sees a driver speed through a traffic light, but decides not to issue a citation. A prosecutor charges a petty thief with disorderly conduct instead of larceny so that the thief may avoid a life sentence under a three strikes law. A grand jury elects not to return an indictment because it believes a police officer's shooting was justified force. And so on. Of course, the state's rules of law guide the exercise of such judgment, but it would be folly to suggest that these rules are complete or detailed enough (or ever could be) to excise the independent moral judgment of the actors who apply them.

This leads in turn to the normative question: Would we *want* to ban private actors from participating in the "infliction" of criminal sanctions, even if we could? Is Harel's idealized divide between public officials and private citizens one that we wish to embrace?

---

* Assistant Professor Law, Brooklyn Law School.

Maybe not. Harel elsewhere analogizes state-centered infliction of punishment to the punishments that parents impose on their children.[1] According to Harel, having the power to punish makes one a better parent because it instills a better appreciation of "what the well-being of [one's child] consists of."[2] Presumably, inflicting sanctions improves the state's stewardardship of our collective interests by teaching it to "govern justly."[3] But the state is neither a parent nor person, and its citizens are not its children. While trying to make the state the best "parent" it can be, Harel has failed to consider the other end of the equation: Is it a good idea for us to conceive of ourselves as children?

Within the last two decades, one of the more interesting developments in law has been the shift toward a type of government that freely moves between the private and public realm. This type of governance, often referred to as either New Governance or democratic experimentalism, purposely ignores the delineations between state and nonstate actors. The New Governance state is the opposite of Harel's idealized state: it invites collaboration, self-monitoring, and the exercise of independent moral judgment from decidedly nonstate actors. Although it is most apparent in areas of administrative law, it has also made crossroads into the criminal realm, most notably in specialized drug courts, which often rely on nonstate actors to carry out multiple goals. However imperfect this new form of governance may be, it demonstrates a growing dissatisfaction with the traditional conception of the state as separate and apart from the people it governs. Moreover, it recognizes that governing nonstate actors as if they are children does them little good.

Harel has done us a great service by forcing us to think about why we feel nagging concerns about the privatization of the criminal justice system. The conception of the state upon which he bases his claim, however, is neither the one we have, nor the one that we want.

---

1. Alon Harel, *Why Only the State May Inflict Criminal Sanctions: The Case Against Privately Inflicted Sanctions*, 14 LEGAL THEORY 113, 123 (2008).

2. *Id.* at 124.

3. *Id.* at 127.

WHY THE STATE MAY DELEGATE THE INFLICTION OF CRIMINAL SANCTIONS

DORON TEICHMAN[*]

In recent years private actors are increasingly involved in punishment. Offenders are being publicly shamed through both primitive means such as wearing T-shirts and more sophisticated technology such as the Internet. In addition, the role of private companies in the incarceration industry has grown: Currently, 7.2 percent of inmates in the United States are incarcerated in private prisons.[1] Alon Harel's core text offers an illuminating new perspective on the subject and presents an argument opposing the use of privately inflicted sanctions. In this brief comment I will highlight some of the difficulties in the argument presented by Harel and point out several issues that Harel did not address.

Harel's thesis presumes a clear distinction between the inevitable negative consequences of a criminal conviction that are brought about by private parties and those that are "encouraged" by the state. The justification for this distinction is questionable. Even without a proactive shaming regime, a criminal conviction could lead to catastrophic consequences ranging from unbearable embarrassment to loss of companionship, work, housing, and so forth. It is unclear against what baseline Harel views the state's acts as "encouraging" private sanctions. There are many instrumental and noninstrumental justifications for a transparent criminal process in which the identity of offenders is public. Yet Harel's argument seems to suggest that the ideal criminal justice system is one in which the identity of offenders remains unknown in order to avoid any negative ramifications beyond those created directly by the state. While one might attempt to defend such a regime, Harel's thesis does not succeed in doing so.

An additional problem with Harel's argument is its lack of pragmatism. The actual moral convictions of people are a matter for empirical measurement. In many areas a general consensus exists among a large part of the community that certain offenders (sex offenders, for example) should be subject to private sanctions. Given the fact that the state knows these beliefs, it can be certain that publicizing the convictions of these offenders will bring about private sanctions. While Harel would like the state to ignore these facts when reaching its own judgment as to the appropriate punishment, I do not find this desirable. The state can calibrate the appropriate mix of both public and private sanctions based

---

* The Joseph H. and Belle R Braun Senior Lectureship in Law, Faculty of Law, Hebrew University of Jerusalem.

1. BUREAU OF JUSTICE STATISTICS, U.S. DEP'T OF JUSTICE, ONE IN EVERY 31 U.S. ADULTS WAS IN A PRISON OR JAIL OR ON PROBATION OR PAROLE AT THE END OF LAST YEAR (2007), *available at* http://www.ojp.usdoj.gov/bjs/pub/press/po6ppuso6pr.htm.

on its judgment of the appropriate sanctions and on its knowledge of expected private sanctions. For example, the state can alter the length of time that the offender will be subject to a shaming sanction. Thus, both private and public actors do in fact judge offenders before deciding if and how much to sanction them.

Another problem with Harel's analysis is that it ignores the possibility of state regulation of private sanctions. For example, take the issue of private prisons: It would seem that Harel believes that the state hands over offenders to these institutions for a given period of time with the instructions "do with them as you please as long as they suffer." In reality, the state scrutinizes every aspect of life in these institutions, from the amount of inmates per square foot to the amount of calories inmates consume each day. In some cases the state may have greater control over the life of inmates when they are incarcerated in private institutions. Similarly, shaming regimes are conducted in the shadow of legal regulation. The state may determine what types of private sanctions are permissible and ensure that offenders are punished in a fitting way.

Finally, I would like to raise two questions that Harel does not address. The first involves state-conferred *benefits* rather than state-inflicted sanctions. In many cases the state has a duty (legal or nonlegal) to confer benefits on its citizens. Education, health care, and national security are some examples. Although I do not think that we have a general obligation to aspire to symmetry in all areas of public policy, Harel should explain if it is permissible to "sever the tie" between the duty to provide public goods and the actual provision of these goods by private actors who are funded by public budgets, and if it is, why the difference between punishment and all other public goods. In other words, why are private prisons different from private schools or hospitals?

Second, Harel should qualify his claim and explain what precisely the scope of his argument is. One of the main justifications for privately inflicted sanctions is instrumental: If one can bring about the same amount of deterrence at a lower cost by using these sanctions, then, all else being equal, one should do so. Thus, assuming that Harel is not oblivious to welfare considerations, at what point can the efficiency of privately inflicted sanctions justify their use?

WHY ONLY THE STATE MAY *DECIDE* WHEN SANCTIONS ARE APPROPRIATE

MALCOLM THORBURN*

Alon Harel's core text raises important and too-long-ignored concerns about the privatization of central features of the criminal justice system. But he does not make sufficiently clear precisely what aspect of criminal sanctions he believes

---

* Assistant Professor, Faculty of Law, Queen's University, Kingston, Canada.

should not be privatized. Sometimes, Harel focuses only on the privatization of the *infliction* of sanctions (something that is at work in both shaming sanctions and private prisons); but at other times, he suggests that the key problem is the privatization of the *decision* that a particular act is wrongful and just how severe a sanction it deserves (something that is sometimes true of shaming sanctions but is not true of private prisons).

The difference is crucial. The infliction of criminal sanctions involves a Hohfeldian legal *privilege*: prison officials are permitted to do things by way of punishment that would normally be criminally prohibited. By contrast, the decision about what conduct is wrongful and what sort of punishment it serves involves the exercise of a Hohfeldian legal *power*: only a court of law can convict someone of a criminal offence and only a sentencing judge can determine what punishment is appropriate in the circumstances. I believe that it is crucial to treat the privatization of these two features separately for reasons I elaborate below.

The aspect of private criminal sanctions that Harel focuses on for much of his core text is the exercise of the legal *power* to decide whether conduct is wrongful, and if so, what punishment it deserves. If that is the part of his argument he wishes to emphasize, then I agree, and I would even push the story further: most state officials are not entitled to make such decisions either. Standard criminal sanctions (such as execution, imprisonment, fines, etc.) usually involve conduct that would be criminal but for the fact that it is being carried out as a criminal sanction. If I decide that a murderer should be "fined" for his wrongdoing and take five hundred dollars from him, this does not turn my action into a criminal sanction—it is just another theft. The same is true if I decide to "imprison" him (this is just wrongful confinement) or execute him (this is just another murder). What is more, even a state-employed prison guard is not entitled to imprison or to execute someone who has committed a crime on her own initiative; she is only entitled to do precisely what she is instructed to do by the order of a sentencing judge.

But if Harel wishes to extend his argument to include private prisons and other cases where state officials maintain a monopoly on the exercise of legal *powers* but find private corporations to carry out specific well-defined tasks, I think that his argument is a good deal harder to maintain. For what sort of argument could support this claim? Because it is officials who carry out punishments, parallels to Biblical requirements that a specific person be the one to carry out a punishment are inapposite (for even in the state case, it is not a specific individual but whoever occupies a certain office that may carry out the punishment). Nor could it be Harel's argument that only state officials carry an "exemption from moral responsibility" when they carry out criminal sanctions. For if officials are exempt in this way, then why shouldn't the employees of private corporations be exempt in precisely the same way if they are given the same sorts of detailed orders by a sentencing judge? Harel's argument for the distinction between the official's position and the private prison corporation employee's position is a mere stipulation: He writes: "It is only by becoming an official of the state that such an abdication of responsibility is justifiable."[1] Why is that so?

In short, although I agree with Harel that the difference between state officials and private actors is important in understanding the legitimacy of criminal sanctions (and of much else besides),[2] I believe that there is a good deal more that needs to be said to explain precisely how that distinction operates. Put in the blunt terms that Harel uses, we are just as likely to mischaracterize the situation by relying on this distinction as we are to clarify things.

---

1. See Harel core text at 135.
2. I develop these arguments about the privatization of legal powers and legal privileges in the context of justification defenses more generally in Malcolm Thorburn, *Justifications, Powers, and Authority*, 117 YALE L.J. 1070 (2008).

WHY DO PRIVATELY INFLICTED CRIMINAL SANCTIONS MATTER?

STUART P. GREEN*

Should the right to inflict criminal sanctions be the exclusive province of the state? Alon Harel says yes, and I agree with much of his reasoning. What I disagree with is his explanation for why the question matters. According to Harel, the state's exclusive prerogative to inflict criminal sanctions has been threatened in recent years in large part by the proliferation of shame sanctions. As I shall argue, however, his focus on shame sanctions reflects confusion about both what it is for sanctions to be "private," and what it means for them to be "inflicted."

Harel says that shame sanctions "privatize both the determination of the severity of the sanction and the infliction of the sanction. The agents who shame select the sanctions they wish to inflict. . . . They are also in charge of inflicting those sanctions."[1] But is that really so? Consider the requirement that convicted sex offenders display a license plate conspicuously identifying themselves as such. The plates are undoubtedly meant to foster condemnation of the defendant on the part of those private citizens who view them. But the sanction is formulated, imposed, and enforced by the government and its officials. Indeed, it is precisely the fact that the *government* is the party that is channeling such unseemly passions that arguably makes shame sanctions objectionable.

---

* Professor of Law and Justice Nathan L. Jacobs Scholar, Rutgers Law School–Newark.
1. See Harel core text at 136.

To the extent that Harel believes it is always inappropriate for criminal sanctions to elicit stigma on the part of private citizens, his argument proves too much. As Joel Feinberg and many others have argued, all criminal sanctions are intended to evoke censure and disapprobation on the part of the citizenry.[2] Shame sanctions simply do it more directly and more emphatically. The only way to avoid having criminal sanctions evoke public censure would be to impose them in private, without public notice.

Harel's analysis also contains a larger confusion: he is unclear about exactly what he means when he talks about privately "inflicted," "initiated," "administered," or "issued" criminal sanctions.[3] At times, it seems as if he disapproves of private involvement in all spheres of the criminal justice system. If so, his argument would again prove too much. While the government has traditionally exercised exclusive control in certain areas of our criminal justice system—e.g., the investigation of suspected criminal activity and the supervision of parole—in other areas private parties have long played the leading role—such as grand-jury indictments, petit-jury verdicts, and capital sentencing. Harel's analysis fails to make clear why private involvement is acceptable in some spheres of the criminal justice system, but not in others.

One contemporary context in which the question is particularly worth asking is the initiation of criminal proceedings. Historically, at English common law, criminal cases were often initiated and carried out by private prosecutors. Over time, this practice has faded away, though vestiges of it remain.[4] In the 2006 case of *Jones v. Whalley*, for example, the House of Lords was presented with a case in which a plaintiff wished to bring a criminal prosecution when the government had declined to do so (instead, police had issued the defendant a written "caution").[5] The defendant argued that allowing such a prosecution would be an abuse of the court's process. In upholding the lower court's decision to bar the private prosecution in this particular case, the Lords acknowledged the complexity of the issue and put off for another day a decision on the broader question whether a private prosecution should ever be permitted under English law.[6]

I assume that Harel would disapprove of the kind of private prosecution that was at issue in *Jones*. In my view, his argument against the involvement of private parties in the criminal justice system would have been more pertinent had it been directed to a case like that rather than to shame sanctions.

---

2. Joel Feinberg, *The Expressive Function of Punishment, in* Doing and Deserving 95 (1970).

3. *See* Harel core text at 129, 130, 133, 134.

4. *See generally* Stuart P. Green, Note, *Private Challenges to Prosecutorial Inaction: A Model Declaratory Judgment Statute*, 97 Yale L.J. 488 (1988).

5. [2006] 3 W.L.R. 179.

6. *Id.* at 187–88.

REPLY

ALON HAREL

Miriam Baer and Doron Teichman challenge my defense of the state's exclusive powers to punish altogether (Baer on principled grounds; Teichman on pragmatic grounds). Malcolm Thorburn and Stuart Green are more sympathetic to my argument but urge me to limit its applicability or scope.

Baer challenges my argument on both normative and descriptive grounds. In her view, the conception of the state described in my paper is "neither the one we have, nor the one that we want."[1] It is not the state we want because new forms of governance or democratic experimentalism dictate that the boundary between public and private is much more fluid than traditionally thought; these new forms of governance ignore the delineations between state and nonstate actors. The New Governance state invites "collaboration, self monitoring, and the exercise of independent moral judgment from decidedly nonstate actors."[2]

I have nothing against these new methods of governance. Yet any cooperation or collaboration between the state and individuals ought to preserve distinct spheres of responsibility. I assume Baer will resist the idea that in the name of democratic experimentalism the government will delegate to individuals the power to make decisions concerning the severity of sanctions or the content of the criminal prohibitions. Cooperation and collaboration ought to be founded on demarcating what the appropriate spheres of responsibility are, and my core text ought to be regarded as providing guidelines for such a demarcation.

Baer also believes that this is not the state we have because public officials exercise judgment and have discretion. Baer wrongly presupposes that such discretion entails that such officials exercise "an independent moral judgment in executing the criminal laws."[3] In contrast, I believe that an official's judgment is not and ought not to be an independent moral judgment. It ought to reflect the values of the system within which they work. Thus, even if a prosecutor thinks that a particular sentence is too severe, she ought not to use this moral judgment in deciding whether to prosecute a person. The official's discretion is thus fundamentally different from an independent moral judgment—the one that ought to guide the citizen.

Teichman draws attention to the difficulty of characterizing the negative consequences of a criminal conviction that are brought about by private parties and those that are "encouraged" by the state. Teichman observes rightly that in my view only the latter raise moral concerns. Teichman argues that given the

---

1. Baer comment at 138.
2. *Id.*
3. *Id.* at 137.

transparency of the criminal process, it is inevitable that the criminal also suffers from the infliction of private sanctions.

Although I have not previously articulated it in these terms, the distinction ought to be understood as a distinction between intending the consequences and foreseeing them.[4] What is impermissible is the conviction of a person with the intention that private sanctions would follow and complement the public ones. It is permissible, however, to punish an individual foreseeing that such punishment would trigger private sanctions.

It is also wrong to assume, as Teichman does, that I am committed to the view that the state ignores the private sanctions inflicted by individuals. Precisely as the punishing state can take into account in calibrating the sanction any personal difficulties facing the criminal resulting from natural forces, so, too, it can take into account personal difficulties resulting from the infliction of private sanctions. Taking into account private sanctions that may be inflicted on the criminal does not mean that such sanctions are regarded as complementary to the state's sanctions in the same way as taking into account the fragile health of the criminal does not mean that the criminal's fragile health complements the sanction inflicted by the state. Economic reasoning typically blurs the distinction between the two, but such reasoning does not reflect either common sense or the values embedded in our system.

Thorburn endorses my claims concerning the exclusive power of the state to decide whether conduct is wrongful and to determine what punishment a criminal deserves. However, he resists the argument favoring the state's exclusive powers with respect to the very infliction of sanctions. Thorburn maintains that while the state may not delegate the power to sentence individuals, it may delegate the power to inflict criminal sanctions whose severity was determined by the state. In his view, if officials are exempted from legal responsibility for inflicting such sanctions, so too should be the employees of private corporations, as long as they get detailed instructions from the state.

In my view, Thorburn is wrong in maintaining that if state officials can be exempted from moral responsibility, so too can employees of private corporations. Employees of private corporations do not have the type of exemption that officials have. Just as an employee of a private corporation is not exempted from moral responsibility in performing his duties for the private corporation, neither should such an employee be exempted when the private corporation serves the state. Such a distinction is evident in our practices. I find it difficult to equate the moral responsibility of a private individual who killed a person on behalf and with the consent of the state with the moral responsibility of an executioner.

---

4. I elaborate on this distinction in Alon Harel, *Why Only the State May Inflict Criminal Sanctions: The Case Against Privately Inflicted Sanctions*, 14 LEGAL THEORY 113, 116–17 (2008).

Green is right in urging me to clarify what I mean by private sanctions. He believes, for instance, that my view necessitates resisting the legitimacy of private prosecutions. I believe he is wrong. The private prosecutor does not inflict a sanction; she is only calling upon the state to inflict one. Green also believes that shame penalties ought to be classified as state sanctions. In his view, shame penalties are penalties "formulated, imposed, and enforced by the government and its officials."[5]

I think this is a mischaracterization of shame penalties. The sanction in cases of shame penalties is not understood to be the state-imposed requirement that sex offenders display a license plate conspicuously, or that the picture of the offender be displayed in public places. It is the stigma resulting from such a display that is understood to be the real sanction. This is in fact the view upheld by both proponents and opponents of shame penalties.[6]

---

5. Green comment at 142.

6. *See, e.g.,* James Q. Whitman, *What is Wrong with Inflicting Shame Penalties?*, 107 YALE L.J. 1055, 1090–92 (1998).

7. RESULTS DON'T MATTER

LARRY ALEXANDER* AND KIMBERLY KESSLER FERZAN**

An actor is culpable for choosing to risk harm to others and their interests for insufficient reasons. In our view, not only does culpability set forth the necessary conditions for blameworthiness and punishment, but also the sufficient conditions. Resulting harm is immaterial.

I. THE IMMATERIALITY OF RESULTS

Our argument against the materiality of results is one of burden shifting. Quite simply, we fail to see how results matter. Moreover, we believe the onus is on those who claim that results matter to explain why results are desert bases.

Before getting to our argument, one caveat is in order. We are retributivists. We are concerned with punishing an actor no more than she deserves. Because we are unwilling to punish the undeserving (or to punish the deserving more than they deserve) in order to serve consequentalist goals, we view arguments that results matter in order advance such goals to be ultimately beside the point.

To understand why one needs an argument about why results matter, contrast causation (or causing results) with choice. The claim that choice is a desert basis is uncontroversial. Even those who wish to punish attempters less than completers still believe that attempts may be punished. That is, choice and acting on that choice are sufficient grounds for desert and punishment. Moreover, it is not difficult to see why acting on a decision to harm or to risk harming someone is sufficient to ground desert and punishment. The criminal law seeks to influence that very choice. Choice is a sufficient condition for punishment.

In contrast, causation is not a sufficient condition for desert. For if causation were sufficient, then even actors who exhibited sufficient concern for others and who exercised maximum care could be held criminally responsible for causing harms. In other words, we would have a strict liability regime. But strict liability runs counter to the very notion of desert because even individuals who care about others will occasionally (often?) harm them accidentally.

* Warren Distinguished Professor of Law, University of San Diego.

** Associate Dean for Academic Affairs and Professor of Law, Rutgers University–Camden. This essay draws from Larry Alexander and Kimberly Kessler Ferzan, with Stephen J. Morse, CRIME & CULPABILITY: A THEORY OF CRIMINAL LAW ch. 5 (2009).

What is interesting about the current debate is that neither of these points is in dispute. Choice is necessary and sufficient for punishment. Causation is neither necessary nor sufficient for punishment. The question is whether culpability *plus causation* has some moral magic that causation itself lacks. Quite frankly, we just do not see how causation suddenly gets this moral power.

Consider the following claim by Michael Moore: "'Causation matters' seems a pretty good candidate for a first principle of morality."[1] Really? It seems to us that "you break it, you buy it" is not a first principle of the criminal law. Rather, the first principle is "treat others with sufficient concern." Now, whatever the actor is going to *do*, the criminal law can only influence the actor by guiding the choice she makes. It is at this point that law and morality guide action, and it is through her choice that the agent controls her action and the results of her action. If the agent does not foresee harm, she is not held responsible for harm just because she caused it. In other words, causation without choice does not matter. So, if the criminal law's power to influence and the agent's power over results occur at the point in time that the actor chooses to act, from where does the result itself derive additional moral power?

The point here is not to argue why causation does not matter, but to point out the need for an argument as to why it should. We do not need an argument. Indeed, we also do not have an argument for why it does not matter if one's victim has eleven toes, or the killing occurs on a Tuesday, or the shooter uses his left hand, or the reckless driver's car is red, and so forth. All we can say is that these things *do not matter* until we hear a compelling argument about why they do. If one is going to punish another person, one needs an account of why that person is deserving of punishment. The arguments for the materiality of choice are powerful. These arguments go to the heart of understanding the purposes of the criminal law, the nature of practical reasoning, and the root of criminal responsibility.

What are the arguments for the materiality of results? The only argument on the table for punishing results more (as a matter of moral desert) is a phenomenological argument. We feel guiltier and blame others more when harm occurs. Before discounting the phenomenology (as we will do in the next section), we wish to note here the contrast between the strength of the choice argument and the weakness of the results argument. The powerful and persuasive reasons that we have in favor of choice simply do not exist with respect to causation of results. Whereas the focus on the actor's choice points to understanding human action as a matter of practical reasoning, the focus on results shifts the emphasis back to our mechanistic causal universe. The very significance of human action is absent from an account that points to harm caused as independently desert enhancing. So, even though we are sympathetic to arguments premised on

---

1. Michael S. Moore, CAUSATION AND RESPONSIBILITY ch. 2 (2008).

emotion and intuition, we cannot find a compelling principle beyond these purported emotions in the case of results.

II. THE INTUITIVE APPEAL OF THE "RESULTS MATTER" CLAIM

Undoubtedly, the man on the street believes that an actor's killing his victim is something worse than an actor's attempt to kill him. Such intuitions have, in fact, been verified empirically.[2] Despite these intuitions, however, we must ask in what respect do results matter, and specifically, do they affect the actor's blameworthiness?

Let's consider an ordinary everyday occurrence. Suppose that two children have been told not to toss and hit baseballs into their neighbor's yard because the ball might hit the neighbor's window. And suppose, while the parents are away, each child, acting alone at different times of day, tosses and hits a baseball into the neighbor's yard. At the end of the day, when the parents return, an angry neighbor appears with two baseballs—one from his yard and one from his house—and one piece of broken glass. Each child, when summoned, admits hitting a baseball into the neighbor's yard, but neither knows if his is the baseball that hit the window.

It seems to us that no parent would spend one second trying to determine which child caused the damage; rather, all parents would punish both children and both children equally. Indeed, if after having grounded both children for two weeks, any parent discovered an eyewitness who knew which child broke the window, we doubt that any parent would believe that he overpunished the one attempter and would therefore seek to make amends, say, by granting the child extra television time. Whether these parents seek to deter future conduct or to punish current conduct, parents will want to punish their children for violating the conduct rule, "do not hit balls into the neighbor's yard," irrespective of which child caused the harm that justifies that rule—"because so doing might break the neighbor's window."

This hypothetical example underscores an important point. We do not claim that harm does not matter. Of course it does. If the children miss the window, the neighbor is not (as) angry, and the parents are not paying for a new pane of glass. (And, alternatively, we often feel guilt for causing harm, even in the absence of culpability, such as when we break something through no fault of our own.) Our criminal laws embody and enforce norms the aims of which are to prevent the unjustified harming of other people. Harm is what the criminal law ultimately cares about.

---

2. Paul H. Robinson and John M. Darley, JUSTICE, LIABILITY, AND BLAME: COMMUNITY VIEWS AND THE CRIMINAL LAW 23 (1995). Importantly, the Robinson and Darley study compares *incomplete* attempts with *completed* crimes.

Notably, simply because preventing the harm may justify the rule does not mean that causing the harm increases the actor's blameworthiness. In any case in which the actor consciously disregards an unjustifiable risk by engaging in reckless action, he displays insufficient concern for causing that harm. The risk of harm an actor unleashes is preventable. The actor's act, and whether it is unduly risky, may be guided by reasons. The results of his act cannot be. These results can only be affected by the choice to act and the reasons that guide that choice.

Criminal law, therefore, is about reducing harm because the occurrence of harm itself is of concern to us. In some sense, it is all that matters. No one doubts that the success of the actor has a significant effect on the victim. The difference between murder and attempted murder is quite simply the difference between death and life. We hope to keep our lives, limbs, and valuables, and to the extent that actors aim at depriving us of these items, it certainly matters whether actors succeed or fail.

Results matter for the most simple of life's decisions and for the most important actions we take. Simply because results matter, however, does not mean that they matter for purposes of moral desert. We make many decisions each day, and the results of these decisions may matter to us, but the results are morally immaterial to an actor's praiseworthiness or blameworthiness. Indeed, imagine a case in which someone tries to rescue a friend from drowning. The praiseworthiness of the behavior is independent of success or failure, despite the fact that success or failure is critically important to the rescuer (and the friend). And although our praise for a successful painter's beautiful work may be greater than our praise of an unsuccessful painter's unsightly one, that kind of praise is not a *moral* judgment about the painters.

III. "RESULTS MATTER" QUANDARIES

For those readers who remain unpersuaded, we wish to turn to the problems with the "results matter" view. Anyone who believes that criminal law should take results into account must be able to offer principled answers to the following questions.

First, if results can increase blameworthiness and punishability, can they also decrease them? Suppose that a would-be killer misses his victim and kills a terrorist who was about to kill 1,000 people. Is there a point at which the actor not only deserves less jail time but also deserves no jail time? A ticker-tape parade? The key to the city? Can the fortuitous results of one's culpable action fully absolve the offender of any blameworthiness whatsoever?

Defenders of "results matter" typically deny that results matter in the absence of culpable mental states (or, in cases where praise and not blame is at issue, in the absence of an intent to bring about a good result). But if results are morally inert in the absence of the requisite mental states, what explains their moral valence in the presence of such mental states? If a person tries to help an old lady across a street, but brings about the saving of 1,000 lives, unaware that he is doing so, is his positive moral ledger enhanced by that result? In other words, defenders of the claim that "results matter" need more than a handful of intuitions; they need an account of *how* choice and causation interact.

There are then the multiple of cause in fact and proximate cause problems that need to be resolved. What should the criminal law do about causal overdetermination cases, alternative causation problems such as *Summers v. Tice*,[3] or the proof problems that gave rise to market share liability in tort law in *Sindell v. Abbott Laboratories*?[4] If *Sindell* were a criminal case, the question would be whether the defendants deserve punishment, and whether the amount that they deserve is dependent upon the harm they actually caused. In our view, we need not await further scientific advances that would allow us to ascertain which manufacturer's diethylstilbestrol (DES) actually triggered a particular victim's vaginal cancer, nor would our attitudes be affected by that knowledge. Rather, we know all we need to know to fix desert.

There are also the cases where the actor causes V's death but also prolongs V's life. One of the most famous puzzles is the three prospectors case. A, B, and C are prospecting. C is going out on his own the next day. A secretly wants to kill C, and while B and C are asleep, A fills C's canteen with poison. Later, while A and C are asleep, B, who also wants to kill C, but who is unaware of what A has done, pours out the contents of C's canteen (thinking that it's water) and fills the canteen with sand. Later, C dies of thirst. A denies killing C, because C did not die of poison. B also denies killing C, because although C did die of thirst as B planned, C died later than he otherwise would have had B not poured out the poison. B actually prolonged C's life. We have no problem with such a case. A and B are both equally culpable, and what happened to C is immaterial. Not so for the "results matter" folks.

The most significant doctrinal and theoretical problem for the "results matter" position is that of proximate causation. Those who adopt the "results matter" position believe that results do *not* matter if the causal linkage between the actor's culpable act and the harmful result that act causes (in fact) is too quirky. But then they are just compounding unprincipled intuitions here—they intuit that results matter, and then they intuit *when* results matter, but they offer no argument in support of either.

There are myriad proximate cause puzzles, but we will offer just one. Consider the story of Pierre and Monique (our entry in the "bad fiction writing" contest):

It was an incredible electrical storm. Lightning was striking every few seconds . . . and some bolts hit right outside the house.

---

3. 199 P.2d 1 (Cal. 1948) (en banc).
4. *Sindell v. Abbott Laboratories*, 607 P.2d 924 (Cal. 1980).

Inside, Pierre's hatred of Monique had reached the flashpoint. She had just informed him—matter-of-factly, dismissively, condescendingly—that no, she would not grant him a divorce so that he would be free to take up with his latest conquest, Bridgette. Her tone as much as her verdict enraged him. And as he looked at her, facing him but totally absorbed in a fashion magazine despite his just having informed her that he wanted to end their marriage, he realized that everything about her now disgusted him. And those body rings! Not only through her nose, but through her lips, her ears, her navel . . . everywhere. She was hideous.

But even as he fought to control his emotions, Pierre concocted a plan. He reached in the desk drawer and took out the loaded .38 he kept there, Monique still absorbed in her magazine and oblivious to his movements. He then aimed the gun at precisely 3°NNW and pulled the trigger.

Two possible endings of this story:

(1) The bullet just missed Monique, as Pierre knew it would. And just as Pierre hoped and believed would happen, Monique, believing that Pierre had just tried to kill her, leaped up and desperately ran from the house. Once outside, however, the metal rings on Monique's body did the work that Pierre hoped and believed they would: They attracted a bolt of lightning, which killed Monique on the spot. Pierre's hastily concocted plan had succeeded.

(2) The bullet just missed Monique because, although he wanted the bullet to kill Monique, Pierre's aim was off. Monique, alarmed at the realization that Pierre had tried to shoot her, immediately ran from the house. However, as she stepped outside, the metal rings on her body attracted a bolt of lightning, which killed her instantly.

In our view, Pierre deserves the same amount of punishment irrespective of how the story ends. The "results matter" position, however, commits one to the claim that Pierre caused Monique's death in (1), but not in (2), and thus is more blameworthy in (1) than (2). For in (1), surely Pierre "caused" Monique's death in whatever way is required for criminal liability; after all, her death occurred just as he had planned. Whereas in (2), if there was ever a "deviant causal chain" that severed proximate from actual causation, this would be an example. *Yet, (1) and (2) differ only with respect to Pierre's mental states preceding the firing of the gun. And these mental states cannot be said to have caused anything in themselves.* Thus, it is difficult to see how (1) and (2) can be distinguished in terms of proximate causation.

IV. CONCLUSION

Results do not matter for blameworthiness or punishability. The law seeks to influence the reasons for which a person acts, but it cannot influence the results of these actions. Thus, when an actor risks harm to others for insufficient reasons, the law's influence has failed, and a culpable act has fully revealed the actor's desert. No further information, such as whether the culpable act caused harm (or benefit), is needed for us to determine the degree of her desert and punishment.

Although many people believe that results matter, there is a distinction to be drawn between results mattering (as they must because they affect the world in which we live) and results mattering for the moral blameworthiness of the actor. We can recognize that some results are harmful, and indeed, that we create laws to prevent such harms, without at the same time committing ourselves to the view that results independently affect blameworthiness.

Because the law currently gives independent significance to the role of resulting harm, criminal law doctrine is flawed. Both cause-in-fact and proximate causation are flawed doctrinal attempts to approximate culpability when causal chains go awry. But if the alternative causers, market sharers, culpable life prolongers, and coincidence contrivers all deserve punishment, it is because of their choices and not because we can concoct a causation test to ensnare them. The better approach is simply to abandon completely any concern with results and causation and attend to choice and culpability directly.

COMMENTS

SOME REASONS WHY CRIMINAL HARMS MATTER

GERALD LEONARD*

Why does the criminal law treat a reckless driver who kills several innocent people far more severely than it treats an identical driver who causes less harm or none? Is there an adequate justification for that use of resulting harm?

I suppose Larry Alexander and Kim Ferzan would say that those questions miss the point, because they are interested only in the question of what each driver "deserves," irrespective of the consequentialist justifications for punishment that the state might offer. Still, they seem to suggest that they are talking about what criminal justice systems should do. So, rather than worry about whether I'm being precisely faithful to the authors' model of culpability, I'd like to offer some reasons why the law justifiably treats the killing driver as subject to greater punishment than the nonkilling driver and along the way suggest why those reasons are consistent with any presently plausible notion of culpability.

An important premise here is that it is all but impossible to specify with confidence what an offender "deserves"; nor is it possible to analyze culpability

---

* Professor of Law and Law Alumni Scholar, Boston University School of Law.

independently from crime prevention. Thus, I hope that everyone endorses the state's rationing of its scarce penal resources in order to minimize harms to an innocent public (each member of which is just as deserving of "justice" as each offender is). That sort of inevitable rationing is necessarily part of the experience that informs common notions of (intuitions about) culpability, such common sense being the closest but still radically imperfect guide to what an offender actually can be said to "deserve." But in reality these authors and other retributivists have progressed hardly at all in giving us methods for determining when any but the most outrageous criminal sentences go beyond what the offender "deserves."

Pursuing public safety within the profoundly uncertain limits of culpability, then, the state might plausibly punish the nonkilling driver less severely than the killing one, first, because only the killer has caused suffering to constituent members of the state, such suffering as must be specifically redressed by the community's collective voice and action. Citizens who suffer wrongs deserve from the state that much solace, that expression of solidarity—even that revenge perhaps—in return for their willingness not to seek justice on their own. Second, the state might punish the nonkiller less severely because its legitimacy requires that it not be seen as cruelly meting out all the punishment it can narrowly justify when, in fact, no one has suffered and no one profits from the punishment. Third, the state may determine (however debatably) that deterrence is more effective when the punishment responds in a measured way to real harm than when it goes overboard in response to mere risk-creation. Presumably, it also matters that the state cannot commonly say with the philosopher's office-bound certainty that two similar choices really did raise identical risks and exhibit equally little concern for others despite their very different results.

I believe these are good, intertwined reasons why criminal law should take results into account, whether under the heading of "culpability" or "justice" or "public safety." Again, I imagine the authors saying that I am off the point, that they are not necessarily saying anything about the legitimacy of the state's punishing offenders *less* than they deserve for any of the above reasons—the core text is ambiguous on this point—that they are only talking about moral desert and thus about the maximum extent to which an actor may be punished. But if I can offer good reasons for harm-based punishment practices that are universally in place, especially if the punishments can't be shown to exceed desert, then what value is there in defining an abstract version of culpability that ignores harms?

More concretely, do an attempted murderer and a murderer both deserve five years? Twenty-five? Life? Death? We aren't told what the punishment for my two drivers above would be, only that they'd both "deserve" the same, just as two drunken child abusers would deserve the same even though one killed and the other did not, just as two reckless sexual actors would deserve the same whether the sexual partner was ultimately thrilled or terrorized by the act. The authors must conclude either that both halves of each of these pairs *must* be punished identically or else that the state commonly and legitimately punishes below the (hazy) upper limit of desert. If the authors approve of differential punishment here, it's hard to see what's useful in the merely semantic assertion that the two offenders nevertheless "deserve" the same. If the authors require identical punishments, then I think they are relying on a notion of culpability that has almost nothing to do with the actual human experience of law and its institutions, experience on which our intuitions about culpability rest in the first place.

WHY CRIMINAL HARMS MATTER

PETER WESTEN*

Larry Alexander and Kim Ferzan claim that an actor's criminal responsibility ought to be solely a function of his disrespect toward the interests of others—and not any harms that may result from his acting on such disrespect. They rest that claim on two premises:

> *Premise 1:* Advocates of harm-based offenses ("harm") possess no *moral* arguments—only historical and sociological arguments.

> *Premise 2:* Advocates of disrespect-based offenses ("disrespect") can rely on an uncontroversial moral argument, namely, that desert is a function of the disrespect with which a person acts, not any resulting harm.

I think both premises are flawed. Before discussing them, however, I will address a separate claim by Alexander and Ferzan that is questionable even if Premises 1 and 2 were valid—namely, that the burden of proof is on harm advocates either to present moral arguments or to lose the debate. That cannot be true. Consider the Trolley Problem, where no moral arguments support turning the trolley versus throwing a fat man on the tracks. Yet, surely, the existence of deep and universal intuitions suffices by itself to justify treating the cases differently.

Now consider Premise 1. Alexander and Ferzan repeatedly assert that harm advocates lack *moral* arguments. But that is not true. The first moral argument of *any* kind on the issue of harm versus disrespect is Plato's argument in support of harm. Plato argued in the *Laws* that the reason communities punish murderers more severely than attempted murderers is that communities are so righteously indignant at the murderer for succeeding that they give him the full punishment he deserves based upon his motivation, while they are sufficiently relieved at an attempter's failure that, appreciating their luck, they are perfectly content to punish him less than he deserves.[1] And they are right to do so. For no

---

* Frank G. Millard Professor of Law, Emeritus, University of Michigan.
1. *See* Peter Westen, *Why Harm Matters: Plato's Abiding Insight in the* Laws, 1 CRIM. L. & PHIL. 307 (2007).

community should be so self-righteous that it punishes more than it wishes to or feels a need to, merely because a subject deserves it.

The problem with Premise 2 is more complex. I agree with Alexander and Ferzan that desert is solely a function of the attitudes that an actor manifests toward the interests of others.[2] I also agree that if punishing harm-causers more severely than attempters consisted of punishing the former more than they deserve, it would be unjust. However, I disagree that the nature of desert suffices to support Alexander and Ferzan's position. Punishing harm-causers more severely than attempters can consist of something that jurisdictions rightly do all the time, namely, punish some offenders less than they deserve when sound political reasons exist for doing so.[3] In short, desert does not do the work that Alexander and Ferzan invoke it to do.

What remains, then, are the several "quandaries" that Alexander and Ferzan pose.

1. *If results increase blameworthiness, do they also reduce it?* Results do *not* increase blameworthiness. Results leave blameworthiness unchanged. Instead, the *absence* of results leaves jurisdictions simply not wishing or feeling a need to give offenders the full punishment they admittedly deserve.

   Can the absence of results leave a jurisdiction not wishing or feeling a need to give deserving offenders any punishment at all? Yes. Indeed, that is what jurisdictions do when they exculpate actors of certain impossible attempts, e.g., attempts to kill by voodoo.[4]

2. *Overdetermination.* It is a fallacy to think that a community's indignation toward an offender for result-based offenses is a function of physical laws such as cause-in-fact. Cause-in-fact is required in criminal law only when it is consistent with the public's indignation toward an offender for result-based offenses.[5] If the public is indignant at two concurrent actors for a single harm, then for the public, both actors "caused" the harm, and nothing supports giving them less punishment than they deserve.

3. *The three prospectors.* The question is, "To whom does the public attribute the death that actually befell C, i.e., death by thirsting?" The answer, it seems, is Prospector B, and, hence, for the public he is the killer.[6]

4. *Proximate cause.* Harm theory does *not* dictate that Pierre is more blameworthy in (1) than in (2). Pierre is equally blameworthy in both.

---

2. *See* Peter Westen, *An Attitudinal Theory of Excuse*, 25 L. & PHIL. 289 (2006).

3. *See* Doug Husak, *Retributivism in Criminal Theory*, 37 SAN DIEGO L. REV. 959 (2000).

4. *See* Peter Westen, *Impossibility Attempts*, 5 OHIO ST. J. CRIM. L. 523 (2008).

5. *Cf.* MODEL PENAL CODE § 2.03 cmt. at 259 (1980).

6. *See* Westen, *supra* note 1, at 325–26.

But harm theory does dictate that when for *any* reason, including quirkiness, the public attributes a death to something other than an actor like Pierre, the public lacks indignation it would otherwise feels and, hence, lacks a wish or need to give him the full measure of punishment that it knows he deserves.

RESULTS DON'T MATTER, BUT . . .

THOMAS MORAWETZ*

I agree emphatically with Larry Alexander and Kim Ferzan that the results of action are morally irrelevant. To the extent that criminal law mirrors morality, the same should be true of criminal law. But does law mirror morality? Should it? My inclination is to agree with Alexander and Ferzan that it should, but the equivalence cannot simply be taken for granted.

As a matter of positive law, a defendant given a lesser sentence for a failed attempt is simply luckier than the defendant who, having succeeded, serves a longer term. A crucial difference between moral evaluation and legal doctrine is the role of luck in the latter. Keep in mind the general character of legal rules. Each provision generalizes over an infinite class of situations. It creates categories of acts and events, and it does so by strictly limiting the features that qualify an act or event for inclusion. In particular, the categories of criminal law omit many considerations that are arguably morally relevant. Accordingly, those who commit unmitigated intentional homicide are eligible to be charged with and prosecuted for murder; it will be irrelevant to this determination whether they act sadistically or whether they act in response to the sadistic acts of others. (I am assuming that the mitigating condition of "extreme emotional disturbance" is not available.) More generally, many defendants with moral, psychological, and circumstantial claims that seem to explain and attenuate their *prima facie* predatory acts may, as a matter of law, be classed with those who have no such claims. Insofar as the law does not recognize their claims as mitigation, they are unlucky—and law and morality diverge.

Alexander and Ferzan are rightly concerned about the evident way in which luck plays a role in criminal action with regard to success and failure. Whether one achieves one's criminal purpose depends on uncontrollable factors: the gun may jam, the bullet may not hit a vital organ. They argue persuasively that success should not be a factor in criminality; two individuals, acting the same way with the same intentions, should be treated the same by criminal law whether they succeed or not.

---

* Tapping Reeve Professor of Law and Ethics, University of Connecticut School of Law.

Consider the same question with regard to transparently reckless (chosen) conduct. Should the reckless driver be seen as culpable to the same degree whether or not she hits or just misses the bicyclist? The clear implication of Alexander and Ferzan's argument is that she should because "results don't matter." But that conclusion is especially hard to square with any reasonable variant of existing practice and is less obviously mandated by morality. Should we punish the driver who misses the bicyclist at the level of reckless manslaughter (which would apply, let us assume, if she killed the bicyclist), or should we treat her when she does indeed kill the bicyclist with the legal response that would be appropriate for reckless driving?

Our moral responses about severity of punishment, about desert, are hardly clear. When we distinguish, indefensibly according to Alexander and Ferzan, between attempt and successes, are we punishing the success more severely than is warranted or are we punishing the attempt too leniently? If morally results don't matter, and legally they shouldn't matter, should the morally justified revision of the law increase penalties for attempts or decrease them for successes?

It is relevant that the attempter or reckless actor who is treated more leniently than the harm-causer is benefiting from good luck, not suffering because of bad luck. To succeed in one's endeavors is neither bad nor good luck, and the criminal actor has success in mind. Given that fact, the moral claim implicit in good luck is very weak.

Lastly, I am puzzled by Alexander and Ferzan's analysis of the events of a dark and stormy night, presumably in France. The authors assume that under their second possible ending Pierre can only be punished for an attempt to kill because there is a "deviant causal chain." But under the Model Penal Code and the law of most jurisdictions, the causal chain is not "deviant" if the causation of the result is not too "remote and accidental." Given the severity of the "incredible" storm, it can easily be argued that Pierre could foresee the dire fate of anyone wearing metal rings outdoors, and therefore he is not off the hook for the ultimate result. We get the same result in both scenarios, just as Alexander and Ferzan want.

ON THE REDUCIBILITY OF CRIMES

JEREMY HORDER*

Forceful though their arguments are that "results don't matter" in the criminal law, there is an element of reductionism in Larry Alexander and Kim Ferzan's analysis. It begins with a request that we "contrast causation (or causing results) with choice," but the contrast does scant justice to the complexity of criminal culpability.

To distinguish causation from choice, without allowing the latter to collapse into mere decision-making, the authors focus on "choosing *to risk harm to others* and their interests for insufficient reasons."[1] This is perilously close to a distinction without a difference. The causing of risk is a consequence of someone's choice, and so a key causal element has not been eliminated. Moreover, if results don't matter, should reasons? I cannot know of all the reasons favoring my choices. So, if there were sufficient reasons for my choice, can I still rely on that lucky fact to justify my conduct even if I did not know of or rely on them?

Further, on the Alexander–Ferzan view of criminal culpability, conduct crimes disappear into the ether even when they reflect choice. Suppose X has mutually participatory and enjoyed sexual activity with one of his mentally deficient patients (Y). That is rape, but the wrongfulness does not lie in X choosing to risk harm to Y. It lies in X's culpable role in what X and Y did together. Similarly, if X and Y agree to commit a crime, X's agreement condemns her even if it is understood that she will play no further role and hence herself risk no harm.

The Alexander–Ferzan choice-focused concept of culpability also sits uneasily alongside their "first principle" of the criminal law: "treat others with sufficient concern." I can easily fail to do that through negligence rather than through choice. To use Antony Duff's memorable example,[2] suppose a man goes out one morning to enjoy himself for a few hours because he has forgotten that it is his wedding day. Does the fact that he did not consciously "choose" to avoid his wedding make us unable to say that he was indifferent to his wedding? Hardly. His forgetfulness manifests his lack of sufficient concern for his intended bride. The many crimes that may be committed through negligence, rather than through choice alone, reflect this insight.

More broadly, the authors overlook the important distinction between reasons (not) to try, and reasons (not) to succeed. I could have a reason to try without a reason to succeed, as when I try to break an unbreakable vase to demonstrate its

---

* Law Commissioner for England and Wales; Professor of Criminal Law and Porjes Trust Fellow, Worcester College, Oxford.

1. *See* Alexander and Ferzan core text at 147 (emphasis added).

2. Antony Duff, INTENTION, AGENCY, AND CRIMINAL LIABILITY 31 (1990).

qualities. Contrariwise, I could have a reason to succeed (by throwing the double six I need to win the game, for example) without a reason to try (I can't "try" to throw a double six). Murder and attempted murder are distinguished because they involve different reasons not to do something (succeed, and try, respectively), even if I cannot commit murder without trying to. The causing of death is not just being gratuitously added on as an aggravating factor to what is the "real" reason not to do something (unjustifiably risk killing). One of Hitler's greatest evils was the authorization of genocide. The authors' analysis casts doubt on that. In their analysis the evil was authorizing conduct that was meant to pose a risk of genocide, not the genocide itself; but without a heinous crime of "genocide," can one make sufficient sense of the evil involve in posing a risk of genocide? I sincerely hope not.

The authors want to be nonconsequentialists and to save the criminal law from instrumentalism. In their view the only action segment of murder that has noninstrumental value is the attempt to kill (or the choice to risk killing), the "consequential" segment—causing death—being improperly included by the law merely to add a dash of instrumental disvalue to the crime. So, must all true nonconsequentialists leave the latter out of the picture, and focus on the attempt segment alone, as the only bit with noninstrumental value? That would be to overlook the difference between the action-reason not to kill and the outcome-reason not to do anything that has someone's dying as a consequence.[3] The criminal law has a number of noninstrumental ways of describing certain actions as wrongs, such as murder, manslaughter, rape, arson, burglary, and theft. The fact that they may be analyzed noninstrumentally means that even nonconsequentialists can accept their legitimacy within a criminal code, alongside crimes of attempting, risking, and so on.

---

3. John Gardner, *On the General Part of the Criminal Law*, in PHILOSOPHY AND THE CRIMINAL LAW 211 (Antony Duff ed., 1998).

REPLY

LARRY ALEXANDER AND KIMBERLY KESSLER FERZAN

We argued that retributive desert turns solely on an actor's culpability and not at all on whether his culpable act causes harm. Further, we argued that the law has failed to come up with a tenable theory of proximate causation, a theory that would be necessary were retributive desert to turn in part on harms caused.

Two of our commentators attempt to justify a distinction based on a principle other than retributive desert. Gerald Leonard appears to believe that it is victims' suffering, not criminals' desert, that justifies state-imposed punishment. It is surely true that when a culpable act causes no harm, there are no victims who suffer, who require the community's solace, and who are primed to take revenge. (On this last point, we express some doubt; but for the sake of argument, we concede it.) And Leonard also argues that we cannot gauge actors' desert with any degree of certainty.

What we fail to see is what these points, even if true, establish. There may be reasons to punish two equally deserving criminals unequally. Our argument does not speak to this point, although it is doubtful that resulting harm will prove to be an adequate reason to distinguish them. Our point in the contribution was that retributive desert does not turn on results, and nothing Leonard says disputes this.

Peter Westen agrees that the attempter and succeeder have the same desert. Nonetheless, he believes that although we do mete out the punishment the succeeders deserve, we mete out less punishment than the attempters deserve, and we do so for a moral reason: Because of our relief at the attempters' failure, we are content to punish them less, and it would be immorally self-righteous to punish them more than we feel the need to merely because they deserve it.

Why our relief at the attempters' failures should make it immorally self-righteous to punish them to the full extent of their desert is never explained, however. If we did wish to give the attempters their full measure of desert, would not that feeling of justifiable indignation at their acts be just as morally valid as our feeling of relief at their failures to cause harm? It is hard to see how one can make the moral case for leniency based on feelings without also making the moral case for deserved severity based on feelings.

Thomas Morawetz appears to concede our point that results do not affect desert from a moral point of view, but he suggests that the law often fails to mirror morality. Moreover, he argues that our analysis leaves open the question whether we are punishing successes too harshly or punishing attempts too leniently.

Morawetz is correct. But we view his point as entirely consistent with our view and in no way a threat to it. It is likely that we think that sometimes successes are punished too harshly, and sometimes attempts too leniently. But these are the issues we should be addressing, once we realize results don't matter.

In contrast, as a matter of retributive theory, Jeremy Horder's view substantially departs from our own. But he is confused about our thesis. First, he argues that our focus on risks requires that we *causally* link the actor's choices with the risks they impose. That is incorrect, however. According to our theory, an actor's culpability turns on the risks he *believes* he is imposing, not on the risks he is actually imposing, which are always one or zero. The risks the actor believes he is imposing turn on his view of what consequences his act might produce.

Horder misunderstands what we mean by "reasons" and asks whether reasons should matter if results don't. But the reasons we believe matter are those the actor is aware of, not those of which he is unaware.

Horder further argues that our view of criminal culpability would eliminate conduct crimes. But if a certain form of conduct is harmful—say, nonconsensual sex—then it can be culpable to risk to a certain magnitude having nonconsensual sex for reasons that do not justify taking that magnitude of risk. And if one believes one is engaging in nonconsensual sex, one's culpability should not turn on the fortuity that, unbeknownst to him, consent was in fact given. (We note, though, that conduct crimes may be better understood as risks to legally protected interests, and *contra* Horder, we do not believe that current special part crimes capture distinct wrongs).

Horder argues that negligence is culpable despite its not reflecting a conscious risking. We answer this argument in our other entry in this collection. And Horder dredges up the distinction between reasons not to try and reasons not to succeed, assuming that one can try to do that which one believes he has no possibility of accomplishing. We deny that assumption. Nor can we see why our view lets Hitler off the hook. By authorizing genocide, he believed he was imposing a very high risk of millions of deaths. What we deny is that his culpability turns on whether and how many deaths occurred.

Finally, we will admit to having no answer to the causation puzzles for which others assert answers without arguments. Westen argues that prospector B is the killer of prospector C, presumably because C died of thirst, not poison. But remember that once A poisoned C's canteen, C was a dead man, and B's act actually lengthened C's life. We're still looking for an argument here.

And Morawetz believes Pierre has proximately caused Monique's death in *both* scenarios. We cannot argue with him, as we have no idea how to resolve proximate cause questions. (Nor is Westen's answer that causation is a function of how the community feels about the matter and not a function of any theory particularly helpful.) All we can say to Morawetz is construct your own hypothetical in which proximate cause fails to obtain, and we will construct a Pierre who planned it that way.

8. POST-MODERN MEDITATIONS ON PUNISHMENT
On the Limits of Reason and the Virtue of Randomization

BERNARD E. HARCOURT*

INTRODUCTION

Since the modern era, the discourse of punishment has cycled through three sets of questions. The first, born of the Enlightenment itself, sought to identify and define a rational basis for punishing. As men freed themselves from the shackles of religious faith, this first question took shape: If theologians can no longer ground political and legal right, then on what foundation does the sovereign's right to punish rest? On what basis does the state have a right to punish its citizens? Naturally, the question was not entirely innocent—no good questions ever are. It was animated by a desire to locate the political and moral limits of the sovereign's punitive power at a time that was marked—at least in the eyes of many of the first modern men of reason—by excessive punishments. The *right* to punish, it turns out, would serve to *limit* punishment. This first line of inquiry endures well into the present, and in the Anglo-Saxon tradition at least, the answers draw heavily on a functional analysis of the criminal sanction.

It did not take long, though, for men of knowledge—as Friedrich Nietzsche described himself—to spot the error in this first line of inquiry. The right to punish, after all, was precisely what defined sovereignty and, as such, could hardly serve to constrain sovereign power. The first question had gotten things backwards: the "right to punish" was what the sovereign *achieved* by persuading its members that it could best promote the legitimate goals of punishment. It was fruitless to look for the right to punish in the purposes, utilities, or functions of the criminal law—whether from a utilitarian or deontological perspective. "[P]urposes and utilities are only *signs* that a will to power has become master of something less powerful and imposed upon it the character of a function,"[1] Nietzsche emphasized. The proper question to ask of the "right to punish," then, was not "on what ground," "of what origin," or "from where" but rather: "How does the sovereign's act of punishing become perceived as legitimate?"

---

* Julius Kreeger Professor of Law and Professor of Political Science, University of Chicago. This core text is drawn from *Post-Modern Meditations on Punishment: On the Limits of Reason and the Virtues of Randomization (A Polemic and Manifesto for the Twenty-First Century)*, 74 J. Soc. Res. 307 (2007).

1. Friedrich Nietzsche, ON THE GENEALOGY OF MORALS 77 (Walter Kaufmann trans., 1967).

With the birth of the social sciences in the late nineteenth century, this critical impulse gave rise to a second line of inquiry. More skeptical, more critical, the questions probed and excavated deeper processes and forces: If the rational discourse over the right to punish is mere pretext and serves only to hide power formations, then what is it exactly that punishment practices *do* for us? What is the *true* function of punishment? What is it that we *do* when we punish? From Emile Durkheim to Antonio Gramsci and the later Frankfurt School, Michel Foucault, and *fin-de-siècle* trends in penology, twentieth century moderns struggled over social organization, economic production, political legitimacy, governance, and the construction of the self—turning punishment practices upside down, dissecting not only their repressive functions but more importantly their role in constructing the contemporary subject and modern society.

A series of further critiques—critiques of meta-narratives, functionalism, and scientific objectivity—would chasten this line of inquiry and nudge it around the cultural turn, helping to shape a third discourse on punishment. This third line of inquiry would focus not on what punishment is doing *for* us, but on what punishment tells us *about* ourselves: What do our punishment practices tell us about *our* cultural values? What is the social meaning of our institutions of punishment? Less meta-theoretical, less critical-theoretic, this final set of questions would build on, while simultaneously trying to avoid, the critique of the construction of knowledge. The questions were intended to be less normative. A description at most. A compelling interpretation. Something to make sense of our world and ourselves. Something to ground, perhaps later, an evaluation of those punishment practices.

Yet even this third line of inquiry could not escape the critiques leveled earlier. Any interpretation of the "social meaning" of punishment practices and institutions told us more about the interpreter and her belief systems, than about the meaning of the practice itself. Surely the semiotic enterprise would reveal more about the modes of reasoning, beliefs, and ethical choices held by the individual interpreter than about the social meaning of the punishment practices themselves. As dusk fell on the twentieth century, the modern discourse of punishment was at a standstill—faced with the painful realization that the same critiques apply with equal force to any interpretation of cultural meaning that we could possibly give to our contemporary punishment practices.

I. THE LIMITS OF REASON

What shall we—children of the twenty-first century—do now? Shall we continue to labor blindly—willfully blindly—on this third set of questions, return to an earlier problematic, or, as all our predecessors did, craft a new line of inquiry? What questions shall we pose of our punishment practices and institutions?

The answer, paradoxically, is that it doesn't matter. The formulation of the questions themselves never really mattered, except perhaps to distinguish the analytic philosopher from the critical theorist, the positivist from the cultural critic—minor differences that reflected little more than taste, desire, personal aptitude, and training. Yes, new questions were formulated and new discourses emerged, but the same problem always plagued those modern texts.

In all the modern texts, there always came a moment when the empirical facts ran out or the deductions of principle reached their limit—or both—*and yet the reasoning continued.* There was always this moment when the moderns—those paragons of reason—took a leap of faith. It is no accident that it was always there, at that precise moment, that we learned the most—that we could read from the text and decipher a vision of just punishment that was never entirely rational, never purely empirical, and never fully determined by the theoretical premises of the author. In each and every case, the modern text let slip a leap of faith—a choice about how to resolve a gap, an ambiguity, an indeterminacy in an argument of principle or fact.

Sometimes, the gaps were empirical. So, for example, punishment theorists relied on rational action theory, yet their claims of deterrence were never properly established. The trouble is, in most research on deterrence, it is impossible to divorce the effects of dissuasion from those of incapacitation. The National Academy of Sciences appointed a blue-ribbon panel of experts to examine the problem of measuring deterrence in 1978, but the results were disappointing: "[B]ecause the potential sources of error in the estimates of the deterrent effect of these sanctions are so basic and the results sufficiently divergent, no sound, empirically based conclusions can be drawn about the existence of the effect, and certainly not about its magnitude"[2] Little progress has been made since then. As Steven Levitt wrote in 1998, "few of the[] empirical studies [regarding deterrence] have any power to distinguish deterrence from incapacitation and therefore provide only an indirect test of the economic model of crime."[3] Yet many of us continue to ground our punishment theories on claims of dissuasion and rational choice.

Another illustration, from the field of modern policing. In the early 1990s, several major U.S. cities began implementing order-maintenance strategies, most notably New York City. These strategies rested on the "broken-windows theory"—the idea that minor neighborhood disorder like graffiti and loitering, if left unattended, would cause serious criminal activity. The proponents declared that the broken-windows theory had been empirically verified; but still today, the empirical claims remain

---

2. Alfred Blumstein, Jacqueline Cohen, and Daniel Nagin, *Report of the Panel on Research on Deterrent and Incapacitative Effects, in* DETERRENCE AND INCAPACITATION: ESTIMATING THE EFFECTS OF CRIMINAL SANCTIONS ON CRIME RATES 42 (Alfred Blumstein, Jacqueline Cohen, and Daniel Hagin eds., 1978).

3. Steven Levitt, *Juvenile Crime and Punishment,* 106 J. POL. ECON. 1156, 1158 n.2 (1998).

purely hypothetical.[4] Ironically, only James Q. Wilson, one of the authors of the broken-windows theory, seems to have fully realized the empirical gap. In a *New York Times* interview, Wilson recently admitted, "People have not understood that this was a speculation."[5] As to whether it is right, Wilson concedes, "God knows what the truth is."[6] Nevertheless, our contemporaries continue to rely on the broken-windows theory to ground their policing practices and punishment theories.

Just as often, though, the gaps are not simply empirical, but derive instead from matters of principle. A good illustration involves the famous Anglo-Saxon harm principle. If one looks honestly at the writings of even its originators, it becomes clear that the harm principle itself cannot resolve the central cases for which it was developed. The case of prostitution is telling. John Stuart Mill framed the question as follows: "Fornication, for example, must be tolerated, and so must gambling; but should a person be free to be a pimp, or to keep a gambling house?"[7] Mill himself never answered the question. "There are arguments on both sides,"[8] Mill suggested. Consistency militated in favor of toleration. On the other hand, pimps stimulate fornication for their own profit and society may elect to discourage conduct that it regards as, in his words, "bad." In the end, Mill refused to take a position regarding the pimp. "I will not venture to decide whether [the arguments] are sufficient to justify the moral anomaly of punishing the accessory when the principal is (and must be) allowed to go free; of fining or imprisoning the procurer, but not the fornicator . . . ."[9] H.L.A. Hart also straddled the fence, finally relying on another principle—the offense principle—to justify prohibiting the public manifestations of prostitution. Faced with a perfect test case to assess the usefulness of the harm principle, both Mill and Hart punt. Why? Because here, as elsewhere, there are harm arguments on both sides of the equation. There is exploitation of women at the very least, and as Catherine MacKinnon has helped us see, significant harm to women in general. Principles alone did not then and do not now resolve the difficult cases in criminal law.

The inevitable space between empirical or theoretical premises and the final judgment derived, in the end, from that imperceptible fissure in human knowledge between the not-falsified, the not-yet-falsified, the apparently unfalsifiable, the verified but only under certain questionable assumptions, and truth. In the

---

4. Bernard E. Harcourt, ILLUSION OF ORDER: THE FALSE PROMISE OF BROKEN WINDOWS POLICING (2001); Bernard E. Harcourt and Jens Ludwig, *Broken Windows: New Evidence from New York City and a Five-City Social Experiment*, 73 U. CHI. L. REV. 271 (2006).

5. Dan Hurley, *On Crime as Science (A Neighbor at a Time)*, N.Y. TIMES, Jan. 6, 2004, at F1.

6. Patricia Cohen, *Oops, Sorry: Seems That My Pie Chart Is Half-Baked*, N.Y. TIMES, Apr. 8, 2000, at B7.

7. John Stuart Mill, ON LIBERTY 98 (Elizabeth Rapaport ed., 1978).

8. *Id.*

9. *Id.* at 99.

empirical domain, no less than in philosophical discourse, proof never followed mathematical deduction but rested instead on assertions—whether empirical or logical—that may well have been true, but for which other entirely reasonable hypotheses could have been substituted. The key issue was always which hypothesis to believe from among the many possible hypotheses, all of which were consistent with the data; which subprinciple to uphold from among all the possible subprinciples that were theoretically coherent with the guiding principle. What the moderns *chose to believe*, ultimately, told us more about them than it did about the world around them.

Those gaps and ambiguities are precisely what have undermined the modern discourse of punishment. Neither the sharpest critics nor the most radical thinkers have ever been able to escape the overpowering urge to build some new construct, a new edifice, some bridge to get to the other side of that epistemological gap. Neither the followers of Emile Durkheim, Karl Marx, or Michel Foucault, nor the cultural critics were able to resist the lure of reconstruction, always cobbling together the "best evidence" to soften their landing.

Many have argued over the ages—and still do—that we should simply continue to muddle and adjust our expectations of truth: that the not-yet-falsified simply *is* the best model—which is, obviously, hard to dispute—and that we should continue to deploy reason to select the most robust empirical inferences and the most coherent deductions of principle. But the idea that we could distinguish between different hypotheses consistent with the data or principles based on what "makes the most sense," "sounds the most reasonable," or "seems the most coherent," is simply fantastic. Those types of judgment are so culturally determined and so highly influenced by our particular time and place, it is inconceivable that any rational being today could possibly continue to make those statements at this late stage of modernity—at least, with a straight face.

No more. It is too embarrassing to watch as one generation after another of moderns, under the banner of reason, hop, jump, and skip over the gaps of knowledge. One would have thought that phrenology would have been sufficient to stop us in our tracks, but, no, instead we get biological determinist theories of social behavior applied to male rape, moral poverty theories of delinquency applied to super-predator Black males, rational action theories applied to suicide bombers—and the list goes on and on of theories that require so many caveats and exceptions that even a child would question our modern claim to rationality. We can no longer leap over the not-yet-falsified. It is no better than turning the clock back and resurrecting faith in divine providence.

II. THE VIRTUES OF RANDOMIZATION

Where does this leave us? The answer must be *randomization.* Where our social scientific theories run out, where our principles run dry, we should leave the decision-making to chance. We should no longer take that leap of faith, but turn instead to the coin toss, the roll of the dice, the lottery draw—in sum, to randomization and chance. And we should do so, I almost hesitate to say, *throughout* the field of crime and punishment.

In the realm of searches, surveillance, and detection, law enforcement agencies should turn either to completeness or to random sampling. The Internal Revenue Service could audit tax returns at random using a social security number lottery system. The Transportation Security Administration could search every passenger at the airport, or randomly select a certain percent based on a computer generated algorithm using last names. The U.S. Occupational Safety and Health Administration could investigate compliance by employers randomly selecting on employer tax identification number. In these and other prophylactic law enforcement investigations, the agency could very easily replace profiling— which rests on uncertain assumptions about responsiveness and rational action—by randomization.

In choosing law enforcement priorities, governmental agencies should begin allocating resources by chance. The local district attorney's office, as well as the federal prosecutor's office, could select annual enforcement targets (as between, for instance, public corruption, insider trading, drug enforcement, or violent crimes) by lottery. State highway policing authorities could distribute patrol cars through a randomized mapping system using heavily trafficked roads and interstate highways. The Bureau of Alcohol, Tobacco, Firearms, and Explosives could choose between equal-impact initiatives on the basis of an annual lottery draw.

And yes, even in the area of sentencing and corrections, courts and prison administrators should—well, perhaps—start thinking about relying more heavily on chance. Judges could impose sentences, following conviction, based on a draw from within a legislatively prescribed sentencing range; the range could easily be determined, for instance, by felony classifications. The department of corrections could assign prisoners to facilities on a random basis within designated escape-risk or security-level categories. Prisoners in need of drug, alcohol, or mental health treatment could be assigned to comparable programs based on a lottery draw.

This is not as far-fetched as it may seem. It does, naturally, assume a sentencing scheme with specified ranges for different degrees of felony. The same kind of randomization, though, could be introduced at the legislative process to decide on actual ranges or to set mandatory sentences (if fixed sentences are preferred to ranges). So, for instance, legislators, having no scientific or principled way to distinguish between six or twelve months of imprisonment for an aggravated assault, could turn to chance. Randomization would allow those legislators to pick a mandatory sentence from within those bounds.

The common gesture running through all this is to question and, ultimately, to reject social engineering through criminal punishment. The desire to stop and refuse to take leaps of faith represents nothing more, in practice, than *stopping to engineer* persons and social relations through the criminal sanction. The central impulse is precisely to resist shaping people by means of punishment—and thereby to wipe the field clean of speculative social science and indeterminate principle.

Critical reason reveals the limit of our reasoning abilities. It brings us to the gap where our predecessors always took their leap of faith. It sheds light on those theoretical constructs that the moderns used to bridge the gaps of knowledge. It should now also allow us to clear the field of these fabrications. It should free us to use the only unbiased device to decide our fate—randomization, lotteries, dice, chance. And the point is not to roll the dice as between different theories, all of which require a leap of faith, but instead to use critical reason to take those theories *off the table*. To eliminate them—and thereby to stop social engineering.

I should emphasize that my central claim here is *not* that we can know *nothing*. No. We have some basic intuitive knowledge that no one can dispute. As an empirical matter, we know that if we execute someone, we are not going to be able to rehabilitate them. As a matter of principle, we know that murdering an innocent person is worse than stealing their wallet. We know that raping someone is worse than spraying graffiti. We know that punishing an entirely innocent person is wrong. And we can use these minimal ingredients of certainty to set limits to the use of chance. So, for instance, we do not draw punishments for murder and pocket-picking—or for rape and vandalism—from the same urn. We do not decide who to accuse by drawing lots. These elementary forms of knowledge allow us to rest our punishment practices minimally on very basic notions of proportionality. For instance, the convicted murderer and the person exceeding a speed limit are not to be treated the same. We impose proportionality constraints on the use of chance. Perhaps we create a category for homicide, another for serious bodily or psychological injury, and another for property damage. There *are* some natural limits to the use of randomization.

We only turn to chance when *our social science and principles run out*. The easy cases are where our social science findings rest on bad evidence, weak data, or faulty models, where there is no scientific evidence at all, or where there are competing and equally plausible hypotheses that are all similarly nonfalsified— in other words, when we do not have reliable social science findings to rely on. This, I take it, can hardly be contested. No one wants to affirmatively and intentionally punish another human being on the basis of bad science or no science at all.

You may ask, naturally, why turn to randomization? There are other alternatives, after all. At the point of making that punishment decision, we could simply stick with what we have done in the past. We could use the same punishments as our mothers and fathers did. We could heed to the status quo. The problem is, their judgments were precisely the product of years and years of uncritical leaps of faith. We will have learned nothing from the exercise of critical reason. Alternatively, we could turn to the democratic process and allow the legislature to decide. But in the end, their vote will reflect nothing more than prejudice, ideology, bias, and, again, leaps of faith. We could decide simply to impose our tastes and aesthetic preferences; but that seems problematic and, perhaps even, irrational.

No, we must turn instead to randomization *because we have no other choice*. We must turn to the lottery because it is the only way to act *within the bounds of critical reason*. We must turn to randomization *by default*. Sure, randomization may have some positive values. It may remind us that our knowledge claims are limited. It may remind us of the frightening role of ideology in our punishment practices. It may help gather information; by using a form of random sampling, we may in fact learn a lot about the world of deviance that surrounds us. Randomization may offer more transparency in our policy-making. And in fact, it may be more efficient than the alternative. But none of these are the reason we turn to randomization. We turn instead because there is no alternative that satisfies critical reason.

III. RESPONDING TO CRITICS

Randomization is by no means foreign to the law. A number of states statutorily prescribe a flip of the coin to resolve election ties. In New Mexico, it's a poker hand that resolves a tie. Courts as well have turned to chance to resolve election disputes, and a number of courts also partition disputed land by lot or chance. Randomness also surfaces across a number of policing strategies, including sobriety checkpoints and the random selection of airline passengers for further screening at airports. Chance also plays a large role in the detection of crime: who gets apprehended and who does not most often turns on luck. Even fixed sentencing schemes have a significant element of chance. A lot turns on the luck of the draw regarding which judge—lenient or stern—presides over the sentencing.[10]

Nevertheless, a call for more randomization will undoubtedly meet with great resistance. Many will instinctively protest that the use of chance is far less efficient than profiling or targeting higher offenders—that it is wasteful to expend law enforcement resources on low-risk offenders. There's no point conducting extra airport security checks on elderly grandmothers in wheelchairs and families with infants—or "Girl Scouts and grannies," as one recent commentator writes.[11] As I demonstrate elsewhere with equations and graphs, however, profiling on the basis of group offending rates may in fact be counterproductive and may actually increase crime even under very conservative assumptions regarding

---

10. Alon Harel and Uzi Segal, *Criminal Law and Behavioral Law and Economics: Observations on the Neglected Role of Uncertainty in Deterring Crime*, AM. L. & ECON. REV. 276, 292 (1999).

11. Paul Sperry, *When the Profile Fits the Crime*, N.Y. TIMES, July 28, 2005.

the comparative elasticities of the different populations.[12] We have no good reason to believe that targeted enforcement would be efficient in decreasing crime and would increase, rather than decrease, overall social welfare.

More sophisticated economists may respond that targeting enforcement on groups that are more responsive, at the margin, would maximize the return of any law enforcement investment.[13] But here, we face an empirical void. What we would need is reliable empirical evidence concerning both the comparative offending rates and the comparative elasticities of the targeted and nontargeted populations. I derive the exact equation for this elsewhere.[14] That evidence, however, does not exist. The problem is not the reliability of the evidence; it's that it simply *does not exist*. If there ever was a place to avoid taking leaps of faith, surely it would be here, where there is no empirical data whatsoever.

The conventional wisdom among law-and-economics scholars is that increasing the probability of detection serves as a greater deterrent to crime than increasing the amount of the sanction because of the high discount rate imputed to criminals. Assuming this is true, the decision to embrace randomization in sentencing should have no effect on deterrence. Using a sentencing lottery to determine the length of incarceration from within a sentencing guideline range, rather than using a grid that places great weight on prior criminal history, gun use, or other factors, would not change the *certainty* of the expected sentence and need not change the *amount* of the expected sentence.

Some behavioral law and economists have argued that the certainty of a criminal sentence—the fact that the size of a criminal sanction is fixed and known ahead of time—may deter criminals more effectively than uncertain sentences and, on those grounds, have argued against sentencing lotteries.[15] However, more recent research involving actual experimental studies suggests that uncertainty regarding a sanction may be *more* effective at deterring criminal behavior. Experiments by Alon Harel, Tom Baker, and Tamar Kugler reveal that a sentencing lottery may in fact be better at deterring deviant behavior than fixed sentences.[16] Other psychological experiments have similarly shown individuals to be averse to ambiguity.[17]

---

12. Bernard E. Harcourt, AGAINST PREDICTION: PROFILING, POLICING, AND PUNISHING IN AN ACTUARIAL AGE 129–32 (2007); Bernard E. Harcourt, *Muslim Profiles Post 9/11: Is Racial Profiling an Effective Counterterrorist Measure and Does It Violate the Right to be Free from Discrimination?* in SECURITY AND HUMAN RIGHTS (Benjamin Goold and Liora Lazarus eds., 2007).

13. Yoram Margalioth, *Looking at Prediction from an Economics Perspective: A Response to Harcourt's* Against Prediction, 33 L. & SOC. INQ. 243 (2008).

14. Harcourt, AGAINST PREDICTION, *supra* note 12, at 133.

15. Harel and Segal, *supra* note 10, at 280.

16. Tom Baker, Alon Harel, and Tamar Kugler, *The Virtues of Uncertainty in Law: An Experimental Approach*, 89 IOWA L. REV. 443 (2004).

17. Harel and Segal, *supra* note 10, at 291.

Randomization in sentencing will likely meet much greater resistance, though, not because of efficiency concerns, but rather because of considerations of fairness, just punishment, and desert. A large body of philosophical and legal literature has grown around the issue of luck in criminal sentencing, some of it tied to the larger debate over what Thomas Nagel and Bernard Williams coined "moral luck." In these debates, most of the commentators oppose the use of chance, in large part, I would suggest, because we all tend to believe that there is a rational alternative. We continue to believe that there is a better way, a more rational way, a more morally acceptable way.

In discussing penal lotteries, R.A. Duff observes that lotteries are generally justified, from the perspective of fairness or justice, only when "there is no other practicable or morally acceptable way of distributing the benefit or burden in question."[18] Lotteries are justified as a default mechanism when there is no other morally justifiable way: "What justifies such lotteries . . . is the fact that it is either impossible to eliminate them, or possible to reduce or eliminate them only at an unacceptably high cost."[19] In this, Duff has it right. What justifies lotteries, morally, is the lack of an alternative. Where he has it wrong, though—and where everyone seems to have it wrong—is in believing that *there is a rational alternative*. The fact is, we have hunches. We take leaps of faith. But we do not have good evidence or determined principles that resolve the sentencing ambiguities. Sentencing lotteries make sense, in the end, precisely because *we have no better choice*.

IV. CONCLUSION

The final triumph of reason is near. Reason has finally reached that state of self-consciousness that will allow it to identify its own limits and stop there. No longer to rely on blind faith to bridge the inevitable gaps, ambiguities, and indeterminacies of human knowledge, no longer to fill that space beyond the nonfalsified hypothesis, reason will relinquish the realm of punishment to chance, the coin toss, the roll of the dice—to randomization.

This would mark, I believe, the end of punishment as a transformative practice—as a practice intended to change humans, to correct delinquents, to treat the deviant, to deter the super-predator. It would usher in a world, effectively, *without punishment*. It would not be a world without anything that could be described as punishment. The person convicted of murder or embezzlement may still be sentenced to a term of imprisonment. But it would be a world in which we have ceased to punish in furtherance of hunches and unfounded theories. A world in which we no longer engage in punishment as a practice of social engineering. A world in which punishment is chastened by critical reason.

---

18. R.A. Duff, *Auctions, Lotteries, and the Punishment of Attempts*, 9 L. & PHIL. 1, 26 (1990).

19. *Id.* at 27.

COMMENTS
GAMES PUNISHERS PLAY

ALICE RISTROPH*

To run a lottery is to choose to prioritize chance. To play the lottery is to make a choice to take a chance. One might choose otherwise. Knowing many aspects of human experience are random, one might still decline to play Russian roulette. Bernard Harcourt's meditations obscure the difference between the inevitably random and the deliberately random*ized*, but do they obscure by chance or by design? Perhaps Harcourt's meditations are best read as Swiftian: a seemingly earnest celebration of random punishment that invites us to reflect on the violence of punishment itself.

Two famous stories illuminate Harcourt's modest proposal that offenders be sentenced to randomly selected punishments. Jorge Luis Borges tells of the Babylon lottery, originally a simple game in which plebians purchased chances to win cash prizes. To stimulate more interest, the lottery was reformed to offer both rewards and punishments: some players would become rich, but others would pay a fine or go to jail. The lottery's administrators—"the Company"—offered chances to "win" increasingly diverse positive or adverse consequences. Enamored of the game, the people asked that the Company assume control of all public affairs. All citizens demanded (or were required?) to participate: the lottery became "secret, free, and general."[1] Now, the drunkard, the dreamer, and the rich man each live as the lottery dictates. But mysteries remain: some say that the Company is eternal, some whisper that it is omnipotent but concerned only with trivialities, and some claim that *the Company has never existed and never will.*[2] A lottery is orchestrated chance, but in this story, the orchestra's conductors appear and disappear. Thus Borges blurs the line between choice and chance.

Shirley Jackson's *The Lottery* is less subtle, and was—at its publication—much more provocative. In a small town, the locals assemble. It is the day of the lottery, and everyone is excited. Children gather smooth, round stones in one corner of the town square. The women gossip and the men talk business or tell jokes. A few townspeople observe that other towns have abandoned their lotteries, but an old-timer scoffs at that foolish notion. "Lottery in June, corn be heavy soon," he says.[3] The lottery begins. The male head of each household selects a paper from a box. They open their papers and discover that Bill Hutchinson has the marked paper. Tessie Hutchinson begins to protest, but the lottery moves to the

---

* Associate Professor of Law, Seton Hall University School of Law.

1. Jorge Luis Borges, *The Babylon Lottery, in* FICCIONES 68 (1962).
2. *Id.* at 71–72.
3. Shirley Jackson, *The Lottery*, THE NEW YORKER, June 26, 1948, at 25.

second stage: five new slips are placed in the box, one each for Bill and Tessie and their three young children. Each family member draws, and now Tessie has the marked paper. As she continues to protest, the townspeople grab stones. The first stone hits Tessie's head, "and then they were upon her."

Tessie Hutchinson is safe from Harcourt. He would inject randomization into policing as well as punishment, but he would not "decide who to accuse by drawing lots."[4] Old-fashioned reason *can* tell us who to punish, Harcourt claims, and it can even dictate a spectrum of appropriate penalties. But it cannot tell us precisely which penalty; to answer that question, Harcourt would have officials select sentences randomly within a prescribed range. This suggestion seems to rest on an assumption that punishment just *is*—it exists and we have no choice but to distribute it one way or another. If social science fails to provide us with a distributive principle, embrace randomization.

But of course punishment isn't just there, in need of some distributive principle. It is a human practice, and there are human punishers. We choose to punish, as Harcourt sometimes acknowledges. "No one wants to affirmatively and intentionally punish another human being on the basis of bad science or no science at all."[5] If this claim is true, one would expect humans to be similarly averse to imposing punishment randomly. Instead, if reason dictates a spectrum of appropriate penalties, why not impose the minimum?

One explanation, implicit in Harcourt's meditations, is that in many persons, the demand to punish is independent of, and indifferent to, scientific knowledge. These punishers have already identified a distributive principle more palatable than randomization. They call it retribution, and it is delightfully nonfalsifiable. Some retributive theories perform the same feat as Babylon's lottery: they depict the Company that orchestrates punishment as the dutiful representative of the people themselves. Retributivists tell the prisoner, like the Babylonian might tell the miserable drunkard, that one's present circumstance is the product of one's past gambles.

For those unmoved by retributive theory, and yet persuaded by Harcourt's critique of social engineering through punishment, there is another option. Some towns have abandoned their lotteries. Some choose not to stone anyone. For some of us, the moment when reason runs out is not the time to roll the dice, but the time to stop punishing.

---

4. Harcourt core text at 169.
5. *Id.*

CHANCE'S DOMAIN

MICHAEL M. O'HEAR*

Bernard Harcourt argues eloquently against the Enlightenment ideal of social engineering through punishment, but his *bête noir* has only a shadowy existence in the real world of American criminal justice. We already have a system that is dominated by chance. With low—sometimes vanishingly small—apprehension and prosecution rates for most categories of crime, it is perfectly clear that luck plays a crucial role in determining which offenders face charges. And, once in the court system, an offender's punishment will be largely determined by the random assignment of judge, prosecutor, and public defender, and by the various bureaucratic and political exigencies they happen to perceive as they exercise discretion over the offender's fate.

Although criminal law theorists may dream of social engineering, and may occasionally persuade policy-makers to embody their schemes in formal law, chance must inevitably play a central role in the administration of criminal justice in a nation that systematically diffuses government power, keeps taxes and public expenditures low, and nonetheless insists on tough responses to whatever is the crime *du jour*. Our criminal justice system lacks the capacity and the will to attempt social engineering at much more than a rhetorical level.

The real question posed by Harcourt is not whether we will have a system driven by chance, but whether we will acknowledge the open secret of randomness and attempt to do randomness in a more principled way. Seen in this light, Harcourt's basic project has much to recommend it. Among legal actors and scholars, the accepted modes of talking about criminal law and process make it difficult to discuss chance as anything but an embarrassing and aberrational feature of the system. Harcourt argues, however, that our desultory efforts at social engineering are what ought to be regarded as the real embarrassment. His project opens space for a conversation about the proper domain of chance, and offers an opportunity to bring our rhetoric into closer alignment with our practices.

But what exactly should be chance's domain? Harcourt does not differentiate adequately among a diverse range of criminal justice decisions. For instance, I find the case for randomization in police investigative decisions far more compelling than the case for randomization in judicial sentencing decisions. No effective mechanism currently exists for public explanation and external review of investigative decisions—the Fourth Amendment jurisprudence might have headed in that direction, but it has not—and given the volume and speed with which officers must make decisions, it is unlikely that such a mechanism will be

---

* Professor of Law and Associate Dean for Research, Marquette Law School.

developed any time soon. In the absence of explanation and review, investigative decisions are widely perceived to be arbitrary, especially in the communities that bear the brunt of law enforcement activity. In this context, making randomization more overt and broadly systematic (e.g., every twentieth car gets pulled over, not every fifth car driven by a Black person) may prove to be a more effective way of dealing with the perception and reality of invidious discrimination than any effort to develop and enforce principled, comprehensive, race-neutral criteria for police decision-making.

In contrast to police investigative decisions, judicial sentencing decisions can be, and typically are, structured around participatory, public proceedings. Moreover, sentencing decisions are explained decisions, and the reasoning process is subject to appellate review. Some judges and some jurisdictions pull this off much better than others, but the sentencing process at least potentially embodies the values that Tom Tyler and other social psychologists refer to as "procedural justice." This is, of course, a "leap of faith" on my part, but I would contend that procedural justice is worth pursuing, both as a good in itself and because it enhances the system's legitimacy. Randomization, however, would radically undermine the social meaningfulness of the sentencing process— indeed, within the framework that Harcourt seems to envision, it is not clear why there would be any sentencing process beyond the selection of a number from the appropriate "urn" (as determined by the offense of conviction).

To be sure, the sentencing judge is routinely guilty of precisely the same offense that Harcourt accuses criminal law theorists of committing: "there always [comes] this moment when the empirical facts [run] out or the deductions of principle reach[] their limit . . . and yet the reasoning continue[s]."[1] An inevitable cost of a meaningful sentencing process may be a final decision that promises a higher degree of rationality that it can actually deliver. If intellectual honesty is a concern—and I agree with Harcourt that it should be—an alternative to randomization may be greater rhetorical humility, with judges admitting where the decisions become difficult and eschewing grandiose claims about the social benefits of the sentences they pronounce.

---

1. Harcourt core text at 165.

THE LURE OF AMBIVALENT SKEPTICISM

ALON HAREL*

Theorists can be divided into those who seek to unearth reasons for social prac-tices and those who raise their hands in desperation and provide reasons why one should not go looking for such reasons—why such search is a futile, or worse, a disingenuous enterprise. Bernard Harcourt falls into the latter camp. What I would like to do is to hoist the latter strategy on its own petard by showing that it is vulnerable to the very same objections it raises against the former strategy.

Harcourt believes that:

> In all the modern texts, there always came a moment when the empirical facts ran out or the deductions of principle reached their limit—or both—*and yet the reasoning continued*. There was always this moment when the moderns— those paragons of reason—took a leap of faith.[1]

Consequently, Harcourt is critical of the very effort to establish a complete and comprehensive "new construct or a new edifice"; namely, a comprehensive justi-fication of punishment.[2] To establish his skeptical outlook, Harcourt criticizes harshly existing theories purporting to provide a comprehensive justification of punishment. A theorist trained in the analytic tradition may be somewhat con-cerned that these criticisms are too sketchy. Yet it would be too hasty to criticize Harcourt for lack of rigor simply because his criticisms of existing theories are sketchy and incomplete. The critical discussion in his core text is only illustrative. It is not meant to persuade the unpersuaded, but only to provide some data for a skeptical reader who ultimately shares Harcourt's skeptical outlook.

But what can we infer from such a skeptical and critical outlook? Harcourt suggests that his critical outlook is not futile; in fact, it generates very specific and concrete recommendations for the policy-maker. Harcourt argues that:

> Where our social scientific theories run out, where our principles run dry, we should leave the decision-making to chance. We should no longer take that leap of faith, but turn instead to the coin toss, the roll of the dice, the lottery draw—in sum to randomization and chance.[3]

The skeptical reader may, as Harcourt notices, turn his skepticism toward ran-domization and ask, "Why turn to randomization?"[4] In response, Harcourt endorses

---

* Phillip P. Mizock and Estelle Mizock Chair in Administrative and Criminal Law, Hebrew University Law Faculty.

1. Harcourt core text at 165.
2. *Id.* at 167.
3. *Id.* at 167–68.
4. *Id.* at 169.

two incompatible answers. First, in an attempt to ground randomization in a moral principle, Harcourt argues that the refusal to ground punishment in theory

> represents nothing more, in practice, than *stopping to engineer* persons and social relations through the criminal sanction. The central impulse is precisely to resist shaping people by means of punishment—and thereby to wipe the field clean of speculative social science and indeterminate principle.[5]

This move is promising but, of course, it is premised upon a moral principle that engineering people through criminal law is wrong. Some people may dispute that an attempt to deter people (even if it is not scientifically sound) is a form of engineering, and others may question why engineering of this type is legitimate when done by education or tort law but not when done by criminal law.

Harcourt may have answers to these questions, and I probably would sympathize with these answers. But it is important to note that by establishing this claim Harcourt is engaged in the very same enterprise that he condemns: namely, unearthing reasons for concrete social practices by establishing the soundness of theoretical premises and deriving from these premises the principle of randomization.

Second, Harcourt takes a different position, defending the view that we "turn to randomization *because we have no other choice.*"[6] Presumably Harcourt means to say that we have no *better* choice. After all, Harcourt's core text itself shows that we have other choices and we often choose them. But lack of better choices requires Harcourt at the very least to establish that randomization is better than any other principle of punishment and establishing such a claim must be premised upon a moral principle or a social science finding of the type Harcourt condemns. Just as moral relativism cannot establish the justifiability of multiculturalism, Harcourt's global skepticism concerning existing theories of punishment cannot justify randomization.

Harcourt therefore faces a dilemma. If he defends randomization, he ought to use the traditional tools of moral theory or social science and abandon therefore his skepticism. If he defends skepticism, he ought to abandon randomization. If I were to choose, I would abandon skepticism for the sake of defending randomization.

---

5. *Id.* at 168–69.
6. *Id.* at 170.

PUNISHMENT MUST BE JUSTIFIED OR NOT AT ALL

KEN LEVY*

Bernard Harcourt is skeptical that punishment can be justified. So he suggests that we should simply give it up. But rather than stopping there, Harcourt offers a positive proposal as well. Harcourt proposes that we conform our law enforcement practices to the ultimate "un-justifiability" of punishment by applying chance or randomization in our allocation of law enforcement resources, annual enforcement targets, post-conviction sentences, and legislatively determined sentence ranges for particular crimes.

We have reason, however, to resist Harcourt's skepticism. First, the argument that he provides in support of his skeptical thesis suffers from both a confusion of power and right, and a misunderstanding of the relationship between sovereignty and the right to punish. Second, we have a very good reason to think that *we must never give up* on justifying punishment.

I understand Harcourt's skeptical argument to run as follows:

1) The attempt to justify punishment is the attempt to determine what gives the sovereign (or State) the right to punish.
2) What defines the sovereign just *is* its right to punish.
3) Therefore it makes no sense to ask where the sovereign *gets* its right to punish. The right to punish is part of its very definition.
4) Therefore it makes no sense to attempt to justify punishment.

The first problem with this argument is that (2) confuses power with right. By definition, sovereigns have the *power*, but not necessarily the *right*, to punish. Sovereigns who do *not* have the right to punish are illegitimate; they came to power illegitimately—e.g., through an undemocratic seizure of power. Conversely, a legitimate authority may have the right to punish but *not* the power if it is stymied in any way—for example, by an elusive suspect or hostile occupation by an invader. Because power and right are conceptually distinct, it still makes perfect sense to ask whether or not a given (legitimate) sovereign, or (legitimate) sovereigns in general, *should* have the power to punish.

The second problem with Harcourt's argument is that even a legitimate sovereign is not necessarily *defined* by its right to punish. What *makes* it sovereign—what *makes* the (legitimate) State *the State*—is not its right to punish but its right to *govern*. Of course, one might respond that the right to govern just *is* the right to punish. But this point is false.

First, it is perfectly possible to imagine a sovereign whose electorate grants it the right to govern but *not* the right to punish. When the sovereign then asks the

---

* Climenko Fellow and Lecturer on Law, Harvard Law School.

electorate how it will enforce the laws that it creates, the electorate has some possible responses: by providing only carrots, no sticks; or by "treating" all lawbreakers rather than punishing them. Second, even if the right to govern *entails* the right to punish, this entailment would not amount to an identity. For the right to govern might entail a number of other rights that are distinct from the right to punish—e.g., the right to legislate. Third, even if governing requires punishing, this would mean only that punishment is a necessary means to the end of governing. And ends are not necessarily, or even usually, defined by their means.

Not only do we have these reasons to reject Harcourt's skeptical conclusion that the project of justifying punishment is futile and misguided, we also have a positive reason to believe that the project of justifying punishment is *morally obligatory* and therefore perfectly sensible. Consider the following argument:

5) People have a strong self-interest in not being punished.
6) People should have legally recognized rights protecting their interests.
7) Therefore people should have a legally recognized right not to be punished.
8) The State should not violate citizens' rights.
9) Most rights, including the right not to be punished, are merely presumptive, not absolute.
10) Therefore the State may punish a citizen if it has a sufficiently strong interest.
11) The State's sufficiently strong interest is its *justification* for inflicting that particular punishment.
12) Therefore the State may punish a citizen only if it has a sufficiently strong justification to do so.

(5) seems difficult to deny, and (11) is merely definitional. (6), (8), and (9) are more controversial because they derive from classical rights theory, which is only one among several plausible political theories. Other plausible political theories might deny the importance of, or need for, individual rights and prioritize instead religion, morality, community, technology, national security, or Gross National Product over the individual. But the timeworn project of justifying classical rights principles is not really necessary here—especially given my sense that Harcourt himself subscribes to them. Rather, I will settle for the less ambitious point that if one accepts classical liberal principles, then one must accept (5) through (12) above and therefore the legitimacy and urgency of the project of justifying punishment, both generally and in its specific applications.

REPLY

BERNARD E. HARCOURT

Alice Ristroph compassionately throws me a lifeline. Perhaps my call for randomization is better understood as Swiftian satire, meant to underscore the extent of arbitrariness in our contemporary punishment practices. How I wish I could grasp that rope to safe harbor! But alas, no, there is no such elegant way out. Critical reason identifies the boundaries of knowledge and there, there we have no choice but to embrace chance.

To be sure, there are, as Alon Harel correctly observes, alternative ways of resolving impasses at points of indeterminacy—we could heed the status quo, leave it to a popular vote, or simply impose our tastes—and there exist positive arguments for choosing randomization over those alternatives. My colleague, Adam Samaha, identifies at least four of those paths to chance. Some theorists— Jon Elster is one—embrace randomization because they believe that, at least in certain limited domains of uncertainty, it may be more honest—and more consistent with rational choice preferences. Others endorse randomization as the only method that produces the equal chance of an outcome. Others embrace chance for pragmatic reasons, and still others, as a form of experimentation—as in the randomized trial.[1]

I embrace chance from a different, a fifth perspective—what may best be described as a critical theoretic perspective.[2] Critical reason exposes the leaps of faith that we regularly take in our empirical and principled reasoning—including, I should note, in the behavioral and rational choice approaches that even lead some, such as Elster, to embrace randomization. Critical reason thus exposes a capacious sphere of indeterminacy, far larger than most imagine.[3] At those points of impasse, I argue, we must turn to chance *by default*, because there is no other way to avoid taking another leap and imposing our preferences, ideology, habits, training, or tastes. From this perspective, chance does not have a *positive* value. It is not more honest, nor more practical. It does not afford the benefits of

---

1. *See* Adam Samaha, *Randomization in Adjudication* (Oct. 24, 2008) (unpublished manuscript, on file with author).

2. Raymond Geuss offers a useful definition of critical theory in *The Idea of a Critical Theory*. *See* Raymond Geuss, THE IDEA OF A CRITICAL THEORY: HABERMAS AND THE FRANKFURT SCHOOL (1981). While Geuss focuses on the Frankfurt School, several other traditions, ranging from Freudian psychoanalysis to contemporary post-structuralist thought, share in this critical tradition.

3. *E.g.*, Jon Elster, *Taming Chance: Randomization in Individual and Social Decisions*, *in* 9 THE TANNER LECTURES ON HUMAN VALUES 105, 157 (Grethe B. Peterson ed., 1988) ("I do not think there are any arguments for incorporating lotteries in present-day criminal law.").

a randomized trial. It is, instead, the only way to avoid another leap of faith beyond the limits of reason.

My commentators mistake my nominalism for skepticism. I am not, foremost, a skeptic. There are things we *can* know—for instance, true facts that can guide our practices of randomization, or veritable limits to reason that delineate the domain of chance. There *is* a difference between innocence and responsibility for human action. Embracing chance need not entail stoning one's neighbor by lot, nor being declared invisible by lottery. I am confident that we can escape these fates by deploying a modicum of knowledge. Rather than skepticism, it is nominalism that guides my position—a sincere belief in the indeterminacy of broad categories, such as harm, order, deterrence, or even deviance. Those categories mask the irreducible individuality of human behavior, naturalize the distributional consequences of endorsing particular theories, and as a result, necessarily impose ideological commitments on our punishment practices.

Does that mean that I am simply "raising my hands in desperation"? I think not. It is, instead, an act of humility. A humble gesture in the face of over three centuries of Enlightenment reason in punishment—of forced sterilization, solitary confinement, chemical castration, eugenics, electro-shock therapy, individual gas chambers and electric chairs, phrenology, and now, mass incarceration. Our track record of enlightened punishments is stunning and, frankly, it humbles me. I contend that it should also chasten our embrace of the alternatives to chance.

Ken Levy urges me to continue the project of *justifying* punishment. The error in my argument, Levy contends, is that it "confuses power with right." Here I must confess—*mea culpa!* But it is no mere accidental confusion. What we believe about *the right to punish* is ultimately the product of complex relations of power that distribute *veridiction*—the production of truth—on the basis of a confluence of forces, including hierarchies of disciplines, ideological drift in discourse, and complex sociologies of professions. These relations of power end up privileging one type of discourse over another—whether it is the psychological language of mental illness, the economists' tool of rational choice, or the retributive notion of just deserts. Our sincere belief in any one of these ways of talking about the *right to punish*, in the end, is inextricably intertwined with relations of power between and among disciplines and professions.

Michael O'Hear acknowledges the significant role of randomness in contemporary punishment practices. But he asks, why not then channel randomization in more pragmatic directions? This sounds entirely reasonable. The trouble is, the domain of chance cannot be set by practical considerations. It is delimited, instead, by the boundaries of knowledge. Others—younger and wiser, perhaps—can explore the advantages of carefully bounded randomization.[4] But I come to

---

4. Adam Samaha is doing just that in *Randomization in Adjudication*. Lior Strahilevitz is also probing the virtues of chance in the law of abandonment—as a potential vehicle to

chance from a different, from a critical theory angle—and from this perspective, it is absolutely crucial not to let ideology slip back in.

The most difficult challenge, in the end, is Alice Ristroph's—captured so brilliantly in the last sentence of her essay, which cut into me like a knife. "For some of us, the moment when reason runs out is not the time to roll the dice, but the time to stop punishing."[5] Indeed, why punish at all when we have reached the limits of reason? Here, I must confess again. I am human, all too human. There is a haunting passage of Nietzsche's that often comes back to me. It is in his *Genealogy of Morals,* where he writes:

> As its power increases, a community ceases to take the individual's transgressions so seriously . . . . It is not unthinkable that a society one day might attain such a *consciousness of power* that it could allow itself the noblest luxury possible to it—letting those who harm it go *unpunished.* "What are my parasites to me?" it might say. "May they live and prosper: I am strong enough for that!"[6]

I aspire to one day believe that our society will achieve that consciousness of power or that degree of strength—for it is strength, I take it, that allows one to thrive along with ones parasites. I fear that I am not yet there. But I so admire Alice Ristroph for keeping the idea alive.

reduce decision costs. *See* Lior Strahilevitz, *The Right to Abandon* (Oct. 23, 2008) (unpublished manuscript, on file with author).

5. Ristroph comment at 174.

6. Friedrich Nietzsche, On the Genealogy of Morals 72 (Walter Kaufmann and R.J. Hollingdale trans., 1989).

9. REMORSE, APOLOGY, AND MERCY

JEFFRIE G. MURPHY*

This core text explores the nature of remorse and the role that remorse might play in decisions to grant legal mercy. The relationship apology bears to remorse is also examined.

I. TWO KINDS OF REMORSE

Some people regard "remorse" and "guilt" as equivalent in meaning. But consider the breaking of an important promise—one of significance, but not one the breaking of which will cause irrevocable harm. In such a case, some nontrivial guilt feelings would surely be expected of a morally serious person, but many would be reluctant to use the word "remorse" to capture these feelings—preferring to reserve the word "remorse" to capture those extremely powerful guilt feelings that are appropriately attached only to grave wrongs and harms.

The difference between some cases of remorse and other instances of guilt is not simply a matter of degree, however. This is because a kind of *hopelessness* is essential to the unconsolable bite of conscience—the *agenbite of inwit*—that is the essence of one kind of remorse. This kind of remorse, although having powerful guilt feelings as a component, seems to involve more than guilt— seems to involve the idea that the wrong one has done is so deep, has involved such a wanton assault on the very meaning of a person's human life, that one can in no sense ever make it right again—such a possibility being permanently lost. Breaking a promise is typically not a wrong of this nature. Blinding a person is—as is murdering a person or that person's beloved child. Rape and torture also come to mind as other examples.

II. REMORSE AND THE CULTURE OF APOLOGY

Must successful apology always be linked with remorse? Surely not. For small wrongs, the mere verbal formulae "I apologize" or "I am sorry" or "Forgive me"

---

* Regents' Professor of Law, Philosophy, and Religious Studies, Arizona State University. This core text is drawn from Jeffrie Murphy, *Remorse, Apology, and Mercy*, 4 OHIO ST. J. CRIM. L. 423 (2007). It drops all references, most of the humor (or at least what I thought was funny), a wonderful cartoon, and significant expansions, qualifications, or defenses of some of the central claims.

or "Excuse me" are generally adequate because their only function is to keep oiled the wheels of civility and good manners. What works for small wrongs is likely to be quite unacceptable for wrongs of greater magnitude, however. Here we normally expect such things as repentance, remorse (in at least one of its forms), and atonement; and we are interested in apologies only to the degree that we believe that they are sincere external signs of repentance and remorse and reliable external signs of future atonement.

Herbert Morris once published a wonderful essay with the title *The Decline of Guilt*, and an alternative title for my essay could have been "The Decline of Remorse"—a decline that I believe is revealed, paradoxically enough, in the increasing prevalence and even celebration of public apology that we find in early twenty-first century America. We now live in what has been called "the new culture of apology"—a cultural movement so pervasive that it has produced satirical essays and a novel (Jay Rayner's *Eating Crow*) and at least one splendid *New Yorker* cartoon.[1]

Some people, of course, find the growing culture of apology a good thing— advancing general social utility and progress and perhaps even exemplifying Christian love and forgiveness. Others—and I count myself among them—fear that it may be little more than a sign of what theologians have called "cheap grace."

Bad people are often quick studies of social trends that can be used to their advantage, and so it is now not uncommon to find such phrases as "it is time to get this all behind us and move forward" or, more recently, "let's not play the blame game" shamelessly and almost instantly on the lips of wrongdoers—often those in high political office.

Added to religious claims or arguments of social utility are, as we might expect in our therapeutic culture, arguments grounded in trendy notions of mental health where such gems of psychobabble as "closure" and "a time for healing" are the order of the day. So sloppy, indeed, is the current state of theology and morality that these shibboleths of pop psychology sometimes simply pass *as* theology and morality.

III. REMORSE, REPENTANCE, AND PUNISHMENT

David Lurie, the central character in J.M. Coetzee's novel *Disgrace*, has admitted sexual harassment of a student but could save his job if he simply apologized and expressed the kind of repentance and remorse demanded of him by the

---

1. The cartoon shows a man of important status (a government official or CEO, perhaps) with a big prideful smile on his face as he talks on the telephone to his wife. He says: "Hi, hon. Guess who's going to be on national television apologizing to the American public."

university disciplinary board that has punitive authority over him. In refusing to give them what they want, he says the following:

> We went through the repentance business yesterday. I told you what I thought. I won't do it. I appeared before an officially constituted tribunal, before a branch of the law. Before that secular tribunal I pleaded guilty, a secular plea. That plea should suffice. Repentance is neither here nor there. Repentance belongs to another world, to another universe of discourse . . . . [What you are asking] reminds me too much of Mao's China. Recantation, self-criticism, public apology. I'm old fashioned. I would prefer simply to be put against a wall and shot.[2]

Lurie identifies the mechanism of legal or quasi-legal punishment as *secular* and claims that talk of repentance (of which remorse is a component) and apology has no business in such a secular context. His point, presumably, is that these concepts are at their core *religious* concepts and that their introduction into a secular context is radically misplaced.

Why might one think this? One possibility is the belief that repentance and remorse are conditions of one's very soul and that the secular state acts wrongly—perhaps even impiously—in presuming to inquire into such private matters and to make secular punishment depend on secular guesses about when these states of character or soul are present. These are, one might think, private religious or spiritual matters between a person and one's God, matters that might be corrupted if the outcome of legal proceedings could depend on them.

Another related consideration here is that issues of deep character are matters about which the state is probably incompetent to judge—it cannot even deliver the mail very efficiently, after all—and which, for that reason and others, might well be regarded as simply none of the state's business. The liberal state might legitimately explore such mens rea conditions as intention, because these define the prohibited act itself; but inquiring into deep character, perhaps even motive on some understandings of that concept, may be viewed as going into matters beyond its legitimate scope.

Let us grant, then, that Coetzee has, through his character of David Lurie, revealed some spiritual and even political dangers that can be present when religious concepts of remorse and repentance are brought into secular tribunals. To the degree that he is suggesting that all concepts of remorse and repentance are religious in nature, however, then it seems to me that he is simply mistaken.

Remorse (as bad conscience) is best understood as the painful combination of guilt and shame that arises in a person when that person accepts that he has been responsible for seriously wronging another human being—guilt over the wrong itself, and shame over being forced to see himself as a flawed and defective

---

2. J. M. Coetzee, DISGRACE 58, 66 (1999).

human being who, through his wrongdoing, has fallen far below his own ego ideal. Shame should provoke repentance—the resolve to become a new and better person—and guilt should (where this is possible) provoke atonement—embracing whatever personal sacrifice may be required to restore the moral balance that one's wrongdoing has upset and to vindicate the worth of one's victim, a worth that one's wrongdoing has symbolically denied.

Why are remorse and repentance of value and worthy of our respect? One of the reasons is, of course, found in those religious perspectives previously discussed but is not limited to them. Even the atheist can believe that the person who is sincerely remorseful and repentant over his wrongdoing exhibits a better and more admirable character than a wrongdoer who is not repentant. Simply having a character properly connected to correct values, even if late in coming, is an intrinsic good—something worthy of our respect quite independently of any external consequences it may have.

Remorse and repentance may also have useful social consequences, and these may matter as well. It is often said, for example, that people who are remorseful and repentant are less dangerous, less likely to do wrong again, than those who are unremorseful and unrepentant. I hope that this is true, but I am not sure. The wrongdoer can be self-deceptive or just honestly mistaken about the sincerity of his own repentance, and even the sincerely repentant wrongdoer can suffer from weak will. It is not for nothing that the term "backsliding" plays a role in both our moral and religious vocabularies, and the concept of weakness of will (*akrasia*) has produced a vast body of philosophical and religious writing.

Another external consequence worth noting is one that may have its most meaningful impact on victims. As I have argued elsewhere, a wrongful act is, among other things, a *communicative* act. When one is wronged by another, a nontrivial portion of the hurt may be the receipt of an insulting and degrading symbolic message delivered by the wrongdoer, the message "I matter more than you and can use you, like a mere object or thing, for my own purposes." The repentant person repudiates this message, stands with his victim in its repudiation, and acknowledges moral equality with the victim—an equality denied by the wrongdoing. It is for this reason that repentance may open the door to forgiveness. If one forgives the unrepentant wrongdoer, then one risks sacrificing one's own self-respect through complicity in or tacit endorsement of the insulting and degrading message contained in the wrongdoing. A repentant wrongdoer, however, eliminates at least this one obstacle to forgiveness. To the degree that the whole community, and not just the individual victim, is a victim of criminal wrongdoing, then repentance on the part of the wrongdoer can have symbolic significance for the community as well.

Another real problem here is not theoretical but is practical, and how one deals with it may depend on one's general attitude toward the human world—on whether that attitude is largely trusting or largely suspicious. The practical problem is obvious—namely, the perpetual possibility of self-serving fakery on the part of wrongdoers. As Michel de Montaigne observed, there is "no quality so easy to counterfeit as piety"—an observation echoed by the Hollywood mogul who said this of sincerity: "Sincerity is the most precious thing in the world. When you have learned to fake that, you've got it made."

So a practical problem with giving credit for remorse and repentance is that they are so easy to fake; and our grounds for suspecting fakery only increase when a reward (e.g., a reduction in sentence, clemency, pardon, amnesty, etc.) is known to be more likely granted to those who can persuade the relevant legal authority that they manifest these attributes of character. To the degree we give rewards for goodness of character, then to that same degree do we give wrongdoers incentives to fake goodness of character. One might even suspect, indeed, that the truly remorseful and repentant wrongdoer—particularly one whose remorse is of the second kind noted previously—would not seek a reduction in punishment but would rather see that punishment as one step on a long and perhaps endless road of atonement. The person who asks us to go easy on him because he is repentant may reveal, in that very request, that he is not repentant. And to the degree that we hand out rewards to those who fake repentance and remorse, then to that same degree do we cheapen the currency of repentance and remorse—making us less likely to treat the real article with the respect it deserves.

The degree to which expressions of repentance and remorse are to be welcomed as grounds for legal mercy will, of course, depend to a substantial degree on the reasons that incline one to favor criminal punishment in the first place.

If one thinks that the main purpose of punishment is special deterrence, then one will favor counting repentance and remorse if one believes that remorsefully repentant people are less likely to commit future crimes—a controversial claim, surely. Such people may also seem to need less in the way of incapacitation. If one places greater weight on general deterrence, however, one may reasonably believe that this is to some degree undermined if it becomes known that one way to avoid serious punishment is to express repentance and remorse.

What about rehabilitation? If we were serious about pursuing this currently unfashionable value, we would surely structure punitive practices in such a way that penance, remorse, and repentance will be encouraged and rendered more likely—something not likely at all, of course, in the present barbaric conditions found in many American jails and prisons, where such horrors as gang rape are the order of the day.

Suppose for the moment that these problems can be overcome and that serving one's sentence in the right sort of penal environment is indeed a route to a valuable kind of remorse, repentance and rebirth. In such a case, we should be particularly skeptical about letting claims of remorse and repentance influence us toward leniency at the time of sentencing, since in the world we are now imagining we will be sentencing people to a kind of punishment that, though it will of course involve the hardship of deserved loss of liberty for them, will also offer them a great good: the possibility of becoming better people. And why would we want to allow the present vice of fake remorse and repentance to deprive us and criminals of the future benefit that a genuinely rehabilitative penal system might confer—the benefit of their becoming better people and better citizens? So, ironically enough, the more that one stresses the reformative value of systems of punishment that will encourage genuine remorse and repentance, the more should one be on one's guard against anything—fake remorse and repentance, for example—that might allow the criminal improperly to avoid such a system or improperly to cut short his time in it.

With respect to clemency decisions, however, the situation in a properly designed rehabilitative world will be quite different. If the goal of the system is itself rehabilitation, and if rehabilitation is thought to be present when remorse and repentance are present, then—if we had a way to recognize a truly remorseful and repentant prison inmate—it can be seen that the system has done its work and release from criminal custody will clearly be in order. This point only holds in theory for an imagined world of pure rehabilitation, of course, since in the actual world rehabilitative goals, however laudable, will likely compete with other values—deterrence, for example.

But suppose that one is not inclined to defend punishment in terms of either deterrence or rehabilitation but is instead a retributivist—one who claims that the purpose of punishment is to give criminals the punishment that they deserve. But what exactly is desert? If one thinks that desert is a function of the legitimate *grievance* that wrongdoing creates for individual victims and for society at large (grievance retributivism), then one might find it hard to see how grievance is lessened by subsequent repentance. If someone assaults me and thereby creates in me a legitimate grievance against him, how is that grievance lessened if the wrongdoer later finds Jesus and repents? *He* may, of course, be a better person because of this, but is *my own* grievance any less? Is society's? If one thinks that the grievance is in part based on the symbolic message of insult and degradation contained in the wrongdoing, then—for reasons earlier discussed—one might indeed think that a grievance is less after repentance, which represents the wrongdoer's withdrawal of the endorsement of that message.

Suppose one is not a grievance retributivist but rather subscribes to character retributivism—that is, one believes the purpose of punishment is to give people the suffering that is proportional to what Immanuel Kant called their "inner viciousness." Most of those holding this view will be strongly inclined to count repentance and remorse in favor of the criminal, because these states of character, if truly present, will be viewed as revealing an inner character that is much less vicious than the character present in the unrepentant criminal.

Even for the character retributivist, however, there will still be the practical problem earlier discussed of distinguishing the genuine article from the fake.

Where, then, do I personally stand on the issue of remorse and repentance as grounds for mercy in criminal law? Given that my own nature (alas) tends to be more cynical and suspicious than trusting, my current inclination—although I am still conflicted about this—is *not* to give much weight to expressions of remorse and repentance at the sentencing stage of the criminal process. I simply see too much chance of being made a sucker by fakery.

With respect to clemency decisions, however, it strikes me that judgments about remorse and repentance may have a much more legitimate role to play. The same noted moral and political values—deterrence, rehabilitation, retribution–are at stake here as are present with respect to sentencing, but the epistemic problems seem—at least to me—less worrisome. Why? Simply because we will have a more reliable evidential foundation upon which to base judgments of sincerity. The writer Florence King, commenting on the Karla Faye Tucker case, gives her reasons for believing that Tucker's conversion was sincere:

> Faith, hope, and snobbery aside, I believe Karla Faye's conversion was sincere, in part because the Born Again stance is so exhausting that no one could fake it for very long. Remember, she was Saved in 1985 and spent 12 years witnessing, praising, and thumping, not to mention perfecting the Pat Robertson art of smiling, laughing, and talking at the same time. "Protestantism," said Mencken, "converts the gentle and despairing Jesus into a YMCA secretary, brisk, gladsome, and obscene." Without the lube job of sincerity working in mysterious ways she would have dislocated her jawbone[3].

Although Florence King is being her usual cynical and funny self, she is tacitly making an important point: Those making clemency decisions have a lot more time and a lot more information upon which to base their decisions than would ever be possible given the time and evidential limits imposed on a criminal trial that culminates in a sentence. Mistakes are still possible in clemency decisions— there is never an ironclad guarantee against being deceived by fakery—but the probability of such mistakes is surely reduced by a nontrivial degree.

IV. APOLOGY AND MERCY

Apology has been lurking in the background of my discussion up to this point, and the time has come to say a few more explicit and direct things about it and the role that it might play in decisions to grant or withhold mercy.

The initial point I want to make is to note that apology is something *quite different* from remorse and repentance. Remorse is an internal mental state and repentance is an internal mental act, both aspects of character that often have external manifestations but are not themselves external. Apology, however, is more complex. In some cases an apology is nothing but a public linguistic

---

3. Florence King, *Misanthrope's Corner*, Nat'l Rev., Mar. 9, 1998, at 72.

performance, a purely external performance that tells us nothing at all about mental states. In other cases, however, an apology is something much more than this—a public linguistic performance, to be sure, but one that leads listeners to form legitimate expectations concerning the presence in the apologizer of certain mental states or mental acts, in particular remorse and repentance.

According to J.L. Austin, if one says "I apologize" or "I am sorry" in the appropriate circumstances—circumstances largely defined by conventional linguistic and social rules—then *one has apologized*, end of story. In this way "I apologize" is like "I promise" or "I do" (in a wedding ceremony). These words are not representing any mental states—this is the very thing that makes them performative and not descriptive—and thus "I apologize" carries with it no commitment to genuine remorse.

Some apologies are, of course, exactly this and nothing more. These are the kind of apologies that are appropriate for trivial wrongs and social gaffes—for example, accidentally bumping into someone in a crowded hall. Here one says "I apologize"—or, more likely, "Excuse me" or "I'm sorry"—merely as counters in social rituals of civility.

Of course, if the apologizer visibly crosses his fingers or says "I'm sorry" in an openly sarcastic way, then the "apology" misfires and fails to be an apology since one of what Austin calls the "felicity conditions" of a successful apology performance is that the public performance not include public behavior normally associated with insincerity. But to require, as a condition of successful performative apology, the absence of public behavior normally associated with insincerity is a far cry from saying that a mental state of actual remorse is being described or represented. So in the kind of trivial social contexts here described, I quite agree with Austin that apologies are mere linguistic performatives.

When we come to the context of serious harms and wrongs, however, Austin's analysis leads us astray since in these cases our expectations for apologies tend to be far more than linguistic in nature. In these contexts, because of social rules and conversational implicatures, we take both promises (at least significant ones) and apologies to involve the representation that one sincerely means what one says—that one really is sorry, remorseful, and repentant in the case of apologies and that one really does plan to do what one says one will do in the case of promises. Here one must, in other words, represent that one is sincere. Indeed, in these cases, what we call "the apology" invariably involves, not merely saying "I apologize" or "I am sorry," but also telling a story about one's behavior—a story in which one acknowledges how terrible it was, explains it without seeking to justify it, and conveys the depth of one's sorrow or even self-loathing over it. We would be quite shocked, I think, if a person attempted to apologize for a grave wrong merely by saying "I apologize" and nothing more. That, we would say, was really no apology at all.

In my discussion from now on, I will be concerned with apologies in a context of seriousness (serious wrong, serious harm) and will thus use the word *apology* in the way I take appropriate to such a context.

One of the reasons that apologies sometimes misfire is because the person supposedly apologizing fails to represent the right kind of sorrow—e.g., saying that he is sorry that you interpreted his (presumably innocent) remark in such a way that your (probably overly sensitive) feelings were hurt. This fails as an apology because, in mislocating the proper object for the sorrow, it fails to acknowledge the genuine wrongdoing that a genuine apology would address.

Even when representations of remorse and repentance are directed to the proper object, however, it is important to remember that representations are simply representations. They are not the same as actual remorse and repentance. The convincing fraud who makes an insincere apology really has apologized in the Austinian sense, but in a context of seriousness we normally take an apology to be something more than an Austinian performative. We take it to represent sincere remorse, and so we may reject the apology as an insulting piece of mere acting—one sense of "performance"—if we believe that there is in fact no remorse, that the representation is nothing but a representation.

Is apology in the absence of genuine sincerity enough so long as it represents sincerity? It all depends on what one wants out of an apology. If one wants admission of and acceptance of responsibility, one can also get that without apology. How? Simply by having the wrongdoer explicitly disclose facts that establish wrongdoing and accept responsibility for what he has done. An apology does that but, in also representing remorse, it does more than that.

There are also some retributive satisfactions that can be gained even from an insincere public apology. To force someone to make a public apology is to subject that person to a social ritual that can be painfully humiliating for that person—particularly, I should think, if that person is *not* sincerely sorry. Some victims of wrongdoing might not care about the sincerity of the apology, however, so long as the making of the apology is painful to the right degree for the person who must deliver it. That it causes deserved suffering might be satisfaction enough for those who are retributively inclined. Thus the public disclosure of wrongdoing, required by the South African Truth and Reconciliation Commission (TRC) as a condition for amnesty, may have had more retributive bite than Bishop Tutu—who likes to think of the TRC as "restorative justice" rather than "retributive justice"—likes to admit. For at least some people it must be quite painful, even if one does not apologize or express remorse, simply to acknowledge in public—including before one's friends and family and fellow parishioners—that, for example, one of the tasks performed as a government police officer was to torture and sometimes even kill suspects or prisoners. Mere humiliating public disclosure without apology can sometimes provide retributive satisfaction to victims—the reason why truth commissions (such as Chile's) that do not publish names of wrongdoers often seem less satisfying to victims than those (such as South Africa's) that do. But if mere disclosure without apology can provide retributive satisfaction to victims, it might be the case that requiring an apology as a condition of amnesty or clemency, even if that apology is insincere or suspected to be so, might provide even more retributive satisfactions to those victims.

Many, of course, might regard the retributive satisfactions afforded some victims by rituals of humiliation—particularly if those rituals require what may be insincere apologies and expressions of remorse—as bought at too high a moral and political price. This is perhaps why, in the Coetzee novel, David Lurie compared the demand that he make a public apology to the humiliating rituals of Mao's China during the Cultural Revolution.

Even if one can imagine a place for public apology as a shaming punishment in certain contexts (for academic plagiarism perhaps), it is not at all clear that one should welcome this in the realm of legal punishment. An academic community may be presumed, without I hope too much self-deceptive fiction, to be bound together by shared values—to be, in short, a genuine community. I fear that many of those who advocate a greater role for apology and expressions of remorse in American criminal law may overestimate the degree of actual community present in our large and complex society with its massive social class and racial and cultural divisions. Such advocates often speak warmly of the capacity of apology to lead to reconciliation and reintegration with the larger community—an idea that makes perfect sense where there is a genuine community but is ludicrous when applied to persons who are so alienated that they have never felt a part of the larger community in the first place. Apology advocates may also have too rosy a picture of the nature of the communitarian society that would make talk of deep reintegration and reconciliation through apology rituals genuinely possible. What was Mao's China, after all, except what might be called communitarianism on steroids?

V. CONCLUSION

It will surely come as no surprise that the skepticism I earlier expressed concerning the possible role of repentance and remorse as grounds for mercy (particularly in sentencing) I now extend to apology as well. A truly sincere apology can be a wonderful, even blessed, thing since it involves the kind of remorse and repentance that often marks a step on the road to moral rebirth, can sometimes provide legitimate comfort to victims, and in the proper sort of cases can indeed lead to a valuable kind of reconciliation. Turn all of that over to the American system of assembly-line justice, however, a system starved for resources and staffed by people who are oppressively overworked and in a hurry to clear cases, and we will—I fear—do little more than cheapen the currency of the real thing and add to the cynicism about our system of criminal law, and indeed about our society in general, that grows greater each passing day. Apology in America may not even be shaming these days—in which case there go even the retributive satisfactions that might be gained by victims from an apology. Just as bankruptcy has generally ceased to be an occasion of shame and has become instead a business or personal planning tool, so might a willingness to apologize if necessary be little more than part of a rational strategy for maximizing one's self-interest.

As with remorse, however, the role of apology strikes me as less controversial in clemency decisions than in sentencing decisions and for the same reason: less risk of mistakes because of the more extensive evidential base that clemency decisions make possible.

Apologies (particularly when sincerely expressive of remorse) can sometimes have many virtues—both individual and social. Our present intellectual culture, however, strikes me as one in which apology and other expressions of remorse are often located (and often overpraised) in the context of a sentimental ideology of therapy and healing rather than an ideology of truth and justice. So some skepticism is surely in order here.

COMMENTS
RETAINING REMORSE

SHERRY F. COLB*

I agree with Jeffrie Murphy that when expressions of remorse pay dividends, the odds of fake apologies increase dramatically. I agree as well that the proliferation of such insincere contrition could have the effect of diminishing the power of true apologies when they come along—in part because people will have become cynical. Nonetheless, I would oppose the elimination of apology and remorse as relevant considerations for a sentencing body.

In the United States, our system places a premium on live witness testimony. Rather than rely on affidavits, the Sixth Amendment protects the right of every defendant to present live people (who may, at his discretion, include the defendant himself) to tell the jury the defendant's story. Such people—including especially the defendant—have incentives to lie. If the defendant is guilty but claims that he is innocent, he may successfully get away with what he has done.

Yet we place our faith in the jury (or judge) to listen to the defendant (if he exercises his right to testify) as well as to other witnesses (who may have their own investments in the outcome) and judge whether it is hearing the truth. We believe that despite its flaws, a group of strangers making up a jury does a decent job of detecting who is and who is not telling the truth, particularly with the assistance of a prosecutor who can point out weaknesses in the defendant's story and reasons (including his status as a party) to doubt his credibility.

To the extent that a jury or a judge at a bench trial is able to distinguish truth from fiction in a live witness, a sentencing jury or judge should be equally capable

---

* Professor of Law and Charles Evans Hughes Scholar, Cornell Law School.

of detecting whether a defendant expresses sincere remorse. The incentives are, as in the context of testifying on one's own behalf, utterly self-serving. If you testify that you are truly sorry, you might receive a lighter sentence. If you either admit that you feel no remorse or say nothing at all, you give up this avenue to leniency. These incentives are as clear to a sentencing body as they are to us. Only the truly remorseful (or the gifted actor, of whom there are unlikely to be an especially large number among convicts) will benefit from their apologies.

For the reasons that Murphy ably identifies for allowing remorse to bear on questions of clemency, it ought to bear on questions of sentencing as well. The distinction he draws, based on the likelihood of fooling the sentencing body, ignores that healthy dose of skepticism that a judge or jury will bring to the task of listening to an apology by someone who stands to gain so much from the enterprise. A sentencing body might, of course, become too skeptical and deny remorse-related leniency to some defendants who have sincerely apologized. But that is a problem that would grow rather than diminish if remorse were no longer "admissible" at sentencing.

INVASIONS OF CONSCIENCE AND FAKED APOLOGIES

STEPHANOS BIBAS*

Jeffrie Murphy does an admirable job cautioning us against viewing remorse and apology as panaceas, cheap cures for crime victims' deep wounds. At the end of the day, though, he views the glass as half empty, and I see it as half full. Though often remorse and apology will not work, they are worth the risks that Murphy notes.

Murphy suggests that the liberal state may not properly probe offenders' characters or perhaps even motives. Of course political theorists have fought this battle for years, but I question whether government should be completely neutral among competing conceptions of the good, especially when it comes to crime. Hate, anger, and bigotry privately held may be matters of inviolable conscience. But when hateful men murder, angry mobs assault, or bigots burn and desecrate, they have already violated the Millian harm principle. They no longer deserve immunity from scrutiny. The state must teach them a lesson; the only question is what and how. Fostering remorse and apology for acts that have already violated others' rights depends on a suitably thin theory of the good to which even a libertarian state could subscribe.

Another objection is that remorse and apology are irrelevant to certain justifications for punishment. Murphy's discussion of rehabilitation, or moral reform

---

* Professor of Law, University of Pennsylvania Law School.

as I prefer to call it, assumes that reform takes place once the offender has already landed in prison. As the therapeutic-jurisprudence movement argues, however, even the way in which we try and convict criminals can itself have therapeutic or antitherapeutic effects. A criminal justice system that rewards or fails to penalize false denials, for example, may harden offenders, while one that vigorously challenges denials may produce confessions. Admitting that one has a problem is one of the first steps toward overcoming it, as Alcoholics Anonymous and other twelve-step programs recognize.

Murphy's analysis of retributivism is particularly important, as he is a leading retributivist theorist. But here too, I think he undervalues remorse and apology. Victims care greatly about remorse and apology, which seem to lessen their grievance. Some victims may see apologies as vindicating them and humiliating wrongdoers; others take remorse and apologies as opportunities to release the weight of their anger and forgive. A classical Kantian would ignore the victim's desires and wishes, viewing punishment as entirely the state's prerogative, but this approach seems too bloodless and theoretical. After all, the victim is the real party in interest, the one most directly harmed whom the state seeks to vindicate and heal. The victim, then, ought to have at least a share and a say in the matter. (Granted, giving victims a say risks introducing inequality depending on whether particular victims are forgiving or hard-hearted, but that cost may be acceptable). If the victim is satisfied, that is a strong argument for at least mitigating the offender's punishment. By expressing remorse and perhaps apologizing, the wrongdoer has at least begun to make amends and suture the wound caused by his crime.

Turning from theory to practice, Murphy is quite right to question the sincerity of many expressions of remorse and apology in the criminal justice system. Defendants know that faking remorse may reduce their sentences, and many are not above lying if it might serve their interests. Others genuinely mean to turn over a new leaf, but can easily backslide the next time temptation presents itself.

Nevertheless, at least some sentencing discounts are worth the risk. First, prosecutors, judges, and juries are no dummies. They know that defendants are tempted to lie and have keen noses for fakery. Second, though it is in their interests to lie, surprisingly many defendants are emotionally invested in denying guilt or minimizing blame. As a prosecutor, I saw countless defendants deny or admit guilt grudgingly, even though their lawyers had tried repeatedly to coach them into expressing remorse and apologizing. These defendants will not express remorse and apologize until they are at least open to the possibility that they were wrong. Third, even an insincere apology has great value. It vindicates the victim, prevents the defendant from persisting in his denial, brings the episode to some form of closure, and may teach others and even the defendant a lesson. As the psychology of cognitive dissonance indicates, a defendant who at first professes something insincerely or half-heartedly may well come to internalize his admission of guilt.

In the end, Murphy's arguments are forceful, but so too are the arguments above. A risk-averse society will side with Murphy and not take chances on potentially dangerous criminals. But one that holds open hope of redemption will take chances, even though many convicts will take advantage of them and disappoint us. Our more humane impulses tug at our hearts to condemn crimes and punish criminals, but then stretch out our hands to forgive.

EVALUATION OF REMORSE IS HERE TO STAY: WE SHOULD FOCUS ON IMPROVING ITS DYNAMICS

SUSAN A. BANDES*

The practical problem with remorse is undeniable—it can be faked. But what should follow from this? As an argument for barring consideration of remorse, it proves too much.

The legal system is irrevocably in the business of determining sincerity and credibility. Definitions of crimes and torts often turn on intent and other states of mind, for example. But on a more basic level, credibility determinations are an essential aspect of the trial system. Legal actors observe the appearance, facial expressions, body language and conduct of witnesses and parties in the courtroom, listen to their testimony (or notice their failure to testify), consider their background, and make decisions about their trustworthiness, integrity, and other character traits.[1]

As Jeffrie Murphy rightly observes, there is no window into the soul. Interpreting outward manifestations of inward states is the only available option, and there is always room for trickery, misinterpretation, and error. Witnesses of all stripes seek to appear credible, and those who evaluate them aren't always good judges of character. In a system devoted to evaluating human behavior, there is no way to avoid judging—and misjudging—internal qualities like integrity and trustworthiness. There is nothing inherently different about remorse. The incentives for displaying it can be very high, but in criminal cases, so are the stakes for displaying trustworthiness, grief, and other outward manifestations of inward affect or character.

It is important to debate the role remorse ought to play in various contexts, such as sentencing and clemency. But as a practical matter, it would be difficult

---

* Distinguished Research Professor of Law, DePaul University College of Law.

1. *See, e.g.*, Michael E. Antonio, *If Looks Could Kill: Identifying Trial Outcomes of Murder Cases Based on the Appearances of Capital Offenders Shown in Black and White Photographs,* in PSYCHOLOGY OF DECISION MAKING (Gloria R. Burthold ed., 2007); Michael E. Antonio, *Arbitrariness and the Death Penalty: How the Defendant's Appearance During Trial Influences Capital Jurors' Punishment Decision,* 24 BEHAV. SCI. & L. 215 (2006).

to bar remorse from the criminal arena, even if we wanted to. The available evidence about decision-making suggests that judges and jurors (and the public) will continue to watch the defendant's demeanor and comportment, and to attempt to assess whether he appears remorseful or arrogant, or whether he evokes sympathy or fear or anger. We would do better to accept that people will try to gauge remorse as an essential aspect of character relevant to criminal responsibility, and to help them do a better job of it—particularly in situations in which there is evidence that people are particularly bad at it. There is evidence, for example, that jurors misjudge demeanor and credibility across racial lines,[2] and that they are poorly equipped to judge the credibility of witnesses with mental disabilities.[3] These problems might be addressed through expert testimony, jury instructions, or other mechanisms.

Murphy asks whether capital cases present particular problems for the role of remorse. My answer to this question draws on something I have long admired about his work. As Murphy teaches us, just as it is hard to see into another's soul, it is difficult to know one's own soul. Fallibility and human frailty are unavoidable parts of the human condition, and we won't excise them from the legal system. But they pose particular problems when the sentence is irrevocable. The death penalty judges not just the act but the worth of the person—the hardened heart, the heinous and depraved character. A death sentence is an assertion that the defendant is irredeemable and no longer fit to live, and that our legal system is capable of ascertaining his unfitness to live. Remorse suggests the possibility of redemption, and the possibility of erroneous judgment about deep character, and before we take a life, we ought to be very slow to discount those possibilities.

---

2. *See, e.g.,* William Bowers, Benjamin Steiner, and Marla Sandys, *Death Sentencing in Black and White, An Empirical Analysis of the Role of Jurors' Race and Jury Racial Composition,* 3 U. Pa. J. Const. L. 171, 244–52 (2001).

3. *See, e.g.,* Georgina Stobbs and Mark Rhys Kebbell, *Jurors' Perception of Witnesses with Intellectual Disabilities and the Influence of Expert Evidence,* 16 J. Applied Res. Intell. Disabilities 107 (2003).

INSINCERE AND INVOLUNTARY PUBLIC APOLOGIES

LISA KERN GRIFFIN*

Jeffrie Murphy deftly analyzes the limitations of apology within the criminal justice process. Authentic apologies do occur, but the institutional pressure of an overburdened and adversarial system pushes in the direction of hollow sound

---

* Professor of Law, Duke University School of Law.

bites. Although I share Murphy's skepticism about public apologies, I disagree with his conclusion that apologies should be inadmissible altogether. Like other socially valuable behavior, such as cooperation with the government, remorse can be relevant to sentencing. And when judges exercise discretion within sentencing ranges, the defendant's apparent level of contrition can serve as a catch-all mitigating factor. Accounting for apologies may generate only marginal returns, but insincere apologies do little harm. Murphy's primary focus on the problem of false apologies is thus misplaced. Forced apologies, however, may produce significant distortions and warrant closer attention.

According to Murphy, we are "interested in apologies only to the degree that we believe that they are sincere external signs of repentance and remorse and reliable external signs of future atonement."[1] But there is a systematic interest in apology as a symbol not just of remorse but also of submission and willingness to engage in a prescribed ritual. Some public apologies are exchanges designed more to enforce authority than to heal discord. It is to this category that we should attend rather than debating the intractable issue of screening for insincerity.

As a practical matter, juries and judges are often quite good at determining whether someone is telling the truth, but they are ill-equipped to discern the underlying motives for speaking or to evaluate matters of conscience. When I served as a federal prosecutor, I witnessed perhaps a hundred conciliatory attempts at sentencing. The majority of them were just the sort of "public linguistic performances" Murphy considers insufficient to apologize for a substantial wrong. Their ultimate utility depended on whether the defense lawyer had artfully coaxed and effectively coached the client to make the conventional gestures. In court, these transactions have minimal transformative power. The most genuine moment of remorse I can recall arose in a case in which the defendant addressed his remarks not to the victims or the judge, but to his young children. Though moving, his statement had no impact on the sentence imposed. Apologies for serious offenses are nuanced, complicated, and ultimately personal. True reconciliation mostly happens outside the courtroom.

Although many in-court apologies are manufactured and misdirected, sentencing courts do not bother to label them as such if they bear outward indicia of credibility. Repeat players like judges, prosecutors, and defense lawyers well understand that defendants may be sorry they got caught but not necessarily sorry for their conduct. Of course, cynical apologies do little cultural work, but even "[f]aked remorse is better than nothing."[2] If "cheap grace" results in small discounts off sentences that already are plenty costly, that strikes me as an acceptable risk.

---

1. Murphy core text at 186.
2. Stephen P. Garvey, *Punishment as Atonement*, 46 UCLA L. Rev. 1801, 1850 (1999).

Involuntary apologies elicited without regard to the distinction between rewarding repentance and punishing silence may not be so innocuous. Murphy argues that apology advocates overestimate the degree of community in our society and the possibility of reintegration. Perhaps they have also underestimated the extent to which forced apology can deepen divisions. As Louis Michael Seidman explains: "There is something degrading about [an apology] ritual, and it is not only the participants who are degraded . . . we cannot help feeling a certain contempt for the weakness of the apologist coupled with fear and envy of the power exercised by the person who extracts the apology."[3] Shame, fear, and envy are not restorative emotions. Forcing apology on top of imposing liability may provide some "retributive satisfactions," as Murphy notes. But it also causes expressive harm in terms of the moral capital of the criminal justice system. Moreover, the abject defeat of a compelled public apology may dehumanize and stigmatize more than it restores. In doing so, it may only alienate the offender further.

Rather than focusing on policing sincerity, it is worth considering how sentencing courts might avoid these counterproductive effects. Public apology will endure in its occasionally redemptive and often mechanistic way. But courts should only account for it while maintaining the distinction between discount and penalty, recognizing the "right to withhold apology,"[4] and exercising caution in those cases in which authority animates the apology and the purported reconciliation is not with any victim but with the government itself.

---

3. Louis Michael Seidman, SILENCE & FREEDOM 26 (2007).
4. *Id.* at 27.

THE SOCIAL MEANING OF APOLOGY

JANET AINSWORTH*

Jeffrie Murphy has contributed greatly to our understanding of the role of remorse and apology in a justice context through his thoughtful and critical analysis. Murphy suggests that Austinian speech act theory is of limited utility to an assessment of the role of apology in criminal punishment because Austin's taxonomy of speech acts—being limited to a consideration of the formal qualities of apologies—does not adequately foreground the crucial role of sincerity in examining apologies. More recent work in sociolinguistics, pragmatics, and discourse analysis on apologies has delved below the surface forms of the language of

---

* John D. Eshelman Professor of Law, Seattle University School of Law.

apology, demonstrating that apologies serve a wide variety of communicative and social functions, not all of which require that the apology be sincere.[1]

Paradigmatic apologies, like expressions of thanks, must be sincerely meant by the speaker.[2] Yet consider the young child urged by a parent to thank his Aunt Agatha for the itchy sweater she gave him as a gift. His grudging "Thank you," is likely to be acceptable to his aunt unless his eye-rolling or tone of voice makes it embarrassingly apparent that he doesn't mean his words of thanks. Now, Aunt Agatha is no fool. Not for a minute does she mistake his formulaic "Thank you," for a spontaneous expression of gratitude. But she will nevertheless accept his thanks as long as his expression is minimally compliant with the social script for gratitude because she shares our social norm that gift recipients ought to thank the giver and that children ought to learn to participate in that social convention.

Expressions of remorse in sentencing are not, of course, on a moral par with thanking someone for an undesired gift. But just wrongful acts are communicative acts sending a symbolic message, so too apologies and expressions of remorse made at sentencing hearings send symbolic messages that transcend their literal propositional content. Sentencing is not a private, bureaucratic assessment of penalty but rather a public, performative ritual of blame and punishment. Sentencings are open to the public, often reported in the newspapers and broadcast into our living rooms. Even in the most cut-and-dried sentencing—one in which a mandatory sentence must be imposed—the full ritual of the formal sentencing hearing must occur. At sentencing, the judge, lawyers, victim, and defendant all have the opportunity to make public pronouncements about the moral and social meaning of the crime and its punishment. Thus, the meaning of what is said at a sentencing is irreducibly social. What is said in this public forum serves as an articulation of our collective values regarding the causing of harm to others and an appropriate reaction to the causing of that harm.

We offer the defendant at sentencing the opportunity to accept responsibility for his actions, to express remorse for the suffering he caused, and to promise to

---

1. *See, e.g.,* Marion Owen, Apologies and Remedial Interchanges: A Study of Language Use in Social Interactions (1985); Bruce Fraser, *On Apologizing, in* Conversation Routine: Explorations in Standardized Communication Situations 259–71 (Florian Coulmas ed., 1981); Robin Tolmach Lakoff, *Nine Ways of Looking at Apology: The Necessity for Interdisciplinary Theory and Method in Discourse Analysis, in* Handbook on Discourse Analysis 199–214 (Deborah Schiffrin, Deborah Tannen, and Heidi Hamilton eds., 2003).

2. Nick Smith notes that a paradigmatic apology articulates the factual nature of the wrong committed, accepts causal and moral responsibility for the harm resulting from the wrong, expresses regret for the harm, and at least implicitly commits to forebear from similar conduct in the future. *See* Nick Smith, I Was Wrong: The Meaning of Apologies 140–42 (2008).

change his ways because we are modeling for him that, whether or not he truly values any of those things, we do. We should preserve the practice of considering apology in sentencing, not because criminals deserve an opportunity to earn a sentencing discount by displaying the proper attitude toward their conduct, but because we as a society need a forum to articulate our beliefs about accepting responsibility for the harm that we cause others.

A defendant, in expressing his remorse, may sincerely share that socially held value, or having apologized publicly, may come in time to share it. Even if he does not, however, our public recognition of the significance of a full apology is worthwhile. It expresses our willingness to reaffirm at sentencing hearings our belief that accepting moral responsibility and expressing sorrow for the harm caused to others justifies lesser punishment. In short, we need apologies and expressions of remorse to matter at sentencing because they are as necessary for us as for the defendant, and we would be the poorer as a society if we marginalized such expressions to the rare and largely unnoticed world of the clemency hearing.

REPLY

JEFFRIE G. MURPHY

Several of my commentators rightly take me to task for not acknowledging that the difficulty of determining the sincerity of remorse and apology may not differ significantly from determining the truth of a variety of other claims at trial and sentencing and that the same mechanisms that lawyers, judges, and juries use to reduce those difficulties will also be available to them with respect to expressions of remorse and apology. As Sherry Colb notes, "a group of strangers making up a jury does a decent job of detecting who is and who is not telling the truth, particularly with the assistance of a prosecutor who can point out weaknesses in the defendant's story and reasons (including his status as a party) to doubt his credibility."[1] My main practical point still stands, however—namely that *much more* is available to minimize mistakes at a clemency hearing.

Moving from a legitimate worry that several of my commentators share, I would now like to respond briefly to a few points made by individual commentators.

Stephanos Bibas claims that I, somewhat surprisingly for someone who is supposed to be a retributivist, undervalue the retributive value of expressions of remorse and apology. I do not think that he is correct about this. I explicitly say that public expressions of remorse and apology, even if insincere, can be painfully humiliating and that this pain can represent retributively deserved suffering. I also say explicitly that such expressions can sometimes lessen the victims'

---

1. Colb comment at 195.

grievances by publicly withdrawing the endorsement of the wrongdoing that might otherwise be allowed to stand.

Bibas also reminds us that "when hateful men murder, angry mobs assault, or bigots burn and desecrate, they have already violated the Millian harm principle [and] no longer deserve immunity from scrutiny,"[2] but surely he does not think I would want to deny this. I did not say that such evil actors should be free of *all* scrutiny but merely expressed skepticism that their expressions of remorse and apology should be given much weight at sentencing. A certain amount of scrutiny—mens rea inquiries, for example—are vital to the criminal process, but inquiring into remorse and repentance could reasonably be viewed as spiritually intrusive and in that sense beyond the legitimate scrutiny of the liberal state. Forced apologies, as Lisa Griffin notes, may be degrading and dehumanizing for the defendant, and it is not at all clear that the liberal state should be in the business of degrading and dehumanizing any of its citizens.

Susan Bandes has more confidence than I do that the death penalty is special in such a way that remorse and apology should be allowed to play a much more significant role in that context than in any other sentencing or clemency context. She gives two reasons for thinking this. First, she notes that a death sentence is *irrevocable*. This is certainly true, but are not *all* criminal sentences irrevocable simply because *the past* is irrevocable? We cannot give an executed person back his life, but neither can we give a person who has wrongfully served twenty years back those twenty years and erase from his mind the no doubt unspeakable conditions (e.g., gang rape) to which he has been subjected during that period— conditions that may have hardened him to such a degree as to undermine any possibility that he might seek and attain redemption. I sometimes wish that some of the passion directed against the death penalty (a fairly rare penalty, after all) could be redirected toward unspeakable prison conditions—conditions that could easily be regarded by some as a "fate worse than death."

Second, Bandes says that "[a] death sentence is an assertion that the defendant is irredeemable and no longer fit to live."[3] This strikes me as too quick. A justification for a death sentence might acknowledge a belief that the defendant is redeemable but might claim that this value is trumped by some even greater value—the value of victim vindication perhaps. Also, clarity is not served if "the defendant deserves to die" or "deterrence will be served by execution of this defendant" are translated simply as "the defendant is no longer fit to live." One might recall Samuel Johnson's observation that nothing so focuses the mind as the prospect of being hanged in a fortnight and come to think that the prospect of being executed may provide the wrongdoer with the very incentive that he needs to bring him toward repentance and redemption. I raise these points not

---

2. Bibas comment at 196.
3. Bandes comment at 199.

because I necessarily agree with them but because I believe that many people who are deeply opposed to the death penalty are sometimes tempted, in their zeal, to skip careful analysis and the careful consideration of arguments on the other side in favor of claims that are more rhetoric than sober argument.

Griffin and Janet Ainsworth insightfully stress, in a way that I neglected to do by my perhaps excessive focus on worries about sincerity, the way in which apologies might be seen as participation in socially valuable rituals. As Ainsworth puts it, "what is said [at sentencing] serves as an articulation of our collective values regarding the causing of harm to others and an appropriate reaction to the causing of that harm."[4]

I think that this was probably once true with respect to apologies, but I am not sure that it still is. The cynicism spawned in our "culture of apology"—where apologies automatically appear on the lips of people trying to avoid responsibility—may have undercut to a substantial degree the social value of the apology ritual. As I noted in my core text, declaring bankruptcy may now be seen as moving from being an occasion of great shame to being simply a business planning tool. So, too, may a willingness to apologize if caught be increasingly seen, not as a willingness to send a socially useful message, but rather as simply a strategy for advancing self-interest. So those who apologize may be seen as merely "playing amid the ruins of forgotten languages."

---

4. Ainsworth comment at 202.

10. INTERPRETIVE CONSTRUCTION IN THE SUBSTANTIVE CRIMINAL LAW

MARK KELMAN*

I. INTRODUCTION

Standard legal analysis requires both an undefended interpretive construction of the facts in dispute *and* some sort of policy analysis of the constructed dispute. I continue to believe that most of what we do when we purport to engage in rational policy analysis is simply rehash a set of largely intractable disputes (and when we don't overtly rehash those disputes, it's most often because we are missing what's really at stake)!

The disputes are almost always in part about legal form: Should we, on any given occasion, accept "rules"—with all their well-rehearsed flaws of under and overinclusiveness—or "standards"—with all their well-rehearsed flaws of inadequate notice and biased or arbitrary administration?[1] They are also (quite often) about whether to interpret people as "determined" objects of circumstances outside their control or as capable of significant degrees of intentional self-governance. We often need to engage this dispute because most persuasive theories of retributive blame are sensitive to whether defendants have more or less capacity to control their behavior, not merely to whether they possess some threshold degree of rational agency. We may need to engage it, too, if we believe that deterrence signals will be largely inefficacious if people are less capable of exercising self-control.[2] We frequently evade the need to get stuck taking one side or the other in these intractable disputes over legal form and the intentionalism/determinism line by subconsciously constructing cases so that they appear "easy."

* James C. Gaither Professor of Law and Vice Dean, Stanford Law School. This core text is based on Mark Kelman, *Interpretive Construction in the Substantive Criminal Law*, 33 STAN L. REV. 591 (1981).

1. On this issue, I have come to believe not that we can reach *resolution*, but that we can at least notice when a particular set of problems is more likely to be bothersome in a particular setting.

2. I believe on this set of issues, theorists who emphasize deterrence and/or incapacitation can have some hope of "making progress" in rational discussion—though I think we have far too little empirical information to say that we have made substantial progress—while the arguments that sound in retribution remain an irresolvable muddled mess.

By interpretive construction, I refer to processes by which concrete situations are reduced to substantive legal controversies: It refers both to the way we construe a factual situation and to the way we frame the possible rules to handle the situation. So we may, for instance, decide (in framing *facts*) to include or exclude events that may have borne on decisions taken at the moment that the actus reus of the crime was committed (time-framing). Or, we may, for example, decide (in framing *rules*) to think of the debate about the propriety of strict liability to consider that strict liability is (merely) an overinclusive rule (with all the flaws, and virtues, of overinclusive rules)—and that it might be more overinclusive in some settings than others, or more overinclusive depending on how the objective offense elements of the crime are defined.

After cataloguing some common "interpretive constructions," I argue that, in a variety of familiar cases, it is easy to reach a "sensible," rationally defensible result *once* the undefended interpretive construction already occurred, but that reaching any defensible result would have been considerably more difficult had we faced the fact that construction itself was not really defensible. There are four fundamentally factual and two fundamentally doctrine-determinative constructions.[3]

II. FOUR UNCONSCIOUS INTERPRETIVE CONSTRUCTS

Unconscious interpretive constructs shape the way we view disruptive incidents, but they are never identified or discussed by judges or commentators. There are basically four forms of unconscious constructs, two dealing with "time-framing" and two dealing with problems of categorization. I discuss unconscious constructs before conscious ones because the former are often used to avoid issues inherent in the latter, issues that legal analysts are most prone to be aware are controversial, perhaps insoluble, and highly politicized.

1. Broad and Narrow Time Frames
We put people on trial. People exist over time; they have long, involved personal histories. We prosecute particular acts—untoward incidents—that these people commit. But even these incidents have a history: Things occur before or after

---

3. My sense is that the factual constructions involving broad or narrow time-framing (whether to include prior occurrences as part of the relevant narrative or not) have proven most interesting to readers over the years. I still believe, with relatively little conviction and even less interest, that other forms of "fact" framing—e.g., whether to separate or unify arguably distinct incidents—may well matter, and I more strongly believe that the "invisibility" of the pervasiveness of the rules/standards dilemma has permitted judges and academics to believe they have resolved issues that they have basically merely skirted.

incidents that seem relevant to our judgment of what the perpetrator did. Sometimes we incorporate facts about the defendant's personal history. Other times, we incorporate facts about events preceding or post-dating the criminal incident. But an interpreter can readily focus solely on the isolated criminal incident, as if all we can learn of value in assessing culpability can be seen with that narrower time focus.

Most often, though not invariably, the arational choice between narrow and broad time frames keeps us from having to deal with more explicit political questions arising from one conscious interpretive construct—the conflict between intentionalism and determinism. Often, conduct is deemed involuntary (or determined) rather than freely willed (or intentional) because we do not consider the defendant's earlier decisions that may have put him in the position of apparent choicelessness. Conversely, conduct that could be viewed as freely willed or voluntary if we looked only at the precise moment of the criminal incident is sometimes deemed involuntary because we open up the time frame to look at prior events that seem to compel or determine the defendant's conduct at the time of the incident.

The use of "time-framing" as an interpretive *method* blocks the perception that intentionalist or determinist issues could be substantively at stake. The interpretive "choice" between narrow and broad time frames affects not only controversial, doctrinally tricky legal cases, but also "easy" cases, because narrow time-framing fends off, at the methodological level, the possibility of doing determinist analyses.

2. Disjoined and Unified Accounts

A second unconscious interpretive construct relating to time involves the tension between disjoined and unified accounts of incidents. Many legally significant situations seem to require a somewhat broad time frame, at least in the sense that we feel we must look beyond a single moment in time and account, in some fashion, for some clearly relevant earlier moment. The earlier "moment" may be the time at which a defendant made some judgment about the situation she was in, some judgment that at least contributed to the ultimate decision to act criminally. For instance, the defendant negligently believes she must use deadly force to defend herself and then she intentionally kills someone, having formed that belief. Alternatively, the earlier moment may simply be the moment at which the defendant initiated the chain of events that culminated in criminal results. For instance, the defendant may shoot at X, but the bullet will miss X and then kill Y, an unforeseeable bystander.

Once we agree to look at these earlier moments, we must decide whether to disjoin or unify the earlier moment with the later moment. We can treat all the relevant facts as constituting a single incident, or we can disjoin the events into two separate incidents.

Once this arational interpretive decision is made, the question of criminal culpability is forever biased. Is a negligent decision to kill followed by an intentional killing a negligent or intentional act? Is the person who misses X and shoots Y someone who commits two crimes—attempted murder of X plus, say, reckless homicide of Y—or one crime—an intentional murder of a person? Sometimes, unifying two arguably separate incidents allows us to avoid making a hard-to-justify assertion that the arguably second incident or decision was determined by the first. Often, other interests are at stake in separating or joining a series of incidents.

3. Broad and Narrow Views of Intent

A third unconscious construct involves broad and narrow views of intent. Each time someone acts, we can say with fair confidence that, in the absence of some claim of accident, he intended to do precisely the acts that he has done. But we have difficulty categorizing those acts, because an individual set of acts may, in the observer's eyes, be an instance of a number of different categories of acts.

For example, when the defendant intends to undertake certain deeds constituting a particular crime, it feels both misleading in significant ways, and perfectly proper in others, to assert that the defendant intended the particular crime. On one hand, it is odd to think of actors as viewing the world in criminal law categories when they act. On the other hand, it is equally odd to think of actors as focusing in their consciousness only on the most precise physical motions they undertake. Thus, when we talk of the requisite intent to commit assault *with intent* to commit murder, it is peculiar to think *either* that the defendant must have mentally focused his conduct on the broadly interpreted *crime* of murder (with all its complications, e.g., that he must intend to act with malice, premeditation, nonprovocation, nonjustification, etc.), or that it is sufficient that he simply focused on the physical *motions* that would predicate the crime (e.g., pulling the trigger on the gun, which we may deem murder if, in fact, he acted with what we call malice, nonprovocation, etc.).

Similarly, a defendant may perform suspicious acts not in themselves criminal or abandon a particular criminal attempt. We wonder whether the defendant, in the first case, can accurately be thought of as intending only the precise acts he committed or whether, in some broader sense, he *intended* some more apt deeds that we would deem criminal acts. Likewise, in the second case, we wonder whether the defendant abandoned only the one criminal incident or abandoned the criminal category of which that incident is but an instance.

4. Broad and Narrow Views of the Defendant

A fourth unconscious construct is that the interpreter may view defendants in broad or narrow terms. Each defendant is a unique individual, with a unique set of perceptions and capabilities. Every crime is committed in a unique setting. At the same time, every defendant has general human traits, and is thus a representative of the broader category of human beings. Similarly, the setting in which a crime is committed is an instance of those settings in which the crime is generally committed, and the features of the more general situation could be ascribed to the particular situation.

III. CONSCIOUS INTERPRETIVE CONSTRUCTS

Just as unconscious constructs shape the way we view disruptive incidents, conscious constructs settle doctrinal issues while obscuring the nondeductive nature of legal discourse. Two forms of such conscious construction involve the choice between intentionalistic and deterministic accounts of human conduct, and the choice between stating legal commands in the form of precise rules or vague ad hoc standards. While judges and commentators seem to be aware of these constructs, they discuss them only as *general* philosophical themes in the criminal law.

But any consciously stated "grand" choices elevating intentionalism or rules, determinism or standards, as *the* solution to legal dilemmas is inevitably partial. The "victory" of one framework or the other is a temporary one that can never be made with assurance or comfort. Each assertion manifests no more than a momentary expression of feelings that remain contradictory and unresolved. Most significantly, arguments based on these explicitly political issues feel less "legal" than arguments grounded in traditional doctrinal categories.

Perhaps more important, the *un-self-conscious* assertion of the inexorability of applying one or the other poles in these controversies to a particular setting settles many doctrinal issues, though the problematic nature of chosen doctrine would become more apparent if the use of interpretive constructs surfaced. In this sense, these interpretive constructs function just like the four unconscious constructs. Though they are conscious political positions when employed at a general level, they may function as unreasoned presuppositions that solve cases while obscuring the dissonant, fundamentally nondeductive nature of legal discourse.

1. Intentionalism and Determinism
Intentionalism is the principle that human conduct results from free choice. An intentionalist interpretation of an incident gives moral weight to autonomous choice and expresses the indeterminacy of future actions. Determinism, on the other hand, implies that subsequent behavior is causally connected to prior events. A determinist interpretation considers behavior by looking backward, and it expresses no (or ambivalent) moral respect or condemnation of these predetermined acts.

2. Rules versus Standards
An overarching conflict within our legal system pertains to the form that legal pronouncements should take. Our legal system bounces fitfully between "clearly

defined, highly administrable, general rules" and "equitable standards producing ad hoc decisions with relatively little precedential value."[4]

Rules seem, on the positive side, capable of uniform and nonprejudicial application. They define spheres of autonomy and privacy and spheres of duty by giving clear notice to citizens of the legal consequences of their conduct. The void-for-vagueness and strict construction doctrines both resonate in the rule-respecting liberal tradition. On the negative side, rules will inevitably be both overinclusive and underinclusive according to the purposes reasonably attributable to the law. This not only leads to random injustice when particular culpable parties are acquitted and nonculpable parties are convicted, but it enables people to calculate privately optimal levels of undesirable behavior that are within the precise confines of the law.

Standards alleviate the problems of nonpurposive applications of legal commands to particular cases. On the other hand, they may be difficult to administer or may be enforced in a biased, unequal, and uncertain fashion. The use of standards in the criminal law is rampant. Whether we are talking about requirements of "malice" in homicide law, looking at regulatory statutes that are openly vague in proscribing *unreasonable* restraints of trade, or considering the use of discretion in prosecution and sentencing, it is difficult to deny that avoiding vagueness is more important as ideology than in practice.

In any argument within our culture, *both* of these modes of framing legal commands are simultaneously appealing and unappealing; neither has killer force. Because neither position can dominate the other, legal arguments about the desirable form of legal commands are not just oscillating, unsettled, and unbalanced, but the choice of one resolution or the other ultimately often feels like a product of whim—a reflection of one's most recent overreaction to the follies of the previously adopted form.

IV. A DISCUSSION OF *MARTIN V. STATE*

In *Martin v. State*,[5] police officers arrested the defendant at his home and took him onto a public highway, where the defendant used loud and profane language. He was convicted under a statute prohibiting public exhibition of a drunken condition. The appellate court reversed, holding that the defendant was involuntarily and forcibly carried to the public place by the arresting officers. The court concluded, uncontroversially, that an involuntary act cannot give rise to

---

4. Duncan Kennedy, *Form and Substance in Private Law Adjudication*, 89 HARV. L. REV. 1685 (1976).

5. 17 So. 2d 427 (Ala. 1944).

liability. But in *People v. Decina*,[6] the court sustained the defendant's conviction for negligent homicide, though at the time his car struck the victims, he was unconscious as a result of an epileptic fit, not voluntarily operating the vehicle. The court held that the defendant was culpable because he had made a conscious decision to drive, knowing that an epileptic attack was possible.

The hidden interpretive time-framing construct becomes visible when one tries to square *Martin* with *Decina*. In *Decina*, the court opened up the time frame, declaring that if the defendant commits a voluntary act at time one that poses a risk of causing an involuntary harm later—for example, drives the car knowing he is a blackout-prone epileptic—then the second act—crashing while unconscious—will be deemed voluntary. But the defendant in *Martin*, as well, may have done *something* voluntarily (before the police came) that posed a risk that he would get arrested and carried into public in his drunken state. Although it is plausible that Martin was arrested on an old warrant (or was arrested utterly without reason) and could not foresee that he would wind up in public on this occasion, it is quite possible that the defendant was arrested for activity he was engaging in at home: for instance, beating his wife.

Why did the court not consider saying that the voluntary act at time one (wife beating) both posed a risk of and caused a harmful involuntary act at time two (public drunkenness) and assessing the voluntariness of the alleged criminal act with reference to the wider time-framed scenario? It cannot be that the involuntary, harmful act at time two was unforeseeable: The probability of an epileptic blackout is almost certainly far lower than the probability of ending up in public after engaging in behavior likely to draw police attention. Arguments that we are less concerned with people "thinking ahead" to avoid public drunkenness than unconscious driving seem inadequate as well; the penalties for public drunkenness are presumably set lower to reflect the relative lack of gravity of the offense. The fact that the police are "human interveners" would not ordinarily break the "causal chain" (even if that were relevant) since they are *duty* bound to take the steps they take. Ultimately, the *Martin* finding of voluntariness "works" not because it is "right," but because all the hard points disappear in the initial interpretive construction of the potentially relevant facts.

Assume though, that we decide that the drunken defendant in *Martin v. State* involuntarily appeared in public. The statute required that perpetrators be publicly drunk *and* boisterous. One interpretation of the court's opinion is that *each* element of the crime must be performed voluntarily; i.e., that it is unjust to punish a person who has not been given *every* chance to avoid the crime. The court thus joined the dissociated elements. It found the drunken boisterous public appearance as a whole involuntary and exculpated the defendant.

---

6. 138 N.E.2d 799 (N.Y. 1956).

But deciding to require each statutory element to be performed voluntarily by the defendant illustrates the framing tension that is present. Courts no doubt would find violations of public exhibitionism statutes even if exposure occurs during an involuntary public appearance. (Just as it is not a defense to a charge that one possesses weapons in jail that one is involuntarily in jail or to a charge that one violates an adolescent curfew that one's status as someone less than 18 years old is not a voluntary act.) The exhibitionism is separated or disjoined from the (earlier, ongoing) involuntary public appearance and judged on its own. In the public drunkenness cases, however, the "incidents" are unified: "Drunken boisterousness in public" is one incident, and if that incident is involuntary, the defendant must be acquitted. There is no principle that explains why this should be the case. It is not obvious that an intoxicated defendant who (arguably) "decides" to be boisterous and profane once involuntarily in public could not be deterred from committing the offense—which requires boisterousness, which occurs subsequent to the intoxicated appearance, to be a complete offense that the state attends to—nor is it obvious he should not be blamed for consummating the offense.

I suspect that both the time framing and the unifying/disjoining techniques are merely useful, dissonance-reducing masks. The narrow time frame permits us to avoid the intentionalism/determinism issue—atypically, here, it is the State that would like to open the time frame to show the presence of choice where the defendant sees constraint.

What is likely at stake is a judgment that acting boisterous when drunk is "*less* intentional" than exposing oneself once in public. The exhibitionist can more easily "avoid criminality," once in public, than can the boisterous drunkard. For the drunkard to be given "adequate" opportunity to avoid the offense, his appearance in public cannot be determined externally, because his boisterousness once drunk is *always* partially determined. Of course, boisterousness is not viewed as so unintentional as to constitute an utterly arbitrary basis for imposing criminal liability—if it were, conviction of boisterous public drunkards in the routine case would be problematic—but rather than face the disturbing reality that we view many things as *partially* determined (and open up the possibility of a general discourse in which we recognize that many things are in some part chosen, but still both explicable and atypically hard to avoid), we simply duck the issue by using disjunctive or unified accounts of incidents.

We also evade the rules/standards dilemma: If we would be drawn to a legal resolution of the case of the form, "don't convict unless the defendant on balance has had 'adequate opportunity' to avoid the commission of the offense," we would be adopting a (difficult-to-defend) standard. We can pretend to maintain our commitment to a criminal law founded in rules by treating this as an easy case in which we forbid punishing those who do not engage in voluntary action, or if (following the Model Penal Code in this regard) we *permit* conviction if liability is based on conduct that *includes* a voluntary act.

V. THE HOSTILITY TO STRICT LIABILITY

Two fundamental points about strict liability are related to "interpretive construction."[7] First, it is often (though by no means always) the case that a person who does not know something at the time he acts (or is not even especially careless/negligent about perceiving facts that are available to him at the moment of criminal conduct) might have learned these facts *earlier* (or that his failure to learn looks more careless when one considers earlier opportunities to learn). Defendants will often seem too sympathetic—look like people convicted though they lack any real opportunity to learn that they were taking steps that ran afoul of the law—if looked at in a narrow time frame. If all that one can do to learn the age of someone one is selling liquor to (or having proscribed sex with) is to look them over or ask, the defendant's mistakes may appear nonnegligent. They may appear considerably more negligent if we expand the time frame (check state-issued documents, ask parents). All I mean to suggest is that the gap between broad time-framed views of negligence and strict liability might (sometimes, not always) be quite small, while the gap between narrow time-framed negligence and broad time-framed negligence might be quite wide.

But this leads to the second problem, the problem that raises the issue of legal form: We need to decide whether to permit juries to make decisions based on relatively unguided negligence standards if (many) juries are likely to substitute a narrow-time framed judgment of negligence for the broad-framed one the legislature prefers them to make, and if, at the same time, the use of the "rule" ("all who make mistakes are conclusively presumed negligent") is (very?) frequently inapt. The inquiry into the rule/standard dilemma in thinking about strict liability versus negligence is a broader one, though, and involves issues that transcend the issue of whether juries make (what legislators would consider to be) systematic errors because they use an (unwarranted) narrow time frame.

Start with mistakes of law—situations in which we are debating whether each particular defendant should be entitled to argue to each jury that his failure to know the law he is charged with violating was nonnegligent. What is at stake here is the legitimacy of conclusive presumptions about what a reasonable person should know (rather than presumptions about what the particular defendant knew). If one believes—as seems pretty obvious to me—that the legislature is entitled to define a belief as reasonable only if it is statistically commonplace, it seems unexceptionable to assert that *anyone* who doesn't know that kidnapping or failing to file a tax return is against the law has believed unreasonably. There is simply no real issue of fact for a fact finder to resolve if asked to find whether the defendant in the courtroom was negligent if he was unaware of the

---

7. These points have been, in my view, the most consistently misconstrued in responses to the original piece.

obligation to file an income tax return (why should a jury know more than the legislature about what is statistically commonplace? why should the issue be resolved differently in different trials?); there is merely room for jury confusion (or misconduct).

Now, of course, the conclusive presumption that all reasonable people are aware of the existence of the particular offense at issue in a given trial *breaks down* in some cases; my point was that using strict liability is far harder to defend in such cases. In each case, we must assess the virtues of the rule against the perils of overinclusiveness, weighing in whatever fashion we would like the risk of convicting someone who was not especially careless (though he might have been more careful still) against the risk of unpatterned and biased acquittals.

The question arises, though, whether this conclusive presumption of negligence is ever appropriate when a person is not negligent merely because he fails to know something that is generally known but because he causes some harm or engages in conduct thought to cause harm. Imagine three distinct ways that a fact finder might use to infer that a liquor license holder has been "unreasonably careless" in purveying liquor to minors.

First, we could direct the fact finder simply to look at the license holder's efforts to avoid illicit sales and judge (without further guidance) whether the efforts are "reasonable." (This is the ordinary negligence *standard*.) Second, we could decide that the license holder's efforts are reasonable only if he has followed some pre-prescribed methods (e.g., checking photo IDs, hiring minors to try to entrap his employees a certain number of times per month, etc.). (This could either be thought of as a predefined, rule-like negligence standard or, as Kenneth Simons says, as enacting a form of strict liability.[8] Failing to check a photo ID, for instance, is at core, then, an attendant circumstance; the conduct element is selling to the minor. But one need not be even negligent as to either the conduct element or the attendant circumstance). Third, and finally, we might tell the fact finder to presume, conclusively, that if the license holder has been caught selling to minors ten times in a month (in a world in which the average number of such illicit sales in an establishment doing the same volume of business is, say, one per year), he will be criminally accountable for the sales, without permitting him to offer any particularized proof that he was just plain unlucky. (This is one version of strict liability).

I continue to believe that there must be *some* (atypically high) number of sales that would make the mandatory inference that the actor is careless rather than unlucky more sensible than allowing fact finders to evaluate the defendant's testimony (with prosecutorial pushback) that he did all a reasonable person should be expected to do, given the problems associated with allowing jurors to make

---

8. Kenneth W. Simons, *When Is Strict Criminal Liability Just?*, 87 J. CRIM. L. & CRIMINOLOGY 1075, 1131 (1997).

such unguided judgments. It might also be more sensible than having some set of (poor-fitting) bureaucratic rules about what one should do to avoid such sales, rules that will inevitably impose needless costs on a subset of purveyors and do too little to avoid problems for some other subset. It might be more sensible to target a particular "output" (a certain maximum number of "violations") than to mandate a detailed code of behavior or to allow people to do whatever they want so long as they can convince relatively unguided fact finders that they did all that could be expected of them.

Of course, it might be *less* sensible, too (particularly if the output target is one that a careful person might be unlucky enough to hit). And *of course* it would seem less sensible if one worries more (than I think anyone has ever satisfactorily defended) about stripping jurors of the power to exercise judgment (rather than simply to find delimited facts) and less sensible if one is more worried about convicting someone who took what reflective people would think of as adequate steps to avoid harm or harmful conduct. But the basic point seems so obvious to me that I persist in thinking that the resistance to it (and constant misinterpretations *of it*) must reflect the problems of interpretive construction (i.e., unduly narrow time framing and failure to see the pervasiveness of the rules-standard problem).

Can the number ever be *one* though? Think about mistakes of victim age in the statutory rape cases. Will a defendant who is as careful as the legislature might want him to be *ever* make a reasonable mistake of age about the age of someone he has sex with (at least in the absence of a pretty elaborate conspiracy to dupe him that DAs exercising discretion to refuse to prosecute outlier cases or jurors exercising nullification powers should arguably attend to)? Legislators not especially moved by the urgency of hook-up sex might sensibly believe that defendants have lots of time and opportunity to check a variety of sources of information about the age of someone he will have sex with. At the same time, (some subset of) jurors will likely believe that asking or deciding the young woman "looked" pretty old is reasonable effort enough, if simply asked to judge whether the defendant is negligent.

Again, we must judge how bad *that* would be (and whether it can be adequately constrained through jury instructions). We must judge how reliable alternative discretion mechanisms are, and how often they would need to be exercised. We must judge how bad it would be if they were not exercised and someone we really thought had been as careful as we want anyone to be to avoid the harmful conduct was nonetheless convicted (given the inevitable presence of some number of wrongful convictions for other reasons).

VI. A VERY BRIEF CONCLUSION

I originally argued that we would see any number of traditional doctrinal puzzles differently if we saw that we had made problems "disappear" through interpretive construction. I hoped at the time, for instance, that the work would help us rethink most of attempt law: Drawing the preparation/attempt line requires resolution of the rules/standards dilemma; thinking about abandonment implicates both issues of defining the breadth of the objects of intention and thinking about the intentionalism/determinism line; thinking about impossibility requires us to worry about the breadth of objects of intention. I also offered substantial treatments of other issues: accomplice liability, nonmerger doctrine in conspiracy, provocation, and imperfect self-defense, for example. I suspect some of the discussions of the particular issues have had some influence on subsequent discourse, but I am dubious that many think they have derived much insight from the application of the general method (or could derive insights about some new set of issues using the same method), except to the degree that they have come to think "time framing" is important and that issues of legal form are more omnipresent than we typically acknowledge.

COMMENTS

UNEXPLAINED, FALSE ASSUMPTIONS UNDERLIE KELMAN'S SKEPTICISM

PAUL LITTON*

Mark Kelman argues that the criminal law is based on contradictory premises that render legal conclusions arational. However, it is Kelman's skepticism about the law's coherence that rests on unexplained, false assumptions about responsibility and control.

Kelman argues that we can simultaneously attribute conduct to an actor's freely willed choice (and thus hold him responsible) and to deterministic forces that "put him in the position of apparent choicelessness"[1] (and thus excuse him). Thus, he assumes that we excuse when we view conduct as causally determined. In his view, responsibility and determinism are incompatible.

Kelman does not argue for this supposed incompatibility. Understandably, he might not want to enter the centuries-old fray over this philosophical issue; nonetheless, Kelman should not simply assume their incompatibility given its central role in his argument. Indeed, Kelman must make a further argument as to their incompatibility because the comments he does make about responsibility are implausible. That prior events caused me to be in my current situation does not imply that I am "choiceless." Even if determinism is true, there is an identifiable difference between actions that I choose and what just happens to me.

---

* Associate Professor of Law, University of Missouri School of Law.
1. *See* Kelman core text at 209.

If prior causes render apparent choices illusory, then Kelman should clarify what "real" choices are and provide reason to think responsibility requires them.

To show the arationality of law based, in part, on incompatibilism, Kelman must show why compatibilism is unpersuasive. Actually, he must also show why incompatibilist views, including libertarianism, are also helplessly unpersuasive. After all, if hard determinism is true, such that no one is ever responsible for what he does or chooses, then the criminal law is *irrational*, not arational, to the extent it is retributive or otherwise based on a nonconsequentialist justification that presupposes the responsibility that hard determinism denies.

Kelman does respond to compatibilism. He states, "[M]ost persuasive theories of retributive blame are sensitive to whether defendants have more or less capacity to control their behavior, not merely to whether they possess some threshold degree of rational agency."[2] But as with his use of "choicelessness," Kelman uses "control" mysteriously, divorcing that concept from practical reasoning. Reason-responsive compatibilists offer an explanation of the kind of control required for blameworthiness. If Kelman's conclusions rest on their supposed failure, then what is his more plausible conception of "control"?

That responsibility rests on our reasoning capacities and what our actions express about our reasoning processes is tied to an essential feature of the criminal law: with minimal exception, we punish only those who acted on or culpably ignored particular reasons. That fact explains why there is no time-framing tension between *Decina* and *Martin*. Our inquiry into events before Decina got into his car is not arational: we assess whether he acted *culpably* at any point. He was *reckless* because he knew he was subject to seizures and ignored the substantial risk he imposed on others. In contrast, *Martin* narrowly focused on the moment police dragged him outside because at no prior time had Martin acted with the mens rea required for conviction. His voluntary drinking posed some risk of appearing drunk in public; but, most likely, the court did not think he *culpably* ignored that risk, considering both the odds of appearing drunk and the seriousness of doing so.

Kelman is not persuaded that Decina's risk-taking was culpable while Martin's was not. He states, "[T]he probability of an epileptic seizure is almost certainly far lower than the probability of ending up in public after engaging in behavior likely to draw police attention."[3] But to assess whether someone's act posed a substantial and unjustified risk, we consider *both* the potential harm's likelihood of actualizing and its seriousness. Decina violated a duty because the risk he posed was far more serious than the risk Martin posed of appearing drunk in public. Kelman responds that the varying seriousness of the harms risked by Martin and Decina, respectively, is already reflected by the different penalties

---

2. *Id.* at 207.
3. *Id.* at 213.

accompanying the relevant crimes. But so what? Their seriousness is also relevant to assessing whether each defendant knew or should have known he was taking a substantial and unjustifiable risk.

Furthermore, laws that punish someone for exposing himself after involuntarily appearing in public or a prison inmate for possessing weapons after becoming incarcerated do not illustrate any framing tension or conflict with *Martin*. The drunkard's opportunity to avoid his offense is not diminished because his public boisterousness was "partially determined." His opportunity is inadequate because inebriation interferes with practical reasoning. If he was not culpable for voluntarily drinking in his home, then it is unfair to punish him for public boisterousness if he is dragged into public in his impaired state. In contrast, though the inmate is in prison against his choice, he has adequate reasoning capacities to refuse to possess weapons, assuming he functions normally. We see here that the alleged intentionalism-determinism and time-framing tensions that Kelman diagnoses are related. However, Kelman fails to show that they exist and render the law arational.

UNCONSCIOUS CHOICES IN LEGAL ANALYSIS

JOHN MIKHAIL[*]

Mark Kelman has a knack for being ahead of the curve. Consider *Consumption Theory, Production Theory, and Ideology in the Coase Theorem*,[1] which captured many of the principal insights of behavioral economics two decades before it emerged as a major presence in legal scholarship. *Interpretive Construction in the Substantive Criminal Law*[2] falls into this category as well. It turns on a set of penetrating observations about standard legal analysis that have not yet been fully absorbed by legal scholars, although they are widely recognized in the cognitive sciences and seem likely to exert a growing influence on legal scholarship in the years ahead.

Kelman's key observation is that the fact patterns that comprise the raw material of standard legal analysis are insufficient by themselves to fix the properties of the mental representations that standard legal analysis presupposes. Rather, these mental constructs are always logically underdetermined. As a result, certain optional *choices* must be made at the front end of the interpretive process before conventional legal reasoning even gets off the ground. These choices are

---

* Associate Professor of Law, Georgetown University Law Center.

1. Mark Kelman, *Consumption Theory, Production Theory, and Ideology in the Coase Theorem*, 52 S. CAL. L. REV. 669 (1978).

2. Mark Kelman, *Interpretive Construction in the Substantive Criminal Law*, 33 STAN. L. REV. 591 (1981).

largely unconscious and rarely subjected to critical scrutiny. Yet they often drive the subsequent doctrinal or policy analysis, so much so that they are frequently outcome-determinative. Moreover, these unconscious choices are not rationally defensible. On the contrary, they are essentially arbitrary. They are also potentially pernicious, insofar as they tend to obscure what is actually at stake and to make difficult theoretical and policy decisions seem easy. It is comforting to think of criminal adjudication as simply a matter of balancing interests or applying preexisting legal rules to facts. Kelman makes a persuasive case that this simple picture is largely a mirage.

I tend to agree, therefore, with one main thrust of Kelman's argument: concepts like voluntary act and proximate cause are interpretive constructs that are imposed on cases like *Martin* and *Decina* in order to render them in a legally cognizable form, to which conventional legal reasoning can then be applied. Why does Martin's public appearance seem involuntary to most judges and commentators? Presumably because they intuitively decide that the police officers are intervening agents who "break the causal chain" between any prior voluntary act and his subsequent appearance in public. No comparable intervention occurs in *Decina*. Reconciling the cases seems easy, therefore, if one adopts this traditional form of legal analysis.[3]

But are these interpretive constructions themselves rationally defensible? This is Kelman's deeper concern, and it clearly poses a much trickier issue. Much depends on what is meant by "rationally defensible" in this context. Here is where cognitive science may offer a useful perspective, for the basic mental phenomena at issue are by no means specific to legal analysis. Rather, they appear in virtually every area of human cognition, including vision, language, causal judgment, and moral reasoning. In visual processing, for example, we know that accurate perception is nondeductive and cannot depend only on the incoming information, due to an underdetermination problem that is functionally similar to the one Kelman identifies. Hence successful perception is possible only because of the operation of internal processing constraints, such as coincidence avoidance, Bayesian inference, and the like. These, too, are unconscious choices that the brain makes to rule out certain logically possible perceptions.[4]

In the case of vision, of course, the relevant "choices" are not really choices at all; rather, they are automatic and essentially mandatory for creatures like us. Nor are they rational in any ordinary sense. Still, they are an intelligent solution to a difficult information-processing problem, given the poverty of the perceptual stimulus and the mental equipment that we do in fact possess.

---

3. *Cf.* Michael S. Moore, ACT AND CRIME 35–37 (1993).

4. *See, e.g.,* Brian Scholl, *Innateness and (Bayesian) Visual Perception, in* THE INNATE MIND: STRUCTURE AND CONTENTS 34–52 (Peter Carruthers, Stephen Laurence, and Stephen Stich eds., 2005).

For legal theory, the critical question is whether the unconscious inferences that Kelman correctly insists must occur at the front end of the interpretative process possess similar properties. Are these inferences under our deliberate control, or are they basically mandatory? To what extent are they informationally encapsulated? Kelman's original article tends to view the residual conceptualism of standard legal analysis through the lens of critical theory, but my guess is that he would agree that evolutionary psychology probably supplies a more useful analytical framework at this juncture, despite its misuse by some theorists. Still, the same normative concerns that drive his original article can be pressed anew in this context, and perhaps are even strengthened when viewed in this light. Why should we allow legal policy analysis to be guided by nonrational modes of cognition that we inherited from our primate ancestors?

INTERPRETIVE CONSTRUCTIONS AND THE EXERCISE OF BIAS

MARGARET RAYMOND*

Mark Kelman's core text provides a useful way to think about a range of perplexing problems in the criminal law. By considering this issue as a problem of criminal theory, however, he treats it more dispassionately than is warranted. In his view, the unconscious choice of interpretive constructs reflects a failure to wrestle adequately with theoretical difficulties, like the balance between determinism and intentionality, or the benefits of the clarity of rules versus the justice of flexible standards. His case study of the problem of voluntariness suggests that addressing these theoretical problems might generate more nuanced, legitimate doctrine. But the interpretive constructions he identifies sometimes conceal not simply a resistance to complex theory, but the opportunity for the exercise of bias.

Consider an example from the law of self-defense, which inevitably presents framing problems. In evaluating a claim of self-defense, should we look back at the actor's prior behavior—in Kelman's terms, expanding the time frame, or unifying what might otherwise be disjointed accounts of unrelated events—to ask whether the person could have avoided the lethal threat he faced? The answer, as it turns out, is "sometimes." And the decision to consider the broader time frame (or not) is not driven by some unvoiced theoretical assumptions; instead, it may reflect a biased assessment about the rights of the actors in the controversy.[1]

---

* Professor of Law, University of Iowa College of Law.

1. I discuss the issues raised in this comment more fully in Margaret Raymond, *Looking for Trouble: Framing and Perceptions of Necessity in the Law of Self-Defense* (Nov. 25, 2008) (unpublished manuscript, on file with author).

Imagine that Joe, the neighborhood bully, tells Frank that he should stay away from the local tavern and that if Frank comes to the tavern, Joe will harm Frank. If Frank goes to the tavern, is set upon by Joe, and responds with lethal force, is Frank entitled to claim self-defense? In this situation, the choice of frame is likely to be outcome-determinative.

In a series of cases with a distinct flavor of the frontier (hence the "O.K. Corral" tone of the hypothetical), courts clearly stated that, in assessing claims of self-defense, the frame should not be expanded to consider an actor's prior opportunity to avoid the lethal encounter. One lawfully minding his own business need not alter his behavior—even in the face of the aggression of another—to be entitled to claim self-defense. "[A] person knowing his life to be threatened . . . is not obliged to remain at home in order to avoid an assault, but may arm himself sufficiently to repel anticipated attack, and pursue his legitimate avocation; and if without fault, he is compelled to take life to save himself . . . the homicide is excusable."[2] The refusal to widen the frame reflected an expansive view of the right of the actor as empowered and entitled.

Contrast these cases with *Laney v. United States*.[3] Laney, a Black man, found himself on the street in Washington, D.C., pursued by a large, violent White mob shouting racist epithets and threats. Fearful for his life, Laney pulled out a gun, which caused the mob to disperse, and ducked into an alley. Believing that the danger was past, Laney returned to the street. The mob resumed its pursuit of Laney, and fired at him. He returned fire, shooting and killing a member of the mob.

The appellate court rejected Laney's claim of self-defense as a matter of law based on its analysis of the framing problem. In the court's view, Laney was required to do "everything in his power, consistent with his safety, to avoid the danger and avoid the necessity of taking life."[4] Because, after his initial encounter with the mob, Laney stepped back into the street even though "he knew his presence there would cause trouble,"[5] he was not entitled to use lethal force. The court implicitly rejected the principles of autonomy and empowerment that drove the frontier cases; its selection of frame definitively determined the issue of justification.

The choice of frame in these cases reflects troubling and significant instances of bias. The outcomes reflect the decision-makers' views of who in society was privileged to travel freely about the streets, and who was required to subordinate his lawful rights to the authority of the mob.

This brings the question back to Kelman. Recognizing the ubiquity of the interpretive constructions he identifies, how should we deal with them if we

---

2. *State v. Gardner*, 104 N.W. 971, 975 (Minn. 1905).

3. 294 F. 412 (D.C. App. 1923).

4. *Id.* at 414.

5. *Id.* at 415.

conclude that they are subject to conscious manipulation in the service of wrongful ends? Ultimately, our recognition of these constructions should be a first step in advancing the just and equitable application of the criminal law.

INTERPRETIVE CONSTRUCTION AND DEFENSIVE PUNISHMENT THEORY

ALICE RISTROPH*

I think it relatively clear that legal analysis, especially in criminal law, involves the sorts of interpretive construction that Mark Kelman identifies. Less clear to me is what it means to say that such interpretive constructions are not "rationally defensible." Attack these interpretive constructions—say, those at work in *Martin v. State* and *People v. Decina*—and someone will usually rush to defend them. Without delving too far into the murky question of the criteria for rational defensibility, I would suggest this much: we engage in interpretive construction, and most of the time we do so unconsciously. But once these constructions are pointed out to us, we can usually give reasons for the ways we have constructed facts in a particular case. Far more difficult, if not impossible, is to prove that a given construction was dictated by reason—that it was not a "mere" construction, but a necessary one. The power of Kelman's insight derives not from the fact that interpretive constructions are indefensible, but from the fact that they are all too defensible—and so, never falsifiable.

To make these claims more concrete, consider the interpretive constructions that shape the assessment of an actor's mental state. Such assessments are often outcome-determinative in the criminal law and elsewhere. "Even a dog distinguishes between being stumbled over and being kicked,"[1] said Oliver Wendell Holmes, Jr., and commentators invoke him to suggest slyly the animal stupidity of anyone who doubts the importance of intentions. The dog's crisp distinction turns mushy under relatively little pressure, as revealed by a quick survey of discussions of the differences between intent and motive, the relative virtues of objective and subjective tests, and the evidentiary challenges of proving mental states. Whether one has been kicked or stumbled over—and which is worse—is probably answerable only after a number of interpretive constructions are in place.

That, it seems, is the point of Kelman's discussion of *Martin* and *Decina*. Emil Decina is punished because his automobile accident is judged more kick than stumble: by choosing to drive while aware of his own history of seizures, Decina

---

* Associate Professor, Seton Hall University School of Law.
1. Oliver Wendell Holmes, Jr., THE COMMON LAW 3 (1881).

chose to risk the lives of others. But the same sort of argument could have been made to punish Cephus Martin: by choosing to drink and to engage in arrest-worthy behavior at home, Martin chose to risk that his loud and profane language would reach the delicate ears of the public. Alternatively, courts could have held that *neither* man was punishable. Martin's objectionable conduct—a public drunken appearance—occurs only after, and because, his will has been overborne by arresting officers. Decina's harmful conduct, if it can be called conduct at all, occurs only after and because his will has been rendered useless by an epileptic seizure. Which of these constructions prevails may turn on instincts, dispositions to dispense harm or mercy, or (as was probably the case in *Decina*) the emotional impact of children's deaths. Bias may produce the prevailing construction. It may just be random. But whatever construction prevails, it will rarely be indefensible. They are *all* defensible.

Either a claim that interpretive constructions are never rationally defensible, or a claim that contradictory constructions are all rationally defensible, leads to a familiar charge of legal indeterminacy. Nonetheless, I think it important to emphasize here the difference between claims that are not defensible and those that are not falsifiable. Interpretive constructions in the criminal law often determine whether a defendant will be punished or not. The defensibility of interpretive constructions helps sustain faith in punishment even as the *over*defensibility of those constructions sustains skepticism.

Justifying punishment is a matter of giving reasons for it, and to note that interpretive constructions are defensible is to acknowledge that punishers will usually be able to give reasons for what they do. Defending punishment is not the hard part. The hard part is to show that only the choices of the punished, and not the nonfalsifiable constructions of the punisher, have produced the penalty. Punishment theory—at least, retributive theory—writes a message from the punisher to the punished: "You, and not I, are responsible for this punishment. I do only what justice requires. Once you committed your crime, it could not be otherwise." It is important to show that in many cases—as in *Martin* and *Decina*—it could have been otherwise. The interpretive construction that determines the outcome will often be defensible, but it will rarely be the only defensible construction. The plurality of defensible outcomes reminds us of the agency of the punisher; it is a critical reminder to those who think they can punish innocently.

REPLY

MARK KELMAN

Paul Litton makes some "big" arguments but also makes "smaller" ones (echoed in Raymond) about the compatibility of *Martin* and *Decina*. Alas, they seem to me to be based on a confusion: *Martin* is about actus reus (voluntary conduct), not mens rea (whether the voluntary conduct was culpable). This is not merely a formalist point for four reasons: (1) First, the court makes no reference to whether Martin was reckless as to a public appearance in doing whatever made him arrest-worthy; Litton's simply imagining an opinion that was never written. (2) Second, the distinction matters in terms of institutional competence: An appeals court would surely not think it reversible error if a fact finder had found the risk of involuntary appearance was one that Martin was aware of and was unduly substantial and unjustifiable. (3) Third, and closely related, the question of whether Martin is reckless (which I clearly indicated in the piece was indeed an additional question) is by no means easy. Of course, risking violating the public drunkenness law may be relatively inconsequential, but the conduct risking that (e.g., domestic violence) is of so little value that almost all risks of further harms (e.g., appearing in public drunk) might be *unduly* high, and second, the probability of the public appearance (conditional on what the arrest-worthy behavior was) might be extraordinarily high. (4) Fourth, conceptually, it seems to me that Litton should care (far more than I do) whether Martin is accurately described as a nonactor (in his words, something to whom something happened) rather than a nonculpable actor (someone who had the capacity to exercise practical reason and chose to exercise it in a fashion that we ultimately decide is not culpable).

Similarly, John Mikhail's "little" point on causation in *Martin* seems unavailing: Intervening actors who are duty-bound to act as they do (as police are duty-bound to remove an abuser from the home) are not causal interveners. If Mikhail thinks that conventional outcome is indefensible, he should explain why.

Are the "interpretive constructs" conscious or unconscious? Margaret Raymond identifies some self-defense cases (that are by no means atypical) in which it seems likely that those making the decisions understood they were picking one of many available "time frames." And I agree with Alice Ristroph that even if lawyers constructed a case without being aware that it might have been constructed differently, they will be able to rationalize either the construction or the outcome it led to if the alternative frame either spontaneously comes to consciousness or is raised by another, but doing so will have the impact she suggests—an increase in the sense of punishers' agency.

But what (inevitably weak) clues might one have that the judges in *Martin* were clueless (about the time frame problem or the conduct requirement of boisterousness)? Well, there is nothing in the opinion that suggests that they see this as a hard case, no reference to alternative constructions. But, of course, it is possible that the judges recognized that a more nuanced opinion would be a murky mess, not that they didn't see how tricky the case was.

I agree with Litton (the "big" point) that I ignore the literature that (arguably) sets out the minimal necessary conditions that trigger blame (either as a mandatory response or a limiting condition on the distribution of punishment). My response would have to be a lot "bigger," too, I suppose, but the reason I've never given the response is because I find the literature advancing these claims so empty at two critical stages that I never know what to address. First, the accounts of the purported mental functioning/capacities of the actors (e.g., the pictures of what practical reasoners do and don't do) seem devoid of tractable cognitive psychological content. Second, the neo-Kantian accounts of our duties to blame seem self-referential and vacuous. It is reasonably easy to see how (in theory, though the empirics are woefully inadequate) an incapacitationist would assess whether acts taken responsive to certain atypical situational pressures ought to be punished (it is all about how likely the situation is to recur or how we infer the defendant will act under some other recurring circumstances), and it is easy to defend the general practice of incapacitation (even if it is not one's preferred punishment rationale.). Both consequentialist and nonconsequentialist explanations for maintaining the general practice of punishing nonconsequentially are infinitely harder to pin down.

The most interesting issues in my mind are raised by Mikhail's response. Is it best to think of the "constructs" not as dictated solely by the "events" in the external world but by the interaction of human cognitive capacities and that world? (An object is invisible in this sense, given the interaction between our perception capacities and its size.) I am finishing a book on the issue now, but suffice it to say, I am skeptical of the sort of massively modularized views of the mind that would make it most plausible that the "constructs" emerged (directly? by analogy? and how does a modularized brain assign novel situations to the apt module?) out of evolutionary pressure in the way many features of perception might have. (This is suggested, in part, by the nonuniversality of the construct responses, in the same way, I think that Mikhail's accounts of universal moral grammar are often belied by the extraordinary divergence of responses by his subjects to the more nuanced Trolley problems). I am also skeptical of accounts of cognition that rely heavily on encapsulation (inability to account for additional cues) that Mikhail's view requires: we seem able to readily rethink issues initially constructed in a particular way. But I think Mikhail is right to suggest that our accounts of what is "rational" often need to be more sensitive to what meets our proximal needs (and "limited" evolved cognitive capacities may meet proximal needs) rather than what is "formally" rational (either in an economist's or logician's sense).

11. CRIMINALIZATION AND SHARING WRONGS

S.E. MARSHALL AND R.A. DUFF[*]

I. INDIVIDUAL AND PUBLIC GOODS

Our concern is with the familiar but still inadequately understood idea that what distinguishes crimes from other kinds of conduct that should not concern the criminal law is that crimes are "public" wrongs. Many crimes, including paradigmatic *mala in se* crimes, are typically directed against individuals rather than against the "public": in what sense, then, are they "public" wrongs?

One answer is that they are public wrongs in the sense that the state should protect certain important individual rights, most obviously those infringed by familiar *mala in se* crimes—rights to life, liberty, and property, for instance. Such a perspective, although it focuses on individual rights and goods, makes room for some "public" goods that the criminal law protects: by punishing attacks on individual *Rechtsgüter*,[1] it assures all citizens that such wrongs will not go unpunished, thus fostering collective security; and crimes of "abstract endangerment" (drunken driving, for instance), protect collective interests in public safety. However, such goods are not, as so far understood, irreducibly public: they may be understood simply as aggregates of individual goods, whose protection is still the criminal law's basic aim.

One objection to this perspective is that it does not show why attacks on individual *Rechtsgüter* should be a matter for criminal rather than civil law.[2] If the wrong done by such crimes as rape or theft is essentially done to the individual victim, why should the state "steal" this "conflict,"[3] by making it a matter of criminal law: why should it not be for the victim to seek redress by bringing a civil case? The state should no doubt provide public assistance for those who wish to pursue such cases, and cases in which there is no individual victim who could bring a suit might need to be pursued by a public authority: but why should

---

* Professors, Department of Philosophy, University of Stirling. This paper is drawn from our *Criminalization and Sharing Wrongs*, 11 CAN. J.L. & JURIS. 7 (1998).

1. The idea of *Rechtsgüter*, significant interests that merit the law's protection, has been central to German discussions of the proper aims and scope of the criminal law. *See* Claus Roxin, STRAFRECHT ALLGEMEINER TEIL i, 8–47 (4th ed., 2006). For critical discussion, see DIE RECHTSGUTSTHEORIE (Wolfgang Wohlers, Andrew von Hirsch and Roland Hefendehl eds., 2003).

2. Another objection is that it cannot do justice to the idea of genuinely collective goods, which are irreducible to aggregates of individual goods. We cannot discuss this objection here.

3. Nils Christie, *Conflicts as Property*, 17 BRIT. J. CRIMINOLOGY 1 (1977).

the default position not be that it is for those directly victimized by the wrongdoing to bring a civil case against the wrongdoer? If we then insist instead that the criminal law must be concerned with genuinely public, or collective, goods, rather than the individual goods and rights on which a *Rechtsgüter* account focuses, we can explain why the protection of such goods should be a matter for the state rather than for individual citizens: but we might then be accused of ignoring, and thus denigrating, the wrongs done to the individual victims of such actions.

Some accounts of "crimes" as "public" wrongs do invite such a criticism: if it is said, for instance, that attacks on individual *Rechtsgüter* should be criminal if and because they cause "social volatility"[4] or because such attackers must be punished in order to incapacitate them from further such attacks or to deter other potential attackers; or because the attacker takes an unfair advantage over all law-abiding citizens. Such accounts do seem to subordinate the individual victim (a concern for their good, or for the wrong done to them) to some supposedly larger social good. The offender's conduct is criminalized, and he is punished, for the sake of that larger good: to which it is appropriate to object that his conduct should be criminalized because of, and he should be punished for, the wrong he does to the individual victim. We do not criminalize rape, and punish rapists, because rape causes social volatility; or because the rapist takes an unfair advantage over his law-abiding fellow citizens: but because of the nature of the wrong that the rapist does to his victims.

We will offer a more plausible account of the idea that crimes should be "public" wrongs, which shows why attacks on individual *Rechtsgüter* should concern the criminal law, as attacks on a common good, without thereby ignoring or denigrating the wrong done to the individual victim. First, however, we must clarify the idea of criminalization.

II. CRIME AND THE CRIMINAL PROCESS

It is worth distinguishing several different aspects of the concept of crime—in part to remind ourselves that criminalization is not a single, simple process.

First, crime involves socially proscribed wrongdoing. Crime is not just conduct that is inconsistent with values held by other members of the community: we may disapprove of many kinds of conduct, without thinking that we have the right or standing, to declare that others ought not to engage in them; for, we may think, they are private matters that are not our collective business. The criminal law, by contrast, is concerned with wrongs that are public in the

---

4. Lawrence Becker, *Criminal Attempts and the Theory of the Law of Crimes*, 3 PHIL. & PUB. AFF. 262 (1974).

sense that they violate norms that claim authority over all members of the community whose law it is—norms that the law itself declares as public norms.[5]

Second, insofar as crime involves wrongdoing, it also involves a wrongdoer— someone who does the wrong and can be held responsible for it. The wrongdoer need not be an individual: we can see corporations, for instance, as agents. But a crime requires a criminal agent, who is (and can be held) responsible for it: who can properly be called, by the community, to answer for that wrong. Crimes are not just undesirable occurrences that a community might wish to prevent; nor are they just "conflicts" that must be resolved. To believe that we should have a criminal law is, therefore, at least to believe that there are some kinds of conduct that the community should declare authoritatively to be wrong; and that they are kinds of wrongful conduct whose agents can properly be held responsible for them.

But how should the community respond to breaches of such norms? That there should be some response follows from the nature of crime as a breach of an authoritative community norm: if we take such norms seriously, we must be ready to respond to breaches of them. Two questions now arise. One focuses on outcomes: should the wrongdoer be liable to censure; to pay compensation to those he has wronged; to punishment? The other focuses on processes: by what kinds of process should such outcomes be determined? This raises the issue of "criminal" as against "civil" processes. Here we focus on the question of who controls the process—the individual victim, or the community.

A "civil" model puts the victim in charge. She, as the complainant, initiates the proceedings against the person who (allegedly) wronged her; it is for her to carry the case through, or to drop it. This is not to say that the community has no role. It declared those norms to which she appeals in claiming that she was wronged; it provides the institutional structure through which her case is decided, the arbitrator or judge who assists in resolving the case or produces an authoritative decision, and enforcement mechanisms to ensure compliance with the decision; it could provide resources to assist the complainant in pursuing her case. But she is still in charge: she decides whether the case is brought and pursued, and whether the decision is enforced; she has no duty to bring a case, and the reasons why she might decide not to pursue it could be quite arbitrary.

A "criminal" model puts the community (the state) in charge. The case is investigated by the police; the charge is brought by Regina, the People or the State; whether it is brought, and how far it proceeds, is up to the prosecuting authority; it is not for the victim to decide whether any decision it produces is enforced. In practice, wrongdoing might be investigated only if the victim first complains to the police, and a charge might be brought and the case pursued

---

5. This covers both mala in se and mala prohibita. *See* R.A. Duff, ANSWERING FOR CRIME chs. 4.4, 7.3 (2007).

only if she is willing that it should be. But the case is still not hers: the community takes it over, and may pursue it or drop it against her will. So there are two aspects to the criminal model. On the one hand, the victim receives more support from the community than she might under the civil model: she is not left to bring the case by herself. But, on the other hand, she loses control of it: it is no longer hers to pursue or not as she see fit.

The question of what kinds of outcome the process might lead to is, to a degree, distinct from that of who controls it. A "civil" process could lead to censure as well as compensation; it can also lead to (a kind of) punishment, insofar as it allows for the award of explicitly "punitive" damages. A "criminal" process need not lead to "punishment," insofar as that is something distinct from censure and compensation. It does seem natural that a "civil" process should lead to victim-directed compensation rather than to punishment. Insofar as punishment is rationalized as a matter of deterrence, incapacitation, reform, or rehabilitation; insofar as it is imposed for the sake of (as well as in the name of) the community: the victim might reasonably argue that it should not be up to her to bring the case to achieve goods for the community—it should be up to the community to pursue such goods. But it is not, we think, so "natural" that a criminal process must lead to punishment: whether it should depends on our understanding of punishment, and on why we think that the "criminal" process is appropriate for certain kinds of cases.

That a response to socially prescribed wrongdoing should involve censure seems obvious enough. We owe it to the victim to take seriously the wrong she has suffered, as a wrong; we also owe it to the wrongdoer, as a fellow member of the community to respond honestly and seriously to her wrongdoing. But even if it is appropriate that, given the social character and the seriousness of the norms she has breached, such censure should be administered through a formal process, this is not yet to say either that it must be administered through a "criminal" process, or that it should be expressed by punishment.

That victims who are harmed by wrongdoing should when possible receive compensation may also seem obvious enough, when the compensation can be genuinely reparative or restorative—although this leaves open, to some degree, the questions of what kinds of wrong can be compensated; of what modes of compensation are appropriate to what kinds of wrong; and of whether that compensation should be paid, either directly or indirectly, by the wrongdoer. But compensation can be the outcome of a "criminal" as well as of a "civil" process; and punishment is distinct from compensation, since as well as expressing censure, it is designedly onerous or painful (whereas compensation is only contingently onerous).

The final, but separable, implication of criminalization is thus that crimes are punished: to ask what kinds of conduct should be criminalized is to ask, in part, what kinds of conduct should attract punishment rather than merely formal censure or liability to pay compensation.

It might be tempting to take the question of punishment as the central question about criminalization: to suppose that the essential distinction between criminal and merely civil wrongs is that the former attract punishment, and that to ask what kinds of conduct should be criminalized is thus to ask what kinds of conduct should be visited with punishment. But this would be a mistake.

To hold that a certain kind of conduct should be criminalized is to hold at least some of the following: that it should be proscribed and condemned by a socially authoritative norm, as a type of wrongdoing for which we can identify a responsible, culpable agent; that it thus merits the censure of the community; that it is appropriately responded to or dealt with by a "criminal" rather than a "civil" process; that it should render the agent liable to punishment rather than to merely formal censure or a duty to compensate.

But while to hold that a certain kind of conduct should be criminalized by our existing legal systems is in effect to make all these claims about it, part of our point in separating these aspects of the concept of crime is to show that one could make some of these claims without making them all. Our aim has also been to show that the different aspects of the concept raise different questions. We need to ask what kinds of conduct merit social proscription; a "criminal" process; punishment—and we cannot suppose in advance either that the answers to these questions will be just the same, or that the considerations relevant to answering each of them will be just the same.

We will argue that by asking why certain kinds of conduct should be dealt with by a "criminal" rather than by a "civil" process, we can see why some notion of the "common" or "public" good is crucial to the criminalization even of attacks on individual *Rechtsgüter*.

III. SHARING WRONGS

Consider rape as an example. Why should rape be a crime? We can agree that it should be socially proscribed and condemned. It is not a "private" matter in which the community has no proper interest, nor is the rape victim simply involved in a "conflict" with her attacker, which they must "negotiate" and resolve: leaving aside problem cases on the borderlines of rape, we should say that rape is a nonnegotiable wrong that the community should declare to be so. This has to do in part with the seriousness of the harm wrought by rape—both the harm contingently consequent upon rape, and the harm intrinsic to it. It also has to do, we suppose, with the idea that it is not difficult for a "reasonable" man to refrain from rape (indeed, that any "reasonable" man should not need to *refrain* from rape); and that any woman ought to be able confidently to expect not to be thus attacked as she goes about her normal life. To say that rape should be criminal is also to say that rapists are (presumptively) responsible for what they do, and can properly be held answerable, and be censured, for it: whatever we may say about the kinds of social structure and attitude that encourage men to see women as mere sexual objects and may thus be said to encourage rape, this does not negate the individual rapist's responsible, culpable agency.

But why should rape be dealt with by a "criminal" rather than by a "civil" process? Why should rape not be defined simply as a civil wrong, so that it is for the victim to bring a case herself (but only if she wishes) against her attacker? Part of the answer will be that the rapist should be punished, rather than being liable only to pay compensation to his victim—and we must ask why we should think that. But there is more to it than that; and that "more" has to do with the kind of interest the community as a whole should take in such wrongdoing—with, we will argue, the sense in which the community should see the wrong done to her as a wrong done to "us."

Of course even if we envisaged rape as only a civil wrong, there are different possibilities. At one extreme it would be for the victim to find the resources herself to bring and pursue the case: the community provides the structure (the civil court) through which she can do so, declares the norms to which she appeals, and will enforce the decision; but no further help is offered. The first step toward some greater community involvement is then to say that the community should at least also offer her resources (advice, help in identifying her assailant and collecting evidence, legal counsel, etc.) to help her bring the case. If we ask why this should be so, we might refer again to the seriousness of the injury she has suffered. We may also say that there is a stronger case for offering such help to citizens when the wrong or harm they have suffered is not one they should be seen as having voluntarily risked suffering, or one that they should be willing to risk suffering (subject to a right to compensation if it is actualized) as a part of their ordinary lives. That is to say, there are certain kinds of wrongful harm that we should be able to expect, categorically, to be safe from; and if we suffer such a harm we should at least be able to expect the community to help us pursue its perpetrator.

Perhaps it is the categorical nature of this requirement that makes the difference here and points us toward a "criminal," rather than a "civil," process. In a civil case, there is room for the idea of "contributory negligence": the defendant can admit that he caused the harm, culpably, but argue that the plaintiff was also at fault—and should thus bear part of the cost. Now judges have, notoriously, sometimes talked explicitly of, or (more often) appealed implicitly to, a rape victim's "contributory negligence": the rapist's culpability (and so his sentence) is thought to be properly reduced by the fact that his victim put herself in danger, or acted in a way that increased the risk of being raped. It is also clearly true that some kinds of conduct—how she dresses, where she goes, how she behaves—in fact create or increase the risk that a woman will be raped; and friends might tell her that she is stupid to behave like that, or criticize her morally if her conduct is intended to stimulate sexual desire or to encourage the prospects of sexual intercourse in a man with whom she has no intention of having sexual intercourse.

We might analogously criticize householders who "encourage" burglary by leaving their houses obviously insecure, or a car owner who "encourages" theft by leaving valuables in view in an unlocked car. But we do not think that this reduces the culpability of the thief, burglar, or rapist: for we think that people should categorically refrain (and should be able to refrain, even if they are tempted) from such wrongs, even if the victim has in fact made it possible or tempting for them to commit such a wrong.

But there is more to the "criminal" process than this. We still need to ask why the community should not merely offer assistance to a victim who wants to pursue a civil case against her assailant, but also take that case over. Does this amount to "stealing" her "conflict" from her; or are there reasons why the case should become the community's ("ours") rather than just hers? We have noted the inadequacy of some answers to this question: answers that appeal to a "public" good distinct from the victim's own individual good, and that thus fail to do justice to the wrong that she has suffered: that wrong must, surely, be integral to the rationale for criminalizing rape and for subjecting the rapist to a criminal process.

But we can offer a more plausible account of the sense in which rape is a wrong against the community, which does not involve ignoring or denigrating the wrong done to the individual victim. Consider how a group of women might respond to a sexual attack on one of them (or how a self-conscious racial group might respond to a racial attack on one of them). They may see it as a collective, not merely an individual, wrong (as an attack on them), insofar as they associate and identify themselves with the individual victim. For they define themselves as a group, in terms of a certain shared identity, shared values, mutual concern— and shared dangers that threaten them: an attack on a member of the group is thus an attack on the group—on their shared values and their common good. The wrong does not cease to be "her" wrong: but it is also "our" wrong insofar as we identify ourselves with her. The point is not just that we realize that other members of the group are also vulnerable to such attacks, or that we want to warn other potential assailants that they cannot attack members of the group with impunity (although the thought that any of us could be attacked and the desire to defend all members of the group are clearly involved): it is that the attack on this individual victim is itself also an attack on us—on her as a member of the group and on us as fellow members.

A group can in this way "share" the wrongs done to its individual members, insofar as it defines and identifies itself as a community united by mutual concern, by genuinely shared (as distinct from contingently coincident) values and interests, and by the shared recognition that its members' goods (and their identity) are bound up with their membership of the community. Wrongs done to individual members of the community are then wrongs against the whole community—injuries to a common or shared, not merely to an individual, good. This, we suggest, provides an appropriate perspective from which we can understand the point and significance of a "criminal" rather than a "civil" process. For suppose we understand a political society not merely as a collection of discrete and separate individuals bound to each other by an imagined social contract, but as a community in this sense (which is what is implied by the communitarian framework of our argument): suppose, that is, that citizens see (or should see) each other as bound together in a way analogous to the way in which members of the women's group or the racial group mentioned in the previous paragraph see each other as bound together see (even if those bonds may be somewhat less intimate). We can then also see how wrongs against individual citizens can be understood as shared wrongs, as wrongs against the whole community, insofar as the individual goods that are attacked are goods in terms of which the community identifies and understands itself.

We can from this perspective begin to see both why the community should bring the case "on behalf of" the individual victim—rather than leaving her to bring it for herself; and why it might sometimes insist on bringing the case even if she is unwilling to do so. For, just as we may say that we owe it to her to associate ourselves with her in this way (to take her wrong as also our wrong), so we may say that she owes it to us to recognize that the wrong was done to us as well as to her. This is not yet to say that the outcome of the case should be punishment—rather than censure, apology, or compensation to the individual victim; and we noted earlier that to justify a "criminal" rather than "civil" process need not be to justify a punitive outcome of that procedure: but we would also suggest that punishment should be understood in terms of the wrongdoer's relationship to the community as well as to the individual victim.

If this is right, it suggests that crimes (as distinct from civil wrongs) must indeed be portrayed as "public" wrongs, against the community (for if they are not public wrongs, it is not clear why they should be dealt with by a criminal rather than a civil process). But it also shows how wrongs done to individuals, attacks on their *Rechtsgüter*, can be understood as being at the same time, and in virtue of their character as wrongs against individuals, wrongs against the community to which the individual belongs. In making the wrong done to the rape victim "ours," rather than merely "hers"; in thus understanding it as an attack on "our" good, not merely on her individual good: we do not turn our attention away from the wrong that she has suffered, toward some distinct "public" good. Rather, we share in the very wrong that she has suffered: it is not "our" wrong instead of hers; it is "our" wrong because it is a wrong done to her, as one of us—as a fellow member of our community whose identity and whose good is found within that community.

It might be objected that the contents of the individual *Rechtsgüter* that (it seems clear) the criminal law should protect—of such goods as life, liberty, property, and health—resist our attempt to "collectivize" such goods: for the contents of those goods are, surely, irreducibly individual interests. But we do not want to deny that these are the interests, and goods, of individuals; nor do we deny that individuals and their goods and interests are important: quite the reverse. Our argument concerns rather the way in which that "importance" should be understood, if it is to provide one ground for a distinction between "criminal" and "civil" law, and one reason for subjecting certain kinds of wrong to individuals to a "criminal" process; it thus also concerns the way in which we should understand the "individual" in relation to, and as a member of, the larger community.

What we want to resist here is an atomistic moral or political ontology that takes "individuals" and their individual goods as basic—as prior to their place in a community—in favor of a more holistic view of individuals as finding their identities and their goods within their relationships to others; in particular, in the context of discussions of the criminal law, in their relationships with each other as citizens of a political community. Any account of the concept of crime and of the proper scope and aims of the criminal law must, we assume, be informed by a political theory (understood in its broadest sense). The political theory to which we would appeal, and on which the idea of community involved in our argument depends, is some version of the "civic republicanism" sketched by Charles Taylor.

> [T]he bond of solidarity with my compatriots in a functioning republic is based on a sense of shared fate, where the sharing itself is of value. This is what gives this bond its special importance, what makes my ties with these people and so this enterprise particularly binding, what animates my "virtue," or patriotism.[6]

Fellow citizens of such a republic will find their individual goods within that republican community, and will see attacks on the central goods of their fellows as attacks on that community; they will share the wrongs that such attacks involve.

To say this is not, of course, to begin to show just what kinds of conduct ought to be criminalized: but it is to show, we hope, what kinds of question we must ask in asking what kinds of conduct should be criminalized. We must ask, in part, what kinds of wrongs should be seen as wrongs against "us"; and this is to ask which values are (which should be) so central to a community's identity and self-understanding, to its conception of its members' good, that actions that attack or flout those values are not merely individual matters that the individual victim should pursue for herself, but attacks on the community.

The argument of this core text and the paper from which it is drawn is only a prolegomenon. There is a very long way to go before we could begin to draw any determinate conclusions from what we have suggested here. We hope, however, that this discussion can help to show the direction in which more concrete discussions about criminalization should proceed, and to provide a framework

---

6. Charles Taylor, *Cross-Purposes: The Liberal-Communitarian Debate, in* LIBERALISM AND THE MORAL LIFE 170 (Nancy Rosenblum ed., 1989).

within such discussions should be set, by making clearer the kinds of question we must ask.[7]

---

7. Since writing the article on which this core text is based, we have made some (so far radically incomplete) efforts to take further the central argument that crimes are wrongs that properly concern all members of the polity, for which we must answer to our fellow citizens through the criminal process. *See, e.g.*, R.A. Duff, S.E. Marshall, Lindsay Farmer, and Victor Tadros, THE TRIAL ON TRIAL III: TOWARDS A NORMATIVE THEORY OF THE CRIMINAL TRIAL (2007); S.E. Marshall and R.A. Duff, *Communicative Punishment and the Role of the Victim*, CRIM. JUST. ETHICS, Summer/Fall 2004, at 39.

COMMENTS

SHARING WRONGS BETWEEN CRIMINAL AND CIVIL SANCTIONS

STUART P. GREEN*

What justifies treating certain kinds of wrongs against private individuals—rapes, murder, thefts, and the like—as wrongs for which a public response in the form of criminal prosecution is justified? According to Sandra Marshall and Antony Duff, the wrongs that constitute crimes are wrongs that can be understood as being inflicted on the community to which the individual belongs. It is not, they say, the community's wrong *instead* of the individual's; it is the community's wrong *because* it is a wrong done to the individual, as a fellow member of the community.[1] In my view, Marshall and Duff's explanation is as good an explanation as anyone has ever offered for how and why private wrongs become the concern of the criminal law. I advance no major critique of it; instead, I want to raise two questions about the precise scope of their theory.

The first question is whether Marshall and Duff intend to view civil and criminal penalties as mutually exclusive. There is some evidence that they do: At various points in their core text, they ask: why "attacks on individual *Rechtsgüter* should be a matter for criminal *rather than* civil law";[2] "why certain kinds of conduct should be dealt with by a 'criminal' *rather than by* a 'civil' process";[3] why rape should "be dealt with by a 'criminal' *rather than by a* 'civil' process."[4]

---

* Professor of Law and Justice Nathan L. Jacobs Scholar, Rutgers School of Law–Newark.

1. Marshall and Duff core text at 235–36.
2. *Id.* at 229 (emphasis added).
3. *Id.* at 233 (emphasis added).
4. *Id.* at 234 (emphasis added).

In reality, however, most kinds of criminal conduct are subject to both criminal and civil remedies, and it is often difficult to say whether one is preferred over the other. The remedies are therefore *complementary* rather than mutually exclusive. Marshall and Duff know this, of course, and elsewhere in their core text they seem to acknowledge it. For example, they state that when a victim is criminally wronged and the state brings a prosecution, the underlying wrong 'does not cease to be "her" wrong,'"[5] and elsewhere, in considering why the community should not merely offer assistance to a victim who wants to pursue a civil case against her assailant, rather than initiating its own criminal case, they ask whether there are reasons why the case should be the community's rather than "just hers."[6] In light of this recognition, I would therefore rephrase their inquiry as concerning why certain kinds of conduct should be dealt with as a matter for the criminal law, typically *in addition to* the civil law.

This in turn raises another question about the scope of their theory—namely, whether it is meant to apply only to crime types or also to crime tokens. To put it another way, is their theory meant to guide only legislatures in their decision to make certain kinds of conduct potentially subject to criminal sanctions, or is it intended to apply as well to the process of criminal investigation, prosecution, adjudication, and punishment, as carried out by police, prosecutors, and courts? On more than one occasion, Marshall and Duff ask about the "kinds of conduct [that] should be criminalized."[7] This would suggest that their focus is primarily on crime types. But there is no reason why their approach could not also be applied to specific crime tokens. In deciding whether to bring criminal charges, or instead allow a case to remain exclusively civil, it makes sense for a prosecutor to consider the extent to which a particular criminal act affects the community at large. One should not assume that every instance of rape or homicide, let alone assault or theft—is necessarily one that the state will be wise to pursue, even though it may have the legal authority to do so by virtue of broadly worded criminal statutes. There might well be cases the prosecutor decides are best left to the civil courts or to private remedies.

If my understanding of Marshall and Duff's intent is correct, I would therefore propose something like the following friendly amendments to their argument. First, that there are certain kinds of conduct that involve wrongs that are properly understood as serious wrongs against the community and, as such, should be potentially subject to criminal penalties, as enacted by the legislature. Second, that such kinds of conduct may, and often do, also merit civil remedies, and that the two kinds of treatment, criminal and civil, should generally be viewed as complementary. And third, that in making the determination whether to bring criminal proceedings or impose criminal penalties in a particular case,

---

5. *Id.* at 235 (emphasis added).
6. *Id.*
7. *Id.* at 232, 233, 237.

it is appropriate for a prosecutor or court to consider the extent to which there has been a serious wrong against not only the individual victim but also the community to which the individual belongs.

VICTIM, BEWARE! ON THE DANGERS OF SHARING WRONGS WITH SOCIETY

SHLOMIT WALLERSTEIN*

Sandra Marshall and Antony Duff argue that society shares the wrong done to the victim. This, they argue, is the public wrong that justifies criminalization and the state's control over how a wrongdoer is to be treated, even though the wrongdoer's conduct is typically directed against an individual. Their argument can be divided into two stages: In Stage I the claim is that society and the victim both share the *same* wrong (through identification with the victim). Subsequently, in Stage II, the claim is that since society has been wronged in a similar way to the victim it can take control over how the wrongdoer is treated, even when its treatment conflicts with the victim's wishes. Because they all share the same wrong, society, being the sum of all members, is better fit to decide how to best respond to the wrong done to them all (victim and society). This argument, however, is troublesome at both stages.

The claim made in Stage I (that both share the same wrong) blurs the unique nature of the wrong done to the victim and her feeling toward it by putting it *on a par* with society's feeling of being wronged. Can we truly say to a rape victim that we can completely understand her and share the same feelings that she does because we were all wronged by her rape? Do we (can we) all feel as violated as she does? Do we all feel the loss of control over one's own life, and the feeling that one's world has been shattered into pieces? Indeed, as Marshall and Duff explain, society's recognition of the fact that the victim has been wronged is an important feature of criminalization, but some distance exists between such recognition and the claim that we all share the same wrong. If it is necessary to show some way in which society at large is being wronged (and I am not sure it is), then it is only right to recognize that the harm done to society is of a secondary order, thereby recognizing the unique features of the wrong done to the victim.

More worrisome is Stage II. Insofar as the course of action chosen by society goes hand in hand with the victim's wishes, no problem arises. However, the notion of shared-wrongs further allows society to demand from the victim that

---

* University Lecturer, Fellow, and Tutor in Law, St. Peter's College and Faculty of Law, Oxford University.

"just as we may say that we owe it to her to associate ourselves with her in this way (to take her wrong as also our wrong), so we may say that she owes it to us to recognize that the wrong was done to us as well as to her."[1] The victim may consider this to be a forceful transfer, through claims of identification with her, of a very personal wrong/harm into public domain. It is not just a hand given to the victim by society in recognition of the wrong done to her. It is a paternalistic claim that we, too, are wronged *in a similar way* and hence are permitted to take control in the name of "shared values" without asking her if she shares, or wishes to share, these values with society in the first place.

Communitarian accounts recognize the existence of shared values in society as constitutive to its existence, but it does not mean that all members of society share these values. Clearly, being nonvoluntary for the most part, mere membership in a state is not proof of implied acceptance of the set of values "shared" by society. There are those who do not share (or wish to share) the same values with society though they are clearly part of it (e.g., anarchists). Marshall and Duff, however, do not merely ask the victim to accept society's decision to pursue criminal procedures against her own wishes. They demand that she recognize the existence of shared values assigned to her (and subsequently, demand her to share the wrong). In taking this position I do not deny that society may, in some circumstances, pursue a criminal prosecution against the victim's wishes. However, insofar as such decisions rest on some public reason (as opposed to attempt to protect the victim who is unable to protect herself), it results from some overriding considerations derived from different "types" of wrongs generated by the criminal conduct. It is important to accurately identify these competing claims, both because society needs to own up to its actions and because the victim deserves to be told the truth about the reasons for acting against her own judgment.

---

1. Marshall and Duff core text at 236.

SHARING THE BURDENS OF JUSTICE

ADIL AHMAD HAQUE[*]

For centuries, both the common law and Islamic law relied on private prosecution by victims or their families to bring most criminals to justice. What justifies a society in controlling the criminal process from start to finish? In particular, how can the public's interest in wrongs to individual victims be sufficiently strong to permit prosecution and punishment of offenders without the victim's

---

* Assistant Professor of Law, Rutgers School of Law–Newark.

consent, yet sufficiently weak that the public does not displace the victim as the source of the underlying claim that prosecution and punishment seeks to vindicate? Sandra Marshall and Antony Duff answer that due to our shared membership in a communitarian polity an attack on one of us is an attack upon us all. As they put it, "it is not 'our' wrong instead of hers; it is 'our' wrong because it is a wrong done to her, as one of us."[1] We have an obligation to the victim to respond on her behalf, and the victim has an obligation to cooperate with our response for our sakes as well as hers.

Having argued elsewhere that retributive justice imposes a duty on communities, owed to their members, to punish those who violate their rights, I am naturally receptive to the authors' position that the reciprocal duties of community membership justify public prosecution.[2] I am also eager to learn how the authors would respond to a few doubts with which I continue to struggle. First, I wonder how Marshall and Duff would characterize the criminal law applied by states to communities that they govern but do not seek or purport to represent: these probably include colonies, occupied territories, and international protectorates and may include some minority-controlled dictatorships and oligarchies. Can a state so divorced from its subjects nonetheless administer a legitimate system of criminal law?

Second, I wonder whether the Marshall and Duff believe that public prosecution is required or merely permitted by community membership. For while states exercise compulsory criminal jurisdiction, the International Criminal Court (ICC) is limited to complementary criminal jurisdiction: states are encouraged to prosecute offenses committed by or against their nationals, and the ICC will step in only where states are unwilling or unable to do so. Complementary jurisdiction is only tenable if shared membership in the international community permits but does not require prosecution by the international community. Yet if complementary jurisdiction is acceptable in the international context, then we must ask why something similar should not be deployed in the domestic context. Why should we not leave it to victims and families to initiate criminal prosecutions in the first instance and expect the state to step in only if some citizens are unable or unwilling to carry out their responsibilities?

I am inclined to say that complimentary jurisdiction is appropriate in the international context and that in the domestic context private prosecution was appropriate in previous eras but domestic public prosecution is preferable in our own historical moment. I believe that the relationship between individuals and states has changed over time and differs in important respects from the relationship between states and the international community. For most of human history the primary responsibility of the state was to protect the negative rights of its

---

1. Marshall and Duff core text at 236.

2. Adil Ahmad Haque, *Group Violence and Group Vengeance: Toward a Retributivist Theory of International Criminal Law*, 9 BUFF. CRIM. L. REV. 273 (2005).

subjects. Only very recently has the state assumed responsibility for discharging the affirmative obligations of its citizens. The modern welfare state is supposed to educate the young, care for the sick, feed the hungry, shelter the homeless, and support the elderly in our names and on our behalf.

I would suggest that just as the modern state acts as a conduit for individual duties of humanitarian assistance and distributive justice, thereby freeing individuals to concentrate on their own lives and happiness, so too should the state relieve victims and their families of the responsibility to seek retribution, a task that distracts them from healing their injuries, from mourning their losses, from moving past their suffering and on with their lives. Private prosecution often requires one to sustain one's anger, hatred, and resentment because such emotions provide the strong motivation necessary to willingly incur future costs to punish past wrongdoing. Yet retributive emotions can be psychologically debilitating, for they require that victims and their families continue to live in the past, constantly revisiting their loss to refresh or reinforce their desire for justice. States do not bear the psychological burdens of retributive justice and this explains why modern states should bear sole responsibility for criminal prosecution in domestic criminal law and primary responsibility for criminal prosecution in international criminal law. I look forward to learning how Marshall and Duff's arresting vision of criminal law applies to such diverse political, historical, and institutional contexts.

CONTRACTUALISM AND THE SHARING OF WRONGS

MATTHEW LISTER*

Sandra Marshall and Antony Duff's novel account of how crimes differ from other sorts of wrongs, and how the wrongs of criminal activity are "public" or "shared" in some way, is based on communitarianism, and as such, depends on society being a community with shared values, ideals, and identifications. But there are good reasons to doubt that this kind of community is either possible or desirable. So we must look to other approaches to answer these questions. A contractualist view, I claim, better captures the important points raised by Marshall and Duff while avoiding the pitfalls of communitarianism. Contractualist approaches also help explain why the law acts as it does in environments where the type of community envisioned by Marshall and Duff is lacking, such as the international realm.

Contractualist accounts vary in form but all involve the idea of society as a system of cooperation for mutual advantage.[1] On this account society doesn't

---

* Law Clerk to Judge Donald Pogue, U.S. Court of International Trade.

1. *See, e.g.,* John Rawls, A THEORY OF JUSTICE 4 (2d ed. 1999). *See also* Samuel Freeman, *Reason and Agreement in Social Contract Views, in* JUSTICE AND THE SOCIAL CONTRACT 17–44 (2007).

need shared values beyond a willingness to cooperate on fair terms. Even this willingness is explained via parties believing they'll be better off if they cooperate then if they act on their own. But cooperation is only rational if each party has reason to believe that the other parties will also cooperate and won't seek to either free-ride or otherwise prey upon those who "play by the rules." Call this the assurance problem.

Criminal law (partially) answers the assurance problem. By banding together and turning over our private right of action to the public we greatly reduce the risk we face from free-riders and predators. This approach also answers questions raised by Marshall and Duff. Crime is a public wrong because, if not prevented or punished, the whole scheme of cooperation threatens to collapse. We no longer see the wrong of criminal activity as the private object of the wronged person because, if we did so see it, she could prosecute the case or not for all sorts of capricious reasons, which would undermine the ability of the criminal law to answer the assurance problem.

Moreover, crimes are distinguished from other harms because other harms either don't threaten cooperation in the same way or are more productively dealt with via other incentives. Civil wrongs based in private agreements, for example, don't threaten general cooperation in the way that crimes do and so needn't be responded to in the same way. Negligence, for example, is distinguished from crime insofar as the one causing harm needn't be seen as taking advantage of others and so is no threat to cooperation in the way crime is. Thus, the contractualist approach resolves the problems set forth by Marshall and Duff without reference to communitarian commitments or shared values beyond those very basic ones needed to make cooperation possible at all. This approach is therefore better, since the deeply shared values and community appealed to by communitarians have little chance of existing in a liberal society. Such community and deeply shared values can persist over time, I contend, only with the use of repressive force of the sort that liberals ought to reject.[2]

Finally, the contractualist approach also helps us see why and how international criminal law can and does work as it does. That criminal law would work at all in the international realm is a mystery on Marshall and Duff's account, since it would seem that here surely there is no community in any real sense. If there is a "community" here, then the term is vapid; it can do no critical work. But if we think of the criminal law as an answer to an assurance problem, then we can explain why international law criminalizes some actions. Because international cooperation is generally less pervasive, less necessary for living a decent life at all, and more modulated by states than is domestic cooperation, we would expect, on a contractualist account, all of these features to show up in the nature

---

2. *See, e.g.*, John Rawls, POLITICAL LIBERALISM 35–40 (1996) and Charles Larmore, PATTERNS OF MORAL COMPLEXITY 40–68, 91–130 (1987).

of international criminal law. And they do. But these features are a mystery on a communitarian approach, showing again why a contractualist approach is superior.

Marshall and Duff have identified some important aspects of the criminal law and pointed us toward important questions. However, contractualism, I contend, gives us a better answer to these questions than does communitarianism.

SHARING REASONS FOR CRIMINALIZATION? NO THANKS . . . ALREADY GOT 'EM!

MICHELLE MADDEN DEMPSEY*

As Sandra Marshall and Antony Duff correctly observe, criminalization puts the community (rather than the victim) in charge of responding directly to wrongdoing, whereas civil remedies leave the victim in the driver's seat. Working from the assumption that many crimes involve wrongdoing that is principally suffered by the victim, Marshall and Duff argue that such wrongs can be shared by the victim's community, thus giving the community standing to pursue a claim directly against the wrongdoer. Absent such standing, the community has no self-sufficient reason to respond to the wrongdoing directly; rather, the community merely has (at most) reasons to support the victim's own claim against the wrongdoer.

I do not believe that wrongs need to be shared in order to provide reasons for criminalization. I lack the space needed to fully defend this claim, so I will proceed instead by framing the question at issue and then offering two counterexamples, both of which suggest the possibility that communities may already have reasons to respond directly to wrongdoing, simply in virtue of the fact that communities consist of human beings and every human being has reason to respond to wrongdoing simply in virtue of being human. If my suggestion is plausible, then a community has no need to jump through the wrong-sharing hoop before it can be said to have reasons to respond to wrongdoing directly through (*inter alia*) criminalization.

According to Marshall and Duff, the reasons a community has to respond directly to wrongdoing are contingent upon sharing the wrong done to the victim. This contingency can be satisfied where there exists "a certain shared identity, shared values, [or] mutual concern" between the victim and community.[1] But what of cases where there are *no* shared identities, values, or concerns?

---

* Worcester College and Faculty of Law, Oxford University.
1. Marshall and Duff core text at 235.

First consider Izzy, the radical individualist, who so despises the idea of being part of any political community that she chooses to leave her home in Homeville and live on a deserted island. She refuses to share any identity, values, or concerns with her fellow Homevillians and, indeed, with any community whatsoever. Izzy is truly a lone wolf. One day Izzy is kidnapped from her island and forcibly taken to Polityville, where she is raped.

Second, imagine a group of people who choose to live on the island of Separatonia, apart from the rest of the world, and who reject the identity, values, and concerns of the "global community." One day, half of the Separatonians set about systematically torturing and exterminating the other half through murder, rape, enslavement, etc. Throughout it all, the victims never doubt their commitment to rejecting the identity, values, and concerns of the "global community." They never once seek help from outside the island, nor do they wish help to be provided. They would sooner be tortured and die than accept help from outside.

In the first case, if Marshall and Duff believe that Polityville has standing to criminalize Izzy's rape based on the mere empirical contingency of her presence within their borders at the time of the assault (and not in virtue of any shared identity, values, or concerns existing between the community of Polityville and Izzy, for *ex hypothesi* none exist), then one may reasonably ask whether there are *any* limits to the contingencies capable of doing the "wrong-sharing" work envisioned by Marshall and Duff. Isn't it more plausible to assume something like the following: Polityville has reason to criminalize Izzy's rapist because rape is wrong, condemning wrongdoing is valuable, the citizens of Polityville are able to realize this value, and thus (*ceteris paribus*) they have reason to do so?

In the second case, Marshall and Duff might explain the "global community's" standing to criminalize the Separatonian genocidaires by reference to the fact that the wrongdoing at issue constitutes "crimes against humanity." To defend this move, however, Marshall and Duff must provide an account of what constitutes a "crime against humanity" that goes beyond the mere declaration that is the sort of wrong that concerns all of humanity (for the very point at issue is, why aren't all wrongs like that?). Isn't it more likely that the global community's standing to respond directly to the genocidaires exists simply in virtue of our shared humanity? In my account, cases involving "crimes against humanity" do not present a special case of criminal wrongdoing: they are simply more serious forms of wrongdoing for which it is therefore more appropriate that there be a global response.

PUBLIC VERSUS PRIVATE RETRIBUTION AND DELEGATED REVENGE

ANDREW E. TASLITZ*

I enthusiastically endorse Sandra Marshall and Antony Duff's emphasis on public, shared wrongs as the basis for deciding whether criminal, as opposed to civil, penalties are appropriate. But they do not adequately explain why victims should themselves want *the public* to impose the punishment. Understanding the retributive emotions corrects this omission. By "retributive" emotions, I mean the desire to make an offender suffer as a way of restoring the victim's social status. Retributive emotions can be felt by the victim or by the community or both.

An individual victim's retributive desire can vary in the degree to which he or she seeks personally to wreak revenge on the offender or instead wants the state to do so. Kenworthey Bilz,[1] drawing on empirical data, has made a strong case for victims often wanting the state—acting on behalf of the community—to impose punishment rather than the victim herself doing so—a preference for "delegated revenge." The special emotional value to the victim of such revenge is precisely that the community, by inflicting punishment, expresses its solidarity with the victim as one of the community's own. For the individual to feel whole, the community's support is necessary.

Other times, however, the individual may be more interested in more directly imposing punishment, and Alan Calnan has made a convincing case that allowing this sense of catharsis from personal vengeance without community breakdown is one important function of the tort system. This is why, argues Calnan, merely compensating a victim from state funds, rather than making the offender personally pay for the harm done, can seem "sterile and impersonal," for the victim "never has an opportunity to return the inconvenience and embarrassment thrust upon him" by the offender.[2] Accordingly, a strong need for reciprocity demands both a "symbolic gesture of the restoration of the moral equality between the parties" *and* "disgorg[ing] from the wrongdoer any gain from her act."[3]

What determines whether the individual will be satisfied with the more private tort response or the more public criminal justice one? One plausible answer

---

* Welsh S. White Distinguished Visiting Professor of Law, University of Pittsburgh, 2008–09; Professor of Law, Howard University School of Law. This comment is partly based on Andrew E. Taslitz, *The Inadequacies of Civil Society: Law's Complementary Role in Regulating Harmful Speech*, 1 MD. J. RACE, RELIGION, GENDER, & CLASS 305 (2001).

1. Kenworthey Bilz, *The Puzzle of Delegated Revenge*, 87 B.U. L. REV. 1059 (2007).

2. Alan Calnan, JUSTICE AND TORT LAW 111 (1997).

3. *Id.* at 115.

lies in the distinction between descriptive and prescriptive social norms. Descriptive norms describe what society expects to occur as "normal" behavior. Prescriptive norms designate what should or should not be done. The separation between the two is not always a sharp one but is useful in understanding retributive behavior.

When descriptive norms are violated, the individual experiences a sense of personal unfairness, of having suffered some individual wrong. The individual's emotional reaction will be distress. But when prescriptive norms are violated, the individual seems to experience a sense that the moral order of the universe has been disturbed—that *social* unfairness has been done—and this breeds intense anger, even rage.[4] Law can be understood as specifying how we ought to behave, thus making all law expressive of prescriptive rather than merely descriptive norms. But a more subtle understanding is possible, namely, that law expresses a continuum of norms, with tort law focusing far more on redressing the sense of personal unfairness, criminal law the rage spawned by egregious social unfairness.

Note that I said "egregious" social unfairness to express the idea that some prescriptive norms are more deeply held, seen more as definitional to the community, than others. Harms to the norms most strongly embraced by the group may thus be experienced by the individual as an attack on herself, thus explaining the rage experienced by individuals suffering not merely personal but also social unfairness.

Similar social processes, however, help to explain the *community's* retributive emotions, for an offense against an individual is a threat to the consensus values that bind the community, thus against the community itself[5]—and this seems to be Marshall and Duff's major point. But I have argued here that their picture is incomplete, explaining only why crime causes public injuries but not why *wronged individuals themselves* seek punishment imposed by the public in response. Understanding the retributive emotions discussed here fills this gap.

---

4. Sarah Maxwell, THE PRICE IS WRONG: UNDERSTANDING WHAT MAKES A PRICE SEEM FAIR AND THE TRUE COST OF UNFAIR PRICING 31–46 (2008).

5. Neil Vidmar, *Retribution and Revenge, in* HANDBOOK OF JUSTICE RESEARCH IN LAW 42–43 (Joseph Sanders and Lee Hamilton eds., 2000).

REPLY

S.E. MARSHALL AND R.A. DUFF

Our commentators have shown how much more we need to do to turn our gestural suggestions in "Sharing Wrongs" into a substantive account of criminalization. We can respond here only, and briefly, on four matters.

First, as to the relation between criminal and civil law,[1] a simple answer would be that they are complementary, serving distinct ends: civil law determines who pays to repair harm that has been caused, or bears costs that have been incurred; criminal law deals with the censure and punishment of (public) wrongs. But civil law clearly, and properly, sometimes provides for a response to wrongs qua wrongs. Between the simple cases of a harm- or cost-focused civil law and a public-wrong-focused criminal law there is therefore room for a semi-private form of criminal law in which the victim of a wrong can decide whether to pursue the wrongdoer for apologetic reparation, but expect public support in doing so: we could, more precisely, think either of a larger category of private prosecutions, or of a category of public prosecutions that would proceed only with the victim's consent or at the victim's request.[2]

The category of purely public criminal wrongs, to be pursued by a public prosecutor, would consist of wrongs that merit or require some formal public response but lack any direct victim distinct from the public at large; and wrongs that have direct individual victims but that the public ought to pursue because it would be a betrayal of their professed values as a polity not to pursue them—a betrayal in which the victim who would prefer not to pursue the wrong would, however nonculpably, share. This is not to claim that we, as the public, share the wrong in the sense that we are all wronged in the very way in which the victim is wronged;[3] rather, we share in the wrong as one that properly concerns us all.

This is to appeal to a set of values that both victim and offender are supposed to share as members of the community; to argue then that in our existing societies we cannot appeal to any such shared values,[4] would be to argue in effect that in such societies criminal law cannot be legitimate. Matt Lister's appeal to a contractualist model cannot help here: if we are to justify the *criminal* law, as an essentially censuring practice that identifies public wrongs, any set of imagined contractors must already see and relate to each other as moral agents in terms of a set of shared values rich enough to ground a system of criminal law.

Second, do we need to appeal to community to justify criminal prosecution and punishment—rather than saying that the polity has reason to realize the good of condemning wrongdoing whenever it is able to do so?[5] This is indeed another possible conception of the role of the criminal law, as discharging the universal and impersonal duty to punish wrongs, though national systems of criminal law are normally limited, for good practical and political reasons, to dealing only with wrongs that are committed within their territory. All we can say here is that this does not seem to us to provide an adequate answer the

---

1. *See* Green comment at 238–40.
2. *See* Haque comment at 242–43.
3. *See* Wallerstein comment at 240.
4. *See* Lister comment at 243–45.
5. *See* Dempsey comment at 245–46.

question of standing: If the wrongdoer asks, "By what right do *you* seek to put me on trial and punish me?" (or, more crudely, "What makes my crime your coercive business?"), we do not think that it is adequate to reply that we—this polity and its courts—are acting as the agents of universal justice: We should rather be able to reply, in most cases, that it is our business because you, the offender, are a fellow citizen and/or because the victim is a fellow citizen and/or because the crime was committed in our civic home (or, which is relevant to Michelle Dempsey's first example, because the victim and/or the offender is a temporary guest, voluntary or not, in the civic home, and is for that reason our concern).

There are also of course cases in which criminal law is applied by states and their officials to colonies, occupied territories and protectorates, without any claim that those applying the law are fellow citizens of those to whom they apply it.[6] Such cases raise serious problems about the legitimacy of the law that is being applied: perhaps the best that can be said for such applications is that the law is being applied in the name of and on behalf of the political community that either does not yet fully exist or is not yet fully able to operate its own criminal law—which of course still raises the question of what gives this state or these officials the right to act in the name of those to whom they apply the law.

Third, this leads to the question of international criminal law (a question on which "Sharing Wrongs" was notably silent—we would like to be able to say that this shows how rapidly the realm of international criminal law has developed in the last ten years): how can an account of this kind explain the moral authority or legitimacy of international criminal courts? In one view, the International Criminal Court (ICC) must claim to act on behalf of the national polities that would ideally deal for themselves with "crimes against humanity" committed within their territories and against their members, but whose courts cannot or will not act (hence the principle of complementarity that governs the ICC)— though that cannot explain its authority in relation to international crimes that lack such a national location. In another view, the ICC acts in the name of universal justice, and is legitimate insofar as it is well suited to the task of punishing those serious kinds of wrongdoing that must be punished.[7] In a third view, the ICC claims to act in the name and on behalf of "humanity," as a normative community whose existence is more a matter of aspiration than of established fact, but which such institutions as the ICC can help to build. Our view of domestic criminal law would fit most easily with a version of the third of these views of

---

6. *See* Haque comment at 242.

7. *See* Dempsey comment at 246. *See also* Andrew Altman and Carl Wellman, *A Defense of International Criminal Law*, 115 ETHICS 35 (2004).

international criminal law; but we realize the difficulty of showing how talk of humanity as a community can amount to more than empty rhetoric.[8]

Fourth, how does punishment fit into this picture?[9] All we can say here is that if criminal punishment is to be justified at all, it must be justified as something that citizens can legitimately do to each other as fellow members of a political community; and that the most plausible way of doing this is to understand punishment as an essentially communicative exercise, which aims to address offenders precisely as fellow members, in terms of the shared values of a normative community to which we and they belong (rather than as an enterprise of either private or public revenge that seeks to satisfy our retributive emotions). However, on our view the criminal trial is also of crucial importance: not merely as a prelude to punishment, but as the formal process through which a polity calls alleged public wrongdoers to answer for their actions to those who have the right thus to call them to account.

---

8. See R.A. Duff, Authority and Responsibility in International Criminal Law, in PHILOSOPHY OF INTERNATIONAL LAW (Samantha Besson and John Tasioulas eds., forthcoming).

9. See Taslitz comment at 247.

12. MONSTROUS OFFENDERS AND THE SEARCH FOR SOLIDARITY THROUGH MODERN PUNISHMENT

JOSEPH E. KENNEDY*

*Whoever fights with monsters should take care that
in the process he does not become a monster.*
—Friedrich Nietzsche[1]

I. INTRODUCTION

Think of the following three terms: drug dealer, child molester, and violent crime. In the abstract, each term is usually taken to refer to the most monstrous offense and offender possible. The term *drug dealer* conjures up an image of an Uzi-toting, gold-chain wearing, remorseless urban predator. The term *child molester* elicits images of a strange man who cruises playgrounds in the hope of luring unattended children into his van, where he commits kidnapping, rape, murder, or all three. *Violent crime* triggers thoughts of a vicious assault, if not a rape or robbery involving a weapon.

In each case, the linguistic category used to describe crime and criminals evokes images of the most serious offenses and offenders. Such offenders do exist, but there are nowhere near as many of them as society imagines, and they constitute a tiny fraction of the actual population of offenders and offenses prosecuted. The monstrous images evoked simply do not correspond with the average offender included in the legal category of offense to which the term refers. For example, most "violent crimes" are simple batteries that involve no physical injury; most injuries sustained in such cases do not require medical treatment; and most cases requiring medical treatment do not require hospitalization. Similarly, the average offender convicted for drug sales is probably a drug user who sells two rocks of crack cocaine in the hope of clearing enough to be able to smoke a third himself, and the average "child molester" is not a stranger but a household member who molests without kidnapping or raping. Why are we so preoccupied with the worst case? Why are we so eager to believe in monsters?

* Associate Professor of Law, University of North Carolina School of Law. This core text is based on Joseph E Kennedy, *Monstrous Offenders and the Search for Solidarity Through Modern Punishment*, 51 HASTINGS L.J. 829 (2000).

1. Friedrich Nietzsche, THUS SPAKE ZARATHUSTRA (Thomas Common trans., 1993) (1883–85).

Monstrous crimes and monstrous criminals provide appetizing fare for a society hungry for agreement and cohesion. Individuals in our society attempt to forge solidarity through the process of punishment by focusing on the worst possible offenses and offenders. Simply put, we exaggerate the worst in order to experience the best: moments when we feel as a society that we have transcended the many differences that keep us apart. The changes, divisions, and tremors in our social and economic structure over the last several decades and the anxieties they have produced about social solidarity have manifested themselves both in the way we speak and think about crime and in the hyperpunitiveness of our criminal justice practices as well.

Crime has served as a rallying cry for a divided and insecure society, and many in our society use the criminal justice system to send symbolic messages reaffirming and defining core values during this time of flux. These anxieties explain a great deal about our move toward a more determinate form of sentencing, the increasing length of the sentences awarded under that system, and a way of thinking that frames society's interest in punishment exclusively in terms of minimizing the risks of recidivism. Criminal punishment has come to serve as a new civic religion for a society worried about its ability to cohere, and the depths of our anxieties about our social solidarity express themselves in our conceptions of crime and in the corresponding severity of our punishment.

By any measure, the 1980s and'90s saw an unprecedented increase in the severity of criminal punishment in the United States. The breadth and depth of the political consensus behind this increase may be without parallel in contemporary political history. Most if not all of the legislative enactments increasing criminal sentences on both the national and state level have commanded widespread bipartisan support.

Ultimately, the severity revolution is best understood as an exercise in scapegoating by people who are desperately trying to forge a greater sense of solidarity in a time of unprecedented change and division: Not just scapegoating in the traditional sense (the demonization of minorities and other outsider groups as the source of criminal activity) but scapegoating in a subtler and more pervasive form as well. The essence of scapegoating is the attempt to identify the sources of social problems as external to the group, and an analysis of some of our society's crime obsessions of the'80s and'90s—drug use, the sexual abuse of children, random violence and serial killers, juvenile "superpredators"—reveals a common pattern. In each case people eagerly believe in the widespread existence of "monstrous offenders" and then project onto those offenders more basic anxieties about social problems that are both widespread and intractable. As a result, the abstract categories of offenses in our penal laws are tied to sentences that are disproportionately harsh for the average offense. We have developed a draconian system of punishment for dealing with the monsters that we have imagined being everywhere, a system that swallows up hordes of lesser offenders.

II. CRIME AND THE SACRED

Emile Durkheim argued that criminal punishment serves as a communicative realm for the expression of sacred values within our society. Talking of the "sacred" in societies as diverse and secular as our own, however, raises conceptual problems for many. The more diverse and secular a society, the greater the need for belief in some set of core values around which its disparate elements can coalesce. These core values constitute what I call the *secular sacred*, and the secular sacred is most easily expressed through stories about its violation. Through punishment, society defines itself by its response to these stories of violation. In this sense, criminal punishment performs a communicative function whose importance deepens in times of flux and acute anxiety about social cohesion. The more we fear division in our society, the more importance we invest in stories about society's response to terrible crimes, and this investment is reflected in the pivotal role which "special crime stories" have played in major criminal justice reforms over the last two decades.

Furthermore, even if one denied the possibility of a shared moral framework in a society as diverse as our own, Durkheim's theory of the process by which modern secular societies *try* to negotiate such a framework is still relevant. There may be no "there" there in the sense of a foundational vision of society upon which most would agree, but perhaps secular societies continue to seek a shared framework of values as meaningful as possible to as many as possible. Durkheim may have identified what amounts to an irrepressible urge for a measure of moral consensus in society, one that some thought we outgrew as our society became more modern and more secular but that persists in ways that the rational, secular outlook of much modern social thought tends to underestimate.

The sense of awe, dread, and outrage that most feel when they read of truly horrible crimes comes from some sense—however inchoate and difficult to articulate—of a violation of something sacred. Consider the following crime, which occurred in a small town. A man becomes angry when he learns that his wife refuses to become pregnant with his child. He plans to murder his wife's infant child by a previous marriage. When his wife is at work he holds a plastic bag over the eight-month-old girl's head until the child turns blue and stops breathing. He chooses this method because he believes that the baby's death will be attributed to Sudden Infant Death Syndrome.

Such a crime does seem to violate something so important to how we see ourselves as human beings that the words "violation of the sacred" seem appropriate. The mere words "right and wrong" seem inadequate in the face of such a crime: they seem too abstract, too detached, too philosophical. What most feel in the face of such a terrible crime is a sense of terrible awe that anyone could watch an infant suffocate inside a plastic bag he was holding over her head. Such a crime produces a sense of horror in the dictionary definition of the word: "a painful and intense feeling of fear, dread, or dismay."[2] A sense also would exist that these emotions would be widely shared ones. Most people reading such a story would feel confident that they could tell this story to a person of any race, class, or political party and elicit the same emotions. Different people might attribute the causes of such behavior differently, but all would feel one in the sense of horror at the crime itself.

Following close upon the sense of awe and horror that such a crime produces would be a powerful anger—perhaps even a sense of hatred—that would demand punishment. People would feel that there would be something deeply wrong with a society that failed to severely punish a person who did such a thing. It is this sort of thirst for punishment that Durkheim has in mind when he argues that we punish violations of the sacred in order to uphold the moral order of a society.

Instrumental arguments about the greater social good could not diminish this desire for punishment. Assume for the sake of argument that this person would never reoffend and would constitute no threat to public safety. Assume further that the sorts of people who commit such crimes simply cannot be deterred. Most people would want this man punished, nevertheless. Although it is easy to label such a sentiment as simply retributive, Durkheim's theory suggests that the retributive impulse to punish is linked strongly to some sense of who we are as a society. There would seem to be something wrong with us if we did not punish this man to some degree; we would have trouble living with ourselves as a society. It is at this point that some public official would probably talk about the *symbolism* of letting such a person go free: when people talk about the symbolic in such a context they are really talking about what signal a specific decision about punishment gives regarding the society's moral framework. The audience for this signal is the society itself, and it is the incontestable nature of the sacred that demands punishment.

Ultimately, Durkheim would probably interpret the severity of our contemporary punishment practices to be a direct result of the widespread and profound anxieties that we harbor about our solidarity as a society. Durkheim recognized that the relationship between social solidarity and punishment could exist in both functional and dysfunctional forms. In a stable society, punishment may help maintain that stability by reinforcing the society's moral framework. An unstable society, however, may express its insecurities through practices of punishment that are overly harsh.

III. CRIME STORIES AND THE SACRED

We live in an era of "special story legislation" in matters of punishment. Vivid stories of individual tragedies have served as catalysts for sweeping changes in

---

2. WEBSTER'S NINTH NEW COLLEGIATE DICTIONARY 582 (1988).

policy a number of times during the'80s and'90s. In California, the passage of the three strikes initiative owes much to the horrifying murder of Polly Klass. In New Jersey, the sexual murder of eight-year-old Megan Kanka by a recently released sex offender resulted in the passage of "Megan's law," which requires public notifications anytime a person convicted of a sex offense is released back into a community. Perhaps the most politically influential story of the period, however, regarded crimes committed by Willie Horton. That story may have influenced the outcome of the 1988 presidential election and established the power of a simple theme in criminal justice policy: any politician, judge, or prosecutor who authorizes the release of a potentially violent offender will be held politically accountable for any future crimes he commits.

Stories of crime and punishment are deeply intertwined with a secular society's search for a collective sense of the sacred because the most powerful stories about the sacred tend to be stories about the violation of the sacred. In part, these may be an extension of the well-known psychological aversion to loss: people respond more powerfully to stories of prospective loss than to prospective gain. In a similar vein, society finds a more powerful experience of its sacred attitudes toward children, for example, in stories of death or injury to children than in stories about the health and welfare of children. The special power of stories of terrible crimes entails more than just the loss of the sacred, however: some element of deliberate human action plays an important role. A busload of children killed by a freak avalanche on a mountain road involves a sacred loss, but that loss has a tragic quality that does not energize people in the same way that a crime does. If some element of human agency can be identified as the cause of a sacred loss, people's sadness turns into outrage. Society has not only a "body to kick," but "a soul to damn."

The deliberate violation of the sacred provides a society with the most powerful and the most unambiguous moments of collective passion about those things that that society cherishes most deeply. Horrible crimes provide moments of communion for a secular society that no longer comes together within the walls of any one church or around any one text. In these moments of communion, society finds respite from anxieties about the things that divide it. Such respites in turn may build confidence that that which binds the society together—a deeply felt and widely shared understanding of "the important things in life"—is stronger than the forces that threaten to pull it apart.

Indeed, the absence of a common philosophical approach to moral questions and the lack of a shared vocabulary for the expression of transcendent principles may make modern secular societies *more* dependent on the stories of violation of the sacred that crime provides. How do the diverse members of large and changing modern societies talk to one another about the important issues of social life in an environment where abstract principles are subject to misinterpretation for linguistic and cultural reasons and where the power of the abstract to command allegiance is accordingly diminished? We communicate most easily in such environments through stories about the violation of the sacred: narratives that create in the listeners a common emotional experience, an experience that more homogeneous societies might be able to create through the mere incantation of some abstract principle or dogma from a shared sacred text.

A moral framework developed principally through stories about violation of the sacred would inevitably have a patchwork-quilt quality, not the finely woven feel of a coherent set of philosophical principles. This piecemeal quality simply reflects in part the limits of language where the interpretive approaches of the various audiences of a social text are not always compatible. In part, this piece-meal quality also might reflect the limited scope of agreement possible in a diverse society regardless of barriers to communication. Stories can serve as cultural resources for discovering the maximal amount of solidarity possible between groups with very different perspectives. Story may permit you to patch together more of a common moral fabric in a diverse society than the more rigor-ous methods of philosophical analysis could weave. In this sense, diverse secular societies may be even more likely to rely on punishment to experience and nego-tiate their shared sense of the sacred than more homogenous societies with more uniform religious beliefs.

IV. DETERMINATE SENTENCING AND RACE

A majority of jurisdictions in this country have moved to a more determinate sen-tencing process through a variety of measures, all of which either constrained or eliminated the judge's discretion at sentencing. There is a revealing irony here. For although legislation is increasingly crafted and passed with compelling narratives about individual cases in mind, the actual sentencing of offenders in individual cases is increasingly determined by the application of a sentencing formula. These formulas are based on determinations made about criminal conduct in the aggre-gate. Criminal justice decision-making has become contextual and story-driven on the macro level but abstract and almost mathematical on the micro level.

Ultimately, the more determinate the sentencing scheme the less opportunity that exists for punishment practices to express the sort of transcendent moral principles that Durkheim saw as central to functional punishment in modern, secular societies. Determinate sentencing largely subordinates moral judgments about the blameworthiness of the individual offender in context to judgments about the harm of the offense to society in the abstract. An inherent tension therefore exists between punishment as pure "crime control" or "risk manage-ment" and punishment as an attempt to express and reinforce a society's moral framework in meaningful ways. Contemporary penalty tries to force punish-ment to serve two incompatible masters.

The one way punishment can be instrumental and expressive of a more tran-scendent morality at the same time is to imagine offenders to be as absolutely evil as possible. The monstrous offender eliminates the tension between a penology based on minimizing risks of harm to society and expressive punishment: monstrous conceptions of crime make the hard reaction to evil embodied in more determinate sentencing processes less controversial. The crimes of the monstrous offender demand harsh punishment, and the failure of the sentencing scheme to consider the past circumstances and future potential of the offender diminishes in importance. Monsters are monsters, whatever the origins of their birth, and the felt need to incapacitate the monstrous offender on the pragmatic grounds of self-protection would bring together those who might disagree on the moral culpability of an offender whose crimes had their origin in racial and socioeconomic inequalities.

Seeing and punishing offenders as monsters could also forge social solidarity between those who disagree about whether punishment should be about moral culpability at all. The harsher punishments that would result from conceiving of offenders as monsters would carry greater expressive force, which would be comforting to those who seek to affirm society's moral framework through punishment. At the same time, those who have lost faith altogether in punishment's expressive moral force—or in the very existence of a moral framework that is actually shared by those subject to the practices of punishment—would be satisfied with the maximal amounts of incapacitation and deterrence achieved by the harsher sentence. Monstrous offenders resolve the schizophrenic tensions of contemporary penalty by allowing society to foster solidarity by being maximally morally expressive while hedging its bet with the greatest degree of self-protection. Problem solved?

Insofar as the monstrous conceptions of crime upon which such a system would be premised are myths, however; the actual effects of such practices on social solidarity would be disastrous, especially in a society such as our own where punishment practices fall disproportionately on communities of color and the poor. Sentences whose severity was based on conceptions of crime more serious than what actually exists and whose imposition ignored the differing potentialities of each offender for good and bad would not be interpreted as being expressive of a shared moral framework by the people and communities most subject to penal practices. In communities of color, a more plausible interpretation would be simple racism.

For example, drug laws that impose draconian prison terms on "drug dealers" would be necessary expressions of a widely shared morality to a White middle class that conceives of drug dealers in the abstract as violent and uncaring sociopaths. People who live in the communities where such draconian drug laws are enforced would see a different reality. The "drug dealers" they would see arrested most frequently would be "runners" who were often addicts themselves and had no history of violence. Watching such offenders sentenced to long prison sentences under mandatory drug laws would probably seem immoral, irrational, and racist. To the White majority, the hostility of communities of color to the prosecution and enforcement of the criminal laws would seem inexplicable. The racial division such punishment causes might fuel further anxieties about the degree to which all members of our diverse society truly share some common moral ground, anxieties that might lead to even more severe punishment practices in a continuous upward spiral.

V. THE MORAL PANICS OF THE EIGHTIES AND NINETIES

Like the alcoholic who lives from drink to drink, our society has gone from one moral panic about crime to another during the last few decades. Many of the public's major crime obsessions of the'80s and'90s have proven to be gross distortions of social reality. Supposed epidemics of child kidnapping, ritual satanic abuse, murders by serial killers, juvenile violence, and crack cocaine addiction have upon closer examination turned out to be more fiction than fact. Each panic was itself an exercise in deep scapegoating. In each case, a monstrous type of offender (or in the case of crack cocaine, a monstrous drug) was imagined to be responsible for committing widespread crime, and hyperpunitive strategies were adopted for dealing with the problem. In each case, however, the problem was constructed in a way that tapped into underlying anxieties about divisive social problems.

It is tempting to blame these panics solely on the efforts of activist groups, the media, or politicians to spread crime fear. To do so, however, might be "scapegoating the scapegoaters." It would divert attention away from our own eagerness to believe the fears being packaged.

Crimes such as school shootings, serial killings, and other monstrous offenses terrify us so because they tap into deep-seated anxieties about the changing nature of social life. People put down their newspaper and wonder "what sort of society are we becoming that breeds children such as these?" The crime is not seen as an aberration: it is seen as expressing something fundamental about social life in America. But you are only prone to see in monstrous crimes some deeper indictment of contemporary society if you are already deeply anxious about society to begin with.

The moral panics of the'80s and'90s have engendered policies that capture far too many small fish. Like a giant dragnet stretched across leagues of ocean, three strikes laws and other mandatory minimum laws have scooped up far too many minor offenders. Each of these moral panics has contributed to the indiscriminate nature of the severity revolution. The crack drug panic lead to the widespread incarceration of drug users and low-level dealers. The juvenile crime scare has resulted in widespread reforms aimed at treating many juveniles as adults and incarcerating them earlier and for longer periods of time. Concerns about random violence have manifested themselves in various "get tough" measures, such as three strikes laws, that have fallen predominantly on minor offenders.

VI. THE MYTH OF THE SOFT-HEARTED JUDGE

An American Studies scholar once described a recurring plot in many contemporary crime novels that reveals something fundamental about how the public sees punishment.[3] A sociopathic killer is hunted by a liberal detective, psychiatrist, or other investigator. Initially, the investigator struggles to understand the killer's lack of empathy for human life, a lack usually rooted in gruesome childhood abuse. The real story of such novels is the liberal investigator's journey from a sympathetic, reformist, or therapeutic perspective to one that permits him to slay the monster he finally chases down. "The hunter is at first reluctant to condemn this pathetic victim of someone else's cruelty but by the end he rises to a murderous rage of his own."[4]

At the root of such stories is a fear that knowledge of the world will disable us from protecting ourselves from it, that the more nuanced one's view of humanity and human behavior, the more likely one is to flinch from the acts necessary for one's own survival. The liberal investigator represents liberal society, and the fear is that our understanding of the roots of criminal behavior in social inequalities or abuse will rob us of the will or the judgment to act in our collective self-defense. In reliving over and over again a story about a sensitive, humane person who nonetheless brings himself to kill, we are reassuring ourselves that we won't be killed ourselves.

The determinant turn in sentencing can be understood in similar terms. The public has cast judges in criminal cases as "the liberal investigator," and public support for more determinate forms of sentencing can be understood as the expression of a fear that judges were unable to identify evil when they saw it because of the moral flux of contemporary times. This fear—and the more determinate sentencing process it has spawned—unfortunately forces the judge to err on the side of seeing every defendant almost exclusively in terms of the harm he has caused or might cause.

In a very real sense, the soft-hearted judge of the public's imagination is the necessary counterpart to the monstrous offender. The public needs an easy, reassuring explanation for why monsters remain loose amongst us. The truth is that offenders already known to be violent have always been dealt with severely by the criminal justice system, and there is simply no way to reliably predict when or if a nonviolent offender will turn violent. The public has not wanted to believe, however, that there is no foolproof way to selectively incapacitate monstrous offenders before they commit a monstrous crime. So they invent a complement to the monstrous offender—the soft-hearted judge.

---

3. Andrew Delbanco, THE DEATH OF SATAN: HOW AMERICANS HAVE LOST THE SENSE OF EVIL (1995).
4. *Id.* at 18.

In the standard script, the soft-hearted judge ignores the clear warning signs of future dangerousness evident in the monstrous offender's past behavior. Instead, he pins society's hopes on the efforts of soft-hearted therapeutic programs to transform a being who is plainly evil at his core.

The mythical soft-hearted judge of the public's imagination was in part a product of the indeterminate sentencing practices of the'60s and'70. Such practices made it easy for the public to believe that judges were ignoring their values and needs. The greatest—and most important—challenge for contemporary practices of punishment is to develop more individualized sentencing processes that won't reinforce this myth and its corresponding anxieties about social normlessness.

VII. CONCLUSION

Nietzsche once said that when you look into the abyss, the abyss looks into you. In staring into the abyss of crime and the suffering it causes, society has seen a reflection of its own anxieties, a picture of itself distorted by the rippling effects of great changes during recent times. This abysmal vision has reached deep into our psyche and has changed punishment in ways that divide us even more. We may not be able to slay our monstrous conceptions of crime until the anxieties that gave them birth have abated. Undoing the work of the severity revolution might begin only when our sense of society's center stabilizes once again. The solution to the severity revolution may therefore lie outside of law and punishment itself. It is also possible, however, that legal practices designed to make punishment more expressive of moral values without conjuring up scapegoats might help an insecure society edge its way back from this abyss.

COMMENTS
DOMESTICATED MONSTERS

MARIANNE WESSON*

Joseph Kennedy's thought-provoking core text suggests a link between our cultural moment and the stunning severity of criminal sentencing in America. But I wonder whether his description of our current middle-class anxieties and our concept of the monstrous offender might be a bit dated.[1] The stranger who

---

* Professor of Law, Wolf–Nichol Fellow, and President's Teaching Scholar, University of Colorado.

1. I mean to qualify what I say here by explaining that I am talking about the anxieties of the American middle class. These are not the only anxieties that deserve attention, but

kidnaps our child, or murders our neighbor, or sexually assaults us or a loved one—is he so much on our collective mind just now? Although American evening television is full of grotesque crimes, my unscientific inventory of these programs' plot lines suggests that the serial killer seems to have been replaced by the family member, or close friend, or romantic acquaintance as the likely perpetrator of the monstrous crime.

These fictional entertainments aside, consider the nonfiction narratives that have riveted us over the last decade and a half. The O.J. Simpson trial led off a parade of spectacles in which it was intimates, not strangers, who were the suspects. A young husband is accused of killing his wife and their unborn child for the insurance money; an Austrian man is found to have imprisoned his own child in a basement and violated her sexually for years; schoolchildren murder the classmates who sat beside them in fifth-period algebra. The difficulty some have had accepting that it may not have been a lover who murdered Chandra Levy, or a family member who killed JonBenét Ramsey, points to the power that the narrative of the devious intimate has acquired over our anxieties. Indeed, the suggestion that a home invader killed the Ramsey child—a suggestion that gained prestige recently when the local district attorney informed John Ramsey that he was no longer under any suspicion—prompted scathing scorn from the vast majority of citizens who posted comments to the news stories.

Of course it is not crime itself that has changed; it is, as Kennedy would argue, the surrounding cultural environment that makes us receptive to some narratives even as it mutes others. And these days we seem to be more anxious about the hidden monstrous capacities of our closest friends and family than about our vulnerability to the drug-addled robber or the random serial killer. Why should this be?

I am no better equipped to answer this question than any random consumer of our culture, but the experience of betrayal seems to be pervasively at large these days. The government we trusted to protect us in a dangerous world has been unmasked as incompetent or worse. The nature we used to experience as benevolent has gone bad on us, producing bewildering violence and destruction and the promise of much worse to come. The economy that once could be counted on to support us and our children has turned unreliable, even cruel.

These events require a narrative that incorporates them into our understanding of the world, for such narratives form part of our strategy for surviving in it. Mistrusting everything, especially that which you once trusted, seems like a decent strategy for these treacherous times. Perhaps the drama of the monstrous friend, the diabolical co-worker, the enemy inside the house, performs the office of reminding us to maintain this vigilance.

---

they will get more than their share, because they are held by those who will, in greater numbers than the poor, vote and contribute to political candidates and write letters to their representatives.

Of course, there is the constant campaign for attention to the threat of terror, with which we are said to be at war. And yet terrorism lacks a compelling individual villain. Saddam Hussein dragged out of his spider hole, Osama bin Laden limping from one inaccessible mountain hideout to another, the first war crimes defendant at Guantanamo, who turns out to be the Al Qaeda equivalent to Don Corleone's chauffeur—there is little there that populates our nightmares. Our anxieties about the intimate stranger haunt us more persistently.

These reflections lead me to some skepticism about Kennedy's account. But more fundamentally, I am not sure that any of our cultural observations, Kennedy's or mine, are genuinely related to American sentencing policy. I would be surprised if most Americans have the slightest idea what terms of imprisonment are typically imposed for the various crimes. Apart from the debate over the death penalty, discussions about how we penalize criminals are exceedingly rare in public discourse. Our mania for crime narratives seems to end once a verdict is pronounced.

"WE HAVE MET THE ENEMY AND HE IS US": COGNITIVE BIAS AND PERCEPTIONS OF THREAT

JANET AINSWORTH*

Joseph Kennedy persuasively argues that deep-seated social anxieties and a yearning for lost solidarity help explain not only our contemporary obsession with horrific crimes (despite their rarity), but also how that obsession has led to draconian increases in sentencing severity for ordinary crimes as well. Kennedy's analysis, however, overlooks the importance of shared cognitive biases in framing our response to horrific crimes. Specifically, powerful cognitive biases favoring a belief in control over threatening occurrences amplify the social response to crime that Kennedy has identified.

Today, our sense of personal well-being and future safety is under assault from many perceived sources of danger. Economically, we are faced with the prospect of once-secure jobs being outsourced abroad, the bursting of the housing bubble causing millions to face imminent foreclosure and others to watch helplessly as the home that they imagined as their nest egg steadily loses value. Threats to the environment from global warming raise terrible specters of rising oceans, inadequate agricultural capacity, catastrophic "super-storms" like Hurricane Katrina, and mass extinctions causing irreparable harm to the ecosystem. Add to that the fear of deadly new infections like severe acute respiratory syndrome (SARS), bird flu, and methicillin resistant staphylococcus aureus

---

* John D. Eshelman Professor of Law, Seattle University.

(MRSA) promising future pandemics, and nervousness over genetically modified organisms, human cloning, and nanotechnology. In addition, many worry that American global power is waning, unable to contain the perceived threat of Islamic fundamentalist extremism and left to fight indeterminate wars with vague and shifting rationales.

What all these threats to personal well-being have in common is that they are diffuse, without easily comprehended causes and without clearly defined ways to avoid or mitigate their potential harm. Moreover, they are agent-less, lacking identifiable villains to be fought and overcome. Instead, they cause a numbing sense of dread and foreboding about the future and a sense that the individual is powerless to do anything about them. Is it any wonder that people yearn for a simpler time when enemies were knowable and could be attacked and beaten?

Social psychologists examining cognitive biases in human thought have identified two that are particularly pertinent here. The first is the tendency to focus unduly on extreme occurrences. We wildly overestimate our odds of experiencing dramatic but low-probability events like winning the lottery, being in a plane crash, or being attacked by sharks at the beach. So, too, we are easily persuaded that horrific crimes are far more common than they truly are. This tendency to overestimate the frequency of dramatic events is amplified when compelling images of these events get disproportionate airtime in the mass media, where the ubiquitous "if it bleeds, it leads" recipe for news presentations guarantees that the pervasive threat of "monstrous offenders" will saturate our collective consciousness.

A second, perhaps less well-known cognitive bias, is termed the illusion of control, or the false sense of personal control over occurrences that are in fact not within our control. The illusion of control is particularly likely to occur in conditions of stress and uncertainty. Although the illusion of control can have positive effects by encouraging personal action when a more realistic perception would sap motivation to act, it can also have negative consequences by encouraging continued irrational and ineffective behavior even in the face of negative feedback.

Together, these cognitive biases help explain not only why "monstrous offenders" are singularly present in the popular imagination despite their rarity and unrepresentative character but also why we respond to them as we do. For example, the rise of eponymous laws, such as "Megan's Law," is an example of action spawned by the illusion of control. By naming the law after a specific victim, we are encouraged to believe that, if only we had enacted the law in time, Megan would have been saved. At least, we assure ourselves, the new law will prevent future Megans from becoming victims.

Likewise, the myth of the "soft-hearted judge" reflects the belief, based in the illusion of control, that monstrous offenders can be identified in advance and that only judicial failure of nerve stands in the way of our incapacitating these monsters before they have a chance to wreak their awful violence. The fact that judges almost certainly overpredict potential future violence is irrelevant. In the illusion of control fantasy, the public comes to believe that we could prevent monstrous violence if only judges had the will to do so.

Monstrous crimes are indeed horrific to contemplate, but the locus of the danger they represent is discrete, and a curative response—capture and total incapacitation of the monsters—appears to be realistically achievable. In a world in which much danger is diffuse, impersonal, and unassailable, there is, ironically, a comfort in the identification of danger that is traceable to specific enemies who can be identified, apprehended, punished, and rendered incapable of future harm.

HAVE GOOD INTENTIONS ALSO FUELED THE SEVERITY REVOLUTION?

DOUGLAS A. BERMAN*

Joseph Kennedy effectively identifies social and psychological realities that help explain the "unprecedented increase in the severity of criminal punishment in the United States."[1] His work helps us understand why the United States has become the world's leader in incarceration. But Kennedy and others have not sufficiently examined how even well-intentioned efforts to address criminal justice problems may also be contributing to the "severity revolution." Indeed, I fear that sensible concerns about wrongful convictions, the death penalty, and sentencing disparity may also be fueling modern increases in U.S. incarceration rates.

1. *Concerns about wrongful convictions.* Revelations of wrongful convictions have prompted new skepticism about the accuracy of criminal justice systems, and the "innocence revolution" should help propel needed systemic reforms. But as David Dow has suggested in a commentary on the death penalty, all the concerns about wrongful conviction of the innocent may eclipse any concern about severe punishment of the guilty:

> [T]he focus on innocence has insidiously distracted the courts. When I represent a client in a death penalty case, judges want to know whether there is any chance that client is innocent. If he isn't, then they are not much concerned about anything else I have to say. Oh, so Blacks were excluded from the jury? So what, he's guilty; any jury would have convicted him. Oh, so police hid evidence? Big deal, there was plenty of other evidence that he did it. Oh, so his lawyer slept through trial? Why does that matter? Clarence Darrow himself couldn't have kept him from the gallows . . . .

---

* William B. Saxbe Designated Professor of Law, Moritz College of Law, Ohio State University.
1. Kennedy core text at 254.

Innocence is a distraction because most people on death row are not in fact innocent, and the possibility of executing an innocent man is not even remotely the best reason for abolishing the death penalty.[2]

As Dow suggests, the focus on innocence can desensitize criminal justice participants to other injustices that afflict the administration of capital punishment. Critically, this desensitization problem extends beyond the death penalty; in my experience, the problem is even more acute when lower-profile offenders challenge long prison terms. Moreover, because defendants immediately after a conviction cannot effectively raise wrongful conviction concerns, legislatures, courts, and prosecutors often countenance procedural shortcuts at sentencing. Lower burdens of proof and limited constitutional and statutory rights at sentencing operate to tilt the criminal justice system toward severe punishments as the "distraction" of innocence fades.

2. *Concerns about the death penalty.* Modern advocacy against the death penalty is another well-intentioned but insidious distraction from concerns about mass incarceration. Capital abolitionists often distract courts, commentators, and would-be reformers from recognizing and assailing severe punishments other than death; they also likely desensitize moderates and conservatives to other problems with the criminal justice system. Because the Supreme Court has restricted the reach of the death penalty, death penalty debates concern only a very small group of the very worst murderers who have been condemned by a prosecutor, jurors, and a trial judge. The alternative to execution in such cases is typically the (arguably more) severe punishment of life imprisonment; indeed, death penalty abolitionists often advocate life without the possibility of parole as a humane alternative to the death penalty. Data now suggest that attacks on the death penalty could be increasing the number of defendants now serving life imprisonment. For every person on death row, fifty others are serving life sentences. But we see precious few critical discussions or serious moral debates over life imprisonment in the United States.

3. *Concerns about sentencing disparity.* Another catalyst for the severity revolution is the law, policies, and rhetoric of modern sentencing reforms. Fueled by cries of disparate judicial exercise of sentencing discretion, modern sentencing reforms have repudiated rehabilitation as a dominant sentencing purpose and have urged greater concern for sentencing uniformity, for imposing "just punishment" and for deterring offenses. Legislatures and sentencing commissions embraced more certain sentencing outcomes and more rigid sentencing rules, placing greater sentencing power in ex ante rule-makers instead of ex post sentence administrators and ensuring that modern sentencing judgments focus on criminal offenders as abstract characters—the threatening figure of a killer or a sex offender or a drug dealer. In addition, structured sentencing reforms often

---

2. David R. Dow, *Death by Good Intentions*, WASH. POST, Oct. 15, 2006, at B07.

mandate (or at least encourage) sentencing judges to focus on offense conduct and to limit consideration of offender characteristics that might justify softer sentences. Though greater uniformity in sentencing is often a worthwhile goal, it encourages a "leveling up" in sentencing outcomes: efforts to make sentences more consistent regularly seek to ensure disparately lenient sentences are more consistently harsh and rarely attempt to make disparately harsh sentences more consistently lenient.

In short, the massive modern increase in incarceration has occurred during the same period in which lawmakers, courts, and commentators have expressed well-intentioned—but perhaps ultimately overstated and misguided—concerns about wrongful convictions, the death penalty, and sentencing disparity. That relationship, I fear, is no coincidence.

REPLY

JOSEPH E. KENNEDY

Marianne Wesson references some of the many high-profile cases involving real or suspected family violence and asks whether seeing society as preoccupied with monstrous strangers is dated. My point is that our fear of monstrous offenders is disproportionate to the amount of crime they commit. To the degree that we are also afraid of violence from family members, that fear is well-grounded in reality. Most female homicide victims are killed by their male intimates. Most children homicide victims are killed by a parent. Most child sexual abuse victims are victimized by household members. Part of what makes our fear of monstrous offenders so inexplicable is that they actually kill and molest far fewer people than our fathers, husbands, and boyfriends. Moreover, greater public awareness of family violence has been cultivated by dedicated activist groups. Our disproportionate fear of monstrous strangers sprang full-grown from our enormous anxieties about social cohesion.

Wesson's second point is to doubt whether American sentencing policy is driven at all by cultural conceptions about offenders. The coincidence of a 500 percent increase in the incarcerated population with a series of moral panics about crime suggests that these conceptions have driven penal policy. More specifically, the circumstances under which measures such as three strikes laws, mandatory minimums in drug cases, and Megan's Laws were rapidly passed in the wake of high-profile crimes that tapped into widespread public fears provide more direct evidence of this connection.[1]

---

1. *See* Joseph E. Kennedy, *Monstrous Offenders and the Search for Solidarity Through Modern Punishment*, 51 HASTINGS L.J. 829, 825–26 (2000).

Janet Ainsworth usefully supplements my sociological story with a psychological account of cognitive biases. These cognitive biases do not operate in a vacuum, however. They become influential in particular social and political contexts. For example, Ainsworth observes that because economic, environmental, biological, and foreign problems are "agent-less, lacking identifiable villains to be fought and overcome. . .they cause a numbing sense of dread and foreboding about the future and a sense that the individual is powerless to do anything about them."[2]

I agree. We take out these unresolved anxieties upon criminals by punishing them harder than we should. Yet these larger problems create such a sense of dread and paralysis largely because we have lost confidence in our capacity for collective action. Anxieties about lack of social cohesion exacerbate these innate tendencies to focus on dramatic events such as monstrous crimes and to delude ourselves about how much we can control crime through incarceration.

Doug Berman brings a useful proceduralist perspective to the policymaking dynamics I address. I agree entirely with his point about the role that concerns formal equality played in the move toward determinacy and severity in sentencing.[3] The move toward more determinate systems of sentencing was, as I've noted elsewhere, driven in part by a desire to make sentencing decisions less visible and thereby less contestable. Ultimately, what determinate sentencing achieved was not a more egalitarian process but one in which the decisions that create racial disparities in sentencing were moved from the visible area of judicial sentencing to the opaque areas of charging and plea bargaining.

Berman also correctly points out that concerns about innocence and the death penalty overshadow concerns about overall severity in punishment. There is an important connection between these concerns and the dynamics I describe in my core text. We are preoccupied with innocence because we have come to see all rights as technicalities. We see rights as technicalities, in turn, because we believe that the evil and guilt of offenders is usually obvious. The reality is that only by observing the "technicalities" can we be confident about our determinations of guilt and innocence or of proportion in sentencing.

2. Ainsworth comment at 265.
3. I make this point in Kennedy, *supra* note 1, at 836–39.

PART II

DOCTRINE

13. AGAINST NEGLIGENCE LIABILITY

LARRY ALEXANDER* AND

KIMBERLY KESSLER FERZAN**

According to the orthodox account, a negligent act is an act that imposes a risk of harm of such a magnitude that imposing it is unjustified given the actor's reasons for so acting—and, crucially, the actor is unaware that the risk he is imposing is of that magnitude. (If the actor were aware that the risk was that high, he would be acting *recklessly*, not negligently). Notably, the negligent actor believes the risk of harm he is imposing is sufficiently low that were he correct, imposing that risk would be deemed justifiable. What presumably makes the negligent actor culpable is that he underestimates the risk his act creates; whereas, a "reasonable"—that is, nonculpable—person would not have underestimated the risk and, as a consequence, would not have acted as did the negligent actor.

I. WHY NEGLIGENCE IS NOT CULPABLE

Here is where the problem lies according to those, like us, who deny that the negligent actor is culpable: The negligent actor appears to be blamed for misperceiving the risk from his act.[1] But misperceiving risk is like misperceiving other things in the world—say, perceiving a stuffed deer to be a live one, or a mirage to be a pool of water. We do not ordinarily blame people for such misperceptions. We realize that how one perceives the world and indeed what influences and beliefs one forms come upon one "unbidden" as it were. And because we cannot control how we perceive, what we infer, and what we believe, we ought not be blamed for these things. "Cannot" defeats "ought to." Otherwise, we are just blaming people for what they are—stupid, obtuse, blind—under the guise of blaming them for what they do.

Because the purpose of the criminal law is to prevent harm by giving us reasons to act and to refrain from acting, the criminal law does not reach the

---

* Warren Distinguished Professor of Law, University of San Diego School of Law.

** Associate Dean for Academic Affairs and Professor of Law, Rutgers University, School of Law–Camden. This core text draws from Larry Alexander and Kimberly Kessler Ferzan, with Stephen J. Morse, CRIME & CULPABILITY: A THEORY OF CRIMINAL LAW (2009).

1. We believe that actors should only be punished if they deserve punishment. But we will not argue here for the retributive justification of punishment that our argument presupposes.

negligent actor *at the time he undertakes the negligent act.* At that time, the negligent actor is not aware that her action unjustifiably risks causing harm, and thus cannot be guided to avoid creating that risk by the injunction to avoid creating unjustifiable risks.[2]

II. FAILED ATTEMPTS TO NARROW NEGLIGENCE

Indeed, because people can make momentary mistakes, and because acts of clumsiness and stupidity hardly seem to be the sort of things for which we wish to hold people criminally liable, even those theorists in favor of punishing for negligence often seek to restrict its reach. That is, even for these theorists, the failure to live up to the "reasonable person" test is not alone sufficient for criminal liability. The challenge for those who wish to punish for negligence, then, is to find a principled way to distinguish those people whose substandard conduct renders them criminally liable from those who do not. We will briefly discuss three attempts to narrow the reach of negligence, none of which we believe provides such a principled distinction.

First, Ken Simons argues that it is appropriate to hold a negligent actor accountable when she is culpably indifferent.[3] Assume Alice and Betty both fail to appreciate a particular risk while they are driving. Alice fails to do so because she is distracted by a call that a friend is in the hospital. Betty fails to do so because she is putting on lipstick using her rearview mirror. Whom should the criminal law punish? According to Simons, the determination should be made using a counterfactual test: if the person had been aware of the risk, would she have proceeded anyway?

Unfortunately, this test raises new difficulties because it conflicts with our conception of free will. It punishes an actor not for what she has done, but for the choice she *might* have made had she been presented with the choice. Under Simons's theory, we should punish Betty if she has the sort of character based on which we would predict that she would choose to take this risk had she adverted to it. Yet, many actors in a given set of circumstances might resort to crime, but we should not punish them until they have actually made that choice and acted on it. Responsibility should not turn on the prediction of future choices. Nor should it turn on assessments of the types of people we are.

---

2. Of course, punishment for negligence may deter the *reckless* actor who would otherwise believe that his recklessness could not be proved at trial. But it does so at the cost of punishing some who are known or believed to be nonculpable.

3. Kenneth W. Simons, *Culpability and Retributive Theory: The Problem of Criminal Negligence*, 5 J. CONTEMP. LEGAL ISSUES 365 (1994).

Simons recognizes that his theory must tie this indifference to the actual harm-causing act.[4] That is, feelings about causing harm are passive, so how does one tie culpable indifference to an act? After all, causing is not enough. A desire may explain an act, but this does not mean that the act was the actor's chosen means of realizing that desire.[5] In his most recent work on the subject, Simons adopts a six-factor test to resolve this "significance in action" problem.[6] We will focus on the one crucial aspect of Simons's argument: the "deflationary" require- ment. "The basis of this prediction [that the actor would have acted in the face of a greater risk] is that when the actor is initially prepared to take the action, he possess the 'higher' mental state of knowledge, but by the time he acts, his mental state has 'deflated' to recklessness."[7] That is, Simons now will only punish an actor for her indifference, if she first was willing to act with knowl- edge, but by the time she does act, she is not practically certain the harm will occur, and is thus only reckless. To Simons, this actor is as culpable as the know- ing actor. In contrast, Simons rejects punishing "inflated" mental states, where we predict the actor would have continued in the face of a greater risk because of "the principle of respecting the actor's autonomy."[8]

This restriction is important. However, for us, it does not go far enough, whereas for negligence proponents, it may go too far. For the latter, Simons's test fails to punish negligent Betty because that would require "inflating" her culpability. Indeed, it is hard to see how this restriction will allow Simons to capture any negli- gent actor. What would it mean to be reckless and then become unaware of the risk? If the "deflation" happens quickly, we might suspect that the actor is still reckless. If the "deflation" occurs over a longer period of time, we may reasonably doubt that the earlier higher mental state should have any bearing on the actor's later negligence. (A decision to kill two years prior to accidentally running someone down does not mean that at the time of the accident, the actor is an intentional killer.) In any event, the typical negligent actor doesn't deflate—he never sees the risk at all.

On the other hand, we fail to see why Simons's reasoning that "the actor should be free to change his mind, even if at one point in time he firmly intends to commit a serious crime"[9] does not apply as well to "deflationary cases" in which the actor *does not act* in the face of a greater risk, but simply the lesser one that he now perceives. In a deflationary case, we may have better evidence about

---

4. *Id.* at 391–94.

5. Michael S. Moore, *Responsibility and the Unconscious*, 53 S. Cal. L. Rev. 1563, 1631 (1980).

6. Kenneth W. Simons, *Does Punishment for "Culpable Indifference" Simply Punish for "Bad Character"? Examining the Requisite Connection Between Mens Rea and Actus Reus*, 6 Buff. Crim. L. Rev. 219 (2002).

7. *Id.* at 275.

8. *Id.* at 280.

9. *Id.*

what an actor would have otherwise done, but punishment in such a case is still punishment for a choice the actor did not make but (very well) might have made under different circumstances. From either perspective, Simons takes an untenable middle position.

Second, Victor Tadros has also sought to identify circumstances under which negligence is criminally culpable.[10] He claims, first, that as agents, what we believe reflects on our character. We are therefore responsible for those things we believe and do not believe if those beliefs are attributable to our virtues and vices. Second, of those beliefs (or lack thereof) for which we are responsible, we should be held criminally responsible for those beliefs that manifest insufficient concern for others' interests.

We have our doubts about both parts of this test. Consider Tadros's argument that we are responsible for the way that we form beliefs. According to Tadros, our belief formation reflects our character, and we are responsible for those actions that reflect our character. He further claims that the "character" for which we are responsible is evidenced by our desires, including not only those desires with which we identify but also those desires that are alien to us if we make no attempt to change them.

But there is a significant gap between our omitting to get rid of a desire and our actually causing harm to another. First, we might ask at what point the actor becomes aware of this vicious trait. Sometimes we learn about our values only when we act. (Nor would hours of navel gazing or therapy usefully help us to divine some of our own values). If we do not know we have a desire, how can we be said to accept it? Second, the very character trait that leads to insensitivity to others may prevent the actor from recognizing her own character flaws. Finally, even if we know we have a particular desire, is it fair to say that we know what its implications are? How often will an actor recognize that her flaws could result in harm to other people?

As for the second part of the test, we are uncertain as to how an act can manifest insufficient concern for others in the absence of some sort of culpable choice by the actor. The driver who believes that she can put on mascara while driving may have a flawed character, but how exactly is it that her action *manifests* her insufficient concern? Tadros has the very same "significance in action" problem that Simons has.

Third, Stephen Garvey has recently produced a sophisticated argument for why some cases of inadvertence to risk are culpable. To the question of how retributive punishment of those who inadvertently create lethal risks can be warranted, Garvey gives this reply:

> The answer I propose is this: An actor who creates a risk of causing death but who was unaware of that risk is fairly subject to retributive punishment if he

---

10. Victor Tadros, CRIMINAL RESPONSIBILITY ch. 9 (2005).

was either *nonwillfully ignorant* or *self-deceived* with respect to the existence of the risk, and if such ignorance or self-deception was due to the causal influence of a desire he should have controlled. The culpability of such an actor does not consist in any choice to do wrong, but rather in the culpable failure to exercise *doxastic self-control*, i.e., control over desires that influence the formation and awareness of one's beliefs. An actor who is nonwillfully ignorant allows desire to preclude him from forming the belief that he is imposing a risk of death when the evidence available to him supports the formation of that belief, while an actor who is self-deceived forms that belief but allows desire to prevent him from becoming aware of it. In either case the actor could and should have controlled the wayward desire, thereby allowing the relevant belief to form and surface into awareness.[11]

Garvey goes on to argue that not just any desire that prevents one from becoming consciously aware of a risk that one either does subconsciously recognize or possesses the information required for recognizing suffices for culpability. He contrasts the case of Walter and Bernice Williams, whose desire not to have their son Walter taken from them by the welfare authorities perhaps prevented them from perceiving Walter's urgent need for medical care and the risk of death he faced, with the fictitious Sam and Tiffany, whose desire to further social climbing by putting on "the party of the decade" caused them to fail to recognize a similar risk to their child.[12] For Garvey, the less admirable desire of Sam and Tiffany, given its causal role in their not adverting to the risk to their son, renders them culpable for their inadvertence, but the Williams case is a much closer call.

Garvey makes it clear that no one deserves punishment merely for possessing base or nonadmirable desires.[13] It is only when the desire interferes with the actor's perception of risk that culpability ensues. The actor in that case is culpable because he does not resist the desire that blocks his formation of the belief about risk that he otherwise would form. The actor has failed to exercise "doxastic self-control."[14] But what puts the actor on notice that he should exercise such doxastic self-control? For Garvey, it is the awareness that his act is somewhat (but not unduly and hence culpably) risky.[15]

All of our acts are potentially risky, however. Suppose Sam and Tiffany recognize that there is *some* risk their son needs prompt medical attention. They would not be any different from any parent who rightfully does not rush her child to the

---

11. Stephen P. Garvey, *What's Wrong with Involuntary Manslaughter?*, 85 Tex. L. Rev. 333, 337–38 (2006).

12. *State v. Williams*, 484 P.2d 1167 (Wash. Ct. App. 1971); Garvey, *supra* note 11, at 333–37.

13. *See* Garvey, *supra* note 11, at 362–63.

14. *Id.* at 365.

15. *Id.* at 368–69.

pediatrician at the drop of a symptom. (Any common complaint—a headache, a sore throat, an upset stomach—*can* be the sign of an emergency, although it usually is not; and we do not deem the average parent, who surmises "it's just a cold," reckless for not seeking immediate medical attention.) So why then would Sam and Tiffany be culpable for continuing with their party planning?

Garvey's argument is fatally circular. One only has a reason to control the desires that might interfere with one's perception of risks if those desires are preventing you from perceiving risks. But if one cannot perceive the risks, one has no (internal) reason to control the desires. The desires may blind the actor to the risks he is imposing. But if they do, they likewise blind him to the reasons he has to control them.

Or, to put the point another way, Garvey's self-deception view conflates a notion of agency that focuses on one's conscious decision-making abilities with a notion of agency that includes conscious and unconscious desires. Blameworthiness, as Garvey concedes, rests on the first notion of agency, but the inappropriate desires are found within the second, broader agency account. Therefore, Garvey cannot maintain (as he does) that the actor is to blame for not controlling his self-deceiving desires, the very existence of which blind him (in the narrow agency sense) to both the desires' existence and the reasons to act otherwise.

III. THE ARBITRARINESS OF THE REASONABLE PERSON TEST

Another angle on negligence is also problematic. The negligent actor is supposed to be culpable for imposing a *risk* of harm. This means that as a theoretical matter, one can be negligent even if no harm results. But if one can be criminally negligent for, say, not realizing that the lane one is driving in is the lane for oncoming cars, then one should be criminally negligent whether or not one's driving in that lane actually results in a collision. Or, put differently, according to this view, if one would have been guilty of negligent homicide had one hit and killed an oncoming driver, one should be guilty of negligently *risking* death or injury when one luckily avoids a collision. It is the inadvertent imposing of the risk of harm, not the harm itself, that is the basis for deeming one culpable.

Risk, however, is an epistemic notion, not an ontic one. That is, it is about beliefs, not reality. Or, to make the same point a different way, from God's epistemically privileged point of view, all risks are either one or zero. When the negligent actor mistakenly drives in the lane for oncoming traffic, God knows whether he will or will not collide with an oncoming car. If he collides, the risk he was imposing from God's point of view was one. If he does not, it was zero.

So suppose he avoids a collision. He estimated the risk of his driving as ordinary—greater than zero, of course, but quite low—because he failed to realize he was in the wrong lane. God, on the other hand, being omniscient, knew the risk he created was zero. Yet, we are supposed to believe the driver is culpably negligent for underestimating the risk. How can that be?

In order for the charge of underestimating the risk to make sense, given that the "real" risk was zero, we must posit as a standard the risk some other actor would have estimated—the so-called "reasonable person in the actor's situation" (RPAS).

However, no principled and rationally defensible way exists to define the RPAS. There is no moral difference between punishing for inadvertent negligence and punishing on the basis of strict liability, and the lack of a moral difference evidences itself in the inability to draw a distinction between strict liability and negligence on any basis other than arbitrary stipulation.

The RPAS has two clear boundary lines. First, the RPAS could be a person apprised of all the facts about the world that bear on a correct moral decision. At the other possible conceptual boundary, the RPAS could be someone with all the beliefs that the actor actually held. Put somewhat differently, where action falls below the standard of recklessness—the *conscious* disregarding of an unjustifiable risk—the action will appear reasonable to the actor and thus to the RPAS if the RPAS has exactly the same beliefs as the actor.

The two possible boundaries that provide the frame for characterizing the RPAS present us with this dilemma. On the one hand, if the RPAS knows all the facts, as God knows, then the RPAS always chooses the action that averts the harm (in the absence of justification, of course). But if this is the standard of the RPAS, then every case of strict liability will be a case of negligence as defined by the RPAS standard. It will never be reasonable not to know. (Notice, as well, that because risk is epistemic, the omniscient actor deals only in certainties: for her, the "risk" of a particular harm entailed by any act is either one or zero. As such, liability would be imposed for every avoidable and regrettable—unjustifiable— harm, but no liability would be imposed when no such harm occurs.). On the other hand, if the RPAS knows only what the actor knows, there is never any negligence either, only recklessness. The RPAS will always act as the actor acted where the actor is not conscious of the level of risk, and will act differently only where the actor is conscious of the level of risk, i.e., is reckless.

In short, at one conceptual boundary, the RPAS collapses negligence into strict liability; at the other, the RPAS collapses negligence into recklessness. The question, then, is where between those boundaries the RPAS should be located.

The answer is that any location between these two boundaries will be morally arbitrary. Between the boundaries, any RPAS will be a construct that will include some beliefs of the actual actor together with beliefs that the constructor inserts. Which beliefs are inserted other than the ones the actor actually had will determine whether the RPAS would act as the actor acted. But there is no standard that tells us which of the beliefs of the actual actor should be left intact and which should be replaced by other (correct) beliefs. The RPAS standard, cut loose from the alternative moorings of the actor's actual beliefs or of the world as it really was at the time the actor acted, is completely adrift in a sea of alternative constructions, none of which is any more compelling than another.

Some commentators at this point assert the possibility that the RPAS is like the actual actor in all material aspects, but that the RPAS "would have" adverted to and properly assessed the risks because the actual actor "could have" adverted to and properly assessed them. But this reply contains an equivocation in the reference to what the actor "could have" adverted to and assessed in the actor's situation. If we take the actor at the time of the "negligent" choice, with what he is conscious of and adverting to, his background beliefs, etc., then it is simply false that the actor "could have" chosen differently in any sense that has normative bite. For although it may be true that the actor "could have" chosen differently in a sense relevant to the free will/determinism issue, it is false that in that situation, the actor had any internal reason to choose differently from the way he chose.

That is, an actor may fail to form a belief (or a correct belief) if he (1) lacks the requisite background beliefs, (2) lacks the intellectual ability, or (3) lacks the motivation to form the belief. With respect to (1), we do not see how it can be fair to say that an actor "could have" believed A if only he had believed B without articulating how it was within the actor's control to believe B. And one would then have to show why it was, at the time belief B was available to him, a *culpable decision* not to form that belief.

In addition, as to (2), we do not see how we can blame an actor who either intrinsically (because of limited intelligence) or extrinsically (because of momentary distraction) fails to be able to form belief A at the appropriate moment. An agent lacks the requisite control over her ability to form the correct belief at the appropriate time.

Finally, with regard to (3), an agent may not be motivated to form a belief for two reasons. First, an agent may simply not see any reason to gather additional information. Suppose someone more epistemically favored than the actor—an epistemically favored observer (EFO), who we shall assume is the equivalent of an RPAS—would estimate the risk that the actor is imposing on others to be higher than the risk the actor actually estimates. The EFO, we shall assume, would be culpable for acting as the actor acts. The problem for the actor, however, is that for him to become an EFO would require the expenditure of resources—time, energy, and perhaps material resources, plus the cost of forgoing of the act in question at the time in question—and given his appraisal of the situation, that expenditure of resources appears unreasonable. After all, the actor does not know what risk the EFO estimates. The risk of harm could be higher than the actor estimates, but it could as well be lower, or the same. (If the EFO is God, then the risk *will* be higher or lower; it will be 1 or 0.) Nothing that the actor is aware of indicates to the actor that he should spend the resources to become an EFO.

Second, a person may fail to appreciate the risk because she is a bad person. However, we fail to see how someone who has no internal reason to form a belief is culpable for not doing so when, for whatever characterological reason, she does not recognize that such a belief should be formed. If the negligence proponent wants to hold us responsible for our characters, he will have to offer some evidence that we have control over them.

IV. CONCLUSION

A culpability-based criminal law will not include liability for negligence. Culpability entails control, and the negligent actor does not have this requisite control. Any control a negligent actor has over her character can only partially and indirectly affect whether the actor will fail to advert to a risk at the requisite time. Moreover, because none of us is perfect, even those with relatively "good" characters will constantly fail to advert to risks that they should have chosen to avoid had they adverted to them.

Moreover, even if we could control these failings, no nonarbitrary way exists to determine the standard against which we should be judged. The reasonable person is neither the actual actor nor the omniscient god, but some construct that lies in-between. Because we have no principled way to determine the composition of this construct, punishment for negligence is morally arbitrary.

COMMENTS
FOR NEGLIGENCE LIABILITY

LEO ZAIBERT*

Very roughly, to act negligently is to fail to show proper care and concern for others. The negligent actor (*wrongly*) thinks that the risk her action creates is so low that it is inimical to the criminal law's (and morality's) concerns. Or, perhaps more commonly, she may simply be unaware of the very existence of the risk, even though she *should* have been aware of it. Yet, even though the second type of negligence is perfectly common, Larry Alexander and Kimberly Kessler Ferzan seem to be interested only in the first type, for they claim that what makes the negligent actor culpable is that she "underestimates" the risk that her act creates.

This "underestimation" quickly morphs into "misperception": Alexander and Ferzan tell us that misperceiving the risks our actions create is like misperceiving any other thing whatever, such as taking a stuffed deer to be a live deer, or a

---

* Copeland Fellow, Department of Law, Jurisprudence, and Social Thought, Amherst College; Associate Professor of Philosophy, University of Wisconsin–Parkside.

mirage to be a real pool of water, etc. Because there exists a sense in which we should not be blamed for our (mis)perceptions, Alexander and Ferzan think that to punish people for their negligent behavior is as normatively indefensible as it would be to punish them for their (mis)perceptions.

The main problem with this argument is that risk is not really analogous to pools of water or stuffed deer. In fact, Alexander and Ferzan are exactly right when they state that risk "is an epistemic notion, not an ontic one" and when they add that "it is about beliefs, not reality."[1] A fortiori, then, to act negligently is not to misperceive things "in the world," but to somehow get things wrong inside our own heads—and this "getting things wrong" is not a matter of perception. The difference between ontic and epistemic notions should be enough to make one abandon the talk of misperception. But if Alexander and Ferzan wish to preserve this talk, they should at least emphasize more than they do now that the misperceptions of the negligent agent concern her own mental phenomena, and not objects in the world. The crucial point is that as a result of this getting-things-wrong-in-her-own-head, the negligent agent fails to form some other mental phenomena that she *should* have formed, and that in turn would have prevented her from acting as she did.

When we blame a loved one for, say, negligently forgetting our birthday, we are not merely blaming her for having misperceived anything, at least not in the usual sense of (mis)perception. We blame her for not having *done* something, namely, remembering our birthday. This forgetfulness says something about her commitment to us—about her not *caring* for us. (It is not necessary to embrace aretaic theories in order to justify blaming people for displaying the sorts of doxastic flaws that are characteristic of negligent actors.) Nothing hinges on the particularities of personal relationships: anyone can show lack of care. We can blame someone, a perfect stranger, for not noticing our foot as she steps on it. And although it is true that we do not ordinarily blame people for misperceptions (say, involving stuffed deer or pools of waters), we do ordinarily blame people for their carelessness. To punish people for their negligence is not to punish them for misperception—even if this negligence was somehow linked to some form of misperception.

Although the preceding remarks perhaps cast doubt on some of Alexander and Ferzan's arguments, they do not by themselves show that the criminal law should in fact punish carelessness. Someone may hold the view that while carelessness is sometimes immoral, it is nonetheless never illegal. Indeed, Alexander and Ferzan seem to lean in that direction, for they think that negligence is above all a matter of "clumsiness and stupidity" of the sort displayed when we mistake a stuffed deer for a real one.

---

1. Alexander and Ferzan core text at 278.

Thus conceptualized, negligence does appear somewhat inapposite in a liberal criminal law. But, as stated, negligence need not be conceptualized this narrowly, and, moreover, one need not share Alexander and Ferzan's commitment to a criminal law whose (only? main?) function is "to prevent harm by giving us reasons to act and to refrain from acting."[2] For to the extent that, in addition to preventing harm, the criminal law is *also* concerned with achieving retributive justice, it should then sometimes punish negligent actors. And the thesis that some negligent actors should be criminally punished would remain true even if Alexander and Ferzan are right in that the "[the?] challenge for those who wish to punish for negligence,"[3] which consists in distinguishing the careless actor who is criminally liable from the careless actor who is not criminally liable, has not been met.

---

2. *Id.* at 273.
3. *Id.* at 274.

THE OBJECT OF CRIMINAL RESPONSIBILITY

MICHELLE MADDEN DEMPSEY*

Unlike Larry Alexander and Kimberly Kessler Ferzan, I think that negligent actors are sometimes morally culpable, and in some legal systems, some of these negligent actors may (properly) be held criminally responsible for some kinds of actions. Although Alexander and Ferzan raise a number of interesting issues, I will limit my comments to their characterization of the object of criminal responsibility (i.e., that for which an actor is held criminally responsible) and the effect this characterization has on our intuitions regarding negligence liability.

As an initial point of clarification, it should be noted that the criminal law does not blame the actor "for misperceiving the risk from his act."[1] Rather, it blames the actor for *causing the harm* at issue: e.g., negligent homicide laws blame the actor *for killing,* not merely for misperceiving the risk that he might kill. So, although I agree with Alexander and Ferzan's intuition that we "do not ordinarily blame people for . . . misperceptions,"[2] it's worth noting that the criminal law does not seek to blame people for their misperceptions—it seeks to blame people for their misdeeds.

In a similar vein, we should acknowledge that the criminal law does not "blam[e] people for what they are,"[3] but instead blames people for what they do.

---

* Faculty of Law and Worcester College, Oxford University.
1. Alexander and Ferzan core text at 273.
2. *Id.*
3. *Id.*

There is, of course, a relationship between what we are and what we do, at least insofar as what we do constitutes what we are (e.g., selfish people possess selfish characters precisely because they habitually act selfishly).

Still, when it comes to the proper object of criminal responsibility, this relationship should not be overstated. An actor is not properly criminalized for being a jerk: but he might properly be subject to criminal liability because, in virtue of being such a jerk, he ended up killing someone else.

If we focus on the proper object of criminal responsibility (actions), limit our cases to those in which serious harm (e.g., death) results from these negligent actions, and direct our attention to negligent actions born of dispositions grounded in vicious character traits, then we will likely find that our intuitions shift away from those suggested by Alexander and Ferzan.

Take the driver who puts on mascara while driving. As Alexander and Ferzan frame it, this case involves a "driver who believes that she can put on mascara while driving . . ."[4] This way of putting it suggests that we are confronted with a driver who believes that she can *safely* put on mascara while driving (i.e., she has averted to the issue of safety in her driving and mistakenly underestimated the risk she poses). If that's what Alexander and Ferzan have in mind, then we may be confronted with a stupid driver, but it is not clear that her stupidity is vicious. And so, if that driver kills someone, I agree it is unlikely that she will be a proper candidate for criminal responsibility.

If, however, a driver never even considers whether she can drive safely while applying mascara, then we may have a very different case at hand. If that driver kills someone while applying mascara, we have identified someone who has caused serious harm to another through an action born of a disposition grounded in what may very well be a vicious character trait. Having been that driver myself in my teen years, I now recognize that my actions were disposed by vicious character traits of (*inter alia*) laziness and vanity. Had I killed someone while applying mascara (or was it lip-gloss?), perhaps I should have been held criminally responsible for my actions.

Distinguishing between culpable and nonculpable negligence and determining which (if any) instances of culpably negligent harm-causing actions merit criminalization is no easy task. We should expect that the lines will vary depending upon the social context at issue and a host of other considerations. Yet, the fact that these lines are difficult to draw doesn't mean they are necessarily arbitrary (as Alexander and Ferzan claim), it just means that the line-drawing exercise should be undertaken with care, in recognition of the grave moral costs of criminalization and with an eye toward minimization. The risk of moral error in delineating criminal negligence does, admittedly, weigh against imposing such liability across a wide range of cases, but it does not (as Alexander and Ferzan

---

4. *Id.* at 276.

would have us believe) condemn all forms of criminal negligence as morally arbitrary.

IS NEGLIGENCE BLAMELESS?

ALAN BRUDNER*

Larry Alexander and Kimberly Kessler Ferzan claim that (1) negligence is not blameworthy because inadvertence is not controllable and 2) there is no nonarbitrary midpoint between the omniscient actor who never errs and the actual actor who did err; hence the standard of the reasonable person in the actor's situation (RPAS) is not a standard shortfalls from which can be regarded as blameworthy. In my view, negligence is blameworthy but not culpable (deserving of judicial punishment). Here I want to say why I think Alexander's and Ferzan's two arguments for the nonblameworthiness of negligence do not work.

Misperceptions are not controllable—Negligence in criminal law, I take it, is the imposition of an unjustified risk of serious harm where the actor had the basic (normal) mental and physical capacities to avoid the risk. That is, any plausible view of negligence liability must adopt H.L.A. Hart's modification of the strict objective standard to take into account abnormal incapacities to conform to the reasonable person standard—incapacities for which the agent is not responsible (e.g., mental retardation, a sudden physiological event). If these are taken into account, the "ought implies can" maxim does not preclude blameworthy negligence.

Many misperceptions are blameless because they are natural illusions or because the actor is not engaged in an activity risky to others. Where we ought to know misperceptions can be dangerous (because we are engaged in an activity where misperception can be injurious), we ought to be on special alert, controlling our inclination to let our attention drift. So to say that we misperceived does not absolve us from blame if our failure to perceive was attributable to inattentiveness (attending to something else) where the activity's riskiness was such that we ought to have focused our attention. It doesn't matter that the actor had no internal reason to advert to the real risk, because the fact that he had no internal reason is precisely what is blameworthy—the external reasons (the dangerousness of the activity) should have been internal. This may be, as Alexander and Ferzan say, to blame someone for being who they are, but there is nothing wrong with blaming someone for stupidity or obtuseness or narcissism, etc. There is indeed something wrong with the state's punishing someone for who they are (even when they are responsible for who they are), but this indicates that negligence is not properly a criminal *level* of fault, not that negligence is blameless.

---

* Albert Abel Professor of Law, University of Toronto.

The reasonable person in the actor's situation is an arbitrary construct—The RPAS is neither God nor the actor. The RP is not omniscient because no one can be fairly blamed for not being God. But neither is it the actor, because, if it were, moral evaluation would be impossible. The question is whether there is a stable standard between God and the actor.

Let's try out the standard of the reasonable person. Not being God, the reasonable person acts in the face of uncertainty, which implies risk. Let's say an unjustifiable risk is a socially extraordinary risk—a risk in excess of that which people reciprocally impose on each other as an inevitable byproduct of social interaction in a certain (technological, urban/rural, etc.) environment. That standard is a legal one that has force independently of the actor's beliefs as to what constitutes an unjustifiable risk, and it is a matter of judgment whether it has been breached—not of the actor's judgment, but of an official's judgment.

Say the judge determines the standard has been breached—the risk was excessive. Is the actor blameworthy for the breach assuming he thought, through misperception of the circumstances, that the risk was within the socially normal? The reasonable person with normal capacities would always be alert to a risk in excess of the socially normal. If the actor had these capacities, he is blameworthy for not adverting as the reasonable person would have done; if not, not. This makes a clear difference from strict liability, where the actor is liable for injury even though he did not take a socially unjustifiable risk. It also makes a clear difference from recklessness, where the actor took what he knew or suspected was an unjustified risk.

There is, I think, a nonarbitrary distinction between actor-characteristics a moral standard of conduct must accommodate and those it may not accommodate. Shortcomings for which the actor is responsible, being themselves blameworthy, cannot absolve from blame; those for which the actor is not responsible do absolve from blame. It is of course a matter of judgment how to apply that distinction, but that doesn't make the distinction itself arbitrary.

FATALLY CIRCULAR? NOT!

STEPHEN P. GARVEY*

If you believe that an actor should be punished if and only if he chooses to do something wrong, it would seem to follow that an actor who unleashes a prohibited risk into the world, but who fails to realize that he is doing so, should not be punished. No awareness of risk, no choice to do wrong, no punishment. So say Larry Alexander and Kimberly Kessler Ferzan. For the most part, I agree.

---

* Professor of Law and Associate Dean for Academic Affairs, Cornell Law School.

Our disagreement boils down to this: They say that an actor should not be punished, all else being equal, unless and until he forms the belief that he is unleashing a prohibited risk into the world. In contrast, I say that it would not be unfair to punish an actor who, though he does not in fact form the belief that he is unleashing a prohibited risk into the world, could and should have formed that belief through the exercise of doxastic self-control. Moreover, if such an actor is punished, he is punished for culpably failing to exercise such self-control when he could and should have exercised it.

Let me flesh this idea out a little more. An actor can only be aware of a prohibited risk if he believes that the risk exists, and he can only believe that a risk exists if he is sufficiently confident that it exists, and sufficiently conscious of its existence. That's what it takes to make a cognitive attitude a belief, and not something else. But an actor's doxastic attitude vis-à-vis a prohibited risk might not rise to the level of belief. It might fall short because it lacks some feature beliefs necessarily possess. It might, for example, fall short because the actor lacks sufficient confidence in the prohibited risk's existence (he merely suspect that it exits), or because he lacks sufficient consciousness of its existence (he is only dimly aware of its existence).

Now, if the evidence available to an actor is enough to cause him to form the full-blown belief that a prohibited risk exists, then why doesn't he form that belief? One answer is desire. Desire can sometimes, somehow get in the way of the smooth operation of an actor's belief-formation process. When it does, the actor fails to see that he is creating and sustaining a prohibited risk. Nonetheless, insofar as the cognitive attitude he does possess vis-à-vis the risk—he suspects that it exists or is dimly aware of its existence—provides him with a reason to exercise doxastic self-control, then he ought to do so. Suspecting that a risk exists, or being dimly aware of its existence, does provide such a reason. It tells the actor to stop and think: to exercise doxastic self-control, thereby deflecting the blinding force of desire and allowing the relevant belief to form. An actor who fails to exercise such self-control is, all else being equal, culpable for that failure.

Alexander and Ferzan detect a "fatal circularity" here. They agree that desires can "blind the actor to the risk he is imposing."[1] But they go onto say, if desires do so blind the actor, then "they likewise blind him to the reasons he has to control them."[2] Well, that's true sometimes, but not all the time. A desire might be such that it prevents an actor from believing that he is imposing a risk, but not such that it prevents him from suspecting that he is imposing a risk, or from being dimly aware of its existence. In other words, it makes noncircular sense to say that desire can preclude the formation of some cognitive attitudes without precluding the formation of others. Moreover, these other cognitive attitudes,

---

1. Alexander and Ferzan core text at 278.
2. Id.

once formed, give an actor a reason to exercise doxastic self-control. Of course, if the offending desire does indeed prevent an actor from even suspecting that he is imposing a prohibited risk, or from even being dimly aware of it, then I agree with Alexander and Ferzan. Such an actor would have no reason to exercise self-control, and so cannot be faulted when he fails to do so.

The foregoing account of the circumstances under which it would not be unfair to punish an actor who fails to realize that he is imposing a prohibited risk no doubt has many problems. But circularity—fatal at that—is not among them!

COGNITIVE SCIENCE AND CONTEXTUAL
NEGLIGENCE LIABILITY

ANDREW E. TASLITZ*

Larry Alexander and Kimberly Kessler Ferzan make original and powerful arguments for flatly prohibiting negligence liability in criminal cases. My own instinct, however, is that the question needs to be more context-specific, for several reasons.

Importantly, central to their argument is their dismissal of how we can be responsible for unconscious thoughts and feelings. Their concern arises partly from a misconception about the nature of the human mind. Cognitive science demonstrates that rather than a consciousness/unconsciousness dichotomy, our mind consists of a spectrum of varying degrees of consciousness. Moreover, conscious thoughts generally begin in the unconscious, and all the different levels interact so that the unconscious can learn from the conscious mind and vice versa in the long run. Thus, for example, though they are correct that introspection is rarely useful, two techniques can provide insight into two sorts of unconscious phenomena—feelings and attitudes. One way to do so is to pay attention to how others react to your behavior. The second is to choose to behave in an admirable fashion, for the unconscious learns from such behavior and becomes admirable. Both tactics have significant empirical and theoretical social science support. Failing to engage in such inquiries thus does indeed reflect a character lacking virtue.

But, they may respond, the fact remains that this individual at the relevant moment has not acted in a way that makes him capable of doing better at the time of the crime, so his potential past character-changing behavior is irrelevant. Yet this seems to me to turn on a misconception of what it means to be a

---

* Welsh S. White Distinguished Visiting Professor of Law, University of Pittsburgh, 2008–09; Professor of Law, Howard University School of Law. This comment is based on Andrew E. Taslitz, *Forgetting Freud: The Courts' Fear of the Subconscious in Date Rape (and Other) Cases,* 17 B.U. Pub. L. Rev. 145 (2007).

"person." Because the conscious and unconscious are so interconnected and interactive, the unconscious cannot routinely be ignored in assigning criminal liability. Moreover, a person *consists of* his past and present. The human mind in fact consists of a series of relatively task-specific modules rather than the unitary mind of folk belief. The appearance of a unitary being arises from each individual's crafting a narrative to explain his thoughts and behavior to himself. For all practical purposes, the person *is* a narrative continuing over time, though observers might interpret that narrative differently than does the subject. The point is this: if we are to hold "persons" responsible for their thoughts, actions, and character, we cannot ignore their past or their unconscious.

This does not mean, however, that every act of negligence creating some minor risk should generate criminal liability. Remember that I said that an individual is most able to change attitudes and feelings, so the possibility of change in those areas is highest.

Furthermore, indifference can often arise from self-deception, the neat but real mental trick of being aware and not aware of something at the same time. There are two kinds of self-deception: semi-conscious and unconscious. The semi-conscious self-deceiver tries to ignore, repress, or minimize inconvenient facts that do indeed, at least dimly and briefly, enter his conscious mind. The unconscious self-deceiver is motivated by self-interest to keep thoughts and feelings residing there from bubbling to the surface, to purge them, or to ignore what it fully expects it would discover if it bothered to investigate. The element of intention in the first sort and the selfishness present in both the first and second sort reveal a particularly reprehensible character.

Additionally, Alexander and Ferzan do not address one sort of risk that I see as a particular danger to creating a fair system of justice: risk of harm to equality values, for example, by treating women or African-Americans as less worthy because of their gender and race. For me, therefore, a self-deceiving man who does not take affirmative steps to inquire whether a woman wants to have sexual intercourse and accurately to understand her answer merits criminal negligence liability because of the combination of an element of intention, a selfish nature, grave risked (and resulting) harm, and injury to equality values. I do not say that this is the only time that negligence merits criminal punishment, but the example makes the point that the question should be a contextual one. On the other hand, Alexander and Ferzan's arguments are sufficiently worrisome that I agree that the default position, absent strong proof like that above, should be no negligence liability.[1]

---

1. As to questions of over-inclusiveness and proof, see *id.* and sources cited therein.

THE DISTINCTION BETWEEN NEGLIGENCE AND RECKLESSNESS IS UNSTABLE

KENNETH W. SIMONS*

In Larry Alexander and Kimberly Kessler Ferzan's view, an actor is culpable for risky conduct only if he is reckless—i.e., only if he is subjectively aware that the risk is sufficiently great that it is unjustified, an awareness that gives him an "internal reason" not to create the risk. But this view must be further elaborated. What constitutes subjective awareness of a risk? How concrete, how specific, how conscious, must that awareness be? And what level of risk must the actor perceive? In answering these qualitative and quantitative questions, the authors then face a dilemma. Either they endorse a super-subjective approach, requiring the actor to form specific beliefs about *all* the legally relevant features of the risky conduct—but then they must endorse a position under which almost no one is ever culpable enough to deserve criminal punishment. Or they acknowledge that any realistic, sensible conception of recklessness requires subjective awareness of only some of the legally relevant features of the risky conduct—but then they must permit judgments of reasonableness of the very sort that they condemn when they critique negligence liability.

Thus, assume for the moment that Betsy realizes that she is posing a significant risk of harm by taking her eyes off the road for several seconds while she is putting on lipstick using her rearview mirror. But suppose she believes that this is a justifiable risk to take; she is a very busy person, after all. Her own judgment of justifiability cannot be conclusive; in applying a recklessness test, it makes some sense to require the actor to be aware that she is posing a significant risk, but we should not require that she subjectively believe that the risk is unjustifiable. So it is implausible to choose the first horn of the dilemma. But if we instead choose the second horn, notice that we are now condemning Betsy not for her subjective beliefs, but for her failure to draw reasonable inferences from those beliefs—here, that the risk she took was unjustifiable. Yet the authors cannot easily endorse this solution, either, for it requires judgments of reasonableness that they otherwise condemn. (It might also run afoul of the "ought implies can" requirement, insofar as they interpret "can" as requiring subjective beliefs about all legally relevant matters).

The sharp distinction that the authors wish to draw between negligent unawareness and reckless awareness is fuzzy and unstable in the other direction as well. To determine that an actor is negligent, we must first find that he is aware of *some* morally and legally relevant features of his conduct and the

---

* Professor of Law, The Honorable Frank R. Kenison Distinguished Scholar in Law, Boston University School of Law.

surrounding circumstances, from which he should have inferred that the risk was substantial and unjustified. Betsy is at least negligent because, from the fact that she is driving and is applying makeup without looking at the road, she should infer that she is posing a risk of harm. If she had no idea that she was driving, or that she was applying makeup, she might well not be negligent at all.[1]

Or consider the interesting phenomenon of an actor who *forgets* the facts that make his conduct risky. Ernest loads his gun in the morning but forgets, when he carries his gun in public in the afternoon, that he loaded it earlier. Is it really unjust to punish him in the afternoon for carrying a loaded gun in public? And yet, under the authors' approach, punishment is unwarranted, for he does not, during his afternoon stroll, have any "internal reason" to take care not to bring his gun with him. Indeed, suppose that Ernest has not forgotten that he loaded the gun, but is simply not giving any thought to whether the gun is loaded when he takes his stroll. Again, their approach appears to entail the dubious conclusion that punishment is unwarranted, because he does not consciously consider the relevant fact, the loaded status of the gun, when he acts.

To be sure, the authors are correct that we should not broadly permit criminal liability for every act that would satisfy a tort standard of negligence. But the concept of culpable indifference justifies criminal liability in a defensible subset of negligence cases. It is also a more nuanced approach than the authors suggest; it encompasses more than the counterfactual test that they critique. For example, an unaware actor can still display culpable indifference when his unawareness flows from:

- inexcusable anger;
- gross insensitivity to the interests of others (suppose D is so focused on his own sexual pleasure that he pays no attention to whether V is consenting to his advances); or
- an illegal or immoral activity or an activity that the actor should know might diminish his ability to perceive risks (e.g., the decision to get drunk).

---

1. *See* Model Penal Code § 2.02(2)(d) (1980) (fact finder must consider the circumstances "known" to the actor in judging whether the actor was negligent).

REPLY

LARRY ALEXANDER AND KIMBERLY KESSLER FERZAN

We claim that criminal law cannot blame and punish for misperception or misestimation. As the first part of our core text argues, theorists cannot articulate a principled standard that distinguishes those instances in which they want to criminally punish individuals from those instances in which they don't. Leo Zaibert and Michelle Dempsey take our complaint to be one of line-drawing. They reply that just because it is hard to draw a line does not mean that no line can be drawn. But our challenge, with respect to their assertions that some people deserve punishment for negligence, is not one of line-drawing. Our claim is that theorists who assert that A (laziness and vanity) is punishable and Z (stupidity) is not fail to offer any principled justification for punishing A. Indeed, Dempsey's comment illustrates just our complaint. She concludes that if she killed someone because of her laziness and vanity, then "perhaps I should have been criminally responsible for my actions."[1] But where is the argument that is presumably embedded within that "perhaps"?

Let us be clear: The arrogant driver who believes he is a safe driver, or believes he poses no risk, or doesn't think about posing a risk, is not deserving of punishment. We have yet to hear the *argument* to the contrary.

In contrast, Alan Brudner accepts that any character trait can suffice for blameworthy negligence (including stupidity or obtuseness), but that in no case does this blameworthiness rise to the level of criminal responsibility. Morally, it is true that we do blame people for their characters. But it should be noted that we only have control over our characters indirectly, and we may not fully know our own character flaws until they eventuate in action. And because individuals have less control or ability to change their characters, the blame cannot be as robust for character flaws as it must be for criminal misconduct. Yes, we blame people for characters, but it is qualitatively and quantitatively different than criminal punishment.

As for Brudner's claim that the RPAS is not arbitrary, we find this to be an assertion without an argument. Brudner posits the "socially extraordinary risk," but we haven't a clue what that is, or by what perspective that is determined. A socially extraordinary risk is relative to some baseline of information, some defined reference class, etc.; but because we can't find a principled way of selecting among alternatives, we still don't know what a socially extraordinary risk is.

Stephen Garvey, Andrew Taslitz, and Kenneth Simons look to the mechanics of the actor's practical reasoning. Our dispute with Garvey boils down to what Garvey takes the relationship between "belief" and recklessness to be. Garvey contends that beliefs require that one must be sufficiently confident of X, and sufficiently conscious of X. When one only suspects that X exists, or is only dimly aware of X's existence, then one does not believe X. But one's dim suspicions (to combine the two) that X will not become a belief that X for a variety of reasons, says Garvey, and one of these reasons is an obstructing desire. (Perhaps the clearest example might be a suspicion that a spouse is cheating that one does not want to allow oneself to believe to be true).

---

1. Dempsey comment at 284.

But with Garvey's claim thus clarified, it isn't circular, but it's semantic and trivial. Our claim is that an actor is reckless and does manifest insufficient concern when she chooses to risk harm to others for insufficient reasons. But an actor who "suspects X" *is aware of X*, and an actor who is dimly aware of X *is aware of X*. That is, these "dim suspicions" do figure in the actor's practical reasoning. The fact that they are not beliefs but only "suspicions" at a level of consciousness and probability[2] does not mean that they are not part of the actor's conscious calculations. And if you only want to punish conscious calculations, then you are on our side, whatever you may "believe."

It is unclear how far apart our view is from Taslitz's, given that he concedes that our arguments are "sufficiently worrisome" that as a "default position" "there should be no negligence liability."[3] Initially, he puts significant emphasis on degrees on consciousness and the way that a "person" consists of his past and his present, his conscious and unconscious. At one point, he says that "if we are to hold 'persons' responsible for their thoughts, actions, and character, we cannot ignore their past or their unconscious."[4] We sincerely doubt, though, that Taslitz thinks that we can be held responsible for, say, dreaming to kill the king; and, of course, this is because we lack sufficient control over our unconscious. In contrast, we have argued elsewhere, opaque recklessness (a combination of conscious and preconscious awareness) can ground recklessness,[5] and we have argued that *prior culpable choices* (is that the person's past?) may also constitute recklessness. So we aren't sure how much disagreement there is here.

Taslitz further argues that indifference can arise from self-deception, and these cases are particularly egregious when one self-deceives oneself with racist or sexist beliefs. Once again, either one is aware of the risk, or one is not. But we still have not heard an argument as to why we may punish for actions arising from character but not choice. But we will say this: If an actor is aware of his racism or sexism, it is an important (and open) question whether he can be responsible (in terms of recklessness) for failing to discharge a duty to rid himself of these beliefs and traits. Provocation's "reasonableness" rule is best seen as a forfeiture rule that the defendant should have rid himself of a violent character trait but failed to try to do so, and we might ask the same question about beliefs. Most pointedly, the question is whether a liberal society committed to freedom of belief *and* to equality can impose a duty on an actor to rid himself of a belief (of which he is aware) that he realizes can potentially harm others in the future. Of course, every belief presents itself as true, so what reason would anyone have (be aware of) for of ridding himself of sincere beliefs?

---

2. Garvey comment at 287.

3. Taslitz comment at 289.

4. *Id.*

5. *See* Larry Alexander and Kimberly Kessler Ferzan, with Stephen J. Morse, CRIME & CULPABILITY: A THEORY OF CRIMINAL LAW ch. 3 (2009).

We would answer Simons's inexcusable anger, gross insensitivity, and illegal/immoral prior activity in just the same way. Ultimately, the work is being done by some ex ante duty to control one's beliefs, desires, and character traits, and if one averts to the fact that they may later cause harm, one may have a duty to do what one can to rid oneself of them. And then there are garden variety cases of genetic recklessness, like forgetful Ernest, who might very well be reckless if it was reckless for him to load the gun, or reckless for him to fail to remind himself that the gun was loaded. When one loads a gun, one likely tells oneself to remember it is loaded (if only for one's own safety), and with that comes a corresponding duty to remind oneself. But there may be reasons that one forgets to remember. And once Ernest has forgotten, he has forgotten.

Simons questions whether we maintain that an actor must also believe that the risk she is imposing is unjustifiable. We do not. But then, Simons argues, we are punishing the actor for the "failure to draw reasonable inferences" from her beliefs. We take it that the heart of this complaint is that an actor cannot control how her reasons come to her any more than she can control her beliefs. That is, how can we punish someone who strongly believes that her time is more valuable than others' but be unwilling to punish someone who fails to form the belief that she is risking harm to others? Well, (1) we doubt that actors truly believe time is more important than others' interests; (2) those who do consistently hold such a belief are likely irrational (can anyone rationally believe lipstick outweighs death?); and (3) we might be willing to grant a limited excuse to those who lacked an opportunity to learn moral codes (e.g., a cultural defense). Acts that are the product of self-preferring weighings of reasons constitute insufficient concern manifested in choice, the very basis of culpability in our view.

Simons may be probing a deeper concern, however, which is at the heart of the free will/moral responsibility debate, when he points out that we cannot control what we take to be reasons for action or the weight those reasons appear to us to carry. All we can say is, that is a different debate. We maintain here merely that factual mistakes are not culpable whereas showing insufficient concern is, even if the latter reflects a mistake about reasons and their weights.

14. RAPE LAW REFORM BASED ON NEGOTIATION
Beyond the No and Yes Models

MICHELLE J. ANDERSON*

In his *Commentaries on the Laws of England*, William Blackstone defined the common law of rape as the "carnal knowledge of a woman forcibly and against her will." "Forcibly" meant that the man used physical force or the threat of physical force to obtain sexual intercourse. "Against her will" meant that the woman did not consent to having sexual intercourse with him, and the common law required that she resist him to the utmost of her physical capacity to express her nonconsent.

Despite some legislative and judicial tinkering at the margins, statutes in the vast majority of states and the District of Columbia continue to reflect the basic requirements of the common law. Although courts have broadened the kinds of coercion that they recognize as force and no longer require that a victim resist to the utmost of her physical capacity, statutes still overwhelmingly require both the defendant's force and the victim's nonconsent before an act of sexual penetration becomes a felony, and the way courts interpret these terms often requires that the victim resist.

Academic proposals for rape law reform have moved well beyond where state laws linger. Arguing that requirements of a defendant's force and a victim's resistance are archaic and unfair, many legal scholars have asserted that the crux of rape is sex without consent. Scholars have offered two interpretive models for this new understanding of rape, which I call the "No" Model and the "Yes" Model.

I. THE NO MODEL

Susan Estrich has advanced the No Model of rape law reform, arguing that proceeding to penetrate someone in the face of a "no" is criminally negligent behavior. "[T]he threshold of liability," she explained, "should be understood to include at least those nontraditional rapes where the woman says no."[1] Similarly, Donald Dripps has advocated criminalizing "sexual expropriation," which he defined as sexual penetration with any person unconscious, mentally incompetent, or

---

* Dean and Professor of Law, CUNY School of Law. This core text is a distillation of Michelle Anderson, *Negotiating Sex*, 78 S. CAL. L. REV. 1401 (2005).
1. Susan Estrich, REAL RAPE 103 (1987).

"known by the actor to have expressed refusal to engage in that act, without subsequently expressly revoking that refusal."[2] Dripps explained, "[T]he intent that matters should be the intent to engage in sex with a person who *says* she refuses."[3]

The No Model attaches great importance to the victim's words of sexual refusal. Unless the defendant employs force or the victim is unconscious or mentally incompetent, a victim has to express her refusal before sexual penetration is criminal. Under the No Model, therefore, sexual penetration is legal unless the woman physically or verbally resists.

II. THE YES MODEL

Stephen Schulhofer has advanced the Yes Model of rape law reform.[4] Schulhofer advocated criminalizing "sexual abuse," which he defined as "an act of sexual penetration with another person, when he knows that he does not have the consent of the other person."[5] He defined consent as "actual words or conduct indicating affirmative, freely given permission to the act of sexual penetration."[6]

Therefore, under the Yes Model, sexual penetration is illegal unless the woman verbally or physically grants permission for it. Schulhofer explained:

> The legal standard must move away from the demand [under the No Model] for unambiguous evidence of her protests and insist instead that the man have affirmative indications that she chose to participate. So long as a person's choice is clearly expressed, by words or conduct, her right to control her sexuality is respected. [7]

Schulhofer provided one example of the kind of conduct that should establish permission: "If she doesn't say 'no,' and if her silence is combined with passionate kissing, hugging, and sexual touching, it is usually sensible to infer actual willingness."[8]

Like the No Model, the Yes Model attaches great importance to the victim's words of sexual refusal. If a woman fails to say "no," one may presume she

---

2. Donald A. Dripps, *Beyond Rape: An Essay on the Difference Between the Presence of Force and the Absence of Consent*, 92 COLUM. L. REV. 1780, 1807 (1992).

3. *Id.* at 1804.

4. Stephen J. Schulhofer, UNWANTED SEX: THE CULTURE OF INTIMIDATION AND THE FAILURE OF LAW (1998).

5. *Id.* at 283.

6. *Id.*

7. *Id.* at 272–73.

8. *Id.* at 272.

consents to penetration. Once she engages in kissing and petting, the Yes Model collapses into the No Model and verbal resistance is again required.

III. PROBLEMS WITH THE "NO" AND "YES" MODELS

Three problems vex the No and Yes Models of rape law reform. First, victims frequently experience peritraumatic paralysis and dissociation during rape. Second, men misinterpret women's nonverbal behavior as indicative of sexual consent. Third, many people engage in heavy petting as a substitute for, or instead of, sexual penetration.

A. Peritraumatic Paralysis and Dissociation

Individuals experience a range of physiological and psychological reactions during traumatic events, what are known as peritraumatic responses. One common reaction to the extreme stress of sexual assault, for example, is the "deer-in-headlights" effect. Like other mammals, humans may respond to great distress with peritraumatic paralysis. One study found that 88 percent of victims of childhood sexual assault and 75 percent of victims of adult sexual assault experienced moderate to high levels of paralysis during the assault.

A second common response to sexual trauma is an alteration in awareness called peritraumatic dissociation. A victim's nervous system can become overwhelmed as it undergoes great emotional distress. During such an episode, one may dissociate from the body as an adaptive means to escape damaging sensory input. As a leading scholar in the field of trauma research explains:

> The person may feel as though the event is not happening to her, as though she is observing from outside her body, or as though the whole experience is a bad dream from which she will shortly awaken. These perceptual changes combine with a feeling of indifference, emotional detachment, and profound passivity in which the person relinquishes all initiative and struggle.[9]

Symptoms of peritraumatic dissociation include confusion, time distortion, and depersonalization, or the feeling that one is outside one's body or in a dream watching an event occur. Memory may be lost and pain thereby ignored. Like physical paralysis, dissociation is a common reaction to sexual trauma.

The No Model allows men to penetrate women who suffer from peritraumatic paralysis and the silence of mental dissociation. A victim who has these common reactions is cut off from her voice and cannot say "no"—she is too shocked to speak or has left her body entirely. Once the Yes Model collapses into the No Model, it suffers from the same deficiency.

---

9. Judith Lewis Herman, TRAUMA AND RECOVERY: THE AFTERMATH OF VIOLENCE— FROM DOMESTIC ABUSE TO POLITICAL TERROR 43 (1992).

B. Male Misinterpretation

A well-developed body of social psychology literature documents that men tend to interpret women's body language as indicative of sexual intent when women have no such intent. Men are more likely to misinterpret a woman's consumption of alcohol as conveying sexual intent. When assessing interpersonal distance, eye contact, and casual touch, men rate women as more seductive and more promiscuous than women rate other women and themselves. Men misinterpret women's friendly body language as indicative of sexual intent when women have no such intent.

Legal scholars routinely label male misinterpretation of women's body language as "miscommunication," which suggests that each party, female and male, is trying to communicate an idea that the other misunderstands. In fact, however, women interpret men's body language and sexual intent toward them with reasonable accuracy.

The No Model ignores male misinterpretation of female body language because it places the burden of stopping sexual penetration on the woman. The Yes Model, though not ignoring the problem, cannot solve it. Schulhofer concedes that under the Yes Model, "Because 'body language' can still count as an expression of consent, this approach (for better or worse) doesn't eliminate all the uncertainties of sexual communication."[10]

So what happens when there are uncertainties? Schulhofer answers that question with resort to the victim's verbal and physical resistance:

> [R]esistance will still be relevant, in some cases, to determining whether consent was given at all. A couple sits side by side necking on a sofa. While kissing his date, the man presses his body forward, so that the woman is pushed back to a reclining position. He then reaches under her dress to touch her genital area. The women might or might not be consenting to these sexual contacts. If she says "no," tries to sit up, and pushes his hands away, we are more likely to think she is unwilling than if she does none of these things. Resistance remains relevant when we are not sure whether the woman gave consent.[11]

Notice that here again the Yes Model collapses into the No Model once a man's sexual initiative begins.

Under the No Model, a man may misinterpret a woman's body language to mean consent to sexual penetration. He has permission to penetrate her until she objects. Under the Yes Model, when there is kissing, hugging, and petting involved, a man may also misinterpret a woman's body language to mean consent to sexual penetration. He may then penetrate her until she objects.

---

10. Schulhofer, *supra* note 4, at 271–72.
11. *Id.* at 131.

C. Heavy Petting

Because of the threat that HIV and other sexually transmitted diseases pose, many people are choosing to engage in sexual behavior that does not include penetration, particularly when they are enjoying casual sexual intimacy or sexual intimacy with a relatively new partner. Young people, for instance, are engaging in more sexual petting and fellatio as a substitute for vaginal intercourse under the belief that these practices maintain technical virginity, avoid pregnancy, and constitute safe sex. Now, more than ever, sexual penetration is a specific act that sexually active people negotiate.

Both the No Model and the Yes Model assume that a woman consents to sexual penetration if she engages in heavy petting, when in fact she may be engaging in heavy petting in order to avoid penetration and the risks associated with it. These models, therefore, are inconsistent with sexual autonomy and sexual health in an age of HIV and other sexually transmitted diseases.

Both models reward willful blindness. Under both models, unless a woman verbally objects, a man who deliberately avoids guilty knowledge by quickly penetrating a woman he is passionately kissing and fondling is a man with consent. Once one understands how sexual trauma can manifest itself as physical paralysis and mental dissociation, it is clear the man cannot assume consent. Once one considers the tendency for men to sense women's sexual intent where there is none, one might want to put the onus on him to check his perhaps overconfident assessment of her behavior against reality. Finally, once one realizes that people routinely engage in heavy petting to avoid penetration and its attendant risks, the No and Yes Models are no longer defensible.

IV. CONSIDERING NEGOTIATION

I propose a new model of rape law reform. I argue that the law should eliminate the requirement of nonconsent. In its place, the law should recognize the centrality of negotiation, in which a person would be required to consult with his or her partner before sexual penetration occurs.

The notions of consent and negotiation are useful contrasts. The *Oxford English Dictionary* defines "consent" as "[v]oluntary agreement to or acquiescence in what another proposes or desires; compliance, concurrence, permission."[12] In the consent model of sexual relations, the man proposes sex and the woman voluntarily acquiesces to his desire. The legal world has concurred with the lay definition. Until 1999, *Black's Law Dictionary* defined consent as "voluntarily

---

12. Oxford English Dictionary 760 (2d ed. 1989).

yielding the will to the proposition of another; acquiescence or compliance therewith."[13]

By contrast, the *Oxford English Dictionary* defines "negotiate" as "[t]o hold communication or conference (*with* another) for the purpose of arranging some matter by mutual agreement."[14] The lay definition of "negotiate," therefore, suggests not acquiescence to another's desire (as "consent" does), but an active consultation with someone else to come to a mutual agreement. The legal world concurs with the lay definition. *Black's Law Dictionary* defines "negotiate" as "to communicate with another party for the purpose of reaching an understanding," or to "arrive through discussion at some kind of agreement."[15]

Negotiation in sexual relations would manifest itself as mutual consultation. The Negotiation Model asks, "Did the person who initiated sexual penetration negotiate with his or her partner and thereby come to an agreement that sexual penetration should occur?" As a model, it seeks to maximize the opportunity for sexual partners to share intentions, desires, and boundaries.

When one wants to engage in penetration, negotiation would minimally require a request for information about another person's desires and boundaries or an expression of one's own with an invitation to respond. Negotiation as a process, therefore, involves an exchange of ideas between people. Unlike the traditional notion of consent, negotiation assumes reciprocal responsibilities between partners and equal authority to direct the sexual interaction, whatever the partners' genders and sexual orientation.

The minimally required negotiation for penetrative acts needs to be specific, but it need not be formal. People rarely say anything like, "I agree to have vaginal sex with you. Let us now proceed." Instead, they say things like, "Kissing you is making me so hot. I want you to be inside me/I want to be inside of you. Do you want that, too?" Though informal, this communication does all the work that negotiation requires. It states a desire and asks the other person for their position, providing the opportunity to express anything from mutual longing to aversion.

Silence would not be adequate to constitute negotiation. Meeting at a party, drinking alcohol, and making out would not constitute a negotiation for sexual penetration. Instead, partners would have to engage in a communicative process—a verbal discussion about what they wanted to do with one another—before penetration occurred.

---

13. BLACK'S LAW DICTIONARY 305 (6th ed. 1990). In 1999, this dictionary changed the definition of consent to "agreement, approval, or permission as to some act or purpose, esp. given voluntarily by a competent person." BLACK'S LAW DICTIONARY 300 (7th ed. 1999). That definition remains in force in the current edition as well. BLACK'S LAW DICTIONARY 323 (8th ed. 2004).

14. OXFORD ENGLISH DICTIONARY, *supra* note 12, at 303.

15. BLACK'S LAW DICTIONARY 1063–64 (8th ed. 2004).

After partners have engaged in a negotiation regarding what they want to do together, each partner may assume the other agrees to engage in the penetrative acts they discussed fondly with one another. Partners need not recite, "I hereby agree to have oral sex with you." Having expressed their mutual preferences is sufficient when the partners engage in what both indicated they wanted between them.

Agreement between partners is dynamic and active. Agreements change over time, and must be sensitive to context and changed circumstance. For example, if two men agree to engage in penetration with each other, begin, and then one changes his mind and expresses a verbal or physical "no" to it, then there is no longer agreement, and his partner must immediately stop. Here the Negotiation Model incorporates an important part of the No and Yes Models—the importance of verbal refusal—but only *after* the partners have agreed to sexual penetration itself. It does not assume penetration is appropriate without consultation.

It is important to note that the risk of rape is highest for people engaging in sexual penetration for the first time. According to crime victimization surveys, the victim and the offender had not previously been intimate with one another in 90 percent of the rapes of females over the age of twelve, and 100 percent of the rapes of males over the age of twelve. Most stranger and acquaintance rapes are the only sexual interaction the two people will have. Therefore, the imperative of verbal negotiation for penetration is especially powerful in new relationships.

Can negotiation and agreement between two people regarding sexual penetration occur nonverbally? Most negotiations regarding specific activities that are to occur in the future happen verbally, of course. Language is ordinarily required to clarify one's desires over time; however, an established custom between two people of engaging in mutually desired behavior in a certain way may itself constitute a negotiation. By repeating the mutually desired activity over time, partners may establish a pattern of sexual behavior that makes explicit discussions unnecessary.

After partners establish a pattern of engaging in sexual penetration that serves as the necessary negotiation, the Yes Model provides sufficient protection for sexual autonomy. A longer-term relationship, therefore, provides a context in which partners may reliably read one another's nonverbal behavior. Without a custom, however, partners have to negotiate penetration verbally.

Therefore, the law should define "rape" as engaging in an act of sexual penetration with another person when the actor fails to negotiate the penetration with the partner before it occurs. The law should define "negotiation" as an open discussion in which partners come to a free and autonomous agreement about the act of penetration. Negotiations would have to be verbal unless the partners had established a context in which they could reliably read one another's nonverbal behavior to indicate free and autonomous agreement. Force, coercion, or misrepresentations by the actor would be evidence of failure to negotiate.

V. NEGOTIATION APPLIED

Two cases featured in many criminal law casebooks are *Commonwealth v. Berkowitz*,[16] and *In re M.T.S.*[17] They provide important points of comparison between the models of rape law reform.

A. *Berkowitz*

Berkowitz and his female victim were twenty- and nineteen-year-old college students, respectively. On the afternoon of the incident, the victim went to Berkowitz's dorm room to find her friend. Berkowitz asked her to stay and she agreed. He asked her to give him a back rub, but she declined. He asked her to sit on his bed, but she refused and took a seat on the floor. Berkowitz then moved to the floor, lifted her shirt, and began massaging her breasts. She said "no" repeatedly. Berkowitz undid his pants and tried to put his penis in her mouth. She again said "no." Berkowitz then locked the door from the inside, pushed the victim down on the bed, straddled and pinned her, and removed her pants and underwear from one leg. He then penetrated her vagina with his penis, withdrew, and ejaculated on her stomach. Both parties agreed that the victim said "no" throughout the encounter.

In assessing the case, the intermediate appellate court in Pennsylvania quoted extensively from the victim's testimony. It pointed out:

> The victim did not physically resist in any way while on the bed because appellant was on top of her, and she "couldn't like go anywhere." She did not scream out at anytime because, "[i]t was like a dream was happening or something."[18]

Note that Berkowitz's victim appears to have been experiencing a dream-like alternation in perception consistent with depersonalization. Despite the fact that the Supreme Court of Pennsylvania found that the victim did not consent to sexual intercourse, it concluded that there was no rape because Berkowitz did not employ force.

Berkowitz is an easy case for the No and Yes Models. Under the No Model, Berkowitz is guilty of sexual expropriation because the victim repeatedly said "no." Under the Yes Model, Berkowitz is guilty of sexual abuse because he penetrated the victim when he knew he did not have her consent.

But what if the victim had reacted to Berkowitz's escalating sexual advances with more powerful symptoms of peritraumatic dissociation? What if she became deeply passive and said nothing? Under the No Model, if she said nothing there would be no crime. Under the Yes Model, Berkowitz would argue that he had "conduct indicating affirmative, freely given permission to the act of sexual penetration." After all,

---

16. 641 A.2d 1161 (Pa. 1994).

17. 609 A.2d 1266 (N.J. 1992).

18. *Commonwealth v. Berkowitz*, 609 A.2d 1338, 1340 (Pa. Super. Ct. 1992), *aff'd* 641 A.2d 1161 (Pa. 1994).

the victim was drinking when she came into his dorm room, she had stopped by intoxicated before, and on a previous occasion she asked him the size of his penis.

Under the Negotiation Model, however, the case changes shape. Berkowitz failed to ask his victim whether he could penetrate her. The fact that she said "no" throughout the encounter simply underscores Berkowitz's failure to consider her desires and boundaries. Even if she never said "no," Berkowitz could not simply press ahead to intercourse based on her passive reaction to his advances and his fantasy about what she meant when she had asked him the size of his penis. He would have to tell her that he wanted to have sex with her and ask if she wanted that, too. His failure to negotiate the sexual penetration with her would constitute rape.

B. *M.T.S.*

Seventeen-year-old M.T.S. was temporarily living with fifteen-year-old C.G.'s family. C.G. accused him of sexual assault, but the two parties disputed the details of what happened on the instance in question.

According to C.G., she awoke early one morning to find her shorts and underwear removed, and M.T.S.' penis already inside her vagina. As soon as she realized what was happening, she slapped him and told him to get off her and get out, which he did. According to M.T.S., the two had engaged in kissing and necking during the three days before the instance in question. C.G. encouraged him to make a surprise visit to her room late that night. When he did, they began to kiss and pet. They then engaged in consensual sex until the fourth thrust when C.G. told M.T.S. to stop, at which point he got off her. C.G. then slapped him.

Faced with this dispute, the trial court found that the "couple had been [consensually] kissing and petting, had undressed and had gotten into the victim's bed and then had sex, but that the actual sex act had not been consented to by the victim." The court also found that there was "no definite expressed refusal by the victim" at the time penetration occurred.[19]

On appeal, the New Jersey Supreme Court declared, "[A]ny act of sexual penetration engaged in by the defendant without the affirmative and freely-given permission of the victim to the specific act of penetration constitutes the offense of sexual assault" and noted that permission "can be indicated either through words or through actions."[20] *M.T.S.* is an important case because it adopted the Yes Model of rape law reform. But, under that model, did it come out the right way?

As the trial court found, C.G. consented to kissing and petting, got into bed with M.T.S., never said "no" or expressed any other form of refusal, and then M.T.S. penetrated her. Under the Yes Model, "[i]f she doesn't say 'no,' and if her silence is combined with passionate kissing, hugging, and sexual touching, it is

---

19. *In re M.T.S.*, 588 A.2d 1282, 1283 (N.J. Super Ct. App. Div. 1991), *rev'd*, 609 A.2d 1266 (N.J. 1992).

20. *In re M.T.S.*, 609 A.2d at 1277–78.

usually sensible to infer actual willingness."[21] C.G. was engaged in exactly the kind of kissing and petting from which it would supposedly be "sensible" for M.T.S. "to infer actual willingness." Under the Yes Model, therefore, without verbal objection, there was no crime: M.T.S. had all the affirmative permission he needed to penetrate her.

Under the Negotiation Model, *M.T.S.* looks different. M.T.S. failed to discuss the sexual penetration with C.G. before he entered her. He neither told her what he wanted to do nor asked about her desires and boundaries. He could not interpret her wishes based on her body language. He could not rely on his assumption that necking meant consent to sexual penetration. He could not engage in sexual intercourse with her without discussing it with her first.

VI. CONCLUSION

The Negotiation Model would require more than any state currently requires from those who engage in sexual penetration. Instead of imposing on the victim a verbal imperative to object, as the No Model does, or allowing a man to imaginatively interpret a woman's body language, as the Yes Model does, the Negotiation Model would require a person who sought to initiate penetration with another to consult with his or her partner, at least until a custom arises between them that would provide a meaningful context in which to interpret body language.

Negotiation would require only what conscientious and humane partners already have: a communicative exchange, before penetration occurs, about whether they want to engage in sexual intercourse. Coupled with extensive popular education, the Negotiation Model of rape law reform would encourage sexual partners to treat each other with humanity.

Still trained too often to acquiesce to male desire, a girl may go along physically with a boy beyond where she feels comfortable. Kissing leads to necking leads to fondling. It has now gone too far, and the girl knows it. She may freeze in terror, or mentally and emotionally leave the scene. At that point, under the common law, the boy may legally penetrate her because he did not have to use force to get there. Under the No Model, he may legally penetrate her because she failed to object verbally. Under the Yes Model, he may legally penetrate her because she engaged in kissing and heavy petting, a functional "yes" in his imagination. Under the Negotiation Model, he may not penetrate her, no matter the kissing and necking shared, nor his hopeful interpretation thereof, until he breaks out of his solipsistic universe and engages the girl—another human being whose desires and boundaries matter—in a conversation.

---

21. Schulhofer, *supra* note 4, at 272.

Rape happens at an alarming rate. It causes devastating emotional and psychological harm. Yet by remaining focused on force and consent, the law has utterly failed to redress the crime. The intimate and serious nature of penetration is why negotiation is so crucial to its legitimacy.

COMMENTS

SELF-DECEPTION AND RAPE LAW REFORM

ANDREW E. TASLITZ*

I. THE PUZZLE

I do not want to challenge Michelle Anderson's fascinating suggestion to replace the element of victim nonconsent in rape cases with a new element requiring the male to engage in negotiation with the woman before engaging in intercourse. Rather, I want to focus on what I see as her implicit embrace of a negligence mens rea requirement. She proposes a standard of behavior deviation from which constitutes, in effect, unreasonable behavior. Under her negotiation model, the man who does not engage in reasonable sexual negotiations commits rape *even if he firmly consciously believed that the woman was consenting*. Failing to negotiate thus effectively serves as a negligence bar to the woman's consent, even though Anderson purports to be eliminating the consent inquiry entirely.

Yet rape is subject to severe punishments, often being a first-degree felony, with potential periods of incarceration matching those for many kinds of murder. It is rare for the criminal law to impose such harsh penalties for negligent behavior. Thus the puzzle: What justifies simple negligence liability for a very serious crime? One answer, I argue, is this: the male capacity for self-deception in sexual matters and the special moral evils it entails.

II. HOW SELF-DECEPTION WORKS

A. Three Types of Mind

Understanding how self-deception works requires recognizing three sorts of minds: the conscious, the unconscious, and the semi-conscious. These three

---

* Welsh S. White Distinguished Visiting Professor of Law, University of Pittsburgh, 2008–09; Professor of Law, Howard University School of Law. This comment is based on Andrew E. Taslitz, *Willfully Blinded: On Date Rape and Self-Deception*, 28 HARV. J. L. & GENDER 381 (2005).

ideal types are not sharply demarcated, being useful tools for describing a continuum. The conscious mind is capable of effortful, deliberative thought. It can for all practical purposes be treated as a unitary entity, though the reality is more complex. Unconscious thought is likely to be rapid, automatic, more reliant on heuristics and stereotypes. Most of our thinking is unconscious, and much of our conscious thought begins in the unconscious. The unconscious can filter certain information from the conscious mind and can bias the interpretation of the data that does reach consciousness.

The semi-conscious mind can be distinguished from the unconscious mind in two ways: first, we are at least dimly aware of semi-conscious thoughts and feelings. Second, semi-conscious thoughts are akin to what some commentators have called the "preconscious": those thoughts that can "easily be made conscious by directing attention to . . . [them]."[1]

Self-deception occurs when semi-conscious or unconscious processes, motivated by an overriding self-interest, suppress from the conscious mind certain thoughts and feelings that might work against that interest. Rather than elaborate on this definition, I will illustrate the techniques that put it into action in the context of rape.

B. The Techniques of Self-Deception in Rape Cases

1. **Semi-Conscious Self-Deception** Imagine a man on a date making increasingly aggressive demands for sexual intercourse. Although he might briefly notice what appears to be discomfort on the woman's part, he chooses to investigate no further because he does not want to risk confirming his concerns ("willful blindness"). He might also choose to think about other things—the smell of the woman's hair or his own irresistible good looks—to distract himself from the moral implications of not inquiring further ("systematic ignoring"). Additionally, he may single-mindedly focus on the goal before him—having sex—as a way of numbing any creeping feelings of concern for the woman that might arise from confronting the suspicion that she is distressed by his behavior ("emotional detachment"). Finally, he may tell himself that her overly religious upbringing or fear of appearing sluttish are leading her to mask her true desire to say yes to him ("rationalization").

2. **Unconscious Self-Deception** Three heuristics may be at work in combination: first, the vividness heuristic—we remember the earthquake better than the bump in the road; second, the availability heuristic—relying on the most easily accessible information rather than investing energy in locating more costly data; and, third, the confirmation bias—the tendency to search more enthusiastically

---

1. Timothy Wilson, STRANGERS TO OURSELVES: DISCOVERING THE ADAPTIVE UNCONSCIOUS 6 (2002).

for data confirming than disconfirming our beliefs. When these heuristics are motivated by self-interest, they constitute self-deception.

Thus information that furthers self-interest may become more vivid and salient, and is given far more attention, than contrary information. In a sense, the unconscious "chooses" to trigger processes that lead to ignoring data briefly perceived, downplaying data remaining, or not seeking out data in the first place because it will not be to the individual's liking. Our conscious mind, however, then needs to explain our behavior, so it crafts explanations consistent with our conscious self-image. Thus the rapist may find signs of the woman's sexual interest (her clothing, mannerisms, willingness to neck) vivid, memorable, and easily available while ignoring signs of the opposite. When he pushes forward, his conscious mind may thus craft a positive misinterpretation of events, read-ing even negative data as supporting the positive conclusion—"she wanted it"—that his self-esteem requires.

There is ample evidence that many men are or easily can be at least dimly aware that their conduct raises the risk of nonconsensual intercourse. This evi-dence includes the publicity given the women's movement, growing educational efforts in schools, the frequent repetition by such men of circumstances where women complain, the chivalry norm requiring men to protect women as the presumably vulnerable and physically weaker sex, and ample empirical data on date rapists' motivations.[2]

III. WHY SELF-DECEPTION IS WORSE THAN ORDINARY NEGLIGENCE

Self-deception is worse than ordinary negligence for several reasons. First, the self-deceiver fails to take action within his power to prevent great harm, harm that he was semi-consciously aware of, or that his unconscious at least briefly perceived but ignored or downplayed—or that it expected to, but in some sense chose not to, find by further inquiry—thus amplifying his culpability. Second, self-deception about sexual consent stems more from feelings and attitudes— that are among the mental states most readily accessible to the conscious mind— than cognitions. Learning to pay close attention to ourselves when we are acting with heat and urgency and to how others then react to us can readily cue us into our real motivations. A man experiencing even the most minor nagging sense of discomfort on his part or the woman's can try to locate the feeling's source rather than ignoring it.

Third, the self-deceiving rapist reveals a personality deeply indifferent to grave human suffering, a violation of basic principles of character morality. Although the semi-conscious self-deceiver may be worse on this score than the unconscious

2. *See* Taslitz, *supra* note *, at 403–13.

one, both display a degree of indifference that, when combined with the other factors noted here, merits harsher punishment than is usual for ordinary negligence. Our unconscious learns from our behavior so that if we want to be sexually respectful, we merely need to commit ourselves to acting in a respectful manner toward women and we will become that respectful person, a tactic that requires no knowledge of our unconscious.

Self-deception about sex is also an act of hypocrisy, defined here as pretending to yourself and to others that you are morally better than you really are. A hypocrite insults us by acting as if he is morally superior to us, or at least our moral equal, when he is no such thing. "Hypocrisy is a parasite, operating by mimicking the attractiveness of virtue, appropriating its rewards," the actors' faux attempts at virtue are "only so much foreplay to their vice."[3]

Relatedly, the self-deceiver fails to live a life of integrity, one in which conscious and unconscious beliefs and values are similar and are consistent with behavior. Research reveals that those living with integrity are less likely to harm others than those living without it.[4]

IV. CONCLUSION

Anderson justifies her theory in ways that reveal it to impose a form of negligence liability on rapists, exposing them to potentially severe sentences. Ordinarily, severe punishment for negligence is unwarranted. Rape cases, I suggest, are an exception.

---

3. William Iam Miller, FAKING IT 20 (2003).
4. *See* Taslitz, *supra* note *, at 433–34.

SEX AS CONTRACT

KIMBERLY KESSLER FERZAN*

Paradigm shifts are difficult to orchestrate. At one time, a woman's sexuality was the property of a man, be it her husband or her father. Now, Michelle Anderson seeks to shift the paradigm to sex as a subject of free and fair negotiation. I want to push on this "sex as contract" model, both to see whether it can survive conceptually and to see how far Anderson is willing to take it.

Anderson seeks to shift from a consent model to a negotiation model. Failure to negotiate is rape. But what does that mean? The criminal law has never

---

* Associate Dean for Academic Affairs and Professor of Law, Rutgers University, School of Law–Camden.

punished breaches or failures to contract. Rather, the criminal law has always defined an interest and then required *consent* as to that interest. That is, the reason why I can be punished for taking your laptop is not because I failed to negotiate but because I acted without consent. Boundary crossings require consent. At the end of the day, I suspect that Anderson's model remains one of consent, albeit in contract's clothing.

Anderson's model is certainly draconian, even if understood as one based on consent. Andrew Taslitz is wrong to think that this model is one of negligence.[1] It is a strict liability model. By defining consent as negotiation, Anderson not only punishes the unreasonably mistaken actor but also the reasonably mistaken actor. That is, consider the proposal to make "no mean no." This wasn't a proposal about how the man *should* interpret "no." Rather, it was a proposal that a woman's saying "no" had the legal effect of making sex impermissible.[2] It proposed to redefine what consent meant legally. Anderson's proposal also seeks to redefine the elements of rape, removing the element of subjective consent and replacing it with one of legal negotiation. A mistake about subjective consent is irrelevant because the law, as Anderson reformulates it, does not care about subjective consent but "negotiation." Hence the crime is one of strict liability with respect to the putative victim's consent.

Specifically, it would help if Anderson would articulate the elements of this crime and how it relates to consent. What if a man has sex with a woman, knowing that he received neither a "yes" nor engaged in a "negotiation," but nonetheless honestly and reasonably believing that he has her consent? Is Anderson willing to punish him in order to prevent acts of unconsented to intercourse? How should one balance the benefits of deterring such conduct against the injustice of punishing a man who has intercourse reasonably believing he has consent? She also needs to say more about grading. Is the failure to negotiate to be treated the same as rape by force?

Finally, to the extent that she is embracing contractual negotiation over our traditional understanding of consent, I wonder whether Anderson is willing to embrace all the implications of a "sex as contract" model. Current law does not punish fraud in the inducement, just fraud in factum. My own view of this disparate treatment is that the criminal law essentially rejects the idea that one can have sex "for" something else. That is, if you know you are having sex, you can't complain that he didn't love you, or he never intended to marry you, or he hadn't planned to take you to Paris, because you can't use sex as a means. Sex is the end in itself. An anticommodification principle is at work.

Anderson's contract model could change this. Fraud in the inducement vitiates consent in contract law. There's no contract if the car dealer lies and says

---

1. Admittedly, I am against negligence liability as well.

2. Peter Westen, THE LOGIC OF CONSENT: THE DIVERSITY AND DECEPTIVENESS OF CONSENT AS A DEFENSE TO CRIMINAL CONDUCT 82–83 (2004).

that J.F.K. rode in the car and that misrepresentation was material to the buyer. So how many material inducements will we have? False claims of love. Lies about marital status or one's religion. Deception about one's career. But these lies go both ways. It's certainly possible that a woman might deceive a man about, say, her age or her use of elective surgery. Does Anderson want to call the woman who lies about her breast augmentation to her "earthy crunchy granola" boyfriend, a rapist?

Perhaps Anderson will embrace this slippery slope. She states that "misrepresentations" are evidence of failure to negotiate.[3] Our preservation of the mysteries of courtship comes at the expense of those who are deceived or violated. Rape no doubt remains a serious problem, and combating its incidence needs serious and creative answers. But before we shift the paradigm, let's make sure we like it.

---

3. Anderson core text at 301.

NEGOTIATING SEX: WOULD IT WORK?

ROBIN CHARLOW*

With so much good to say about Michelle Anderson's proposal on rape law reform one hesitates to offer any criticism at all. My pause in wholeheartedly embracing her idea stems mostly from hesitation about its implementation.

Anderson's proposal presents practical advantages over the current regime. Using prevailing definitions of rape, countless disputes arise over the meaning and nature of both core components, force and consent. Moreover, in the typical scenario, we need to know not only whether a woman consented, but also whether a man was cognizant in some fashion of her nonconsent, resulting in difficult contests regarding mens rea. By making consent turn on a particular kind of overt conversation, a defendant's subjective belief about consent becomes much less important.

So why hesitate? For one thing, the very virtue just mentioned could present a problem. By reducing or eliminating the significance of mens rea, the negotiation model runs counter to the general principle that the more serious a crime, the higher the required culpable mental state. This is meant to ensure sufficient blameworthiness to justify the level of punishment imposed. Thus, a serious crime (rape) usually necessitates proof of significant subjective awareness of the problematic nature of one's act. By obviating the importance of the defendant's subjective appreciation about consent, a negotiation model strays from the usual rules on mens rea. Some maintain that most American jurisdictions already

---

* Professor of Law, Hofstra University School of Law.

effectively apply an objective, negligence standard regarding nonconsent for rape (which Taslitz champions), so the change to a negotiation model, in which the evidence regarding consent is put into stark terms, might not make much difference. But does all sex without negotiation, even with an apparently willing partner, necessarily suffice for the culpability associated with a serious felony?

In addition, criminal law is most successful when it attempts to reflect rather than shape social norms. Our general societal practice is not, and probably never has been, to negotiate noncommercial sex. Anderson states that most rapes involve people who have not previously been intimate with one another. Given the awkwardness of newer relationships, especially among the young, open discussion about the desire for intercourse might be less likely to occur in initial sexual encounters. Anderson's negotiation model would require it. Failing to do so would result in the commission of a serious crime. Are we going to imprison a generation of young men, for felony rape, until enough of them get the message?

Anderson suggests extensive popular education about the need for negotiation. At a minimum, such education should be a prerequisite for adopting her proposal, as should a delay in its implementation sufficient to publicize the rule and effect the education. But I'm not sure even that would serve to alter what is usually intimate, unwitnessed, undiscussed behavior, behavior that currently comports with near-universal social conventions. Possibly the most vulnerable population would be teens and young adults, who are notoriously resistant to teaching about social ills and consequences, even those involving crime (consider drug use or shoplifting). And since the certainty of conviction is what usually has greatest behavior-altering effect, the fact that the overwhelming majority of nonnegotiators would not likely face prosecution is not an encouraging sign. If education does not work, how many of those who failed to learn the lessons of public service announcements would end up in jail for long periods? Would they disproportionately be members of poorer socio-economic classes, or young African-American men, a population already experiencing high levels of imprisonment for behaviors that do not conform to criminally-enforced norms?

Finally, the negotiation proposal would not eliminate all disputes about rape. Controversies would remain over whether the required negotiation occurred, what the negotiating statements meant, or whether negotiated consent was coerced or withdrawn. Because Anderson posits that a pattern of engaging in sexual penetration would obviate the necessity for negotiation, disputes might also arise about implied consent between repeat partners. Hopefully, the number of disputes would decrease. But if behavior did not readily change, we might not see a marked reduction in the ambiguous situations that Anderson rightly decries, in which men believe they have consent and women believe they have not consented.

Perhaps the time has come to take a radical step forward and switch the default rule regarding who bears the burden of ambiguity about sex. If so, let's do it carefully, in a manner most likely to succeed, and without unwarranted or undesirable sanction.

CONVERSATION BEFORE PENETRATION?

SHERRY F. COLB*

In 1993, Antioch College adopted a "Sexual Offense Prevention Policy" that required express permission for each stage of sexual intimacy. Comedians and others ridiculed the policy and its implication that men would have to say things like the following to partners: "I would like to escalate our intimacy from kissing your mouth to licking your ear." Such seemingly bizarre scripting of sexual contact struck most people as political correctness run amok.

Students in a seminar I taught in feminist legal theory shared the negative assessments of Antioch's Code, with one notable exception. Most women in the class thought that men should have to obtain express permission before penetration. Smiling uncomfortably, women said that they did not believe that kissing and petting should be read as "consent" to intercourse. At the same time, women sensed that partners often felt entitled to penetration once intimacy had begun, seemingly uninterested in whether or not intercourse was mutually desired. Some women felt silenced and unable to say "no" and wondered why the law treated aroused men like runaway trains that simply move along their tracks if not stopped from the outside.

Michelle Anderson's wonderful core text reminded me of my students' reactions. The silence of which they spoke might well have reflected trauma resulting from a man's apparent obliviousness to his partner's wishes. A caring man would make a point of ensuring that he has accurately assessed his partner's desires. But for the narcissist, a rule that says "ask whether she wants you to enter her and refrain from acting unless she says yes" could be the only thing that protects a woman's bodily integrity from unwanted assault.

The difficulty with Anderson's proposed reform is that the criminal law can only be as effective as jurors' willingness to enforce it. Because explicit requests for consent are the exception rather than the rule, the men serving on juries might well see themselves reflected in the defendant "led on" by kisses and fondling. As prosecutors confirm, getting a conviction for acquaintance rape is not easy, even when the accused uses force and the victim explicitly says "no." Many people still believe that a woman who places herself in a compromising position "asks for" what she gets. In other words, many jurors and potential jurors have, in their own lives, implemented a "waiver" approach to the right against coerced sexual intercourse that excuses or even justifies forcible, nonconsensual rape when a woman invites a man into her home.

An older family friend of mine, a woman, indicated in the early 1990s that she was frightened for her son, a young man in his 20s. She was worried, she

---

* Professor of Law and Charles Evans Hughes Scholar, Cornell Law School.

said, that an unscrupulous woman could seduce her son and then ruin his life with a false accusation. If she and others who share her worries sit on juries, one could expect an increase in jury nullification if rape were prosecuted under a negotiation statute. The odds of jury nullification would appear to be greatest when the law demands more of a defendant than jurors are prepared to demand of themselves (or their sons).

I believe that Andrew Taslitz is correct to suggest in his comment that much of what happens in coerced sexual encounters is the product of negligence and willful blindness. I also agree with both Anderson and Taslitz that it is fair to punish people harshly for disregarding a risk of grave harm in the pursuit of self-deception that strokes the offender's ego. I therefore do not share the worries about subjecting well-meaning people to prosecution for failing to negotiate consent.

What worries me is that we might, paradoxically, make it more difficult than it already is to get a conviction for acquaintance rape if the standard we present to the jury appears to condemn conduct of which jurors not only approve but in which they have likely engaged themselves.

Consider an analogy. I am a vegan. I believe that it is wrong to torture and kill animals for our consumption. I also suspect that many people who consume animals and animal products tell themselves that the animals are treated humanely. They are aided in this self-deception by the invisibility of slaughterhouses and feedlots that would expose the grotesque reality of farmed animals' lives. Yet for now I reject the idea of criminalizing the use of animal products.

Though the struggle for women's sexual autonomy has made greater progress than have efforts to protect nonhuman animals' freedom from torture and killing, the two movements may nonetheless share one limit in common: If the law advances too far ahead of social norms, it will likely be ignored, by jurors, by prosecutors, and ultimately by the perpetrators at whom it is aimed.

YOU CAN'T GET AWAY FROM CONSENT

MARIANNE WESSON*

I admire very much Michelle Anderson's thoughtful critique of various efforts to mend the law of sexual assault and her provocative alternative proposal. Her critique seems unanswerable, but even so I wonder if her proposal really solves the problem of acquaintance rape or merely relocates it. Lately I have come to believe that rape law may present a more intractable problem than its reformers have acknowledged.

---

* Professor of Law, Wolf–Nichol Fellow, and President's Teaching Scholar, University of Colorado School of Law.

What would be the elements of rape under Anderson's definition? They would appear to be sexual penetration and failure to negotiate on the actus reus side (failure to negotiate being an omission for which liability may be imposed); but what, exactly, on the mens rea side? Andrew Taslitz's suggestion that rape ought to be treated as a crime of negligence is a helpful one, but if we accept this suggestion, what is gained by treating the "failure to negotiate" as the second actus reus element rather than "without consent"?

Of course the notion of "consent" is, as Gollum (in *The Lord of the Rings*) would say, tricksy. The casebooks are full of cases that reinforce this point. But it appears to me that "failure to negotiate" is at least as slippery. Unless one is to follow the much-derided Antioch College proposal and require particular words to be employed, one must acknowledge (as Anderson does) that a variety of gestures, verbal and nonverbal, may be put forward with a plausible claim that they constituted "negotiation" (just as a variety of gestures have been argued to constitute, and not to constitute, consent).

Anderson refers to "custom between them" together with "body language" as possible proof of negotiation between a couple for whom it is not the first time, although she would require verbal negotiations for first-time sexual partners. But surely she is not suggesting that an act of penetration that has been preceded by a discussion can never constitute rape? It seems necessary to stipulate that some discussions would fail to legitimize an ensuing sexual encounter because one of the discussants chose to conclude the negotiation without consenting to the encounter. Apparently one cannot get away from "consent" and its dissatisfactions.

If this is the case, why do we not address the problem as satisfactorily as it can be addressed (which is not very satisfactorily, I agree) by defining rape as sexual penetration committed by one in the absence of consent by an actor who is (criminally) negligent about the victim's lack of consent? I wish there were some knife to cut this Gordian knot, but I do not think there is. I am unpersuaded that reformulating the lack-of-consent element as failure-to-negotiate simplifies the problem or leads to better outcomes.

REPLY

MICHELLE J. ANDERSON

Traditional rape law asks: What did she do to suggest acquiescence to penetration? It focuses on the victim. The Negotiation Model asks: What did he do to obtain her agreement before he penetrated her? It focuses on the actor. An actor would rape purposely or knowingly when he penetrated someone realizing that he had not engaged in negotiation leading to agreement beforehand. He would rape recklessly when he penetrated someone while consciously disregarding a substantial and unjustifiable risk that he had failed to negotiate an agreement about penetration beforehand. He would rape negligently when he penetrated someone honestly but unreasonably believing that he had engaged in negotiation beforehand.

Taslitz elucidates the self-deception often involved in rape, and argues that it warrants "severe punishments," with "periods of incarceration matching those for many kinds of murder."[1] I agree with his analysis on self-deception, but note that nonnegotiated penetration deserves less punishment than rape exacerbated by an extrinsic attack (commonly known as rape by force). Ferzan claims the Negotiation Model is a "sex as contract" model, and wonders whether I wish to import contractual negotiation principles into the criminal law. I do not.[2] I only wish to emphasize the importance of mutual consultation. Ferzan argues further that the Negotiation Model establishes a "strict liability" crime with regard to the victim's "subjective consent." As indicated, however, rape law under the Negotiation Model continues to require customary mens rea. Like the No and Yes models of rape law reform, the Negotiation Model limits speculation about the victim's state of mind. Scholars have criticized the traditional focus on subjective consent as tending to put the victim on trial instead of the defendant.

The core objection the commentators (Ferzan, Charlow, and Wesson) raise is, what happens to a man who has sex with a woman without negotiating the penetration but who nonetheless believes she consented? Here I split with (at least) Ferzan on what justifies penetration. I reject consent as requiring nothing but passive acquiescence. Honestly and even reasonably believing one has mere acquiescence on the part of one's partner—she will not put up a fight—does not justify penetration. Penetration requires an assessment of active desire.

We also split on reasonable mistake. Although acquiescence may be inferred nonverbally, specific wishes ordinarily cannot. It is unreasonable to assume desire for penetration without consultation. Because people may become frozen in fear when they are assaulted, it is unreasonable to assume desire from passivity alone. Because men have a propensity to misread women's nonverbal behavior (a point Taslitz augments with self-deception), and because people engage in lesser intimacy in place of penetration, it is unreasonable to assume desire for penetration from nonpenetrative intimacy alone. Specific wishes around penetration should be gleaned from mutual consultation.

Charlow and Colb both contend, however, that people do not consult with one another about whether they want sexual penetration. A shared premise leads them to opposite conclusions. Colb worries about underenforcement. She posits that a rape statute under the Negotiation Model might increase jury nullification.

---

1. Taslitz comment at 305.

2. Like the No and Yes Models of rape law reform, under the Negotiation Model, some fraudulent inducement, though not all, would establish rape. Wherever the line is drawn, however, it is safe to say that someone who "lies about her breast augmentation" to obtain sex, the hypothetical that Ferzan poses, would not be guilty of rape.

Charlow worries about overenforcement, particularly against poor and African-American young men.

First, I am not sure about the shared premise. Mores in this area are changing and people increasingly do consult with one another about whether they want sexual penetration. Eighty-four percent of sexually active adolescents and young adults have had a discussion with their partners about what they feel comfortable doing sexually.[3] Negotiation need not even include a full discussion. A woman whispers that she wants to go down on her date and he whispers back, "Wow, that sounds like fun." Two men agree not to have sex because neither brought a condom with him. A boy tells his girlfriend, "You really turn me on but I don't want to have sex because we're too young," or "You really turn me on and I want to have sex with you," and in either case, she says, "I feel the same way." One may not think of these interactions as negotiations but they are exactly that. Anytime partners confer about sexual desires and boundaries regarding penetrative acts, they are engaging in mutual consultation.

Second, I am not sure that the Negotiation Model poses too great a risk of underenforcement or overenforcement. I advocate substantial education about the social and legal importance of discussing desires and boundaries before the Negotiation Model becomes law, which would help with both potential problems. Regarding underenforcement, juries, prosecutors, and judges may resist reform; some have resisted the No Model as it has been adopted. I do not see any reason, however, why rape law requiring mutual consultation would not earn the same acceptance over time. Regarding overenforcement, further rape reform will not likely exacerbate the disproportionate incarceration of men of color. Those incarcerated for rape are more likely to be White than those incarcerated for other offenses,[4] which may speak to the devaluation of women of color victimized by this overwhelmingly intra-racial crime.[5]

Ferzan asks how one should balance the Negotiation Model's potential benefits against its potential injustices. The Model benefits those who consult with their partners before they engage in penetration. It burdens those who do not wish to express their own sexual desires, but the risk is that they will not get the sex they want. My guess is they will learn to speak or go without. It risks a rape conviction for those who penetrate without consultation. If they penetrate without consultation because they do not care about their partners' desires, they are culpable actors and conviction is not an injustice. In order to avoid the injustice

---

3. HENRY J. KAISER FAMILY FOUND., NATIONAL SURVEY OF ADOLESCENTS & YOUNG ADULTS: SEXUAL HEALTH KNOWLEDGE, ATTITUDES, & EXPERIENCES 19 tbl.13 (2003).

4. Lawrence Greenfeld, BUREAU OF JUSTICE STATISTICS, U.S. DEP'T OF JUSTICE, SEXUAL OFFENSES, AND OFFENDERS 21 (1997). Those incarcerated for sexual assault are substantially more likely to be white. Id.

5. In about 88 percent of reported rapes, the victim and the offender are the same race. Id. at 11.

of convicting someone who penetrates without consultation because he does not understand the process or importance of consultation, I advocate extensive education about how and why to negotiate sex. Unlike Charlow, I don't think youth are resistant to teaching on these issues. Studies indicate that young people want more education about how to engage in sexual communication.[6]

Unlike Charlow and Ferzan, who contend that the Negotiation Model is radically different from the status quo, Wesson believes it is more or less the same. She argues that failure to negotiate is just as slippery as nonconsent, pointing out that some dialogues between sexual partners will not suffice as negotiations leading to agreement, and disputes will arise around the content of those dialogues. She concludes that we cannot get away from consent. I agree that we cannot get away from all ambiguity in language, but I disagree that the Negotiation Model preserves the status quo. Mere acquiescence implied by nonverbal cues is how the law usually interprets consent. Requiring agreement forged through meaningful (presumptively verbal) communication is a step forward. The Negotiation Model provides a transformative lens to analyze these cases, getting to yes—or no—by a process of discourse.

---

6. Henry J. Kaiser Family Found., *supra* note 3, at 2.

15. PROVOCATION
Explaining and Justifying the Defense in Partial Excuse, Loss of Self-Control Terms

JOSHUA DRESSLER*

I. INTRODUCTION

From an early time in Anglo-American common law, homicides committed in the heat of passion have been treated differently from the premeditated variety. The latter constituted murder. The former was denominated as the lesser crime of manslaughter. Today it remains a lesser crime than murder in England, the United States, and in other portions of the world. But why is the impassioned killer consistently treated more leniently than the calm killer?

The doctrine was developed by common-law judges in order to mitigate the harshness of the mandatory death penalty that previously was invoked in all homicides. This rationale, however, fails to explain the doctrine's continued viability in the Anglo-American world in which capital punishment has been abolished or, at least, is no longer mandatory. The common law itself sheds little light on the doctrine's rationale. It has been observed that the doctrine "suffers from the common defects of a compromise."[1] Until relatively recently, scholars demonstrated remarkably little interest in entering the quagmire to search for a legitimate rationale for this widespread doctrine.

A careful analysis of the language and results of common-law heat-of-passion cases demonstrates that there is uncertainty whether the defense is a subspecies of justification or of excuse. The uncertainty is well expressed by J.L. Austin.

> Is [the provoker] partly responsible because he roused a violent impulse or passion in me so that it wasn't truly or merely me "acting of my own accord" [excuse]? Or is it rather that, he having done me such injury, I was entitled to retaliate [justification]?[2]

---

* Frank R. Strong Chair in Law, Michael E. Moritz College of Law, The Ohio State University. This core text brings together portions of two earlier articles on the subject: Joshua Dressler, *Rethinking Heat of Passion: A Defense in Search of a Rationale*, 73 J. CRIM. L. & CRIMINOLOGY 421 (1982), and Joshua Dressler, *Why Keep the Provocation Defense? Some Reflections on a Difficult Subject*, 86 MINN. L. REV. 959 (2002) [hereinafter Dressler, *Why Keep the Provocation Defense?*].

1. ROYAL COMMISSION ON CAPITAL PUNISHMENT REPORT, CMD No. 8932, para. 144 (1963).

2. J.L. Austin, *A Plea for Excuses*, 54 PROC. ARISTOTELIAN SOC'Y 1, 2–3 (1956–57), *reprinted in* ORDINARY LANGUAGE 43 (V.C. Chappell ed., 1964).

Unfortunately, courts have often failed to coherently state which doctrinal path is involved; or worse, they have rationalized the doctrine under both theories.

II. PROVOCATION AS A JUSTIFICATION DEFENSE

An argument for treating provocation as a (partial) justification is that "the defence entails a denial that the defendant's actions were entirely wrongful in the first place."[3] Indeed, some aspects of the common-law doctrine can best (or, perhaps, only) be explained on justificatory grounds. For example, the old English rule that a husband's sight of his wife's adultery constitutes adequate provocation to kill the paramour, which mitigates the homicide to manslaughter, but that a similar sighting of unfaithfulness by a fiancé does *not* result in mitigation, can be explained on the antiquated patriarchal ground that, because adultery was considered the "highest invasion of [a husband's] property,"[4] the deceased's paramour's actions constituted "a form of injustice perpetrated upon the killer . . . , whereas 'mere' sexual unfaithfulness out of wedlock [did] not."[5] According to this approach, the husband was justified in protecting his property, but the excessiveness of his efforts reduced the justification to a partial defense only. When one understands the basis of this old rule of law, it is easy to consider repealing the provocation defense. But, of course, nobody would take seriously the wife/fiancé property law distinction today in the United States, and in any case, if the defense is seen in *excuse* terms, as it should be, this distinction evaporates.

Even when one moves away from such antiquated reasoning, there is additional evidence that courts and legislatures sometimes treat the doctrine as if it were a justification defense. The common law and, often, statutory "misdirected retaliation" rule—namely, that the defense only applies if the provoked party seeks to kill the provoker and not an innocent third party—is best explained on justificatory grounds. For example, in an Australian case, a father observed his son knocked down and injured by a car driven by Dibbs. The father, enraged by the driver's actions, moved toward Dibbs with a knife, intending to attack him, but was prevented from doing so by an innocent bystander, whom the father thereupon killed. The trial judge refused to instruct the jury on provocation, a ruling approved by the Victoria Supreme Court, even as it hinted that had the father killed Dibbs, a provocation claim would lie.[6]

Applying an excuse theory (at least, the type I advocate below), the court's refusal to allow the jury to consider the provocation claim was wrong, but it is

---

3. Finbarr McCauley, *Anticipating the Past: The Defence of Provocation in Irish Law*, 50 MOD. L. REV. 133, 139 (1987).

4. *Regina v. Mawgridge*, [1707] Kel. J. 119, 137, *reprinted in* 84 Eng. Rep. 1107, 1115.

5. Dressler, *Rethinking Heat of Passion, supra* note *, at 440.

6. *Regina v. Scriva* (No 2), [1951] VICT. L. REV. 298.

correct if one views provocation as a justificatory doctrine premised exclusively on the ground that the deceased's wrongful conduct caused the killer's violent outburst and, critically therefore, that the deceased—but not an innocent bystander—(partially) forfeited his right to life, (partially) deserved to die, or is less socially valuable than an innocent person (and, thus, the social harm from his death is less).

Although as with all moral arguments one may dispute the point, I consider such justificatory reasoning morally objectionable. This is not to suggest that such reasoning cannot be found elsewhere in the literature in regard to well-recognized justification defenses, because it can be. But in those circumstances in which such reasoning has justified homicides, the deceased's conduct involved life-threatening behavior or, at least, conduct that would have justified the death penalty upon arrest and conviction. In provocation cases, however, the deceased's alleged behavior is apt to involve nothing more than highly insulting or offensive conduct, or immoral but physically noninjurious conduct (e.g., adultery); and, even in the more extreme cases, the provocation typically consists of noncapital criminal conduct (e.g., rape of a family member) that may justify severe punishment of the wrongdoer/provoker after a fair trial but does not serve as the basis for privately imposed capital "punishment."

There is another way one might try to understand provocation in justificatory terms. Jeremy Horder has provided a fascinating account of English provocation doctrine. His explanation of early provocation law is based on "Aristotelian notions of just retribution for . . . unjust losses [of personal honor] attributable to provocative wrong-doing."[7] Horder writes that in the seventeenth century and earlier in England

> [n]atural honour [as distinguished from acquired honor] was the good opinion of others founded in the assumption that the person honoured by the good opinion was morally worthy of such esteem and respect . . . . To treat a man with irreverence, disdain, or contempt, to poke fun at him or to accuse him (even in jest) of failing in point of virtue, was, accordingly, to fail to treat him with respect; it was to undermine or disregard the supposition, at the heart of natural honour, that he was not deficient in any principal virtue.[8]

The Aristotelian man of honor not only was expected to retaliate against the offender, but he was supposed to do so without reluctance. Indeed, the honorable man was morally justified in responding to provocation (or, at least, to those forms of provocation recognized in early common law) in anger, but with a specific type of anger: "anger as outrage,"[9] rather than anger based on loss of

---

7. G.R. Sullivan, *Anger and Excuse: Reassessing Provocation*, 13 OXFORD J. LEGAL STUD. 421, 422 (1993) (explaining Horder's thesis).

8. Jeremy Horder, PROVOCATION AND RESPONSIBILITY 26–27 (1992).

9. *Id.* at ch. 4.

self-control. The hot-blooded response of the man of honor was *not* an out-of-control response to an affront, but was a morally justified hot-blooded and *controlled* rational retaliation in proportion to the nature and degree of provocation involved.

What if the man of honor responded *disproportionately* to the provocation? Then the offense was manslaughter if the actor's response was only slightly excessive; it was murder if the response was grossly excessive, i.e., the taking of life in response to very trivial provocation (in common-law terms, "inadequate provocation").

One could try to take Horder's account and argue that provocation is a partial justification founded on an actor's *right* (justification) to respond with moderate violence to a serious attack on honor, which right is reduced because of the excessive (homicidal) response.[10] Such a conclusion strikes me as conceptually wrong. Either a person has a right to act in a certain manner or he does not. Even if one has a right to respond to provocation with nondeadly force (and, thus, be acquitted), a homicide—doing what one does *not* have a right to do—should be explained in excusatory terms. In any case, even if Horder's account explains seventeenth century (and earlier) English attitudes, it is not proper (although perhaps understandable) today in the United States for a "virtuous person" to respond violently—even to commit a battery—in mere defense of one's honor.

III. PROVOCATION: WHY THE LAW PARTIALLY EXCUSES THE HOMICIDE

I contend that the provocation defense is an excuse defense, albeit a partial one, but one that may (but need not) have a justification-like component.

My best effort to explain basic provocation law runs as follows: An intentional homicide is not mitigated to manslaughter unless certain conditions are met. First, there must be a provocative event that results in the actor feeling rage or some similar overwrought emotion. It is important here to understand why the provocation does—and does *not*—result in anger. It is not that the provocation "touches a nerve" as, for example, when a person drops a cup when he is stung on the hand by a wasp. The act of dropping the cup—the wasp almost literally hitting a nerve—is a physiological action (in legal terms, an involuntary act) and not one "mediated by judgment and reason." In the provocation context, however, anger is preceded by some judgment by the provoked party, even if it occurs instantly, that he or another to whom he feels an emotional attachment has been wronged in some manner by the provoker. In the ordinary provocation case, for example, when the provoker spits in another's face, or uses insulting racial

---

10. Horder, however, does *not* make this claim. He couches the defense in excuse terms and, thereafter, proposes that the provocation doctrine be abandoned. *See id.* at 186–97.

epithets, or wrongs the individual by assaulting him, or commits some harm to a loved one, the provoker sends a disparaging message (or, at least, the provoked party reasonably interprets it this way) or commits a seeming injustice, which incites the victim of the provocation to fury.

But fury is not enough to activate the defense. The law considers some provocations "adequate," and others not, to reduce a homicide to manslaughter. If we believe that the provocation is the type that *entitles* a person to feel anger or, even more strongly, if we feel that the provocation *should* make a person feel anger or outrage—e.g., when a person is verbally insulted or spat upon—then we may characterize the emotion as, in some sense, "justifiable" or appropriate. In this very limited way the heat-of-passion doctrine potentially contains a "justificatory" feature.

But the basis for mitigation does not require a finding that the provoked party's anger or outrage is one of which we approve or find appropriate ("justifiable"). Assuming that it makes sense to talk about the experience of an emotion as "blameworthy" or not, it is enough that we are prepared to "excuse" the actor for feeling as he does or, perhaps more precisely, we empathize with the actor's feelings. We must remember that the provocation defense is based to a considerable extent on the law's concession to ordinary human frailty, so the ultimate question is whether we (or the jury) consider the provoked party's anger within the range of expected human responses to the provocative situation. Put somewhat differently, we must decide if the provocative event might cause an ordinary person—one of ordinary and neither short nor saintly temperament—to become enraged or otherwise emotionally overcome. Speaking here in terms of the ordinary person, rather than the "reasonable" person (the term most courts use), avoids the oddity of describing a "reasonable person" as one who acts on occasions in a rage, rather than with due deliberation (though use of the word "reasonable" reinforces the important point that the objective standard contains a normative component and is not purely descriptive).

For example, consider a person's emotional upheaval in being informed by his long-time married paramour that she intends to end the relationship and return to her husband. A jury may be unwilling to think of the man's anger or other passionate emotions as justifiable. After all, the woman had every right— indeed, perhaps moral duty—to call off the relationship, and thus the man had no right to expect the woman to continue the relationship. But a jury could (not necessarily would) consider the man's emotional outburst "excusable" ("empathizable"?), even if it were not prepared to characterize it as appropriate. That is enough to meet the first ingredient of the provocation defense.

But it must be kept in mind—critics of the provocation doctrine often do not— that "justifying" or "excusing" the provoked party for his emotional upset does not in itself entitle the defendant to mitigation for a killing. My use of the term "emotional outburst" in the last paragraph was purposeful: it points us in the direction of the reason why provocation is an excuse defense, and not a justification.

The modern defense is not about justifiable and controlled anger as outrage to honor, *but about excusable loss of self-control*. It is not enough simply to say that a defendant's anger, which was mediated by judgment and reason, was, in the sense I have explained, justifiable or excusable: the provocation must be *so* serious that we are prepared to say that an ordinary person in the actor's circumstances, even an ordinarily law-abiding person of reasonable temperament, might become sufficiently upset by the provocation to experience impairment of his capacity for self-control and, as a consequence, to act violently.

Under no circumstances is the provoked killing justifiable *in the slightest* and, indeed, the actor's violent loss of self-control is unjustifiable. Moreover, the loss of self-control is not totally excusable, because the law's assumption is that the provoked party was not *wholly* incapable of controlling or channeling his anger. If he were totally incapable, a *full* excuse would be defensible. Instead the defense is based on our common experience that when we become exceptionally angry— and remember we are not blaming the person for his anger—our *ability* to conform our conduct to the dictates of the law is seriously undermined, hence making law-abiding behavior far more difficult than in nonprovocative circumstances.[11] It is this understandably greater difficulty to control conduct that appropriately mitigates a provoked actor's blameworthiness and, therefore, his responsibility for a homicide.

IV. FEMINIST ABOLITIONIST CHALLENGES TO THE DEFENSE

Feminist critics of the provocation defense fall into two general categories: those who would abolish the defense and those who would substantially narrow it, particularly in those circumstances in which the defense affects women most notably, e.g., adultery cases. Due to space limitations, I will limit my comments here to the abolitionist position, which basically runs as follows.

Provocation is a male-centered and male-dominated defense. Although the defense is supposedly founded on compassion for ordinary human infirmity, it is really a legal disguise to (partially) excuse male aggression by treating men "as natural aggressors, and in particular *women's* natural aggressors."[12] Men who are provoked desire to inflict retaliatory suffering on those who have attacked their self-worth. More often than not, the self-worth "attackers" are women. In studies of battered women, for example, violence is prompted by male possessiveness and sexual jealousy; a male's feelings of self-worth require "absolute possession

---

11. For reasons why provocation is better understood as a partial excuse based on an actor's partial loss of the capacity to exercise self-control, rather than on any unfairness in the opportunities available to him to exercise self-control, *see* Dressler, *Why Keep the Provocation Defense?*, *supra* note *, at 974 n.68.

12. Horder, *supra* note 8, at 192.

of a woman's sexual fidelity, or her labour, and of (on demand) her presence, love, and attention in general."[13] In reality, therefore, the defense simply reinforces precisely what the law should seek to eradicate, namely, "men's violence against women, and their violence in general."[14]

These observations are accurate in many respects, but they fail to justify abolition of the defense. Feminists are correct, of course, that the defense largely benefits men. But let's put this in perspective. First, the *victims* of male violence are more often than not other men, rather than women. Second, it is true that the provocation defense benefits men, but so do all other excuse and justification defenses, most of which are not considered controversial, for the simple reason that men, far more often than women, kill people for *all* reasons. Finally, in relation to the specific issue at hand, it should be remembered that the provocation defense is raised in a not insignificant number of cases that do *not* involve male-on-female (or same-sex) intimate violence.

The fact that the provocation defense is primarily invoked by males is insufficient reason to repeal it unless we are prepared to call into question all the other defenses, including self-defense, that are more often claimed by men than by women. If there are legitimate grounds for the defense, as I have sought to show— reasons, it ought to be pointed out, that apparently strike a responsive chord with female jurors, too, since manslaughter verdicts require juror unanimity—we ought to retain the defense.

Furthermore, lest we forget, *women* sometimes claim the provocation defense. Indeed, provocation represents the only (or, at least, best) *partial* defense to murder available to battered women who kill their abusers in nonimminent quasi-self-defensive circumstances in many jurisdictions. To abolish the defense is to deny some women (battered or otherwise) the ability to claim provocation on the Holmesian utilitarian ground that "justice to the individual is rightly outweighed by the larger interests on the other side of the scales."[15] For those who advocate retributive just deserts, however, that is not a satisfactory reason for denying women the opportunity to assert their excuse claim, even assuming the accuracy of the controversial premise that abolition of the defense will have a positive general or specific deterrent effect on male domestic violence.

In any case, utilitarian critics of the provocation doctrine miss the real point of the defense. The provocation defense is about human imperfection and, more specifically, impaired capacity for self-control. The defense recognizes the fact that anger (and other emotions) can affect self-control. The defense does not exist to justify or condone male violence or female victimization, nor even to justify or condone any particular emotion. Instead, the defense recognizes a rather ordinary fact: that in provocative circumstances, ordinary people become

---

13. *Id.* at 193.
14. *Id.* at 194.
15. Oliver Wendell Holmes, Jr., THE COMMON LAW 48 (1881).

angry, self-control in such circumstances is more difficult, and in some cases twelve jurors, probably both men and women, will determine that the provoked person who kills is less culpable than one who kills in control. We ought to trust the jury system to distinguish between the legitimate and illegitimate claims of provocation, just as we do with other exculpatory claims by defendants.

V. CONCLUSION

Provocation law raises difficult and troubling issues. Although I do not believe that the defense is intended to justify or excuse domestic violence, it is undeniable that its effect is to permit some violent men to avoid the harshest punishment available for their crimes. Nonetheless, the provocation defense plays an important role in homicide law. Particularly with serious felonies like criminal homicide, the law is well-served by partial excuses that permit juries to finely tune levels of criminal responsibility on the basis of differential culpability. As long as people get angry and that anger affects one's capacity for self-control, there will be a need for a partial legal excuse that recognizes the fact that even people who possess normal levels of self-control sometimes "lose it."

Manslaughter is not a trivial offense. Those convicted of this crime do *not* avoid significant societal condemnation and they can receive significant punishment for their offense. It is wrong, however, to stigmatize, condemn, and punish a person to the extent that we do a murderer simply because that individual only lives up to the standard of the ordinary law-abiding but imperfect person in similar circumstances. We may want people to be better than they are, but the criminal law is not meant to make people virtuous or punish them for being less than that.

COMMENTS

HE HAD IT COMING: PROVOCATION AS A PARTIAL JUSTIFICATION

SUSAN D. ROZELLE*

Joshua Dressler's piece straightforwardly lays out current conventional wisdom regarding the provocation defense: provocation is about excuse, not justification. Indeed, that this is now the conventional wisdom on the topic is largely due

---

* Associate Professor of Law, Capital University Law School. This comment draws from Susan D. Rozelle, *Controlling Passion: Adultery and the Provocation Defense*, 37 RUTGERS L.J. 197 (2005).

to Dressler. Nevertheless, the conventional wisdom here is mistaken; provocation is properly viewed as a justification, not as an excuse.

Beginning at the theoretical level, Dressler dismisses utilitarian perspectives on the defense wholesale. If provocation is an excuse, then he is right to do so: not only would pure utilitarians not mitigate murder to manslaughter for a heat-of-passion killing, they would actually *increase* the sentence. If these defendants are control-impaired, then warnings will not stop them, and punishment will not teach them. Far from justifying a lesser punishment, those with impaired control will require greater rehabilitation or incapacitation than the more in-control killers, who might be reasoned with. Yet provocation is not really about excuse. It is about justification. Moreover, insofar as justifications send messages that affect behavior, the consequences associated with having the defense matter; insofar as consequences matter, utilitarian perspectives on the defense cannot be so easily dismissed.

But how can provocation be a justification? Do we really want to rest provocation mitigation on the idea that the victim "had it coming"? I submit that we do, and that this understanding of the defense entails significantly narrowing the class of cases to which provocation applies. Because provocation is better conceived of as a partial justification, it ought to be available only to those defendants who were legally entitled to use some amount of force when they killed.

As an empirical matter, provocation cannot be founded on excuse, because ordinary, reasonable, otherwise law-abiding people—the people to whom provocation ostensibly applies—in fact do control themselves, even when faced with provoking events. Consider the numbers: Almost half of all spouses in this country cheat on their mates, but the number of murder and nonnegligent manslaughter convictions involving a "romantic triangle" ranges from only 97 to 129 per year. The conclusion is inescapable: The vast majority of people who discover that their spouses are cheating somehow manage not to kill them. Control is distributed along a bell curve, and the bulk of that curve—those ordinary, reasonable, otherwise law-abiding people to whom provocation ostensibly applies—have enough that they will never avail themselves of provocation's mitigation.

So provocation cannot rest on excuse. Justification, though, makes perfect sense, at least when drastically limited. Dressler suggests that the concept of partial justification is wrongheaded: people either have a right to act in a certain way or they do not.[1] But sometimes the law permits the use of nondeadly force: in defending against the unlawful use of nondeadly force, for example, or in resisting unlawful arrest, both classic examples of adequate provocation. What if people in these situations use deadly force instead? They had the right to use *some* force, just not as much as they actually used. Here, it makes perfect sense to offer a discount: the amount of force used, discounted by the amount of force

---

1. *See* Dressler core text at 322.

that would have been permitted, resulting in a compromise verdict. Rather than punish such defendants for the full amount of force used, which would result in a murder conviction, we punish for the amount used less the amount that would have been permitted, to arrive at a manslaughter conviction.

Of course, the law does not often permit force at all—certainly not in the most controversial provocation cases, like adultery or homosexual advance. To my mind, provocation has no place in those cases. Rather than viewing provocation erroneously as an excuse, we should recognize it for the justification it is, and limit it accordingly to those who were legally entitled to use nondeadly force when they killed.

PROVOCATION: NOT JUST A PARTIAL EXCUSE

VERA BERGELSON*

Why does the defendant who killed his provoker deserve leniency? Is it only because his self-control was impaired when he did the killing, or is it also because killing the provoker, wrongful as it is, is still less wrongful than killing an innocent bystander? I believe the correct answer is the latter. The doctrine of provocation includes numerous elements that can be explained only from the perspective of partial justification. Consider some of them.

First, if the defense of provocation were purely excusatory, we would not care who or what was the source of the defendant's provocation. Thus, we would have to grant the defense to a man who, say, strangled his wife because he was aggravated by Lou Dobbs's TV show, and the poor woman—unlike Lou Dobbs—happened to be in arm's reach. However, most American jurisdictions disallow provocation mitigation whenever the intended victim is not the actual provoker.[1] The so-called "misdirected retaliation" rule clearly derives from the justification principle: mere loss of self-control is not enough. The defendant may successfully plead provocation only when the person who suffered harm was, in part, responsible for it.

Second, the defense of provocation is available only when the provoking event is serious enough to provide a "reasonable explanation or excuse" for the defendant's emotional disturbance. Why would the law require a reasonable explanation for one's loss of self-control? Partly for evidentiary purposes—in order to establish its genuineness. However, if the only rationale for the provocation defense were excusatory, the defense should also be available to a defendant who could prove his honest but unreasonable rage. The fact that the law asks not only how badly the actor was distressed, but also *why* he was so badly distressed,

---

* Professor of Law, Robert E. Knowlton Scholar, Rutgers School of Law–Newark.

1. *See, e.g.*, Wayne R. LaFave and Austin W. Scott, Jr., CRIMINAL LAW § 7.10(g) (2d ed. 1986).

implies that only a person who was *justifiably* outraged may be entitled to the defense of provocation.

Finally, had the rationale for the defense of provocation been simply the loss of self-control, it would not matter how the defendant lost it. Perhaps he was upset because his favorite soccer team had lost a game or his roommate had left a mess in the shower. If we exculpate a person because he was not quite himself, we should not care about the reason for his distressed condition and should eliminate the very requirement of provocation. All we need to establish is that he truly was extremely distressed, mentally or emotionally.

Neither should we care whether the defendant could be blamed for his distressed condition. After all, if a person develops a mental impairment, which qualifies him for the defense of insanity, we do not deny him this defense simply because the impairment is a result of his own irresponsible conduct. In contrast, current law (with which Dressler agrees) would extend the provocation defense only to those perpetrators who cannot be blamed for their anger and with whose raw feelings we can empathize.[2] This "clean hands" requirement implies that the rationale for the defense is, in part, justificatory: We are interested not only in the defendant's disturbed state of mind but also in the circumstances that make the defendant somewhat "right" and the victim somewhat "wrong," i.e., circumstances that reduce the wrongfulness of the defendant's transgression.

All told, these considerations suggest that the provocation defense cannot be adequately explained in excusatory terms alone, and as such, that it is more than just "concession to ordinary human frailty."[3]

---

2. *See* Dressler core text at 323.

3. *Id.*

REFRAMING THE ISSUES: DIFFERING VIEWS OF JUSTIFICATION AND THE FEMINIST CRITIQUE OF PROVOCATION

MARCIA BARON*

Without entering the debate on whether provocation should be classified as an excuse, a justification, or a hybrid, I want to note that Joshua Dressler's argument against classifying it as a justification relies on a contested view of justification. To say that D was (partially) justified in killing V does not, as Dressler suggests, necessarily entail that V "(partially) forfeited his right to life, (partially) deserved to die, or is less socially valuable than an innocent person

---

* Rudy Professor of Philosophy, Indiana University.

(and, thus, the social harm from his death is less)."[1] One may hold instead that provocation is a partial defense in the following sense: D acted somewhat wrongly in killing V, but not wrongly enough that the homicide should be considered a murder (where "wrong" is understood formally, not materially).[2]

I turn now to Dressler's discussion of the feminist challenge, my interest here being the question of what should be considered a strong feminist objection. Although his initial presentation is apt, his reply seems to assume that the gist of the feminist objection to the provocation defense is that it is primarily invoked by males. That does not do justice to the feminist challenge, which he nicely sums up elsewhere as holding that "at its core [the defense] assumes that 'men will be men,' that men should be partially excused for acting like men, and that the Reasonable Man is, first and foremost, a man."[3] The feminist objection is not that the defense benefits men more than it benefits women (nor—though this would be somewhat more plausible—that it benefits men who kill more than it benefits women who kill). It would be bizarre to suppose that a defense had to benefit men and women equally, or even that it had to benefit in the same proportion men and women who sought to avail themselves of the defense.[4]

The key point, rather, is that the defense, although purporting to be a concession to human frailty, is a concession primarily to certain misconduct associated with masculinity, misconduct which, moreover, is not particularly deserving of leniency. The defense is much better suited to the case of a man who kills upon discovering his wife's adultery than it is to a battered woman's killing of her batterer. Yet surely adultery is a less grave provocation than ongoing physical and emotional abuse. So the defense seems to be in need of modification insofar as it facilitates mitigation in the less meritorious cases, and is less available (in some jurisdictions, unavailable) to battered women who kill in a state of desperation (perhaps tinged with fear and anger) rather than in the classic "sudden heat."

A related problem is the tendency of the provocation defense to abet long-standing "discounting" of violence of men toward their female partners (or ex-partners). As Jeremy Horder writes,

---

1. Dressler core text at 321.

2. Formal wrongness is keyed to what the agent knew or should have known; material rightness reflects the benefit of hindsight. Thus my action may be formally right, yet turn out to be deeply regrettable. *See* Marcia Baron, *Justifications and Excuses*, 2 OHIO ST. J. CRIM. L. 387 (2005).

3. Joshua Dressler, *When "Heterosexual" Men Kill "Homosexual" Men*, 85 J. CRIM. L. & CRIMINOLOGY 726, 737 (1995).

4. In Dressler's defense, I want to acknowledge that there is a lot of bad scholarship, and a lot of pretty good scholarship that is marred by some incautious statements. I have no doubt that he has encountered such an objection to the provocation defense. I merely seek to correct any impression that what he presents is the main, or a central, feminist objection.

[T]he vast majority of killers are male. Even in the domestic context, men are much more likely to have been the serious aggressors whether they are ultimately killers or victims. These grim facts might at one time have been regarded as part of the natural order of things which it is the function of the law to reflect. One must now ask whether the doctrine of provocation, under the cover of an alleged compassion for human infirmity, simply reinforces the conditions in which men are perceived and perceive themselves as natural aggressors, and in particular *women's* natural aggressors.[5]

If one holds, as Horder does, that the answer is a clear "Yes," that is a serious objection to the defense. That more men receive the defense than do women, or that more male killers receive the defense than do female killers, is not. It is only a symptom of the serious problems.

---

5. Jeremy Horder, PROVOCATION AND RESPONSIBILITY 192 (1992). For proposed modification aimed at addressing these and related problems, see LAW COMM'N, MURDER, MANSLAUGHTER, AND INFANTICIDE (Nov. 28, 2006).

TOLERATING THE LOSS OF SELF-CONTROL

JOAN H. KRAUSE*

Joshua Dressler has made a strong argument for provocation's provenance as a partial excuse based on the actor's loss of self-control. Yet a closer analysis suggests that Dressler's rejection of provocation as a justification has deeper moral roots—roots that share some common ground with the feminist calls to abolish the defense.

Dressler's argument is complicated by the fact that several historical aspects of the doctrine can be explained only if provocation is a justification. Dressler acknowledges that the misdirected retaliation rule, in particular, makes little sense if the defense is an excuse: If the defendant has genuinely and understandably lost his self-control, it should not matter whether the deceased was the source of the provocation. Viewing the defense solely as an excuse, then, may require us to explain away traditional elements of the law.

Yet Dressler's discussion of the misdirected retaliation rule provides a deeper insight into his concerns. He admits that the rule makes sense as a justification if, by virtue of his wrongful provocative conduct, the deceased (partially) forfeited his right to life—and thus the social harm of his death is less than the death of an innocent person. Dressler candidly admits that he finds "such justificatory reasoning morally objectionable," and argues that it applies to other defenses

---

* George Butler Research Professor of Law, University of Houston Law Center.

only when the deceased's conduct is either life-threatening or constitutes a crime that would have justified the death penalty upon conviction.[1]

There, I think, lies the crux of Dressler's objection. Dressler has consistently rejected the moral theory of forfeiture as a justification for killing.[2] I sense that he is concerned not so much with justification per se, but rather with the *behaviors* the doctrine may be used to justify. In short, I think Dressler is profoundly uncomfortable (for good reason) with the notion that, over time, society has come to accept that certain offensive but non-life-threatening actions give others the right to kill in response.

Perhaps counterintuitively, here is where Dressler actually has something in common with the feminist abolitionist approach. Feminist commentators likewise reject the provocation doctrine not so much in the abstract as in how it has been *applied*: in cases of traditional male-on-female violence in which the doctrine so often affords a partial defense. Critics note that a significant number of cases involve a man killing a wife or lover whose provoking "act" was expressing an intention to *leave*—homicides that more closely fit the domestic violence model than the "sudden heat of passion." Indeed, Victoria Nourse's research suggests that efforts to modernize the defense have in fact exacerbated this problem: It is easier for men to invoke the defense based on the emotional upset caused by a romantic partner's departure in jurisdictions that follow the Model Penal Code's "extreme mental or emotional disturbance" formulation than in jurisdictions that limit the defense to traditional common-law categories of provocation.[3]

In light of Dressler's concerns, this aspect of the doctrine should give him pause. Although portraying provocation as an excuse does send the message that the defendant's conduct is not "right," it nonetheless *tolerates* that conduct—by offering the defendant not only our sympathy, but also a significant reduction in punishment. Dressler argues this reduction is warranted because the defendant is merely acting as a flawed, emotional human being—"the ordinary law-abiding but imperfect person." But the criminal law should require more. If the only constraints on our behavior were that we should act as imperfect human beings are wont to act, we would need significantly fewer criminal laws. Achieving safety for the

---

1. This may not always be the case: Few would dispute that a woman has the right to use self-defense against an attempted rape that threatens severe (but not life-threatening) injury, yet the Supreme Court has made clear that such crimes are not death-eligible. *See Kennedy v. Louisiana*, 128 S. Ct. 2641 (2008) (Eighth Amendment prohibits death penalty for rape of child where crime did not result, and was not intended to result, in the victim's death); *Coker v. Georgia*, 433 U.S. 584 (1977) (Eighth Amendment prohibits death penalty for rape of adult woman).

2. *See, e.g.*, Joshua Dressler, *Battered Women and Sleeping Abusers: Some Reflections*, 3 OHIO ST. J. CRIM. L. 457, 465–67 (2006) (rejecting "the forfeiture theory as morally unacceptable").

3. Victoria Nourse, *Passion's Progress: Modern Law Reform and the Provocation Defense*, 106 YALE L.J. 1331, 1334–38, 1343–49 (1997).

greatest number of people in society requires instead that we *prevent* ourselves from acting in accordance with our baser instincts—and refuse to tolerate such conduct by others—no matter how sympathetic such actions may be. We should demand no less of ourselves, or of the criminal law.

EXCUSE DOCTRINE SHOULD ESCHEW BOTH THE REASONABLE AND THE ORDINARY PERSON

KENNETH SIMONS*

Joshua Dressler provides a strong argument for a partial excuse conception of provocation. In the course of the argument, he suggests jettisoning the "reasonable person" component of the provocation test adopted by the Model Penal Code and by a number of state criminal laws, and replacing it with the ordinary person: "[W]e must decide if the provocative event might cause an ordinary person—one of ordinary and neither short nor saintly temperament—to become enraged or otherwise emotionally overcome . . . . [T]he provocation must be *so* serious that . . . an ordinary person in the actor's circumstances . . . might become sufficiently upset . . . to experience impairment of his capacity for self-control and, as a consequence, to act violently."[1]

I agree that provocation doctrine, and excuse doctrine more generally, should eschew the reasonable person. At the same time, finding a suitable replacement is difficult, for the law also should (as Dressler acknowledges) decline to adopt either a purely subjective test ("Did the defendant actually lose self-control due to strong provocation?") or an objective test that is purely descriptive ("Would the average person, or would most people, lose self-control due to that provocation?"). Rather, it would be best, in doctrines of complete or partial excuse, to employ a criterion that directly appeals to the excusatory rationale.

The "reasonable person" makes three principal appearances in the criminal law: (1) in defining the conduct or culpability requirements of a crime (such as negligent homicide); (2) as part of a defense of justification (e.g., the requirement that defensive force be supported by reasonable beliefs); and (3) as part of a defense of complete or partial excuse (e.g., in duress, the person of "reasonable firmness"; and in provocation, the "reasonable person" who might lose self-control, or an extreme emotional disturbance for which there is a "reasonable explanation or excuse."). But "reasonableness" means very different things in these different contexts.

---

* Professor of Law, The Honorable Frank R. Kenison Distinguished Scholar in Law, Boston University School of Law.
  1. Dressler core text at 323, 324.

In the first two contexts, the reasonable person describes an ideal standard of behavior—such as proper care in conducting a risky activity, or well-founded beliefs and proportional response in using defensive force. The ideal is action-guiding: It explains how we would like law-abiding citizens to act and to form beliefs. But in excuses such as duress and provocation, reasonableness plays a different role: It constrains a subjective test (of subjective coercion or subjective loss of control) that would otherwise permit too broad a defense. Excuses, by definition, involve conduct that is *wrongful and regrettable*. So the reasonable person cannot possibly serve as an action-guiding norm here.

Moreover, the Model Penal Code's standard requiring a "reasonable" explanation or excuse for the emotional disturbance encompasses not only provocation cases, but also diminished responsibility cases in which the killing results from an *unprovoked* serious mental disturbance. In the latter cases, "reasonable" is especially obscure. By employing this single standard, the MPC awkwardly fuses two quite different mitigations, a purely subjective partial excuse for abnormal mental disturbance (a quasi-insanity defense) and a partially objective partial excuse for more normal types of emotional distress due to provocation.

So what should we do?

In duress, rather than asking whether a person of "reasonable firmness" would be able to resist the threat, we should ask whether it is understandable and forgivable that the defendant, faced with a sudden coercive threat, engaged in criminal conduct, even though a reasonable and law-abiding person would not. In provocation, similarly, we should ask whether it is understandable and *somewhat* forgivable that the defendant, faced with a serious provocation, had impaired powers of self-control and thus reacted with deadly violence. Even if we think principles of justification as well as excuse underlie provocation, provocation is only a partial defense, so we should still abjure the rhetoric of "reasonableness" with its implication that the defendant must act in an ideal or permissible way; at most, the test should explicitly refer to a "somewhat justifiable" or "good" reason for losing self-control.[2]

But why not let the "ordinary" person replace the "reasonable" person in excuse standards? Because even an ordinary or average person would not actually *kill* in response to a coercive threat or a provocation, at least not in all the cases where we wish to provide a mitigation. But could we qualify the ordinary person criterion, requiring only that an ordinary person *might* kill, or would be *tempted* to kill, in response to a provocation? This is better. Still, the italicized terms are extremely vague. Does a 10 percent chance that the ordinary person would kill suffice? 2 percent? We also must clarify that "ordinary person" refers, not to

---

2. Consider this proposed language from the English Law Commission report, requiring that the defendant "acted in response to . . . gross provocation . . . which caused the defendant to have a justifiable sense of being seriously wronged." LAW COMM'N, MURDER, MANSLAUGHTER, AND INFANTICIDE (Nov. 28, 2006).

ordinary behavior, but to ordinary *capacities* for self-control, rationality, and the like. (In some communities, the ordinary person is homophobic.)

Thus, it is best to eschew both the reasonable and the ordinary person, and to embrace an explicit excusatory criterion.

GET RID OF ADEQUATE PROVOCATION!

STEPHEN P. GARVEY*

I find myself in broad agreement with Joshua Dressler's account of why provocation is a partial defense. Dressler puts it in terms of an actor's having partially lost his capacity for self-control. I might put it instead in terms of an actor's having exercised self-control but having failed to achieve it. The differences between these two formulations do not seem too terribly important. The issue I want to press here deals with the adequate provocation requirement. In particular, I want to suggest that the law should get rid of any requirement of adequate provocation.

As I see it, the adequate provocation requirement is a forfeiture rule. It withdraws the defense from an actor who acquires an occurrent desire to kill as a result of something the victim has done if and because the actor should not have acquired that desire. He should not have gotten *that* angry, one might say. The causal path from the victim's conduct to the actor's desire to kill varies. Perhaps the actor believes that he has suffered a grievous wrong at the victim's hand, and acquires the desire to kill straightway. Or perhaps the actor believes that he has suffered some lesser wrong at the victim's hand, and as a result acquires a desire to *hit* the victim in retaliation. But the actor's desire to hit in turn causes him to believe that the victim's conduct was actually more egregious than he had initially believed, and so on, until at last the actor finds himself wanting to kill.

An actor can stop a desire, including a desire to kill, from becoming his strongest desire, but can he stop himself in the here-and-now from acquiring that desire in the first place? If he can, would it be fair to demand that he do so? All I have room to say now is that I have my doubts. I doubt, in other words, that any actor can exercise synchronic self-control so as to prevent himself from acquiring an occurrent desire, including the desire to kill; or if he can exercise such self-control, I doubt that it would be fair to insist on its exercise. Consequently, I doubt that any actor can fairly be held responsible at any moment in time for finding himself possessed of a desire, including a desire to kill. But that, it seems, is precisely what the adequate provocation requirement does. It presupposes that an actor is responsible for finding himself in the grip of a desire to kill,

---

* Professor of Law and Associate Dean for Academic Affairs, Cornell Law School.

and if a reasonable person would not have been so gripped, then the actor loses the opportunity to claim the provocation defense altogether.

Consider the following two cases:

V does φ to A. As a result of V's φ-ing, A acquires an occurrent desire to kill V. A tries hard to control this desire. Regrettably, his attempt fails. His desire to kill becomes his strongest desire, and as such he ends up forming a volition that translates his desire to kill into bodily movement the result of which is V's death. A's acquisition of the desire to kill V is (we agree) unreasonable. The provocation that caused A to acquire the desire to kill is therefore inadequate. Thus, despite having done his best to control his desire to kill, A is convicted of murder.

V does α to B. As a result of V's α-ing, B acquires an occurrent desire to kill V. Like A, B tries hard to control this desire. Regrettably, his attempt fails, too. His desire to kill becomes his strongest desire, and as such he ends up forming a volition that translates his desire to kill into bodily movement the result of which is V's death. But unlike A's acquisition of the desire to kill, B's acquisition of that desire is (we agree) reasonable. The provocation that caused B to acquire the desire to kill is therefore adequate. Thus, having then tried his best to control his desire to kill, B is convicted of manslaughter.

How do these cases differ? The difference is that B's acquisition of the desire to kill was "reasonable," whereas A's acquisition of it was not. But if neither A nor B can fairly be held responsible for acquiring the desire to kill in the first place, then it is hard to see why the acquisition of that desire, whether or not a reasonable person would likewise have acquired it, should be a ground upon which A is denied a mitigation to which he would otherwise have been entitled. After all, A, like B, did his level best to control his desire to kill once he found himself in its grip.

Let me be provocative: The adequate provocation requirement must go! Would Dressler agree?

ENFORCING VIRTUE WITH THE LAW OF HOMICIDE

MARIANNE WESSON*

Joshua Dressler's thoughtful analysis carried me along so skillfully that at first I found no seam where I might lodge an objection. Yet at the end I remained less persuaded than he is of the moral case for continuing to recognize a partial defense based on provocation. Perhaps his last sentence holds the clue to my

* Professor of Law, Wolf–Nichol Fellow, and President's Teaching Scholar, University of Colorado.

resistance: "*We may want people to be better than they are, but the criminal law is not meant to make people virtuous or to punish them for being less than that.*"[1]

Isn't it? When we impose criminal sanctions for acts of gross negligence, isn't our purpose to punish heedless actors for being less than virtuous? When we disallow a self-defense claim for those who actually but unreasonably believed that they were compelled to resort to force to protect themselves, don't we display our readiness to hold ourselves and others to a standard of virtue, rather than one of "empathizability"? (Yes, some jurisdictions do allow for a partial defense in such cases, on the rationale Dressler articulates for a voluntary manslaughter doctrine—but most do not.) And those who respond lethally but "unreasonably" to provocations dearly felt by them are still deemed murderers. We expect them to be virtuous.

The expectation that young men will be able to control their sexual behavior, even when desire is overwhelming and even when it is produced in part by the "provocative" behavior of their companions, has produced a salutary and morally useful reexamination of the law of rape. This reexamination was undertaken in the hope and expectation that it would change behavior in the world, not just the words on the pages of our statute books. Why do we not bring to the law of homicide this same conviction that the law matters, even in moments of extreme metabolic pressure toward its disregard?

Dressler would likely reply that we cannot expect to deter provoked homicide because by definition the actor is out of control—meaning precisely unable to respond to the threat of any legal sanction. I wish I had a better sense of what that means: "out of control." I have similar doubts about the notion that one can "lose it," and have never been sure what the "it" signifies in that expression. What scientific basis is there for the segregation of human behavior into the categories "in control" and "out of control"? (I am not talking about the distinction between voluntary and involuntary acts, nor is Dressler.) Today's science does not take us so far, and it is not customary for murder trials (unless an insanity defense has been pleaded) to feature testimony by any sort of expert witness who can elucidate this question for the jury.

One consequence of the opacity of this notion of "control" is opening the door for juries to apply their own notions of rough justice (or to compromise with fellow jurors) when invited by their instructions to choose between a verdict of murder and one of manslaughter. That might be acceptable to some, but in that case why worry about whether the law of manslaughter rests on (partial) excuse or (partial) justification? If there is no shared meaning to the term "out of control," then (in most cases) I do not see a way to enforce an understanding that it is the former and not the latter that the jurors should seek to administer.

---

1. Dressler core text at 326.

As Dressler observes at the beginning of his core text, the manslaughter formula was originally invented to mitigate the harshness of a regime that imposed capital punishment for all felonies. Other formulas have now taken its place as the angels of this mercy, and I believe that provocation is now a rule in search of a defensible justification.

REPLY

JOSHUA DRESSLER*

I have said that provocation is a "difficult subject."[1] The seven thoughtful comments on my essay by respected scholars, published above, support that proposition. I will respond to some of their observations, but I hope the conversation continues.

Susan Rozelle asserts that provocation "cannot"—not just *should* not—"rest on excuse. Justification, though, makes perfect sense, as least when dramatically limited."[2] Why can't provocation excuse? Rozelle makes the empirical claim that ordinary, otherwise law-abiding persons *do* control themselves when seriously provoked, as evidenced by the relatively few "romantic triangle" homicides that occur. The problem with this reasoning is that the standard of adequate provocation only requires that the provocation would "*tend* to cause"[3] the ordinary person to act out of passion rather than reason, or "*might render* ordinary men . . . *liable* to act rashly . . . ."[4] Even if most people *do* control their passions in a specific situation, the legal standard of provocation can still be met, and there is no reason why a jury that wishes to mitigate the homicide in such circumstances must do so on justificatory grounds.

As for justification, Rozelle is blunt: provocation mitigates because the victim "had it coming."[5] She would limit the partial defense to cases in which the actor was permitted, as the result of the provocation, to use *non*deadly force against the provoker. When the defendant uses excessive (deadly) force, he would receive a penal "discount" in the form of a manslaughter conviction. This "provocation defense" apparently is available to the defendant in the absence of passion or difficulty of self-control (indeed, why require such elements if the victim had it

---

* Frank R. Strong Chair in Law, The Ohio State University, Moritz College of Law.

1. Joshua Dressler, *Why Keep the Provocation Defense? Some Reflections on a Difficult Subject*, 86 MINN. L. REV. 959, 988–89 (2002).

2. Rozelle comment at 327.

3. *Girouard v. State*, 583 A.2d 718, 722 (Md. Ct. App. 1991) (emphasis added).

4. *Maher v. People*, 10 Mich. 212, 220 (1862), *overruled on other grounds by People v. Woods*, 331 N.W.2d 707, 725 (Mich. 1982).

5. Rozelle comment at 327.

coming?). Thus, Rozelle is not limiting the provocation defense, as she claims—she is abolishing it, and expanding the doctrine of "incomplete" or "imperfect" justification. Many states reduce a homicide to manslaughter when an actor *unreasonably* believes the facts support the use of deadly force. Rozelle would allow a partial defense even when the defendant calmly, in full control of his actions, *and in full awareness of the factual circumstances*, exceeds his legal authority to use force. Sorry. I, for one, would not (partially) justify such a killing.

Vera Bergelson states that provocation cannot be explained *solely* in excusatory terms. She points to the "misdirected retaliation" doctrine, which is defensible only on partial-justificatory grounds. True enough. I pointed this out in my core text.[6] This rule, as well as other justificatory-based rules (e.g., the defense applies to observation of adultery but not unfaithfulness outside of wedlock) should be abolished. My argument for provocation-as-an-excuse is meant to be prescriptive as well as descriptive.

Bergelson also reasons that the requirement of *adequate* provocation suggests that "only a person who was *justifiably* outraged may be entitled to the defense of provocation."[7] Yes, and no. As I argued, the provocation must be such that the actor's anger or outrage, *as distinguished from the killing*, is either justifiable or excusable. Therefore, I agree that many cases of adequate provocation involve justifiable anger. The killing, however, remains no more than partially excusable.

Marcia Baron says I have mischaracterized the essential feminist critique of the provocation defense: the true objection is not that the defense is primarily invoked by males, but rather that it provides a concession to only certain types of human frailties, those "associated with masculinity."[8] Baron says the defense as currently constituted is better suited to the case of the man who kills after observing adultery than to the battered woman who kills her abuser. To the extent her point is that adultery is a much less serious provocation than ongoing abuse, I wholeheartedly agree. That is why I have argued that the battered woman who is not under immediate attack (and thus cannot assert self-defense) should be able to argue for a *full* defense based on duress.[9] And, of course, the battered woman who kills in sudden passion *is* entitled to claim provocation (whether Baron would characterize such conduct as masculine or feminine), provided her passion is the result of adequate provocation.

Joan Krause asserts that I should be allied with feminist abolitionists because of my general opposition to use of deadly force in nonlife threatening circumstances.

---

6. I also pointed it out in my first article on provocation. *See* Joshua Dressler, *Rethinking Heat of Passion: A Defense in Search of Rationale*, 73 J. CRIM. L. & CRIMINOLOGY 421, 440 (1982).

7. Bergelson comment at 329.

8. Baron comment at 330.

9. Joshua Dressler, *Battered Woman and Sleeping Abusers: Some Reflections*, 3 OHIO ST. J. CRIM. L. 457 (2006).

Why should I go along? Krause reasons that, although the provocation defense as an excuse sends the proper message that the homicide is wrong, its *effect* is to tolerate provoked killings. To achieve safety for the greatest number of people, we should not tolerate such conduct and, therefore, abolish the defense. This is also the underlying point of Marianne Wesson's comment, in which she argues that the purpose of the criminal law is (contrary to my assertion) to make people virtuous (or, at least, deter them from nonvirtuous activity). She eloquently reminds us that the law can and does change behavior in the world.

To these critics, what can I say? I have already conceded that if we grade offenses on utilitarian grounds, the provocation defense might be objectionable.[10] I believe, however, that the partial defense is and should be based on retributive concepts of moral desert. And, lest we forget, the killing is *not* tolerated: the provoked killer will spend significant time in prison.

Kenneth Simons and Stephen Garvey, in general agreement with my analysis, offer other suggestions. Simons advocates avoiding the "reasonable person" standard in provocation law (and all other criminal doctrines of excuse). In the provocation context I prefer the "ordinary person" standard used by some courts because it avoids the oddity of telling a jury that a "reasonable person" sometimes acts in rage rather than with due deliberation. However, Simons's broad point—that the concept of the "reasonable person" plays different roles depending on whether it is used in the definition of an offense, in justification analysis, or in the excuse context—is correct and requires greater attention.[11] I am unsure, however, whether his intriguing suggestion that we ask jurors whether the provoked killer's loss of self-control is "understandable and forgivable"[12] is the best language. I am concerned with the term "forgivable": forgiveness is something that can only be granted by the victim (or, here, the victim's family) and not a jury; and it is an inappropriate emotion until the wrongdoer repents and seeks forgiveness from the victim. Those who understand forgiveness as I do may be unwilling to forgive a provoked actor, but might nonetheless be willing to mitigate his crime to manslaughter on other grounds.

That leaves Garvey. He cautiously presents a radical idea (can one cautiously offer a radical idea?), which is that the "adequate provocation" requirement be abolished. He writes that "[a]n actor can stop a desire, including a desire to kill, from becoming his strongest desire, but can he stop himself in the here and now from acquiring that desire in the first place? If he can, would it be fair to demand

---

10. Dressler, *supra* note 1, at 966 ("The point is that if the provocation doctrine is analyzed through the utilitarian lens, the case for the . . . defense—*indeed for excuses generally*—is questionable") (footnote omitted).

11. In this regard, *see* Peter Westen, *Individualizing the Reasonable Person in Criminal Law*, 2 CRIM. L. & PHIL. 137 (2008).

12. Simons comment at 334.

that he do so?"[13] His tentative answer is "no" to both questions. Therefore, if one cannot be blamed for acquiring an intention to kill, even as the result of trivial provocation, how can we blame one who, now in rage, is unable to control that desire to kill?

I don't believe this is how we should think about the provocative event. Instead, I see the event this way: V provokes D; D becomes enraged by the provocation; *while in the rage*, D develops an intention to kill; finally, as a result of his anger-produced weakened self-control, D kills V. What makes us willing to mitigate D's offense is that we consider the provocation, which led to the anger and *subsequent formation of the intention to kill*, so outrageous that we are unwilling to treat him as a murderer when his self-control fails him. There is good reason, therefore, for retaining the "adequate provocation" requirement.

---

13. Garvey comment at 335.

16. OBJECTIVE VERSUS SUBJECTIVE JUSTIFICATION
A Case Study in Function and Form in Constructing a System of Criminal Law Theory

PAUL H. ROBINSON*

It is not likely to be controversial to suggest that the goal of criminal law theory ought to be to construct the theoretical system that can provide the best foundation for criminal liability and punishment rules. Central to this enterprise is identifying those distinctions that are most important and useful to serve criminal law's purposes. Of course, the distinctions that are "most important and useful" will depend upon the system's distributive principles. A system that seeks to distribute liability and punishment according to desert obviously would rely upon a different set of distinctions than one designed to distribute liability according to dangerousness, or according to efficient general deterrence, and so on.[1]

The following analysis of the distinctions on which the criminal law ought to rely assumes, among other things, that the criminal justice system cares about whether the actor's conduct causes a harm or evil, about the blameworthiness of the actor, and about legality virtues such as giving fair notice. Although some academics may disagree with one or all of these assumptions, the assumptions do nonetheless represent the overwhelming view of current American criminal justice systems. The larger point here is that form ought to follow function. There is no universal conceptualization for criminal law that everyone everywhere must accept, but the system of criminal law theory that one constructs necessarily depends on what one seeks to achieve in the real-world operation of one's criminal justice system.

In the context of general defenses, the most important and useful distinction may be that between justification and excuse. In both instances a defendant is acquitted even though his conduct violates a prohibitory norm. However, the theory underlying the acquittal is quite different in the two instances. The gist of the justification acquittal is that the defendant did the right thing, and that we would be happy to have others do the same thing in the same situation in the

---

* Colin S. Diver Professor of Law, University of Pennsylvania. This core text is drawn largely from Paul H. Robison, STRUCTRUE AND FUNCTION IN CRIMINAL LAW ch. 5C (1997); Paul H. Robinson, *Competing Theories of Justification: Deeds vs. Reasons, in* HARM AND CULPABILITY 45–70 (A.T.H. Smith and A. Simester eds., 1996).

1. *See generally* Paul H. Robinson, DISTRIBUTIVE PRINCIPLES OF CRIMINAL LAW: WHO SHOULD BE PUNISHED HOW MUCH? (2008).

future. In contrast, the gist of the excuse acquittal carries the opposite implication for our view of the defendant's conduct. We excuse the actor because of his blamelessness, but condemn his act, and would not want others to do the same thing in the same situation in the future.

Enter the problematic case of the actor who reasonably believes that her conduct is justified but is incorrect in that belief—she burned the cornfield to save the town from the oncoming forest fire when in fact the fire was a controlled burn by the forest service, or, more commonly, she kills another in what she believes is necessary self-defense when in fact the person she kills was not threatening her or not threatening her with the kind of harm sufficient to justify lethal force.

Those who advocate a "reasons" theory of justification and correspondingly a subjective formulation of justification defenses—one is "justified" if one reasonably "believes" that justifying circumstances exist—will want to treat this mistake-as-to-a-justification case as a case of "justification." In other words, they are happy to minimize or deny the significance of the distinction between actual objective justification and a mistaken belief in justification. They believe that mistake-as-to-a-justification cases are most usefully grouped with the objective justification cases, with these two kinds of justification cases standing in contrast to excuse defenses.[2]

Those who advocate a "deeds" theory of justification and correspondingly an objective formulation of justification defenses—one is "justified" only if one's conduct does actually avoid a greater harm or evil—will want to treat this mistake-as-to-a-justification case as an excuse. (Logic and law require, of course, that the mistake be reasonable to fully excuse.) In other words, they think it important to maintain and indeed highlight the distinction between actual objective justification and a mistaken belief in justification. They think the mistake-as-to-a-justification cases are most usefully grouped with other excuse defenses, with all of these excuses standing in contrast to objective justification defenses.

Are there meaningful differences between each of these three kinds of cases and, if so, is dividing line A or B more important?

	A	B
Objective Justification (the right deed)	Subjective (Mistaken) Justification (the right reason)	(Other) Excuses (general mistake and disability defenses)

---

2. I will refer to a "subjective" versus an "objective" approach to formulating justification defenses, but they could as easily be referred to as a "reasons" versus a "deeds" approach, respectively, or a "defendant" perspective versus an "omniscient" perspective.

The objective "deeds" approach distinguishes all three cases and sees distinction A as being far more important than B. The subjective "reasons" approach denies the existence of distinction A, or at least denies that there is anything meaningful in it, and argues instead for using only distinction B. The analysis below hopes to show that the objective deeds approach is a dramatically more useful and clarifying conceptualization than the subjective reasons approach.

I. THE FUNDAMENTAL IMPORTANCE OF THE DISTINCTION BETWEEN ACTUAL, OBJECTIVE JUSTIFICATION AND SUBJECTIVE, MISTAKEN JUSTIFICATION

As already noted, there is an obvious and important difference between cases of objective justification—the actor's conduct in fact avoids a greater harm or evil—and cases of subjective, mistaken justification—the actor's conduct in fact brings about a net harm or evil, although the actor is blameless in doing so (because his mistake is reasonable). This is distinction A above, which the deeds theory highlights and the reasons theory ignores.

A. Effectively Announcing Rules of Conduct Ex Ante

The distinction has a variety of important practical implications of which a system of criminal law theory must take account. Perhaps most fundamentally, the distinction between these two kinds of cases is important in performing the two primary, and sometimes conflicting, functions of criminal law: setting the rules of acceptable conduct ex ante and adjudicating violations of those rules ex post.

Although either a deeds or reasons approach will properly exculpate the blameless actor, thereby serving the latter function, only the objective formulation of justification defenses under the deeds approach can effectively serve the former function. Imagine a swarm of police after a car chase beating a Black motorist for his refusal to follow police directions for surrender. Further assume the beating is objectively unjustified, as unnecessary and excessive, but that the officers are not sufficiently blameworthy to deserve criminal punishment, perhaps because of their poor training to deal with the adrenaline and fear from such a confrontation with an arrestee they think is on PCP. An acquittal under a subjective formulation, holding the conduct "justified," serves to affirmatively confuse the conduct rules rather than to clarify and reinforce them. Both citizens and other police may take such a "justified" finding as approving of the beating that seems so excessive. In contrast, an acquittal under an objective formulation, holding the actor "excused," would not be seen as approving the conduct but rather condemning it—just the message the system needs to send to reinforce its conduct rules for other officers in the future.

To deny the importance of distinction A above as the subjective formulation does—that is, to mix together cases of actual objective justification and mistaken belief in justification—is to undermine the law's ability to effectively communicate ex ante the rules of conduct. Such an approach fails to effectively tell people what they can and cannot do when the same situation as the case at hand arises in the future.

B. Providing a Workable Definition of the Trigger for Defensive Force

A different kind of problem for the subjective formulation of justification defenses is found in the practical need for criminal law to define when defensive force may lawfully be used. There is no disagreement here as to the desired rules: A person ought not to be able to lawfully defend against objectively justified aggressive force, but one should be able to lawfully defend against an attacker who only mistakenly believes he is justified (even if the attacker's belief is reasonable). An analogous point may be made with respect to assisting aggression. A person should be able to lawfully assist an actor who is objectively justified, but not lawfully assist an actor who only mistakenly believes he is justified.

The difficulty here is that the subjective formulation of justification defenses—one is "justified" if one reasonably "believes" one is justified—makes it difficult to define the force that one may lawfully resist or assist. Because the subjective formulation has tainted the term "justified" to include not only conduct that is actually, objectively justified (and therefore cannot be lawfully resisted) but also conduct that the actor only mistakenly believes is justified (and therefore can lawfully be resisted), the legal rule cannot simply say "one can defend against unjustified conduct, but one cannot defend against justified conduct." The subjective formulation must find some other means by which to distinguish objective justification from mistaken justification. This is distinction A above, which the subjective approach has otherwise sought to deny.

In contrast, the objective approach can use that simple rule: "One can defend against unjustified conduct, but cannot defend against justified conduct." A reasonable mistake as to a justification is excused under a separate excuse provision. In part because of this advantage, this is the approach taken by the National Commission for Reform of the Federal Criminal Laws and adopted by some states that codified their criminal laws after the National Commission's 1971 Report.[3]

The subjective formulation has a serious problem here. In order to define the triggering conditions for defensive force, it must distinguish between objective justification and subjective mistaken justification, but having defined "justification" subjectively, it has worked hard to affirmatively obscure the distinction. Thus, it must improvise some other mechanism, which has given rise to what is probably the most obscure and troublesome provision in the Model Penal

---

3. *See, e.g.,* N.D.Cent. Code §§ 12.1-05-03–12.1-05-12; Final Report of the National Commission on Reform of the Federal Criminal Law §§ 603–08 (1971).

Code (MPC), § 3.11(1). The MPC's defensive force justifications allow one to use force to defend against "unlawful force,"[4] which is defined in § 3.11(1) to mean:

> force, including confinement, which is employed without the consent of the person against whom it is directed and the employment of which constitutes an offense or actionable tort or would constitute such offense or tort except for a defense (such as the absence of intent, negligence, or mental capacity; duress; youth; or diplomatic status) not amounting to a privilege to use the force. . . .

Come again? To translate, what the provision is trying to do is this: Because it no longer can use the term "justified" to refer exclusively to the situation of actual justification, it must find some substitute term to perform that role. It borrows from tort law the concept of "privilege," so it can then provide that one cannot defend against force "amounting to a privilege." But this is not much of a solution, for what the drafters borrow from tort law still is defined nowhere in the MPC. Further, one can imagine the difficulties that will come from a rule that tells people that they *can* use force to resist "justified" conduct.

Finally, the subjective formulation has tainted the concept of "excuse" as much as it has the concept of "justification," and that, too, comes back to haunt them. They want to tell people that they *can* use force to defend against an excused actor but, having muddied the justification-excuse distinction, the MPC cannot simply state the rule in that simple form, "one can use force to defend against an excused attack." Without access to a clean justification-excuse distinction, the drafters are left to give examples of the kinds of defenses they have in mind—"mental incapacity; duress; youth"—and to hope that the user will have the conceptual clarity to extrapolate from these examples of excuse defenses when needed to include excuse defenses not listed (a conceptual clarity that they, the drafters, apparently did not have).

It is, of course, this same self-made problem that has thrown some academics into agonizing over "the perplexing borders of justification and excuse."[5] If one would like a clean border between justification and excuse, which seems important for the reasons discussed above, it would seem a bad strategy to begin your program by assuming a conceptualization of justification that makes it difficult to distinguish objective justification from mistaken justification.

C. Summary

To conclude, given how essential distinction A is to the effective operation of criminal law's liability rules, the objective formulation of justification is preferable because it highlights the distinction rather than denies it, as the subjective

---

4. *See, e.g.*, Model Penal Code § 3.04(1), § 3.06(1)(a).

5. Kent Greenawalt, *The Perplexing Borders of Justification and Excuse*, 84 Colum. L. Rev. 144 (1984).

formulation does. The significance of the three different kinds of cases might be summarized this way:

	Objective Justification (the right deed)	Subjective (Mistaken) Justification (the right reason)	(Other) Excuses (general mistake and disability defenses)
1. Defense basis	Conduct causes no net harm	Conduct does cause a net harm, but the actor is blameless	
2. Criminal law function served	ex ante setting of rules of conduct	ex post adjudication of rule violation	
3. Do we want to tell others they can do the same thing in the same situation in the future?	yes	no	
4. Can one lawfully defend against?	no	yes	
5. Can one lawfully assist?	yes	no	
6. Labeling under objective formulation	justified	excused	
7. Labeling under subjective formulation	"privileged" (MPC §3.11(1))	justified	excused

II. THE LIABILITY ERRORS GENERATED BY THE SUBJECTIVE FORMULATION

What has been said above focuses on matters of labeling clarity in liability rules and effectiveness in announcing ex ante the rules of conduct. What some people will see as a more direct criticism of the subjective approach is found in the erroneous liability results that such an approach generates.

In cases of mistake as to a justification, the subjective approach may well invite error. The complexity and opacity of the MPC's attempt to make the defensive force provisions work using § 3.11(1) illustrates the point. Any code that takes the subjective approach will have the same difficulties. But at least the MPC is trying to get to the proper liability result.

The same cannot be said for the liability results in the reverse sort of cases—where the actor believes that her conduct is not justified but in fact it is objectively justified. The actor burns a neighbor's cornfields as a lark, only to find out later that it provided a needed firebreak that saved the town from an oncoming forest fire.

Should the actor be fully liable for property destruction, or is the case conceptually analogous to an impossible attempt, thus calling only for attempt liability? What supports a finding of liability here is not a resulting harm or evil—in this instance there is a net good—but rather the actor's demonstrated willingness to break the law, the precise point of punishing impossible attempts. Attempt liability is not only a good fit conceptually but also matches people's intuitions. The empirical evidence on the community's intuitions regarding the unknowingly justified actor is clear. He is not punished at the full liability level, as if the absence of the net resulting harm were irrelevant, but rather is punished at a reduced level that matches that typically given for attempt liability.[6]

The subjective approach to justification defenses generates the wrong result in these cases. Because the actor does not "believe" his conduct is justified, the existence of the objective justifying circumstances and the absence of a net harm are treated as irrelevant and full liability is imposed. The objective approach, in contrast, gives a justification defense for the burning—the act is justified because it avoids a greater harm—but imposes liability under the standard attempt offense for the actor's manifest intention to commit the offense.[7]

Indeed, that's not the end of the liability problems for the subjective formulation. Imagine that the owner of the cornfield cares more for his property than for the town and, even though he knows of the approaching forest fire, he would like to use force to resist the burning. The subjective formulation, by taking away the justified status of the burning, gives the owner that right—to resist the burning that will save the town. Similarly, a bystander who knows the true situation and who seeks to help in the burning and to resist the owner's interference with it, cannot lawfully do so—the owner's interference is not "unlawful" force and thus will not trigger a right to use defensive force.

The point here is that, to properly control the right of resistance and assistance in situations of justification, the law must look not to the subjective state of

---

6. Paul H. Robinson and John M. Darley, *Testing Competing Theories of Justification*, 76 N.C. L. Rev. 1095, 1124, esp. tbl.3 (1998).

7. *E.g.*, MODEL PENAL CODE § 5.01(1)(a) and (b). Of course, if one believes that resulting harm is insignificant and that all attempts should be punished the same as the substantive offense, then this is not a liability error that will be of concern—an example of the differences that might flow from a disagreement with the basic assumptions described at the beginning of this core text. Even for these academics, however, the subjective formulation's liability results still suffer the other problems noted in the text immediately following.

mind of the original actor but to whether the original conduct is objectively justified. Because the subjective formulation of justification defenses focuses on the original actor's state of mind, it generates the wrong results in each instance—results that undermine society's interest in having the firebreak burned and that are inconsistent with the community's intuitions of justice.

The objective formulation, in contrast, recognizes the justified nature of the original conduct and thereby prohibits interference with it and authorizes assistance of it. The field's owner cannot lawfully interfere with the burning, and the bystander can lawfully assist in the burning and resist interference by the owner, the correct results on all counts—results that advance society's interests in having the firebreak burned and that are consistent with the community's intuitions of justice.

The discussion above might be summarized as shown in the following table.

	Under an Objective Formulation	Under a Subjective Formulation
1. *Liability for actor who makes a **reasonable** **mistake as to justification**?*	**no liability,** defense under a separate excuse for mistaken justification	**no liability,** "justified"
2. *Liability for actor whose conduct is **unknowingly** **justified**?*	**conduct justified, but liable for attempt** *—consistent with community intuitions* *—right result to advance societal interests*	**unjustified, full liability** *—inconsistent with community intuitions* *—wrong result to advance societal interests*
3. *Liability for actor who, knowing of justifying circumstances, **interferes** **with unknowingly justified** act?*	**liability** (unjustified in resisting justified conduct) *—consistent with community intuitions* *—right result to advance societal interests*	**no liability** (justified in resisting unjustified conduct) *—inconsistent with community intuitions* *—wrong result to advance societal interests*
4. *Liability for actor who, knowing of justifying circumstances, **assists** **unknowingly justified act** **or interferes with resistance** **to it**?*	**no liability** (justified in resisting unjustified conduct) *—consistent with community intuitions* *—right result to advance societal interests*	**liability** (unjustified in resisting justified conduct) *—inconsistent with community intuitions* *—wrong result to advance societal interests*

III. OBJECTIONS TO THE OBJECTIVE FORMULATION

Against these advantages of the objective formulation of justification, what do the proponents of the subjective formulation have to offer? There is a small literature on this, of course, but the responses seem to commonly come down to one of three lines of argument.

A. Announcing Conduct Rules Through the Defendant's Mistaken Perspective

Some people may dispute the claim that an objective formulation is needed to properly announce and reinforce the system's rules of conduct for future use. After all, they suggest, the subjective formation can advertise the proper rule of conduct, but it does so by looking at the situation *from the defendant's perspective*. The law judges the propriety of the conduct but *under the circumstances as the defendant believed them to be*.

The problem with this approach is that it does not take account of how the ex ante communication process actually works. Consider that in most cases of justification, the justifying circumstances actually exist and the actor knows of them—shooting an attacker in self-defense. Thus, even under a subjective formulation, the public naturally comes to associate the term "justified" with actually, objectively justified. When a mistaken justification case arises, as with the excessive beating of the Black motorist, it is natural enough that people take a finding of "justified" to have the same meaning as they have observed it to mean in the past—that the conduct is being judged objectively justified. There is no mechanism under the subjective formulation by which they are specially signaled that this case is different from the previous cases where "justified" conduct was objectively justified.

Further, even if most cases were instances of mistaken justification, it is unrealistic to think that the public will take their conduct-rule lesson from what is in the defendant's head rather than from the objective facts. As with the video tape of the beating of the Black motorist, it is easier to know the objective facts and more difficult to know the more complex story by which we may decide to exculpate based on the mistaken belief in justification. Only those with special familiarity with the trial are likely to understand the more obscure subjective mistake claims. Objective facts are billboards; mental states are long speeches. Effective communication of the rules of conduct is most common and most effective through the former, and less likely through the latter.

Part of the subjectivist's confusion may arise from a mistaken belief that a future actor will use the cases of mistake as to a justification to guide her conduct—she needs to know which mistakes will be excused and which won't. But this approach misconceives the perspective of the future actor. It fails to see that the future actor will always think the circumstances actually are as she believes them to be. She does not know at the time that she is mistaken. From her perspective, it is only the objective rules of conduct that govern her actions.

The rules governing mistake-as-to-a-justification may be relevant to others but not to her.

B. The Need to Announce a Defense for a Reasonable Mistake as to a Justification

It might be argued that people at least need to know that a mistake as to a justification excuse exists because, if it does not, then they may refuse to act in the face of justifying circumstances for fear that they might, for unknown reasons, be mistaken. True enough. However, this argument does not support a subjective formulation of justification defenses. First, it has no application where the actor has an independent motivation to act, as is common in justification situations. If the alternative to a person acting is her getting injured, she won't spend much time worrying about the availability of a mistake defense.

More importantly, even if the future actor has no independent motivation to act—such as the person deciding whether to set the firebreak to save a town of strangers—the actor can be as effectively assured of a reasonable mistake defense by the existence of an independent excuse defense for a reasonable mistake as to a justification. There is nothing in *formulating justification defenses subjectively* that advances this goal. Indeed, one could argue that the availability of such a mistake defense might be better advertised by an independent defense provision titled "defense for a mistake as to a justification" than by the subjective formulation of justification defenses.

In any case, neither this line of argument nor the one above does anything to address the problem of the erroneous liability results, discussed previously in Section II.

C. The Unfairness of Labeling as Only "Excused" an Actor Who Reasonably Believes She Is Justified

Another worry that seems to motivate those supporting a subjective formulation goes something like this: The reasonably mistaken actor has done the right thing from his point of view and is blameless, so it would be unfair to categorize him as only "excused" and not "justified." But of course all cases of a reasonable-mistake excuse, whether concerning mistake as to a justification or mistake as to a prohibition, involve people who think they are acting lawfully because of their mistaken view of the circumstances. When a person votes in the mistaken belief that it is lawful for her to do so because an election official told her so, she is in the same moral position as a person who burns the firebreak mistakenly believing her conduct is justified by a coming forest fire that does not in fact exist. They both made a reasonable mistake in believing that their conduct was lawful. If we are happy to hold the illegal voter excused, as she would be under Model Penal Code § 2.04(3)(b)(iv), on what grounds does the field burner have grounds to complain about being only "excused"?

The complaint (of the unfairness of being given only an "excuse," not a "justification") works only if one begins with the assumption that the term "justified" has a prior fixed meaning that includes "acting for the right reason." But this produces an obvious circularity problem. We must formulate justifications subjectively because the concept of justification is subjective.

Not all moral philosophers take this view, but it seems to be only philosophers who do. Some apparently assume that the term "justified" has an independent and fixed meaning that criminal law is obliged to follow—a view that may reflect a larger view that criminal law theory, and thereby the criminal justice system's legal rules based upon that theory, must adhere to a previously existing meaning of terms (as found in the philosophical literature, for example). If one sees criminal law theory as an intellectual game without important real-world consequences, this is an easy mistake to make. What lawyers know, and some philosophers forget, is that the formulation of criminal law rules can have dramatic real-world consequences. A better view is that criminal law theory ought to be constructed to produce the best real-world results and nothing else.

In this connection, Parts I and II have suggested two serious kinds of problems that arise from formulating justifications subjectively, which can be avoided by formulating them objectively. The only persuasive response can be to show that the cited problems do not exist or to show that they are outweighed by equally or more damaging problems that would follow from an objective formulation. In either case, the currency of debate must be making criminal law more effective in performing its functions, not aesthetic consistency with some other literature.

In the context of justification defenses, the arguments in Parts I and II suggest that effective performance of criminal law's functions means purging the concept of justification of any meaning regarding the particular defendant's moral status and having it speak instead only to the desirability of the actor's conduct. Justification defenses should be used to approve the conduct that people see, in the situation as they see it, as appropriate for another actor to repeat in the same situation in the future. In other words, every adjudication ought to provide an opportunity to broadcast and clarify the relevant conduct rule, rather than to create a worrisome risk of muddling it. With the ex ante educative function thus performed by the justification defenses, the excuse defenses can be applied to judge ex post the moral status of the actor at hand.

COMMENTS

A PLATONIC JUSTIFICATION FOR "UNKNOWING JUSTIFICATION"

PETER WESTEN*

The measure of any normative theory is (1) its formal simplicity as compared to rival accounts, (2) its ability to prevent inadvertent normative errors, and (3) its ability to produce correct normative outcomes. I believe that by each of those measures, Paul Robinson's "deeds" theory of justification is superior to the Model Penal Code's "reasons" account, though not always, or only, for the reasons Robinson gives.

Simplicity. Robinson and the Model Penal Code both agree that when an actor, A, who has knowledge of the facts is attacked by another, B, the permission of A to use force against B is entirely a function of B's deed, even when B reasonably but mistakenly believes that underlying deeds give him permission to harm A. Robinson and the MPC also use "justification" to refer to A's permission to use force against B—Robinson because of A's deed, and the MPC because of A's "belief." Yet because the MPC bases justification on belief, it is also obliged to classify B as "justified." Consequently, as Robinson points out, in defining which of the two actors is permitted to use force (and which of them a knowledgeable third party may assist), Robinson can adopt a rule based upon the single conception of "justification," viz., "An actor is justified in defending himself or others against unjustified conduct but not against justified conduct." In contrast, because the MPC treats both actors as "justified," it is obliged in § 3.11(1) to devise two conceptions—namely, "justification" and "privilege"—to explain which of the two actors is permitted to act.

To be sure, jurisdictions can reasonably disagree with Robinson and the MPC that an actor, A's right to defend himself is entirely a function of deeds, e.g., where A deceives B into mistakenly thinking that A is mortally attacking him thus causing B mistakenly to resort to self-defense. And jurisdictions can reasonably disagree that a third party's right to assist is entirely a function of deeds, e.g., where a third party, C, knowing that a workman on the tracks is allowed to turn a runaway trolley into another in order to save *himself*, contemplates helping turn the trolley. In that event, however, jurisdictions would have to amend both Robinson's and the MPC's rules.

Inadvertent normative mistakes. Consider Robinson's hypothetical situation: A, being unaware of an approaching fire that renders burning his neighbor B's cornfield a lesser evil to save a town, undertakes to burn B's field out of malice;

---

* Frank G. Millard Professor of Law, Emeritus, University of Michigan Law School.

B, aware that burning his field is the lesser evil under the circumstances, undertakes to use force against A to prevent the burning; a third party, C, knowing all the facts, decides to help B resist the burning. Surely the MPC does not wish to exonerate B and C. Yet because it looks only to A's beliefs and, hence, treats A's act as unjustified, the MPC inadvertently finds itself without a rule to prohibit B and C's conduct.

Correct normative outcomes. Robinson believes that his theory produces better normative outcomes of two kinds: (1) better ex ante communication of acceptable conduct, and (2) better treatment of "unknowing justification."

I would agree with Robinson about ex ante communication if I thought the public learned about criminal law by reading penal codes or if juries were required to return special verdicts on justification and excuse. But because the public learns about criminal law by observing general verdicts in notorious cases, I doubt that any ex ante educative function is served by teaching which theory penal codes to adopt.

I agree that Robinson's theory produces better results in unknowing-justification cases. But I disagree that the issue comes down to a contest between philosophical principle (which supposedly favors reasons theory) and widespread practice and public intuition (which favors deeds theory). Philosophical principle also favors the deeds view.

Plato argued in the *Laws* that the reason communities punish murderers more severely than attempted murderers is that communities are so righteously indignant at the murderer for succeeding that they give him the full punishment he deserves based upon his motivation, whereas they are sufficiently relieved at an attempter's failure that, appreciating their luck, they are perfectly content to punish him less than he deserves.[1] And communities are right to punish him less. For no community should be so self-righteous that it punishes more than it wishes or feels a need to, merely because a subject deserves it.

By that measure, Robinson is correct about unknowing justification, because although the unknowingly justified actor's motivation is fully as evil as any murderer, he unwittingly does what society wishes under the circumstances, and hence, like all attempters, is the lucky beneficiary of society's having no wish to give him the full punishment that it knows he deserves.

I am curious to know how Robinson would resolve the hypotheticals in the third paragraph above (wherein A deceives B into mistakenly thinking that A is mortally attacking him, and where C, knowing that a workman may turn a trolley to save himself, contemplates helping the workman turn the trolley), and eager to know if he embraces Plato's rationale for objective justification.

---

1. *See* Peter Westen, *Why Harm Matters: Plato's Abiding Insight in the* Laws, 1 CRIM. L. & PHIL. 307 (2007).

THE THIRD, COMBINED, THEORY FOR JUSTIFICATIONS

SHLOMIT WALLERSTEIN*

Paul Robinson presents two opposing positions for justifications: the subjectivist ("reasons") theory and the objectivist ("deeds") theory, arguing for the latter. I argue that both reasons and deeds are essential for understanding justifications. Moreover, although I agree with Robinson's conclusion (though not with his reasons) that mistake-as-to-justification cases are cases of excuse, I contend that unknowingly justified cases are cases of neither justification nor excuse.

For Robinson, a deeds theory is based on the conduct actually avoiding greater harm or evil. In my view, not all justifications are in fact based on the fact that the actor's conduct produces the lesser evil.[1] But in any event, a deeds theory need not be based on lesser evils. A deeds theory only needs to account for the reality that, *in fact*, the circumstances were such as to justify the defensive conduct. Because justifications *derive from* the existence of certain circumstances (e.g., the imposition of an unjust and immediate threat for self-defense), the existence of these circumstances *in fact* is essential to the recognition of a justification. At the same time, the beliefs and intentions of the actor are also an important part of the circumstances or situation. When a person commits an otherwise criminal act, the reasons for her act are central to our assessment of that *act*. It is further possible to use such subjective components to set a workable ex ante rule. Thus, I agree with Robinson's conclusion that cases of mistaken justification are cases of excuse, but I disagree with him that the objective component on its own is sufficient to warrant it a justification.

In situations of unknown justification (the farmer's example), Robinson argues that the reasons formulation reaches the wrong result with respect to the various participants: the arsonist, the interfering farmer, and the helpful bystander. First, he argues that the arsonist (who is unknowingly justified) attracts too much liability under the reasons approach. This argument is based on the premise that no crime is committed when no net harm results. Hence the arsonist did not commit a crime in setting the field on fire. However, the fact that the burning of the field ended up saving the town does not negate the fact that the arsonist did succeed in burning the field, which is *a wrong* (even if not a "net" harm): She has fulfilled the actus reus of the offense with the relevant mens rea.

---

* University Lecturer, Fellow, and Tutor in Law, St. Peter's College and Faculty of law, Oxford University.

1. *See* Shlomit Wallerstein, *Justifying the Right to Self-Defense: A Theory of Forced Consequences*, 91 VA. L. REV. 999, 1029–30 (2005) (rejecting lesser evils as a justification for the justificatory defense of self-defense).

As such, liability for the complete offence of arson is a fair label for what she has done, and fair labeling is more important than the "community's intuition."

Second, Robinson argues that the reasons approach is wrong not to impose liability on the interfering farmer, and wrong too when it does impose liability on the bystander who comes to the aid of the unknowingly justified arsonist. In my view, the farmer should be permitted to resist the arsonist. Indeed, he may interfere with anyone who wrongs him (as the arsonist does). At the same time, a reasons formulation (as well as one that includes the actor's beliefs and intention within the assessment of his act) would characterize as justified the conduct of the bystander, not by reference to the arsonist's conduct and the subsequent resistance of the farmer, but rather as a conduct justified in terms of the defense of others. Thus, the bystander has an independent reason for burning the field—to save the town. This reason exists even when the arsonist is "the other" (such as when the bystander burns the field to save the arsonist's home). The right to defend others is not limited by the fact that that "(an)other" is in fact acting on, or even *aware of*, her right to defend herself. When the bystander intervenes and exercises her right to defend others, the farmer (who is permitted to interfere with the arsonist) is not permitted to interfere with the bystander's (justified) actions.

IN DEFENSE OF SUBJECTIVE JUSTIFICATIONS

MITCHELL N. BERMAN*

In this comment, I criticize Paul Robinson's principal arguments against reasons formulations of justification defenses. I also contend that Robinson misconceives the basis for the reasons approach, and I advance one argument against his deeds approach.[1]

First, Robinson wrongly claims that the reasons formulation cannot effectively announce ex ante conduct rules for mistaken justification. In most reasons theories, justifications announce that people who believe that specified circumstances obtain may violate offense prohibitions, if such beliefs are deemed reasonable ex post. Thus, Robinson's Rodney King example is inapt, for few reasons-based formulations would hold the police conduct justified. The reasons theory requires that the defendant genuinely and reasonably believes his conduct necessary to achieve some lawful end—e.g., self-protection or effectuating a lawful arrest. Robinson's hypothetical does not satisfy these criteria.

---

* Richard Dale Endowed Chair in Law.

1. For elaboration, see Mitchell N. Berman, *Justification and Excuse, Law and Morality*, 53 DUKE L.J. 1 (2003).

A better test case involves a robbery victim who shoots a robber whose gun turns out to be unloaded. To communicate that we "condemn his act, and would not want others to do the same thing in the same situation," Robinson would grant this victim-defendant only an excuse. Subjectivists think the shooting unfortunate but condemnation inappropriate. Furthermore, we believe that "situation" can include beliefs and intentions. Therefore, say subjectivists, the legal system *should* tell others: "If you're in a situation like this—i.e., you genuinely believe someone intends to kill you—you may shoot first." Although objectivists disagree, their dispute is not over whether justifications are conduct rules, but over what such rules should be, and when condemnation is appropriate.

Second, in contending that reasons formulations cannot provide a workable definition of the force one may lawfully resist, Robinson mistakenly intimates that subjectivists can't improve on the MPC formulation. We can. A first pass: "An actor may use force against an individual to protect against what he believes is either unjustified force or force that would be unjustified but for the individual's mistaken belief that justificatory circumstances exist." Further refinement might be required, and the final version won't be as crisp as that of the objectivists. But I'd bet it would be adequately clear and workable.

Third, Robinson's contention that reasons formulations generate too much liability when an actor is unknowingly justified takes community intuitions too seriously. That the reasons theory licenses punishing defendants with unknowing justifications more than "the community's intuition" warrants doesn't entail that it "generates the wrong result." Conformity with popular desert judgments should not be decisive lest the criminal law be rendered hostage to existing community sentiments. Besides, empirical desert considerations can be accommodated at sentencing.

Fourth, Robinson's belief that reasons formulations necessarily generate wrong liability results when third parties resist or assist unknowingly justified actors is simply mistaken. A subjectivist penal code could provide, say, that "an actor may not use force against an individual engaged in conduct that the actor believes would be lawful were that individual to correctly apprise the relevant circumstances." Under this formulation, Robinson's farmer would not be permitted to forcibly resist the burning of his cornfield, and bystanders would be permitted to resist the farmer's resistance. In Robinson's second chart, rows three and four thus misdescribe the outcomes a subjective formulation directs. Liability would mimic what the deeds theory provides.

Fundamentally, Robinson contends erroneously that the reasons approach grounds justifications and excuses alike on the actor's blamelessness. As I have emphasized, at least some subjectivists conceptualize justifications as announcing what conduct the criminal law permits. Sharing Robinson's view that justifications are ex ante conduct rules, we merely urge that the conduct in question be conceived in an epistemically sensitive way. Thus, we disagree with most characterizations of our position in Robinson's first chart. We'd complete the "mistaken justification" column like this: (1) Conduct is permitted. (2) Ex ante conduct rules. (3) Yes. (4) No. (5) Yes.

Accordingly, the major difference between the approaches is captured in line 1: Robinson thinks conduct justified when and because it causes no net harm, whereas some subjectivists conceptualize justifications as permissions or exemptions. But an example undermines the no-net-harm conception.[2] Under both subjective and objective formulations, a dying misanthrope who kills one hundred aggressors who unjustifiably threaten his life is justified (criminally speaking) even if each aggressor solely supports ten toddlers with special needs. Yet it is implausible that the misanthrope produces "no net harm," or "did the right thing." No, he is legally justified because we grant justifications when we think it wiser on balance to permit conduct than to prohibit it—even if we sometimes prefer the permission not to be exercised. And permissions better serve their function when subjectivized because people can only be expected to act in accordance with their beliefs.

---

2. *See* Mitchell N. Berman, *Lesser Evils and Justification: A Less Close Look*, 24 L. & PHIL. 681, 689–700 (2005).

CONSTRAINING THE NECESSITY DEFENSE

JOHN MIKHAIL*

Although I am sympathetic to Paul Robinson's general approach to justification, particularly his emphasis on the need for clear ex ante rules and a sound conceptual distinction between justification and excuse, there is one aspect of his approach to this topic that I find puzzling: his assumption that objective justification should be equated, simply and without further qualification, with conduct that actually avoids the greater harm. A different theory of justification, which ample evidence suggests corresponds more closely with the community's sense of justice, also turns on the causal *means* by which the greater harm is avoided and requires that those means exclude battery, homicide, or certain other wrongful acts. Most individuals—upward of 90 percent as suggested by some well-publicized studies—simply do not believe that the end always justifies the means, at least when the end is preventing death or serious bodily harm to a relatively small number of persons, and the means is purposeful battery that results in knowing homicide to the person who is battered for the sake of this objective. That, at any rate, appears to be the relevant lesson for the substantive criminal

---

* Associate Professor of Law, Georgetown University Law Center.

law of the family of so-called "trolley problems" and other familiar psychological experiments.[1]

Consider an actual case. In February 2008, a Stanford-trained physician was indicted for prescribing excessive doses of drugs in order to hasten a patient's death and accelerate the harvesting of his organs, thereby performing much-needed transplants.[2] To keep things simple, let us suppose, contrary to the apparent facts of the case, that the patient was not already about to die, but rather had several weeks to live, albeit with a clear prognosis of impending death. Suppose further that purposeful battery (including lack of consent), knowing homicide, and the necessity of the act (i.e., no less harmful alternative) are clear and provable, and the only relevant question at trial is whether the doctor was justified in preventing the deaths of two other patients in this manner, which he did in fact manage to do, because the transplants were successful. Should the doctor be acquitted on this ground?

If I understand Robinson correctly, he would answer this question affirmatively, because by hypothesis the doctor's conduct did in fact avoid the greater harm. Likewise, if one makes the further assumption that the doctor reasonably believed hastening death was necessary to save the lives of the other two patients, § 3.02 of the Model Penal Code would also apparently hold the doctor's conduct to be justified. Despite their differences, Robinson's "deeds" approach and the MPC's "reasons" approach seem to agree on this point. LaFave and Scott would also apparently concur, as John Yoo famously sought to exploit on several occasions to justify battery, torture, and even homicide of certain incapacitated persons.[3] Common sense rejects all these lines of reasoning, however, and holds the doctor's conduct to be wrong and unjustified. Although the doctor might be excused or escape blame, the community's sense of justice would presumably resist a justification acquittal. Nor would most individuals want others to do the same thing in the same situation.

The foregoing example, which the experimental literature has shown can be generalized across many contexts, suggests that although the principal distinction on which Robinson relies might be a useful starting point for criminal law theory, it is too simple to capture the complexity of ordinary moral and legal thought. Neither the "objective" deeds theory nor the "subjective" reasons theory appears to be descriptively adequate with respect to an important subset of actual

---

1. *See, e.g.*, John Mikhail, *Universal Moral Grammar: Theory, Evidence, and the Future*, 11 TRENDS. COG. SCI. 143 (2007). *See generally* Greg Miller, *The Roots of Morality*, 320 SCIENCE 734 (2008); Steven Pinker, *The Moral Instinct*, N.Y. TIMES MAG., Jan. 13, 2008.

2. Jesse McKinley, Surgeon Accused of Speeding Death to Get Organs, N.Y. TIMES, Feb. 27, 2008.

3. *See, e.g.*, *Memorandum for Alberto R. Gonzalez Counsel to the President, August 1, 2002*, *in* THE TORTURE PAPERS: THE ROAD TO ABU GHRAIB 208 (Karen J. Greenberg and Joshua L. Dratel eds., 2005).

cases of necessity, because both fail to take into account the means by which otherwise justifiable objectives are sought and actually produced. Criminal-law scholars should therefore consider whether, and if so how, to narrow the scope of the necessity defense to exclude certain impermissible means, such as purposeful battery. Common moral intuitions do not have the last word on this matter, of course, but they are an important source of information and deserve a place in this debate, as Robinson and John Darley have persuasively argued.[4]

---

4. *See, e.g.*, Paul H. Robinson and John M. Darley, *Testing Competing Theories of Justification*, 76 N.C. L. Rev. 1095, 1105–07 (1998).

REPLY

PAUL H. ROBINSON

As a preliminary matter, consider John Mikhail's comment, in which he agrees with the general approach to justification proposed but objects to one aspect: what he says is its "assumption that objective justification should be equated, simply and without further qualification, with conduct that actually avoids the greater harm." He criticizes the Model Penal Code for taking the same approach.

Unfortunately, his comment is based on a false premise. As my treatise and other writings make clear, it is not my view that the balance of interests in justification defenses is limited to a comparison of the tangible harms. Indeed, it is commonly intangible interests that make the difference.[1] In the standard self-defense case, for example, the competing tangible harms are a life for a life. It is the intangible interest of society's abhorrence of aggression that tips the balance in favor of allowing force against the aggressor. Mikhail does the same disservice to the Model Penal Code. The drafters have no intention of limiting the balance of interests to tangible harms, even under the broad balancing of §3.02.[2] That is why the provision uses the phrase "harm *or evil*" (indeed, the section is titled "Lesser *Evils*") and why the commentary speaks of "weighing conflicting *values*"—and why I was careful to use the phrase "harm *or evil*" in the first paragraph of my core text. Mikhail may be forgiven his error, however, because it is a

---

1. *See, e.g.*, Paul H. Robinson, Criminal Law 408, 422–3, 428, 443 (1997). And some would argue that some intangible interests are so important that they can never be outweighed.

2. *See* Model Penal Code § 3.02 comment (1985). For example, see comment 4 at 17, discussing the "weighing of conflicts values" and disagreements over "which values are absolute or relative."

common one, even among serious criminal law theorists, including here both Mitch Berman (his last paragraph) and Peter Westen (his third paragraph).[3]

Turning to the main points of attack on the objective theory of justification, consider the comments in terms of the two arguments the core text makes in support of that theory. First, it argues that the distinction between actual, objective justification and subjective, mistaken justification is an important one. This is so because ignoring the distinction, as the subjective theory of justification does, makes it more difficult both (1) to announce clear ex ante rules of conduct and (2) to define the conditions triggering a right to use defensive force.

Shlomit Wallerstein appears to agree that the actual-mistaken distinction is an important one and that mistaken actors ought to be excused, not justified. Westen also agrees, but rightly points out that the resulting benefits can be realized only if the system adopts special verdicts that advertise the distinction in case adjudications. I have urged such special verdicts.[4]

Berman disagrees that the objective theory makes easier the law's ex ante function of announcing rules of conduct. He makes the standard Type 1 error discussed in Section III.A: He fails to appreciate that future actors will not know of their errors at the time they act, and thus will use the objective, actual justification rules as their guide, not rules relating to mistaken actors. As to the problem of an effective triggering condition for defensive force, he appears to concede that the Model Penal Code's subjective approach has a problem, but argues that it can be improved and offers a rewrite. But remember that this rule must serve as a rule of conduct for laypersons facing threats and as such should be neither complex nor intricate. His rewrite is as ineffective in performing this function as Model Penal Code language. What is required here is the simple, almost intuitive rule that only the objective theory provides: "one can defend against *unjustified* conduct."

Second, the core text argues that the objective theory of justification ought to be preferred over the subjective theory because the former gives correct liability assessments—attempt liability for the unknowingly justified actor, no defense for knowingly resisting an unknowingly justified actor, and no liability for knowingly assisting an unknowingly justified actor—while the latter gives incorrect results. Its results are "correct" because they are consistent with community intuitions and provide the correct incentives to advance societal interests.

Westen agrees that the objective theory results are preferable. His complaint is that I don't give enough credit to moral philosophy, where some have long supported these results, such as Plato. Wallerstein, who supports the "mixed" theory of George Fletcher, in which justification requires that both objective and

---

3. *See* Berman comment at para. 359; Westen comment at para. 354.

4. *See, e.g.,* Paul H. Robinson and Michael T. Cahill, Law Without Justice 210–12 (2006); Paul H. Robinson, Structure and Function in Criminal Law 204–07 (1997).

subjective requirements be satisfied, prefers contrary results but offers no explanation for why they ought to be preferable. She would have the law authorize the farmer to prevent the firebreak that the farmer knows is needed to save the townspeople, a result contrary to common sense, if not more.

Berman concedes that the objective theory has the right results with regard to assisting and resisting the unknowingly justified actor, but argues that the subjective theory also could come to these results. The core text, he complains, "misdescribes the outcomes a subjective formulation directs."[5] This seems something less than fair, however, given that the core text describes the results that people have always assumed the subjective Model Penal Code provides. It turns out that what Berman is really suggesting is that one could construct a special rule to alter the Model Penal Code's results to match those of the objective theory.

In contrast, with regard to liability for the unknowingly justified actor, Berman would create no special rule and defends the Model Penal Code's full liability. However, he offers no explanation for why people's intuitions and society's interests should be sacrificed. Indeed, even under the deontological analysis that he seems to prefer, the unknowingly justified actor is in a morally analogous position to the impossible attempter. Neither actor has injured society (indeed, the unknowingly justified actor has benefitted from it), but both mistakenly believe that they have. On what grounds can one justify punishing the unknowingly justified actor more?

Note also the peculiarity of Berman's position here: The unknowingly justified actor is not justified, while the person assisting him is justified. So much for Berman's earlier claim that his theory would do better in announcing an ex ante rule of conduct. What rule of conduct is one to draw from these conflicting dispositions about the permissibility of the burning?

A broad view of the debate suggests that the best critics can do is to argue that the subjective theory of justification is not quite as bad as claimed or that, with some special rules, its problems can be minimized or fixed. But why bother?

What is missing in the attacks is an argument for why the subjective theory should be preferred despite its problems. In the end, I suspect that support for the subjective theory lies in the standard Type 3 error discussed in Section III.C: that people commonly start with a premise that justification must be subjectively defined because it has been so in some previously existing literature, then set themselves to defend that unreasoned premise.

---

5. Berman comment at 358.

17. SELF-DEFENSE AND THE PSYCHOTIC AGGRESSOR

GEORGE P. FLETCHER* AND LUIS E. CHIESA**

Can one justifiably kill a faultless, insane assailant to save oneself or another from imminent and serious harm? Although scholars on both sides of the Atlantic agree that the person attacked should not be punished for defending herself from the psychotic aggressor, they disagree as to whether the defensive response should be considered justified or merely excused. Furthermore, among those who argue that the appropriate defense in such cases is a justification, they disagree as to whether the specific ground of acquittal should be self-defense or necessity.

I. THE PROBLEM

The hypothetical case of the psychotic aggressor was first put forth by one of us more than thirty-five years ago:

> Imagine your companion in an elevator goes berserk and attacks you with a knife. There is no escape: the only way to avoid serious bodily harm or even death is to kill him. The assailant acts purposively in the sense that he rationally relies on means that further his aggressive end. He does not act in a frenzy or in a fit, yet it is clear his conduct is nonresponsible. If he were brought to trial for his attack, he would have a valid defense of insanity.

In general form, the problem is whether force may be justifiably exerted against excused but unjustified aggression. More specifically, the case of the psychotic aggressor poses two basic questions. First, if the actor defending against the attack defends himself and kills the aggressor, should he be acquitted? Secondly, if a third party, a stranger, intervenes on behalf of the defender and kills the aggressor, should he be acquitted?

The answer to the first question is relatively easy: it is hard to see either the justice or efficacy of punishing someone who kills for the sake of self-preservation.

* Cardozo Professor of Jurisprudence, Columbia Law School. This core text draws on and further elaborates upon the ideas first espoused in George P. Fletcher, *Proportionality and the Psychotic Aggressor: A Vignette in Comparative Criminal Theory*, 8 Isr. L. Rev. 367 (1973).

** Associate Professor of Law, Pace Law School.

The more difficult issue is whether third persons should be allowed to intervene without risking criminal conviction. If one party to the affray must die, either the insane aggressor or the actor defending against his attack, why should an outsider be encouraged to take sides? Neither is morally at fault; neither deserves to die. Yet it is hard to deny the pull in the direction of favoring defender and permitting intervention to restrain and disable the aggressor.

II. FIVE FAILED APPROACHES

A. Necessity as an Excuse

It is easy to solve the first-person case as a matter of necessity understood as an excuse. The claim would be that even though killing the insane aggressor is wrong, it is the natural expression of the human instinct for survival. The claim seems sound; no one can be blamed for killing to save his own life.

The problem with this approach is that it fails to account for our intuition that if a third-party stranger had to choose between you and the aggressor, he would be right and proper in favoring you, the innocent defender facing death, over the aggressor endangering your life. Reducing the defender's claim to an excuse is to concede that killing the psychotic aggressor is wrong. If killing the aggressor is wrong, why should anyone have a right to voluntarily intervene on behalf of the defender? An excuse of necessity in such cases would be limited to parties who stand in a close relationship with the person being attacked.

These implications conflict with our sense of justice in the situation. If anyone should be assisted, it is the party struggling to save his life against the psychotic aggressor, not vice versa. These counterintuitive results derive from conceding that resisting the psychotic aggressor is wrongful though excusable. An adequate theory, one that would permit third parties to intervene against (and not for) the psychotic aggressor, would have to hold that resistance was not merely excusable but indeed justifiable.

B. Self-Defense as an Excuse

Larry Alexander has argued that "when the aggressor is morally innocent, then self-defense, if it exonerates, cannot always be treated as a matter of justification."[1] Thus, he contends that an "attack by innocent aggressors is better characterized as a case of duress that excuses homicide, not a case of Wrong that justifies it."[2] Alexander's view is driven by his belief that no morally relevant reasons should lead us to assume that the interest in survival of the defending party outweighs the interest in survival of the insane aggressor.

---

1. Lawrence Alexander, *Justification and Innocent Aggressors*, 33 WAYNE L. REV. 1177, 1187 (1987).
    2. *Id.*

Insofar as Alexander's solution is premised on excusing the killing of the psychotic aggressor, it gives rise to the same counterintuitive results that were discussed in the previous section. Furthermore, by focusing on the relatively narrow question of whether the interests of one party outweigh the interests of the other, Alexander fails to acknowledge one very important feature of the case: that the actor defending against the psychotic aggressor's attack does not lose his right to be free from unwarranted invasions of his living space merely because his assailant is insane. The focus should be on examining the comparative *rights* of the parties, not on undertaking a balancing of their relative interests in survival.

In a sense, it is unfortunate that the psychotic aggressor has to suffer an invasion of his sphere of autonomy so that the defender can vindicate her rights. Insane assailants are, after all, innocent aggressors. However, it would be much more unfortunate if the law were to adopt Alexander's view and tell the defender that she cannot lawfully defend herself from an insane assailant's unjustified attack. No one has a duty to capitulate to wrongful aggression.

C. Necessity as a Justification

Although excusing the killing of the psychotic aggressor leads to counterintuitive results, perhaps we can avoid such implications by *justifying* his killing under a theory of necessity. The problem with this approach is that one would have to find that taking the life of the psychotic aggressor constituted the "lesser evil" under the circumstances. Yet the most that can be gained from the killing is the saving of one's life. If it is life against life, it is hard to see why we should say that it is justifiable for one person to live and the other to die.

The fact is that in the case of the psychotic aggressor, we are inclined to favor an acquittal even if the loss to the aggressor is greater than the gain to the defendant. Indeed, as the problem is stated, that is the case. For all the defending party knows, he might possibly die if he does not resist. To fend off this possibility, he chooses certain death for the aggressor. When relevant probabilities are included in assessing the competing interests, the defendant clearly engages in conduct with a higher expected loss (certain death) than expected gain (a probability of death). We could decrease the threat to the defendant without altering our intuitive judgment about the desirability of an acquittal. Would it make any difference if the defendant were threatened with loss of limb, rape, or castration? One would think not. As the problem is treated in the literature, it is assumed that justice would require acquittal in these cases as well.

Perhaps those that look at the problem as one of justifiable necessity think that the life of the insane aggressor is worth less than the life of the defendant who is standing his ground. One finds analogies between psychotic aggressors and attacks by wild animals. If one thinks of the psychotic aggressor as subhuman, one might be able to justify the defensive killing as an act preserving the greater value. This is an intriguing if startling approach, but one that is apparently inadequate. Among its other defects it fails to account for the case of temporary psychosis. If the aggressor is a brilliant but temporarily deranged scientist, it would seem rather odd to say that his life is worth less than that of the defender, who for all we know might be a social pariah.

D. Interest-Balancing Approaches to Justifiable Self-Defense

One could be tempted to adopt an interest balancing approach to self-defense that justifies conduct when the interest preserved by the defensive action outweighs the interest harmed. As such, it constitutes a variation on the choice of evils defense. This approach is well-equipped to explain the justifiable nature of standard cases of self-defense in which the aggressor acts culpably. In such instances, the culpability of the aggressor is used as a rationale for diminishing the interests of the assailant relative to those of the defender. By depreciating the culpable aggressor's interest in the balancing process, the use of defensive force can be justified even when the physical harm averted by the defender is of equal value to the one visited upon the aggressor.

Yet with culpability as its pinion, the interest balancing approach to self-defense cannot solve the problem of the psychotic aggressor. By definition the psychotic aggressor is not culpable and thus this conception of self-defense fails to explain why his interests should be worth less than those of the defender.

E. Passive Necessity as a Justification

Continental scholars have increasingly turned to passive necessity whenever their traditional theories of choice of evils and self-defense fail to justify conduct that they believe ought to be considered lawful. The claim of passive necessity, which has yet to find legislative or scholarly support in common-law jurisdictions, maintain that conduct aimed at neutralizing the source of the threat is justified as long as the harm caused is not disproportional to the harm averted. The defense is confined to cases that do not qualify for justification under a theory of self-defense.

Recently, Mordechai Kremnitzer and Khalid Ghanayim argued that self-defense should justify the use of force only when it is necessary to repel a wrongful *and* culpable aggression.[3] They did so by defending an interest balancing approach to self-defense akin to the one described in the previous section. The novelty of their argument, however, lies in their contention that wrongful but nonculpable threats should trigger a right to use justifiable force pursuant to a claim of *passive necessity* rather than self-defense.

The gist of the proposal consists in adopting a theory of necessity that attaches considerable weight to determining which of the conflicting parties is the source of the threatened harm. This consideration proves decisive in the case of the psychotic aggressor. Although the harm inflicted by killing the insane assailant (death) is equal or greater to the concrete harm averted by the defender (serious

---

3. Mordechai Kremnitzer and Khalid Ghanayim, *Proportionality and the Aggressor's Culpability in Self-Defense*, 39 Tulsa L. Rev. 875 (2005).

bodily injury or death), the fact that the psychotic aggressor was the source of the threat tips the balance in favor of the defender.

The rationale underlying this proposal appears to be that mere aggression, regardless of whether it is unjustifiable or culpable, provides a basis for diminishing the interests of the assailant in the balancing process. Yet this argument does not survive critical examination. Why should someone's interest be diminished by virtue of conduct that cannot be characterized as either wrongful or culpable? One can understand diminishing an aggressor's interests if he acts wrongfully or if he is to blame for the encounter, but it is hard to see why he should be worth less merely because his body is the *locus* of the threat. Ultimately, this argument places too much emphasis on motion and nonmotion. Without consideration of whether the actor's conduct is wrongful or blameworthy, the mere fact that one party's body is moving toward the body of another seems to be a morally irrelevant feature of the conflict.

III. AN AUTONOMY-BASED THEORY OF SELF-DEFENSE AS A JUSTIFICATION

What is it about the aggression that prompts us to think that the defender and the third person ought to be able to kill the psychotic aggressor? The underlying judgment must be that the defender has a right to the integrity and autonomy of his body and that he has a right to prevent encroachments upon his living space. Respect for another person's autonomy is one of the foundational principles of our society. In each and every one of our interactions with another human being we are under a duty to not interfere with their autonomy. The duty, of course, is reciprocal, for others are also under a duty to respect our freedom.

The notions of individual freedom and the right to protect autonomy underlie a theory of self-defense that is not grounded on the balancing of interests. According to this theory, the crux of the aggressor's attack is that it unjustifiably threatens to encroach upon the victim's autonomy. Because an aggressor who engages in an unjustified attack has breached his duty to respect the rights of the defender, the defender's reciprocal duty to respect the aggressor's rights wanes. Thus, insofar as the aggressor unjustifiably impinges upon the defender's autonomy, the defender is no longer required to abstain from interfering with the assailant's liberty and is instead entitled to use whatever force is necessary to repel the attack. The innocent defender is assumed to have a right to prevent any unwarranted encroachment upon his personal space. As German scholars have put it, the right should never yield to the wrong.[4]

---

4. It is generally held that the phrase first appeared in U.F. Berner, *Die Notwehrtheorie*, Archiv des Criminalrechts 546, 557, 562 (1848), though the maxim derives straight

This theory provides a vehicle with which to clearly distinguish between the justifications of self-defense and necessity. Whereas in cases of self-defense the conduct that threatens to impinge on the defender's freedom amounts to a breach of a duty to respect the defender's rights, in cases of justifiable necessity it does not. Thus, the person acting under necessity is still required to fully respect the rights of the person who is the source of the threat. Since none of the parties in a conflict that gives rise to a situation of necessity has infringed their duty to respect the other's rights, there is no reason to afford less protection to the autonomy of the actor whose conduct originated the threat. As a result, justification in cases of necessity can only follow when the good achieved by interfering with the autonomy of one of the parties outweighs the harm caused by doing so. The situation is different in cases of self-defense. Given that the aggressor has breached his duty to respect the autonomy of the defending party, the attack may be repelled even when doing so entails causing more harm than the one averted (e.g. the victim may kill the aggressor in order to avoid serious bodily injury or rape).

This approach to self-defense is espoused by many German, Spanish, and Soviet criminal theorists. It also found expression in the early common law. Sir Edward Coke insisted that no "man shall (ever) give way to a thief, etc., neither shall he forfeit anything."[5] John Locke supported the same theory of an absolute right to protect one's liberty and rights from encroachment by aggressors.[6] Among the various accounts of this version of self-defense, one finds the common theme that the act of aggression puts the aggressor outside the protection of the law. Locke, for example, speaks of the aggressor's being in a "state of war" with the defender.[7] The argument is that the aggression breaches an implicit contract among autonomous agents, according to which each person is bound to respect the living space of all others. The unwarranted intrusion upon someone's living space itself triggers a justified response.[8]

Only aggressions that amount to a breach of a duty to respect the defender's autonomy should trigger the right to use force in self-defense. This is the gist of the Model Penal Code's § 3.04 requirement that self-defense only be exerted in response to the use of "unlawful force" against the defender's person. According to the Model Penal Code, force employed against another person is unlawful if it is constitutive of an "offense" or an "actionable tort." The requirement is sensible,

---

from the conceptual framework of Kant's theory of law. *See* George P. Fletcher, *Law and Morality: A Kantian Perspective*, 87 COLUM. L. REV. 533 (1987).

5. Edward Coke, THE THIRD INSTITUTE OF THE LAWS OF ENGLAND 55 (1642)

6. John Locke, TWO TREATISES ON CIVIL GOVERNMENT 120–27 (1690).

7. *Id.* at 126.

8. The same doctrine finds expression in the rhetoric of the American Revolution. The slogan "Don't Tread on Me" expresses the claim that treading on someone else in itself entails a justified response.

for only conduct contrary to the criminal or civil law amounts to a breach of a legal duty to respect the rights of others. We find the same requirement in Continental criminal codes, which condition the use of force in self-defense upon the existence of a "wrongful" (*rechtswidrig* in Germany, *ilegítima* in Spain) aggression. The rationale for this proviso is clear. The wrongful invasion of the defending party's vital interests authorizes him to temporarily neglect his duty to respect the autonomy of the aggressor to the extent that doing so is necessary to ward off the threat.

However, some threats that interfere with another person's autonomy do not trigger a right to use force in self-defense. This is most obviously the case when someone interferes with another person's freedom as a result of a justified course of action. Take, for example, the case of a police officer who is effectuating a lawful arrest. Even though the conduct certainly impinges upon the freedom of the arrestee, it would be mistaken to claim that the officer has violated his duty to respect the rights of others. Given that the officer's aggression is justified, the arrestee has an obligation to tolerate the interference with his or her liberty.

Aggressions that lack human agency constitute another example of nonwrongful attacks that should not justify using force in self-defense. Causal processes that are not the product of human will are akin to natural events, even if they originate within the confines of a human body. Therefore, claiming that acts not reflective of human agency are wrongful is as erroneous as asserting that a threat that originates in a natural event amounts to unlawful force. If there is no "act," there can be no wrongful attack.

On the other hand, excused aggression qualifies as a wrongful attack that gives rise to a claim of self-defense. We ought to be able to demand that others abide by their duty to respect our autonomy regardless of their personal limitations and mental conditions. Our legal system reflects this idea. As a perfunctory examination of the tort law demonstrates, the mentally ill are under a duty to respect the rights of others in much the same way as sane people are. There are good reasons for this to be the case. Our right to be free from unlawful interferences with our person should not be compromised merely because the threat to our autonomy originates in the acts of an inculpable person. The defender does not have to pull his punches merely because the aggressor is mentally ill. In such a confrontation on the street, the aggressor loses the protections that he would get during a trial, that is, the right to plead excuses such as insanity or duress.

IV. CONCLUSION

Once we recognize that even a psychotic aggressor is under a duty to respect the autonomy of others, one can see why his aggression can be justifiably warded off in self-defense. In light of the wrongful nature of the attack, the defender's reciprocal obligation to show consideration for the psychotic aggressor's auton-omy weakens. As a result, the law affords him a right to use whatever force is necessary to repel the unlawful aggression.

The fact that the psychotic actor would be acquitted on grounds of insanity if he were tried for his aggression is beside the point, for excuses such as insanity do not negate the wrongfulness of the act. Ultimately, the roots of the right to use defensive force are not in the culpability of the aggressor, but in the unjustifiable invasion of the defender's autonomy. Furthermore, given that the defender's use of force against the psychotic aggressor is justifiable rather than merely excus-able, third-party intervention on behalf of the defender should be considered lawful as well.

COMMENTS

"SELF-DEFENSE AND THE PSYCHOTIC AGGRESSOR": WHAT ABOUT PROPORTIONALITY?

BOAZ SANGERO*

The main disadvantage of an autonomy-based theory is the absence of a propor-tionality requirement. Autonomy isn't a sufficient rationale for self-defense as a justification. We shouldn't be excited about the saying "right should never yield to wrong." Such an approach has led to one German Supreme Court judgment—supported by German scholars—holding that a person was justified in shooting, and seriously wounding, a youth stealing fruit from his garden.[1] A theory failing to take proportionality into account should be rejected ab initio.

When balancing the interests of the aggressor and the attacked person, it is important to take into consideration not only the physical harms caused or expected, but also three abstract factors, none of which is sufficient on its own to justify self-defense: the *autonomy of the person attacked*, the *aggressor's guilt*, and the *social-legal order*.[2] The use of necessary and proportionate defensive force against a culpable aggressor protects both the autonomy of the attacked person and the social-legal order.

---

* Head of the Department, Criminal Law and Criminology, Academic Center of Law and Business, Ramat Gan, Israel.

1. George P. Fletcher, *Proportionality and the Psychotic Aggressor: A Vignette in Comparative Criminal Theory*, 8 Isr. L. Rev. 367, 381 (1973) (Reichsgericht [RG] [Federal Court of Justice] Sept. 20, 1920, 55 Entscheidungen des Reichsgerichts in Strafsachen [RGst] 82) (F.R.G.)).

2. Boaz Sangero, Self-Defence in Criminal Law 93 (2006); *see also* Boaz Sangero, *A New Defense for Self-Defense*, 9 Buff. Crim. L. Rev. 475 (2006).

A culpable aggressor can choose to stop his attack. A nonculpable aggressor has no such choice. It is proper to view the use of defensive force against a psychotic aggressor as an excuse, like necessity or putative self-defense, and to place restrictions on the defender, like a duty to retreat and a stronger requirement of proportionality than usual.

The fact that the innocent aggressor isn't trying to exploit the attacked person is morally significant. In addition to his lack of culpability, he isn't causing any serious harm to the social-legal order. That isn't to say that the attacked person must capitulate. One must obviously be allowed to defend oneself. However, greater compassion should be shown to the innocent aggressor.

If we abandon the requirement of the aggressor's guilt, then the unique nature of self-defense—characterized not only by the aggressor's attack, but also by his guilt and the use of defensive force against him—is lost in comparison to the other defenses of constraint: necessity and duress. We would be left with a very weak justification for self-defense; so much so that it doesn't make much sense to isolate self-defense from the broader defense of necessity. Indeed, if self-defense also includes the use of lethal defensive force against an innocent aggressor, then the moral justification for the defense is weakened to such an extent that we lose the significance of characterizing it in law as a justification, as opposed to an excuse.

The fact that self-defense cannot appropriately be characterized as a justification in the case of an innocent aggressor is illustrated by the need to establish special rules in legal systems where it is accepted as such. Thus, for example, even in German law, where the autonomy of the victim is emphasized as the sole rationale for self-defense, and where a duty to retreat isn't generally imposed, such a duty has been imposed in the special case of an innocent aggressor.

George Fletcher and Luis Chiesa believe that most people would agree with their intuitions that a person attacked by a psychotic has a right to self-defense, as a justification; and that a third party has a right to intervene on behalf of the attacked person. But my intuitions are different. I agree that the attacked person isn't required to capitulate, and that he shouldn't be held responsible for the harm resulting from his use of defensive force. But this doesn't necessarily mean that his act is justified. It is more proper to grant him an excuse of necessity or putative self-defense—as the case may be. Since the defender is granted an excuse, a third party would indeed not be justified if he intervenes on the defender's behalf, but it is possible that he, too, would be excused.

In such a tragic situation, it may also be possible for the innocent aggressor to be excused for resisting the defender. After all, from his perspective the attacked person has become an aggressor. While contradictory justifications are impossible by definition, contradictory excuses aren't. Excuses deal with human weaknesses, not with rights. Anyone who remains unconvinced should consider, instead of the case of a psychotic aggressor, the threat of a young child innocently playing with a loaded gun. In such a case, what does our intuition tell us: that the use of defensive force against such a threat should be encouraged by a justification, or that an excuse is sufficient?

SELF-DEFENSE AGAINST WRONGFUL ATTACK: THE CASE OF THE PSYCHOTIC AGGRESSOR

JOHN MIKHAIL*

George Fletcher and Luis Chiesa are surely correct that one may use force, including deadly force if necessary, to resist a violent attack by a psychotic aggressor. If the victim of such an attack defends herself and thereby kills the aggressor, she should be acquitted, assuming other relevant conditions are satisfied. Fletcher and Chiesa also seem correct to hold that the appropriate defense in such a case is one of justification rather than excuse, and of self-defense rather than necessity.

Still, because the psychotic aggressor is morally innocent, and cannot be held criminally liable because he has an excuse of insanity, why is his attack wrongful? The answer given by the law of torts is simple: his act still constitutes both intentional battery and negligence. It is battery because by hypothesis he performs a voluntary act with the intent to cause a harmful or offensive contact with the victim, which does in fact ensue and is neither consensual nor privileged. Because negligence is an objective standard of reasonable conduct, which looks to the conduct itself rather than the actor's state of mind, the act is also negligent, insofar as its expected costs exceed its discounted expected benefits.[1]

For the criminal law, the relevant question is why the victim is justified in using force, perhaps even deadly force, to repel this wrongful attack. Here I share the authors' conviction that self-defense is a distinct and adequate ground on which to justify what otherwise would be a purposeful battery and knowing homicide on the part of the victim. Neither consent nor necessity is a viable alternative in these circumstances, in light of how those defenses are usually conceived. Of course, the victim's right to use force against the psychotic aggressor is limited. Her objective must be to prevent an impending battery or other harmful contact, or to stop one that is in progress, not to retaliate, punish, or attack preemptively. Further, deadly force may only be used to defend against deadly force, with all of the usual caveats and restrictions.

Surprisingly, Fletcher and Chiesa imply that a tortious act is not merely sufficient to justify using force in self-defense, but also necessary. They write: "Only aggressions that amount to a breach of a duty to respect the defender's autonomy should trigger the right to use force in self-defense."[2] This proposition

---

* Associate Professor, Georgetown University Law Center.

1. For a formal analysis of the concepts of *expected cost* and *discounted expected benefit* as they would likely apply in this context, see John Mikhail, *Moral Grammar and Intuitive Jurisprudence: A Formal Model of Unconscious Moral and Legal Knowledge*, in MORAL JUDGMENT AND DECISION MAKING (Brian H. Ross et al., eds., forthcoming).

2. Fletcher and Chiesa core text at 370.

seems untenable. Self-defense is a strong enough principle to warrant the use of force against both tortious and nontortious threats to one's life, at least in many circumstances. For example, no one is compelled to become collateral damage in another's justified effort to rescue third parties. Rather, an innocent bystander who is threatened in this manner may justifiably use force to defend herself.

Moreover, I am inclined to think that Fletcher and Chiesa risk confusing matters by relying on complex principles like autonomy and reciprocity to identify the precise contours of the right to self-defense in these circumstances. Although these principles do provide a useful philosophical gloss on this situation, they cannot easily function as premises of an argument that generates the relevant considered judgments in these cases. Their correct definition and application to different fact patterns is simply too contested and uncertain, and codified law properly eschews them whenever possible for just this reason. The authors' emphasis on the aggressor's breach of duty to the victim also seems somewhat misplaced, for similar reasons. Wrongfulness must be defined independently of breach of duty if one is to avoid circularity, as Henry Terry pointed out long ago.[3]

---

3. *See* Henry T. Terry, *Negligence*, 29 HARV. L. REV. 40 (1915).

JUSTIFYING HOMICIDE AGAINST INNOCENT AGGRESSORS WITHOUT DENYING THEIR INNOCENCE

SHERRY F. COLB*

George Fletcher and Luis Chiesa have written an excellent analysis of moral responses to the psychotic aggressor. They persuasively reject excuse-based arguments in favor of justification. The right that they embrace—of defending one's own bodily integrity and autonomy against attack—is an appealing description of the moral intuitions involved. I am puzzled, however, by the authors' choice of a "breach of duty" account of why we distinguish between the self-defensive homicide by the would-be victim (justified) and the unprovoked attack by the psychotic aggressor (merely excused). A better approach combines the authors' insights about autonomy with the recognition that the psychotic aggressor does not and need not breach any duty to his target to trigger a right of self-defense.

The difficulty one encounters in justifying the killing of the psychotic aggressor is the latter's blamelessness in his aggression. Ordinarily, we associate the right of self-defensive homicide in part with a forfeiture of sorts by the aggressor

---

* Professor of Law and Charles Evans Hughes Scholar, Cornell Law School.

who, by unjustifiably threatening another's life, temporarily reduces the imperative on others to respect his own. The psychotic aggressor, by hypothesis, cannot be said to have made such a forfeiture because he has not behaved culpably. Repelling his actions, under these circumstances, cannot rest on notions of desert, because he does not deserve retribution for his sickness. He is innocent. Yet our intuitions tell us that self-defense is nonetheless permissible against the psychotic aggressor.

At the same time, however, we do not authorize people to kill, "in self-defense" or otherwise, whenever their own survival requires them to take a life. Consider, for example, the patient who needs a heart transplant immediately. Neither he nor his loved ones are justified in shooting the next compatible would-be donor who comes along. A seemingly essential component of killing in self-defense is that the person to be killed is, at the time of the killing, posing a threat to the life or limb of the killer, a threat that will dissipate if he is killed.

Recognizing that the person to be justifiably killed must have himself posed an unjustified threat, Fletcher and Chiesa suggest further that there must be misconduct of a tortious sort associated with that threat. In defining the psychotic aggressor, they say that his acts are purposive (though not criminally culpable) and that there must be an act (in the actus reus sense) rather than simply a fit or a frenzy. The reason for this narrow definition of the aggressor's impairment becomes clear when Fletcher and Chiesa present their hypothesis that the actor against whom homicide in self-defense is permissible has breached a duty and thereby reduced the sanctity of his autonomy interest relative to that of his would-be victim.

This focus on a purposive act (by a psychotic actor) seems arbitrary. I would not distinguish between the psychotic aggressor and the epileptic aggressor, for purposes of triggering a right of self-defense in their respective targets. If a person poses a threat to your life, you may justifiably terminate that person's life as necessary to protect your own. Indeed, Fletcher and Chiesa appear to be headed toward that conclusion but then suggest that a right of self-defense turns on the psychotic aggressor's having breached his duty to respect the rights of others and thereby effected the forfeiture (or "waning" of others' duty toward him) necessary to authorize the use of deadly force against him.

But could we not justifiably defend ourselves against a sleep-walking or hypnotized aggressor? If the right of self-defense requires that there first be a breach of duty by an aggressor, moreover, then a psychotic aggressor's actions should not trigger the right either. After all, if truly insane, he is as incapable of fulfilling a civil duty as he is of understanding and following a criminal prohibition.

The insight that Fletcher and Chiesa surface so beautifully is that the justification of self-defense does not appear to depend on an aggressor's blameworthiness. If someone threatens us and the threat is not justified, then we have a right to defend ourselves, period. Fletcher and Chiesa seemingly back away from this notion, however, when arguing that "[w]ithout consideration of whether the actor's conduct is wrongful or blameworthy, the mere fact that one party's body is moving toward the body of another seems to be a morally irrelevant feature of the conflict."[1] I respectfully disagree. There is a fundamental distinction between defusing a threat that one faces, however innocent the source, and harming people who pose no threat. This distinction provides the moral foundation for the justification of self-defense.

---

1. Fletcher and Chiesa core text at 369.

TWO FLAWS IN THE AUTONOMY-BASED JUSTIFICATION FOR SELF-DEFENSE

SHLOMIT WALLERSTEIN*

George Fletcher and Luis Chiesa advance self-defence as an autonomy-based justification. They argue that an unjustified attack is a breach of the aggressor's duty to respect the rights of the defender, which wanes the reciprocal duty of the defender to respect the aggressor's rights. This explanation accounts for a justification-based claim of self-defence against nonculpable aggressors (e.g., the psychotic aggressor) because what matters is the unjust—or to use their term, "wrongful"—aggression that encroaches upon the defender's personal space. The culpability of the aggressor does not matter.

This explanation assumes that the defender's duty to respect the aggressor's rights is *based on* reciprocity. This would be true if the rights in question rested on an explicit or implicit undertaking to respect the corresponding rights in another. But even if we accept the authors' starting proposition that "the duty [not to interfere with other people's autonomy] . . . is reciprocal, for others are also under a duty to respect our freedom,"[1] it does not follow that the recognition of personal autonomy *originates* out of any explicit or implicit contractual relationship. Consider the duty not to lie to my friend. Though this duty is reciprocal, in that my duty not to lie to my friend is similar to his duty not to lie to me, the ground for this duty is *not* the fact that he has a duty not to lie to me, but rather the fact that lying is morally wrong.

Yet Fletcher and Chiesa move without explanation from the claim that the right to personal autonomy is reciprocal to the claim that the existence of one right originates from, and depends on, reciprocity. This move is unsound. For one thing, personal autonomy is often regarded as being intrinsically valuable

---

* University Lecturer, Tutor, and Fellow in Law, St. Peter's College and Law Faculty, Oxford University.

1. Fletcher and Chiesa core text at 369.

because of the value in allowing people to choose how they live, and our recognition of autonomy is based on this intrinsic value (rather than on reciprocity). But more importantly, the core "rights" to which the authors refer (and which they describe as autonomy-based rights) seem to be the rights to life and physical integrity. These are natural (or human) rights. As such, they do not rest on "mutual" respect or reciprocity any more than they originate out of contractual, quasi-contractual, status-relational, or other contingent and variable circumstances.[2] Thus, for example, many people argue that torture—a violation of the right to life and physical integrity—is wrong even when the person tortured has done something wrongful (e.g., kidnapped another person).

Fletcher and Chiesa go on to argue that what matters is unjust aggression because this wrongful invasion of the defender's vital interests is what authorizes him to neglect his duty to respect the autonomy of others. Therefore, excused conduct, such as that of the nonculpable aggressor, triggers the right to self-defense, but aggression that lacks human agency (the nonagent aggressor) is outside the scope of this justification. A nonagent's aggression cannot be "wrongful" insofar as a nonagent aggressor is akin to a natural event, and hence talk of such conduct as "wrongful" or "unjust" is misplaced. Yet, once Fletcher and Chiesa recognize that the blameworthiness of the aggressor is irrelevant,[3] the only sense in which the aggression is morally "wrongful" is the fact that he has threatened to violate vital interests of the defender without any justification. Thus, cases of nonagent aggressors are similar to nonculpable aggressors in that in both the threat to the defender's interests is *not justified*. The nonagent aggressor has no privilege to threaten the vital interests of the defender.

Moreover, even if we accept Fletcher and Chiesa's claim that the nonagent aggressor is like a threat from natural events (thus owing no duties), natural events are objects, and objects have no entitlement to claim from others to avoid their destruction in an attempt to save life. In contrast, Fletcher and Chiesa's claim is that at the time of the act of aggression the aggressor is both an object that owes no duties and a subject owed a duty simply by virtue of her humanity. If the aggressor is akin an object, then one ought to be able to treat her similar to the way other objects are treated.

---

2. *See* Hugo Bedau, *The Right to Life*, 52 MONIST 550 (1968).

3. A point with which I agree, though for other reasons. I argue that causal responsibility is the relevant factor. *See* Shlomit Wallerstein, *Justifying the Right to Self-Defense: A Theory of Forced Consequences*, 91 VA. L. REV. 999, 1029–30 (2005).

PROBLEMS FOR THE AUTONOMY THEORY OF SELF-DEFENSE

WHITLEY R.P. KAUFMAN*

George Fletcher's *Proportionality and the Psychotic Aggressor* is one of the seminal legal essays of the twentieth century, and it is an honor to comment on his and Luis Chiesa's newly updated version of it. Still, though I agree with the conclusion that exercising defensive force against the psychotic aggressor is permissible, I want to raise some concerns about the structure of the argument.

First, Fletcher and Chiesa assume that third-party intervention is permissible only if defensive force is justified, not if it is merely excused. Although this position has some historical precedent why we should follow it is not clear. Indeed, if it is excusable for the defender to kill the psychotic aggressor, it would seem to be excusable for a third party to do so *for the very same reason* (or, contrariwise, if it is wrong for the third party, why isn't it equally wrong for the person being attacked)? Only if one adopted an extremely and implausibly narrow definition of excuse (e.g., one that excused the defender because he was overcome by an irresistible impulse of self-preservation) would the third-party restriction obviously follow.

Second, and more fundamentally, I have my doubts about whether the analysis of self-defense in terms of "rights" is very helpful.[1] The case of the innocent aggressor is one in which the rights to life of two innocent parties conflict. Why should we allow the defender to "vindicate" his right by violating the right to life of another innocent person? Nor does it resolve the question to declare that the defender has no "duty to capitulate."[2] The question is not whether there is a "duty to capitulate," but whether there is a right to kill an innocent person to save one's own life. One might have thought that a rights theory would insist that the answer is "no": what could be a more serious violation of rights than killing an innocent person? The argument verges on paradox: it seems that the possibility of an innocent person being killed is so bad that it justifies killing an innocent person to prevent it! (Furthermore, this is to trade a merely *possible* death (or even serious bodily harm) of an innocent for a nearly *certain* death).

The authors tell us that killing the psychotic aggressor is permissible because of his "breach of a duty to respect the defender's rights."[3] But if the psychotic aggressor's blameless use of force against the victim is a failure to respect the victim, then why isn't the victim's blameless use of force against the psychotic

---

* Professor, Department of Philosophy, University of Massachusetts—Lowell.

1. I have developed this critique in detail in Whitley R.P. Kaufman, *Is There A "Right" To Self-Defense?*, CRIM. JUST. ETHICS, Winter/Spring 2004, at 20.

2. Fletcher and Chiesa core text at 367.

3. *Id.* at 370.

aggressor a failure to respect the psychotic aggressor? It seems the authors are trying to have it both ways: the psychotic aggressor is innocent but also sufficiently culpable to justify the loss of his right to life.[4] We are further told that "[t]he wrongful invasion of the defending party's vital interests authorizes him to temporarily neglect his duty to respect the autonomy of the aggressor to the extent that doing so is necessary to ward off the threat."[5] The word "neglected" seems inappropriate, as it implies a careless failure to attend to the right (indeed, it suggests the language of excuse, not justification), whereas killing the psychotic aggressor is hardly "neglecting" the right but rather deliberately violating it. In any case, one would have thought that a right to life is not the sort of thing that ought to be neglected.

It is equally puzzling to learn that the duty to respect others somehow "wanes" as a result of the aggression. It is typical of rights-based theories to develop creative new vocabularies in their attempts to explain how there can be a right to life that can nonetheless be violated. Here, the claim seems to be that the duty to respect the rights of others may be "temporarily neglected" when that duty has "waned." But we will want a much more detailed explanation of what it means for a duty to "wane," and when, how, and why waned duties may be "neglected."

Finally, the authors raise an intriguing parallel in the field of tort law, where an insane person may sometimes be held to an ordinary standard of reasonable care. In cases where such liability is permitted, however, the stated policy reasons are entirely utilitarian: to encourage caretakers to control their patients, and to avoid the need for adjudications of the mental competence of defendants. Whether either of these reasons would be relevant to the psychotic aggressor case is unclear. More importantly, to accept them would be to adopt a straightforwardly utilitarian justification for killing an innocent person—something a Kantian, rights-based theory would hardly be able to endorse!

---

4. The various references given *supra* at 370 are not applicable because they all refer to cases of culpable aggressors. This includes the "Don't Tread on Me" slogan, which referred to perceived deliberate British wrongful aggression, not aggression in general (even if George III was perhaps an insane aggressor!).

5. *Id.* at 371.

REPLY

GEORGE P. FLETCHER AND LUIS E. CHIESA

Boaz Sangero agrees with us that the person threatened by the psychotic aggressor should not be held criminally responsible for employing force to repel the insane assailant's attack. However, he believes we are wrong to claim that the use of force in such cases is justified. Because the psychotic aggressor is not culpable, is not trying to exploit the defender, and causes no harm to the social-legal order, Sangero argues that the force used to repel his wrongful but inculpable aggression is excused, not justified. He also claims that accepting his proposition does not mean "that the attacked person must capitulate," for "one must obviously be *allowed* to defend oneself" against attacks from insane assailants.[1] It appears to us, however, that Sangero is attempting to have his cake and eat it too.

It is inconsistent to claim that the use of force against a psychotic aggressor is merely excused while simultaneously contending that the defender must be *allowed* to thwart the inculpable attack. Actors are not permitted to use excused force against the person of another, for excusable conduct is, by definition, impermissible, prohibited, and wrongful. Thus, if it is true, as Sangero claims, that the defender's use of force against the psychotic aggressor is merely excused rather than justified, it simply cannot be the case that the defender is "allowed" (i.e., permitted) to repel the attack.

Toward the end of his comment, Sangero enjoins us to contemplate whether our intuitions would lead us to justify or merely excuse an actor who employs defensive force to repel a wrongful attack from a young child with a loaded gun. Assuming that the only way for the actor to repel the child's aggression is to use defensive force against him, our intuitions regarding the case are no different from the case of the psychotic aggressor: The use of force against the child is justified and third-party intervention on behalf of the defender should be permitted. Although there is no way to reconcile our intuitions with Sangero's, it should be pointed out that many, if not most, of the Anglo-American and Continental scholars who have directly addressed this question believe that it is justified to use of force against inculpable aggressors, psychotics and children alike.

John Mikhail agrees with our conclusion that the use of defensive force against the psychotic aggressor is justified. He takes issue, however, with our claim that the right to self-defense should only be triggered by conduct that amounts to a breach of a duty to respect the defender's autonomy. Mikhail argues that "self-defense is a strong enough principle to warrant the use of force against . . . nontortious threats to one's life."[2] He cites as one such example a case where an innocent person is threatened with the use of force that is the product of "another's justified effort to rescue third parties."[3]

Suppose, for example, that a police officer must shoot at and through an innocent person being used as a human shield in order to avoid the deaths of third parties who are being threatened by terrorists. Mikhail would contend that in such cases the innocent human shield is not "compelled to become collateral damage"[4] in the police officer's efforts to save the lives of third parties. Although we agree

---

1. Sangero comment at 373 (emphasis added).
2. Mikhail comment at 375.
3. *Id.*
4. *Id.*

with this observation, we fail to see how it undermines our conclusions. According to the theory of self-defense that we espouse, justifiable defensive force may not be used against the human shield because the officer is not being wrongfully attacked by the shield. Thus, the police officer's attempt to kill the shield amounts to wrongful aggression that may be justifiably warded off in self-defense. It thus seems that our theory is perfectly compatible with Mikhail's intuitions regarding such cases.

Sherry Colb disagrees with our assertion that "[w]ithout consideration of whether the actor's conduct is wrongful or blameworthy, the mere fact that one party's body is moving toward the body of another seems to be a morally irrelevant feature of the conflict."[5] Therefore, she claims that one may justifiably defuse in self-defense any threat, *however innocent the source*. The problem with Colb's proposition is that it proves too much. If we are entitled to ward off threats without considering their wrongfulness or their blameworthiness, it follows that we should be allowed to defend ourselves against justifiable attacks. Colb, however, is not willing to go that far, since she qualifies her position by requiring that the threat that triggers the right to self-defense be unjustified. This admission gives away the game. Once it is admitted that the justifiable or wrongful nature of the threat is relevant to determining whether the right to use defensive force is triggered, it is clear that, contrary to what Colb wants to argue, the threat/ nonthreat distinction does not provide the moral foundation for the justification of self-defense.

Shlomit Wallerstein has qualms about our contention that the right to self-defense should only be triggered by threats that are reflective of human agency. Her objection is grounded on the fact that "cases of nonagent aggressors are similar to nonculpable aggressors in the sense that the threat to the defender's interests is *not justified*," given that "the nonagent aggressor has no privilege to threaten the vital interests of the defender."[6] As a result, Wallerstein appears to suggest that one may justifiably use force in self-defense against an unjustified aggressor regardless of whether his conduct was reflective of human agency.

While Wallerstein is right to point out that nonagent and nonculpable aggressors are similar because their attacks are unjustified, she fails to note that they are also different because legal norms do not prohibit aggressions that originate in a nonagent whereas they do prohibit attacks stemming from a nonculpable person. This difference is not inconsequential. Attacks lacking human agency are simply not of the same moral quality as acts that reflect human agency. This is the lesson to be learned from Oliver Wendell Holmes Jr.'s oft-cited assertion that "even a dog distinguishes between being stumbled over and being kicked." It is also telling that the distinction found its way into the tort law, which

---

5. Fletcher and Chiesa core text at 369.
6. Wallerstein comment at 378.

compensates harm caused by a nonculpable agent,[7] but does not compensate for damages caused by nonagents.[8]

Whitley Kaufman argues that we are "trying to have it both ways" by claiming that the psychotic aggressor is innocent while also contending that he is "sufficiently culpable" to justify killing him in self-defense.[9] This mischaracterizes our position. We never suggested that defensive force may justifiably be used against the insane assailant because of his culpability. According to our theory, the roots of the right to self-defense lie not in the culpability of the aggressor but rather in the *wrongfulness* of the aggression. Thus, we would focus less on the mental state of the attacker and more on the lawful or unlawful nature of the attack. This, as Kaufman concedes, is compatible with the tort law's insistence that insane defendants be held liable for the damages caused by their conduct. What matters in such cases is the breach of the duty owed to the defender, not the aggressor's moral innocence.

This rule, contrary to what Kaufman contends, is not justified solely in virtue of utilitarian considerations, but also as a result of the nonconsequentialist conviction that "where one of two innocent persons must suffer a loss it should be borne by the one who occasioned it."[10] This principle also underlies our theory of self-defense, although we would qualify it by asserting that in any given conflict between two innocent persons, the loss should be suffered by the party that unlawfully generated the conflict.

---

7. *See, e.g., Ellis v. Fixico*, 50 P.2d 162 (Okla. 1935).

8. *See, e.g., Cohen v. Petty*, 65 F.2d 820 (D.C. Cir. 1933).

9. Kaufman comment at 380.

10. *Breunig v. American Family Ins. Co.*, 173 N.W.2d 619, 624 (Wis. 1970).

18. SELF-DEFENSE AGAINST MORALLY INNOCENT THREATS

JEFF MCMAHAN*

I. TWO PROPORTIONALITY CONSTRAINTS

Suppose you are unjustifiably attacked by a person you know to be morally inno-cent and entirely blameless. Let us refer to this person, and to all others who pose a threat to another, and against whom defensive force might be directed, as a *Threat*. Suppose that the threat he poses is nonlethal and that you have several options for defending yourself. If you do nothing, he will break your arm. You could avoid all harm to yourself by breaking both of his arms. Or you could exer-cise restraint and divide the harm between you—for example, by breaking one of his arms, but allowing yourself to suffer a broken finger.

If he were fully culpable for the threat he poses, you would be morally justified in breaking both his arms to prevent him from causing any harm to you. But given that he is morally innocent, it is arguable that you ought to choose the intermediate option of inflicting the lesser injury on him, thereby accepting a small injury to yourself. If that seems plausible, it suggests that his moral innocence is relevant to the stringency of the proportionality constraint on self-defensive action.

There are, in fact, two proportionality constraints that govern the morality of self-defense. They are well illustrated by the example of Bernard Goetz, who in 1984 shot four men on the New York subway who had crowded around him in a menacing way and demanded that he give them money. His action raised two issues of proportionality. The men clearly meant to be threatening Goetz and were liable to some sort of defensive action. But it seems that the harm he inflicted on them was excessive. This is a judgment of "narrow" proportionality—a judg-ment about how much harm it can be proportionate to inflict intentionally on a Threat as a means of self-defense. This narrow proportionality judgment is sen-sitive to the severity of the harm threatened, the probability that the harm will be inflicted in the absence of defensive action, and also, it seems, the degree to which the Threat is culpable. The suggestion that you might be required to suffer a broken finger to avoid breaking both arms of a Threat who is morally innocent is a claim about narrow proportionality.

* Professor of Philosophy, Rutgers University. This core text is based on Jeff McMahan, *The Basis of Moral Liability to Defensive Killing*, 15 PHIL. ISSUES 386 (2005).

Goetz's action not only intentionally harmed the men who threatened him but also unintentionally endangered the innocent people who were in the enclosed space of the subway car in which he fired his bullets. It seems that the risks to which he exposed those people were also excessive in relation to the threat he faced from the four men. This is a judgment of "wide" proportionality—about side-effects on people other than those who are liable to defensive attack. Because individual self-defense seldom has significant side-effects, discussions of proportionality in self-defense tend to focus on the narrow constraint. Yet in discussions of war the focus is almost exclusively on the wide constraint.

It is important to keep the narrow and wide proportionality restrictions distinct, for the considerations that are relevant to each are different and it is best to know precisely what is being claimed when an act is judged to be proportionate or disproportionate.

Suppose now that the morally innocent person who threatens you in an objectively unjustified way poses a *lethal* threat. And suppose there is no way to divide the threatened harm between the two of you: either he will kill you or you must kill him in self-defense. The commonsense intuition is that you are morally justified in killing him. While his moral innocence may affect the proportionality calculation when the threat he poses is nonlethal, and there are various options for self-defense, in this case it makes no difference at all.

Although this is the commonsense view, it is not immediately obvious how it is to be justified. There is, it seems, a strong moral presumption against intentionally killing another person, so that for killing to be justified there must be a positive justification sufficiently strong to override this presumption. The mere fact that someone threatens your life is insufficient to ground a justification for killing him in self-defense. If, for example, you are morally liable to be killed, you have no right of self-defense. A rampaging murderer who sees that he is about to be killed by a police sniper will be guilty of one more murder if he kills the sniper in self-defense.

II. THE RIGHTS-BASED ACCOUNT

The theory of self-defense that is perhaps most prominent today, which I will call the *Rights-Based Account*, offers a way of distinguishing morally between the police sniper and many other Threats who are also morally innocent but seem to be legitimate targets of defensive action. According to this theory, what makes a Threat a legitimate target is that he threatens another's *rights* and thus he *lacks* a right not to be prevented, by necessary and proportionate means, from violating those rights. Thus, if the only way a police officer can prevent a murderer from killing yet more innocent people is to kill him, the murderer cannot have a right not to be killed, and this explains the permissibility of killing him. Moreover, because the police sniper does not threaten to violate the murderer's rights, he retains his own right not to be killed, and this explains why the murderer has no right of self-defense against him.[1]

Yet, unlike the police sniper, other Threats who are morally innocent may threaten other people's rights and thus may be legitimate targets of defensive attack. Here is one example.

The Resident. The identical twin of a notorious mass murderer is driving at night in a remote area when his car breaks down. He is nonculpably unaware that his twin brother has within the past few hours escaped from prison in this area, and that the residents have been warned of the escape. The murderer's notoriety derives from his invariable modus operandi: he breaks into people's homes and kills them instantly. As the twin approaches a house to request to use the telephone, the resident of the house, reasonably believing himself to be defending his family from the murderer, takes aim to shoot him preemptively.

According to the Rights-Based Account, the resident threatens the twin's right not to be killed; therefore the twin is justified in killing the resident in self-defense, despite the resident's moral innocence, and the resident has no right of defense against the twin.

To discuss this and other examples, we need to draw some distinctions. First, I distinguish between permission and justification in a way that may not be familiar. An act is morally permitted when, in the circumstances, it is not wrong to do it. Justification is a species of permission. Not only is a morally justified act permissible, but there is also positive moral reason to do it. Not all acts that are permitted are justified, for there are indefinitely many acts that are not wrong that there is nevertheless no moral reason to do.

Second, there are objective and subjective accounts of both permissibility and justification. An act is objectively permissible or justifiable when what explains its permissibility or justifiability are facts that are independent of the agent's beliefs. An act is subjectively permissible or justified when two conditions are satisfied: first, the agent acts on the basis of beliefs, or perhaps reasonable or justified beliefs, that are false, and, second, the act *would* be objectively permissible or justified if those beliefs were true.

Although the resident's belief about the twin is false, it is epistemically justified in the circumstances. If it were true, his action would be objectively justified. He is therefore blameless. According to a subjective account of permissibility, his action is justified, though according to an objective account, it is impermissible. I will refer to those who, like the resident, pose an objectively wrongful threat on the basis of epistemically justified but false beliefs as *Innocent Threats*. (Note that this is different from the way the term is usually used in the literature,

---

1. The classic defense of this view is Judith Jarvis Thomson, *Self-Defense*, 20 PHIL. & PUB. AFF. 283–310 (1991).

where it tends to refer to all those who pose objectively wrongful threats but are nonetheless morally innocent.)

Even though an objective account of permissibility judges that the resident acts wrongly, it acknowledges that he is blameless and thus fully excused. There are other excusing conditions, such as duress, that can also absolve a person who poses an objectively wrongful threat of all culpability. If you kill an innocent person because someone has put a gun to your head and credibly threatened to kill you if you do not, both subjective and objective accounts of permissibility coincide in judging that you act impermissibly. But both may also agree that you acted blamelessly and are fully excused. I will refer to those who pose an objectively wrongful threat but are nonetheless morally innocent because they are fully excused as *Excused Threats*. The categories of Innocent and Excused Threats obviously overlap. The resident, for example, is an Excused Threat according to an objective account of permissibility but an Innocent Threat according to a subjective account.

A further and more problematic category is exemplified in the following case, taken from Judith Thomson.

> *The Falling Man.* A fat man is enjoying a picnic on a cliff directly above the deck on which you are lying with your leg in traction. Suddenly a villain pushes him off the cliff. If he lands on you he will kill you, but he will survive because you will cushion his fall. You cannot move aside but can save yourself by hoisting your sun umbrella and impaling him on it.[2]

Thomson, the leading exponent of the Rights-Based Account, claims that it is permissible to kill the falling man because he will otherwise violate your right not to be killed. Because most people agree that you may permissibly kill him, this is a welcome conclusion. Yet it is not clear that it is actually an implication of the theory. According to Thomson, a right "that X has against Y . . . just is a moral fact equivalent to Y's behavior's being constrained" in a certain way.[3] Yet a person cannot be morally constrained from being involuntarily acted upon by physical forces. So no one can have a right against a person that he not be hurled or fall through the air; therefore the falling man does not threaten to violate your right, even though he will kill you if he falls on you. The falling man is what I call a *Nonresponsible Threat*—that is, a person who without justification threatens to harm someone in a way to which she is not liable, but who is in no way morally responsible for doing so.

---

2. *Id.* at 287. In the story as she tells it, you can use your awning to deflect him past the edge of the deck onto the road below. Since there are accounts of the distinction between killing and letting die that would classify deflecting him as allowing him to die rather than killing him, I have altered the example in a way that makes your act uncontroversially an instance of killing.

3. Judith Jarvis Thomson, THE REALM OF RIGHTS 77 (1990).

I noted earlier that the commonsense view is that it is permissible to kill any person who, without objective justification, will otherwise kill you, even if he is morally innocent. Nonresponsible Threats challenge that view. For there seems to be no morally significant difference between a Nonresponsible Threat and an innocent bystander, and most of us believe that it is impermissible to kill an innocent bystander as a means of self-preservation, even if that is the only way to save one's life. The only difference between a Nonresponsible Threat and an innocent bystander is that a Nonresponsible Threat is causally implicated in the threat one faces. But by itself that is just a fact about his position in the local causal architecture and is no more a ground of *liability* than the parallel fact about an innocent bystander that her position in the causal nexus makes killing her the only means of saving one's life.

If this is right, what Nonresponsible Threats show is that it matters to the permissibility of killing a morally innocent person in self-defense why, or on what grounds, he is morally innocent. Some reasons why a person who poses an unjustified threat is morally innocent are compatible with his being liable to be killed. This is true in the case of the resident. By contrast, the reason why the falling man is innocent is also a reason why he cannot be liable to be killed in self-defense.

That the Rights-Based Account does not provide a justification for killing the falling man is not an objection to the theory. It merely makes it less appealing intuitively than it would be if it could justify the commonsense intuition. But there is another case that does ground a strong objection to the theory. It is familiar from discussions of the Doctrine of Double Effect.

The Tactical Bomber. A bomber fighting in a just war has been ordered to destroy a military facility located on the border of the enemy country. He knows that if he bombs this facility, the explosion will kill innocent civilians living just across the border in a neutral country. But this would be a proportionate side-effect in relation to the contribution the act would make to the achievement of the just cause. The civilians cannot flee but do have access to an anti-aircraft gun.

The traditional question is how the tactical bomber can be justified in bombing the facility when it would not be justifiable for a terror bomber to drop a bomb in the same spot, producing the same effects, with the *intention* of killing the civilians. My question is different. Assuming that the tactical bomber would be objectively morally justified in dropping his bomb, are the civilians permitted to shoot him down in self-defense?

To explain why this case challenges the Rights-Based Account, I need to distinguish two ways of acting against a right. When one impermissibly does what another has a right that one not do, one *violates* her right. When one permissibly does what another has a right that one not do, one *infringes* her right.[4] Defenders

---

4. I draw this distinction differently from the way Thomson does. *See id.* at 122.

of the Rights-Based Account have failed to provide guidance in cases involving infringement rather than violation. For example, in her exposition of the Rights-Based Account, Thomson does not discuss whether a person loses his right not to be attacked when he threatens to infringe the rights of another. Yet it is reasonable to suppose that when a person threatens to infringe rights through action that is objectively *justified*, the justification exempts the agent from liability to defensive action. In criminal law, one who acts with justification is exempt from liability to punishment and in tort law one who acts with justification but causes a loss to another is exempt from liability to pay compensation except in a limited range of cases governed by a standard of strict liability. It seems that a justification should similarly exempt a person from liability to defensive action.

The tactical bomber is what I call a *Justified Threat*: someone whose objectively justified act nevertheless threatens to harm someone who is not liable to be harmed and who will thus be wronged by the action. Because the tactical bomber acts with justification, he will merely infringe the civilians' rights. If it is correct that liability to defensive action is defeasible by a justification, he retains his right not to be killed. According to the Rights-Based Account, therefore, the civilians may not kill him in self-defense.

But this is hard to believe—unless, perhaps, his mission is so important that they are morally required to sacrifice themselves for the sake of its success (in which case it is not necessarily his right that morally constrains them: he might be liable to attack and yet it would still be wrong to attack him). Can the Rights-Based Account accommodate the intuition that the civilians may kill the tactical bomber in self-defense? It cannot be claimed that his right is overridden by morally weightier considerations; for the stipulation that his act would be proportionate entails that the failure of his mission, which would be a consequence of their killing him, would be worse from an impartial perspective than their being killed.

Perhaps, then, contrary to the common assumption, one may lose rights by threatening to infringe rights, even with justification. If so, the fact that the tactical bomber will otherwise infringe the civilians' right not to be killed means that he lacks a right not to be killed by them—that is, he makes himself liable to be killed by them. But this too is hard to believe. For if he has lost his right not to be killed by them, it seems that he can have no right of self-defense against them. Yet intuitively it seems that, just as it is permissible for the civilians to kill the tactical bomber in self-defense, so it is also permissible for the tactical bomber to kill the civilians in self-defense. This apparent symmetry is, however, incompatible with the implications of the Rights-Based Account.

III. THE CULPABILITY ACCOUNT

The case of the tactical bomber challenges other theories of permissible defense as well. According to one theory, which I will call the *Culpability Account*, culpability for causing an objectively unjustified threat is both necessary and sufficient for moral liability to defensive action. The tactical bomber acts with justification and is in no way culpable; therefore he is not liable to attack on this account. The innocent civilians, it seems, have no right of self-defense against him.

Despite its harsh implications for the civilians, the Culpability Account has considerable intuitive appeal because of the strong link between culpability and liability. When a person is both causally responsible and culpable for an objectively unjustified threat, it is intuitively uncontroversial that he is liable to necessary and proportionate defensive action. Many people's intuitions suggest that culpability may in certain cases be sufficient for liability even in the absence of causal responsibility for a threat. This is true in some cases of wrongful attempts. Here is an example.

The Culpable Attempter. Aware that a villain plans to kill you, you begin to carry a gun. On one occasion you have the opportunity to empty the bullets from his gun and you do so. Immediately thereafter, he confronts you in an alley and tries to fire. As he continues to pull the trigger in frustration, you see that a second villain is preparing to shoot you from behind a narrow basement window (it is a tough neighborhood). Unable to flee in time and also unable to fire with accuracy through the tiny window, you can save yourself only by shooting the first villain, causing him to slump in front of the window, thereby blocking the second villain's line of fire.

Many people accept that it is permissible to kill the first villain to save yourself from the second, despite the fact that he has no causal role in the threat to you. His culpable attempt is sufficient for liability. The problem with this suggestion, however, is that if we reject the requirement of causation, there seems to be no principled point at which culpability of any sort ceases to be a basis of liability to harm in the service of saving the lives of the innocent. Suppose, for example, that the first villain was just strolling peaceably through the alley but had made a culpable attempt on your life ten years ago. Would it be permissible to kill him now to preserve your life? Would it be permissible to kill someone who is making a futile but culpable attempt on your life as a means of securing his organs for transplantation?

A further problem with the Culpability Account is that it implies that Excused Threats and Innocent Threats, such as the resident, are not liable to defensive attack. This is intuitively implausible. And there is a theoretical basis for holding the resident liable, despite the fact that he acts reasonably in the light of his epistemically justified beliefs. For he voluntarily chooses to try to kill someone, knowing that there is a possibility of mistake (for example, it might be that the perceived murderer is wounded or seriously ill and poses no threat, or, as is in fact the case in the example, that the person is not the murderer at all). When one chooses to kill another person, one renders oneself vulnerable to the possibility of mistake, and if one is in fact mistaken, even if only through bad luck, one is liable to suffer the bad consequences of one's choice.

There is, indeed, a basis for liability even in cases in which an Innocent Threat (in the sense stipulated above) does not choose to harm or kill but merely engages in an activity that is known to have a very small risk of causing serious harm.

The Conscientious Driver. A person who always keeps her car well maintained and always drives carefully and alertly decides to drive to the cinema. On the way, a freak event that she could not have anticipated occurs that causes her car to veer out of control in the direction of a pedestrian.

If it were possible for the pedestrian to defend his own life by killing the driver, it would be permissible for him to do so. His justification would be that the driver had made herself liable by choosing to set a couple of tons of steel in motion as a means of pursuing her ends, knowing that this would involve a very small risk of killing an innocent person. Again, a voluntary choice with a foreseeable risk (of error in the case of the resident, mishap in the case of the driver) is the basis of liability to defensive action. The basis for liability is in fact stronger in the case of the driver, since she acts with only subjective permission, whereas the resident acts with subjective justification.

Some will claim that this view makes the driver's liability depend on moral luck, and thus on factors over which she has no control. There were countless other drivers who acted no differently from the way she did but whose cars did not go out of control. Why should she alone be liable?

This objection would have more force if the issue were who should compensate the pedestrian ex post. That burden could in principle be divided among all those who impose risks through driving. But this is a case of defense, and the issue is whether it is permissible to kill the driver or whether the pedestrian must be allowed to be killed. In this choice, it is not unfair to hold the driver liable. What she lacked control over is comparative: that her car when out of control whereas those of other drivers did not. But the basis of her liability is her choice to impose a risk, and over *that* she did have control. That she ended up liable to defensive action while the others did not may seem unfair, but it is no more unfair than that some gamblers leave the casino with losses while others leave with winnings.

IV. THE RESPONSIBILITY ACCOUNT

The examples and arguments reviewed thus far suggest a different criterion of liability to defensive action. According to what I will call the *Responsibility Account* of permissible defense, the basis of moral liability to defensive action is moral responsibility for an objectively unjustified threat of harm.

There are various noteworthy features of this view. Notice, first, that one may be morally responsible for a threat without *posing* the threat. One may be responsible through action done in the past for a threat that has arisen only now.

Suppose, for example, that I tampered with the brakes of your car last week. If, as a result, the brakes have now failed and your car is about to go off a cliff, you may permissibly steer the car into me if that is the only way to save yourself. Even though stopping the car by running it into me is not literally defensive, because at this point I am no part of the threat to you, I am nonetheless liable to be harmed in this way by virtue of my moral responsibility for your present predicament.

Second, because moral responsibility for a threat is a matter of degree, so too is liability to defensive action. It may, however, be hard to see how that could be so. Either one is liable or one is not. How could one be more or less liable? The answer is that variations in the degree of a Threat's liability are manifest in the stringency of the narrow proportionality restriction, as I indicated earlier in the opening paragraphs. The greater the degree to which a Threat is liable, the more harm it may be proportionate to cause him through necessary defensive action.

Third, on this view, culpability is not a condition of liability; hence Excused Threats and Innocent Threats, such as the resident and the driver, may be liable to defensive attack. Yet some other Threats who are morally innocent are not liable. The falling man is one example. Because he is in no way responsible for the threat he poses, he cannot be liable to defensive action according to the Responsibility Account. This is of course counterintuitive, but I think it is correct. Liability arises from what we choose to do as morally responsible agents; it cannot arise solely from what happens to us (though of course *duties* can). There may be a justification for killing the falling man in self-defense, but it cannot be that he is morally liable to attack.

In some cases there may be uncertainty about moral responsibility. Here is an example.

> *The Cell Phone Operator.* A man's cell phone has, without his knowledge, been reprogrammed so that when he presses the "send" button, the phone will transmit a signal that will detonate a bomb, killing an innocent person.

According to an objective account of permissibility, this man acts impermissibly but is fully excused—that is, he is an Excused Threat. According to a subjective account, he acts permissibly and is thus an Innocent Threat. Suppose the only way to prevent him from detonating the bomb is to kill him. Is he liable to be killed in defense of the person who will otherwise be killed by the bomb? According to the Responsibility Account, this depends on whether he is morally responsible for the threat he poses.

The cell phone operator is relevantly different from the resident and the conscientious driver. Although all three act in "invincible ignorance" of relevant facts (that the phone is a detonator, that the approaching figure is the murderer's twin, that there is an undetectable problem that will cause the car to go out of control), only the cell phone operator makes no choice to inflict a harm or to impose a risk of harm. Although his act does impose a risk, it is unforeseeable that it will cause harm in this way, or indeed in any way at all. What is singular about him is not that he is nonculpably and invincibly ignorant of some relevant fact—a characteristic he shares with the resident and the driver; it is, rather, that he is nonculpably and invincibly ignorant that he poses any kind of threat or risk of harm to anyone. And this, I think, absolves him of all responsibility for the threat he poses. He is an Innocent Threat who is also a Nonresponsible Threat. The cell phone operator, like the falling man, is not liable to defensive attack.

Finally, like the Rights-Based and Culpability Accounts, the Responsibility Account implies that the tactical bomber is not liable to defensive attack. He is of course responsible for the threat he poses, but because his action is objectively justified, there is no basis for liability.

Intuitively, the Responsibility Account gives the wrong answers in the cases of the falling man, the cell phone operator, and the tactical bomber. Yet in the case of Nonresponsible Threats, it is our intuitions that are mistaken, not the theory. They are overgeneralizations of our intuitions about standard cases of self-defense. But the case of the tactical bomber is different. He knowingly threatens the lives of innocent people. If these people would not be required to sacrifice themselves for the sake of his mission, they seem entitled to defend their lives.

One possibility is that innocent people are permitted to defend their rights not only against violation but also against justified infringement—that is, they may defend them even when they are overridden. On this view, the civilians are permitted to attack the tactical bomber in self-defense, even though he is not liable to attack. Because he is not liable, their defensive action, if successful, will infringe his rights; therefore he retains his right of self-defense and is permitted to attack them preemptively. In short, each party to the conflict is permitted to attack the other.

There are, however, various problems with this suggestion. I will mention only one, which is that defensive action by the civilians would seem to be dispro-portionate in the wide sense. Because the action of the tactical bomber is by hypothesis justified, it is proportionate—that is, the harm to the civilians is outweighed by the importance of achieving his mission. Self-defense by the civil-ians would therefore involve the intentional killing of an innocent person for the sake of the lesser good, impartially considered.

The problem of Justified Threats, exemplified by the case of the tactical bomber, therefore continues to pose a vexing challenge to all theories of permissible defense.

COMMENTS

RIGHTS AND LIABILITIES AT WAR

ADIL AHMAD HAQUE*

Jeff McMahan's "Responsibility Account" of liability to defensive force seems to entail that civilians may not defend themselves from being killed by a military attack conducted using just means in the service of a just cause. McMahan struggles to resist this result, which he admits is highly counterintuitive. I would like to suggest that the case of the tactical bomber exposes a deeper problem with McMahan's approach to the topic of defensive force, namely that, for McMahan, the permissibility of defensive force turns on the attacker's innocence rather than on the defender's innocence. McMahan believes that an attacker's responsibility for an unjust threat makes her liable to defensive force. On the contrary, a defender's responsibility for an unjust threat deprives her of the right to use defensive force. The right to use defensive force can be lost through the unjustified acts of the defender, but it cannot be taken away by the justified acts of the attacker. In this sense the very language of "liability to defensive killing" is misleading.

As I read McMahan's example, neither the civilians nor the tactical bomber are responsible for an unjust threat: the threat posed by the tactical bomber to the civilians is justified as a necessary and proportionate side-effect of an attack on a legitimate military target; the civilians pose no threat to the tactical bomber and are not responsible for the unjust threat posed by their government. In McMahan's view this means that neither the tactical bomber nor the civilians are liable to defensive force. In fact this means that both sides retain their right to use defensive force. McMahan reasons that (1) neither the bomber nor the civilians are liable to defensive force; (2) the killing of the civilians is justified by the balance of moral reasons while the killing of the bomber is not; and therefore (3) the bomber may kill the civilians but the civilians may not kill the bomber. On the contrary, (1) both sides retain their right to use defensive force; (2) both sides are permitted to exercise that right (whether or not doing so is "justified" in McMahan's sense); and therefore (3) the civilians may defend themselves from the bomber and the bomber may resist any defensive force from the civilians.

McMahan suggests that the civilians are not permitted to resist the tactical bomber because such resistance would involve "the intentional killing of an innocent person for the sake of the lesser good, impartially considered," and would therefore be "disproportionate in the wide sense."[1] Now, the killing of an attacker need only be proportionate in the narrow sense that one may only

---

* Assistant Professor of Law, Rutgers School of Law–Newark.
1. McMahan core text at 396.

defensively kill an attacker to prevent a comparable harm to oneself. It is only if the use of defensive force against an attacker would also harm innocent bystanders that we must ask whether the harm to the bystanders is proportionate in the wide sense. But McMahan does not state that the use of defensive force against the tactical bomber would harm innocent bystanders, only that the tactical bomber's mission is supported by the overall balance of moral reasons. True, civilians cannot use defensive force if doing so would kill a disproportionate number of equally innocent bystanders. But civilians may use defensive force even if doing so would delay or prevent the triumph of a just cause. The moral prerogative to act contrary to the balance of moral reasons (though not contrary to the rights of others) forms part of the very essence of liberty-rights such as the right to self-defense, and it is this prerogative that makes us ends in ourselves rather than mere means to the achievement of the greater good.[2]

Criminal law scholars in particular should recognize the overgeneralization implicit in McMahan's seemingly familiar position that justified attackers may not be resisted. It is true that, under domestic criminal law, aggressors can be resisted by defenders but defenders cannot be resisted by aggressors. In McMahan's view this is because aggressors are unjustified and therefore liable to defensive force while defenders are justified and therefore not liable. In fact this is because aggressors have lost their right to use defensive force whereas defenders have not. These two accounts generate very different implications for innocent bystanders. In McMahan's view, justified actors are not liable to defensive force either by wrongful aggressors or by innocent bystanders. In fact wrongful aggressors forfeit, but innocent bystanders retain, their right to use defensive force. Conflicts between rights are rarely confronted by domestic criminal law, but the potential for such conflicts is an inevitable feature of war.

---

2. *See* F.M. Kamm, 2 MORALITY, MORTALITY 229 (1996).

WHY CAUSAL RESPONSIBILITY MATTERS

SHLOMIT WALLERSTEIN*

Jeff McMahan draws the line between nonculpable aggressors (*Innocent and Excused Threats*), who can be killed in self-defense, and nonagent aggressors (*Nonresponsible Threats*),[1] who, together with innocent bystanders, cannot be. In my view, McMahan draws the line in the wrong place. Contrary to McMahan,

---

* University Lecturer, Fellow, and Tutor in Law, St. Peter's College and Faculty of Law, Oxford University.

1. I prefer to use the term *nonagent* aggressor over the term *nonresponsible* threat because the latter does not distinguish between moral and causal responsibility.

nonculpable and nonagent aggressors may be killed in self-defense, but innocent bystanders may not.

Talking about aggression that lacks human agency (the *Falling Man* example), McMahan argues that "no one can have a right against a person that he not be hurled or fall through the air; therefore the falling man does not threaten to violate the defender's right."[2] This position is based on the fact that the nonagent aggressor is similar to an object and as such not subject to duties. Indeed, we do not talk of rights with regards to objects and natural events. Thus, we do not think of a rock as "violating" a person's right to life, but neither do we talk of the Rock as "infringing" that right. We also do not talk of a rock as being "permitted" (nor "justified") to injure a person. Moral concepts and the terminology of rights have no application with regard to objects and natural events, but that also means that such a threat to the defender's life cannot be *justified*, so as to prevent him from defending himself. Note that the requirement for self-defense is commonly referred to as the "unjust" threat and *not* as the "wrongful" threat. Thus, unless the threat is positively justified (!) the defender should be permitted to use self-defense, whether the threat is not justified because it is wrongful, or because moral assessment of the threat is inapplicable.

McMahan argues that this position is untenable. The fact that a person is causally responsible is irrelevant because "by itself that is just a fact about his position in the local causal architecture, and is no more a ground of *liability* than the parallel fact about an innocent bystander that her position in the causal nexus makes killing her the only means of saving one's life."[3] Indeed, causal connection is only a fact about the nonagent aggressor's position in the local architecture but that fact is significant.

Situations involving nonagent aggressors (and nonculpable aggressors) are situations in which due to some "bad luck" the aggressor becomes the locus of an unjust threat to the defender's life and inevitably either the aggressor or the defender will have to bear the costs. Fairness requires that the aggressor not transfer his "bad luck" in becoming an *unjust* threat to another person and not demand that the defender (or another) be the one to suffer the consequences.[4] Self-defense is about repelling the threat and preventing the aggressor from transferring the consequences of his "bad luck" to another. If, while falling, the falling man becomes able to shift himself so that he will not hit the defender, no doubt he has an obligation to do so. For him, to use the defender to avoid his own death amounts to using an innocent bystander and that is wrong—even according to McMahan's position (transforming into an innocent threat).

---

2. McMahan core text at 388.

3. *See id.* at 389.

4. For further examples in support of this position, see Shlomit Wallerstein, *Justifying the Right to Self-Defense: A Theory of Forced Consequences* 91 Va. L. Rev. 999, 1029–30 (2005).

But McMahan says that the defender has "no right not to be hurled" by the falling man. Why should that change just because mid-fall, the falling man becomes able to shift himself? The falling man's obligation can only make sense if we recognize the existence of other pertinent considerations that do not originate out of culpability or McMahan's responsibility.

The explanation suggested above is also the basis for the distinction between the nonagent aggressor and the innocent bystander. Since the innocent bystander is not the locus of the threat the defender cannot use him to avoid the threat to his life. Killing the innocent bystander to save himself would not serve to prevent innocent bystander from transferring "bad luck" to the defender. On the contrary, if the defender kills the bystander he would be transferring to the innocent bystander his own "bad luck" in getting into a situation in which his life is threatened—something that he is not allowed to do. Our intuition about the availability of self-defense where human agency is lacking is not due to overgeneralization of core situations of self-defense. It results from our attitude toward the distribution and transfer of consequences forced on a person.

CAN'T SUE; CAN KILL

KIMBERLY KESSLER FERZAN*

Jeff McMahan advances a "Responsibility Account" of self-defense. What is perhaps most unique about McMahan's view is that he believes he can draw a principled distinction between different types of innocent aggressors and threats. Unlike psychotic aggressors, children, and human projectiles, the Innocent Threat can be responsible for the threat he poses, and therefore liable to defensive killing. An Innocent Threat is responsible for the threat he poses if and because he engages in risk-imposing activity, provided his conduct *foreseeably* imposes a risk of harm.

Unfortunately, both the "risk-imposing activity" and foreseeability criteria are problematic. First, McMahan's example of a driver against a pedestrian conceals difficult questions inherent in the idea of a "risk-imposing activity."[1] What would McMahan say about a driver who is not swerving at a pedestrian but another driver? They have both run the very same risks, so can one kill the other? McMahan has two options. A more fine-grained analysis, such that an out-of-control Civic

* Associate Dean for Academic Affairs and Professor of Law, Rutgers School of Law–Camden.

1. Cf. Heidi M. Hurd, *Nonreciprocal Risk Imposition, Unjust Enrichment, and the Foundations of Tort Law: A Critical Celebration of George Fletcher's Theory of Tort Law*, 78 NOTRE DAME L. REV. 711 (2003).

would not be liable to a defender Hummer, or a coarse-grained option, where among reciprocal risk-takers there is no liability.

But even once the conceptual boundaries are clear, how can this sort of conduct ground McMahan's claim that merely engaging in such conduct is sufficient to render one "liable" to being killed? McMahan's risk-imposition condition is a form of strict liability that extends to activities beyond those recognized even in tort law. But how can it be permissible to kill someone whom we can't even sue in tort, let alone punish? The actor who, going through a life that always imposes risks, behaves in a cautious and admirable way hardly seems to have somehow assumed a risk of being killed defensively more than an actor who is insane, or is a child, or is involuntarily thrown down a well. What distinguishes the sudden onset of a psychotic breakdown from the inexplicable malfunctioning of a perfectly maintained car? How is one responsible for one risk more than the other when functioning in this society could bring about either breakdown?

The other problem for McMahan is that many activities do risk (and will cause) harm whether we know it or not. To address this problem McMahan adds a restriction: foreseeability, as illustrated by the case of the cell phone bomb. But the problem for McMahan is that foreseeability, properly applied, will likely slide him back to a negligence standard. Foreseeability will always be a matter of (1) the selection of the description of the harm and (2) the selection of the information available to the assessor. (All harms that occur are foreseen by the omniscient, even the cell phone.) It is true that driving seems risky (people die in car accidents), but it isn't true that we would say that safe driving with a well-maintained vehicle is risky vis-à-vis a mechanical malfunction. Which description governs?

Moreover, does McMahan require that the harm be foreseen by the actor? Would it matter if Fearless Fred never thinks that any harm can come from driving his car? Conversely, what if Nervous Nellie reads the literature on self-defense and becomes convinced that we are in the midst of an epidemic of Innocent Projectiles? Will her mere appearance in public now be a risk-imposing activity because she believes it is? Conversely, if the governing perspective is not the actor's then how does McMahan justify importing some artificial, epistemically limited perspective into his objective test? And importantly, how can morality speak through a construct that mirrors neither the actor's perspective nor the omniscient's?[2]

One renders oneself liable to defensive killing through one's choices, and specifically through one's culpable choices, which create a moral asymmetry between the aggressor and the defender. In my view, by causing the victim to fear attack, the attacker renders himself liable to be killed *defensively* vis-à-vis the

---

2. *See id.* at 722–23.

perceived threat that the Culpable Attempter poses.[3] The value of the Culpability Account is that it provides a principled explanation as to who is liable to defensive killing and who is not.

McMahan correctly notes that Innocent Projectile cannot be said to have created a moral asymmetry between the projectile and the defender such that killing the projectile may be justified. But the same can be said of all nonculpable threats. McMahans's Responsibility Account is just a line in the sand between innocents.

---

3. I cannot defend the Culpability Account here, though I will say that the question of whether one may appropriate the Culpable Attempter for one's use rests on a far broader principle of moral forfeiture than the Culpability Account requires.

CAN "MORAL RESPONSIBILITY" EXPLAIN SELF-DEFENSE?

WHITLEY R.P. KAUFMAN*

Jeff McMahan provides us with a thought-provoking examination of the problem of self-defense. His critique of the Rights Account and the Culpability Account seem to me quite correct. McMahan's suggested alternative is the Responsibility Account, according to which liability to defensive force is based on "moral responsibility for an objectively unjustified threat of harm."

But the problem is to explain how one can lack culpability and yet have sufficient moral responsibility to be liable to being killed. A good example of this problem is the Conscientious Driver, who has taken every conceivable precaution to avoid harming pedestrians, but who through a "freak event" becomes a danger to a pedestrian; the pedestrian is (McMahan argues) permitted to shoot the driver. Saying that every driver knowingly accepts a risk of harming others seems unconvincing, especially given that this extremely low-probability event was totally unforeseeable. Suppose, for example, that the probability of this freak event was equivalent to or even smaller than that in the cell-phone case. Does that change the conclusion? What if the cell-phone user had some inkling of the potential danger but ignored it?

As to the Tactical Bomber, McMahan thinks that his theory prohibits the civilians from using defensive force against Tactical Bomber. But if the Conscientious Driver is liable to defensive force given that driving involves a foreseeable risk of harming innocents, then why isn't the Tactical Bomber liable to defensive force

---

* Professor, Department of Philosophy, University of Massachusetts–Lowell.

on the same grounds, since dropping bombs involves a far greater risk of harming innocents than does merely driving? Indeed, in the Tactical Bomber case it is stipulated that the harm to innocents is not merely foreseeable but actually foreseen. Even more troubling, it is in fact problematic whether Tactical Bomber is justified in his bombing mission at all under McMahan's Responsibility Account: Because the civilians have no responsibility at all, pose no threat, and are not causally implicated in any harm, it would seem that harming them is simply impermissible. We cannot of course simply assume that the Tactical Bomber is "objectively justified"; the question at issue is whether and why such a mission is permissible given the foreseeable harm to innocent civilians, in contrast with the Terror Bomber who deliberately harms the same number of civilians. If the Terror Bombing is wrong, why is the Tactical Bomber's equally harmful action permissible? In both cases, the civilians are equally not morally responsible and hence not liable to harm on this theory.

One might also wonder how the Responsibility Account is to distinguish between Innocent Aggressors and Innocent Threats (e.g., the Falling Man). For McMahan, the Falling Man is not liable to defensive force because he has no responsibility. But how does this case differ from the Psychotic Aggressor, who is caused to harm you by organic changes in his brain chemistry? He would seem to be no more responsible than Falling Man, yet intuitively it is permissible to kill the Psychotic Aggressor. The same holds for all Innocent Aggressors: Why should the fact that they are "acting" make a moral difference, if they are equally morally blameless and equally causally responsible as the Innocent Threat? Again, it does not seem that the unspecified concept of "moral responsibility" can provide much guidance here. Indeed, one might say that the very problem of self-defense is determining what constitutes sufficient moral responsibility to be liable to defensive force—or for that matter, whether moral responsibility is required at all, as in the case of Innocent Aggressors.

More fundamentally, what is it that determines if one is morally responsible, especially given that culpability is not required? Presumably responsibility requires *causal* responsibility for a given harm, but just why is that, especially given that the criminal law does not require causal responsibility (e.g., attempted murder)? Further, we are told that causal responsibility is not sufficient, but why does causal responsibility plus nonnegligent activity (e.g., driving a car) render one liable to be killed? This sort of synergistic effect needs to be explained, given that neither alone renders one liable to being harmed.

Ultimately, the notion of "moral responsibility" seems too vague to be very helpful, since each person might have a different sense of who is morally responsible. Suppose, for example, that it seems to me that the Conscientious Driver is *not* morally responsible in any meaningful sense. How would the theory help us resolve this dispute? (Or suppose someone thinks that only *culpable* actors are sufficiently morally responsible to be liable to defensive force: then the account collapses into culpability.) We will have to await a fuller explication of the idea of "moral responsibility" before being able to evaluate McMahan's Responsibility Account.

DOUBTS ABOUT THE RESPONSIBILITY PRINCIPLE

VICTOR TADROS*

Jeff McMahan refines what I will call the *responsibility principle* in the following ways:

1) A person becomes liable to have force used against them as protection from a threat only if she caused that threat.
2) The threat that the person causes must have been foreseeable.
3) The person who caused the threat must have acted voluntarily in bringing it about.
4) The person creating the threat need not have been culpable.
5) If the threat that the person poses is objectively justified, she is not liable to be harmed.

I claim that the responsibility principle is both too permissive and too restrictive. First, consider how it is too permissive:

Lifesaver. Harry is walking by a lake and sees a boy drowning. He is the only person who can save him. He jumps in a motorboat, at some risk to himself, and races out into the lake. He gets the boy into the boat, but through exertion falls unconscious. He falls against the accelerator and the boat heads for Jake, threatening his life. The only way for Jake to save himself is to shoot Harry in the head, knocking him off the accelerator.

According to the responsibility principle Jake is permitted to shoot Harry. That is counterintuitive. What might explain the intuition? Perhaps this: unlike in the driving cases that McMahan considers, Harry had no *moral* choice but to get in the boat, with all the risks involved. Getting in the boat was *required* rather than merely permissible or justified. He takes on a risk to do his moral duty, and that risk should not be exacerbated by making him liable to be killed in self-defense by people in Jake's position.

The same might be true in some cases not involving doing one's moral duty. McMahan's account has plausible results in the case of the out-of-control car. But if we slightly alter the scenario, the account looks less attractive. Consider:

Runaway Racing Car. You are a racing driver and lose control of your car completely accidentally on a difficult bend. Your head is jammed against the

---

* Professor, School of Law, University of Warwick.

steering wheel and the only way to divert the car away from me, and thus to save my life, is to shoot you in the head. I would not have faced this threat had I not jumped over a safety barrier to keep spectators away from the race track.

The responsibility principle indicates that it is permissible for me to shoot you in the head. But that seems wrong, even though driving a racing car is merely permissible. For in this case, I had adequate opportunity to avoid the threat. McMahan may reply that I am responsible for being threatened. True enough. But now we need a richer account of the principles underlying responsibility than McMahan provides.

The responsibility account is also too restrictive. Consider:

Double Hit Man. Barry hires a hit man to kill Yolanda. Cynthia has also hired a hit man to kill Yolanda. Cynthia's hit man arrives first. Yolanda uses Barry as a shield to protect herself against Cynthia's hit man.

and

Double Hit Man 2. Evelyn hires a hit man to kill Wayne. Fred has also hired a hit man to kill Wayne. Both hit men arrive at the same time. Because of where they are standing, Wayne can only use Fred as a shield against Evelyn's hit man and Evelyn as a shield against Fred's hit man. He manages to do that, causing the deaths of Evelyn and Fred.

Surely Wayne doesn't have to allow himself to be killed in *Double Hit Man 2.* That would be an extreme consequence of the responsibility principle. If that is true, Yolanda is permitted to use Barry as a shield in *Double Hit Man.*

Does this lead to the permissive consequences of the culpability account that concern McMahan? Consider:

Transplant. Ursula points a pistol at Larry and pulls the trigger, falsely believing the pistol to be loaded. Larry is dying of heart failure. Larry forcibly transplants Ursula's heart into himself, killing her.

However, we can distinguish this case from the *Double Hit Man* cases. If everyone did their moral duty, Larry would die of his heart condition. If he were permitted forcibly to transplant Ursula's heart into himself, he would be a beneficiary of her unjust attack. But now consider:

Transplant 2. The same as *Transplant* except Larry's condition is a consequence of a moral wrong.

Is Larry now entitled to perform the transplant? I'm not sure. We need arguments to restrain the scope of self-defense, but the responsibility principle is surely too constraining in the *Double Hit Man* cases.

REPLY

JEFF MCMAHAN

I find it reassuring that Haque and Wallerstein find my account of self-defense too restrictive, Ferzan and Kaufman find it too permissive, and Tadros thinks it is both. It would be more discouraging had they all agreed in their criticisms.

For Haque, the claim that each person has a right of self-defense unless she forfeits it is morally foundational. Yet he does not discuss the relation between the right of self-defense and the right against attack. As his discussion of the tactical bomber shows, it does not follow from a person's having a right of self-defense that it is wrong to attack her. Suppose that my life is threatened by a Nonresponsible Threat and that I have not forfeited my right of self-defense. In Haque's account, I may kill the Nonresponsible Threat. But does the Nonresponsible Threat retain her right of self-defense? Do I retain a right against defensive attack? Haque's account seems silent.

Suppose that to preserve my life, I must kill an innocent bystander. According to Haque, the bystander retains her right of self-defense. But do I retain mine? Or do I forfeit my right of defense when I attack an innocent bystander in self-preservation, though not, as most people think, when I attack a Nonresponsible Threat in self-defense? If so, what explains the difference? Haque's account gives no answer. We require an independent theory of forfeiture—that is, of liability. The Responsibility Account provides that, but an account that appeals only to the rights of self-defense of innocent victims does not.

Haque is right about proportionality. How a bad side-effect is caused may matter to how it affects proportionality. If a defender's means of self-defense also kills an innocent bystander, that death counts differently from that of an innocent person whom the attacker would later have saved had he not been killed by the defender.

Wallerstein's view is closely related to Haque's, though she offers a criterion of liability to defensive attack. The reason it is permissible to kill a Nonresponsible Threat in self-defense but not to kill an innocent bystander in self-preservation is, on her view, that the former but not the latter is liable by virtue of being causally responsible for an unjust threat. Causal responsibility is relevant because it is connected with the ownership of bad luck. Just as a person under lethal threat may not transfer his bad luck to an innocent bystander by killing the bystander in self-preservation, so a person who has the misfortune to threaten the life of another without being responsible for posing that threat must bear the costs of her own bad luck.

It is, however, not the falling man who has bad luck. If no one does anything, he will not be harmed, for there is a cushion below him. It is that cushion, an immobilized person, who has bad luck. May he transfer that bad luck to an innocent person, the falling man, by killing him? To override the presumption against killing, there must be a basis of liability. That basis is lacking in this case, just as it is when a person can save himself only by killing an innocent bystander. Of course, the person beneath the falling man is not liable either; thus, if the falling man can shift himself in midair, he must do so to avoid killing. But if he has that power and does not exercise it, he is no longer a Nonresponsible Threat.

Ferzan and Kaufman challenge not only the Responsibility Account's distinctions among morally innocent Threats but also its distinction between those who innocently pose a threat and those who engage in the same activities but have better luck and do not pose a threat. In the case of the latter, I accept an option Ferzan does not mention: that among reciprocal risk-imposers, moral luck can determine liability. Among morally innocent Threats, I do attempt to distinguish those who are responsible from those who are not, and to distinguish degrees of responsibility and liability among the former.

But Ferzan and Kaufman are right that the distinctions are difficult to draw with precision and sometimes seem to have only slight moral significance. They are also right that there is no identifiable threshold above which acts foreseeably impose a significant risk but below which they do not. There is also no precise line separating acts that culpably impose a significant risk from those that do not. Yet Ferzan and Kaufman seem to accept that a culpability criterion of liability is coherent nonetheless. One function of courts is to adjudicate difficult cases in the areas of indeterminacy within which vague thresholds for responsibility, culpability, and foreseeable risk seem to lie.

In the well-known hypothetical example in which a hiker in a snowstorm breaks into a cabin and burns some furniture, the hiker is not liable to defensive force but is liable to pay compensation. There may also, contrary to Ferzan's suggestion, be cases in which a person is liable to defensive force but would not be liable to pay compensation—for example, when it is unavoidable that one of two persons must die, one bears a slight degree of responsibility for this while the other bears none, and all other things are equal. Because tort law must be formulated to satisfy requirements other than those of corrective justice, liability in tort law may diverge from liability to defensive action.

Like Ferzan and Kaufman, Tadros argues that the Responsibility Account is too permissive. Yet the conclusion it implies in his Lifesaver example, which he says is counterintuitive, is the commonsense conclusion. While Harry acts admirably, he does not act with *objective* justification when he poses a threat to Jake; for it is not permissible to save the boy if that involves killing Jake. Tadros is right that his second case requires a richer account of responsibility than I have provided. But it can be given. It would have to take account of the contributory negligence of the spectators and the assumption of risk by the person under threat.

In my discussion of the Culpable Attempter, I questioned the Responsibility Account's assumption that causation is necessary for liability. Tadros's Double Hit Man 2 brilliantly strengthens that challenge. Intuitively, the Responsibility Account seems too restrictive here. This case may be morally distinguishable from the Transplant cases because the instigators are culpably responsible for a continuing unjust threat, while the culpable agent in the Transplant cases in fact poses no threat at all. But there are other cases in which the Responsibility Account becomes excessively permissive in its implications in the absence of the causal requirement. Notice, though, that Double Hit Man 2 challenges *all* accounts of self-defense. Any account that relaxes the causal requirement in that case must identify an alternative constraint on permissible killing in self-preservation.

19. SELF-DEFENSE, IMMINENCE, AND THE BATTERED WOMAN

WHITLEY R.P. KAUFMAN*

We are currently in the midst of a major debate about the scope and limits of self-defense, and in particular about the so-called imminence rule, which restricts the use of defensive force to situations where the threat is imminent. Some critics question the appropriateness of applying the imminence rule to women who claim to have been subject to repeated domestic abuse, and who kill their abuser during a lull in these attacks, even (in some cases) when he is asleep or unconscious. They argue that in such "battered woman" situations, applying the imminence restriction is unfair, since doing so would undermine her claim of justified self-defense when she in fact resorted to the only available option for self-protection.

Addressing this question is difficult given that, remarkably, there is no clear consensus at all as to why the traditional doctrine of self-defense requires that the threat be imminent. As George Fletcher says, the "existing literature of criminal law has done a woefully inadequate job in constructing a case for the imminence requirement."[1] This core text defends the imminence rule as an important limitation on the individual citizen's right to use force, even in the case of the battered woman. The rule is designed to protect the state's monopoly on all force, except when used in immediate self-defense.

I. BATTERED WOMEN AND THE IMMINENCE RULE

The *Norman* case is the most widely-cited example of a battered woman prevented from claiming self-defense solely by an application of the imminence rule.[2] Judy Norman at the time of the incident had been married for twenty-five years and had several children. She testified that her husband had begun drinking and abusing her about five years after they were married; numerous times he threatened to kill or maim her. Eventually she decided to take matters into her own hands. Her husband had been asleep for some time; Ms. Norman walked to

---

* Professor, Department of Philosophy, University of Massachusetts–Lowell. This core text is based on Whitley R.P. Kaufman, *Self-Defense, Imminence, and the Battered Woman*, 10 NEW CRIM. L. REV. 342 (2007).

1. George Fletcher, *Self-Defense and Relations of Domination*, 57 U. PITT. L. REV. 553, 569 (1996).

2. *State v. Norman*, 378 S.E.2d 8 (N.C. 1989).

her mother's house, obtained a gun, and then returned and shot her husband three times in the back of the head while he slept, killing him. At trial, Ms. Norman claimed self-defense, but the courts refused her plea on the sole ground that she could not have been under an imminent threat at the time of the shooting, since her husband was asleep. Ms. Norman was convicted of manslaughter and sentenced to six years imprisonment.

The *Norman* case has served as the rallying point for the movement to revise or eliminate the imminence rule. Advocates for battered women have argued that the law of self-defense, including the imminence rule, is constructed with men in mind, based on the paradigm of two strangers of equal size and strength in a public place. Furthermore, social institutions are not well designed for protecting abused wives: Police are reluctant to interfere in private domestic matters, restraining orders are not easy to enforce, and the presence of children in the home further complicates matters. Hence these advocates have claimed, it was necessary for Norman to act even in the absence of an imminent threat. For these reasons, the imminence rule is said to be discriminatory against women and should be modified or rejected, at least for battered women.

In order to address such an argument, we need to ask just why the law limits defensive force to cases involving an imminent threat. I begin by considering the two leading accounts of the purpose of the imminence rule.

II. IS THE IMMINENCE RULE REALLY NECESSARY?

In the first view, the imminence rule is merely a measure of whether force was really necessary. The imminence rule, on this view, has no independent significance, but is merely a "proxy" or an "indicator" or a "translator" for necessity (we will henceforth call this the Proxy Thesis). This thesis, however, is mistaken, for the imminence and the necessity rules are logically independent. Imminence and necessity are of course closely related, in that ordinarily when a threat is not yet imminent, it will not be necessary yet to resort to defensive force. Similarly, in most cases where the use of defensive force is judged to be necessary, it will typically be the case that the danger is either imminent or actual. The explanation for this close connection is obvious: the further off in the future a potential threat lies, the less likely it is that it will be necessary to counter it with present force, since there is ample time to find other (nonviolent) responses. Further, because temporally distant harm is usually highly uncertain and even speculative, it is harder to justify a claim that a violent response is necessary right now.

However, imminence and necessity sometimes diverge. It is easy to conceive of situations in which the threat is not imminent and yet the use of force is necessary. Indeed, such divergence is the reason for the current debate: the case of the woman who has been repeatedly abused in the past and has no alternative for protecting herself against future harm than to attack her abuser preemptively.

It is true that in general the further off in the future is the threat, the less likely it will be necessary to act now. However, sometimes the best or indeed the only time to act defensively is before the threat ripens into an imminent danger, and in such cases it is perfectly reasonable to assert that it is necessary to act now, rather than risk disaster by waiting too long. This is precisely how commentators typically interpret the case of Judy Norman: that in her judgment, it was necessary to act decisively, as the police were unable or unwilling to help her, and to wait until the moment of attack by her husband would be to risk serious abuse or even death if she did not take the opportunity to act preemptively.

Furthermore, the Proxy Thesis fails to recognize how our legal system handles cases where imminence and necessity diverge. Where the use of force is necessary, but the threat is not imminent, the individual is not permitted to resort to force herself. However, this does not mean she must passively surrender to the threat or wait until it becomes imminent before she can act. Rather, the law requires that she turn to the authorities for protection, i.e., call the police. Crucially, the lack of an imminent threat does *not* entail that the police or courts are prohibited from using force (or the threat of force) as necessary to protect the individual. The authorities may use all necessary and proportionate force to protect the woman, including, for example, arresting the abuser or issuing a protective order (backed by the threat of force). Thus the imminence rule is no mere indicator of necessity, but establishes a strict division of the right to use force. Just why there exists this division of labor has, of course, not yet been established and will be discussed below.

Kimberly Kessler Ferzan provides another account of the imminence requirement.[3] Ferzan argues that the "compelling need to aid battered women has made the self-defense argument too easy." She insists that imminence is "more than a proxy for necessity," and has an independent ethical basis. Her argument is based on the conceptual distinction between self-defense and self-preference. The distinctive feature of self-defense, according to Ferzan, is precisely that it is a defense against an act of aggression: "Self-defense is only understandable as a response to another's aggressive conduct." And imminence is the measure of aggression. This prior-aggression requirement is a moral one: "[T]he moral assessment of both the aggressor's and the defender's rights hinges on some notion of aggression." One who invokes self-defense before a threat is imminent loses the moral high ground and thus the justification for his act: "The aggressor's action 'starts it.'" The imminence requirement ensures that the force really is defensive and therefore morally justified.[4]

The problem for this view is that an act of aggression does not suddenly become unjust at the moment of imminence. Someone who is planning and

---

3. Kimberly Kessler Ferzan, *Defending Imminence: From Battered Women to Iraq*, 46 ARIZ. L. REV. 213 (2004).

4. *Id.* at 257–62.

preparing an unjust attack on me is already in the wrong, and I have the high moral ground against him even before he commences his attack. It is not plausible to insist that I must in every case wait until the attack is about to happen in order to be morally justified in taking action to protect myself. It is certainly true that the earlier one intervenes, the more likely it will be that one is mistaken about the purported attacker's intentions. However, it is equally true that the longer one waits before resorting to defensive force, the more one risks missing the window of opportunity to protect oneself. Surely there are some cases where preemption against a planned aggression is morally justified. Indeed, this is just the argument of the battered woman: it is unreasonable to expect her to wait until an actual or imminent attack in order to protect herself.

Equally problematic for this thesis is the fact that, as Ferzan recognizes, the state is *not* prohibited from acting preemptively in the use of its police power. But this would make no sense if morality requires that the use of force not take place until the moment of imminence. It is compelling evidence against her argument that morality does not in fact require police to wait until an attack is imminent, nor do we think that the police thereby become immoral "aggressors." Quite the opposite: We insist that the state intervene as early as possible, once it is determined that an unjust aggression is underway (i.e., there is some sort of overt act). That is just what the state is *supposed* to do in protecting the battered woman—its failure to do so is precisely the reason that has been given for allowing the woman to use force herself. But then, of course, there is no intrinsic *moral* argument against the morality of preemptive force. Why should the state be permitted to act preemptively but not the individual?

III. THE IMMINENCE RULE: POLITICAL, NOT MORAL

My thesis is that the imminence rule is independent of the necessity rule, and that it derives not from morality but from political theory. As so often, George Fletcher correctly grasps this point: "[T]he requirement properly falls into the domain of political rather than moral theory. The issue is the proper allocation of authority between the state and the citizen."[5] Fletcher here invokes what is traditionally called the "Public Authority" restriction on the use of force. The basic idea is that the state claims a "monopoly on force," under which no individual or any nonstate group is permitted to resort to force without the state's authorization. There is, however, one major exception to this monopoly. Where the danger is present and immediate, and there is no time to resort to a central authority, the individual is permitted to resort to force without seeking the state's prior authorization. Self-defense thus remains a private right for just this reason.

---

5. Fletcher, *supra* note 1, at 570.

But all preemptive force—before there is an imminent threat and punitive or restorative force after the threat has ceased to be imminent—belongs entirely to the authority of the state.

Some critics have mistakenly thought that this allocation simply follows from the necessity rule: It is not necessary for the individual to use force because the state is able to do so. But such a view reflects a misunderstanding of the necessity rule, for it would entail absurdly that the state cannot use force either, for the very same reason (since the individual could use it instead of the state). Indeed, any time two parties are under attack, neither would be permitted to use force because it would not be strictly necessary for either of them so long as the other could use force. When more than one party is capable of using force, then the necessity rule does not dictate who is the proper one to use it. Rather, we need some other explanation for the allocation of force as between the state and the individual, one best sought in history.

The rise of the imminence rule is bound up with the historical rise of the state monopoly on violence, especially retaliatory violence, but also preemptive force in anticipation of future dangers. The state monopoly on force, with the sole exception for individual self-defense against an imminent threat, only gradually became established during the crucial formative period of the modern world order in the sixteenth and seventeenth centuries, the period of "transition from feudal Europe to the modern Europe of sovereign states."[6] The many jurists and philosophers who contributed to this modern synthesis included Francisco Vitoria and Alberico Gentili, but especially Hugo Grotius, who limited the individual's use of violence to one type of case: where "our lives are threatened with immediate danger." When under an immediate threat, the individual is unable to invoke the protection of the state, and so has entered what is in effect a state of "private war," justifying him in using extreme force. Although we today no longer recognize the idea of "private war," we have inherited this rule of self-defense, grounded in the essential limitation to cases of imminent threat, where government assistance is not available.

The imminence rule thereafter became a fixture in the discussions of the private resort to violence. It is found in Samuel Pufendorf's *On the Duty of Man and Citizen*, in John Locke's *Second Treatise of Government*, and in Charles Montesquieu's *The Spirit of the Laws*. William Blackstone's extraordinarily influential *Commentaries on the Law of England* stated the imminence rule as part of English law:

> This right of natural defence does not imply a right of attacking: for, instead of attacking one another for injuries past or impending, men need only have recourse to the proper tribunals of justice. They cannot therefore legally exercise this right of preventive defence, but in sudden and violent cases; when certain

---

6. George Clark, THE SEVENTEENTH CENTURY 140 (1961).

and immediate suffering would be the consequence of waiting for the assistance of the law.[7]

Following Blackstone, the imminence restriction first starts appearing in legal treatises in the late eighteenth century, where it has remained ever since.

This particular allocation of the authority to use force is a response to the fundamental political concern of regulating and controlling the use of violence in society. Private violence constituted a constant threat of internal anarchy. As Grotius and others recognized, the deep moral and political problem is the need to ensure as far as possible the objectivity and disinterest of those who are authorized to use force, or else it will result in an endless cycle of violence. As Grotius declares, "it is much more conducive to the peace of society for a matter in dispute to be decided by a disinterested person, than by the partiality and prejudice of the party aggrieved."[8] The Public Authority restriction thus ultimately rests on the venerable natural law principle (also dating back to ancient Rome) that no one should be a judge in his own case; the decision to use force against another person must be made by an objective and disinterested authority. The use of force must be justified by an objective authority in a position to decide without bias or interest in the case. The state reserves the right to the use of retaliatory (punitive) force against past harm, as well as preemptive/preventive force against future threats. The single exception to this principle is where the immediacy of the threat rendered it impossible to resort to external protection and thus licensed self-help.

IV. IMMINENCE AND THE BATTERED WOMAN

The imminence rule creates a powerful presumption against the individual using force in her own protection. Even if one accepts this thesis, however, it is possible to argue that certain individuals are entitled to a waiver of the imminence rule. For an important corollary of the thesis has not yet been made explicit: If the imminence restriction is premised on the fact that the state can otherwise provide protection against violence, it follows that if the state is unable to do so then the imminence rule is suspended. In that case, the right to use preemptive (or even retaliatory force) could, it might be argued, revert back to the unprotected individual or group. Hence one way of interpreting (or reconstructing) the position of advocates of battered women is that they can endorse the thesis of this core text, but claim that battered women are not adequately protected by the state and hence should be exempted from the imminence rule.

---

7. William Blackstone, 4 COMMENTARIES *184.

8. 10 Hugo Grotius, THE RIGHTS OF WAR AND PEACE 55 (A.C. Campbell trans., Elibron Classics 2003) (1625).

However, to adopt such a view has risks of its own, for it entails abandoning the clear, bright-line imminence rule in favor of a more vague and subjective standard. Consider, for example, the standard that some commentators have suggested for suspending the imminence rule: When the state is not "effective" in protecting the individual, she may resort to violent self-help. The problem is that the notion of "effectiveness" is so vague and open-ended, it would exceedingly complicate jury trials, resulting in lengthy, complex debates over how to define "effective," whether the state was effective, and just how effective it had to be before force was justified. It is doubtful that such a standard could constrain the danger of vigilante violence. It creates a slippery slope at the end of which are cases such as that of Bernhard Goetz, who felt justified in resorting to vigilante justice on the grounds that the state was not effective in keeping the streets safe. It is worth recalling that the lynching of Blacks in the South was widely defended on the grounds that state punishment was too lax and too slow to adequately protect Southern women from rape. Whereas in cases of an imminent threat, the individual's judgment is least susceptible to bias or wrongful motives as the danger is clear and unmistakable because immediate (it is also more easily susceptible to proof of necessity after the fact), the very opposite may be said of an open-ended standard such as "effectiveness."

Unfortunately, the literature on battered women rarely acknowledges these inevitable limitations and distortions of human judgment. Indeed, advocates of battered women repeatedly insist on these women's enhanced and superior ability to recognize imminent threats that would not be perceptible to the ordinary person, by purportedly entering into a state of "hypervigilance," which permits them to recognize subtle signs of danger. Yet despite repeated assertions that research supports the existence of such extraordinary perceptual capacities, remarkably little attention has been given to producing studies demonstrating such abilities, or if they exist, to measuring their effectiveness. Such sweeping generalizations in effect bypass the imminence rule by stipulating the presence of a danger that only the battered woman, with her supernormal capacities, can recognize. Indeed, it is equally possible that victims of repeated abuse develop the opposite tendency, becoming hypersensitive to signs of "dangers" that do not exist.[9]

It bears emphasizing that the very rationale for a bright-line rule (or at least as bright a line as can reasonably be drawn) in the case of violent self-help is to minimize the room for the exercise of human judgment as to when and how much to impose harm on others in order to protect oneself. Without it, people

---

9. In fact, the concept of "hypervigilance" as used in discussions of post traumatic stress disorder (PTSD) more generally, outside the context of Battered Women's Syndrome, seems typically to be used so as to emphasize the increased *unreliability* of perception of danger due to repeated stress. Thus, Jonathan Shay describes the hypervigilance of returned soldiers as the "inappropriate reaction to perceived risk" and as the loss of trustworthiness of perception. Jonathan Shay, ACHILLES IN VIETNAM 172–74 (1995).

are likely to overestimate future risks and to err in the direction of acting preemptively "regardless of cost to others."[10]

Equally important, the imminence rule serves to limit the influence of retaliatory motives. Women no less than men are of course influenced by retaliatory motives, a fact that must be kept in mind even for cases of battered women. Indeed, there is evidence of a retaliatory motive even in the Judy Norman case: Her therapist testified that the day before the killings, Norman expressed "considerable anger toward her husband" and said she should kill him "because of the things he had done to her"—i.e., for past wrongs rather than future threats.[11] The imminence rule thus serves to ensure objective, publicly available evidence that the claimed danger was real and immediate. This has the double purpose of preventing mere retaliatory attacks in the guise of self-defense and also limiting the use of self-serving and unverifiable testimony regarding the individual's unique capacity to detect a risk of danger for which there is no independent evidence.

V. CONCLUSION

In recent years we have seen a major attack on the imminence rule, especially in its application to battered women. The wide range of proposals for modifying the imminence restriction for battered women include eliminating the rule entirely, subordinating it to necessity, modifying it, supplementing it, making it more flexible, subjectivizing it, contextualizing it, broadening it, and so forth. My purpose here has been to sound a cautionary note.

Although there may well be some genuine cases where the application of the imminence rule serves an injustice (and perhaps here, a pardon is the ideal response), one ought to be very careful in tinkering with a crucial historical limitation on the right to violent self-help. This is particularly important given the serious doubts that have been raised about whether the proposed reforms would have much impact on battered-women homicides. As Holly Maguigan emphasizes, the existing law of self-defense in most jurisdictions is "consistent with the self-defense claims of battered women who kill"; to the extent there is a problem, it has to do with the "unfair application of existing law," not with the current standards of self-defense per se.[12]

---

10. David Gauthier, *Self-Defense and Relations of Domination: Comments on George Fletcher's* Domination in the Theory of Justification and Excuse, 57 U. PITT. L. REV. 615, 617 (1996).

11. *Norman*, 378 S.E.2d at 10–11.

12. Holly Maguigan, *Battered Women and Self-Defense: Myths and Misconceptions in Current Reform Proposals*, 140 U. PA. L. REV. 379, 458 (1991).

The imminence rule is an independent restriction on the individual right to resort to violence against others, especially deadly violence. The first task of the state is the control of violence, and restricting the use of individual violence to cases of genuine emergency—cases in which recourse to state protection is impossible—is crucial to establishing this monopoly on violence. Civil life is, as Pufendorf warned, "too fragile to allow each man to exact what he believes to be his due by violent self-help."[13] Moreover, the rule of law requires that each person—even batterers—have a right to due process of law, especially when their lives are at stake. If the rules of self-defense permit an exception to this principle in the case of imminent danger, it is an exception that is best kept to an absolute minimum. As Joshua Dressler cautions, "we should hesitate long and hard before we promote a criminal defence that categorically justifies the taking of life before it is immediately necessary."[14] Before we proceed with any modification (let alone elimination) of the imminence restriction, we had better consider very carefully the implications of such a radical change in the long-established and highly effective principles controlling the private resort to violence.

---

13. Samuel Pufendorf, ON THE DUTY OF MAN AND CITIZEN ACCORDING TO NATURAL LAW 156 (James Tully ed., Michael Silverthorne trans., Cambridge Univ. Press 1991) (1673).

14. Joshua Dressler, *Battered Women Who Kill Their Sleeping Tormentors*, in CRIMINAL LAW THEORY 215, 275 (Stephen Shute ed., 2002).

COMMENTS

THE REAL LINK BETWEEN IMMINENCE AND NECESSITY

GIDEON YAFFE*

Whitley Kaufman objects to the Proxy Thesis—the view that the imminence of an attack by an aggressor matters to self-defense because it is evidence that an attack by the aggressor will actually take place. Imminence, on this view, silences doubts to the effect that something will prevent the attack, such as change of mind by the aggressor, or intervention by another, or something else that takes time to materialize. The thought is that generally speaking, although not always, only imminent attacks require violence against the aggressor right now. The advocate of the Proxy Thesis, then, holds that imminence only matters to self-defense because it often matters to necessity which, in turn, matters to self-defense.

---

* Associate Professor of Philosophy and Law, University of Southern California.

Kaufman's criticisms of the Proxy Thesis are predicated on the claim that imminence is not a logical condition of necessity. As he notes, cases involving battered women seem to demonstrate that this is so. Defendants in such cases often have no reason to doubt they will be killed or seriously injured by the batterer, despite the fact that the attack is not imminent. However, the cases involving battered women show only that imminence is not a necessary condition *of its being true that the aggressor's attack will take place.* As I will argue, imminence is a logical condition of the *reasonableness of the belief* that the attack will take place. So, imminence matters to self-defense only because necessity does, but the relevant connection between the two is not the one described in the Proxy Thesis, and not of the sort that allows for Kaufman's objections.

A defendant arguing self-defense must show both that he thought he would be attacked and that he had sufficient reasons for that belief. To show the latter, he must show that the various possible grounds for doubt about whether the attack would take place were properly silenced. But this is not all he needs to show. A person who is aware, for instance, that he's paranoid, and so regularly believes that he's about to be attacked, might have no reason at all to think that something will prevent the aggressor's attack. Still, he ought to stop and say to himself, "Sure, I have no doubt that I'm about to be attacked, but I'm often wrong about such things." In order to reasonably believe that he must do violence to the aggressor to avoid being attacked, doubts must be silenced not just about the aggressor's resolve and about the absence of third-party intervention; doubts about the reliability of the defendant's beliefs must also be silenced. We need to ask not only whether the world provided the defendant with good signs that he was going to be attacked but also whether he had reasons to doubt that he read the signs correctly.

Now it's reasonable to rely on beliefs derived directly from present sensory experience. It's reasonable to trust your eyes. But only beliefs about things that are actually impinging on the senses can give rise to perceptual beliefs. Beliefs about far future events are at best indirectly derived from present sensory experience. Thus, a belief to the effect that one is to be attacked can only be directly derived from present sensory experience if the attack one believes will take place is also imminent. The imminence requirement limits the affirmative defense of self-defense to those who are relying on the immediate deliverances of their senses for their beliefs about what is going to happen to them if they do not do violence to another. It is a high bar for the reasonableness of that belief, but it is not implausibly high. The thought is that when one is about to do violence to another, one must be as certain that one is to be attacked as one is certain that things are as they appear.

Kaufman rightly notes that the imminence requirement is rooted in sixteenth- and seventeenth-century philosophy influential in Britain. He misidentifies, however, the relevant strain of thought from the period. The relevant strain is not concerned with the proper allocation of state powers, but instead with the proper grounds of our beliefs. Francis Bacon, Thomas Hobbes, and John Locke, among others, were concerned to defend the view that although all our beliefs are ultimately derived from the senses, some of them are nonetheless sufficiently certain for all of the affairs of ordinary life. Those that are sufficiently certain, they thought, are those directly derived from sensory experience. With Bacon's, Hobbes's, and Locke's efforts to defend empiricism, then, we find the view that when a great deal is at stake and something close to certainty is required, as in self-defense, we should only rely on what our senses tell us directly. This is the real purpose of the imminence requirement.

IN DEFENSE OF THE PROXY THESIS

MARCIA BARON[*]

Whitley Kaufman argues that what he calls the Proxy Thesis is "mistaken, for the imminence and the necessity rules are logically independent."[1] The Proxy Thesis claims that imminence is significant primarily as an indicator of necessity. A lack of imminence thus provides no more than a presumption that it was not necessary to use force. I agree that the imminence and necessity rules are logically independent. But why think that the fact that neither rule entails the other shows the Proxy Thesis to be mistaken? That a requirement of necessity does not entail a requirement of imminence would seem to support the Proxy Thesis. It puts the burden on those who favor retaining the imminence requirement to say why (assuming the requirements for self-defense other than imminence are met) the fact that it is necessary to use force in self-defense is not enough and imminence should also be required.

Another objection Kaufman lodges is that the Proxy Thesis "fails to recognize how our legal system handles cases where imminence and necessity diverge."[2] But the point of the Proxy Thesis is to explain why and to what extent imminence is important, thus providing a basis for abolishing or modifying the imminence requirement. It is no argument against the Proxy Thesis that it fails to recognize how our legal system handles certain cases when the Proxy Thesis does not aim to provide an account that leaves in place how the system handles such cases. Indeed, proponents of the Proxy Thesis are more likely to favor expanding our picture of how legal systems handle such cases by looking at other, generally similar, legal systems; Canada and Australia, for example, have no imminence requirement for self-defense.

---

* Rudy Professor of Philosophy, Indiana University.
1. Kaufman core text at 408.
2. *Id.* at 409.

Probably the strongest objection against the Proxy Thesis is that the imminence requirement serves vital functions that would not be well served if we replaced it with a necessity requirement (even if we added that if the danger was not imminent, there is a presumption—but a rebuttable one—that the use of force was not necessary). One version of this argument is that because killing another human being is a terrible thing, any defense to murder has to be sharply restricted. To weaken the imminence requirement by treating imminence as only a marker for necessity is therefore unwise. But this argument is hard to take seriously given the absence in the U.S. of a robust retreat requirement. Why allow people to kill rather than safely retreat, and yet insist on imminence even if it means one is then unable to defend oneself against an aggressor?

Another version of the argument is that the imminence requirement serves to confine the defense to cases in which it is clear that the danger is real. But why suppose that imminence guarantees that the danger is real? One can't help wondering if those who speak as if it does are beguiled by an ambiguity in "imminent." We sometimes use "imminent" to mean that the event is about to happen, emphasizing not just immediacy but inevitability. By contrast, "imminent" in the imminence requirement means only that D reasonably believed that the danger was immediate (or virtually so), not that it really was. The imminence requirement can be met even if, unbeknownst to D, A's gun is not loaded.

It might be countered that although imminence is no guarantee, it greatly reduces the risks of mistakes. No doubt it does reduce the risks somewhat, but it is important not to exaggerate the reduction, or to forget the cost: where the danger is not imminent yet D cannot defend herself if she waits until it is, D is, legally, out of luck.

Kaufman claims that the imminence requirement "serves to limit the influence of retaliatory motives."[3] This is true, but only because (a) retaliatory motives are highly unlikely when the attack is by a stranger; and (b) when the attack is not by a stranger, the imminence requirement renders it more difficult for defendants to legally use force in self-defense (particularly when the attacker is physically much stronger than his victim). In addition, retaliatory motives are not incompatible with D's killing in self-defense. They should be a concern only if (a) they tainted D's judgment, so that D did not act on a reasonable belief that the use of force was necessary, or arguably (b) they are the real reason D killed. In any event, imminence is no guarantee that one will perceive the situation accurately, and retaliatory motives are not the only way one's judgment may be tainted; to give but one of many obvious examples, racist views distort one's perception of immediate danger.

---

3. *Id.* at 414.

THE VALUES AND COSTS OF IMMINENCE

KIMBERLY KESSLER FERZAN*

Whitley Kaufman defends the imminence standard in self-defense for what he believes are political reasons—the imminence rule exists to maintain the state's monopoly on the use of force.

At the outset, it seems as though much of the debate over imminence in the context of battered women is profoundly misguided. The imminence debate begins with claims that the battered woman cannot escape and may at some time be subjected to deadly force. She is assumed to be stuck and then the question is how close to completion a deadly threat must be before she can act and defend herself. Judy Norman is the anti-imminence poster child.

But imminence only applies if the defender is not currently subjected to a threat or injury sufficient to warrant the use of deadly force. But Norman was subject to an enduring injury that *did* justify the use of such force. First, no one does the math. Judy was barely fifteen (and, you guessed it, pregnant) when she married J.T. Second, to say that she "worked as a prostitute" ignores that she was really being raped, repeatedly. So, the question is, why does this person—deprived of any sort of meaningful life—need a deadly threat before she can act? Let's assume that J.T. never planned to kill her, just to whore out this captive slave of his that he knocked-up at fourteen. Does Judy have to submit to this life?

Of course, Norman's case is the extreme, and that gets us back to imminence more generally. As Kaufman notes, I defend imminence, claiming that we need the imminence requirement to distinguish offense from defense. In response, Kaufman claims that "an act of aggression does not suddenly become unjust at the very moment of imminence," because "[s]omeone who is planning and preparing an unjust attack on me is already in the wrong."[1] Fair enough. But consider the question I was answering: Is the defender's *need* sufficient to ground self-defense? My reply is "no." The need to act in self-preservation exists independent of the putative attacker's intent or current capabilities. That isn't self-defense. Self-defense requires aggression; and an important function of the imminence rule is that it serves as an actus reus for aggression. If one wants to debate whether that actus reus is too stringent, that's fine. But recognize that imminence is not just a proxy for necessity.

---

* Associate Dean for Academic Affairs and Professor of Law, Rutgers University, School of Law–Camden. My views on this subject are more fully set forth in Kimberly Kessler Ferzan, *Defending Imminence: From Battered Women to Iraq*, 46 ARIZ. L. REV. 213 (2004), and Kimberly Kessler Ferzan, *Self-Defense and the State*, 5 OHIO ST. J. CRIM. L. 449 (2008).

1. Kaufman core text at 409–10.

Kaufman claims that imminence has a separate political grounding. In my view this explanation is really a moral (consequentialist) justification for imminence, and the relationship between imminence and necessity that Kaufman identifies is simply an example of the rules/standards problem. Kaufman claims that imminence and necessity are logically independent. But that does not mean that they are morally independent. The value of imminence is that it best approximates the moral rule that the individual act only when necessary. Kaufman's historical citations do nothing to undermine the presupposition that the reason *why* the state requires imminence is because those are the only times it is necessary for the individual to act. The state can have a monopoly on violence specifically because the presupposition is that the state can otherwise intervene effectively.

The fact that imminence and necessity sometimes come apart is entirely consistent with the overinclusive nature of rules themselves. We use rules (like imminence) when and because they are, all things considered, better at guiding action and adjudication than standards (like necessity). As Kaufman acknowledges, "the very rationale for a bright-line rule (or at least as bright a line as can reasonably be drawn) in the case of violent self-help is to minimize the room for the exercise of human judgment as to when and how much to impose harm on others to protect oneself."[2]

But here is the puzzle that Kaufman must then solve. Imminence is a rule that provides all the consequentialist values that rules have (e.g., clear answers in instances of epistemic uncertainty). But what of the battered woman? What if the underlying justification for the imminence rule would permit her to kill, but the rule, designed to prevent error over the run of cases, is in her case overinclusive and would prohibit her from killing? The battered woman is a moral innocent: she has engaged in morally permissible conduct. Those who are morally innocent ought not to be punished. The rule of imminence nonetheless binds her to the altar of consequentialist values. I, for one, don't think society ought to plunge that knife.

---

2. *Id.* at 413.

IMMINENCE RECONSIDERED: ARE BATTERED WOMEN DIFFERENT?

JOAN H. KRAUSE*

Whitley Kaufman offers a compelling rationale for maintaining the imminence restriction on the use of defensive force, particularly as applied to battered women

---

* George Butler Research Professor of Law, University of Houston Law Center. This comment is based in part on Joan H. Krause, *Distorted "Reflections" of Battered Women Who Kill: A Response to Professor Dressler*, 4 OHIO ST. J. CRIM. L. 555 (2007).

who kill in nonconfrontational circumstances. In contrast to commentators who defend the rule primarily on moral grounds as a means of protecting the sanctity of human life,[1] Kaufman provides an intriguing historical account of imminence as a construct of political theory, a rule "designed to protect the state's monopoly on all force, except when used in immediate self-defense."[2]

Although elegant in theory, this approach fails to account for the practical ways in which imminence has functioned in self-defense cases. Imminence is only one of the legal requirements for the use of deadly defensive force. Other well-established rules have the effect of expanding, not restricting, the individual's ability to act in circumstances where alternatives may exist. Take the example of retreat: If we permit individual force only when there is no recourse to state protection, jurisdictions uniformly should require individuals to retreat (and seek such protection) before responding. Yet the majority of jurisdictions do *not* require retreat, and those that do often recognize exceptions such as the castle doctrine. It may be logical to give individuals greater leeway to respond with force in their own homes, either on a property-rights theory or because of the practical difficulties of obtaining assistance there. But my point is that the law of self-defense considers the Public Authority restriction merely as one among several competing values, not as the doctrine's core principle.

In fact, recent trends suggest an ever-expanding sphere in which individuals are free to engage in self-help. While controversial, several states have enacted so-called "shoot first" laws that permit the preemptive use of deadly force without retreat against intruders and extend the castle exception to virtually any location in which the defendant has a right to be present.[3] Such laws pose a much greater threat to the state's monopoly on force than do the few battered women who seek to argue this defense.

Moreover, if imminence is a temporal criterion that permits self-help only where "there is no time to resort to a central authority,"[4] it should arise primarily in nonconfrontational cases in which a time lag exists between threat and deadly response. Yet Victoria Nourse's detailed study of self-defense cases found that the vast majority of imminence disputes—both in general (84 percent) and for battered women in particular (70 percent)—arose in *confrontations*, suggesting that imminence was being interpreted to have a broader meaning than time alone.[5] Far from being the bright-line standard that Kaufman posits, imminence appears to suffer from the same vagueness as the "effectiveness" rule he rejects as a substitute.

---

1. *See, e.g.*, Joshua Dressler, *Battered Women and Sleeping Abusers: Some Reflections*, 3 OHIO ST. J. CRIM. L. 457, 466 (2006).

2. Kaufman core text at 407.

3. *See, e.g.*, FLA. STAT. ANN. § 776.013 (West 2005).

4. Kaufman core text at 410.

5. V.F. Nourse, *Self-Defense and Subjectivity*, 68 U. CHI. L. REV. 1235, 1252–54 (2001).

Finally, Kaufman unfairly rejects the possibility that at least some battered women may satisfy the corollary to the imminence rule, as is suggested by a fuller recitation of the *Norman* facts. Putting aside Judy Norman's twenty-year history of abuse by her husband J.T., the following events occurred just in the *24 hours preceding the killing*: Police were called to the Normans' home and advised Judy to take out a warrant, but she told them that J.T. would kill her; police were called back to the home a short time later, after Judy overdosed on pills, and J.T. interfered with emergency medical personnel; after J.T. threatened to kill Judy, her mother, and grandmother, the officer chased J.T. away; Judy was taken to the hospital; when Judy returned home the next day, J.T. threatened and beat her in front of witnesses; once again Judy's mother "called the sheriff's department, but no help arrived at that time."[6] The fact that the violence escalated so much in the final day that Judy attempted suicide and law enforcement personnel responded twice—and *failed to show up* a third time—demands a deeper analysis of whether, at that point, the state had proven it truly was incapable of protecting her.

Indeed, battered women advocates ask for nothing more than the *opportunity* to make the argument that the use of defensive force was valid. The problems raised by nonconfrontational killings are not unique to battered women, but rather are inherent in our fragmented approach to the use of deadly defensive force. If the state's monopoly on the use of preemptive force is endangered, and the ratio of private to public force in need of rebalancing, we should not do so on the shoulders of battered women.

---

6. *State v. Norman*, 366 S.E.2d 586, 588 (N.C. Ct. App. 1988), *rev'd*, 378 S.E.2d 8 (N.C. 1989).

THE "IMMINENCE" REQUIREMENT, BATTERED WOMEN, AND THE AUTHORITY TO STRIKE BACK

JEREMY HORDER*

Whitley Kaufman does a fine job in distinguishing between the requirements respectively of necessity and of imminence in the defense of self-defense. I agree with much of what Kaufman has to say about the danger of suspending or setting aside the so-called imminence rule for any category of defendant. The need to avoid self-help remedies when resort could be had to state protection (whether or not subjectively judged adequate) is of paramount importance. However, I doubt

---

* Law Commissioner for England and Wales; Professor of Criminal Law and Porjes Fellow, Worcester College, University of Oxford.

whether this justification for avoiding self-help through the use of force is best expressed through an "imminence" rule. This is only a legal term of art and may mislead if taken too literally. The relevant principle should be interpreted as a requirement that there be "no reasonable opportunity" to resort to state protection (whether or not subjectively judged adequate).[1] In my view, that gives adequate expression to the political principle at stake, but can be more readily seen as applicable to the hostage situation—and to the situation of at least some battered women controlled by violent partners—than the imminence requirement.

My main concern with Kaufman's argument is whether it is right to suggest that a more generous treatment of the battered woman who kills a passive abuser "creates a slippery slope at the end of which are cases such as that of Bernhard Goetz, who felt justified in resorting to vigilante justice on the grounds that the state was not effective in keeping the streets safe."[2] This might of course happen. However, the real question is whether the two situations can and should be distinguished, at least in some cases. I think that the two situations can sometimes be distinguished, theoretically and in practice.

The problem with Goetz's use of his own initiative was well-explained by John Finnis some years ago: "Such an ambitious attempt as the law's can only succeed in creating and maintaining order, and a fair order, inasmuch as individuals drastically reduce the occasions on which they trade off their legal obligations against their individual convenience or conceptions of the social good."[3] Goetz claimed for himself the right or authority to take (violent) action against persons supposed to would-be criminals, in a situation in which he had no claim to such an authority. As I have elsewhere explained the point:

> No one is a moral island or morally omniscient, and a willingness to submit to legal rules—as communal solutions to complex and/or recurrent problems with wide-ranging ramifications—is to demonstrate one's practical reasonableness as a citizen, ruling out (inter alia) morally simplistic "Robin Hood" solutions to injustice and other social problems.[4]

Goetz's conduct arrogantly asserted a right to depart from the practically reasonable demand that crime must be addressed through official law enforcement, on no better basis than his own moral and political convictions (the "Robin Hood" solution).

By way of contrast, the battered woman may (in exceptional circumstances) have an authority-based claim to take action herself. One important basis for the law's authority is that the law is normally in a much better position than any

---

1. Jeremy Horder, *Killing the Passive Abuser*, in DOCTRINES OF THE GENERAL PART 283, 289–90 (Stephen Shute and A.P. Simester eds., 2002).

2. Kaufman core text at 413.

3. John Finnis, NATURAL LAW AND NATURAL RIGHTS 319 (1980).

4. Jeremy Horder, EXCUSING CRIME 219 (2004).

individual to account for the reasons for and against permitting or prohibiting certain types of action. This is arguably not true of the situation facing some battered woman. Kaufman may be right to argue that battered women do not have "enhanced and superior perceptual capacities" such that they can recognize threats that cannot reasonably be tackled through resort to the authorities. However, their intimate knowledge of the individual abuser, knowledge not based on any superior "capacity," but just on experience, may mean that they— quite reasonably, and in a way that can be explained to a jury—believed that resort to the authorities for protection could not reasonably have been expected of them (to use my terminology) in the circumstances. Quite simply, Goetz had no such superior knowledge, as well as not being effectively "trapped" by his victims and hence unable to seek the assistance of law enforcement authorities.

Even if one accepts this argument, that still leaves open the question whether intentional killing was a reasonable response, as opposed to a seriously disabling injury (e.g., blinding), but there will be rare cases in which even such an extreme step can be justified.

REPLY

WHITLEY R.P. KAUFMAN

There is no easy answer to the problem of imminence and battered women. If we retain the imminence rule, some victims of domestic violence will suffer as a result; if we relax the rule, it will likely result in unnecessary or vindictive killing under the rubric of self-defense. It is worth reiterating that my argument is intended merely as a cautionary note against an overhasty abandonment of a long-standing rule.

Gideon Yaffe claims to be able to deduce the imminence rule from principles of empiricist epistemology, on grounds that one cannot have "direct" evidence of a danger unless the threat is imminent. It is difficult to evaluate this claim because he does not define the term "direct." Of course, there is an obvious though trivial sense in which knowledge of future events must be indirect. However, this is irrelevant. Inasmuch as an imminent threat *also* refers to a future event (albeit in the near future), one would not, by Yaffe's standard, be justified in using force against an imminent threat either. Moreover, the law nowhere requires that one's knowledge of a danger be "direct,"' nor does the law endorse the British empiricism as a general matter. Indeed, Yaffe misleadingly implies that the imminence rule derives from British sources, when in fact my core text makes it clear that the rule's origin is, if anything, more grounded in the Continental tradition (Francisco Vitoria, Alberico Gentili, Hugo Grotius). Most important of all, if one reads the relevant historical passages, it is clear that the central concern was the allocation of the right to use force, rather than concerns about epistemological limitations. Indeed, the state is subject to the same epistemological limitations as the individual, yet it can use force even absent an imminent threat.

Marcia Baron is correct that imminence can and often does serve as a useful proxy for necessity; however, I disagree that this is the imminence rule's primary function, which is rather to ensure that all use of force be limited to the state, wherever possible. Hence in cases where force may be necessary yet there is no imminent threat (as in some cases of battered persons), the use of force should be restricted to the police. I am puzzled as to why she thinks the logical distinction between imminence and necessity is an argument *for* the Proxy Thesis rather than against it; clearly, the more independent the two are, the less useful one can be as a proxy for the other.

As to my argument that we need to look at how the legal system works, this was (obviously, I hope!) not meant to suggest we should simply assume that our system's status quo is right, nor that we should ignore other legal traditions. Rather, the point was that the Proxy Thesis fails to capture how the imminence rule actually functions within our legal system, which is not as a proxy for necessity but as a means of distributing the right to force. Nor does the evidence from other countries undercut this thesis. Canada is a rare example of a country that recently abandoned the imminence rule, but it is no objection to my argument, since the Canadian courts rejected the rule only by explicitly relying on the (mistaken) Proxy Thesis. Indeed, this action illustrates just the hasty reliance on questionable new theories that worries me. Finally, Baron mistakenly assumes as to the retaliation question that the only cases at issue are those in which self-defense is legitimate but in which retaliatory motives are *also* at work. But the real concern is with cases in which the need for defensive force is questionable or nonexistent, but the person uses it anyway, under the influence of retaliatory motives for past wrongs. It seems uncontroversial that requiring an imminent threat will severely limit any such abuses.

Kimberly Ferzan argues that the issue here is one of adopting a rule rather than a standard, given that the use of a rule will keep stricter control on the use of violence.[1] She argues for the Proxy Thesis, that the "value of imminence is that it best approximates the moral rule that the individual act only when necessary."[2] But this leaves us with the puzzle of why the *state* can act when there is a nonimminent threat, given that the state is bound by the necessity rule as well. Moreover, it is unclear how to square the Proxy Thesis with her "conceptual" argument that self-defense is impermissible unless there is an imminent threat. Ferzan also claims that the retention of the imminence rule "punishes" women.

---

1. However, the fact that an argument in favor of a rule over a standard refers to consequences does not make it "consequentialist." Consequentialism is the doctrine that morality is concerned *only* with consequences.

2. Ferzan comment at 420.

This criticism is puzzling, given that she herself calls for retaining the imminence rule without considering this to be equally (in her unfortunate metaphor) "plunging the knife" into the battered woman. The purpose of the imminence rule, as I argue, is to prevent anyone from plunging the knife into anyone else, and to restrict the use of violence to the state unless the threat is imminent, where the state cannot intervene in time.

Joan Krause claims that defensive force is not subject to the necessity principle, i.e., that it can be used even where there are alternatives, such as retreat. However, this is a common fallacy (found in Marcia Baron's comment as well). The rationale for the no-retreat rule is to protect the right to be where one is legally permitted to be. This is not to defend the rule, but merely to explain that it is *not* in fact an exception to the necessity rule. The necessity rule holds that you may not resort to force unless there is no alternative means of protecting *a given value*; here, the value of exercising your right of freedom of movement. Whether the right to go where one pleases is sufficiently important to justify the use of force is a different question, one of proportionality, not necessity. Nor do I claim that the Public Authority principle is the "core" principle of self-defense; quite the contrary, to the extent self-defense has a core principle, it is necessity. Finally, I would certainly agree with Krause that victims of abuse should, like everyone else, have the "opportunity" to argue that their defensive force was valid; in fact, they already do. The question is rather whether their use of force should be subject to a different set of rules than is applied to everyone else.

I am sympathetic to Jeremy Horder's suggestion that a "no reasonable opportunity" rule would be a possible alternative to the imminence rule, especially given that time is not the only relevant factor in determining whether self-help is justified. However, in the vast majority of cases, time will in fact be the determining factor. Moreover, in hostage cases, even if there is no imminent threat to one's life, one already has a right to use deadly force in self-defense, due to the deprivation of one's freedom. A temporal standard is much more objective than a vague "reasonable opportunity" standard, and as such the latter will in practice be likely to license substantially more private violence than the former. Moreover, Horder does not address the likelihood of misuse of the relaxed rule, where a person's claim to have had access to special signs of impending violence is both self-serving and unverifiable. The presumption, I would suggest, should be in favor of limiting the use of private violence as much as possible and of protecting abuse victims by societal means rather than by licensing further violent self-help.

20. REASONABLE PROVOCATION AND SELF-DEFENSE
Recognizing the Distinction Between Act Reasonableness and Emotion Reasonableness

CYNTHIA LEE*

All of us can empathize with the individual who has just found out that his or her intimate partner has been unfaithful. Anger, outrage, sadness, a feeling of worthlessness, depression—all are understandable emotional responses to the betrayal of trust that comes with infidelity. It is eminently reasonable to feel these strong emotions. Provoked killers, however, go beyond *feeling* outraged. They *act* on their emotions in the most extreme way—by taking a human life. Most of us would not kill, even if we were extremely upset. Yet the provocation doctrine partially excuses an act of killing if the defendant's emotional response is considered reasonable. If a reasonable person in the defendant's shoes would have been provoked into a heat of passion, then the provoked killer is acquitted of murder and convicted of the lesser offense of voluntary manslaughter. The provoked killer receives this mitigation even if the reasonable person would not have acted the way he did because the provocation doctrine does not require that his act be reasonable.

We can also empathize with the individual who is afraid of being physically harmed by another person. An individual can have differing degrees of fear depending on the situation. In *The Gift of Fear*, Gavin de Becker describes a woman with a gut feeling that the stranger who has offered to carry her groceries has an ulterior motive for being so nice.[1] It would be foolish if that woman ignored her gut feeling. Ignoring one's intuition can place one in harm's way. There is, however, a difference between preventive action, such as refusing the suspicious offer of assistance, and preemptive action, such as shooting the man. It would hardly be reasonable for the woman to take out a gun and shoot the stranger before he did anything to confirm her gut feeling.

As these examples suggest, there is a difference between reasonable emotions (fear, anger, outrage) and reasonable action. Even if a particular emotion is reasonable under the circumstances, this does not mean that acting on that emotion by using deadly force is also reasonable. It may be reasonable to feel anger at one's unfaithful partner, but not reasonable to act on that anger by killing the

* Cynthia Lee, Professor of Law, George Washington University Law School. This core text is based on Cynthia Lee, MURDER AND THE REASONABLE MAN: PASSION AND FEAR IN THE CRIMINAL COURTROOM ch. 10 (2003).
1. *See* Gavin De Becker, THE GIFT OF FEAR 1–7 (1997).

partner. It may be reasonable to fear an attack, but if that attack is not imminent or if one can avoid that attack by running away or disabling the attacker, then killing is not a reasonable response.

It makes sense to engage in separate inquiries regarding the reasonableness of a given action and the reasonableness of the emotions leading to that action. Yet jurors in provocation and self-defense cases are usually instructed to focus upon the reasonableness of the defendant's emotions (or beliefs), and thus pay little or no attention to the reasonableness of the defendant's acts.

I. PROVOCATION

In modern jurisdictions, the key issue in a provocation case is whether legally adequate provocation was present. Legally adequate provocation is said to exist if the defendant was *reasonably* provoked into a heat of passion. One could interpret this ambiguous language as requiring what I call "act reasonableness," a finding that a reasonable person in the defendant's shoes would have responded or *acted* as the defendant did. An unscientific survey of model jury instructions used in the fifty states, however, indicates that only a few states require act reasonableness. Most states require what I call "emotion reasonableness," a finding that the defendant's *emotional* outrage or *passion* was reasonable. An example of "emotion reasonableness" is found in Illinois' model jury instructions, which tell jurors that legally adequate provocation is "conduct sufficient to excite an intense *passion* in a reasonable person."[2]

The reluctance to require act reasonableness stems from the belief that the act of killing in the heat of passion is never reasonable. I agree. The provoked killer's actions are wrongful as a matter of law, which is why he does not receive a complete acquittal. We do not want others to emulate the behavior. We mitigate the charges only because we feel sympathy for the provoked killer. But requiring the jury to focus on the reasonableness of the defendant's actions does not mean they must find it was reasonable for the defendant to kill. Rather, act reasonableness can be satisfied if the provoking incident would have provoked an ordinary person to violence.

Jeremy Horder provides a useful explanation of the difference between reasonable feelings of anger (reasonable emotions) and reasonable action in anger (reasonable acts). According to Horder, a reasonable feeling of anger means "being angered for the right reason, at the right time, to the right extent, and so on."[3] In other words, one's emotional response is considered reasonable if one has the right amount of anger and outrage relative to the provoking incident.

---

2. Illinois Pattern Jury Instructions (Criminal), No. 7.03 (4th ed. 2000) (emphasis added).

3. Jeremy Horder, PROVOCATION AND RESPONSIBILITY 44 (1992).

For example, if someone kidnaps your family and tortures them, a reasonable emotional response is to be very angry. If you are only moderately angry, your emotional response is not reasonable because it is too small. If, on the other hand, you feel violently outraged at a baby's persistent crying, your emotional response would probably be perceived as unreasonable and excessive.

In contrast, reasonable *action* in anger means proportional retaliation against the person who has wronged you. "For men of honour . . . , to *act* justly in the face of an affront or other injustice is to inflict proportional requital, retaliation of the correct amount, on the perpetrator of the injustice."[4] In other words, reasonable action in provocation means action that is proportionate to the provocation. For example, if V slaps D for no reason at all and D responds by hitting V once or perhaps even twice, one can say that D's response is proportionate to the initial wrong, and therefore reasonable. If D were to instead take out a knife and stab V to death, his response would likely be deemed unreasonable because a fatal stabbing is grossly disproportionate to a slap.

Under a proportionality principle, the reasonableness of the provoked defendant's action depends on the type of force and degree of force used in relation to the triggering provocation. Proportionality does not mean that the provoked defendant must respond with force equal to the force used by the provoker because provocation doctrine partially excuses the use of deadly force even when the provoker does not use any force at all. The defendant's act, however, must be seen by the jury as commensurate with the wrong inflicted by the provoking party.

Some would reject a proportionality requirement in provocation doctrine on the ground that once a person has been provoked into a heat of passion, he cannot control the mode or degree of force he uses to retaliate against his provoker. This criticism might be persuasive if the presence of passion completely obliterated the ability to control one's actions. The law, however, assumes that there are degrees of loss of self-control. If the provoked killer completely lacked the capacity to control his acts, then it would not be just to punish him at all. But we do punish provoked killers, albeit less severely than murderers. The treatment of provocation as only a partial defense reflects the assumption that the provoked killer's loss of self-control is not complete.

Act reasonableness does not mean the defendant's response must be strictly proportionate to the alleged provocation. Proportionality is merely suggested as a tool to help jurors think about whether the defendant's acts should be deemed reasonable.

II. SELF-DEFENSE

A similar distinction between emotion reasonableness and act reasonableness exists in the self-defense arena. Even though act reasonableness is implied in

---

4. *Id.* at 51.

self-defense doctrine's proportionality requirement, jury instructions on self-defense tend to focus only on emotion (or belief) reasonableness. Jurors are instructed to find that the defendant reasonably *believed* (or reasonably feared) deadly force was necessary to counter an imminent threat of death or grievous bodily injury. Jurors are not instructed to separately find that the defendant's *act* of shooting or stabbing or beating the victim was reasonable.

This focus on reasonable beliefs reflects the presumption that a defendant who reasonably fears imminent death or grievous bodily harm acts reasonably when he resorts to deadly force. In most cases, a correlation between reasonable fears and reasonable acts will exist. However, just because someone has a reasonable belief that another poses an imminent threat of death or serious bodily injury does not *necessarily* mean a particular action leading to death is reasonable.

For example, in *State v. Dill*,[5] two men in the parking lot of a bar a little before midnight were having trouble getting their truck to start because of a low battery. One of the men, Terry Greenwood, walked over to another car in the lot and asked the three occupants whether they could give him a jump. One of the passengers in that car offered to give Greenwood a jump for $5. Offended that the men would not help him for free, Greenwood began to argue loudly with the passenger and then walked toward the driver's side of the car. Defendant Dill was sitting in the driver's seat with the window down. Suddenly, Dill saw Greenwood lunge toward the open car window with a knife. Dill responded by reaching for a loaded gun from between the seats of the car. He opened the car door and shot Greenwood in the head. Greenwood died a short time later.

Dill was charged with Greenwood's murder. At trial, Dill argued he shot Greenwood in self-defense. Like most self-defense statutes, Louisiana's statute focused exclusively on the reasonableness of the defendant's beliefs, providing that a homicide is justifiable "[w]hen committed in self-defense by one who *reasonably believes* that he is in imminent danger of losing his life or receiving great bodily harm and that the killing is necessary to save himself from that danger. . . ."[6] Rejecting Dill's claim of self-defense, the jury found Dill guilty of manslaughter.

In affirming Dill's conviction, the Louisiana Court of Appeals found that even though Dill's *belief* in the need to act in self-defense was reasonable, his *act* of shooting Greenwood was not. The court explains why Dill's fear was reasonable in the following passage:

> There is no question that the two men were engaged in a heated argument at the time of the shooting. The victim approached the car during the encounter to continue the altercation. From the relative sizes of the two men it appears that Dill (5′4, 145 lbs.) would have received the worst end in a fight, even if the

---

5. *State v. Dill*, 461 So. 2d 1130 (La. App. 1984).
6. *Id.* at 1133 (emphasis added).

victim (6'o, 200 lbs.) had been unarmed. *Accordingly, [Dill's] apprehension of receiving great bodily harm could be deemed reasonable.*[7]

Even though Dill's *fear* of bodily harm was reasonable, the appellate court affirmed Dill's conviction because Dill's *act* of shooting Greenwood in the head at close range was not reasonable. In drawing this conclusion, the court pointed to several less fatal alternatives Dill might have employed to avoid the threatened harm.

> In the present case, it would appear that the trier of fact could readily conclude that the defendant possessed the ability to retreat or withdraw from the impending conflict. He was in an automobile. It was possible to have driven off or at the very least, rolled up the window to prevent any attack by the victim . . . it was likewise evident that deadly force was not mandated by the situation. By the defendant's own admission he issued no warning to the victim. Nor, apparently when firing at a close range did he aim for a less vital area than the head.[8]

State v. Garrison likewise illustrates the difference between reasonable fear of great bodily harm and reasonable action in self-defense.[9] Jessie Garrison went to visit his sister at her apartment. Jeremiah Sharp, his sister's former boyfriend, showed up drunk and belligerent and began arguing with Garrison's sister. Garrison intervened, and his sister left the room. During the argument, Sharp reached for a pistol in his waistband. Because of Sharp's intoxicated state, Garrison was able to remove the pistol from Sharp's waistband. Sharp then grabbed a steak knife and advanced toward Garrison with the knife raised high. Garrison backed up and, using the pistol he'd just retrieved from Sharp, fired at Sharp's left ankle. Garrison then fired one more shot, which killed Sharp.

Garrison was charged with manslaughter in the first degree with a firearm. At trial, Garrison argued that he acted in self-defense. The trial court could have found that Garrison's *fear* of grievous bodily harm was reasonable since Sharp was advancing toward Garrison with a knife. Nonetheless, the court rejected Garrison's self-defense argument on the ground that Garrison's *act* of shooting Sharp was unreasonable. According to the trial court, Garrison's act of shooting was unreasonable because less drastic alternatives were available to avoid the threatened harm. Garrison could have retreated or he could have again disarmed Sharp, especially after Sharp was shot in the left ankle.

A person who honestly and reasonably *fears* imminent death or great bodily harm does not necessarily *act* reasonably if he uses deadly force in self-defense. The type and degree of force used by the defendant to ward off the threat may or

---

7. *Id.* at 1137 (emphasis added).

8. *Id.* at 1138.

9. *State v. Garrison*, 525 A.2d 498 (Conn. 1987).

may not be reasonable depending upon the gravity of the threatened harm and whether less deadly alternatives were available to deal with the threatened harm. Recognizing the distinction between reasonable beliefs and reasonable acts would go a long way toward ensuring that outcomes in self-defense cases reflect appropriate judgments about the use of deadly force.

III. CONCLUSION

With respect to self-defense, what I propose is not a radical reform of current doctrine. Self-defense doctrine already includes a reasonable act requirement. The defendant's response to the aggressor's threat must be reasonably necessary to avert that threat, and it must be proportionate to that threat. Implicit in both the necessity and proportionality requirements is the notion that the defendant's acts must be reasonable in light of the threat. The problem is that most model jury instructions on self-defense fail to tell jurors that they should scrutinize the reasonableness of the defendant's actions. My proposal would simply make explicit that which is implicit in current self-defense doctrine.

With respect to provocation, only a few jurisdictions currently require jurors to consider the reasonableness of the defendant's acts. Therefore, unlike self-defense doctrine, which already includes a reasonable act requirement, requiring act reasonableness in provocation doctrine would constitute a departure from current practice in most jurisdictions. This departure is well worthwhile. Requiring act reasonableness in the form of relative proportionality serves to remind jurors that one who takes a human life and claims he was reasonably provoked should expect some scrutiny of his or her claim of reasonableness.

COMMENTS

MAKING WAVES: RADICALIZING ACT REASONABLENESS

SUSAN D. ROZELLE*

Cynthia Lee puts forward a truly modest proposal: Remind jurors to consider the reasonableness of defendants' actions, in addition to the reasonableness of their emotions, in self-defense and provocation contexts. As she points out, this marks only the slightest change in self-defense doctrine, which already contains an

---

* Associate Professor of Law, Capital University Law School. This comment is based on Susan D. Rozelle, *Controlling Passion: Adultery and the Provocation Defense*, 37 RUTGERS L.J. 197 (2005).

act-reasonableness requirement in the form of proportionality and necessity: her proposal would simply make explicit the task jurors are already asked to undertake. And although provocation doctrine generally contains no such act-reasonableness, there too her proposal is a modest one. She suggests only that the provoked actor's behavior be "proportionate"—and, she hastens to add, not even strictly so. "Proportionality is merely suggested as a tool to help jurors think about whether the defendant's acts should be deemed reasonable."[1]

If anything, Lee's proposal is too modest. In response to the objection that her proposal would limit provocation to situations in which defendants faced physical violence or threats thereof, she insists that proportionality should not be so strictly construed. Fair enough, but I would urge Lee to tell us how flexible her proportionality requirement can be. Much of the criticism of the provocation defense has centered on the potential for, and occasional reality of, unjust results in cases in which the defense is raised. When sentences are reduced because homicide victims danced with someone else at a party, announced they were leaving the relationship, or invited a homosexual flirtation, something is wrong. Better to propose a change more likely to, well, change things.

I agree with Lee that the proper starting place is our focus on emotion-reasonableness to the exclusion of act-reasonableness. I would urge her to make waves in the existing doctrine, however, and tell us more precisely what act-reasonableness means. Lee has suggested elsewhere that jurors be instructed to mentally "switch" sex, race, sexual orientations, and so forth, in order to examine whether any unconscious biases might be driving their sense of reasonableness in the case before them.[2] I wish that were enough, but I can hear the indignant replies of jurors so instructed all the way from here: "That's different!" If the male defendant had been a woman, if the Black defendant had been White, well, these jurors insist, naturally they would have felt differently about the reasonableness of the action in question. That would have been a completely different situation. Bias is bias—by its nature, impervious to reason.

I submit that an alternative approach stands a better chance. Rather than asking jurors whether they believe the act was sufficiently reasonable to justify mitigation, ask when the law already sanctions the use of nondeadly force. If the law would permit some less-than-deadly amount of force to be used in response to the provoking event, then it makes sense to punish the use of deadly force in response to that same event at a discount (in other words, mitigating murder to manslaughter, just as the provocation defense does). Punishment for murder under those circumstances would be excessive, because some of the force used was legally sanctioned. Rather than punish for the full amount of force used, we

---

1. Lee core text at 429.

2. Cynthia Lee, MURDER AND THE REASONABLE MAN: PASSION AND FEAR IN THE CRIMINAL COURTROOM 277 (2003).

punish for the amount used less the amount that would have been permitted: manslaughter, rather than murder.

This suggestion puts real boundaries on the definition of act-reasonableness in the provocation context. Self-defense requires more than proportionality; it also requires necessity. If an actor can defend against deadly force with non-deadly force, he is required to do so. This additional limitation restricts proportionality in the self-defense context, resulting in real guidance for the juror trying to decide whether the use of force in a given case was reasonable. Similarly, provocation requires more than proportionality. Adding the requirement that some lesser amount of force would have been permitted would provide jurors with real guidance in trying to decide if provoked defendants' actions, not just their emotions, were in any part reasonable.

Having redirected our attention to the distinction between act-reasonableness and emotion-reasonableness, Lee insists her proposal barely leaves a ripple in the legal-theory waters. With reasonableness defined as some general sense of proportionality between the provocation and the defendant's action, she is right. Sometimes, though, it is better to make waves.

IS AN ACT REASONABLENESS INQUIRY NECESSARY?

CARISSA BYRNE HESSICK*

Cynthia Lee frames her distinction between act reasonableness and emotion reasonableness as a proposal for proportionality. But the act/emotion distinction also reflects Lee's dissatisfaction with the decision-makers who approve as "reasonable" reactions that are clearly irrational and unreasonable. These reactions highlight the racist, sexist, and heteronormative biases of modern American society: fearful White citizens kill young African-American men, husbands and boyfriends kill their female partners out of jealousy, and straight men kill gay men who make sexual advances. The defendants in these cases successfully plead provocation or self-defense, despite having committed quite troubling crimes.

The judges and juries who accept self-defense and provocation claims in these cases are simply giving the wrong answers to questions of reasonableness. Did Bernhard Goetz have a *reasonable* belief that he was in imminent danger of losing his life when four young African-American men asked him for five dollars? Was Hipolito Martinez *reasonably* provoked into a heat of passion when he saw his former girlfriend dancing with another man? Lee discusses these cases

* Associate Professor of Law, Sandra Day O'Connor College of Law, Arizona State University.

because it seems as though the answers should be "no," and she proposes the act/emotion distinction as a way to elicit that answer from jurors.

Lee acknowledges that the self-defense doctrine already includes a reasonable act requirement. Self-defense is available only to those defendants who can show that their actions were *necessary* to save themselves from a threat of death or great bodily harm. If an action is necessary, it is doubtlessly also reasonable. What Lee's proposal really amounts to in this context is giving jurors a second bite at the reasonableness apple—essentially asking them "are you *sure* that this behavior was reasonable?"

Although Lee's act/emotion distinction in the self-defense context seems more an effort to remind jurors of the requirements of self-defense, the distinction in the provocation context could alter the legal landscape. In some jurisdictions, including those influenced by the Model Penal Code, legislators and judges have passed the burden of determining the adequacy of an alleged provocation to jurors. Jurors are given broad discretion to determine whether the circumstances in a particular case would have provoked a reasonable person to a heat of passion. Because jurors are given little legal guidance, their views of reasonableness tend to reflect majority norms and biases, and thus their verdicts are sometimes troubling.

Although Lee's focus on the reasonableness of a defendant's actions may lead to different outcomes in these provocation cases, we might be able to obtain more palatable jury verdicts without shifting our focus from emotions to acts. In some of the more troubling modern provocation cases, jurors seem to treat emotion as binary—i.e., was the defendant angry or not? There are, however, varying degrees of emotion: I get angry when another car cuts me off in traffic, but I would be far angrier if I saw my neighbor intentionally kill my cat. In the first instance, a reasonable person would be somewhat angry with the other driver, but in the second situation we would expect the reasonable person's anger to be significantly greater and more intense. By asking jurors to determine whether the *intensity* of a defendant's emotion was reasonable, rather than whether the defendant's actions were reasonable, we might receive more palatable juror verdicts without facing the problems that the other commentators have noted (e.g., commensurability and eliding the justification/excuse distinction).

When a matter is committed to the jury's discretion, as is the case with questions involving reasonableness, it is difficult to ensure that jurors will make normatively palatable choices. And even when we can alert jurors to their own prejudice about race, gender, and sexuality, other entrenched beliefs are likely to remain. For example, the widespread fear of strangers is likely to affect juror deliberations in self-defense cases, and the traditional views about violence as a semi-legitimate method for settling personal disputes is likely to affect provocation decisions. Those of us who find these dominant views troubling are likely to be continually dissatisfied with the jury verdicts in such cases.

DIFFERENTIATING COGNITIVE AND VOLITIONAL ASPECTS OF EMOTION IN SELF-DEFENSE AND PROVOCATION

TERRY A. MARONEY*

Cynthia Lee sees a hidden consistency underlying self-defense and provocation doctrine: both involve assessments of *act* reasonableness and *emotion* reasonableness. Although dividing the objects of "reasonableness" determinations in this way has much value, the concept of emotion reasonableness should be divided still further.

Self-defense doctrine is primarily concerned with the cognitive aspects of emotion—that is, with underlying beliefs—while provocation doctrine additionally is concerned with its volitional aspects—that is, with the behavioral aspects of emotion. The emotion-reasonableness inquiry is thus more limited for self-defense and more expansive for provocation. The more expansive concept applicable to provocation conceptually includes act reasonableness. Although Lee urges a separate act-reasonableness inquiry, this finer-grained understanding of the volitional aspect of emotion reasonableness provides a sounder basis for the rough "proportionality" she desires in provocation cases.

Lee elides the distinction between belief and emotion in the context of self-defense. Lee says that jurors must assess whether "the defendant reasonably *believed* (or reasonably feared) deadly force."[1] This is incorrect. Self-defense doctrine is primarily concerned with the actor's beliefs, not the emotions they produce. So long as one's belief that her life is imminently threatened is sincere and reasonable, she is entitled to use deadly force in self-defense, whatever her emotional state at the time she exercised that force. But Lee is, of course, correct to point to a strong correlation between fear and an actor's belief that she is facing imminent deadly force. Richard Lazarus, in his highly influential theory of "core relational themes," proposed that a cognitive assessment that one is facing "immediate, concrete, and overwhelming physical danger" will necessarily spur fear.[2] Although other emotions—surprise, anger—also may be experienced, fear is good evidence of the sincerity of the relevant belief, which can then be judged reasonable or not. Thus, the emotion-reasonableness inquiry in self-defense relies on a normative assessment of the cognitive aspect of emotion.

---

* Assistant Professor of Law, Vanderbilt University Law School.

1. Lee core text at 430.

2. Richard S. Lazarus, *Universal Antecedents of the Emotions, in* THE NATURE OF EMOTION: FUNDAMENTAL QUESTIONS 163, 164 and tbl.1 (Paul Ekman and Richard J. Davidson eds., 1994).

An actor's emotional experience resulting from that belief is significant only insofar as it constitutes evidence of the belief's sincerity.

In contrast, the emotion-reasonableness inquiry in provocation cases implicates both the cognitive and the volitional aspects of emotion. Provocation doctrine, like self-defense doctrine, cares whether the actor's beliefs—*my wife is cheating, that man raped my child*—are sincerely held, and whether they are reasonable—*when one's wife has cheated or one's child has been raped, it is appropriate to be extremely hurt and angry*. But it also cares about the influence of emotion on behavior. Intense emotion can be experienced as an overpowering, even externally driven force; it may act as an attention funnel, limiting the inputs to which one attends and magnifying their importance; and it biases a person's physical response toward typical actions, such as fleeing or striking out.

A juror in a provocation case will assess these aspects of emotion as well, asking whether a sane, more-or-less ordinary person confronting the particular indignity the defendant confronted would feel at the mercy of her emotions, lose perspective, and perceive a significant loss of control over her actions. If so, not only is the underlying belief—the cognitive aspect—reasonable, the influence of the resulting emotion on the actor's behavior—the volitional aspect—is understandable. But the law still punishes an actor's failure to rise above these challenges and exercise appropriate emotional regulation and behavioral control. Thus, the law of provocation—unlike self-defense—requires jurors to assess not only the reasonableness of the beliefs giving rise to emotion, but also the understandability of the actor's failure to control the influence of emotion on her actions.

This dissection of the emotion-reasonableness inquiry is better suited to provocation than is a separate act-reasonableness one. As Lee acknowledges, the provocation defense presupposes that the killing was unreasonable. But she suggests that it might still be assessed against a metric related to reasonableness—being "roughly proportionate" to the precipitating affront. Proportional retaliation sits comfortably within self-defense but has an apples-to-oranges feel in provocation, which presumes that the killing was disproportionate. In contrast, a focus on the cognitive inputs to, and volitional impacts of, emotion fits comfortably within the doctrine's historical focus on self-control and at the same time contains tools for evaluating whether we can understand, if not condone, the defendant's actions. This focus delivers the rough proportionality Lee seeks. Rather than import a separate act-reasonableness inquiry into provocation, we should broaden the emotion-reasonableness one.

NORMS, PROPORTIONALITY, PROVOCATION, AND IMPERFECT SELF-DEFENSE

CAROLINE FORELL*

Cynthia Lee proposes that provocation and self-defense jury instructions, and the law they reflect, should explicitly require "act reasonableness" as well as "emotion reasonableness." According to Lee, most states' provocation instructions only refer to emotion reasonableness—that it was reasonable for the defendant to suffer the emotional outrage or passion that led him to kill; most states' self-defense instructions require proportionality but fail to sufficiently emphasize that this means act reasonableness. Lee correctly identifies a common problem with provocation and self-defense: both put too much emphasis on emotions.

When the partial defense of provocation is being considered, the jury should be instructed to assess the act as well as the emotion. As Lee suggests, "if the provoking incident would have provoked an ordinary person to violence," but not deadly violence, then manslaughter is the correct outcome.

However, the problem provocation presents is not limited to how a jury should be instructed to assess the act of killing. It is also that provocation simply covers too much ground. In most jurisdictions, provocation appears to cover both rage and fear of serious physical harm. Yet, when critiquing current provocation doctrine Lee, like most commentators, only refers to provocation examples involving jealous rage, outrage, or revulsion. Lee gives the examples of finding one's spouse in bed with another and discovering that someone has kidnapped and tortured one's family.

In fact, the *Dill* and *Garrison* cases,[1] the examples Lee gives where complete self-defense is not made out despite proof of emotion reasonableness, are also examples of provocation or some other partial defense even though the term "provocation" goes unmentioned in describing them. In both cases the reasonable emotion was fear of serious bodily harm; violence was a proportionate response; deadly violence was unnecessary and therefore unreasonable; and thus the appropriate crime of conviction was manslaughter. Most likely, provocation isn't even discussed in such cases because, unlike jealous rage, allowing a partial defense for killing out of reasonable fear of bodily injury is clearly acceptable.

To make provocation a more coherent defense it should be limited to emotions other than fear of serious physical injury or death. My research suggests that if it is so limited, juries will usually apply prevailing social norms to reject

---

* Clayton R. Hess Professor of Law, University of Oregon School of Law.

1. *State v. Dill*, 461 So. 2d 1130 (La. App. 1984); *State v. Garrison*, 525 A.2d 498 (Conn. 1987).

the defense when the killing is based on jealous rage.[2] Juries will often conclude that even if the emotion of jealous rage is understandable, a violent response is not. As a result, successful provocation claims based on jealous rage or revulsion (such as gay panic cases) will over time likely simply disappear, leaving provocation for much rarer cases, such as Lee's kidnap and torture example[3] in which the emotion of rage and a nondeadly violent reaction would clearly satisfy social norms.

For situations in which a defendant experienced a reasonable fear of serious bodily injury and violence was therefore understandable, but killing was an unnecessary and therefore unreasonable act, the defense of imperfect self-defense should be more widely adopted as a partial defense separate from "heat of passion"/provocation. This defense would cover cases like *Dill* and *Garrison*, as well as cases in which battered women kill out of fear and despair but are unable to prove perfect self-defense. A number of Australian jurisdictions are to good effect drawing this distinction between the emotions of rage (on the one hand) and fear of serious bodily harm (on the other) through the analogous defense of excessive self-defense or the crime of "defensive homicide."

Regarding Lee's specific recommendations, her proposal that juries be instructed to assess the act as well as the emotion, would make the defense of provocation, and imperfect self-defense if it is adopted, more just. But requiring that the jury be instructed to assess the acts involved in these cases in terms of *reasonableness* would go too far. Instead, incorporating the term "proportionality" into the instruction would allow the jury to assess the act without being put in the untenable position of determining whether it was reasonable. By definition, the act was unreasonable if either provocation or imperfect self-defense is the correct defense. In order to help a jury understand what proportionality means in this context, it might also be helpful, as Lee suggests, to instruct its members that the partial defense is only available if the defendant's resort to deadly violence was an unreasonable response and resort to nondeadly violence would have been a reasonable response.

Finally, as Lee notes, self-defense already incorporates act reasonableness through its requirement of proportionality. Adding an explicit instruction mandating act reasonableness is a sensible tweak. However, it does not address the more pressing problem of bias in current norms that, as Lee has powerfully demonstrated,[4] still infects self-defense, especially when men of color are killed or battered women kill. To remedy this problem, juries should be expressly

2. Caroline Forell, *Gender Equality, Social Values and Provocation Law in Australia, Canada, and the United States*, 14 Am. U. J. Gender, Soc. Pol'y & L. 27, 59–61 (2006).

3. Lee core text at 429.

4. *See* Cynthia Lee, Murder and the Reasonable Man: Passion and Fear in the Criminal Courtroom 138–60 (2003).

instructed that they must apply outsider norms in self-defense cases where dominant norms are unjust.

DIFFERENT WAYS TO MANIFEST REASONABLENESS

JEREMY HORDER*

Cynthia Lee develops a clear analysis of an issue that troubles theorists of defenses in criminal law. The issue can be presented in different ways. Let me try to express it using Lee's terminology of "act reasonableness" and "emotion reasonableness":

> The infliction of (lethal) harm must be reasonable, in the circumstances, before it can be excused or a fortiori justified. The reasonableness of inflicting harm may be judged against two sets of criteria. The infliction may be "act reasonable" if it is a right or permissible thing to do. Alternatively, it may be "emotion reasonable," in that it proceeds from the experience of emotions—such as fear—that understandably led to violence.

Modern discussion of this issue goes back a long way.[1] Earlier thinkers took it that so-called "act reasonableness" was an action-guiding notion. More accurately, it is something to do with normative (justificatory) rules, tied to what is right or permissible (or wrong or impermissible). In the provocation context, as J.L. Austin might have put it, act reasonableness carries the connotation that the provoked person is or would be justified in retaliating as he or she did. By contrast, he would have regarded "emotion reasonableness" as offering no guidance on appropriate actions, because it is a kind of ascriptive (blaming) rule.

In Lee's analysis, this relatively sharp distinction becomes lost, because she does not use the act/emotion reasonableness difference to track the distinction between justification and excuse. In relation to provocation, she argues that a defendant's acts may be normatively reasonable if the defendant's response bears a reasonable relationship to the provoking act or incident.[2] This was, perhaps, a defensible view centuries ago when provocation was linked to physical attacks on the person or property, where some physical force might be justified to repel the aggressor. However, now that provocation theoretically covers insults alone, this view is less defensible. Even if V needles D beyond endurance by making racist remarks day after day, until D finally explodes with violence and

---

* Law Commissioner for England and Wales; Professor of Criminal Law and Porjes Trust Fellow, Worcester College, Oxford University.

1. J.L. Austin, *A Plea for Excuses*, in PHILOSOPHICAL PAPERS 375 (3d ed. 1990). *See also* Eric D'Arcy, HUMAN ACTS (1963).

2. *See* Lee core text at 429.

kills V, the cumulative nature of the provocation does nothing to *justify* killing V (act-reasonableness). It only goes to show that D was (emotionally) fully justified in "losing self-control," or "blowing his top," etc.: what I have called engaging in "demonstrative" anger.[3]

Turning to Lee's analysis of self-defense, let it be granted that an action in self-defense is "act reasonable" if, other things being equal, it is reasonably proportionate to the perceived threat.[4] Nonetheless, one is dealing with a different phenomenon from that encountered in provocation cases. An analysis of a reaction to a threat, in terms of (lack of) proportionality in the response, is predominantly normative ("Did D act as he or she was permitted, normatively, to do, or go beyond that limit and if so, how far?"). By contrast, an analysis of a reaction to provocation is predominantly ascriptive ("Given the degree of provocation, how much to blame was D in exploding into lethal violence?"). Such an analysis presupposes that D has no normative leg to stand on (his or her conduct was unjustified, period), and the focus is hence on the degree of blame for engaging in that unjustified action.

A final point. Should self-defence be analyzed, at a theoretical as opposed to an "ordinary case" level, as turning in part on an element of "emotion reasonableness," even if they are mostly about "act reasonableness?" I believe that, if you are going to use this kind of approach, it would be more accurate to speak of "cognitive reasonableness"—reasonableness of *belief*—rather than "emotion reasonableness," as what self-defense cases in part turn on, at a theoretical level. Of course, in practice self-defensive action will involve fear motivating the defensive action; but that does not make fear central to the theory, as opposed to the reality, of self-defensive action.

---

3. Jeremy Horder, PROVOCATION AND RESPONSIBILITY 194–97 (1992).
4. *See* Lee core text at 432.

REQUIRING REASONABLE BELIEFS ABOUT SELF-DEFENSE ENSURES THAT ACTS CONFORMING TO THOSE BELIEFS ARE REASONABLE

KENNETH W. SIMONS*

Cynthia Lee makes a valuable basic point: Legal doctrine and jury instructions should be more explicit in requiring that the defendant's *acts*, and not merely his

---

* Professor of Law, The Honorable Frank R. Kenison Distinguished Scholar in Law, Boston University School of Law. This analysis is largely drawn from Kenneth W. Simons, *Self-defense: Reasonable Beliefs or Reasonable Self-Control?*, 11 NEW CRIM. L. REV. 51 (2008).

emotions and beliefs, satisfy legal standards of self-defense. It is not enough that the actor reacts while in a state of fear, believing that he is about to be attacked. He must also *act* reasonably: He may use only proportional force in response and must refrain from inflicting force when safer alternatives exist.

However, although this emphasis on the legal requirement that acts as well as beliefs (or emotions) be "reasonable" is useful, it can also be misleading. First, the proportionality and necessity requirements associated with self-defense are typically articulated, not in the form of a general standard (that the force must be "reasonably" proportionate or "reasonably" necessary), but instead in the form of a rule—for example, the defendant may only use deadly force if faced with deadly force, rape, or kidnapping; or may only use force if the threat is imminent (on one version) or immediately necessary (on another); or must retreat in circumstances X but not Y (or alternatively, is never required to retreat).

Second, the actual cases that Lee cites as proof of a need for an independent reasonable *act* requirement seem instead to illustrate that the law should more explicitly require honest and reasonable *beliefs*—specifically, beliefs about necessity and proportionality and not merely beliefs about the existence of a threat. Lee aptly criticizes the courts' overemphasis on honest and reasonable beliefs that one is being threatened, and their neglect of the question whether the actor should have used lesser (or no) force in response. But that neglected question can and should be posed by requiring the actor to honestly and reasonably believe *both*:

(a) that the degree of force he is using in response is not disproportionate (e.g., he must reasonably believe that he will only inflict nondeadly harm in response to a threat that the jurisdiction would consider nondeadly); *and*

(b) that the response is necessary to protect himself (e.g., he must reasonably believe that the threat is imminent and that no effective nonviolent alternatives are available).[1]

Thus, a reasonable act requirement adds little to the traditional requirement that the actor honestly and reasonably believe a specified set of facts that legally suffice to provide a defense. Indeed, adding an independent act requirement is in tension with the well-accepted doctrine that one can make a reasonable mistake about a required element of self-defense yet obtain a full defense.

Still, I do agree that an act requirement of a *modest* sort is implicit within self-defense tests—namely, the requirement that the actor's forceful response be *in conformity* with his honest and reasonable beliefs. Suppose I honestly and reasonably believe that I am threatened with nondeadly force, that my forceful response is necessary, and that it will cause only nondeadly harm. Now suppose that my use of force causes the death of the aggressor. How could this happen?

---

1. In the *Dill* case upon which Lee relies, the court quotes another decision holding that defendant must *reasonably believe* that deadly force was necessary. The court never explicitly distinguishes actual necessity from reasonable belief in necessity.

First, perhaps I tried to use nondeadly force but accidentally caused more harm than I reasonably expected. This is a case of reasonable mistake; I did act in conformity with my beliefs, so I should receive a full defense. Second, perhaps I got carried away and just chose to kill the aggressor. In this case, of course, although my initial beliefs were honest and reasonable, my final decision to kill was not in conformity with those beliefs, so they cannot provide a defense.

This last, implicit act requirement is indeed scanted in self-defense doctrine. This requirement is a little-noticed instance of criminal law's broader requirement that mental states and acts "concur." "Purposely" killing another is murder, but only if the purpose concurs with the homicidal act. "Knowingly" killing another is also murder, but only if the knowledge coincides with the homicidal act, not if the actor recognizes the act's lethal potential only after the death occurs. And satisfying the "honest and reasonable belief" requirements of criminal law defenses should only provide a defense if the actor incorporates these beliefs into his conduct.

A final comment. Lee appears to endorse a similar "reasonable act" requirement for both self-defense and provocation. But the meaning of reasonableness in the provocation context is quite different: Here, it does not refer to justifiable conduct, but to either partially justifiable or (more plausibly) partially excusable conduct. What she means to emphasize, I believe, is not that the killing must be reasonable or commensurate to the provocation, but that it must not be *greatly* or *extremely disproportionate*. In almost all instances when mitigation is warranted, the deadly response is at least *somewhat* disproportionate to the provocation. By contrast, if the killing is roughly proportionate, often the actor should be acquitted.

REPLY

CYNTHIA LEE

Susan Rozelle argues that my proposal is too modest, and that it is unlikely to change results in troublesome provocation cases. She writes, "Lee insists her proposal barely leaves a ripple in the legal theory waters."[1] I do not so insist. While my proposal in the self-defense context is not a radical reform of current doctrine, requiring act reasonableness in the provocation context would constitute a major departure from current practice in most jurisdictions and would likely make more than a ripple of difference in outcomes. For example, say a defendant charged with murdering a gay man claims he was provoked into a heat of passion because the victim made an unwanted non-violent homosexual advance. If jurors are asked to focus simply on the question whether it was reasonable for the defendant to become upset, offended, even outraged, they are

---

1. Rozelle comment at 434.

likely to say yes if they think the average heterosexual man would be upset and offended by a homosexual advance. If, however, jurors have to consider the additional question of whether the defendant's conduct was reasonable—whether killing was a reasonably proportionate response to the gay man's non-violent homosexual advance (and if they are asked to engage in a role reversal exercise of the type outlined in my book)—they are likely to come to a different conclusion.

Rozelle proposes that instead of asking whether the defendant acted reasonably, jurors should ask whether the law would sanction the use of non-deadly force in response to the provoking event. If so, then Rozelle would allow the manslaughter mitigation. Rozelle does not provide any examples of when the law would permit an individual to use non-deadly force in response to a provoking incident. This is probably because such examples would be difficult to find. Most legislators do not want to encourage citizens to use force of any kind (deadly or non-deadly) against other citizens, so they are unlikely to pass legislation saying, for example, that it is permissible to hit someone who has spit on your car. Rozelle's proposal is thus unlikely to provide jurors with any more concrete guidance than that provided by my proposal or current doctrine.

Rozelle correctly notes that I have elsewhere suggested that jurors be instructed to engage in a simple mental exercise in which they would switch the race, gender, or sexual orientation of the defendant and victim in order to make salient any unconscious bias that might be driving their legal decision-making.[2] Rozelle argues that my switching proposal does not go far enough because jurors infected with unconscious bias are not likely to rise above that bias even if that bias is made salient to them. Recent social science on race and implicit bias, however, suggests that making racial bias salient can and does help reduce what would otherwise be automatic stereotype-congruent responses. In several experiments, social scientists have documented the positive effects of making bias salient. In cases where such bias was made salient, subjects were less likely to engage in biased behavior.[3] In contrast to Rozelle, who thinks my proposal does not go far enough, Carissa Hessick argues that my proposed act-emotion distinction in the provocation context "could alter the legal landscape."[4] Hessick suggests that we needn't go so far. Rather than focusing on the reasonableness of the defendant's *actions*, Hessick would ask jurors "whether the *intensity* of a defendant's emotion was reasonable."[5] The problem with Hessick's proposal is that it may end up partially excusing defendants who perhaps shouldn't be excused. Using Hessick's example, I might be very upset if my neighbor intentionally kills my cat (and my upset might be justified), but it would not be

---

2. Cynthia Lee, MURDER AND THE REASONABLE MAN: PASSION AND FEAR IN THE CRIMINAL COURTROOM 252–53 (2003)

3. *See* Cynthia Lee, *The Gay Panic Defense*, 42 U.C. DAVIS L. REV. 471 (2008).

4. Hessick comment at 435.

5. *Id.*

reasonable for me to retaliate by killing my neighbor. Focusing on the reason-ableness of the intensity of my emotions rather than on the reasonableness of my conduct allows me to receive the manslaughter mitigation, which may not be the right result in such a case.

Terry Maroney sees value in my drawing a distinction between act reason-ableness and emotion reasonableness, but proposes a more expansive under-standing of the concept of emotion reasonableness in provocation doctrine. Specifically, Maroney argues for recognition of both the cognitive and volitional aspects of the provoked killer's emotional response. Under Maroney's proposal, a defendant would be entitled to the provocation mitigation if the cognitive aspects of her emotion (the beliefs motivating her passion) were both sincere and reasonable *and* the defendant lacked volitional control over her emotions. I agree with Maroney's assessment that provocation law ought to care about both the cognitive or belief-driven aspects of emotion and the volitional aspects of that emotion. Jurors, however, may find such an analysis too complex.

Maroney also suggests that I elide the distinction between belief and emotion in the context of self-defense. As support for this, Maroney writes "Lee says that jurors must assess whether 'the defendant reasonably *believed* (or reasonably feared) deadly force,'"[6] and then states, "This is incorrect."[7] The quoted material is conveniently taken out of context. What I said was:

> Even though act reasonableness is implied in self-defense doctrine's propor-tionality requirement, jury instructions on self-defense tend to focus only on emotion (or belief) reasonableness. Jurors are instructed to find that the defendant reasonably *believed* (or reasonably feared) deadly force was neces-sary to counter an imminent threat of death or grievous bodily injury. Jurors are not instructed to separately find that the defendant's *act* of shooting or stabbing or beating the victim was reasonable.[8]

If the distinction between beliefs and emotions in self-defense doctrine is being conflated, it is being conflated by those who draft model jury instructions on self-defense.

Caroline Forell proposes limiting the provocation defense "to emotions other than fear of serious physical injury or death."[9] While Forell's proposal might work in jurisdictions that have adopted the defense of imperfect self-defense (ISD), limiting the provocation defense in the way that she proposes could work injustice in jurisdictions that have not embraced ISD. For example, the battered woman who kills her sleeping abuser, honestly fearing that he will kill her when he awakens, cannot receive a jury instruction on self-defense in a jurisdiction

---

6. Maroney comment at 436 (quoting Lee core text at 430).

7. *Id.*

8. Lee core text at 429–30.

9. Forell comment at 438.

that strictly construes the imminence requirement.[10] If the jurisdiction does not recognize the partial defense of ISD, and provocation is limited to emotions other than fear of death or serious bodily injury, this defendant is likely to be convicted of murder unless she can claim some kind of mental defect.[11]

Jeremy Horder recognizes that the distinction between act and emotion reasonableness I propose has the support of early thinkers like the British moral philosopher J.L. Austin. Horder contends, however, that early thinkers saw act reasonableness as having "something to do with normative (justificatory) rules" and saw emotion reasonableness "as a kind of ascriptive (blaming) rule."[12] Horder suggests that "this relatively sharp distinction" between act reasonableness as justificatory and emotion reasonableness as ascriptive becomes lost in my analysis of provocation, because "[I do] not use the act/emotion reasonableness difference to track the distinction between justification and excuse."[13]

Horder is correct that my proposal to recognize act reasonableness as separate and distinct from emotion reasonableness does not track the distinction between justification and excuse. This is because I do not think it necessary to characterize act reasonableness in justificatory terms and emotion reasonableness in excuse terms. Under my proposal, act reasonableness in the provocation context would not serve to justify a provoked killer's conduct. It would merely force the fact finder to consider whether the defendant's reaction was reasonably proportionate to the provoking incident. As discussed more fully in *Murder and the Reasonable Man*, current provocation doctrine, while widely characterized as a partial excuse, already contains elements of both justification and excuse.[14] My proposal for recognition of an act-emotion distinction would not change any of this. Nor would my proposal turn provocation into a justification defense, notwithstanding Horder's suggestion to the contrary.[15]

---

10. *See, e.g., State v. Stewart* 763 P.2d 572 (Kan. 1988) (holding that it is not reasonable for an abused women to fear an imminent attack from her sleeping husband).

11. Forell also argues that my proposal "does not address the more pressing problem of bias in current norms that . . . still infects self-defense." Forell comment at 439. As explained in my reply to Rozelle, I also propose a role reversal jury instruction which more directly addresses the problem of bias.

12. Horder comment at 440.

13. *Id.*

14. *See* Lee, *supra* note 2, at 227–29.

15. *See* Horder comment at 440–41 ("Even if V needles D beyond endurance by making racist remarks day after day, until D finally explodes with violence and kills V, the cumulative nature of the provocation does nothing to *justify* killing V (act reasonableness)."). If I were to track the distinction between act reasonableness as justificatory and emotion reasonableness as ascriptive, as Horder suggests would be appropriate, then Horder's suggestion that my proposal would turn provocation into a justification defense might have some persuasive force.

Horder next attacks my suggestion that a defendant's acts may be normatively reasonable "if the defendant's response bears a reasonable relationship to the provoking act or incident,"[16] a notion that finds support in Horder's own work.[17] Horder tries to distinguish my use of proportionality from earlier uses on the ground that proportionality, though perhaps a sensible limitation on the provocation defense centuries ago when provocation was limited to physical attacks, makes less sense now that provocation theoretically covers insults alone.

Although Horder may be correct as a theoretical matter, he is not correct as a matter of existing law. Most modern jurisdictions have retained the early common-law rule that mere words cannot constitute adequate provocation, except perhaps in cases where the words are spoken by a woman to her husband and convey the fact of adultery or are perceived as an insult to his sexual abilities.[18]

Finally, Horder argues that it is more accurate in self-defense cases to speak of cognitive reasonableness—reasonableness of belief—rather than emotion reasonableness. I agree that self-defense at a theoretical level deals with cognitive reasonableness, not emotion reasonableness. However, most model jury instructions on self-defense elide the distinction between beliefs and emotions, utilizing the language of emotion (fear) rather than the language of belief. My proposal simply calls attention to the fact that most model jury instructions focus on the reasonableness of the defendant's emotions or beliefs, not the reasonableness of his acts.

Kenneth Simons and I agree with each other far more than we disagree. Simons argues that the reasonable person test in self-defense law focuses too much on the *cognitive* fault of the actor (the reasonableness of his or her beliefs) and too little on whether the actor exercised reasonable self-control. I agree with Simons on this point. Simons's reformulation of self-defense doctrine to require the actor to honestly and reasonably *believe* that his response is proportionate and necessary, however, provides inadequate attention to whether the actor's *conduct* was reasonable.[19]

---

16. Lee, *supra* note 2, at 268.

17. Jeremy Horder, PROVOCATION AND RESPONSIBILITY 51 (1992).

18. *See* Cynthia Lee and Angela Harris, CRIMINAL LAW: CASES AND MATERIALS 373–83 (2005).

19. Simons is correct that one can make a reasonable mistake about a required element in self-defense and still be fully justified. My proposal does not change this well-established principle. My proposal does not require actual proportionality or necessity; it merely requires reasonable proportionality and necessity.

21. AGAINST CONTROL TESTS FOR CRIMINAL RESPONSIBILITY

STEPHEN J. MORSE*

I. INTRODUCTION

Let's be clear. In commonsense terms, it is true that some people have more difficulty than others controlling their conduct in general or in specific contexts, and "lack of control" has meaning. The rationale for an independent control test for criminal responsibility is that some defendants allegedly do not have rationality defects, and therefore cannot satisfy cognitive tests, but they nonetheless cannot control their conduct and therefore deserve excuse or mitigation on desert and deterrence grounds. The question for the law is whether an independent control test for excuse or mitigation is conceptually sound and practically feasible. This core text suggests that at present there is no need for the law to adopt an independent control test.

II. FALSE STARTS AND DISTRACTIONS

This section addresses four false starts or distractions that bedevil clear thinking about the necessity for a control test: 1) the belief that allegedly uncontrollable behavior is not action; 2) the belief that behavior must be out of control if it is the sign or symptom of a disease; 3) the belief that the metaphysical argument about free will and responsibility has any relevance to the criminal-law problem of whether a control test is necessary; and 4) the belief that causation at any level of causal explanation, including abnormal causation, is per se an excusing condition or the equivalent of compulsion.

Control test cases uniformly involve human action and not mechanism. A control test is an affirmative defense to or a mitigation of prima facie guilt. If the defendant's conduct is a literal mechanism, such as a reflex, or if it is

---

* Ferdinand Wakeman Hubbell Professor of Law and Professor of Psychology and Law in Psychiatry, University of Pennsylvania. This core text is derived from four previous articles: *Culpability and Control*, 142 U. PA. L. REV. 1587 (1994); *Rationality and Responsibility*, 74 S. CAL. L. REV. 251 (2000); *Uncontrollable Urges and Irrational People*, 88 VA. L. REV. 1025 (2002); *Genetics, Addiction and Criminal Responsibility*, 69 L. & CONTEMP. PROBS. 165 (2006).

performed in a state of substantially clouded or divided consciousness, then the defendant does not act at all and there is no need for a control test. Cases in which a control test seem necessary often have the feature that the relevant conduct, such as seeking and using drugs, is allegedly the symptom of a disease, but that does not mean that the defendant is not acting. Seeking and using drugs are quintessentially intentional human actions, and at least potentially subject to the control of reason.

Conduct is not per se out of control simply because it is the symptom of an alleged disorder. Most signs and symptoms of diseases are literally mechanisms and not human action. Once the disease process begins, one cannot stop it simply by intentionally deciding to end it. In contrast, the signs and symptoms for which a control test are allegedly necessary are per se human actions and simply refraining from acting in the objectionable way is sufficient to end the sign of the disease. If actions that are signs and symptoms of a disease are to be excused because they are involuntary, involuntariness or compulsion must be independently demonstrated to avoid begging the question.

Control tests have nothing to do with free will understood as contra-causal freedom or agent origination. All criminal law responsibility doctrines are compatible with the truth of determinism. Control problems must be demonstrated independently of the external, metaphysical debate about free will and responsibility because doctrines of excuse are internal to law. Control and its lack must be understood in the folk-psychological terms upon which all law is based. Moreover, if some behavior is randomly caused or the product of indeterminacy, this would not be a secure foundation for responsibility or nonresponsibility. Even if it were, there is no reason to believe that random or indeterminate causation plays a greater role in supposed control test cases.

Causation of behavior is not per se an excusing condition and it is not the equivalent of compulsion or involuntariness. To believe otherwise is to make the "fundamental psycholegal error." In a causal universe that is massively regular, that satisfies what philosopher Galen Strawson terms the "realism constraint,"[1] all behavior is presumably caused by necessary and sufficient conditions. If causation were per se an excuse or the equivalent of compulsion, then no one could ever be responsible for any behavior. Causation is not the equivalent of compulsion because the nonliteral compulsion that control tests address is normative. It applies only to some defendants. All behavior is caused, but only some behavior is compelled. The external critique of all responsibility practices based on universal causation does not explain or improve understanding of positive law.

Even if the causal process is considered "abnormal," it does not follow that the caused behavior cannot be controlled. For example, the dominant biological

---

1. Galen Strawson, *Consciousness, Free Will, and the Unimportance of Determinism*, 32 INQUIRY 3, 12 (1989).

theory of addiction hypothesizes that persistent use of rewarding substances usurps the brain's normal mechanisms of reward. Even so, lack of control must be proven independently by showing how this usurpation translates into a folk-psychological excusing account.

Lack of control must be explained and understood in the terms of folk psychology. Folk psychology refers to the theory of explaining behavior that treats mental states, such as desires, beliefs, intentions, and reasons, as genuinely causal and that treats people as agents who can potentially be guided by reason. It is the law's implicit theory of action because all legal criteria presuppose folk psychology. Evidence concerning action, disease, or disorder mechanisms, and causation may be relevant to the proof of whether a control problem exists, but the definition of and the criteria for a control problem must be folk psychological.

III. WHAT IS A CONTROL PROBLEM AND HOW DO WE KNOW ONE EXISTS IN INDIVIDUAL CASES?

Proponents of a control test for criminal responsibility believe that it is necessary to do justice when the defendant seems otherwise rational. How can it be either fair or consequentially justifiable to blame and punish a person for behavior he cannot control? Proponents often point to cases in which there is clearly a cognitive problem, however, such as those in which the agent's antisocial desires are inexplicable and seem to serve no purpose other than their own satisfaction, or those in which strong emotions impair the agent's ability to exercise good judgment. Nonetheless, people use locutions like "I can't help myself" to characterize situations in which they subjectively experience (or ascribe to others) an inability to act differently. People genuinely feel that way and in such situations, it is harder to control oneself. If there is no apparent cognitive problem, a control test seems intuitively appealing. Nevertheless, its conceptual basis and criteria must be provided.

An adequate, independent folk-psychological account of loss of control must fulfill at least five criteria. First, it must be a capacity account. Otherwise, simple failure to exercise the capacity for self-control the agent possesses would be sufficient for excuse, which would be a morally and legally indefensible result. Second, the account must be distinguishable from weakness of will, which is considered a moral failure. Drawing this distinction will be difficult because the definition of weakness of will is fraught. Third, loss of control must be a continuum capacity. It is virtually inconceivable that control capacity would be all-or-none. Fourth, the capacity should be applicable in an ordinary environment broadly conceived. An agent's ability to restrain himself if extraordinary restraining influences were present does not entail that he can control himself under ordinary circumstances. Fifth, the criteria must be folk psychological because the law is resolutely folk psychological. To claim that folk psychology is "wrong" or unscientific is an external attack on all current conceptions of law. Such critiques should be addressed directly and should not be smuggled in partially through a control test.

Virtually all proposed loss-of-control theories already meet all or most of these criteria, except perhaps the second and last. Finally, a nonconceptual criterion is that the capacity must be practically subject to reasonably objective application.

A. Conceptual Problems

Let us begin with the phenomenology. Suppose that a person has a powerful desire to do something that is unwise, immoral, or illegal. That is, the agent really, really, really wants to do something wrong. Desires, whether "normal" or "abnormal," may be strong or weak, persistent or sudden. It is of course easier, in the colloquial sense, to behave wisely, morally, and legally if an agent does not have suddenly arising, strong desires. Moreover, failure to satisfy strong desires can cause very unpleasant feelings, such as tension and anxiety. The agent's instrumental practical reason may seem unimpaired when powerful desires arise and virtually all agents who yield to strong and even sudden or surprising desires to behave unwisely, immorally, or illegally fully recognize that yielding is wrong. What does it mean to say that an agent "can't help it" when the agent yields?

Consider the example of addiction. How do we know or why are we justified in believing that the addict's seeking and using is "compulsive"? The most objective means to assess this is by observing the person's behavior. Common sense suggests that an addict is "out of control" when he persists in seeking and using substances although such behavior causes the agent profound physical, interpersonal, financial, and legal problems, and when the person is ambivalent about and in many cases condemns his behavior. Unless the agent affirmatively wants to destroy himself—which might betoken a rationality problem—why doesn't the agent quit if he could? Addicts also often report a buildup of subjective, visceral craving between occasions of use. A "control" problem is plausible in such cases, but, again, what are the folk-psychological processes that explain loss of control?

The plausibility of the commonsense account of control problems among addicts has motivated the biological, psychological, and social sciences to identify the "underlying" literal mechanisms that might causally explain such otherwise puzzling behavior. There are theoretical and scientific problems with all these explanations, however. Nonetheless, some of them are certainly on the right track, and future discoveries will inevitably clarify our understanding of addicts' self-destructive behavior.

The problem of control remains, however, because the science furnishes mechanistic causes, and causation per se, at any level of causation and whether or not it is "normal," is not an excusing condition nor the equivalent of compulsion. Humans clearly have "stop" folk-psychological processes that are

influenced by mechanistic causes. Successful human interaction would otherwise be impossible. Nevertheless, we still need an adequate, independent folk-
psychological account of why the addict or anyone else has trouble controlling
himself.

A common approach is to conceive of loss of control as motivational compulsion, as occurring when a desire has too much motivational force to be resisted
under ordinary circumstances. The analogy is to overwhelming physical force,
but rather than being compelled by external force majeure, the agent is compelled
by his own "overpowering" desires. Some desires are stronger than others, but
desires are not like external physical forces that physically overwhelm the agent's
ability to resist. If this were true, the claim would be no action. The agent who
loses control acts.

There are not "forces" of desire. Physical forces can bypass intentionality and
assent; desires cannot. It is more likely that strong desires redirect rather than
bypass intentionality. Resisting the desire causes the agent so much effort and
discomfort that resisting is not worth the effort, even though it is possible, so the
agent collaborates with the desire. This account also fails to distinguish between
strong desires because all strong desires appear to be sources of loss of control.
Focusing on "abnormal" desires will not solve the problem because "normal"
desires may be equally strong and abnormal desires may be weak. Moreover,
once the desire is considered resistible with effort, how is this case different
from weakness of will? The motivational compulsion account of loss of control
leaves all the important issues unresolved.

Another theory hypothesizes that compulsion arises from a conflict between
first-order desires, what the agent wants to do now, and second-order desires, the
desires that the agent reflectively has about what he should want. Conflict
between first and second order desires may make it more difficult to avoid acting
on one's first-order desires, but this theory has weaknesses and why it is a theory
of compulsion is unclear. The observation that an agent is in conflict does not
mean that the agent cannot control his conduct unless there is an account of why
that conflict produces lack of control.

A promising approach to control difficulty is based on "reasons responsiveness." If an agent cannot be persuaded, actually or hypothetically, to avoid acting
by good reasons not to, or if he cannot bring those reasons to bear, then
the agent probably cannot control himself. The reasons must be ordinary
reasons or the criteria would be too demanding. A gun at the head would constitute an extraordinary reason. If the agent can control himself in such circumstances, it would not follow that the agent could control himself in ordinary
circumstances.

Although this account is subject to objections and difficulty distinguishing
compulsion from weakness of will, it is intuitively appealing because it does not
suffer from the disanalogy to physical force and because it provides a commonsense folk-psychological process for loss of control. Nonetheless, to the extent it

is valid, it is a rationality account. The capacity to grasp and be guided by good reason is the heart of normative rationality.

A final theory for an independent self-control failure is the analogy to the two-party excuse of duress, but we do not excuse in these cases because the agent had a volitional or control problem. The agent's reasoning is intact, and his will operates effectively to save him from the threat. We excuse the agent because he faced a dreadfully hard choice for which he is not responsible, and we could not fairly expect him not to yield.

The agent faced with the threat of frustration of strong internal desires is essentially claiming an "internal duress" excuse. But is the frustration of desire the equivalent of the experience of death, grievous bodily harm, or agonizing pain? The metaphorical involuntariness of duress is a continuum concept. Painful psychological states are unpleasant, but even if the desire and its strength are not the agent's fault, the agent must be threatened with enormous but difficult-to-assess psychological pain plausibly to consider an agent not responsible for serious crime. This theory is more appealing, however, if the agent commits a lesser offense.

Almost all agents predisposed to yield to strong desires to do wrong, especially serious wrongs, would be considered responsible because the threat of psychological pain will seldom be sufficiently great to excuse. And again, there is no control defect. Moreover, even if the agent were not responsible for having the untoward desire, agents with continuing "control problems" know that they will face pain caused by strong desires in the future. Rationally unimpaired agents will be responsible if they fail to take the steps necessary to avoid placing oneself in such a condition. Duress does not obtain if the agent is at fault in placing himself in the threatening situation, a limitation that ought to apply equally in one-party cases.

Proponents of an independent control test have not yet provided a persuasive folk-psychological account independent of a rationality problem. In addition, control tests suffer from the defect that I have termed the "lure of mechanism," the tendency to analogize allegedly out-of-control agents to literal mechanisms. Sophisticated proponents do not do this, but many academic lawyers, practitioners, and mental health experts do. The usual basis is the mistaken belief that if behavior is caused, the agent could not have acted otherwise. Control tests inadvertently fuel this pernicious problem because they mask the difference between the folk-psychological sense of loss of control and the metaphysical question of whether determinism or universal causation undermines all deontological responsibility.

B. Practical Problems

Control tests also raise difficult practical problems. Even the American Psychiatric Association supported the movement to abolish control tests on the ground that it was impossible to evaluate lack of control objectively. Lack of control was recently revived, however, in *Kansas v. Crane*,[2] which required "serious difficulty" controlling oneself as a criterion necessary to justify involuntary quasi-criminal commitment of mentally abnormal sexually violent predators. Justice Breyer provided a typically thin and seemingly commonsense test.

> [W]e did not give to the phrase 'lack of control' a particularly narrow or technical meaning. And we recognize that in cases where lack of control is at issue, 'inability to control behavior' will not be demonstrable with mathematical precision. It is enough to say that there must be proof of serious difficulty in controlling behavior.[3]

It would have been harder for Justice Breyer to do better. There is no consensual scientific definition or measure of lack of control. Nor is there yet an adequate folk-psychological process that has been identified as normatively justifiable for legal purposes.

Justice Breyer's vague and unhelpful "serious difficulty" control criterion was the wrong test. How would a fact finder know if the defendant had serious difficulty controlling himself except on the bases of the defendant's self-report and observations of the defendant's seemingly self-destructive conduct? Justice Scalia's dissent observed that the test would give trial judges "not a clue" about how to charge juries. Justice Scalia speculated that the majority offered no further elaboration because "elaboration . . . which passes the laugh test is impossible."[4] Justice Scalia wondered whether the test was a quantitative measure of loss-of-control capacity or of how frequently the inability to control arises. In the alternative, he questioned whether the standard was "adverbial," a descriptive characterization of the inability to control one's penchant for sexual violence. The adverbs he used as examples were "appreciably," "moderately," "substantially," and "almost totally."[5] Justice Scalia's commonsense criticism of the test was apt. To date, advocates of an independent control test have not demonstrated the ability to identify "can't" versus "won't."

IV. IMPAIRMENT OF RATIONALITY EXPLAINS CONTROL DIFFICULTIES

Cognitive tests provide a distinct folk-psychological mechanism for excuse or mitigation, including the inability to attend to the proper considerations for guiding conduct in a specific context and the inability to use those considerations actually to guide conduct. An agent who lacks these abilities for any nonculpable reason has a rationality defect. This section suggests that such explanations make

---

2. 534 U.S. 407 (2002).

3. *Id.* at 413.

4. *Id.* at 423.

5. *Id.* at 423–24.

sense of the commonsense claim that a defendant could not control himself. The rationality standard is a genuine and limiting condition of nonresponsibility rather than a metaphoric ground. It can be applied workably and fairly and leaves room for moral, political, and legal debate about the appropriate limits on responsibility.

If we consider the legal and moral standards of responsibility, it is clear that the capacity for rationality is the primary criterion. Only lack of rational capacity can explain the diverse conditions that undermine responsibility, including, among others, infancy, mental disorder, dementia, and extreme stress or fatigue. Reflection on the concept of the person that law and morality employ and on the nature of law and morality suggest that the capacity for rationality must be the central criterion. What distinguishes human beings from the rest of the natural world is that we are endowed with the capacity for reason, the capacity to use moral and instrumental reasons to guide our conduct. Law would be powerless to achieve its primary goal of regulating human interaction if it did not operate through the practical reason of the agents it addresses and if agents were not capable of rationally understanding the rules and their application under the circumstances in which the agent acts. The central reason why an agent might not be able to be guided by moral and legal expectations is that the agent was not capable of being guided by reason. It is sufficient if the agent retained the capacity for rationality even if the capacity was not exercised on the occasion.

Compulsion or duress is also an excusing condition, but as we have seen, not because the agent lacks rationality or is out of control. If the situation of compulsion or duress is so deranging that it renders the agent irrational, then the core irrationality criterion of nonresponsibility will obtain. Most duress standards in criminal law are extremely limited, do not apply in the vast majority of cases in which an agent claims an excuse, and the duress analogy is not a successful strategy for analyzing one-party cases of compulsion or loss of control.

Lack of rational capacity is a familiar standard applicable in a wide variety of legal, moral, and everyday contexts. The commonsense notion of rationality is a congeries of abilities, including the ability to perceive relatively accurately, to reason instrumentally, to evaluate one's actions in the light of reasons, to weigh appropriate considerations, and the like. It also includes the capacity to feel appropriate emotional responses and to use those emotions to guide action. Sometimes undesirable emotions intrude, however, undermining the agent's capacity to bring reason to bear. If such emotions are not culpably caused, the agent has a potential irrationality excuse.

The lack of a consensual, technical definition of rational capacity does not compel the conclusion that the law should abandon the everyday understanding that we all apply routinely and successfully, including in moral evaluation. A demand for a more precise definition of rational capacity would be unreasonable. The commonsense concept is grounded in ordinary human experience and in our understanding of practical reason and its critical role in human interaction.

It is a normative standard that is always open to revision. It could not be otherwise for creatures like ourselves. To require more in ordinary human interaction, including the operation of our legal system, would be impossible and unnecessary. Indeed, successful human interaction would be impossible if people were generally unable to understand the practical reasoning of others and to make assessments of the capacity for rationality. The rational capacity account of responsibility also does not entail any particular political, moral, or legal regime of responsibility. It makes normative debate about how much capacity is necessary for responsibility possible by providing the proper criteria for such debate.

In contrast, although we also talk colloquially about and appear to have an everyday understanding of loss of control, we do not, in fact, have a good understanding. Moreover, successful human interaction does not depend on successfully assessing control capacity. Rationality assessment is crucial to human existence; control assessment is not. Even when we appear to be making commonsense, ordinary judgments of lack of self-control, the psychological process is unspecified. If it were analyzed, a rationality impairment would appear. The burden of persuasion should be placed squarely on those who wish to adopt an alternative test.

If one examines most cases of alleged "loss of control," they raise claims that, for some reason, the agent could not "think straight" or bring reason to bear. The "control" language used in *Crane* and in other cases and statutes is metaphorical and better understood in terms of rationality defects. Human beings control themselves by using their reason. "Stop" mechanisms are primarily cognitive. If agents cannot use their reason, it is difficult to behave properly, and this is why some people seem "out of control."

Consider the responsibility of addicts, who are a core case for a control test. Most addicts are firmly in touch with reality and fully aware of the applicable moral and legal rules. Furthermore, although an addict's desire for legal and controlled substances and related behavior may be statistically abnormal and morally objectionable, addicts are virtually always instrumentally rational when they satisfy those desires. Perhaps some desires are irrational, however, and we do talk colloquially about "abnormal" desires, especially if the desire is the symptom of a disorder. The claim that some desires are themselves abnormal or irrational in a normative sense would strengthen my argument, but, as most philosophers concede, these claims fail.

Suppose, however, that an agent's desire is so powerful and insistent that it compromises the agent's ability to think straight, to bring reason to bear on the reasons not to act. Some people in the throes of intense desires may be virtually unable to think of anything except satisfying the desire. Indeed, some addicts, for example, describe seeking and using in almost automaton-like terms. Their minds are blank, and seeking and using "just happens." This is a textbook example of irrationality. Moreover, the build-up of the desire and its nonsatisfaction may cause further distracting psychological states. Fundamental components of rationality, such as the capacities to think clearly and to evaluate self-consciously one's reasons for action, may be severely compromised. Agents in such states will find it difficult to behave well because they have severe difficulty contemplating alternatives or coherently weighing alternatives. These are rationality problems.

Assuming that intense desires can compromise rationality and responsibility, a fundamental question remains: Is the agent suffering from a rationality defect nonetheless responsible because he failed to avoid the situation in which rationality may be compromised, and he is aware of the usual consequences of diminished rationality? The agent knows during more rational moments that he is at risk for acting in such a state of defective rationality in the future. The agent must take all reasonable steps to prevent himself from acting wrongly in an irrational state in the future. If the agent does not take such steps, the agent may indeed be responsible, even if at the moment of acting he suffers from substantially compromised capacity for rationality. The situation would be analogous to the case of a person who suffered from a physical disorder that recurrently produced irrational mental states or blackouts during which the person caused harm, but who did not take sufficient steps to prevent such harm in the future. We would surely not excuse such an agent.

In some cases, however, an agent's capacity for rationality may be generally rather than intermittently compromised, or he may find himself unforeseeably in a compromised state. A straightforward general irrationality excuse or mitigation would apply in appropriate cases. In the case of addicts, for example, stress, declining health, malnutrition, and other factors may undermine the agent's capacity for rationality.

Lack of rational capacity also may be easily and more reliably evaluated than loss of control. It is an ordinary, everyday standard that we use all the time to evaluate the behavior of ourselves and others. Lay people may not know the causes and correlates of substantial rationality defects, but they surely can recognize such problems. Rationality defects are the core of a mental health professional's clinical expertise, and rationality standards will permit professionals comprehensibly to explain the precise behavioral grounds for inferring that an agent has such defects. Rationality tests also will help experts avoid the unscientific, conclusory reasoning that marks opinions about control deficits, and aid legal evaluation uncontaminated by metaphorical evidence that confuses action and mechanism.

Cognitive tests as currently construed are often too narrow to achieve justice. They result in the unfair convictions or failures of mitigation in cases in which the agent's rationality is seriously compromised. If the agent's material reasons for action were caused by a rationality defect or if the agent cannot grasp and be guided by reason, the agent should be excused or mitigated. If this is correct, the answer is reform or better understanding of these tests rather than adding a control test.

Consider the following example. Andrew Goldstein, who had an extensive psychiatric history of severe disorder, killed a young woman by pushing her into the path of a subway train. In his confession, he said that the act was a "fit." He knew she would be killed, knew it was wrong, and was horrified by his own conduct. Nonetheless, he described himself as under the sway of an alien and overwhelming urge to do it. He did not think about pushing her. It just happened, like a random variable. Narrowly speaking, Goldstein did know the facts and the moral and legal rules, but excusing him does not require a control test. He was unable to bring reason to bear to hinder acting on his desire. It is a case of core irrationality that any adequate rationality test should address. If knowledge of what one is doing or knowledge of right and wrong cannot be interpreted broadly enough to encompass this case, a broader formula, such as the incapacity to grasp and be guided by reason, will have to be devised.

V. CONCLUSION

The burden should be on the proponents of control tests to identify and to defend the folk-psychological foundation for lack of control as an independent excusing condition. Cognitive tests do indicate the relevant psychological process, such as lack of knowledge of right and wrong, and explain control difficulties. It is insufficient for proponents of control tests to point out the potential defects of even reformed cognitive tests. No legal test will ever be perfect and rationality evaluation is at the heart of human social life.

I have no personal stake in the matter. My goal is to ensure that the criminal law does not blame and punish or overpunish those who do not deserve such a response. If proponents of control tests can provide an independent standard, I will be delighted and will no longer write articles entitled, *Against Control Tests*. At present, however, my analysis of control tests suggests that they cannot meet a conceptual, empirical, and practical test for adequacy and that they invite confusion and misapplication. I suggest, therefore, that rather than adding an inadequate test to already barely adequate cognitive tests, the law should reform the cognitive tests.

COMMENTS

THE FOLK PSYCHOLOGY OF SELF-CONTROL

STEPHEN P. GARVEY*

The fact that an actor lacked the capacity to control himself should not provide a basis in law for a full excuse to criminal liability, nor should the fact that an actor suffered from a diminished capacity to control himself provide a basis for a partial excuse. So says Stephen Morse. Why? The problems with such excuses, Morse says, are both conceptual and practical. Leaving the (big) practical problems to one side, the conceptual problem, as I understand Morse to say, is that we so far have no adequate folk-psychological analysis of what it means to say that an actor lacked the capacity, or suffered from a diminished capacity, to control himself. Let me take a very rough stab at it, drawing liberally on the work of others.[1]

An actor suffers from a *diminished capacity* to control himself (i.e., a diminished capacity for self-control) at time *t* if he suffers from a diminished capacity at that time to act as he believes he ought to act, and he suffers from a diminished capacity to act as he believes he ought to act if the number of nearby possible (or counterfactual) worlds in which he succeeds in so acting is small (and the smaller the number of such worlds the more diminished his capacity). Similarly, an actor *lacks the capacity* to control himself (i.e., lacks the capacity for self-control) at time *t* if he lacks the capacity to act as he believes he ought to act, and he lacks the capacity to act as he believes he ought to act if the number of nearby possible worlds in which he succeeds in so acting is vanishingly small.

Apply this analysis to the addict. An addict who manages to resist his desire for the object of his desire in virtually no nearby possible world lacks the capacity to control himself, even if he may succeed in resisting it in some remote world, such as one in which he will suffer instant death if he acts to satisfy his desire. An addict who succeeds in resisting his desire in some nearby possible worlds suffers from a diminished capacity to control himself inasmuch as the number of such possible worlds is small, and the smaller the number of such worlds, the more diminished his capacity.

Morse suggests that any analysis of what it means to say that an actor lacked the capacity to control himself, or suffered from a diminished capacity for such control, will in the end reduce to, or depend on, some claim to the effect that the actor suffered from a lack of rationality, or a diminished capacity for rationality. Or, as one might otherwise put it, rationality defects are always somehow analytically at the root of putative control defects (or defects of will). But I see no

---

* Professor of Law and Associate Dean for Academic Affairs, Cornell Law School.

1. *See, e.g.*, Michael Smith, *Rational Capacities, in* ETHICS AND THE A PRIORI 114 (2004).

such reduction or dependence in the analyses offered above. If not, do they provide the sought-after, nonmetaphorical analyses of the folk psychology of nonexistent capacity and diminished capacity for self-control?

Reasonable minds may of course disagree when faced with the facts of any particular case, whether the number of nearby possible worlds in which the actor succeeds in controlling himself is so small that we should say he lacked the capacity for self-control (at that time), or whether we should say instead that his capacity was merely diminished, or whether we should say instead that it was neither lacking nor diminished. But the existence of such disagreement does nothing, so far as I can tell, to render incoherent or unintelligible the idea that the capacity of some actors to achieve control over a wayward desire, and thus to control what they do, is sometimes (though perhaps exceedingly rarely) nonexistent, or (more likely) sometimes diminished. Nor can one sidestep or otherwise avoid questions about the course of events in nearby possible worlds: those questions arise *whenever* we ask about the existence or extent of an actor's capacity, including his capacity for rationality. What happens in nearby possible words is what makes claims about an actor's capacity—*any* capacity—true or false.

One last point. Morse says that folks who believe the criminal law should recognize control excuses ought to bear the burden of persuasion on the question. But why? Insofar as talk of control and lack of control constitute long-standing ways in which the folk evaluate one another's actions, insofar as the folk believe that such talk makes sense (even if they cannot give an adequate folk-psychological analysis that makes sense of their talk), shouldn't the burden be on folks like Morse who would banish such talk from the criminal law altogether?

MORSE ON CONTROL TESTS

MICHAEL LOUIS CORRADO*

I will start with a distinction. There are two ways in which an actor may lack the capacity for rational action (with respect to a given action at a given time): She may be (a) unable to acquire accurate information or to draw the correct conclusions from the information, or (b) unable to turn her correct conclusions into conforming actions. There is the possibility of a dangerous elision here. The first defect is properly called a defect of cognition or a defect of reason. The second would be a defect of control (assuming that there are such defects; I don't mean to beg the question here). The fact that either may result in irrational behavior doesn't make them both defects of reason.

---

* Arch Allen, Jr., Distinguished Professor of Law and Professor of Philosophy, University of North Carolina School of Law.

Thus I believe Stephen Morse is mistaken when, discussing "reasons respon-siveness" theories, he says, *"[T]o the extent it is valid, it is a rationality account.* The capacity to grasp and be guided by good reason is the heart of normative rationality."[1] The capacity to grasp is indeed an element of rationality; but the capacity to be guided by reasons is a control notion. An action may be irrational either because the reasoning that leads to it is defective, or because it does not conform with the agent's reasoning. When there is a failure to conform because the agent lacks the capacity to conform, that's a defect of control, not of reason.[2] To treat them both as defects of reason vindicates the rationality hypothesis, but only by redefining defects of reason to include defects of control.

Morse challenges us to come up with a "folk-psychological" (FP) explanation of control and control tests. What exactly does he mean? He means, I think, that many of the distinctions we find in the law are based on a commonsense view of human action. He offers an FP explanation of rationality defects and insists that no FP explanation of control defects is possible. To this claim, a number of points.

First, it is impossible to give an FP account of control only if we limit FP terms to labels for intentional entities like beliefs and desires, and insist on a reduction of talk about control to talk about such intentional entities. For if we admit ordinary talk about control and unavoidability and difficulty, we do seem to have an FP account. (If mentalistic terms are not the basic terms of folk-psychological discussion, then I would ask Morse to tell us what the basic terms are. If there are no basic terms, if FP discussion is not that precise, then how can it exclude notions like control and avoidability?)

Perhaps Morse is looking for something deeper, perhaps an FP account of *how* someone controls his behavior or lacks control. But I'm not sure that folk explanations can be pushed so far. After all, what is the FP explanation of a belief? Of a desire? Belief and desire are the building blocks of FP explanations, regardless of whether a deeper explanation of those ideas is itself possible.

The notion of folk psychology has this much going for it: *The law, as it stands, is based upon the ordinary conception of how human beings operate.* Part of this ordinary conception is that some human beings understand their behavior and its consequences and others do not, and (I would add) that some human beings can avoid behaving in certain ways and others cannot. But the principle of respon-sibility, which ties together these folk notions with punishment, is not a folk-conception. It is a principle of morality superimposed upon commonsense notions of human action. But if those notions happen to be false, the principle does not change: If we were to find out that the common conception of human behavior is false and that no one is rational, or that no one can control her behavior,

---

1. Morse core text at 453–54 (emphasis added).
2. I reject reasons-responsiveness theories, for different reasons.

we would be committed to the conclusion that Morse dreads, that no one is responsible and no one may be punished.

Finally, the notion that causation will excuse leads to universal excuse only if in fact all actions are caused. If it makes any sense at all to talk about folk psychology and its importance for the criminal law, then it makes sense to acknowledge that in the layman's conception of human action most people can, at most times, avoid doing what they did, under the very conditions under which they did them. In other words, the layman is not a compatibilist. Compatibilism would be an appealing way to avoid the path to universal excuse for one who accepts what Morse (following Galen Strawson) calls "the realism constraint," but so far compatibilism is merely a program, not yet a solution.

SOMETIMES A CONTROL TEST IS JUST A CONTROL TEST

SUSAN D. ROZELLE[*]

Stephen Morse argues that control tests of responsibility reduce to rationality tests, and therefore that a proper rationality test would obviate any need for an independent control test. Although some theorists use the language of control when what they really mean is reason, sometimes a control test is just a control test.

Certainly without an action (or culpable inaction), there is no crime, and hence no need for an excuse at all. Morse dismisses the equation of lack of control with lack of action,[1] but as he points out, control exists on a continuum.[2] As a matter of folk psychology, it seems those who could not exercise any control whatsoever over their "actions" did not act. These poor souls would not need an excuse, as they would not have committed the necessary actus reus. But most people have some measure of control, falling somewhere along the continuum between full capacity and no capacity; that is enough to establish an act. Of course, the fact of action does not end the inquiry. A control test posits that where there is sufficient impairment in control, there ought to be a concomitant excuse or mitigation.

How much impairment should trigger an excuse will necessarily involve line-drawing. Though capacity-for-control falls along a continuum, the law is fully capable of declaring that X amount of control is sufficient to hold a person fully responsible, while X–1 amount of control is not. Nor should the real-life imprecision in quantification present a bar. Limits like "appreciably" or "substantially"

---

* Associate Professor of Law, Capital University Law School.

1. *See* Morse core text at 449–50, 453.

2. *See id.* at 451.

appear throughout our legal system, and fact finders regularly manage to apply them.

The last preliminary objection Morse raises regards the difficulty of separating "can't" from "won't."[3] The American Psychiatric Assocation (APA) famously recommended against a control test on this very ground, pointing to the difficulty of distinguishing between twilight and dusk. Clearly these defendants *did* not control themselves; but whether they *could have*, we cannot say. Because control tests necessarily ask whether these defendants *could have* controlled themselves, Morse proposes that, as a practical matter, no test can ever satisfy: we are, he believes, asking an unanswerable question.

I disagree. We routinely ask fact finders to peer into the mists to discern mental states and capacities equally inaccessible by objective indicators. How are we to decide whether someone intended X, knew Y, was aware of the risk of Z? In each of these scenarios, we are forced to rely on "the defendant's self-report and observations of the defendant's . . . conduct."[4] And though the truth may never be known with certainty, we often entrust fact finders with determining whether it was twilight or dusk. That this is a difficult job, not subject to objective verification, does not trouble us in other circumstances; it ought not trouble us here.

At the center of his piece, Morse unintentionally smuggles control into his proposed rationality test. Andrew Goldstein knew he was pushing his victim in front of a train, knew that would kill her, knew that was wrong, and was horrified to see himself doing it nonetheless. Morse describes this as a "case of core irrationality" and suggests that if rationality tests do not yet cover it, they should.[5] Because Goldstein knew what he was doing and that it was wrong, the standard rationality tests do not excuse him. Morse's suggested broadening, to include "the incapacity to grasp and be guided by reason," smuggles a control test into his proposed rationality test. The capacity to *grasp* reason surely is a rationality test; that is reflected in the current standard of understanding what one is doing. The capacity to be *guided* by reason, however, is the essence of that folk-psychological explanation of control for which Morse has been seeking.

Rather than "the heart of normative rationality,"[6] a failure to be guided by reason tends to show an impairment in control, presuming the person's rationality is unimpaired. Return to Goldstein: his rationality was not impaired. He knew he was pushing his victim under a subway train, and he knew that doing so would kill her. He also knew that doing so was wrong, and he was horrified at the thought. But he did it anyway. Given that he understood what he was doing and its implications, and given his horror and lack of desire for that outcome, the fact that he did it anyway makes us—at a folk psychology level—wonder why.

---

3. *Id.* at 454–55.

4. *Id.* at 455.

5. *Id.* at 459.

6. *Id.* at 454.

The answer comes to us at the same folk-psychological level: It may be that although his rationality was intact, his ability to conform his conduct to the dictates of that rationality was impaired. Sometimes a control test really is just a control test.

WHY IS A FOLK-PSYCHOLOGICAL ACCOUNT OF LOSS OF CONTROL NECESSARY (AND WHAT PRECISELY IS IT)?

TERRY A. MARONEY*

Stephen Morse may be correct that the behavioral phenomena targeted by control tests can be adequately, or better, accommodated within a more generous rationality test. But is "folk psychology" the relevant frame?

Morse asserts that any adequate account of excuse or mitigation "must be folk psychological because the law is resolutely folk psychological."[1] Insofar as criminal law relies in large part on the unschooled ideas of regular folk about how people think, feel, and behave—what is generally meant when speaking of naïve or folk psychology—he surely is right. Inability to articulate a theory of responsibility, excuse, or justification in folk terms is a death knell, for people will neither understand nor implement it. But this cannot be Morse's real gripe with control tests, for—as he acknowledges—everyday talk is replete with references to being unable to help one's thoughts, feelings, and actions. That people have differential capacity for self-control and that such capacity varies with situational factors, such as the presence of strong emotion, is firmly enshrined in folk psychology.[2]

This is not to say that a notion is correct just because it is commonly held. Folk psychology is more likely to be accurate where it concerns everyday, consciously accessible phenomena; it is less likely to be so where it concerns complex or nonconscious ones or the thoughts, feelings, and behavior of dissimilar others. Morse presumably would not advocate enshrining into law a patently false notion because of its folk pedigree. For example, though many believe that no rational

---

* Assistant Professor of Law, Vanderbilt University Law School. The ideas in this comment are drawn from Terry A. Maroney, *Emotional Common Sense as Constitutional Law*, 62 VAND. L. REV. 101 (2009).

1. Morse core text at 451.

2. One of the most common folk accounts of "being emotional" entails a feeling of loss of control. *See* W. Gerrod Parrott, *The Heart and the Head: Everyday Conceptions of Being Emotional, in* EVERYDAY CONCEPTIONS OF EMOTION: AN INTRODUCTION TO THE PSYCHOLOGY, ANTHROPOLOGY, AND LINGUISTICS OF EMOTION 73, 80 (J.A. Russell et al. eds., 1995).

person would falsely confess to a serious crime unless he were physically tortured, this is not true, and law should not pretend that it is.

So if, as Morse suggests, folk-psychological articulation is a threshold requirement, control tests meet it. But, as he must agree, crossing that threshold does not mean that folk accounts of control tests are sufficient, for they may be off-base.

This seems to be Morse's real gripe. He frequently uses "folk psychology" in accord with its general meaning, but also suggests that he really means to refer not to all law-relevant lay beliefs but to one in particular.[3] As a rejoinder to arguments (based on the contemporary mind sciences) that determinism will come to dominate criminal law, Morse elsewhere has argued that a nondeterministic view of human agency is among the most common folk-psychological beliefs, that such view necessarily underlies criminal law, and that no advance in the mind sciences will alter that view.[4] By here asking us to focus on this particular folk-psychological belief, he signals that his core argument is that control tests—even if commonly articulated in regular talk—are fundamentally incompatible with first-order principles of agency.

Morse has not yet made a strong enough case for this claim. He can't define control tests away by (a) requiring that any theory of excuse meet his subdefinition of "folk psychology" and (b) pointing out that this definition says nothing about control. He points our attention to "commonsense" notions of rationality and its defects, which notions are legitimate, he argues, by virtue of being "grounded in ordinary human experience and in our understanding of practical reason and its critical role in human interaction."[5] But he also acknowledges the "commonsense plausibility" of control tests, and his claim that everyday life relies on commonsense assessments of rationality but not control is asserted rather than defended. If common sense supports both rationality and control tests, it sheds little light on the distinction. Further, it is not clear whether Morse regards "common sense" to be a virtue or vice.[6]

What Morse is really saying is that tests based in rationality are correct as an account of human reality—that is, empirically—and as an account of the human agency we must assume for law to function—that is, theoretically—and that ones based in volition are not. He can make that case, but the frames of folk psychology and common sense are not helpful in doing so.

---

3. *See* Morse core text at 451 (defining folk psychology as "the theory of explaining behavior that treats mental states . . . as genuinely causal and . . . people as agents").

4. *See, e.g.,* Stephen J. Morse, *Determinism and the Death of Folk Psychology: Two Challenges to Responsibility from Neuroscience,* 9 MINN. J. L. SCI. & TECH. 1, 2–5 (2008).

5. Morse core text at 456.

6. *See id.* at 455 (criticizing Breyer's *Kansas v. Crane* opinion as establishing a "typically thin and seemingly commonsense test" and praising Scalia's "commonsense criticism" in dissent).

COGNITION, RATIONALITY, AND RESPONSIBILITY

ROBERT F. SCHOPP*

Recall when you were five years old and hit your sister. She screamed, "S/he hit me." You yelled, "I didn't mean to." She screamed, "S/he did it on purpose," and you responded with the alternative defense, "I couldn't help it." Even then, you thought that an adequate conception of responsible agency required some volitional component.

Stephen Morse argues that the types of impairment that apparently provide plausible bases for volitional excuse or partial excuse in fact undermine the capacity for rationality due to impaired cognitive capacity or due to emotion or stress that prevents the actor from bringing relevant cognitive capacities to bear on the criminal act. He contends that the lack of capacity for rationality may be easily and reliably evaluated. He refers to addiction as one example of impairment that this approach accommodates.

Consider two variations of one controversial category of cases:

Alice suffers post-partum depression of psychotic severity. She hears God's voice informing her that Satan will dominate the world for one hundred years. Her infant daughter will be subject to the horrors of life under Satan's domination, and after death she will endure eternity in hell. If Alice kills her daughter now, however, her daughter will spend eternity in heaven with God. Alice kills her daughter, believing that she has a moral obligation to do so according to God's instructions although she will spend eternity in hell for killing her daughter.

Bertha suffers from chronic and severe but not psychotic depression. Her experience includes chronic anhedonia (the inability to experience pleasure) and serious depressive pessimism regarding the possibility that life can improve. She frequently considers suicide to escape her ongoing misery. She is aware that her mother experienced similar depression, and she expects her infant daughter to experience life as she and her mother have. She kills her daughter to spare her the misery of life, believing that doing so is evil but a moral obligation she must fulfill to protect her child.

Alice would provide a strong candidate for the insanity defense under common variations of the *M'Naghten* standard, and many readers would conclude that Alice should not be held criminally responsible. Bertha might present a very difficult case. Different opinions about Bertha's criminal responsibility might partially reflect difficulty in understanding the nature and degree of impairment involved in anhedonia or depressive pessimism, as well as the differences

---

* Robert J. Kutak Professor of Law, Professor of Psychology and Philosophy, University of Nebraska.

between these forms of impairment and the psychotic distortions experienced by Alice or the serious pessimism manifested by some individuals who do not qualify for any clinical diagnosis.

Alice and Bertha simultaneously believe that they have an obligation to kill their daughters and that doing so is evil. It is difficult to understand how they can hold these contradictory beliefs, but it is also unclear how these contradictory beliefs differ from the perception of conflicting obligations that unimpaired people sometimes experience. The differences in opinions might also reflect the lack of clarity regarding the type and degree of capacity for rationality that is required for criminal responsibility. The traditional ignorance of wrongfulness standards arguably represent a misguided interpretation of the type of cognitive impairment that undermines responsible agency because these standards seem to frame responsible agency as possession of certain information and the corresponding lack of responsible agency as ignorance regarding that information.

Although Morse contends that "[l]ack of rational capacity also may be easily and more reliably evaluated than loss of control,"[1] these offenders suggest that accurately assessing an offender's capacity for rationality for the purpose of criminal responsibility requires the integration of at least two distinct lines of inquiry and the application of that integrated inquiry to specific offenders and offenses. The first line of inquiry requires more detailed description and explanation of various types of clinical impairment and of the similarities and differences among them. The second requires an account of the most defensible conception of accountable agency as the minimal capacities that render one eligible for the expression of condemnation inherent in criminal punishment. The principled application of that institution to various offenders requires that we pursue clear, consistent, and defensible explanations of: the capacities that fulfill the minimal requirements of responsible agency for the purpose of justified punishment, the functional impairment manifested by individuals who suffer various forms of psychopathology, and the justificatory significance of the latter for the former.

In short, at age five, you realized that the familiar cognitive standards were inadequate, but defensible revision of those standards requires precise integration of various forms of psychopathology with a clearly articulated account of the capacities of responsible agency. Then, as now, regarding conduct that fulfills the Model Penal Code's provision addressing those who lack substantial capacity to conform, "I couldn't help it" meant "I'm not responsible, but I can't explain why."

---

1. Morse core text at 458.

REPLY

STEPHEN J. MORSE

Despite my challenge to do so, none of the four commentators who argue for a control test provides a conceptual or practical account, and only Stephen Garvey purports to try. None directly addresses the implementation problems. None claims that the distractions I identify are not false starts and distractions, and all accept the centrality of folk psychology, albeit one is ambivalent. Once again, I have no stake in rejecting independent control tests. If someone provides an adequate folk-psychological explanation of them and a workable test for them, I'll argue for their legal implementation.

Garvey's "counterfactual" test for deciding *if* an agent has some capacity defect is an excellent way to proceed. I use it myself. But Garvey has not described the defective folk-psychological process that explains *why* a criminal would fail to behave properly in nearly all counterfactual worlds. A positive conceptual and practical account is still needed.

Michael Corrado and Susan Rozelle claim that the ability to guide one's behavior is a control standard, but neither suggests the folk-psychological process that explains *why* a criminal who is able to grasp the relevant reasons to refrain is unable to be guided by them. Simply to assert that the ability to be guided is a control notion, or that criminals who aren't guided cannot control themselves, begs the question and permits finders of fact to reach a legal conclusion without guidance. Corrado wonders if folk psychology can describe how someone controls his behavior. Rozelle correctly notes that fact finders often assess subjective mental states. Nonetheless, the fact finder needs criteria for those subjective mental states in order to assess them. If we cannot describe the process, however, what is the fact finder supposed to evaluate? Even admittedly murky judgments about excusing conditions must be based on some nonconclusory criteria.

All the commentators implicitly or explicitly agree that the law's model of the person and its criteria of responsibility are folk psychological. Corrado says, however, that responsibility is not a folk-psychological conception. He is right that it is a principle of morality we apply to practical reasoners. Unless one is a strong metaphysical moral realist, however, morality is a matter of practical and not theoretical reason. This is not the occasion to reenter the determinism debate, with which Corrado closes his comment, but it is worth noting that a practical-reasoning account of human behavior is compatible with libertarian, compatibilist, and hard determinist metaphysics.

Terry Maroney's title raises two excellent questions: Why is a control test necessary? What is it? But she answers neither. Instead she offers an ambivalent, indeed downright grumpy, set of worries about folk psychology. She characterizes practical reasoning as my preferred "subdefinition" of folk psychology (and folk psychology generally as "unschooled"), but practical reasoning is the indispensable core of any folk-psychological account. This claim needs no further defense. One can dispute the precise details of an adequate account of practical reason, but nothing in psychology or the allied sciences remotely indicates that human beings are not practical reasoners. As the philosopher of mind, Jerry Fodor, says, if we're wrong about intentional folk psychology, "that's the wrongest we've ever been about anything."[1]

Maroney is right that many commonsense judgments we make turn out to be false, but this is just a dispute about details. She asks why I want to exclude control tests even though we do talk colloquially about control. The reason is not, as she claims, that I believe lack of control is incompatible with "first-order principles of agency." Rather, the reason is the same as her sensible reason for wishing to abandon demonstrably incorrect folk-psychological notions. The law should not use criteria for blame and punishment that employ concepts we can neither explain nor reasonably implement. Maroney says that I think a nondeterministic folk-psychological view of agency necessarily underlies criminal law, but the cited passage says the opposite. Legal-responsibility doctrines are entirely consistent with the realism constraint.

Robert Schopp is with the program. He does not argue for a control test, but he usefully shows that rationality-defect tests can produce difficult line-drawing problems that require thick behavioral description and a full account of the minimal capacities required for accountability. I agree and have tried to provide them in the papers cited in the core text. Could I do more? Sure, but the work must address rationality criteria that will fill the gap in our explanation of excuses that some people improperly try to fill with a control test.

Schopp and Maroney use the term "volition" or "volitional" as a synonym for "control capacity," but this usage is ill-advised because there is immense philosophical dispute about the meaning of volition. According to one influential theory of volitions as executory intentions, people with an alleged control problem do act volitionally. Let's stick with "control."

Lack of rational capacity is still the most plausible candidate for an agent's failure to grasp and be guided by good reason. Rational capacity is a normative concept about which we can disagree, but there is a lot of common ground about the criterial mental states, such as knowledge, awareness, beliefs, and intentions. Consequently, we can provide a folk-psychological test a fact finder could use. For example, did the defendant know right from wrong? Although we can argue normatively about the precise criteria, and there will be line-drawing problems, at least we know what we're talking about when we talk about everyday rationality. Our normative concepts and human behavior are both complex. These are

---

1. Jerry A. Fodor, PSYCHOSEMANTICS: THE PROBLEM OF MEANING IN THE PHILOSOPHY OF MIND xii (1987).

not grounds to adopt a standard that can be neither explained nor implemented. They are reasons to work harder at developing and assessing rationality criteria.

I also suggest, contra Corrado, that it is the task of psychology and allied sciences to discover the nature of rationality problems and how they affect behavior. The more we learn, the more rationality problems seem to be at the heart of the matter. For example, the expanding findings concerning addiction, which is the strongest case for the plausibility of a control test, indicate that addictive behavior is a result of substance-induced cognitive defects of attention, memory, and judgment. Influential accounts based on an addict's hyperbolic or steep time discounting consider these rationality problems. For another example, Andrew Goldstein was not able to access and use his evaluative judgments at the moment of the crime, another classic rationality defect.

If it turns out as science develops that we are not genuinely practical reasoners, that our mental states do no causal work in explaining our behavior, then all current notions of responsibility—including rationality tests and control tests—would almost certainly wither away. I doubt that it will ever happen, but until it does, focusing on rational capacity is the most promising route conceptually and empirically to pursuing justice in the realm of excuses.

22. ABOLITION OF THE INSANITY DEFENSE

CHRISTOPHER SLOBOGIN*

I contend that, both morally and practically, the most appropriate manner of recognizing the mitigating impact of mental illness in criminal cases is to recast mental disorder as a factor relevant to the general defenses, not to treat it as a predicate for a special defense.

I. THE INTEGRATIONIST ALTERNATIVE

The starting point for this claim is the retributive principle that blameworthiness should be the predominate guidepost of the criminal law's attempt to define the scope of liability. My central assertion is that the insanity defense does not adequately carry out this task. At least in its modern guises, the insanity defense is overbroad. Instead, mental disorder should be relevant to criminal culpability only if it supports an excusing condition at the time of the offense that, under the subjective approach to criminal liability increasingly accepted today, would be available to a person who is *not* mentally ill. The three most prominent such conditions would be: (1) a mistaken belief about circumstances that, had they occurred as the person believed, would amount to a legal justification; (2) a mistaken belief that conditions exist that amount to legally-recognized duress; and (3) the absence of intent to commit crime (i.e., the lack of mens rea defined subjectively, in terms of what the defendant actually knew or was aware of). I call this approach "integrationist," because it eliminates the special defense of insanity while providing people with mental disability the same defenses available to everyone else.

The criminal law (especially under the Model Penal Code) has tended toward increasing subjectivization, both with respect to mens rea and with respect to the affirmative defenses such as self-defense, provocation, and duress. As a result, in a sizeable number of jurisdictions today, anyone—mentally ill or not—who makes a mistake as to result or fact or who believes he is confronted by circumstances that would lead to justification, provocation, or duress may have a defense. Thus, the universe of excuses has expanded to the point where many of

* Milton Underwood Professor of Law, Vanderbilt University Law School. This core text is drawn from Christopher Slobogin, *An End to Insanity: Recasting the Role of Mental Disability in Criminal Case*, 85 VA. L. REV. 1199 (2000), which also appears in a revised version in Christopher Slobogin, MINDING JUSTICE: LAWS THAT DEPRIVE PEOPLE WITH MENTAL DISABILITIES OF LIFE AND LIBERTY ch. 2 (2006).

those who would be acquitted under an insanity defense could also succeed under another doctrine. For example, a criminal defendant who did not know the nature and quality of the criminal act will usually lack mens rea if the latter is subjectively defined, while a person who didn't think the act was wrong will often have a subjective justification. Although the subjectification trend pioneered by the Model Penal Code has its detractors, it has also been vigorously defended, and my analysis will be premised on the assumption, without further discussion, that it represents the morally appropriate view.

One could conclude from all of this that the insanity defense is no longer needed. If, as I eventually propose, general ignorance of the law is added to the list of excuses recognized in the Model Penal Code, the subjectively defined defensive doctrines provide a broader basis for exculpation than both the pre-*M'Naghten* formulations of the insanity defense and the *M'Naghten* test itself (at least if literally interpreted). Thus, if the latter formulation is morally sufficient for purposes of recognizing the exculpatory effect of mental disorder, the integration approach should be as well.

However, some defendants who might be acquitted under more modern versions of the insanity defense would not be entitled to a defense under these other subjectively defined doctrines. For instance, those whose beliefs, if true, would not amount to justification (e.g., John Hinckley, who believed killing President Ronald Reagan would unite him with Jody Foster) would not be acquitted under any of the subjectified defenses; an insanity plea under the American Law Institute (ALI) or a similarly broad test would provide the only hope of avoiding conviction in such situations. Likewise, those who exhibit only volitional impairment would generally have a defense only under the volitional prong of the insanity test. The question thus becomes whether there are normative reasons for recognizing a separate, special defense in such situations.

I answer this question in the negative. Current insanity tests that are based on lack of appreciation or volition, if taken literally, move too far toward the deterministic reductio ad absurdum that no one is responsible. The rationality test favored by a number of scholars begins to deal with the problem, because only a small percentage of offenders are truly irrational, but it, too, is overinclusive: it fails to explain why irrational reasons are necessarily exculpatory. Allowing subjectively defined defensive doctrines to do the work better captures the universe of people who should be excused.

II. THE FAILURE OF EXISTING TESTS AND PROPOSED TESTS FOR INSANITY

A. The Volitional Test

At least three insanity formulations focus on lack of volition: the "irresistible impulse" test, the ALI's prong excusing substantial inability to conform behavior, and the *Durham* case's product test. Applied literally, the first test is the narrowest and the last test the broadest. But for present purposes the differences between these formulations are not important. The key point is that, given the wide array of mental disorders that can be said to affect volition, these tests open the door to excusing so many people that punishment becomes hard to sustain as a meaningful enterprise.

The usual volitional impairment claim is that the offender "felt compelled" to carry out the offense. For instance, the psychotic individual who hears voices telling him to kill may experience a powerful urge to commit a crime. Unfortunately, however, that compulsion claim does not distinguish him from a large number of other, less "ill" individuals. From what we can ascertain, the subjectively felt urges of pedophiles, repeat rapists, and thieves who steal to feed an addiction are at least equal to the impulses experienced by people with manic-depressive and other psychoses. The same can probably be said of people with other types of nonpsychotic disorders such as borderline personality disorder and attention deficit disorder. Even the greedy corporate executive who manipulates accounts, or the teenage boy on a Friday night who wants to have intercourse with an underage girlfriend, may feel as compelled as the psychotic offender. A criminal justice system that recognized an excuse in all, or even just in many, of these situations would begin to look whimsical.

The volitional test is even more insidious, however, because it countenances not only the subjective urge claim but the predisposition claim. The latter goes something like this: "I have characteristics or have experienced events that are highly correlated with criminal behavior; therefore I am compelled (or strongly predisposed) to commit crime." Defendants who assert the "extra male chromosome" defense, an abnormal brain pattern, or the rotten social background defense are making this type of claim. Note that these people do not say they did not intend the criminal act, or that they committed it for "crazy" reasons. They are stating instead that their criminal behavior is caused by factors outside their control. Recognition of an excuse here would not just disrupt a culpability based system, but spell the end of it.

A proponent of the volitional test might object to all of this by reminding us that, as a historical matter, the test was only meant to excuse offenders with a "severe" mental disease or defect. That is true, as an historical matter. But no logical basis for that limitation exists. Recent research indicating that people with serious mental illness are no more likely to commit crime than the general population reinforces the conclusion that the urges of a person with mental illness are not provably greater than the urges of people we would never think of excusing. If an offender truly finds it hard to stop himself from committing a crime, there is no ground for distinguishing between different disorders, or even requiring that the person have one. A psychosis-only limitation, or anything similar, is justified at best by a bare desire to cabin the insanity defense.

In sum, the volitional test, assuming it is not arbitrarily limited, creates a huge potential for chaos in a culpability based criminal justice system. There are two solutions to this problem. One is to reject the culpability orientation of the criminal justice system. The other is to retain that orientation and reject volition-ally based insanity claims entirely. But the latter stance may strike some as unfair: If we are willing to recognize an excuse for those coerced by external sources (the duress defense), how can we fail to recognize a defense based on internal compulsions? In other words, how can a culpability oriented system legitimately ignore credible claims that crime was caused by factors outside the criminal's control?

The best attempt at reconciling this tension comes from Michael Moore. To the determinist claim that all of us are volitionally impaired and thus cannot be held responsible, Moore responds, "causation is not compulsion."[1] Moore *assumes* that all behavior is caused by biological, characterological, unconscious, or environmental factors. But, he argues, none of those causes necessarily disrupt one's ability to generate reasons for one's actions, based on one's desires and beliefs. These reasons, Moore demonstrates, are also causes of behavior, even if they themselves are caused by biological or other factors. Thus, when a person acts for reasons, he is, so to speak, the "proximate" cause of his actions and generally should be held responsible for them (unless the reasons are irrational).

Stephen Morse, another irrationality theorist, bolsters these arguments with observations about the incoherence of the traditional volitional impairment inquiry.[2] Aside from reflex events, Morse argues, everyone, no matter how compelled they feel, has choices at the time they act. When the pressure to act is external, as when someone puts a gun to one's head and orders a crime be committed, an excuse may make normative sense. But Morse suggests that when the pressure to act is internal, as might be the case with a drug addict or pedophile, a separate volitional excuse generally cannot be sustained for practical and conceptual reasons.

First, "it will often be too difficult to assess the degree of threatened dysphoria that creates the hard choice." As Morse has elsewhere noted, "[t]here is no scien-tific measure of the strength of urges." Second, "it is simply not clear that the fear of dysphoria would ever be sufficient to excuse the breach of important expectations, except in precisely those cases in which we would assume naturally that the agent's rational capacity was essentially disabled." For example, Morse says, the "policeman at the elbow" test, which limits the volitional prong of the insanity defense to situations in which the urge to commit crime is so strong that not even the presence of a law enforcement official disinhibits the person, "is . . . better interpreted as a rationality test."

---

1. Michael Moore, *Causation and the Excuses*, 73 CAL. L. REV. 1091, 1130 (1985).

2. Morse's arguments appear in several fora. His most elaborate exegesis on the point in the text is Stephen J. Morse, *Culpability and Control*, 142 U. PA. L. REV. 1587 (1994), but this brief summary will come from several of his works.

Moore and Morse make a solid argument against the contention that deter-minism defeats the law's effort to attribute culpability, as well as a convincing case for looking at a person's desires and beliefs at the time of the crime in decid-ing when culpability should be imposed. If one accepts their arguments, the volitional test can legitimately be discarded as a contender for the insanity defense, meaning that only the appreciation, rationality, and integrationist tests are left standing. Moore and Morse endorse the rationality test. Before discuss-ing that approach, it will be useful to examine the appreciation test, because an understanding of its flaws helps explain why the rationality test is superior, and why the integrationist test is even better.

B. The Appreciation Test

The ALI's appreciation-of-wrongfulness formulation is the most popular insan-ity test today. Thus, it is particularly unfortunate that, if applied honestly, the appreciation test, like the volitional test, would excuse numerous offenders whom most people would not want excused. Modern knowledge about behavior leads irrevocably to the conclusion that the appreciation test, like its volitional counterpart, would upend the criminal justice system, if it is taken seriously. The same is true of the *M'Naghten* test, to the extent the word "know" in that test is applied in the deeper, affective sense. In the following discussion, however, I will assume there is a distinction between the appreciation test and the "literal" *M'Naghten* test (as well as the integrationist test), and highlight that distinction, so the differences can be better understood.

Exhibit A in the case against the appreciation test is the psychopath, virtually everyone's paradigm of the "evil" person who should be punished if he commits crime. Dr. Robert Hare, the leading researcher on this particular phenomenon, summarizes it as follows: "[Psychopaths] seem unable to 'get under the skin' or to 'walk in the shoes' of others, except in a truly intellectual sense. . . . [They] are glib and superficial, lack remorse or guilt, lack empathy, have shallow emotions and lack responsibility."[3] This type of person, if he commits crime, clearly does not meet a literal *M'Naghten* test, because he knows his act is criminal and not justified. For the same reason, he would not be excused under the integrationist test. But he would meet the appreciation test, if honestly applied. People with psychopathic personalities do not internalize the enormity of the criminal act. *By definition*, they do not emotionally appreciate its wrongfulness.

Another class of people who commit a large amount of crime is comprised of people with mild retardation, having IQs between 50 and 70. Consider this observation about their cognitive capacities: "Mildly retarded persons may be able to distinguish right from wrong in the abstract, but they have difficulty

---

3. Robert D. Hare, WITHOUT CONSCIENCE: THE DISTURBING WORLD OF THE PSYCHOPATHS AMONG US 34, 44 (1993).

applying abstract concepts in specific actual settings and are unable to appreciate the wrongfulness of what they do."[4] If this statement is accurate, people with mild retardation, while generally sane under a literal *M'Naghten* test and the integrationist test, should be found insane under the appreciation test. Yet the latter result would be repugnant to many people, including some advocates for people with mental retardation. Criminals with mild mental retardation should escape execution, but few should escape conviction.

The appreciation test, honestly applied, also excuses many people whose principal dysfunction appears to be volitional rather than cognitive. Here, for example, is an excerpt from testimony in *State v. Companaro*,[5] involving a person who was found insane under the appreciation test for embezzling money to support his pathological gambling habit:

> Well, here's a man who is a law enforcement officer, who knows the law well, who knows about right and wrong, [and therefore would not meet the literal *M'Naghten* test or the integrationist test] but who is in a desperate strait. He's under a tremendous amount of stress at that point, does not consider right and wrong. I don't think that becomes part of the thinking process. His process then is to survive. He's losing his job, his family, his children, his reputation, everything is going down.

Companaro illustrates how the appreciation test permits volitional impairment to be described in terms of cognitive impairment: People under stress, the argument goes, do not think through the consequences of their actions, and thus do not appreciate the wrongfulness of their act. If that argument is allowed, prohibition of volitionally based claims will accomplish very little, because many volitional impairment cases can be recharacterized as cognitive impairment cases. Even many people who do not have mental disorders (for instance, those who offend in a "blind rage") might not "consider right and wrong" at the time they commit a crime.

Again, as with the volitional test, one could try to solve these problems by limiting application of the appreciation test to cases of psychosis and like disorders. Although this type of move may conform with the intuitions of most people, the rationale for privileging "severe" mental illness over other forms of mental disorder is no more obvious in this context than it is when looking at volitional claims.

In any event, even if the appreciation test is limited to cases of gross mental disorder, it may excuse people who should not be excused. Take the case of Ted Kaczynski, a.k.a. the Unabomber. The people to whom he mailed letter bombs all were somehow involved with technology. Kaczynski, who was clearly suffering

---

4. C. Benjamin Crisman and Rockne J. Chickinell, *The Mentally Retarded Offender in Omaha–Douglas County*, 8 CREIGHTON L. REV. 622, 646 (1975).

5. Union County Indictment (no. 632079) (Sup. Ct. N.J. Crim. Div. 1981).

from schizophrenia, picked these individual targets because he wanted to send a message that if his victims and people like them failed to curb society's reliance on sophisticated machinery, computers, and the like, the world as we know it will come to an end. His crimes were his way of preventing this destruction of the world by technology. He knew it was wrong to kill people and he knew that sending the letter bombs would result in other people's deaths, so he did not meet the literal *M'Naghten* Test. But there is a strong argument that he did not appreciate the wrongfulness of his actions, because in his confused state he felt they were necessary.

If one believes that Kaczynski *should* have been excused for his crimes, the problem then becomes distinguishing him from other less "crazy" offenders who convinced themselves their crimes were justified, such as John Wayne Gacy, who believed he was doing the world a service when he killed over twenty men he thought were homosexual prostitutes. Similarly, many pedophiles rationalize their molestations on the ground that the children somehow benefit. The only basis for refusing to excuse these latter type of offenders while excusing people like Kaczynski is that he somehow held his self-justificatory beliefs more intensely. That distinction is footless, for reasons best developed in connection with the Rationality Test, which more squarely raises the issue.

C. The Rationality Test

At first glance, an insanity test based on irrationality would seem even more likely to open the floodgates of exculpation than either the volitional test or the appreciation test, because virtually all criminal behavior could be labeled "irrational." But as Michael Moore defines the term, irrationality should not be equated with inaccurate, abnormal or bad judgments. Rather, it exists only when a person exhibits unintelligible desires, strongly held but inconsistent beliefs, and incoherent thought process.[6] This, of course, comes close to the traditional definition of psychosis. So defined, it is not surprising that the rationality test justifies, better than either the volitional or appreciation tests, a threshold for insanity that puts the psychoses on one side and most other disorders and mental phenomena on the other. As a result, the Rationality Test is preferable to either of these other two tests as a legal response to the challenges of modern behavioral science.

Yet the same type of question asked in connection with the volitional and appreciation tests is germane here as well. Why is irrationality (qua psychotic-like symptoms) singled out? What is it about irrationality that makes it the excusing condition? Proponents of the Rationality Test do not give a sufficient answer

---

6. Michael Moore, Law and Psychiatry: Rethinking the Relationship 100–08 (1984).

to this question. Moore's entire case for an insanity test that focuses on irrationality is as follows:

> Only if we can see another being as one who acts to achieve some rational end in light of some rational beliefs will we understand him in the same fundamental way that we understand ourselves and our fellow persons in everyday life. We regard as moral agents only those beings we can understand in this way.[7]

Morse offers a somewhat different rationale: Irrationality is the preeminent excusing condition because, in his words, it "make[s] it too hard" for a person "to grasp or be guided by good reasons not to offend."[8]

One can concede Moore's point that we view irrational people differently without being forced to reach the conclusion that they thereby deserve exculpation from criminal offenses they commit. In fact, his explanation is tautological on the question of who should be considered responsible; it simply declares that irrational persons are not "moral agents." To bolster his point, he notes the medieval tendency to equate mentally disordered persons with beasts and infants, whom he says we do not regard as moral beings. But that equation applies only in those cases in which the medieval cases applied it: When the offender did not know the nature and quality of the act (and thus lacked the capacity to form intent, or at least was ignorant of the law in the general sense, as might be the case with infants and severely retarded individuals). People who know they are harming another cannot so easily be consigned to the "nonmoral being" category, assuming such a category should exist in the first place.

Morse provides a more cogent reason for using irrationality as the test, but in doing so engages in the same reasoning he criticizes in those who support the inquiry into volition. How do we know when, to use Morse's language, it is *"too hard . . . to grasp or be guided by good reasons not to offend?"* The assumption that irrational individuals find it more difficult to obtain or process information than do other people sounds remarkably like the proposition that mentally ill people find it more difficult to control their behavior than do other people. But Morse rejects the latter proposition, in large part because it is empirically unverifiable. Morse's assertion about the link between psychosis and the difficulty of accessing the right reasons for acting should likewise be rejected.

Consider a real case, involving a man we shall call Ralph. Ralph killed his father because he believed the father was sleeping with Ralph's wife and daughter. This information, which was clearly wrong, had been communicated to Ralph through "voices" that let him know everything his father did. On the day of the offense, Ralph woke up and, in his words, "found a knife by the side of my bed." He drove to his father's house, met his father outside the house, and

---

7. *Id.* at 244–45.

8. Stephen Morse, *Immaturity and Irresponsibility*, 88 J. Crim. L. & Criminology 15, 30 (1997).

stabbed him twelve times. During a post-offense interview, Ralph stated that he knew it was not "right" to kill his father for sleeping with his wife, but mentioned that his father had abused him as a child and that the voices continually harped on his father's indiscretions with Ralph's wife and daughter. It is impossible to know whether this person's ability to be guided by good reasons was any more diminished than either that of a mentally ill person with similar beliefs who doesn't kill his "tormentor" or that of a nonmentally ill person who kills when he discovers that his father *is* sleeping with his wife and daughter. As Dr. Drew Ross, a psychiatrist who has spent years evaluating murderers, notes, "psychosis may enhance and enact the drama already present, and the drama is not necessarily an innocent one."[9]

Examples can easily be multiplied that lead one to question whether rationality makes sense as the culpability threshold. Some people with paranoid schizophrenia harm those whom they inaccurately perceive are harassing them while other paranoid individuals, also irrationally fearful, do not. At the same time, those who are generally not irrational may be just as likely as people with paranoid schizophrenia to react disproportionately to perceived threats. The law books are full of cases in which sensitive but otherwise normal people are convicted, albeit sometimes only of manslaughter, when they kill a person who has slighted them. In short, just as the existence of a disorder cannot tell us how hard it was for the offender to *do* what is right, the existence of irrationality usually cannot tell us how hard it was to *perceive* what is right.

IV. INTEGRATIONISM REPRISED

For all of these reasons, the linchpin of culpability analysis should not be volition, appreciation, or rationality. The linchpin should instead be the mens rea and subjective justification inquiries that form the basis for determining criminal culpability when mental disability is not involved. Two questions about this rule remain: First, what role should mental illness play when negligence is the mens rea? Second, when, if ever, should ignorance of the criminal law due to mental disorder be an excuse?

For now, I will only provide brief answers to these questions, without supporting argument. On the first question: Mental disorder can be exculpatory even when negligence is the mens rea, if negligence is defined in the semi-subjective manner endorsed by the Model Penal Code (MPC).[10] However,

---

9. Drew Ross, Looking into the Eyes of a Killer: A Psychiatrist's Journey Through the Murderer's World 87 (1998)

10. Model Penal Code § 2.02(d) (Proposed Official Draft 1962) ("The risk must be of such a nature and degree that the actor's failure to perceive it, considering the nature and purpose of his conduct *and the circumstances known to him*, involves a gross deviation from

congruent with various defensive provisions in the MPC (e.g., the denial of a defense to those who create their own necessity), exculpation should not be based on avoidable mental disorder. On the second question: Exculpation can be based on an incapacity to grasp the *concept* of criminal law (as might occur with an infant), but should not be based on a mistake as to a particular criminal-law doctrine (e.g., self-defense or the law of burglary), again congruent with the MPC's analogous provisions.

Putting all of the foregoing together, the Integrationist Alternative might read something like this:

> A person shall be excused from an offense if at the time of the offense [by reason of mental disease or defect] he or she (a) lacked the subjective mental state for the conduct, circumstance, or result element of the crime; (b) believed circumstances existed that, if true, would have justified the offense; (c) believed circumstances existed that, if true, would have amounted to duress; or (d) was unaware of the general prohibitions of the criminal law, provided that he or she did not cause any of these mental states by purposely avoiding treatment aware that such states would occur without such treatment.

---

the standard of care that a reasonable person would observe in the actor's situation.") (emphasis added).

COMMENTS

NO EXCUSE FOR YOU

SUSAN D. ROZELLE*

Christopher Slobogin may have proved too much. In his zeal to discredit each of the leading rationales grounding the insanity defense (for impairments of volition, appreciation, or rationality, respectively), he manages to explain that no one, under any circumstances, merits an excuse.

Not that he means to say so. Indeed, he explicitly provides that although he would dispense with an insanity defense as such, persons should be excused if they lack mens rea; believe facts that, if true, would support a justification or a duress claim; or are generally ignorant of the law, all regardless of their mental health status. But this explains who should be excused, not why. And by discrediting the whys that underlie the insanity defense, Slobogin manages to discredit the whys underlying his own proposal as well.

---

* Associate Professor of Law, Capital University Law School.

The first prong of his proposed excuse is dispensed with easily. Those who lack whatever mens rea is required for a given crime are not guilty of the prima facie case. Since they lack an essential element of the crime, these individuals do not need an "excuse" to avoid conviction.

In the remaining prongs, he proposes excusing a variety of other defendants: those who wrongly believed they were defending themselves or another against an unlawful harm, or who wrongly believed they were facing a hard choice would, for example, be excused under the integrationist proposal. So much for whom to excuse. But why? What rationale underlies the integrationist excuse?

Those who labor under a mistaken belief that they are being attacked are generally understood to merit an excuse because such people lack appreciation of what they are doing, or perhaps lack rationality, depending on why they formed the mistaken impression. If Joe reasonably mistakes a midnight visit from a drunken friend as a burglar's break-in, then the conventional wisdom probably would explain that he ought to be excused because he failed to appreciate, through no fault of his own, the nature of his action.[1] He was not in fact defending himself from unlawful force, but instead was unlawfully attacking his friend. If his mistake was unreasonable, but arose from a mental illness such as paranoid schizophrenia—perhaps he believed his friend was about to attack him because, to take a suitably schizophrenic example, his friend was wearing a wristwatch—then the excuse probably lies in his lack of rationality, which again arose through no fault of his own.

Those who labor under a mistaken belief that they are being coerced are generally understood to merit an excuse because such people suffer from impaired volition. The choice is too hard for us to fairly blame these defendants for giving in; any of us would have done likewise if faced with the same choice.

Provocation does not make it into Slobogin's proposed integrationist excuse offered at the end of his piece, but he mentions it as an excusing condition early on. The conventional wisdom on provocation is that, like duress, it is based primarily on an impairment of volition. Having suffered a wrong so grievous that any of us would have found it difficult to contain ourselves, the provoked defendant's action is less blameworthy than it would have been in the absence of the provocation.

Finally, Slobogin proposes an expansion of current law to include a defense for those who suffer from a general ignorance of "the *concept* of criminal law (as might occur with an infant)." Again, we ask why this form of ignorance should

---

1. Of course there may be a better grounding than conventional wisdom offers for any given defense. *See, e.g.*, Susan D. Rozelle, *Controlling Passion: Adultery and the Provocation Defense*, 37 RUTGERS L.J. 197 (2005) (offering alternative to conventional wisdom in provocation); Susan D. Rozelle, *Fear and Loathing in Insanity Law: Explaining the Otherwise Inexplicable* Clark v. Arizona, 58 CASE W. RES. L. REV. 39 (2007) (offering alternative to conventional wisdom in insanity).

merit an excuse, and again, the answer I suspect we would most often receive is that such people lack appreciation or rationality.

I am afraid Slobogin's project is misguided. He offers his integrationist approach on the same footing as the volitional, appreciation, and rationality approaches, but they seem to be apples and oranges. Integrationism identifies *who* should be excused (those who lack mens rea, or whose mistakes would provide them with a justification or duress defense, or who are ignorant of the concept of criminal law). The volitional, appreciation, and rationality approaches explain *why* we excuse these defendants.

Having done his best to discredit the volitional, appreciation, and rationality approaches to the insanity defense, Slobogin offers no grounding for his preferred integrationist excuse. Moreover, if that excuse must ultimately be grounded in the volitional, appreciation, or rationality approaches that Slobogin rejects, the result is a proposal that undercuts its own girders, unintentionally advocating not only the abolition of the insanity defense, but the abolition of all excuses—including the integrationist one.

NOT BY COGNITION ALONE

SHERRY F. COLB*

Christopher Slobogin's integrationist approach reduces the complexity of excuse doctrine and coherently "integrates" mentally ill defendants who deserve to avoid punishment with similarly situated others. One important aspect of his proposal, however, troubles me—his refusal to recognize volition-based excuses.

Slobogin's litmus test for determining whether a mentally ill defendant has an excuse is to ask whether his conduct would have been justified (or excused under duress) if the defendant's beliefs about the conditions under which he committed his crime had been accurate. If my client suffers from schizophrenia and believes his sleeping roommate has pointed a gun at him, my client has an excuse for shooting the roommate. If your client is mentally well but operates under the same misapprehensions, your client, too, is excused. The illness provides no morally relevant distinction between our clients.

Slobogin would, however, reject an excuse for mentally ill defendants whose factual beliefs—if true—would *not* justify or otherwise excuse their conduct. My client suffers from schizophrenia and believes that his roommate is the Antichrist. Under the criminal law, even if his roommate *were* the Antichrist, killing him would be prohibited. Therefore, my client has no excuse. By the same token, your mentally well client—who belongs to a religious group that

---

* Professor of Law and Charles Evans Hughes Scholar, Cornell Law School.

classifies people like the roommate as enemies of God—also lacks an excuse for homicide.

In this example, many would have differing intuitions regarding our respective clients. My client's "belief" that his roommate is the Antichrist is a symptom of his mental illness, not the product of his approach to life or his value system. This makes his conduct meaningfully different from that of a religious fanatic who deems some people to be the enemies of God. Yet there is no acceptable way to translate an excuse for my mentally ill client into a justification for the accurate assessor of reality.

Consider two real-life illustrations: Juan J. Gonzalez, a.k.a. the "Staten Island Slasher," and Andrea Yates, the woman who drowned her children.

Gonzalez suffered from paranoid schizophrenia. When he felt himself becoming "dangerous," he visited a hospital and sought admission. Asked whether he felt suicidal, he said no and was consequently permitted to stay only a few days, despite his statement that "Jesus wants me to kill." Shortly thereafter, Gonzalez—operating under the influence of command hallucinations—brought a sword onto the Staten Island Ferry and began hacking people with it, killing two and injuring nine. Family members of the victims agreed with the defense that Gonzalez should be deemed not guilty by reason of insanity, and he was subsequently committed to the State mental hygiene department.

Yates suffered from post-partum psychosis. According to all reports, she had loved her five children but became increasingly depressed and psychotic after the birth of her youngest. Prior to the killings, her psychiatrist inexplicably took her off her medication and told her to think "happy thoughts." Yates waited until no one was home with her and her children and then successively drowned all of them. She was operating under a delusional belief that if she did not kill her children, they would all go to hell.

With respect to both Gonzalez and Yates, their beliefs—had they been accurate—would not have justified their conduct. If God had really told Gonzalez to kill ferry passengers or if Yates's children had truly been headed for hell, the law would still have prohibited both killers' actions. There is no justification for acts performed under actual orders from God.

Nonetheless, Gonzalez and Yates were widely understood to be nonculpable due to the impairments associated with their respective mental illnesses. Contributing to that understanding was the fact that both felt *compelled* by their pathologically distorted thinking to act as they did. One index of that compulsion is the reality that both of them experienced regret and otherwise behaved in a manner demonstrating that their conduct on the particular occasion represented an extreme departure for each of them.

Slobogin correctly observes that volitional impairments are difficult to verify or quantify, difficulties that pose a challenge for those who would apply a volitional standard. Nonetheless, to the extent that people like Juan Gonzalez and Andrea Yates suffer from mental illness that seems to take over their psyche and their will, it would be unjust to hold them criminally responsible for their actions. That victims' families in both cases recognized as much argues for the inadequacy of a purely cognitive integrationist approach. Cognition, emotion, and volition are—at least in the case of the severely mentally ill—inextricably bound.

AGAINST INTEGRATIONISM

PAUL LITTON*

Christopher Slobogin's criticisms of insanity tests that track irrationality are misguided, and integrationism is morally inferior to systems that retain an insanity defense.

Slobogin surprisingly attributes minimal arguments to rationality theorists despite their extensive justifications. Moore, Morse, and other theorists systematically examine the excuses we recognize in law and morality, and argue that the most coherent account of our practices includes the principle that responsibility requires the capacity for rationality. Such inquiry reveals our firm belief in the unfairness of punishing those who lacked the capacity to grasp and apply reasons that support our obligations. Indeed, the law treats mental abnormality as significant precisely because abnormality often signifies irrationality.

Yet without inquiry into the basis of responsibility, Slobogin favors integrationism because it supposedly "better captures the universe of those who *should* be excused."[1] "*Should*" according to what criteria? He states that the "linchpin of culpability analysis"[2] should be mens rea and subjectively defined defenses, but that approach is inadequate. Children act with prohibited mens rea, and we can assess whether they acted justifiably or under duress assuming their factual beliefs were true. Slobogin cannot explain why the law would exempt children. The reason it exempts children is that they are insufficiently rational, and for that same reason the law must excuse irrational adults.

Slobogin's only other responsibility criterion is popular sentiment about individual cases. He argues that existing insanity standards would excuse some agents who should not be excused, and the reason they should not be excused is that most people would not excuse them. But without any account of responsibility's basis, Slobogin cannot answer the objection that most people might be unaware of the implications of their firm commitments regarding responsibility. This inability to respond is particularly problematic because many people might feel a vengeful urge to punish murderous defendants (like Charles Manson or

---

* Associate Professor of Law, University of Missouri School of Law.
1. Slobogin core text at 474.
2. *Id.* at 481.

Ted Kaczynski) without considering what our principles of responsibility imply. Widespread intuitions about particular cases are important to theorizing and evaluating proposed standards, but especially when controversial, they neither control unconditionally nor necessarily trump our general commitments.

Nonetheless, according to Slobogin, those who say that Kaczynski or Manson might plausibly be insane will face an insuperable challenge: namely, that it is impossible to distinguish them from criminals who are uncontroversially responsible, like Gacy and the pedophile who thought their victims benefited, both of whom believed their actions were justified. He argues that under the "wrongfulness" version of the appreciation test, the "only basis" for excusing the former pair but not the latter is that the former "held their self-justificatory beliefs more intensely."[3]

But that is not the only basis. The relevant question is not whether a defendant felt justified and thereby actually failed to appreciate the wrongfulness of his conduct. The question is whether he lacked substantial *capacity* to appreciate its wrongfulness: could he recognize reasons to refrain from his crime? Among defendants who believed their crimes justified, some had that capacity; others did not. These cases pose no problem for the appreciation or rationality tests.

Slobogin argues that, unlike integrationism, existing insanity tests require "impossible" and "unprovable" judgments about defendants' capacities. But first, even under integrationism, jurors must get into the defendant's head to determine what he believed and then apply difficult legal standards, like whether a defendant alleging duress lacked a fair opportunity to avoid crime. Second, integrationism does *not* eliminate all need to consider a defendant's capacities. For example, under the MPC's subjectivized self-defense standards, a successful defendant must believe lethal force was necessary, which involves knowing he cannot retreat. Imagine a defendant who used lethal force and denies that he knew he could retreat, even though a normal-functioning adult would have known retreat was possible. Jurors then would assess his claim of ignorance and determine whether he would have recognized the possibility of retreat. That decision involves determining his capacities—what he *could* have recognized.

Finally, integrationism is unjust. First, it does not permit adequate consideration of disturbed reasoning processes. A defendant may possess bizarre beliefs that, even if true, would fail to render his action justified or excused. Integrationism holds him responsible even though he may be unable to reason logically, avoid focus on irrelevant facts, draw reasonable conclusions from evidence, or form abstract concepts correctly. Second, even under the MPC, a severely irrational defendant could be convicted of negligent homicide if his belief in the necessity of lethal force was unreasonable, even though he lacked capacity to judge reasonably. A defendant should have the opportunity to argue that his beliefs and reasoning processes were so disturbed that he should not be punished.

---

3. *Id.* at 479.

JUSTIFYING DEFENSES

MATT MATRAVERS*

Christopher Slobogin's strategy is to test various rationales for the insanity defense against examples of cases that should clearly be—or, more often, not be—excused. Any insanity defense that would excuse in cases where Slobogin thinks the accused should be punished is found wanting.

I have a comment on one example of this argumentative strategy (the case of the psychopath), but first it is worth making a general point about Slobogin's method. Of course, in legal philosophy—as in moral and political philosophy—one important way in which we assess the plausibility of a theory is by testing it against our strongly held convictions. A theory of justice, no matter how well worked out, that declared slavery to be just would be suspect, and we would know it to be suspect precisely because it does not match our belief that slavery is unjust. Nevertheless, were we only to test our theories against our convictions, and always favor the latter, we would diminish the possibilities offered by philosophical reflection. The point is that we must work both ways. Sometimes our best efforts at theoretical reflection will contradict our convictions and that will be reason to reflect again. However, we should be open to the thought that it might be time to revise our convictions. Slobogin is sure that he knows the right answers, and this certainty blunts his critique of the alternatives to his integrationist thesis.[1]

A particularly egregious example of Slobogin's method is displayed in his discussion of the "appreciation test." "Exhibit A in the case against the appreciation test," Slobogin writes, is "the psychopath, virtually everyone's paradigm of the 'evil' person who should be punished if he commits crime."[2] Slobogin offers no evidence for this empirical claim (or for any other) and the addition of "virtually" makes it impossible to assess. Suffice to say, then, that the philosophical literature on psychopathy is replete with examples of people who think that psychopaths should *not* be held responsible or punished.[3]

The critical issue in the philosophical literature is whether psychopaths have the *capacity* to appreciate the moral wrongness of their actions. The underlying thought here is a simple one: It is unjust to hold people responsible for, say, not performing action X if they lack the necessary capacity to perform X. Unpacking

---

* Professor of Political Philosophy, Department of Politics, University of York, United Kingdom.

1. Obviously, this paragraph owes a debt to Rawls's discussion of "reflective equilibrium." *See* John Rawls, A THEORY OF JUSTICE 20–21 (1971).

2. Slobogin core text at 477.

3. For a very recent discussion (and further references), see the symposium on psychopathy in 14 PHIL., PSYCH., & PSYCHOL. (2007).

that simple thought is unfortunately complex. Different moral theories have different understandings of what it is to have the capacity to appreciate moral wrong. Kantians, for example, locate the relevant incapacity in a cognitive failure (an inability to apply a certain type of practical reasoning); Humeans in an inability to feel a special kind of "sympathy"; and Aristotelians in an inability to reason properly in a manner that combines intellect and emotion.[4] All, though, would agree that if a person lacks the capacity—however defined—then it would be wrong to hold him responsible.

Slobogin's response to this is to invoke his method of comparing putative results with his convictions along an increasingly steep slippery slope: If we excuse the psychopath, then what about the mildly retarded, the person who just does not think properly, the Unabomber and the serial killer? I do not have the space here to discuss each of these in turn and in any case, as mentioned above, it would require that I first offer an argument for one version of the capacity to appreciate moral wrong.

Nonetheless, the analysis above points in the direction of how we should go about the discussion. It seems to be likely that the accused in *Companaro* had the capacity to appreciate the wrongness of what he was doing, even if he did not in fact do so. The same may well hold for the Unabomber and the serial killer. They may *believe* that their actions are justified, all things considered (because of the need on the one hand to warn the world of the dangers of technology and on the other to get rid of homosexual prostitutes), but that is not the point (nor is it to the point to wonder about the intensity of their beliefs). The point is one about their capacity to understand their actions as moral wrongs.

---

4. This paragraph draws on Matt Matravers, *Holding Psychopaths Responsible*, 14 PHIL., PSYCH., & PSYCHOL. 139 (2007).

REPLY

CHRISTOPHER SLOBOGIN

Susan Rozelle is technically correct in suggesting that I do not explain why the Integrationist alternative excuses. I simply assume a consensus that an excuse should be granted to people who do not have the requisite subjectively defined mens rea or think they are experiencing a threat that, if true, would justify their act. Others, including those who drafted the Model Penal Code, have defended this approach to criminal liability against the objectivists, and I decided not to replicate that effort.

But Rozelle is wrong to suggest that debunking the appreciation, rationality, and volitional tests destroys the foundation for the integrationist test as well. The appreciation and rationality tests should be rejected because they provide an excuse to people who *do* intend their crimes and *don't* believe they are threatened. These latter people would not have a defense if they are not mentally ill and should not have a defense if they are. Similarly, the volitional tests merely require a strong impulse, which does not excuse those who are not mentally ill and should not excuse those who are.

Sherry Colb takes issue with this last statement. Note first that the cases she uses to illustrate her argument—an offender who believes God has ordered murder (Gonzalez) and an offender who believes her children will go to hell if she doesn't kill them (Yates)—are best described in terms of *cognitive*, not volitional, impairment. More importantly, relabeling religious motivations as delusions (and the line between the two is much fuzzier than many suppose) should not change the exculpatory inquiry, however bizarre it might sound: if God *did* command a person to hack innocent people to pieces or if one's children *will* go to hell if they're not killed, should one who acted on those thoughts have a defense? In my view, Yates might well be excused under the integrationist test, given the options she believed she had. In *Gonzalez*, a jury might reach the opposite result: God only *pretends* to command the death of innocent people, as a test of faith (e.g., Abraham and Isaac); moreover, to recognize the contrary claim would give an excuse to fundamentalist terrorists as well.

A huge number of offenders—ranging from child molesters to addicts—feel compelled to do what they do. Granting them an excuse would upend the criminal justice system. Unless the "compulsion" is so great that the offense is literally unthinking or the related thoughts lead one to believe that harm is imminent, even mental illness should not excuse. If the concern is that someone like Gonzalez needs treatment, that goal should be pursued through prison reform, not a criminal law doctrine that affects only a fraction of those with mental problems.

Paul Litton's comments go more directly to the viability of the integrationist test. The Moore/Morse position to which he subscribes boils down to the proposition that people should be excused if they cannot grasp the right reasons for acting because, to use Litton's words, they are "unable to reason logically, avoid focus on irrelevant facts, draw reasonable conclusions from evidence, or form abstract concepts correctly."[1] Litton is right that a subset of people with these characteristics—those who intend their crimes and do not feel threatened when they commit them—would not be excused under the integrationist test.

And they should not be. Many people with psychosis, although generally irrational, commit serious crime out of greed, jealousy, or hatred (e.g., perhaps Kaczynski and Manson). Conversely, many offenders who do not have psychosis and whom we would not want to excuse nonetheless do not "reason logically," etc., at the moment of their offense (e.g., domestic abusers, hotheads, and a host

---

1. Litton comment at 487.

of other "spur-of-the-moment" offenders; some people with psychopathy and mild mental retardation; people like Jeffrey Dahmer who act for "bizarre" reasons). Any definition of excuse that includes such people is too broad, not only because the populace thinks so but because a functioning criminal justice system couldn't countenance excusing so many people.

These points also respond to Matt Matravers's objection that the integration-ist approach would permit conviction of those (including psychopaths) who lack the "capacity" to carry out the mental functions necessary for liability. Psychopaths might lack capacity to care about the wrongness of their acts. But at the time of their crime and probably much of the rest of the time, so did the Unabomber, Gacy, and many others whom we don't feel comfortable excusing. Matravers (and Litton) are correct that I make no deeper, more "philosophical" claim than this comparative one. But as a practical matter it is a powerful claim; psychopaths alone comprise perhaps 20 percent of our prison population. The only other option is to jettison the retributive enterprise and adopt a preventive regime.

Finally, it should be noted that the integrationist proposal would still excuse a significant number of individuals. Contrary to Litton's suggestion, children below six or seven usually don't have mens rea or are ignorant of mala in se criminal prohibitions. Most people with psychosis who commit crimes against persons do so because they honestly feel threatened. Even psychotic people charged with negligent homicide could be acquitted under the Model Penal Code, given the MPC's threshold inquiry in negligence cases into whether the actor should have refrained from crime "considering the circumstances known to him."

23. ENTRAPMENT AND THE "FREE MARKET" FOR CRIME

LOUIS MICHAEL SEIDMAN*

Few people wanting to learn about the entrapment defense would start their research by reading *Lochner v. New York*,[1] and yet it is with the *Lochner* tradition that a real understanding of entrapment doctrine must begin.

In *Lochner* itself, the Supreme Court invalidated a New York statute that regulated the hours bakers could be required to work. The case has come to stand for a broader jurisprudential position, however, that equates market allocations with freedom and treats redistributive departures from market baselines as coercive and problematic. Criticism of that tradition, in turn, takes two forms. The substantive critique claims that *Lochner*'s philosophical commitments are flawed. On the one hand, substantive critics have disputed the fairness, voluntariness, and inevitability of market distributions. On the other, they have disputed the premise that market distributions can really be separated from government choice. The procedural critique does not necessarily embrace the substantive criticisms, but recognizes that there is enough to them to justify placing issues about redistribution in the discretionary, political sphere rather than in the mandatory, constitutional sphere.

When the police entrap a suspect, they redistribute the cost of crime control from outcomes produced by the "ordinary" market for criminal acts. Instead of accepting privately established market rates for crime as a baseline, they influence the market, thereby shifting the cost of deterrence onto people who might not otherwise become entangled with the criminal law. When judges, in turn, resist these efforts, they are insisting that the market distributions are natural and sacrosanct. They are, in other words, embracing the *Lochner* tradition and ignoring the substantive critique of that position.

With regard to the procedural critique, it is significant that entrapment doctrine is often a judicial creation. To be sure, at least some aspects of judicially fashioned entrapment rules are subject to legislative revision, and to this extent the rules are compatible with the procedural critique. Some forms of entrapment seem to be constitutionally impermissible, however, and even with respect to the subconstitutional parts of the doctrine, strong inertial forces sharply limit

* Carmack Waterhouse Professor of Constitutional Law, Georgetown University Law Center. I am grateful to Luis Miguel Dickson, Steven Goldberg, Martin Lederman, Richard McAdams, and Silas Wasserstrom, for help in thinking through some of the problems addressed in this core text.

1. 198 U.S. 45 (1905).

the realistic possibilities of political correction. To this extent, entrapment doctrine also runs afoul of the procedural critique.

Entrapment doctrine, then, provides yet another example of how *Lochnerism* survives in the world of criminal law and procedure long after it has supposedly been discredited elsewhere.[2] All of this was, I hope, implicit in an analysis of entrapment I published more than a quarter of a century ago.[3] Since then my analysis has been subjected to some penetrating and subtle criticisms, which have helped me think more clearly about the problem. I am especially grateful to Richard H. McAdams[4] and to the team of Ronald J. Allen, Melissa Lutrell, and Anne Kreeger (hereinafter ALK),[5] whose insightful and generous treatment of my work has caused me to understand the ways in which it was flawed, incomplete, unclear, or simply muddled. Perhaps out of stubbornness, I still want to insist that the main lines of my argument were correct. The criticism has nonetheless convinced me that my argument might have been more persuasive had I made the connection between entrapment and *Lochnerism* explicit rather than merely implicit.

I. BLACK LETTER ENTRAPMENT AND ITS DIFFICULTIES

Superficially, the "black letter" of federal entrapment law seems easy enough to comprehend.[6] Supposedly as a matter of statutory construction, the Supreme Court has read federal criminal statutes to prohibit punishment of a defendant, not previously disposed to commit a crime, who is induced to commit it by a government agent. Although the defendant has the burden of production on the issue, once he introduces some evidence of "inducement," the government must then demonstrate beyond a reasonable doubt that the defendant was in fact predisposed—a burden that it can meet by introducing evidence of the defendant's reputation, character, prior convictions, and prior bad acts. Except in the very rare case where the government can offer no evidence of predisposition, the defense then goes to the jury.

---

2. I discuss this point at greater length and with reference to other aspects of criminal law and procedure in Louis Michael Seidman, *Points of Intersection: Discontinuities at the Border of Criminal Law and the Regulatory State*, 7 J. CONTEMP. LEGAL ISSUES 97 (1996).

3. Louis Michael Seidman, *The Supreme Court, Entrapment, and Our Criminal Justice Dilemma*, 1981 SUP. CT. REV. 111.

4. Richard H. McAdams, *The Political Economy of Entrapment*, 96 J. CRIM. L. & CRIMINOLOGY 107 (2005).

5. Ronald J. Allen, Melissa Luttrell, and Anne Kreeger, *Clarifying Entrapment*, 89 J. CRIM. L. & CRIMINOLOGY 407 (1999).

6. Much of what follows in this section is drawn directly from Seidman, *supra* note 3.

Although state law is split on the issue, the success of the federal defense does not depend on the reasonableness of the inducement that the government offers. Even if the government offers an "excessive" inducement, the defendant will not prevail if he is in fact "predisposed." The federal defense is thus subjective; its focus is on the defendant's preinducement state of mind. A bare majority of the Supreme Court has maintained, however, that the defense should be supplemented by objective, constitutionally based restrictions. When truly outrageous government conduct is proved, the Due Process Clause apparently prohibits conviction of even predisposed defendants.

As many commentators have noted, this black-letter law is very nearly incoherent. The core problem is that it makes no sense to separate the question of predisposition from the level of inducement. Potential criminals, like most other people, do not work for free, and their willingness to work depends on the return on their labor. Thus, when juries are instructed to determine whether the defendant was abstractly "predisposed" without reference to the level of inducement offered to him, they are asked a meaningless question.

I have argued that one might nonetheless make some sense of the doctrine if "disposition" were understood in the sense of "temperament" or "character" rather than "tendency." In everyday life, we sometimes categorize individuals in terms of the specific acts they perform (which is the way in which the criminal law usually treats defendants), but we also sometimes categorize them in terms of their general demeanor. We are especially prone to this tendency when we use demeaning stereotypes. "Trailer trash" does not necessarily categorize people according to their abode, and "Starbucks Democrats" need not drink coffee. These terms refer to ways of life or thought rather than to specific acts. So, too, when we say that a person has a "criminal disposition," we may mean that his general lifestyle and pattern of behavior is associated with stereotypic preconceptions of what criminals are like rather than with any specific act. Such a person is simply one of the usual suspects.

I make no claim that the Supreme Court intends for "predisposition" to be understood in this way, but there can be little doubt that this is what the term means in practice. The jury in an entrapment case does not have the luxury of deciding an issue as concrete as what the defendant did, or even what he was thinking when he did it. The jury must speculate on what the defendant would have done in a different, nonexistent world. The jury must make this decision by utilizing instructions that are, for reasons I have already explained, incoherent and impossible to apply in a principled manner. Moreover, once the defendant raises an entrapment defense, special rules of evidence apply. The prosecution is permitted to undertake a broad-scale inquest into the defendant's character and reputation. Normally, of course, this evidence is inadmissible, precisely because it distracts the jury from deciding what acts the defendant performed and causes it to focus instead on the defendant's character. Can it be doubted, then, that when this evidence is admitted on a question as nebulous as entrapment under a test as confused as predisposition even the most conscientious jury ends up making a judgment about the kind of person it perceives the defendant to be?

II. *LOCHNER*, ENTRAPMENT, AND DISTRIBUTING THE COSTS OF DETERRENCE

Why should courts, often in the absence of any legislative encouragement, mandate these judgments? Although the Supreme Court has occasionally suggested otherwise, the entrapment defense cannot be justified on retributive grounds. The retributive problem is not, as some commentators have argued, that an entrapped defendant has caused no harm. We regularly punish and hold blameworthy people who have not caused harm, as when, for example, a person intending to kill fires a gun into an empty bed. The problem, instead, is that we have no general retributive principle that excuses individuals when they are motivated by very tempting offers. We know that this is true because there is no defense when these offers come from private sources. To be sure, in extreme circumstances, we sometimes exculpate individuals when threats make obedience to law very difficult, but we make no similar allowance for offers, as when, for example, a public official is led astray by a very generous bribe that is too good to refuse.

The failure of retributive theory to justify an entrapment defense has led commentators to suggest two other arguments, one based on efficiency, the other on the risk of political abuse.

A. The Efficiency Rational

Building on earlier suggestions by Richard Posner and Steven Shavell,[7] ALK argue that it is inefficient to punish individuals who receive above-market offers to commit crimes.[8] Richard McAdams elaborates on and qualifies ALK's theory by distinguishing between "true offenders," who commit offenses in the real world; "false offenders," who commit offenses only in the artificial world created by government inducements; and "probabilistic offenders," whose willingness to offend depends upon fluctuating preferences and opportunities.[9] He adds to this a persuasive account of why the police might be motivated to entrap false offenders even when doing so produces little law enforcement gain.

Although some of the argument supporting it is complex, the basic insight driving the efficiency argument is clear enough: There is no need to incapacitate

---

7. *See* Richard A. Posner, ECONOMIC ANALYSIS OF LAW 255 (5th ed. 1998); Steven Shavell, *Criminal Law and the Optimal Use of Nonmonetary Sanctions as a Deterrent*, 85 COLUM. L. REV. 1232, 1256 (1985).

8. *See* Allen et al., *supra* note 5, at 415–21.

9. *See* McAdams, *supra* note 4, at 126, 150.

individuals who respond to offers unlikely ever to be made in the real world, and punishing these individuals adds nothing whatever to the deterrent threat that already exists against individuals who respond to more realistic offers.

It must be noted at the outset that none of these authors claims, and there is no reason to suppose, that the actual entrapment defense bars only these supposedly inefficient, above-market offers. For reasons explained above, the actual defense operates primarily to exculpate individuals who do not fit our stereotype of the criminal class. Suppose, though, that an idealized entrapment defense of the sort that ALK and McAdams advocate were put in place. Could such a defense be justified on efficiency grounds?

McAdams demonstrates his deterrence point with a simple numerical example.[10] Imagine that in the absence of entrapment, one hundred individuals respond positively to the market rate for criminal activity and that ten of these individuals are apprehended. The chance of apprehension is therefore 10 percent. Now suppose that of the original one hundred individuals three, who would not otherwise be apprehended, are entrapped at market rates. The chance of apprehension goes up to 13 percent, and, if potential offenders perceive this change, there is a deterrence gain. Suppose, however, that the three entrapped individuals are "false offenders" in the sense that they are responding only to an artificially inflated price. If they are entrapped by above-market rates, McAdams claims, their apprehension has no additional effect on individuals who are responding to market rates. For this group, the odds of apprehension remain at 10 percent. McAdams concludes that because "individuals care only about the probability of their own detection, which they judge from the probability of detecting the class of individuals like themselves," the claim that above-market inducements advances general deterrence is "erroneous."[11]

There are several problems with McAdams's argument. First, the argument fails to account for the fact that some true offenders will nonetheless think, rightly or wrongly, that they will be able to take advantage of an entrapment defense by convincing the jury that they are false offenders. Given how amorphous the defense is, and given the fact that, once an inducement is shown, the government will have to prove the absence of entrapment beyond a reasonable doubt, this possibility is far from fanciful. Suppose, then, that individuals think that if they respond to government inducements, they will have a 25 percent chance of prevailing with an entrapment defense, even if they are true offenders. This means one-quarter of our original three percentage point gain in deterrence from the entrapment strategy has been eaten away by the mere existence of the defense even if the government never entraps a false offender.

---

10. *See id.* at 129–30. I have modified the example slightly for expository purposes.
11. *Id.* at 130.

Second, the entrapment defense is costly because it raises the cost of the government making its case. Oddly, McAdams himself seems to recognize this point. He analogizes entrapment to what he calls "proxy" crimes. He uses the example of a statute that makes it a criminal offense to have an opened alcohol container in an automobile.[12] One might say that just as punishing individuals who respond to above-market offers adds no deterrence for individuals responding to market offers, so, too, punishing individuals who do not drink from open containers adds nothing to the deterrence already directed against individuals who do drink. It is obvious, though, that the government is better able to deter those who do drink if it does not have to prove that they do. The same point applies to individuals who accept market offers to commit criminal acts.

Finally, McAdams's argument assumes that if there is an entrapment defense, the government will accurately calculate the market price and, having done so, will refrain from making above-market offers. If either of these assumptions is wrong, then the defense again produces a loss of deterrence. If the government itself is not deterred by the rules prohibiting above-market incentives, some individuals who would have responded to those incentives and been convicted will instead respond to above-market incentives and be acquitted. How often would the police make this kind of mistake? There is no way to know, but the difficulty of accurately calculating the market rate for crime as well as the factors that sometimes cause police to be more interested in arrests than convictions provide reason for concern.

An analogy to the Fourth Amendment exclusionary rule is useful here. If the police always obeyed the Fourth Amendment, the exclusionary rule would impose no costs because no evidence would ever be excluded. But we know that the exclusionary rule does impose costs caused by the fact that the police do not always obey the Fourth Amendment. When they disobey it—because they make a mistake, or because they think they will not be caught, or because they are uninterested in securing evidence—the disobedience sometimes leads to the acquittal of guilty defendants. There is no reason to think that entrapment rules operate any differently.

None of this demonstrates that McAdams and ALK are necessarily wrong about the putative efficiency losses imposed by some kinds of entrapment. It is at least possible that the effects I identify are swamped by the incentives police have to entrap individuals even when the entrapment serves no law enforcement purpose. Moreover, if one focuses on incapacitation rather than merely on deterrence, it seems obvious that there are inefficiencies inherent in incarcerating individuals who are unlikely to receive offers that will lead to crime.

There are, of course, well-known problems with the incapacitation strategy, which I will not discuss here. Moreover, it is worth emphasizing again that the

---

12. *See id.* at 158.

idealized entrapment defense that McAdams and ALK describe bears little relationship to the actual defense we have. But suppose that we put all these problems aside and assume, for the sake of argument, that McAdams and ALK are right and that some kinds of entrapment impose costs that are not paid for by crime prevention. Even on this assumption, I think that these costs are smaller than McAdams and ALK suppose. For the reasons I have just explained, allowing an entrapment defense also imposes costs. Nonetheless, our supposition, for the sake of argument, is that when we net out the various costs, it is more expensive to make above-market offers than not to make them.

Does this concession establish the case for an entrapment defense? Only if one definitionally excludes distributive concerns from the efficiency analysis. It is here that the arguments of the *Lochner* Court and its critics take hold. Just as government regulation of the labor market redistributes goods from those who benefit from market pricing to those who do not, so, too, entrapment redistributes the cost of deterrence from those who bear that cost when the market prices criminal conduct to a new class that bears it when government conduct helps set the price.

The key insight is that if, as I have already argued, above-market prices deter to at least some extent, then we can achieve some of our law enforcement purposes by redistributing the cost of deterrence to a different group of people. This will be true even if the same level of deterrence could be achieved by market offers. In other words, the question is not, as McAdams supposes, whether above-market offers buy *additional* deterrence, but whether they buy *as much* deterrence as market offers. If they do, then we are in a position to redistribute the cost of crime control. Of course, the redistributive effort will impose costs. In the post-*Lochner* world, it is widely assumed that the political branches are nonetheless permitted to impose those costs for the sake of social justice.

Why might redistribution of the cost of crime prevention promote social justice? The critique of *Lochner* again provides an explanation. For nineteenth century liberal theorists, freedom of contract was just that—free choices made by, for example, workers and holders of capital to exchange service for pay at rates set by large numbers of autonomous transactions. So, too, a *Lochnerian* conception of freedom might treat criminals as deserving their punishment because of their free choice to accept market rates in exchange for criminal activity.

In the context of the economic regulation, critics of *Lochner* have responded by arguing that supposedly autonomous bargains in the labor market are in fact dictated by prior entitlements. Workers accept low wages not because they want to but because the pattern of prior entitlements force them to. Precisely the same point can be made about the criminal market. Imagine that there is a good called crime-resistance capital that is unequally allocated at or shortly after birth. This capital might consist of early training in impulse control, plausible noncriminal paths toward wealth and happiness, inculcation in mainstream values, and so forth. It is easy to see that, through no fault of his own, a person with little crime-resistance capital is differently situated from a person with a great deal of this capital with respect to ability to obey the law. Whereas the low-capital person might respond to a market inducement, it might require an above-market inducement to tempt the high-capital person.

Without entrapment, or with only market-level entrapment, we force the low-capital person to bear the entire cost of deterring criminal conduct. This distribution is no more natural and inevitable than the distribution that forced the *Lochner* bakers to work ten hours per day. A government interested in social justice might sensibly intervene in both markets to produce more just distributions even if the intervention also imposed some cost.

B. The Political Rationale

McAdams supplements his economic rationale with a political theory. He has both a macro and a micro concern. On the macro level, he persuasively argues that police will have incentives to use an entrapment strategy even when doing so does not advance crime control.[13] On the micro level, he worries that the police may select the particular individuals to entrap for illegitimate reasons.[14]

McAdams is right to worry about these possibilities, but his remedy for them turns out to be upside down. To see the problem, we need, once again, to connect the entrapment controversy to *Lochner* and its history. From the outset, *Lochner*'s defenders have relied on a theory of politics as well as a theory of freedom. As noted above, part of their defense was rooted in the claim that market ordering was the product of consensual decisions by market participants. But another part of the defense was based on the belief that government could not be trusted to allocate resources in a fair and efficient fashion. Like McAdams, they had both macro and micro concerns. On a broad scale, familiar defects in political markets were likely to lead to regulation that benefited powerful minorities rather than served the public good. On the individual level, government bureaucrats might use their power to punish unpopular minorities or political enemies.

Lochner's opponents had both a response to this argument and a strategy for reducing the extent of the problem. The response amounted to confession and avoidance. It was true, they acknowledged, that whenever the government regulated markets, the power to regulate might be abused. The problem was that there was no escape from government regulation.

Opponents of *Lochner* pointed out that supposedly private markets were themselves inevitably formed by background government decisions allocating entitlements. Markets could be "regulated" as much by adhering to these earlier decisions as by departing from them. A government decision "not to regulate," thereby leaving politically powerless individuals to the mercy of the markets

---

13. *Id.* at 153.
14. *Id.* at 149–56.

formed by earlier government decisions, was itself a form of regulation. Moreover, this regulation, like its more overt cousin, might result in oppression. Defects in the political process and prejudice against unpopular groups might just as easily produce laissez faire as interventionist policies.

The strategy for reducing the extent of the problem was famously foreshadowed in *United States v. Carolene Products*,[15] decided in the immediate aftermath of *Lochner*'s demise. Several generations later, John Hart Ely elaborated on it with great sophistication.[16] The basic idea was to prevent government oppression by yoking the interests of the powerful to the interests of the powerless through the Equal Protection Clause. By requiring the regulation to apply to a larger group of people, the Court could assure that the usual political processes that prevent repression would come into play.

Of course, requiring broader application makes the regulation less efficient for the very reason that more people are burdened by it. Nonetheless, this price might be worth paying if it produced political safeguards against tyranny. Consider, for example, the Supreme Court's treatment of automobile stops on less than reasonable suspicion. The Court has prohibited the police from stopping some people but not others, but permitted the police to stop all people at police roadblocks.[17] From an efficiency standpoint, this "misery loves company" rule seems perverse. In this context, the purpose of the Fourth Amendment is to protect individual freedom of movement from government interference. Yet the Court's doctrine requires more restrictions on movement when the police might be able to achieve their goals with less. The Court has nonetheless thought the trade worth making in part because widening exposure to the restrictions links the interests of the politically vulnerable to the politically powerful, thereby harnessing political processes to guard against oppression.

How does this analysis apply in the entrapment context? Whatever entrapment doctrine we adopt, the government will inevitably be regulating the market for crime. Even if it conducts no undercover operations at all, its decisions concerning, say, monetary and fiscal policy, trade, education, and family autonomy affect the distribution of crime-resistance capital. Just as even a laissez-faire government necessarily forms economic markets, so too even a government with no police force at all will form criminal markets.

McAdams's concern is not just with these large-scale macro effects, though. He also worries about government singling out of individuals on the micro level. But it is hard to see how his proposal solves this problem. Even if the government is barred from making above-market offers, it can still target individuals.

---

15. *See United States v. Carolene Products*, 304 U.S. 144, 1532 n.4 (1938).

16. *See* John Hart Ely, DEMOCRACY AND DISTRUST (1980).

17. *Compare Michigan Dept. of State Police v. Sitz*, 496 U.S. 444 (1990), *with Delaware v. Prouse*, 440 U.S. 648 (1979).

If it dangles market offers before a particular person with low crime-resistance capital, it can virtually guarantee that she will offend.

The only difference an entrapment defense makes is that it reduces the size of the pool of people subject to individualized political abuse. Whereas the government can ensnare people with both low and high crime-resistance capital without the defense, the pool of victims is limited to those with low crime-resistance capital with the defense. If we take the *Carolene Products* strategy seriously, this reduction in the size of the vulnerable pool is a step in the wrong direction. People with little crime resistance capital tend to be the same people who have little political capital. They are just the people most at risk of political abuse. Just as we might want the police to stop more motorists at checkpoints even if it leads to some inefficiency, so too we might want more people subject to the risk of entrapment.

This line of argument leads to something like the reverse of McAdams's policy proposals. As counterintuitive as it seems, perhaps entrapment should be allowed *only if* the government offers above-market inducements and *only if* the inducements are offered widely enough to attract individuals with high crime-resistance capital. Requiring above-market inducements ensures that the pool of people potentially subject to government abuse is broad enough to trigger a political response. Spreading the cost of deterrence is not only just from a blameworthiness perspective; it also helps the built-in *Carolene Products* safeguards against tyranny to operate.

III. CONCLUSION

I have no illusions that my above-market incentive proposal will be adopted anytime soon. The very fact that the proposal will strike almost everyone as ludicrous reinforces another point I made many years ago: Our society's judgments about the population appropriately put at risk of criminal sanction cannot be justified by a coherent theory of blame. It rests, instead, on deeply ingrained presuppositions about the class of people that should be treated as criminal and the class that should be treated as law-abiding. For just this reason, it is simply inconceivable that the government might be required to adopt a policy putting "ordinary" rather than "predisposed" citizens at risk of criminal sanction.

Standing alone, the entrapment defense is an insignificant contributor to the network of legal rules that reflect this presupposition, and to be clear, I don't suppose that abolition of the defense would somehow set us down a path leading inexorably toward social justice. The defense is worthy of study only because it is a particularly egregious and conspicuous example of how our assumptions about the appropriate class of criminals blind us to allocational injustice.

But the entrapment defense does not stand alone. It is indeed part of a network—a network that is all the more powerful because it operates outside our conscious perception. We pay a price for the protection of this network. It helps produce a downward spiral begun by the deep, and in my view, wholly justified resentment felt by the criminal class. Embittered by what they perceive as unfair treatment, they turn away from mainstream norms and commit still more crime. The law-abiding class responds to these depredations with increased fury and imposes still more concentrated and draconian punishment on the criminal class, which in turn becomes even more alienated.[18]

When I described this phenomenon a quarter century ago, I did not imagine that the spiral would lead to the incarceration of more than two million of our fellow inhabitants. The number is growing, and there is no obvious solution to the problems that our own anger and failure of empathy have produced. It is anybody's guess how many of our people will be locked up a quarter-century from now.

---

18. I provide a more complete description of this dynamic in Louis Michael Seidman, *Soldiers, Martyrs, and Criminals: Utilitarian Theory and the Problem of Crime Control,* 94 YALE L.J. 315 (1984).

COMMENTS

MAKING SENSE OF ENTRAPMENT LAW AFTER THE DEATH OF *LOCHNER*

SHERRY F. COLB*

By comparing entrapment doctrine to *Lochner v. New York*,[1] Louis Michael Seidman introduces a fascinating lens through which to view government sting operations. As Seidman explains, critiques of the public-private distinction that have been leveled at the constitutionalization of a largely unregulated free market can apply with equal force to the presumption underlying the entrapment defense. The criminal law typically treats crime as a creature of private criminal behavior rather than a function of how the government distributes and protects entitlements. That this treatment fails to reflect reality may have important implications for how we ought to define, prevent, and punish crime. I disagree, however, with Seidman's suggestion that rejecting the empirical and moral underpinnings of *Lochner* entails rejection of the entrapment defense.

There are two reasons for rejecting *Lochner*. Proponents of *Lochner*-style freedom of contract take the view that a contractual agreement almost always reflects the wishes of the parties better than an alternative framework that the government

---

* Professor of Law and Charles Evans Hughes Scholar, Cornell Law School.
1. 198 U.S. 45 (1905).

might design. This view assumes that private agreements express the parties' true preferences. To prohibit some agreements, on this approach, is to reduce the collective well-being of the population by interfering with consensual exchanges that result from supply and demand in their purest form.

One critique of *Lochner* points to the "baseline problem," as Seidman notes. In a free market, the government is not absent but forcefully protects the property interests that have accumulated over time (in part as a result of oppressive legal arrangements of the past) and uses its might to enforce agreements. Free marketeers too often overlook the fact that without a functioning state, there is no "free" market.

Critics of *Lochner* also offer a second line of attack that focuses less on the role of the state in giving rise to (and protecting) bargaining inequities and more on the responsibility of the state to guard the weak against exploitation by the powerful. This second critique, which points to the "justice" problem, does not require us to attribute causal responsibility to the government for having contributed to the poverty, hunger, and desperation of a person willing to work long hours under dangerous conditions in exchange for paltry wages. Upon finding this state of affairs, however, the justice critique demands that the state not stand by and allow such exploitation to occur. It must (or at least can, consistent with the Constitution), refuse to enforce the contract and perhaps provide enough of a safety net to prevent such bargains from tempting workers in the first place.

Rather than attack the presumed "private" baseline against which labor laws intrude, the justice critique of *Lochner* suggests that government is obliged to protect people from exploitation, regardless of whether or not the opportunity for exploitation came about due to state action.

Seidman proposes that just as seemingly private-market transactions reflect the impact of background government activity, so too do seemingly private criminal transactions. If the government may regulate conduct in the market (on the theory that its regulations have created the free market in the first place), it may also "entrap" people into engaging in criminal transactions, on the theory that it has already manipulated criminal conduct by setting and protecting background conditions in which "private" crime occurs. Thus, the baseline problem infects both "free market" transactions and "private" crime.

The justice problem, by contrast, does not manifest itself the same way in the market and criminal contexts. The substantive justice critique of life in a pure free-market economy leads to the conclusion that refusing to enforce some kinds of agreements serves the needs of workers more effectively than enforcement would have done. But there is no reason to think that permitting entrapment (by eliminating the entrapment defense) will do much to serve the needs of people whose oppressive lives have led them to perpetrate crimes or the needs of those who—often part of the same disadvantaged group—find themselves differentially targeted by criminals. Expanding the class of actualized criminals (to include those of the privileged class) by legalizing entrapment could, in fact, increase such victimization while simultaneously diverting scarce enforcement resources toward inducing rather than detecting ongoing crime.

To the extent that we feel aggrieved by the conditions under which some people are driven to crime and others are not, the best way to approach such grievances is to reexamine the content of the criminal law or redistribute the crime-resistance resources that put people at risk. Noting the baseline problem is a significant contribution, because it liberates government to intervene when it might otherwise be reluctant to do so. But it does not dictate the content of that intervention.

ENTRAPMENT AND THE QUANDARY OF THE UNDERCOVER INVESTIGATION

MIRIAM BAER[*]

In his provocative discussion of the entrapment doctrine, Louis Michael Seidman suggests that society's unease with entrapment is a variant of the view that the government should keep its hands out of private markets, even illicit ones: "When the police entrap a suspect, . . . [i]nstead of accepting privately established market rates for crime as a baseline, they influence the market, thereby shifting the cost of deterrence onto people who might not otherwise become entangled with the criminal law."[1] According to Seidman, this anathema to government intervention has resulted in an incoherent doctrine not much better than the Supreme Court's much-criticized decision in *Lochner v. New York*.[2]

What then to make of the potential government abuse that fuels this doctrine? Seidman floats the rather surprising suggestion that courts should *permit* only those government inducements that are so above the criminal-market price that they persuade ordinarily law-abiding persons to break the law. Because Seidman's proposal reaches a wider and more powerful group of people than the members of the "criminal class" who usually fall for the antics of the police, these above-market offers presumably create a reaction that eventually tamps down government abuse. The more people who feel the sting of government power, the greater likelihood they will do something about it.

Sadly, Seidman's proposal likely would backfire even on its own terms. Allowing the government to use only above-market inducements to catch those who usually resist the urge to commit crime might alter our impression of the "entrappees" rather than the entrappers. Having concluded that there is less

---

* Assistant Professor of Law, Brooklyn Law School.

1. Seidman core text at 493.

2. 198 U.S. 45 (1905).

resistance to crime than we thought, we might use more resources to set *more* traps.

Seidman's strategy is also mired in the old paradigm of relying on judicial doctrines to regulate law enforcement agencies. The key concern fueling the entrapment doctrine is not with the resultant "price" that the government sets for crime, but with the means it uses to infiltrate the market in the first place: the undercover operation. The undercover operation is one of law enforcement's best tools for apprehending wrongdoers who engage in nonobvious criminal conduct. It incapacitates wrongdoers and increases the costs of doing criminal business as offenders must expend resources to protect themselves from stings.

Yet we are understandably uncomfortable with the notion that our next conversation may be with someone who is not who she says she is. We like to think of our society as one built on trust and contributing to the collective good, but sting operations fuel the distrust and selfishness that arises when individuals dissociate from one another. Entrapment's threat comes not from government's failure to set the "proper price" for criminal conduct, but from its ability to chip away at the social norms that restrain wrongdoing in the first place.

The judicial entrapment doctrine reaches only the edges of our discomfort and does so in an entirely inefficient way. Defendants have plenty of reason to avoid contesting the government's methods (if they are even aware of them) and seek what relief they can in plea bargaining. Where defendants do seek relief in court, they are hobbled by the fact that they are doing so ex post, already altered (in the eyes of the court) by the sting itself.

When Seidman first wrote on entrapment, he could not have predicted the technological breadth and expertise that have come to characterize undercover law enforcement efforts. What he did recognize, however, was the entrapment doctrine's failure to protect against government abuse of power. In this case, doctrinal failure masks institutional failure. We would do far better to use explicit legislative and binding administrative tools to determine the proper scope of undercover police power. Although Congress briefly considered this following the U.S. Department of Justice's ABSCAM investigation in 1982, it effectively ceded the regulation of undercover investigations to federal and state agencies, whose actors follow self-made guidelines.

Some may argue that those who fall within Seidman's "criminal class" are as politically powerless to effect legislative change as they are to obtain judicial relief. Perhaps; perhaps not. As our technological improvements render undercover techniques cheaper and more broadly available to a wider class of enforcement agencies, however, we owe it to ourselves to reconsider the methods by which we regulate these types of investigations.

AN ENFORCEMENT POLICY PERSPECTIVE ON ENTRAPMENT

BRUCE HAY*

Louis Michael Seidman's paper has many insightful things to say about entrapment from the standpoint of policy, politics, and constitutional law. I'd like to stick with the policy side of the problem, and to see whether I can clarify matters by breaking things down a bit more analytically, without focusing specifically on the details of Seidman's argument. Let's take, as a random example, a sting operation in which the police pose as buyers and/or sellers of some unlawful item like child pornography.

First question: Why would we ever allow them to do this? The reason, I take it, is that a sting operation of this kind may be more effective than alternative methods of combating the crime. If stings are prohibited, police will have to resort to alternatives such as opening people's mail, spying on the Internet, peering in people's windows, and so on, which is (1) more costly and intrusive, and (2) probably less effective than the sting method at ferreting out the criminals.

Second question, opposite the first: Why not simply allow unfettered use of sting operations? Here the answer also seems pretty clear: It would be silly to have the police spend lots of time trying to induce ordinary law-abiding citizens into committing crimes they otherwise never would have committed. Aside from the obvious ancillary costs (trials, ruined lives, pervasive fear of agents provocateurs), law enforcement itself has an obvious opportunity cost. Better to focus resources on "genuine offenders," which I define as people who are likely to participate in the genuine market for child pornography. Such a focus is better because (1) it yields more incapacitation of offenders, and (2) deterrence is concentrated on the right target rather than being diluted on people who don't need to be deterred.

The optimal point then will lie somewhere between these poles of zero stings and indiscriminate stings; that is, it will involve "discriminate" stings that try to concentrate on genuine offenders. There are two ways of discriminating: (1) gathering independent information about someone, and (2) using an inducement in the sting that is unlikely to attract anyone but a genuine offender. The first of these, of course, corresponds to the "predisposition" test; the second corresponds to the prohibition on "above-market" inducements. The better we can gauge predisposition, the less important regulating inducements is; the harder it is to devise foolproof inducements, the more important gauging predisposition will be. Obviously this will vary from crime to crime. But it's difficult to imagine being able to dispense entirely with either method of discrimination.

---

* Professor of Law, Harvard University Law School.

Final question: Who decides on the appropriate type and degree of discrimination? Put aside constitutional issues and think purely in policy terms. There are three possibilities: (A) The legislature specifies the amount of predisposition required and the amount of inducement allowed. (B) The choice is delegated to the executive, with no judicial second-guessing, i.e., no entrapment defense in court (entrapment objections would be directed at the executive). (C) The choice is delegated to the executive in the first instance but with second-guessing by the courts, which can allow an entrapment defense if they think the right type of discrimination has not been undertaken.

Each alternative has familiar drawbacks: A is bad because legislation is hard to fine-tune; B is bad because executive discretion may be used irresponsibly; C is bad because courts lack expertise and accountability on matters of optimal criminal-enforcement resource use. I do not think the choice among them is obvious, though, or that any of them can be struck from the list as plainly dominated by the others.

I would note in particular that C is not obviously dominated by B. It is all very well to tout the executive's comparative advantage over the courts in determining law enforcement resource allocations. But those are not the only resources being allocated! As I mentioned before, the costs associated with chasing after ordinary law-abiding citizens are not just the opportunity costs to law enforcement, but also: the costs of trials, of lives ruined by imprisonment, of trust eroded in an atmosphere where everyone may be an agent provocateur trying to lure neighbors into committing crime. To put it mildly, the executive is not the obvious entity to have the last word on how these things should be weighed, with no judicial input.

So where does this leave us? I suppose the best answer is: The analysis doesn't clearly take us anywhere from the status quo. It makes sense to discriminate among targets by focusing on predisposition and regulating inducements; and there is no obvious reason courts should not play a role in the task of discrimination. This makes me skeptical of calls for an overhaul in the basic structure of entrapment doctrine. Without claiming that the present arrangement is optimal, I doubt the optimal arrangement would differ in any systematic way from the present one.

THE ENTRAPMENT DEFENSE DEFENDED

RICHARD H. MCADAMS[*]

Louis Michael Seidman's work is the classic critique of the entrapment defense, but I am unpersuaded by the central point of his text, an analogy between the entrapment defense and the Supreme Court's decision in *Lochner v. New York*.[1] I agree that one can creatively characterize undercover police operations as a form of governmental intervention in the market—a redistribution of the criminal opportunities and temptations that citizens face. But the analogy is otherwise inapposite. Just because *Lochner* is wrong does not mean that every governmental intervention—including every undercover operation—is right.

The substantive critique of *Lochner* is merely a reason to reject the particular rights-based reasons that underlie its holding. Once one sees that that there is no "natural," nonregulatory position for government to take on labor conditions, one is still perfectly free to reject particular market interventions on other grounds. Consistent with the substantive critique of *Lochner*, one may reject a minimum wage of $25/hour, not because it violates the natural rights of individuals to sell their labor free from government constraint, but because such a high wage would cause high unemployment. Also consistent with the *Lochner* critique, one can reject certain undercover operations for their adverse effects on human welfare.

The substantive critique of *Lochner* is irrelevant to the entrapment defense because no one seeks to justify the defense with *Lochner*'s natural-rights framework. I certainly do not claim that individuals possess a "right" not to have the government expose them to temptations that do not exist in the market.[2] Nor do I claim that there is anything "natural" or "sacrosanct" in the distribution of criminal temptations the market creates. To the contrary, I reject a possible fairness rationale for the defense by asserting that the initial distribution of criminal temptations is "arbitrary," not fair.[3] Quite obviously, government inevitably regulates those temptations not only in the ways Seidman describes, e.g., "monetary and fiscal policy," but more fundamentally by the fact that the government creates criminal prohibitions. If cocaine trafficking were legal, for example, the distribution of criminal temptations would be radically different than what it is.

---

[*] Bernard D. Meltzer Professor of Law, University of Chicago Law School. I thank Margareth Etienne, Andy Leipold, and Anna Marshall for discussions on these topics.

1. 198 U.S. 45 (1905).

2. Richard H. McAdams, *The Political Economy of Entrapment*, 96 J. CRIM. L. & CRIMINOLOGY 107 (2005).

3. *Id.* at 144–45 (noting that fairness might require more undercover operations that tempt the affluent).

Instead, my defense of the entrapment defense is consequential: that without the defense, police would waste society's resources seeking valueless arrests of individuals who would offend in sting operations but not in the real world; that the system would inflict needless suffering by punishing such people; and that the unfettered power to target individuals in sting operations presents the danger of political abuse. Far from saying that the government is not allowed to redistribute criminal temptations, my claim is that government *should* redistribute such opportunities when it advances social welfare, as by apprehending those who offend outside undercover operations, but not otherwise. Even where I advocate (with qualifications) limiting government to "market-based" inducements,[4] the point is solely that such limits will work pragmatically to separate those who offend outside undercover operations from those who don't. The substantive critique of *Lochner* has nothing to say about the truth or falsity of my claims, any more than it helps decide what the minimum wage should be.

Nor is the procedural critique of *Lochner* pertinent. As Seidman acknowledges, where state legislatures have codified the entrapment defense, there is no issue of judicial interference with legislative primacy. Even where the entrapment defense is judicially created, however, as in the federal system, it is an interpretive gloss on criminal statutes, leaving legislatures free to repeal the defense. That no legislature has even curtailed the defense over the decades since its creation, despite the salience of the issue and the constant legislative expansion of criminal law, shows that legislatures acquiesce in the defense.

The one possible exception is that there are a (very) few cases holding that an undercover operation for which there is no entrapment defense nonetheless violates the Due Process Clause. But even here, courts are directly constraining the power of police (and their informants), not legislatures. There is no reason to believe legislatures approve of the few undercover operations that the courts find so shocking as to constitute a Due Process violation.[5] In sum, neither the substantive nor procedural critique of *Lochner* illuminates the entrapment defense.

Seidman's other most provocative point concerns the just distribution of criminal liability. He claims that, in childhood, individuals acquire different levels of "crime-resistance capital." The government might "produce more just distributions" by increasing the temptations for those with more resistance. He suggests that this redistribution requires permitting undercover operations "*only if* the government offers above-market inducements and *only if* the inducements are offered widely enough to attract individuals with high crime-resistance capital."[6]

This reformulation raises problems. How do we identify individuals "with high crime-resistance capital" so we can apply the proposed test? Seidman might

---

4. *See id.* at 179–82.
5. *See, e.g., State v. Lively*, 921 P.2d 1035 (Wash. 1996).
6. Seidman core text at 502.

mean to use socio-economic factors, but surely there are people with low levels of education and income who have high-resistance capital and affluent, educated people with low-resistance capital. Above-market inducements will perversely ensnare more law-abiding members of economically disadvantaged groups. Similarly, when sting operations target *only* the economically privileged, such as those aimed at bribery, what is the point of above-market prices? One can't possibly justify punishing law-abiding members of the privileged class in order to be "fair" to non-law-abiding members of the privileged class. Finally, even if we achieve distributional equity *between* groups with different resistance capital, the use of above-market prices ensures that police can target political enemies and scapegoats *within* each group.

The more central issue, however, is the nature of the distributional problem Seidman raises. One possibility is that police disproportionately target and juries too readily convict poor and minority groups. Though he offers no data, I suspect that drug buy-and-busts are the most common sting operation and that their targets are frequently racial minorities and the poor. Yet other sting operations—those offering bribes—ensnare those outside the stereotypic criminal class; operations aimed at pedophiles cut across economic class. Thus, if race and class are the issue, a better solution than above-market undercover inducements is the reallocation of policing resources away from the war on drugs.

But perhaps Seidman does not mean his distributional point to turn on race and class, but entirely on the unfairness of targeting people who, for reasons beyond their control, have low crime-resistance capital. In the end, the problem here is the strange sense of justice that requires locking up some citizens who do *not* risk harming others through crime in order to be fair to those who do. I never sought to defend the entrapment defense "from the ground up," but only by assuming our standard criminal law commitments and asking whether the entrapment defense is consistent with them.[7] Those commitments rule out punishing people who, by virtue of a strong ability to resist criminal temptations, present no risk to society.

By contrast, Seidman rejects these core principles, saying that there is "no coherent theory of blame" to justify our punishment practices. Though I agree that the criminal system is in some ways pathological, I have serious doubts about Seidman's underlying critique, but that debate will have to take place elsewhere.

---

7. McAdams, *supra* note 2, at 123–24.

REPLY

LOUIS MICHAEL SEIDMAN*

I agree with Sherry Colb when she writes that "there is no reason to think that permitting entrapment . . . will do much to serve the needs of people whose oppressive lives have led them to perpetrate crimes."[1] She is also right when she says that "the best way to approach such grievances is to reexamine the content of the criminal law or redistribute the crime-resistance resources that put people at risk."[2]

As I tried to make clear in my original text, I have never thought that entrapment doctrine was somehow a central pillar holding up the structure of inequality that is our criminal justice system. I think that study of entrapment doctrine is nonetheless worthwhile because it reveals our *Lochner*-like commitment to market outcomes. This commitment gets in the way of achieving social justice, not just (or primarily) with regard to entrapment doctrine, but also with regard to the kinds of broader and more important redistributive efforts that Colb and I favor.

Miriam Baer argues that entrapment is problematic because "[w]e like to think of our society as one built on trust and contributing to the collective good; yet [entrapment] fuels the distrust and selfishness that arises when individuals dissociate from one another."[3] Although I am certain that she does not intend to do so, Baer's argument demonstrates her own commitment to *Lochner*-like thinking. Yes, when the police entrap or engage in other undercover activity, they erode trust. The problem is that criminals also erode trust, and entrapment, when it works, prevents criminals from engaging in trust-eroding activities. Baer neglects this point because she treats private-trust erosion as natural and "just there," and public-trust erosion as requiring justification. But without presumptive baselines rooted in the private sphere, it becomes an empirical question whether entrapment erodes more trust than it protects.

Bruce Hay begins his comment by stipulating that "it would be silly to have the police spend lots of time trying to induce ordinary law-abiding citizens into committing crimes that they otherwise never would have committed."[4] Perhaps, but the thrust of my argument is that this tactic is not silly at all.

In standard economic or utilitarian theories of deterrence, punishment is a cost, justified only by the larger benefit in crime prevention that it produces. Like all costs, the cost of punishment must be distributed. If above-market offers directed at "ordinary citizens" produce as much, or nearly as much deterrence as punishment

---

* Carmack Waterhouse Professor of Constitutional Law, Georgetown University Law Center.
1. Colb comment at 504.
2. *Id.* at 505.
3. Baer comment at 506.
4. Hay comment at 507.

of citizens who are somehow not "ordinary," then we need to consider whether this alternative distribution makes sense from the standpoint of social justice. I argue that it does make sense because, from a moral point of view, people with low crime-resistance capital who respond to ordinary inducements are no "worse" than people with higher capital who respond only to above-market inducements. Perhaps this position is wrong, but surely it requires an argument to show that it is wrong. Labeling the position "silly" should not be confused with an argument.

I agree with Richard McAdams that rejecting *Lochner* does not entail accepting all redistributive programs, no matter how foolish. It does, however, entail a rejection of market distributions as a presumptive baseline with the burden of proof placed on those who want to depart from this baseline. As applied to entrapment, the anti-*Lochner* position (or at least the version of the anti-*Lochner* position to which I am attracted) means that there is no reason to assume that a "free market" in crime is the baseline that presumptively produces the right distribution of punishment costs.

Of course, McAdams is correct that if redistribution away from market outcomes "waste[s] society's resources,"[5] it is probably a mistake. But McAdams's implicit endorsement of a *Lochner*-like presumptive baseline is revealed by his failure to ask the complementary question: whether market distributions "waste society's resources." My argument is that market distributions are wasteful so long as one counts distributive justice as an important element of the equation.

McAdams responds that it is a "strange sense of justice that requires locking up some citizens who do *not* risk harming others through crime in order to be fair to those who do."[6] But there is nothing "strange" about a redistributive program that requires costs to be borne equally among two groups of people who are equally culpable. Perhaps it bears repeating that these groups *are* equally culpable because both groups are willing to engage in criminal behavior and because the difference in the prices to which they respond often results from differences in crime-resistance capital, the possession or nonpossession of which is not an appropriate ground for praise or blame.

McAdams's ultimate response to all this is to note that he "never sought to defend the entrapment defense 'from the ground up'" and that his argument assumes the validity of "our standard criminal law commitments."[7] Although he has "serious doubts"[8] about my underlying critique, he puts off a debate on the subject. This is really a shame. The point of my original text was, precisely, to raise questions about "our standard criminal-law commitments." Putting off discussion of those commitments is putting off the one criminal-law conversation that we urgently need to have.

---

5. McAdams comment at 510.

6. *Id.* at 511.

7. *Id.*

8. *Id.*

PART III

ADMINISTRATION

24. THE POLITICAL ECONOMY OF CRIMINAL LAW AND PROCEDURE
The Pessimists' View

RICHARD H. MCADAMS*

In *The Pathological Politics of Criminal Law*, Bill Stuntz provides a powerful critique of the modern American criminal justice system. Other commentators have criticized legislatures for constantly adding to an already overbroad set of criminal prohibitions. Stuntz explains the political dynamic that makes this outcome inevitable. The ultimate result is that the modern prosecutor defines what is criminal by her selection of cases to charge, while criminal legislation is a mere "side-show." Stuntz concludes that this state of affairs is "lawless" and pathological. As a solution, he proposes that courts resurrect or expand certain constitutional doctrines to reclaim some of the power now wielded by prosecutors. In this core text, I summarize and comment on Stuntz's argument.

I. THE PATHOLOGICAL POLITICS OF CRIMINAL LAW

A. The Political Economy of Overcriminalization

Commentators contend that the scope of criminal law is unnecessarily broad and constantly expanding. Stuntz illustrates the point by counting the stark increase in the number of criminal offenses in a sample of jurisdictions. He notes how trivial some newer crimes are, such as negligent assault or endangerment or possession of burglar's tools. Federal crimes include the unauthorized use of an image of "Woodsy Owl" and, under one interpretation of (mail) fraud, the awarding of graduate degrees to students whose work was plagiarized.[1] Let me add that federal crimes occur in what must be very common situations: knowing misstatements on mortgage or student loan applications, misapplying student loans or unauthorized use of food stamps, tax evasion, marijuana possession, and violation of copyright.

---

* Bernard D. Meltzer Professor of Law, University of Chicago Law School. The core text is based on William J. Stuntz, *The Pathological Politics of Criminal Law*, 100 MICH. L. REV. 505 (2001). Stuntz is the Henry J. Friendly Professor of Law at Harvard Law School. I thank Adam Cox, Adam Samaha, and Margareth Etienne for helpful comments on an earlier draft.
   1. Stuntz, *supra* note *, at 523–26.

The constant creation of new offenses increases prosecutorial power in two ways. First, because it is impossible to prosecute anywhere close to the letter of the law, criminal overbreadth creates enormous discretion to select offenders. Second, overcriminalization enables "charge stacking," where prosecutors charge multiple overlapping crimes for what is intuitively a single act. Double Jeopardy law adopts a technical view of what is the "same offense" for which one cannot be punished twice. As a result, when the legislature enacts multiple provisions that apply to a single act, the prosecutor can often choose to bring a multitude of charges. For fraud, a federal prosecutor may combine mail fraud and wire fraud statutes with more specific crimes for health care fraud, bank fraud, computer fraud, etc. Drug offenses often involve separate conspiracy, gun "use," and money-laundering crimes. When any one offense carries only a mild or moderate punishment, stacking charges allows the prosecutor to threaten a far more severe punishment, one that even the prosecutor considers to be disproportionate to the offense. Prosecutors threaten what by their own lights is unjust punishment to induce risk-averse defendants, even those with a good chance of acquittal, to plead guilty.

Where the first effect of overcriminalization—overbreadth—is that prosecutors decide what is criminal, the second effect—what we might call "overdepth"—is that prosecutors decide what punishment the defendant receives. Overbroad crimes circumvent the role of the legislature. Police and prosecutors effectively define what is prohibited by their discretionary decisions to arrest and charge individuals. Charge-stacking circumvents the role of the jury by inducing defendants with strong cases to waive their right to a jury trial. Both shifts also circumvent the judge by taking away sentencing discretion. Unless changes are made, "we are likely to come ever closer to a world in which the law on the books makes everyone a felon and in which prosecutors and the police both define the law on the street and decide who has violated it."[2]

Stuntz explains these developments by examining the incentives of the significant players in the criminal justice system. Legislators care about their constituents' preferences, which concern less the content of criminal statutes than the outcome of crime. Unlike most legislative domains, there is little organized pressure to narrow criminal statutes because it is stigmatizing even to show concern that one may be accused. Police and prosecutors seek to maximize arrests and convictions (weighted for crime type); prosecutors also care about their win rate at trial. Both groups are an important lobby pressuring the legislature to expand criminal liability. The federal system presents a special case because unelected federal prosecutors are less responsive to the public than local prosecutors.

---

2. *Id.* at 511.

These incentives explain the "one-way ratchet" of ever widening criminal liability. Prosecutorial discretion is not the mere byproduct of resource constraints. Instead, legislatures intentionally write statutes to reach conduct they do not generally want punished because doing so makes it easier for prosecutors to reach actors the legislatures do want punished. Legislators do not worry about the downside of overbreadth—that prosecutors charge individuals for behavior the public believes is unobjectionable—because (a) elected prosecutors tend to avoid such prosecutions, and (b) if the prosecutions occur, the public will blame the prosecutor rather than the legislature. Thus, legislatures fear blame if statutory underbreadth allows some bad actor the public wants punished to escape criminal liability, but not if the law is overbroad. As a result, legislatures prohibit more and more, delegating to prosecutors the decision of what conduct is criminal.

Here, it is important to see exactly how statutory overbreadth makes prosecution easier. Stuntz explains:

> Suppose a given criminal statute contains elements ABC; suppose further that C is hard to prove, but prosecutors believe they know when it exists. Legislatures can make it easier to convict offenders by adding new crime AB, leaving it to prosecutors to decide when C is present and when it is not. Or, legislatures can create new crime DEF, where those elements correlate with ABC but are substantially easier to prove. . . . When [prosecutors enforce these crimes, they] are engaging in informal adjudication: they are not so much redefining criminal law (the real crime remains ABC) as deciding whether its requirements are met, case by case.[3]

Thus, because burglary is hard to prove, the legislature authorizes criminal punishment for possession of burglar's tools (which are just any tools useful for a burglary, e.g., a screwdriver) with intent to commit a burglary. Because drunken driving is hard to prove, legislatures punish the driver for the presence of open alcohol containers in her vehicle, whether or not she consumed alcohol. Because some of the traditional elements of fraud are hard to prove, Congress criminalizes the open-ended "intangible rights" standard which omits those elements.

In other work, Stuntz claims that legislatures circumvent constitutional rules of criminal procedure by expanding criminal law.[4] The same process occurs here. The more straightforward way to make ABC easier to prove would be to lower the evidentiary standard to something below "proof beyond a reasonable doubt." But because the Supreme Court interprets the Constitution as mandating

---

3. *Id.* at 519.
4. *See* William J. Stuntz, *The Uneasy Relationship Between Criminal Procedure and Criminal Justice*, 107 YALE L.J. 1 (1997); William J. Stuntz, *Substance, Process, and the Civil-Criminal Line*, 7 J. CONTEMP. LEGAL ISSUES 1 (1996).

the higher standard,[5] legislatures respond by changing the elements of the crime. To give a concrete example, assume that proof beyond a reasonable doubt means more than 90 percent likely. Suppose also that a person's having committed AB or DEF proves a 75 percent probability that she committed the original crime ABC. Requiring the prosecutor to prove AB or DEF beyond a reasonable doubt (to a 90 percent certainty) is the equivalent (assuming statistical independence) of proving ABC to a mere 67.5 percent probability (90 percent times 75 percent). If the legislature later makes DE a crime, and the existence of DE proves ABC to only a 50 percent certainty, then proof beyond a reasonable doubt of DE proves ABC only to a 45 percent probability (90 percent times 50 percent). Perhaps a standard so low—the defendant is more likely than not innocent of the original offense—seems implausible, but these percentages are merely averages. Stuntz's point is that the legislature trusts the prosecutor to use her discretion to prosecute only that individual whom she believes (with some unspecified probability) is guilty of the original offense ABC.

B. The Pathology of Overbroad and "Overdeep" Criminal Laws

One might reasonably ask what is wrong with the state of affairs Stuntz describes, given that the public might prefer this outcome. Stuntz offers two main reasons for calling the current system "pathological,"[6] one substantive and one procedural.

Substantively, the current system does an increasingly poor job of sorting the guilty from the innocent. If criminal statutes condemned only behavior the public wants punished, then statutes would facilitate sorting. In the example above, if our real object of concern is behavior ABC and we only prohibit ABC, then we don't have to rely too much on the prosecutors' judgment. At least that is true if prosecutors cannot stack charges to the point where they easily induce guilty pleas from defendants with a good chance of acquittal. Without that ability, the system would sort out innocents because prosecutors would find it much harder to convince juries to convict the innocent of ABC than to convict the guilty. Under the current system, however, prosecutors find it about as cheap to convict the innocent. The key is that they exercise discretion in ways that are largely invisible to the public. When prosecutors convict someone of (what I call) "proxy" crime AB, no outside observer knows if the prosecutor had good reason

---

5. *See* In re *Winship*, 397 U.S. 358 (1970).

6. Stuntz presents two other arguments I regard as secondary, though important. First, the current system leaves no room for the expressive function of criminal law because criminal statutes cannot signal condemnation of conduct if they routinely ban conduct that the public regards as undeserving of punishment. Second, the system facilitates the existence of vice crimes, such as prostitution and gambling, which the majority may favor only if it can choose targeted enforcement against political minorities over even-handed enforcement.

to believe that omitted element C existed. When prosecutors stack charges to induce a guilty plea, outside observers don't know if the prosecutor had good evidence of the defendant's guilt. That no one knows when prosecutors do a bad job gives them no strong incentive to do a good job.

Procedurally, the system fails on rule of law grounds. Our ordinary procedure for regulating government officials involves the separation of power into different branches. Yet we are evolving to a system where prosecutors possess plenary power. Legislators delegate to prosecutors the power to select the small subset of formal prohibitions that will be enforced—to decide what is criminal. The prosecutor acts as the adjudicator when deciding whether to stack charges and thereby bring overwhelming pressure to plead guilty. In the few cases that go to trial, the jury decides whether the easily proved proxy crime—AB—exists but the prosecutor is the ultimate fact finder on whether the crucial omitted element—C—exists.

Vesting such power in prosecutors stands on its head the distinctive criminal law idea of the principle of legality, which demands advanced legislative definition of crime. One justification for the Anglo-American common law's rejection of judicial crime creation (even while allowing judicial tort creation) is the need to give individuals notice of what conduct is criminal. But overbroad statutes and standardless prosecutorial discretion provide no better notice than retroactive crime creation. A second standard justification is the need to restrain arbitrary and discriminatory enforcement. Police can arrest and prosecutors can charge only when there is "probable cause" to believe the suspect has committed a crime, but if the category of crime is open to further judicial creation, then police and prosecutors could arrest and charge anyone on the grounds that they did something that a court might later recognize as criminal. Yet this justification also fails if police and prosecutors essentially decide what is criminal.

To sum up the diagnosis: "Criminal law is . . . not law at all, but a veil that hides a system that allocates criminal punishment discretionarily." Stuntz immediately adds, "Not quite," noting that defendants can go to trial and "sometimes win . . . by arguing that someone else committed the crime charged." But in the final analysis, "[p]rosecutors decide what is a crime."[7]

C. How to Return to the Rule of Law

Finding the patient diseased, Stuntz offers a dose of pessimism about potential cures. He rejects as unworkable the possibilities of eliminating prosecutorial discretion and de-politicizing criminal law through deference to experts. As the best of a limited set of options, he proposes that courts constitutionalize more of criminal law, curtailing legislative supremacy in that realm. He recommends three doctrinal mechanisms. The first tool is to expand the Due Process holding

---

7. Stuntz, *supra* note *, at 599.

of *Lambert v. California*,[8] requiring an element of notice of criminal liability. "[T]he question is not whether the defendant knew he was violating this particular statute, but rather whether the defendant knew that his behavior was, in some more general sense, out of line."[9] Thus, where the legislature bans activity that an ordinary citizen would not think of as criminal, the government would have to prove some functional notice. Second, Stuntz proposes that courts enforce a doctrine of desuetude, rendering criminal statutes void if they are not enforced for a period of time. Finally, Stuntz proposes that courts retain, under the Eighth Amendment, the discretion to give sentences that they regard as proportionate, even if less than a statutory minimum (or presumably more).

II. COMMENTARY AND CRITIQUE

A. The Principal-Agent Problem in Criminal Law

Stuntz's methodology is a global analysis of the political economy of the criminal justice system. He not only steps back from the legal doctrine and the idealized role of legal actors to examine their actual incentives and motivations, but he also attempts to perform his sophisticated description holistically, without holding any particular part of the system constant.

I want to emphasize Stuntz's investigation of "agency costs." These are costs that principals must incur monitoring and controlling their agents.[10] Economists view the agency problem as central to some areas of law, such as corporations. Yet the concept mysteriously plays only a peripheral role in the economics of criminal law, which instead focuses on identifying optimal sanctions. A few papers apply agency theory to a particular actor, such as the prosecutor. By contrast, Stuntz considers the interaction of multiple agents—police, prosecutors, courts, and legislators. If one is going to apply agency cost theory, then surely it is correct to recognize that the criminal justice system consists of a complex set of agents with overlapping but partially independent domains of authority.

Indeed, the problems of *governmental* agents are arguably more severe than the ones that dominate corporate law scholarship because, first, market discipline is probably more reliable than electoral politics at driving into extinction an entity that is bad at controlling agency costs. Second, most agents in a firm are hierarchically arranged so that higher agents—e.g., corporate officers—can fire the agents below them; possessing formal power over others, CEOs cannot pass blame on subordinates nearly as effectively as they could if the other agents were independent. Although there are some hierarchies of agents in criminal law

---

8. 355 U.S. 225 (1957).

9. Stuntz, *supra* note *, at 590.

10. *See, e.g.*, Eric A. Posner, *Agency Models in Law and Economics, in* CHICAGO LECTURES IN LAW AND ECONOMICS 225 (Eric A. Posner ed., 2000).

(e.g., chief and line prosecutors), most criminal justice agents are aligned horizontally, operating without formal control by others.

To understand the problem fully, we should consider all the agents whose unreviewable discretion can block or impede an offender's punishment. We must address not only the agents Stuntz identifies—police, prosecutors, courts, and legislators—but also some he neglects—grand and petit juries (who can refuse to indict or convict), the chief executive (who can pardon), and prison authorities (who determine actual confinement conditions), not to mention private parties, such as the media, private police, and bounty hunters. Our federalist system magnifies the problem because governmental actors exist at the federal, state, and local level. There is more to say about the complex motivations of police, which must differ throughout different levels of the bureaucracy and according to whether the force is unionized. There is also much left to explain about the *principal* in this principal-agent framework, i.e., the public, which Stuntz describes as savvy in some ways (e.g., understanding prosecutorial discretion) but naïve in others (e.g., thinking that anything Congress prohibits is a serious problem).

In any event, Stuntz points the way toward a comprehensive analysis of the massive agency problems in the criminal system. His approach seems more economically fundamental than much of the law and economics scholarship, given that the multiplicity of agents means there is no one social planner to implement economic theories of optimal enforcement, nor any obvious way to coordinate among different agents.

B. Are We (Almost) All Felons?

Is Stuntz exaggerating when he says that the current system is "lawless," that criminal statutes are a "side-show," that we are coming "ever closer to a world in which the law on the books makes everyone a felon"? Stuntz is surely right about the direction of movement, that statutes grow in breadth and depth and therefore that prosecutors increasingly wield powers that at one time were allocated to different branches. But what we really want to know is (1) precisely how far we are along the continuum and (2) how much further we will slide down the continuum before some political force pushes back.

As to the first question, we are somewhere on a scale defined by these endpoints: an ideal criminal code that does the best job possible of avoiding underinclusion and overinclusion, and the truly lawless nightmare of state actors who can decide at any point to impose an extended prison sentence on any citizen. Where exactly we are between them is an empirical issue. We need to know what percentage of Americans could now be convicted of a felony or some other category of offenses subject to serious punishment (committed within the relevant statute of limitations). Or, for what percentage is there a sufficiently plausible case that a prosecutor could induce a guilty plea? However rough the estimate, this is a key inquiry.

The second issue is how far down the continuum we will go. Stuntz implies that one day virtually everyone will be a felon. I am skeptical. Criminal law has been expanding for decades. Why is there no state law yet that simply makes lying of any sort a crime? Or failing to keep one's promises? Indeed, there is a trend to *narrow* statutory rape laws to require an age gap between the perpetrator and victim. Stuntz also underestimates how much lobbying there is against expansion of criminal laws, given how much those laws regulate industry. And he may overestimate how far the public is willing to go. If a legislator proclaimed that a proposed bill would make 85 percent of her constituents felons, but that law-abiding citizens would benefit from giving prosecutors the discretion to target those she knows are deserving of punishment, I suspect that the public would oppose the bill. An optimist might say that the public prefers criminal law expansion for the purpose of effectively lowering the evidentiary standard from proof beyond a reasonable doubt (as explained above) and therefore the system will reach political equilibrium once we reach the desired lower standard for all crimes.

Perhaps Stuntz would plausibly counter that the public is unaware of the trend of criminal overbreadth, which occurs beneath the radar of media scrutiny. If the problem is the accumulation of low-salience statutes each one of which makes a felon of only, say, 5–20 percent of the public, then perhaps Stuntz's dire prediction is accurate. In the end, this, too, raises empirical questions.

For now, I want to emphasize one of Stuntz's related insights—the growth of proxy offenses. This strikes me as vitally important. I have argued for understanding "undercover" offenses exactly this way.[11] There is significant agreement that we should not punish individuals who commit crimes in a sting operation that they have not and likely would not commit outside a sting operation. If so, then the best explanation for why we generally do punish individuals who offend in sting operations is that their undercover offense is evidence of an "external" offense. In Stuntz's terms, selling drugs outside undercover operations is crime ABC, while selling drugs in undercover operations is DEF; we punish the otherwise harmless behavior DEF because we think it is correlated with ABC. What obscures this point, in my view, is that the undercover offense usually does *not* prove an external offense beyond a reasonable doubt. Yet that turns out to be perfectly ordinary under the proxy approach. It would obviously be constitutional for the legislature to criminalize selling drugs *in undercover operations*, even if the only reason to punish the behavior is that it proves to some lesser evidentiary standard something else—an external offense—we want to deter.

Many theorists miss the pervasiveness of proxy offenses, that is, of the fact that modern criminal statutes commonly reach behavior that is merely correlated

---

11. *See* Richard H. McAdams, *The Political Economy of Entrapment*, 96 J. CRIM. L. & CRIMINOLOGY 107, 158–64 (2005).

with the true object of concern. Consider three examples. Heidi Hurd and Michael Moore criticize hate crime penalty enhancements as violating retributivism.[12] In response to claims that hate-motivated crimes involve greater wrongdoing or harm than the same crime without the hate motive, they assert that the posited relationship is merely contingent, i.e., that the hate motivation is only a "proxy" for the additional wrong or harm. Because "[p]roxies are almost always both over- and underinclusive of the phenomena for which they are proxies," they are retributively unjustifiable.[13] Paul Robinson and John Darley claim that, to maximize compliance with criminal law, criminal statutes should correspond to common intuitions about the moral wrongfulness of behavior.[14] They therefore criticize criminal statutes that deviate from the pattern of moral intuitions they discover. Eric Posner and Adrian Vermeule criticize a common view about torture: that we should ban it without exception but allow ex post forgiveness in extreme situations that justify its use.[15] They say instead that the case for specifying ex ante when torture is permissible "is identical to the argument in favor of the rule of law, an argument that appears to be decisive in every other setting."[16] They propose applying to torture the "baseline regime" of criminal law, where "the circumstances in which serious harms may be inflicted are specified ex ante, rather than being remitted solely to the discretionary mercy of juries, judges, and the executive after the fact."[17]

Yet if Stuntz is right about criminal overbreadth and the existence of proxy offenses, then these scholars are misguided. Hurd and Moore may be right that proxies are retributively unjustifiable, but nowhere do they acknowledge that modern criminal law is rife with overbroad proxy offenses, i.e., that their retributivist critique throws out a lot more than hate crimes. Similarly, if the public is content with overbroad criminal statutes that create vast prosecutorial discretion, then Robinson and Darley are wrong to claim that the moral authority of criminal law depends on its *statutes* matching the public's moral intuitions. If the public focuses on legal outcomes, such as whom prosecutors convict, then public intuitions need only match those outcomes. Finally, if Stuntz is correct, then Posner and Vermeule are wrong to claim that the rule of law carries the day in "every other setting." To the contrary, it is a regular feature of modern criminal law—part of the "baseline"—that our prohibitions are overbroad and that we

---

12. Heidi M. Hurd and Michael S. Moore, *Punishing Hatred and Prejudice*, 56 STAN. L. REV. 1081 (2004).

13. *Id.* at 1086.

14. *See, e.g.*, Paul H. Robinson and John M. Darley, JUSTICE, LIABILITY, AND BLAME (1996).

15. Eric A. Posner and Adrian Vermeule, *Should Coercive Interrogation Be Legal?*, 104 MICH. L. REV. 671 (2006).

16. *Id.* at 695.

17. *Id.* at 707.

avoid undesirable punishment solely through "the discretionary mercy" of various agents in the system, particularly prosecutors. That the law prohibits all torture, without specifying some rare exception that could justify its use, makes torture exactly like scores of modern offenses.

C. Is More Constitutional Law Better?

Assuming Stuntz is correct in his descriptive claims, is it appropriate to call the current system *pathological?* And do his proposed solutions offer a cure? Related to both points is an ambiguity in Stuntz's account of the public. I read Stuntz as sometimes suggesting that the public is getting what it wants in the criminal justice system. If so, that raises both the normative question of why the public's tradeoffs are objectionable and the prescriptive question of how a little more constitutional law could finally suppress majoritarian forces. If, for example, the public is committed to prosecutors having maximal discretion, then surely the legislature will simply reenact any law that the desuetude doctrine threatens to invalidate.

Yet Stuntz's normative critique is, I believe, sound. The concern for the rule of law and for "sorting" the guilty and innocent are different sides of the same coin. Beyond some point, giving agents more power undermines their incentives to act in the public interest. Because the public has limited information about prosecutors, for example, it monitors simple facts like the total number of prosecutions, the trial-win percentage, and the conviction of high-profile defendants. If prosecutors have sufficient power, to the point where they can convict the innocent almost as easily as the guilty, they can easily ensure a large number of convictions, a high trial win rate, and the conviction of specific individuals the public wants convicted. But they can accomplish these goals without paying much attention to sorting the innocent and guilty. At the same time, unchecked power is something subject to abuse, as where prosecutors target people they do not like or extract bribes from the innocent to refrain from prosecution.

Keith Hylton and Vic Khanna emphasize the last point—the danger of corruption—in justifying pro-defendant rules of criminal procedure.[18] An individual with unchecked powers of criminal-law enforcement can credibly threaten the innocent with punishment in order to extract bribes. They point to the criminal standard of proof—proof beyond a reasonable doubt (PBRD)—as constraining this corruption by making it more costly for the prosecutor to convict the innocent than the guilty. Hylton and Khanna also recognize that prosecutors could circumvent PBRD by prosecuting an individual serially, wearing her down with the state's superior resources. Thus, they justify the double jeopardy limitation as a mechanism to prevent this circumvention. Yet Stuntz shows how the

---

18. *See* Keith N. Hylton and Vikramaditya Khanna, *A Public Choice Theory of Criminal Procedure*, 15 SUP. CT. ECON. REV. 61 (2007).

Double Jeopardy Clause (as interpreted) is not sufficient to serve this end. Instead of prosecuting defendants again after an acquittal, charge-stacking allows prosecutors to wear down defendants by threatening them with a series of charges *all at once*, prompting the risk-averse to plead guilty even if they stand a reasonable chance of acquittal at trial.

There is no reason to think that the public desires this state of affairs. More likely, the public is unaware of the new power that prosecutors exercise. This is why I said previously that, if a legislator advocated a bill on the grounds that it would make felons of 85 percent of the public, thus creating even more prosecutorial discretion, then most of the public would oppose it. Thus, if we are moving ever closer to that result, there is no reason to think it satisfies some public desire.

If the public is unaware of the current trend toward prosecutorial power, then there is also reason to believe that courts could succeed in halting the trend. Contrary to my suggestion above, the public will not circumvent a desuetude doctrine by supporting reenactment of old statutes if they do not actually support limitless prosecutorial power. Similarly, Stuntz's proposed notice requirement would usefully force the government to publicize unconventional crimes. He doesn't say how, but in some contexts the government provides notice via public service announcements, the posting of signs, and the practice of merely warning first offenders. Thus, prosecutors could no longer extract guilty pleas from defendants for "nonintuitive" crimes that they and the public did not know nor have reason to know existed.

Requiring reenactment of unused statutes and publicity for unconventional crimes arguably reinforces democracy by ensuring the popularity of criminal enforcement. However, Stuntz's sentencing limitation is more troubling to majoritarian ideals because it is easier to believe the public supports higher sentences than the judiciary. Yet the sentencing proposal is essential to prevent charge-stacking, which the first two solutions seem not to address. The good news is that a little bit of second-guessing on sanctions could go a long way. Courts might effectively undermine charge-stacking by lowering the sentences only in the few such cases that go to trial. If judges refuse to impose the full sentences authorized or even required by multiple overlapping charges, they will rob prosecutors of the leverage that induces guilty pleas even from defendants with a good chance of acquittal. Nonetheless, to justify this solution requires addressing the arguments for the ideal of majoritarianism.

In the end, Stuntz's work raises but does not fully answer an essential empirical question: What percentage of Americans could today be convicted of a felony? Stuntz suggests that the percentages are already sufficiently high that prosecutors now effectively decide who is a criminal. I am enough of a pessimist to find this answer plausible, but only further research can answer the point with confidence.

COMMENTS

THE ENDURING PATTERN OF BROAD CRIMINAL CODES AND A PATH FOR STRUCTURAL CHANGE

DARRYL K. BROWN*

The result of the dysfunction in American criminal justice that William Stuntz and Richard McAdams identify is substantive criminal law's greatly—and they suggest newly—excessive scope. But even when codes were short, criminal law was always quite broad. Consider, at the beginning of the nineteenth century, the range of conduct in the average person's life that was criminally regulated. Private, consensual sex lives were limited by fornication, adultery, and sodomy felonies. Choices of whether to work on Sundays, whether to work at all, and even whether to attend church, were often dictated by criminal law. Basic market transactions were barred by criminal law—selling goods outside a designated market or purchasing goods for resale. Ordinary, pervasive regulation was enforced criminally—rules setting wharf sizes or banning gunpowder storage and wooden buildings (to prevent fire). No First Amendment doctrine constrained the Sedition Act that in effect (but ineffectively) criminalized political criticism. Save for market regulation, little had changed by the early twentieth century.

In contrast, we have an arguably impressive history of *decriminalization*. Legislatures decriminalized birth control, some gun possession regulation, gambling prohibitions, and—with the collapse of Prohibition—anti-alcohol crimes and "blue laws" barring Sunday commerce. In the nineteenth century, there was a mini-wave in state legislatures of death penalty abolition (a path revived recently in New Jersey). Legislatures and courts both contributed to decriminalization of sodomy and other consensual sex crimes; the Supreme Court largely led the way on decriminalizing speech crimes in the twentieth century.

In this account, it is not clear that our criminal law is a "one-way ratchet" that grows only more burdensome. Nonetheless, this history hardly means one should be more sanguine about our criminal law than Stuntz and McAdams suggest. The breadth of criminal law is still vast, and it can be vast in pernicious ways, especially in punishing relatively innocuous conduct. And although legislatures are capable of decriminalization when social movements push and cultural mores shift, they sometimes lag those forces significantly. Moreover, legislatures' decriminalization track record is best on culturally salient issues. Less visible crimes, which are often more pernicious, can endure with little public notice.

---

* Professor of Law and David H. Ibbeken Research Professor, University of Virginia School of Law.

For solutions, Stuntz looks to courts to play a stronger role in providing notice and apportioning punishment. He also urges a rule of desuetude that goes to the core of criminal lawmaking's two-part problem—the political ease with which legislatures create new crimes, and legislatures' failure to monitor and repeal outdated crimes, especially those of little political salience. A desuetude rule helps solve the second part. But what about the first? The fundamental dynamics of criminal lawmaking that Stuntz identifies are largely unchanged.

Even Stuntz cannot devise a full solution because, as American criminal lawmaking is now structured, none is feasible. Criminal lawmaking is too democratic. Criminal law is unusually free of influence by specialized or expert lawmakers outside of legislatures. Narrower bodies of substantive law—say, contracts—are governed largely by judicial lawmaking and specific codes (such as the Uniform Commerical Code) effectively drafted by specialized bodies that legislatures adopt mostly unchanged. This is mostly true also of specialized procedural codes—civil and criminal procedure, evidence, etc.: experts do most of the drafting and thereby guide legislation. It is true also of narrow bodies of substantive law often enacted by way of "uniform acts."

Criminal law sprawls over a much wider range of conduct. Its closest analog may be administrative law, which also governs a very wide collection of activities (and many of same activities), from financial market dealings to environmental damage to workplace safety. But note the difference in administrative and criminal lawmaking. In the former, legislatures delegate much more lawmaking to experts—to agencies that draft the details of substantive rules as well as exercise enforcement power. (And note that agencies are structured with different lawmaking procedures and political incentives than our elected prosecutors, and have obligations for articulating public reasons for their lawmaking.) The Administrative Procedure Act provides some structure for how agencies make law. Nothing comparable usually exists in criminal law. Legislatures control criminal lawmaking process, largely unmediated by commissions, experts, or agencies.

Criminal law has had occasional moments when it moved, briefly or modestly, toward this model. The most prominent historical moment, of course, was the wave of reform prompted by the Model Penal Code. To really address the problems Stuntz identifies, criminal lawmaking needs to be more thoroughly delegated to, and mediated by, agencies that play a substantial drafting and agenda-setting role. Until that sort of structural change occurs, second-best remedies by courts are likely at best to mitigate the harms of sprawling criminal codes that have long burdened American jurisdictions.

THE SOURCES OF OVERBREADTH

SAMUEL W. BUELL[*]

William Stuntz is a master at getting the many parts of the criminal justice system moving together in a picture that seems to explain all that is happening—and all that is wrong—in the politics of crime in America. Still, a conspicuous actor is practically missing from Stuntz's portrayal: the criminal, or at least the professional offender. I will illustrate with a stylized example, in which Stuntz's fixed variable of the criminal actor is dynamic. The example is designed to show how those engaged in behaviors subject to regulation can exert expansive pressure on liability rules.

Suppose that at time t_1 society determines that it cannot tolerate infrequent but horrific maulings of people by enraged pit bulls. It chooses to ban something like "knowing possession of a pit bull prone to attack humans" by sanctioning such possession with fines and, given the meager assets of many pit bull hobbyists, imprisonment. The ban does not work. Deadly pit bull attacks continue. Some of these attacks are a dog's first attack on a human, allowing hobbyists who trained their pit bulls to attack the chance to claim that the training was aimed at other dogs and not expected to cause human injury. Other hobbyists learn to train pit bulls in secret, leaving no evidence to prove the owners' knowledge of their dogs' violent tendencies.

At time t_2, society concludes that the value of pit bull ownership under any circumstances is outweighed by the harm from pit bulls that attack. Seeing no alternative but to regulate more broadly than the ill at issue, lawmakers amend the ban to cover "knowing possession of a pit bull," defined as any animal with at least 50 percent pit bull lineage. With a few generations of breeding, or perhaps some genetic engineering, the hobbyists, and the breeders who profit from the hobbyists' avidness, develop a new dog that has less than 50 percent pit bull blood but is equally amenable to aggressiveness training. The attacks on humans continue.

At time t_3, society could try to update the legal regime to define the prohibited animal to meet the innovations of the hobbyists and breeders. Having seen what has occurred and having considered emerging breeding technologies, lawmakers are soberly pessimistic about this approach. Society therefore chooses another course. It enacts a ban on "knowing possession of a dog of any breed or from any lineage, which breed or lineage has a history of attacking humans." Now the law may have the attack dog enthusiasts where it wants them: They must choose between abandoning their pursuit and proceeding at risk of heavy sanction. Yet the law is now overbroad. Thousands, perhaps millions, of innocuous

---

[*] Associate Professor, Washington University School of Law.

pet owners are "technically"—that is, actually—in violation of the ban. Only enforcement discretion remains to confine the ban to its intended target of owners of dogs likely to wound or kill humans.

This is not quite the political economy Stuntz describes when he says that legislatures frequently define real crime ABC as legally consisting of AB to make it easier for prosecutors to obtain guilty pleas, and secure in the knowledge that prosecutors generally will indict and take pleas only in the cases in which they conclude C is actually present. In my scenario, the third element remains in both the crime and its legal definition but is allowed to vary, probably by ex post judicial application, in a range between say C and F. The justification for this flexibility is that the offender controls the criminal act, operates in the shadow of the legal regime, and can too easily avoid liability if the element's meaning is fixed at C.

The cost, however, is overbreadth. Some cases of ABD, ABE, or ABF will not involve offenders who present dangers, cause harms, or exhibit blameworthiness equivalent to offenders in cases of ABC. There will still be worries about controlling agency costs among prosecutors. But the sources of this form of overbreadth in liability rules, and the agency costs that result, will be very different. If the cause of the problem is genuine efforts by regulators to keep pace with the subjects of regulation, there may be different avenues and new promise for controlling those costs.

Is there reason to think this different model fits at least some instances of expanding criminal liability rules? If one examines the path of federal racketeering, money laundering, fraud, and obstruction of justice law over the past twenty years—and particularly the role of the federal judiciary in expanding those laws—one can find abundant evidence of efforts by legislators, judges, and prosecutors to expand liability rules not simply to broaden prosecutorial powers for their own sake but to keep pace with the activities of a range of sophisticated actors engaged in innovative forms of professional crime.[1]

---

1. *See* Samuel W. Buell, *The Upside Of Overbreadth*, 83 N.Y.U. L. REV. 1491 (2008).

WHY HERE AND WHY NOW? BRINGING HISTORY AND SOCIOLOGY TO BEAR ON PUNITIVE PATHOLOGY

JOSEPH E. KENNEDY*

William Stuntz and Richard McAdams have made a brilliant case for why our politics of crime are pathologically punitive. It is so convincing, however, that we must ask ourselves why our crime politics have not always been so, and why similar societies don't suffer the same pathology. Ultimately, the dynamics Stuntz and McAdams identify are only a partial explanation for the pathology they diagnose. A less reductionist and more contextual account is needed to understand why at this point in its history (and not earlier) American society (and not Western European societies) has become so pathologically punitive.

With respect to the ongoing debate about the causes of mass incarceration in the United States, Michael Tonry once observed that explanations emphasizing factors peculiar to American society failed to answer the "why now" question.[1] If Americans are culturally punitive, why is mass incarceration a relatively recent phenomenon? In a similar vein, Tonry observed that explanations emphasizing the social conditions and structures of modernity failed to answer the "why here" question.[2] Why is the United States alone embracing mass incarceration when Western European societies experiencing many of the same social dynamics have not? The incarcerated population in this country seems to have stabilized around two million people, so why here and why now remain the two-million person questions.

The political dynamics that Stuntz and McAdams identify undoubtedly supply part of the answer. Aspects of our political system—most notably the election of prosecutors and increasingly of judges—distinguish us from most Western European societies. That helps with why here. Sociologists and political scientists have explored in some depth how certain approaches to crime politics become institutionalized over time in a cumulative way.[3] That helps with the why now.

---

* Associate Professor of Law, University of North Carolina.

1. Michael Tonry, THINKING ABOUT CRIME: SENSE AND SENSIBILITY IN AMERICAN PENAL CULTURE 21–41 (2004).

2. *Id.*

3. Marie Gottschalk, THE PRISON AND THE GALLOWS: THE POLITICS OF MASS INCARCERATION IN AMERICA (2006); Jonathan Simon, GOVERNING THROUGH CRIME: HOW THE WAR ON CRIME TRANSFORMED AMERICAN DEMOCRACY AND CREATED A CULTURE OF FEAR (2007).

Still, very big pieces of the puzzle are missing. Perhaps the most obvious is race. Some of the pathologies Stuntz and McAdams describe have an obvious racial dimension. For example, during our nation's first real drug war in the 1920s, racial disparities were relatively small and the punishments were relatively light, notwithstanding the fact that narcotics addiction had been at very high levels and was seen as a very serious social problem.[4] After the civil rights era, racial disparities associated with our drug wars have been stark and the punishments harsh. Living in a desegregated society seems to have changed the relationship between race and punishment in a way that makes us more punitive.

A complete account of our pathological crime politics needs to attend to race, as well as to other historical and sociological features characteristic of modern-day America. Reductive analyses, such as that of Stuntz and McAdams, neglect these features. For all their analytical elegance and power, accounts of contemporary punitiveness that slight social and historical factors in favor of relatively timeless and placeless political dynamics neglect essential parts of the story. Why have these punitive pathologies taken root in the U.S. during this particular time? More specifically, what role has race played in their operation? These are questions worthy of concern.

---

4. Joseph E. Kennedy, *Drug Wars in Black and White*, 66 LAW & CONTEMP. PROBS. 153 (2003).

THE POLITICAL ECONOMY OF PROSECUTORIAL INDISCRETION

ANDREW E. TASLITZ[*]

I endorse Richard McAdams's recommendation to publicize (re)enactment of silly or outdated crimes as a way to create political pressure to constrain legislatures' "criminalize everything" attitude. He is correct to say that that attitude accounts for much of the growth of largely unregulated prosecutorial discretion. But substance and procedure are not so easily separable. Limits on how prosecutors exercise their discretion and on how sentencing laws, not merely substantive crime definitions, amplify that discretion are also necessary.

---

* Welsh S. White Distinguished Visiting Professor of Law, University of Pittsburgh School of Law, 2008–09; Professor of Law, Howard University School of Law. This comment is based upon Andrew E. Taslitz, *Prosecutorial Preconditions to Plea Negotiations: "Voluntary" Waivers of Constitutional Rights*, 23 CRIM. JUST. 14 (2008).

Plea bargaining is an important illustration. The practice resolves at least 90 percent of criminal cases in most American jurisdictions. Yet the bargaining process takes place in secret, the subsequent in-court guilty plea colloquy revealing only the final terms of the agreement. Prosecutorial power in bargaining is huge. Under the federal sentencing guidelines (even though they are technically now "advisory," as a practical matter they govern most cases), the only way for many defendants to get past mandatory minimum sentences or to obtain a guideline departure is to cooperate with the prosecution in building cases against other offenders. The severity of these and other sentencing laws make going to trial a dangerous defense gambit. Prosecutors frequently have more information about the state's case but often have no obligation to share most of it. Indeed, constitutional mandates requiring prosecutors to reveal exculpatory evidence *do not apply in advance of a plea agreement*. Prosecutors can rely on the police to conduct investigation, whereas frequently underpaid and underresourced defense counsel have little incentive or ability thoroughly to investigate cases.

Psychological processes further enhance prosecutorial power. Most people, and thus most defendants, are loss-averse, worried more about what they might lose than gain. They also suffer from "time-discounting," undervaluing future harms. They may likewise engage in selective perception, perceiving or greatly weighing only information fitting their preconceptions. These impediments to sound defendant decision-making are still worse for juveniles and the mentally impaired. Defendants facing high offers from prosecutor thus worry more about the threatened enormous loss in liberty than about the benefits of hard-line bargaining, do not fully appreciate the future suffering from lower but still lengthy sentences, and may give more weight to the strengths than weaknesses in the prosecutor's case. For example, a defendant facing a twenty-year sentence may minimize his lawyer's advice that there is a good chance of acquittal at trial, consequently readily perceiving an offer, this time of ten years, as a great deal, only to find later that the ten years were a lot harder than he thought and that he should have listened to his counsel in the first place.

Defense attorneys only partially compensate for these weaknesses. Research suggests most defense lawyers have personality types favoring predictability, decisiveness, and the resolution of ambiguity. Time pressure and mental fatigue also increase this need for closure. Defense attorneys also work in an environment in which pleas are processed more through a "courtroom team" approach than the truly adversarial one sparked only by going to trial. The massive press of cases leads to assembly-line justice in which defense counsel are forced to rely on stereotypes and quick categorizations of a case as being of a "certain kind," with a certain "going rate." Combined with defense counsel's reduced access to information relative to the state, these factors still leave most represented defendants with limited bargaining power.

Case law places few limits on prosecutors' ability to insist on waivers of defendant's statutory and constitutional rights. The law would thus permit a prosecutor to refuse to negotiate until a defendant first waives his rights to receive exculpatory evidence, to challenge certain forms of prosecution evidence at trial, to bring later ineffective assistance of counsel claims, to raise prosecutorial misconduct objections, to waive any post-conviction right to raise claims of innocence, and even to waive the right to keep admissions made during negotiations from the jury at trial. A defendant who refuses these waivers goes to trial, risking harsh retaliation at sentencing if he is convicted. Yet if he waives these rights and no deal is reached, the chances of his being convicted at trial skyrocket. Catch-22.

There is something amiss in a system that gives the prosecutor nearly unlimited discretion, acting in secret, to extort waivers of rights supposedly necessary to justice, to dictate sentences, and to take unfair advantage of defense vulnerability. Limiting the number and scope of substantive crimes or advertising the legislature's failure to do so, as McAdams suggests, will alone do too little. We must also reform sentencing laws and reduce the secrecy and vast power disparities that characterize the plea bargaining process. In a political world in which harsh crime control policies become an aid to electability and a means of governance, that will be a difficult task indeed.

AN OUNCE OF PREVENTION: REALISTIC
TREATMENT FOR OUR PATHOLOGICAL POLITICS

RACHEL E. BARKOW*

William Stuntz is a master diagnostician, lining up the symptoms of our diseased criminal justice system to identify all that is wrong with it. We owe an intellectual debt to Stuntz for focusing our attention to politics and institutional design as key elements in thinking about criminal law. If one were to seek a second opinion, it would not be about Stuntz's brilliant diagnosis but his prescribed cure.

Stuntz turns to the judiciary as the solution to what ails criminal justice. And Stuntz is surely right that greater court oversight would be a valuable corrective. The problem is that judges lack the incentives to take on this function in light of the costs. More judicial oversight would mean more work for judges and more clashes with their political overseers. That is why courts have remained on the sidelines while the pathological politics run their course.

But the judiciary is not the only answer. Other mechanisms may prove more realistic means of relief, even if they are also more modest. The appropriate

---

* Professor of Law, New York University School of Law.

mechanism depends on whether the pathological politics one hopes to correct exist at the state or federal level.

At the state level, politics may actually end up being the most realistic fix for its own pathologies. Even though the federal government now incarcerates more people than any single state, incarceration costs remain a minuscule part of the federal budget. States, in contrast, know that they bear the primary responsibility for prosecuting crime, and incarceration costs are a substantial portion of state budgets.[1] As incarceration costs have increased and state budgets have tightened, state legislators have recognized that the constant expansion of criminal liability comes at a price. At some point, that price is too expensive. That is why approximately half the states have reformed their criminal laws in recent years, repealing or lowering penalties for certain offenses. It is also why so many state legislatures defer to sentencing commission proposals to reduce the penalties for certain offenses, especially nonviolent ones.[2] Prosecutors may want tougher sentences on the books to use as bargaining chips, but when that practice leads to ballooning incarceration rates and overcrowded prisons, political pressure pushes in the opposite direction, forcing legislators to find ways to reform the law and lower the costs.

At the federal level, the politics are unlikely to self-correct because of Congress's lack of concern with costs. But a closer look at administrative law offers another possible check. Administrative law's central task is to check institutions that combine powers—and the accretion of lawmaking, executive, and adjudicative powers in prosecutors is, of course, the very danger that Stuntz identifies. Administrative law checks combined powers not just with judicial review, but with institutional design. Specifically, it separates functions among different actors within the same agency so that the same person does not enforce the law and make adjudicative decisions. U.S. Attorney's Offices have the resources to split authority along similar lines.[3] Specifically, these offices could prohibit the same prosecutor who makes investigative and advocacy decisions from making adjudicative decisions in the same case, with adjudicative decisions including the decision to charge, whether to accept a plea, and whether to file a substantial assistance motion. Separating functions would allow someone who has not formed a judgment about the case to assess it with a fresh set of eyes and an appreciation of the adjudicative nature of the task.

Like Stuntz's judicial proposal, this solution relies on two decision-makers, not one. The difference is that prosecutors are not as neutral as judges, so this

---

1. I have explained this dynamic in greater detail elsewhere. *See* Rachel E. Barkow, *Federalism and the Politics of Sentencing*, 105 COLUM. L. REV. 1276 (2005).

2. Rachel E. Barkow, *Administering Crime*, 52 UCLA L. REV. 715, 804–12 (2005).

3. Rachel E. Barkow, *Institutional Design and the Policing of Prosecutors: Lessons from Administrative Law*, 61 STAN. L. REV. 869 (2009). This solution may work in some district attorney offices, too, depending on resources.

solution is not as robust. On the other hand, this corrective has a more realistic chance of being adopted because it would increase the ability of U.S. Attorneys to control line prosecutors by placing adjudicative decisions with supervisors or other trusted personnel.

Neither of these proposals is a cure for all that is wrong with the politics of crime, but both are viable mechanisms that provide modest improvement. Richard McAdams notes that Stuntz "offers a dose of pessimism" about potential cures that rely on checking prosecutorial discretion or using experts. But Stuntz reached that conclusion by considering options that sought to operate outside the political system and structures, not the reforms suggested here, which aim to work within them.

PROSECUTOR ELECTIONS AND OVERDEPTH IN CRIMINAL CODES

RONALD F. WRIGHT[*]

Richard McAdams and William Stuntz offer a panoramic view of criminal justice institutions at work. This vantage point reveals why legislators are the reliable friends of prosecutors. Together, they have every reason to expand both the breadth and depth of the criminal law.

But prosecutors and legislators are more than just friends or co-conspirators. Prosecutors exercise power that legislatures delegate to them, and both serve as agents of the same principal: the public. Just as the U.S. Congress passes a statute that sets environmental standards and empowers the Environmental Protection Agency to enforce those standards and to give them further meaning, legislatures do much the same with prosecutors. They pass criminal statutes, create prosecuting agencies, appropriate their annual budgets, and authorize them to enforce the criminal laws and to give those laws further, more detailed meaning.

One reason that the public accepts the delegation of power from legislatures to regulatory agencies is because the agencies follow a process that promotes public review and input into their decisions—think of the notice-and-comment rule-making process, enforced by judicial review. This source of legitimacy, however, is attenuated when it comes to criminal prosecutors.

Prosecutors do not routinely seek public input as they select their priorities or refine the meaning of the directions they receive from the legislature. They do not follow the administrative process that other agencies must use when they

* Professor of Law and Associate Dean for Academic Affairs, Wake Forest University School of Law.

adjudicate disputes or make rules. The prosecutor's work is also less visible than the work of the typical administrative agency, because open records laws generally do not apply to criminal prosecutors.

Yet prosecutors do have a powerful claim to democratic legitimacy: most prosecutors in this country are elected rather than appointed. Moreover, they are elected at the local level, where accountability to voters should be strongest. The state prosecutors in 47 jurisdictions are locally elected, and there are 2,344 separate chief prosecutors in the state courts, each the final authority on the application of criminal laws in his or her jurisdiction.

We know astonishingly little about the impact of prosecutor elections on the institutional dynamics that Stuntz explores. Do voters value crime control over other government priorities, and push their elected prosecutors to favor broader and deeper criminal codes, in an effort to suppress crime? Or do elections, other things being equal, push prosecutors toward more restrained use of legal and correctional resources?

Our constitutional structure operates on the assumption that government agents who answer to the public can limit one another. As James Madison put it in *Federalist 51*, "the great security against a gradual concentration of the several powers in the same department, consists in giving to those who administer each department the necessary constitutional means and personal motives to resist encroachments of the others.... Ambition must be made to counteract ambition."[1] Does this insight not apply when two agents—legislators and prosecutors—compete for the affections of the public in matters of crime and punishment? Shouldn't prosecutors object when legislators try to duck all responsibility for an overreaching criminal law?

Elections hold the potential to set the ambition of prosecutors against the ambition of legislators, particularly when it comes to the depth of criminal codes. The "overdepth" problem—the presence of multiple code sections and multiple punishments that could all apply to a single defendant based on a single criminal transaction—gives prosecutors a powerful say in the total amount that the state spends on criminal punishments. Prosecutors often overspend the available budget by filing charges and requesting sentences that the state cannot afford. At least in theory, the voters could hold prosecutors responsible both for crime control and for effective use of the crime budget. In such a world, chief prosecutors might be reluctant to accumulate more legal tools that line prosecutors would use to overspend the budget.

There are, however, two problems with this hopeful theory. First, the voting public receives little useful information during election campaigns about the aggregate charging decisions of the prosecutor's office. Voters learn even less about the chief prosecutor's impact on the state corrections budget. Better information about

---

1. THE FEDERALIST NO. 51, at 322 (James Madison) (Clinton Rossiter ed., 1961).

office performance would have to appear before prosecutor elections could change prosecutor ambitions for the better.

Second, prosecutor elections target the wrong voting public. These elections happen at the local level, while the money for the most expensive criminal punishments comes from the state level. Local voters have no reason to ask their own prosecutors to spend more carefully the revenue from other taxpayers around the state. Voter interests and taxpayer interests must be better aligned.

Does the best answer to the overbreadth of criminal codes lie in reform of state and local election law?

REPLY

RICHARD H. MCADAMS

Consider first the comments regarding Stuntz's description of the pathologies of criminal law. Darryl Brown offers some important historical perspective: Compared to the early nineteenth and twentieth centuries, criminal law has at least in some respects narrowed rather than expanded. We have fewer sex crimes, permit fewer restraints on speech and religious practices, and are less likely to regulate market prices.

Stuntz avoids much of this counter-history, however, because his thesis concerns only the past few decades rather than all of American history. Also, where the courts are responsible for the contraction, as by ruling that the First Amendment and Due Process Clause prevent the state from punishing certain activity, the contraction is consistent with Stuntz's thesis that recent *legislative* action favors constant expansion. Nevertheless, as Brown indicates, the trend is more complex than Stuntz allows. In the few decades before *Lawrence v. Texas*,[1] some state legislatures decriminalized sodomy, and as I noted in the core text, statutory rape law has also contracted recently. Yet, in the end, Stuntz's claim survives; it is difficult to find many other examples in the past half century that cut against the enormous expansion of criminal statutes he identifies.

Samuel Buell raises the possibility that criminal overbreadth is functional because it addresses the problem of the professional offender. He illustrates with the problem of dangerous dogs. Clever offenders will respond to criminal regulation by seeking a means of circumvention, to remain just out of the statute's reach. The only way to keep up with those dedicated to creating fighting breeds is to expand criminal liability to the point of overbreadth.

I'm not sure that Buell's argument actually contradicts Stuntz's claim. As common ground, Stuntz's view, and my own, concedes that the overbreadth of criminal law makes it easier (cheaper) for prosecutors to convict dangerous or

---

1. 539 U.S. 558 (2003).

blameworthy criminals, people whom the public wants punished. That is why legislatures embrace it. The problem is that the same power overbreadth grants to punish those whom the public thinks (or would think if it considered the matter) are deserving of punishment also includes the power to punish those whom the public thinks (or would think) are undeserving of conviction, individuals who are neither blameworthy nor dangerous. As a result, we depend on the prosecutor to make unobserved adjudicatory decisions about which offenders are "professional" criminals who deserve to be prosecuted. I'm not sure Buell disagrees with the point—he is just claiming there are advantages as well as disadvantages to overbroad statutes.

The possible disagreement is whether the evil of overbroad laws is *necessary* to reach the conduct of the professional criminal. At one level I agree that it is necessary: If we fix the costs of conviction and the prosecutor's budget, then (even with plea bargaining) there will be some maximum level of convictions she can obtain. If we employ any new mechanism to lower the cost of conviction, then we will create extra convictions; to achieve those "extra" convictions, the new mechanism is strictly *necessary*. Overbreadth lowers the costs of convictions and thus necessarily produces some convictions that are otherwise too costly to achieve.

But at another level I disagree. As my core text explains, overbreadth accomplishes indirectly what we would accomplish directly by lowering the prosecutor's burden of persuasion from "proof beyond a reasonable doubt" to something else. Because the courts block this approach, legislatures achieve the same results by removing difficult-to-prove elements from the statutory definition of crime. But if overbreadth circumvents the criminal proof standard, then the argument for overbreadth should include an argument *against* that burden. Only if the evidentiary standard is unjustified should we approve its circumvention.

This is a difficult issue—the correct trade-off between wrongful convictions and wrongful failures-to-convict is the subject of considerable commentary. Stuntz's point is that, when the issue *covertly* arises in the form of overbreadth, the legislative process is not at all likely to get the trade-offs correct. When prosecutors testify that they need more overbreadth to get the "bad guys," legislatures too happily concede that power because they don't think they'll get blamed if the prosecutors use the power to go after "good guys." No one gets blamed when the public fails to discover that a person it would regard as undeserving of punishment pleads guilty. When the public does make this discovery, it blames the prosecutor instead of the legislature. So there is no reason to think that legislatures employ overbreadth only when the benefits—e.g., convicting more professional criminals—outweigh the costs—i.e., punishing the innocent. The political dynamic makes it likely that the legislature will keep expanding criminal law beyond any optimal point.

Joseph Kennedy suggests that there is an alternative cause of the pathological punitiveness of American criminal justice: the effects of race. Similarly, Rachel

Barkow says that politics may eventually solve the problem at the state level because the costs of prison is causing the public to back away from the harshest punishments. These claims may be right, but I would distinguish the common complaint of excessive punitiveness from Stuntz's claim of excessive criminalization. A society could assign severe punishment for each crime it creates yet still define its crimes very narrowly. Conversely, a society could have overly broad and excessively overlapping crimes and yet punish violations only mildly.

Although much attention is justifiably paid to American punitiveness, Stuntz's point is about excessive breadth and depth of criminal law. Thus, even if the cost of prison or other factors cause politicians to decrease criminal sanctions, it may not cause them to define crimes more narrowly. In addition, Ronald Wright observes a complication in Barkow's account about politics at the state level: prison costs are incurred at the state level, but the prosecutors whose decisions determine the number of state prisoners are elected at the local level.

Let me now turn to comments directed toward the solutions to the criminal law's pathologies. In this connection, Brown proposes that legislatures delegate their power over criminal law content to administrative agencies. Andrew Taslitz identifies the source of criminal law pathologies in plea bargaining and suggests, as a solution, reforms that "reduce the secrecy and vast power disparities"[2] in the process. Wright identifies the source of the problem in the politics of prosecutorial elections and suggests that we look for electoral reforms. At the federal level, Barkow advocates a reform of prosecutors' offices to allocate to different individuals the functions of advocacy (building a case against an individual) and adjudication (deciding whether to prosecute and what plea and sentence to accept).

These are all interesting ideas. Even in a democracy, we sometimes reach a consensus that too much responsiveness to popular opinion is bad, so we delegate some decisions—e.g., the money supply and military base closings—to agencies or commissions with either unreviewable discretion or the power to make proposals on which the legislature will vote up or down without modification. Perhaps criminal law is such a policy area. But the pessimist doubts that legislatures will ever tie their hands this way. Stuntz notes that we tried this approach with the American Law Institute's Model Penal Code, and it failed (in that immediately after recodification, legislatures began adding crimes in disregard of MPC principles).

The other proposals focus on prosecutors. Taslitz may be right about the problems of plea bargaining, though the question is exactly what reforms are both sufficient and politically plausible. Wright raises an interesting area for reform—the electoral process for prosecutors. Though the ideal is to make the public a better monitor of prosecutors, I remain pessimistic, given that the public

---

2. Taslitz comment at 535.

pays even less attention to prosecutorial elections than many others. Finally, although no one solution will work by itself, Barkow's institutional idea strikes me as having the merit of being politically plausible. As Barkow notes, separating the investigative and adjudicative parts of the prosecutor's workload offers to make the U.S. Department of Justice conform to the institutional structure used in many other federal bureaucracies. That seems like a good start.

25. AGAINST JURY NULLIFICATION

ANDREW D. LEIPOLD[*]

Jury nullification occurs when the defendant has been proven guilty beyond a reasonable doubt but the jury decides to acquit anyway. Perhaps the jury thought it unfair to prosecute this defendant when the law was routinely violated by others (think public drinking on New Year's Eve). Perhaps the jury was worried that the defendant had already suffered enough (the elderly man who mercifully kills his beloved but terminal wife), or the law was unfair (the glaucoma patient who possessed marijuana), or that the victim was the real bad actor (the battered spouse who killed her abuser). Juries have unfettered power to "acquit against the evidence," and we all have examples of cases that either outrage or please us when that power is exercised.

Juries don't nullify very often, so it's easy to treat the topic like we treat meteors hitting the earth—spectacular when it occurs, but rare enough that it is not worth worrying about. But jury nullification has a surprisingly large impact on the criminal law, *especially* in cases where the jury does not exercise its power. Whatever benefits flow from the few cases where a jury acquits against the evidence, they pale in comparison to the doctrine's undesirable collateral effects that flow from the many procedural rules that protect the nullification power against encroachment.

I. THE SCOPE AND COSTS OF JURY NULLIFICATION

The power to nullify is ultimately the general power to frustrate a legislative judgment that certain behavior should be punished as a crime, and the more limited ability to frustrate an executive judgment that this defendant should be punished for doing so. And although freeing the guilty is not intuitively appealing, we tolerate it, even celebrate it, for two intersecting reasons.

First, the alternatives to allowing juries to nullify sound worse than the power itself. We love the vision of juries as a black box, where twelve average citizens meet behind closed doors to reach common ground on questions of life and liberty. Peeking behind the doors to see why juries made their decisions would be chilling, and we are loathe to do it even in the most compelling circumstances.

* Edwin M. Adams Professor, University of Illinois College of Law. The full-length presentation of these ideas appears in Andrew D. Leipold, *Rethinking Jury Nullification*, 82 VA. L. REV. 253 (1996).

Second, many are convinced the nullification power is an affirmative good. It can round off the sharp edges of the law, keep prosecutors honest, signal to legislators that certain crimes have become too removed from community sentiment, and allow juries to do individual justice without affecting the law generally.

Each of these reasons is incomplete, speculative, or just wrong. When we compare the undeniable costs of jury nullification against its speculative benefits, it becomes easy to see why the doctrine is in need of reform.

A. The Costs: No Error-Correcting Devices

Nullification proponents correctly assume that juries acquit against the evidence very rarely, but incorrectly infer from this that the effects of the nullification doctrine are small. To the contrary: The real impact of nullification lies in the procedural rules whose purpose is to ensure that this power is not infringed, but whose effect is to make trials and verdicts less accurate.

The primary impact of current nullification law is to prevent the courts from employing procedural devices designed to correct jury error. The civil law offers judges numerous chances: judgments on the pleadings, judgments as a matter of law, new trial motions, and appellate review are all based on the unremarkable notion that sometimes a verdict is based on passion or confusion, and sometimes a verdict is tainted by bad evidentiary rulings or bad jury instructions.

Not so in criminal cases. A judge can never direct a verdict for the prosecution, nor can the government appeal an acquittal. These rules apply even though criminal defendants can be "wrongly" acquitted in the same way that they are wrongly convicted. Because error-correcting devices are unavailable to the prosecution, however, mistakes that lead to acquittals are left in place, and a guilty defendant goes free.

The lack of error-correcting devices can be traced to the jury's power to nullify.

1. **No "Judgment of Conviction"** Everyone knows that the judge may not bypass a jury and enter a judgment of conviction. The reason given is that a defendant's right to a jury would be violated if the court did so. This makes superficial sense: The Sixth Amendment guarantees a jury, and if the judge prevents or overrules a favorable defense verdict, that guarantee has apparently been violated.

Of course, the Seventh Amendment guarantees a jury in civil cases, yet there judgments as a matter of law for either party are constitutional. Because nothing in the text of the Constitution requires a different rule in criminal and civil cases, some unique feature of criminal verdicts must make bypassing the jury singularly illegitimate.

The only important distinguishing feature is the power to nullify. A criminal jury is also expected to find the facts and apply the law, but it is then given the additional power to decide whether this particular defendant should be acquitted, regardless of the evidence. This authority, unavailable on the civil side, makes acquittals untouchable: A judge can never legitimately say that the prosecution is "entitled" to judgment as a matter of law, because the jury always has the power to return a verdict that disregards the law.

So when courts say that directed verdicts for the prosecution would violate the right to a jury, they are preserving the jury's right to decide not only whether the defendant *committed* the crime, but also whether he should be *convicted* of it. Only the power to nullify explains this additional role.

2. No Appeals of Acquittals When a defendant is acquitted, the prosecution may not appeal even if trial errors are plain on the record. Here the relationship to nullification is oblique, because courts cite the Double Jeopardy Clause to support the rule: The prosecution cannot appeal because if the acquittal were overturned, there would be a second trial and the defendant would again be put in jeopardy for the same offense.

Double jeopardy explains a lot, but here the explanation is too broad. If preventing multiple verdicts were our chief concern, it would be hard to explain the many instances where the government is already permitted to try a defendant more than once. A second trial is typically allowed when the defendant successfully appeals a conviction; when the defendant moves for a mistrial; when the prosecutor moves for a mistrial and there is a "manifest necessity" for granting it; when defendant moves to dismiss on grounds other than innocence; and when the first trial was by a different sovereign.

Given this, the rule on acquittals must protect some value that can be realized only if a flawed acquittal is placed beyond review. The value that best fits this description is preserving the power to nullify. An appeal necessarily would require a claim by the government that a trial error led to an "erroneous" verdict, that is, a verdict that did not follow from the evidence. But because the jury *might* (legitimately) have acquitted against the evidence, we can never say for sure that an acquittal was influenced by the trial error. To protect the jury's ability to acquit for any reason at all, the rule makes it impossible for an appeals court to correct even the clearest errors that favor the defendant.

B. Other Costs

The inability to employ error-correcting devices is not the only cost to consider. Other rules and incentives have evolved to protect the nullification power, each of which detracts from the accuracy or efficiency of trials.

1. No Special Verdicts Properly used, special verdicts would allow courts to frame complex jury decisions to make them more logical and consistent. Special verdicts are discouraged in criminal cases, however, because courts fear that if juries had to answer questions about the verdict, their independence would be unduly compromised. As one court put it, "[t]here is no easier way to reach, and perhaps force, a verdict of guilty than to approach it step by step. A juror, wishing to acquit, may be formally catechized. By a progression of questions, each of which seems to require an answer unfavorable to the defendant, a reluctant juror may be led to vote for a conviction which, in the large, he would have resisted."[1] Or as another court put it directly, "[s]ome of the antipathy toward special verdicts in criminal trials has its roots in the doctrine of 'jury nullification.'"[2]

2. Tolerating Inconsistent Verdicts When identical evidence is introduced against two codefendants, and the jury acquits one and convicts the other, part of the verdict is plainly in tension with the evidence. Likewise, when a single defendant is convicted of using the telephone in the commission of a felony, but in the same verdict is acquitted of the felony itself, something is obviously amiss.

A court could interpret inconsistent verdicts as proof the conviction was tainted—how could there be reasonable doubt on one count but not on the other? The Supreme Court and most state courts, however, typically will not construe inconsistencies as evidence that the conviction is flawed, because the acquittal portion of the verdict *might* have reflected a decision to nullify.

As a result, a defendant appealing a conviction has lost a potentially valuable argument that the jury failed to find proof of each element beyond a reasonable doubt. For the prosecution, an inconsistent verdict could be evidence that the jury acquitted because of some trial error, yet no appeal is permitted to correct it. The theoretical possibility of nullification thus can harm both parties, even where there is no credible argument the jury intended to acquit against the evidence.

3. Skewed Judicial Rulings The party's asymmetric ability to appeal puts uncomfortable incentives on judges. All judges hate to be reversed, and so a judge faced with a difficult trial ruling might be inclined to err in favor of the defense. If the ruling for the defense was erroneous and the defendant is still convicted, no harm was done because the government has nothing to complain about. If the ruling was erroneous and the defendant is acquitted, no appeal is permitted, so the chances of being reversed are again zero.

On the other hand, the current structure may tempt judges to err in the prosecutor's favor, particularly if the evidence of the defendant's guilt is strong. The judge may be reluctant to rule for the defense if it might lead to an acquittal, knowing that the prosecutor will not have another chance to convict. And if the defendant is convicted after the court rules for the government, he can always ask the court of appeals to fix the error. Ultimately, it doesn't matter whose ox is gored, only that the absence of the government's ability to appeal can affect the course of trials in troublesome ways.

II. THE WISDOM OF NULLIFICATION

Jury nullification is like free speech: it is given "breathing room" to make sure the core power is not even potentially infringed. Unlike speech, however, the

---

1. *United States v. Spock*, 416 F.2d 165, 182 (1st Cir. 1969).
2. *United States v. Desmond*, 670 F.2d 414, 416 (3d Cir. 1982).

necessity and desirability of the core activity are far from clear. Moreover, any doctrine that imposes burdens such as those imposed by jury nullification should bring with it commensurate benefits, or at least be required by the Constitution. Neither is true for jury nullification.

A. Right versus Power

Lurking in the background of the arguments over nullification is an assumption that juries have a "right" to acquit against the evidence. If there is such a right, it is well-hidden. There is no stable claim that the right is constitutionally based: there is little indication in the usual sources that the Framers debated, discussed, or even thought about nullification when drafting Article III or the Sixth Amendment. Even if they did, later events have discredited the claim of right: The one time the Supreme Court has addressed the issue,[3] it rejected the view that juries have the right to "find the law," and no federal court has seriously suggested otherwise since. (There also is something odd about claiming that defendants have a "right" to be tried by a jury with the power to nullify, but jurors can't be told of this right.)

It is more accurate to say that nullification is a *power* that juries have, not a right. Juries of course have the raw ability to acquit for any reason, in large part because the opacity of general verdicts makes it impossible to know when a jury nullified rather than simply rejected the prosecutor's evidence. More importantly, because acquittals cannot be reviewed, even if instances of nullification could be identified, a court would be powerless to stop it.

But once we conclude that nullification is not an enforceable right, we can fairly examine the doctrine and ask if the benefits of nullification outweigh the costs of change.

B. Flawed Assumptions

Consider the cancer patient who buys illegal treatment drugs from overseas; a member of a low-stakes poker game; the defendant charged with statutory rape although he later married the victim; or the defendant caught by outrageous police conduct that stops just short of entrapment.

When cases like these arise, nullification is nearly irresistible. Some laws are stupid, some were once sensible but have outlived their usefulness, and sometimes prosecutors bring foolish charges. Because we know of cases where juries did justice when no one else would, it is easy to embrace nullification as a necessary and desirable tool.

But arguments in favor of nullification generally are built on two flawed assumptions. The first is that juries have enough information to make a reasoned decision to nullify. When jurors acquit a distraught father charged with

---

3. *Sparf & Hansen v. United States*, 156 U.S., 51, 102 (1895).

manslaughter who failed to put his child in a car seat, they may feel that justice required mercy. What they may not know is that the father had two previous convictions for child abuse, or that the father had drugs in his system at the time of arrest, evidence that was suppressed on Fourth Amendment grounds. The jury also might assume that the actual sentence the father faced was much higher than the one he actually faced. This information is kept from the jury because it is inadmissible to prove the crime charged, yet it might be highly relevant to a decision to acquit against the evidence. But because nullification is never the subject of argument or instructions, juries nullify in the dark, based on incomplete and even misleading information.

The second erroneous assumption is that when juries nullify the result is a fair and compassionate verdict. But for every case where the jury extends mercy to a deserving defendant, there may well be one (or two, or five) others where the verdict is based on improper considerations. The archetypical case occurs when the acquittal is based on race or ethnicity: the victim was Hispanic and jurors considered the harm done less than if the victim were White, or perhaps the jury was biased in favor of a defendant because of his race. Nonracial examples are also easy to imagine: a jury believes the rape victim was "asking for it" because of her behavior or the way she dressed.

Here the nullification doctrine is at its worst. The rules continue to protect the right of juries to "vote their conscience," even when their conscience is not offended by views that have been repudiated in every other area of the law. From the refusal of the post–Civil War juries to convict those who attacked newly freed slaves to the refusal to treat assaults against homosexuals as a serious crime, juries have at times shown a willingness to acquit on the basis of factors that would render a decision arbitrary or unconstitutional in any other official context.

Right-thinking people should be repelled by these examples, but the power to nullify is hard to limit to cases that we find satisfying. Once we sanction the ability to reach a verdict on extra-legal grounds, we must accept as legally legitimate all these decisions, good and bad. And while it is unclear how often juries give in to these biases, the lack of data hardly makes the affirmative case for the doctrine's protected status.

The capacity for mischief is not limited to verdicts based on impermissible grounds. There are cases in which community views are sharply split, where the decision to nullify turns on the luck of the draw in jury selection. Charges against pro-life advocates who block abortion clinics, environmentalists who interfere with logging efforts, and antiwar protesters who picket too close to politicians are cases where an acquittal against the evidence would be welcomed by some and denounced by others. The lack of consensus in these cases reinforces the arbitrariness of nullification, with no necessary correlation between community values and an acquittal.

III. WHAT ALTERNATIVES?

A better system would have two features. First, the legislature should turn jury nullification into an affirmative defense, to address the worst features of the current practice. Second, courts should permit the government to make use of error-correcting devices, including the authority to appeal from acquittals, under the same rules that now govern appeals of convictions, to lower the unnecessary costs of the doctrine.

A. An Affirmative Defense

The first step is to recognize that nullification is a close cousin to existing affirmative defenses. Self-defense, duress, necessity, insanity, and entrapment all involve defendants who committed the actus reus and had the mens rea but are not punished because they were justified or excused. So it is with nullification: The jury has concluded that the defendant has satisfied the elements of the crime, but still should not be convicted.

Existing defenses have the political legitimacy of a statute, and all relevant evidence concerning the defenses is presented to the jury. To prevent the jury from being distracted, the judge requires the defendant to present some threshold showing of the defense before the court will allow argument or give the jury instructions on the issue. Nullification has none of these qualities, and restructuring the power into an affirmative defense would be a step in the right direction. Juries would be free to act largely as they do now, but would have more guidance and would make better-informed decisions if the issues were placed before them honestly rather than by hint and indirection.

One attraction of the affirmative defense idea is its flexibility, with the grounds for nullification being as broad or as narrow as desired. Jurisdictions might, for example, adopt a defense patterned after Model Penal Code's § 2.12, which allows the judge to dismiss charges where guilt is clear but defendant's conduct "did not cause or threaten the harm or evil sought to be prevented by the law defining the offense, or did so only to an extent too trivial to warrant the condemnation of conviction." That same provision also permits dismissal where extenuating circumstances make the defendant's conduct such "that it cannot reasonably be regarded as envisaged by the legislature in forbidding the offense." The nullification defense would give this same authority to jurors, a power they already have whether they know it or not.

A legislature could fashion a defense as it wished, but it would make the defense available to all similarly situated defendants, not just those who stumble upon a jury that knows of the nullification power. Just as important, a statutory defense would make it clear that those reasons for nullification that are *not* included are illegitimate and could be subject to further review.

B. Making Error-Correcting Devices Available

Once nullification loses its protected status, the rules whose justifications are tied to the nullification doctrine should be alterable at will. Most significantly, if the government believed that an acquittal was influenced by a trial error, it could appeal. If the prosecutor thought that an erroneous exclusion of evidence or an erroneous jury instruction led to an unfair acquittal in the first trial, the prosecutor could raise the issue in the appellate court in hopes of winning a new trial. This change would allow the prosecution to have one error-free opportunity to prove guilt, just as the defendant is entitled to a trial free of serious error before he is convicted.

The idea of government appeals is radical, but in practice the system is unlikely to be. As the appellant, the prosecution would have the burden of showing that the error substantially influenced the verdict and that, absent the error, a rational jury could have found guilt beyond a reasonable doubt. The grounds for appeal would invariably be legal errors; given the government's trial burden, there would be few, if any, cases where the prosecution could make a plausible "sufficiency of the evidence" argument.

The likely infrequency of successful appeals is not grounds for rejecting the proposal. The costs of erroneous acquittals is great, and the benefits of protecting the nullification power remote, so that even a marginal shift could lead to a modest improvement in the justice system.

IV. CONCLUSION

How we feel about nullification ultimately turns on our view of juries generally. If we view juries as independent actors, separate from and uncontrolled by the government, nullification is a critical power. Juries may be the last outpost of a skeptical citizenry, one that prevents too much power from pooling in the hands of officials by reminding prosecutors who has the last word on who can be punished.

But nullification also is a form of unreviewable power, with all the risk such power entails. It should not violate our romantic vision of juries to permit some oversight of their decisions; it merely reflects an understanding that sometimes mistakes are made, mistakes that we should correct if we can. It is this vision of the jury—as an institution constrained by the limits that the democratic process imposes on the rest of the criminal system—that is worth preserving and strengthening.

COMMENTS

JURY NULLIFICATION CHECKS
PROSECUTORIAL POWER

RICHARD H. MCADAMS*

Andrew Leipold's masterful critique of jury nullification pushes the debate from an evaluation of the individual cases where nullification occurs to an assessment of the nullification power's systemic effects. He concludes that the nullification power's "undesirable collateral effects," which occur even when the jury does not nullify, exceed the benefits "from the few cases where the jury acquits against the evidence."[1] But as he identifies the systemic costs, Leipold takes less seriously the possibility of systemic benefits. He acknowledges that nullification might prevent "too much power from pooling in the hands of officials, by reminding prosecutors who always has the last word."[2] But Leipold does not explore this insight as relentlessly as he examines the institution's undesirable effects.

To investigate the systemic benefits of the nullification power, one might begin with Bill Stuntz's claim that the "pathological" politics of criminal law drives legislatures to delegate to prosecutors the power to decide what is criminal.[3] Legislatures intentionally and pervasively enact overbroad statutes that criminalize conduct that neither the public nor the legislature believes merits punishment. Legislatures make felons of huge segments of society in order to lower the costs of conviction. The legislature trusts prosecutors to use their power to go after "bad actors" who have done something worse than the technical offense.

Stuntz does not identify nullification as a check on prosecutors, but points instead to the restraining effect of electoral politics: Elected prosecutors wish to avoid bringing cases the voters do not want treated as crimes. But politics, by itself, will fail to constrain the prosecutor in most cases. The public is notoriously inattentive to these matters, especially in the absence of media coverage. When the media cover a case, the public is likely to defer to a prosecutor's assertion that the defendant has done worse than the technical crimes alleged. Even if they generally work, electoral pressures disappear when the prosecutor faces no

---

* Bernard D. Meltzer Professor of Law, University of Chicago Law School.
1. Leipold core text at 543.
2. *Id.* at 550.
3. *See* Richard McAdams, *The Political Economy of Criminal Law and Procedure: The Pessimists' View, in* CRIMINAL LAW CONVERSATIONS 517 (Paul Robinson, Stephen P. Garvey, and Kimberly Kessler Ferzan eds., 2009) (explaining Stuntz's thesis).

real political challenge or decides not to seek reelection. Finally, in the federal system, prosecutors aren't elected.

Enter the jury. In this institution, citizens learn the details about a case and the prosecutor's charging decision. If the legislature is no longer in the business of defining crimes limited to what the public thinks is worthy of punishment, then the jury's view is our best estimate of where the public would draw the line if it considered the matter. Given rampant overcriminalization, the effect of nullification is not generally, as Leipold puts it, to "frustrate a legislative judgment that certain behavior should be punished as a crime,"[4] but to frustrate a *prosecutorial* judgment that certain technical violations frequently left unpunished should be treated on the present occasion as criminal. The idea that, on rare occasions, we need jury nullification to prevent the law's application to an unusual set of facts the legislature did not anticipate is quaint. Instead, we need the threat of nullification *every day* to deter prosecutors from enforcing the intentionally overbroad parts of the law in cases where the public would not approve.

Of course, nullification is a highly imperfect means of checking prosecutorial power. Leipold rightly observes that the jury often lacks the evidence it needs to decide whether to nullify. We might add that some juries will be too timid to resist applying the law as instructed, even though they regard their verdict of conviction as unjust. Still, in many cases, the jury will notice the triviality of the violation or the absence of facts that seem morally important despite being irrelevant to the overbroad statute. Fortunately, even a low risk of nullification may deter a significant amount of prosecutorial overreaching simply because prosecutors hate so much to lose at trial. Even if prosecutors are still *likely* to win a guilty verdict in purely technical cases, they are *less* likely to win these cases than the ones that conform to jury beliefs about criminality. The effect is to push prosecutors to pursue cases that correspond to jury intuitions about what should be treated as a crime.

No doubt nullification is "a form of unreviewable power"[5] subject to abuse. But also subject to abuse is the modern prosecutor's unreviewable power to select, among many who commit technical violations of overbroad statutes, the few to charge. The Constitution separates and diffuses powers among the branches of government, but prosecutors exercise legislative power when they decide what parts of an overbroad statute to enforce and adjudicative power when they base charging decisions on their determinations of morally relevant facts not required by an overbroad statute. However imperfect, the jury's absolute power to acquit stands as one of the last remaining checks on this expanding power.

---

4. Leipold core text at 543.
5. *Id.* at 550.

SCULPTING THE SHAPE OF NULLIFICATION
THROUGH JURY INFORMATION AND INSTRUCTION

CAROL S. STEIKER*

Andrew Leipold performs a valuable service by exploring the downsides, systemic and individual, of the jury nullification power. Leipold's account, however, is oddly removed from the current social, political, and legal context, which is characterized by a crisis of mass incarceration, an upward spiral of penal sanctions, and the virtual disappearance of jury trials. In a government supposedly regulated by a system of checks and balances, who is checking and balancing our penal policies? Not our legislatures or prosecutors. Not sentencing judges, either: their discretion to treat each case on its individual merits has been curtailed by the growth of mandatory penalties and sentencing guidelines. Executive clemency is on the decline as well, in the White House and governors' offices around the country. At such a moment, the possibility of jury nullification—warts and all—looks more, rather than less, attractive.

What Leipold's account glosses over is just how much jury nullification we *don't* have. Juries generally do not know about their nullification power; judges refuse to instruct juries about nullification and forbid defense lawyers from arguing or introducing evidence about it; and juries who express a willingness to nullify are struck for cause from the jury pool. These limits place enormous constraints on the nullification power, and that is probably a good thing. The power that Leipold fears is well cabined by these limits, despite the lack of judicial review or reversal. Rule of law values *should* focus the jury primarily on the charges before them, and refusing to convict despite the evidence *should* feel exceptional. The constraints currently in place provide assurance that this is indeed the case.

But in this moment of excessive punitiveness, we need a revival of jury nullification, and not necessarily along the lines of the affirmative defense proffered by Leipold. Offering protection to defendants in cases of "trivial" harm or in cases not "envisaged by the legislature," as Leipold suggests,[1] would do little to stem the power of most conscientious prosecutors or the excesses of most tough-on-crime legislators. The protection we need is from overpunishment and excessive sanctions for cases of *real* harm that *were* envisaged by the legislature. Mandatory ten- and twenty-year sentences for drug mules, for example. Or mandatory five- and ten-year sentences for downloading child pornography. Or fifty years for a repeat offender who stole nine videos from K-Mart. How could we

---

* Howard and Kathy Aibel Professor of Law, Harvard Law School.
1. Leipold core text at 549 (echoing the Model Penal Code).

revive nullification in such cases without opening the Pandora's Box of unfettered jury power that is kept pretty tightly closed by the limits we now have?

I propose two relatively small changes. Without touching the rules we currently have about excluding explicit nullifiers from the jury or limiting what can be introduced or argued, we could make two changes that would take us pretty far. First, Leipold is undoubtedly right that juries lack access to much information relevant to the nullification decision. But in an era of skyrocketing sentences and mandatory penalties, the single most relevant piece of evidence is simply the sentence that the judge may or must impose upon conviction of an offense.[2] This is a fight worth fighting because such a change could yield the kind of check on our excessive penal policies that we most need, generating more jury trials, more acquittals, and more reasonable plea agreements.

The second change is again a modest one, already in place to some extent in some jurisdictions throughout the country. Instead of instructing juries, as is commonly done, that they "must" convict if the prosecution proves all of the elements of the offense beyond a reasonable doubt, juries should be instructed that they "may" convict under such circumstances (though they "must" acquit if the prosecution fails to carry its burden of proof on any element). Eliminating language that absolutely forbids nullification opens the door just a crack to jury recognition of their power. Combined with information about the applicable penalties, this small departure from current practice could move us more toward a world in which juries can serve as a check on overpunishment.

The relative attractiveness or scariness of jury nullification will always be a product of its times. Nullification can certainly take on a frightful aspect, and Leipold has done a good job of showing us its horns and tail. But in our times, the alternative—an unending spiral of mass incarceration—looks a lot worse.

---

2. *See, e.g., United States v. Polizzi,* 549 F. Supp.2d 308, 449–50 (E.D.N.Y. 2008) (Weinstein, J.) (setting aside jury verdict on Sixth Amendment grounds for failure to instruct on sentencing consequences).

JURY NULLIFICATION AND ERRONEOUS ACQUITTALS: GETTING THE CAUSATION BACKWARDS

SHERRY F. COLB[*]

Andrew Leipold takes an interesting approach to jury nullification, treating it as a legal right (albeit one that lacks a coherent foundation) with undesirable incidental effects. He believes that "[l]urking in the background of the arguments

---

* Professor of Law and Charles Evans Hughes Scholar, Cornell Law School.

over nullification is an assumption that juries have a 'right' to acquit against the evidence."[1] It is not apparent, however, that the law and those who debate jury nullification treat it as a right. Accordingly, Leipold may be mistaken in describing our judiciary's refusal to correct erroneous acquittals as a byproduct of jury nullification.

As Leipold recognizes, traditional accounts of prohibitions against judicial correction of jury acquittals rest on the Fifth Amendment Double Jeopardy provision and the Sixth Amendment jury trial right. Leipold finds these accounts unconvincing and makes persuasive arguments for rejecting the Supreme Court's interpretation of the relevant amendments. Such arguments, however, do not demonstrate that what is really going on is the erection of "procedural rules" intended to "protect the nullification power against encroachment."[2]

Indeed, as Leipold suggests in criticizing nullification, juries frequently lack the evidence necessary to an informed decision to nullify. The rules of evidence prevent defense attorneys from offering evidence whose only relevance is to support acquittal despite a defendant's demonstrable guilt. Excluding such evidence would be strange in a system that extends procedural protection (presumably including the law of evidence) to nullification as a "right." Its exclusion is not at all surprising, however, in a system that considers nullification an incidental byproduct of other rights (such as double jeopardy and trial by jury). If we assume that the jury is not *allowed* to nullify (despite the fact that it can), it becomes sensible to exclude evidence that would facilitate nullification.

If, as Leipold claims, moreover, existing procedures were aimed at protecting a jury's right to nullify, it would be difficult to justify the dismissal-for-cause of any juror who says she is unwilling to apply the law as instructed to her by the judge. A juror, in other words, who admits that she intends to nullify (or even that she believes it is her prerogative to nullify) would not automatically disqualify herself from the job if nullification were treated as though it were a right.

The prosecutor's inability to obtain a directed verdict or to appeal an acquittal appears to rest on a vision of the lay jury as the best and least corruptible fact finder to protect innocent criminal defendants from being railroaded into an undeserved prison term or death sentence. The assumption here—which is certainly subject to debate—is that if the government wants to deprive a person of his life or liberty for a crime, it should be able to do so only if a jury of his peers—with its superior ability to assess facts with common-folk wisdom—accepts the government's version of events. Allowing a judge to question a jury's acquittal might suggest that the judge is better suited than the jury to assess whether the facts justify a guilty verdict.

---

1. Leipold core text at 547.
2. *Id.* at 543.

The sacred quality of an acquittal, in other words, appears to have much to do with protecting the process by which a jury properly reaches an acquittal—lay fact-finding by nongovernment officials—and little to do with the desire to protect a jury's disregard of its directive to apply the law to the facts. The jury has the last word when it issues an acquittal because we trust a jury (and, absent waiver, only a jury) to review the evidence and decide that a conviction is proper.

Nullification, of course, does become a possibility if we do not allow anyone to second-guess an acquittal. Though the jury is not supposed to acquit against the evidence, it *can* do so, and no one has the ability to stop it. Leipold is therefore right to discuss nullification in the same breath as the procedural devices that protect the finality of jury acquittals. And his critiques of the wisdom of nullification (on grounds of incomplete information, the possibility of prejudice, and the arbitrariness of which jurors happen to wind up on a particular defendant's jury) are quite convincing and well-taken.

By treating the finality of acquittals as a byproduct of nullification, however, Leipold is allowing the tail to wag the dog. Furthermore, at least some resistance to his most significant proposals—that we allow judges to reverse acquittals (at trial and on appeal)—are likely to come from quarters not at all wedded to the protection of a jury's right to nullify.

ACCURACY AND LEGITIMACY

JOSH BOWERS*

Andrew Leipold sees jury nullification as the reason for the finality of acquittals, and he sees the finality of acquittals as a barrier to accurate adjudication of criminal cases. His controversial proposal to fix this perceived problem is to make "error-correcting devices" available to the prosecution. I wish to put to one side the constitutional and deontological objections to judicial "error-correcting devices" and raise instead the question of whether the lack of such devices even promotes inaccuracy in the first instance. Put concretely: Are the utilitarian costs real? The answer turns on a second question: Relative to what?

Few civic determinations are as solemn as the decision about whether to brand another person a criminal or, alternatively, to return her to the community. In short, criminal juries exercise terrific power. From this power comes responsibility—a sense of ownership. And this sense of ownership undergirds communal perceptions of systemic legitimacy. Entrusted with weighty and complex decisions, juries take seriously their obligations to carefully assess evidence under applicable legal standards in order to reach informed and accurate conclusions. Juries are diligent

---

* Associate Professor of Law, University of Virginia School of Law.

precisely because they know that their decisions carry significant consequences (and they may even know that their acquittals are final). If juries come to believe that professional jurists are micromanaging their lay decisions, then these juries may treat their diminished roles as consisting of only rote exercises that are less meaningful and less deserving of considered deliberation. Error rates would increase.

Moreover, it's not clear whether the increased errors would more likely be Type I (erroneous convictions) or Type II (erroneous acquittals). It could be that wrongful convictions (conventionally thought to be the worse error type) would increase as juries relied less on application of facts to law and more on hunch, intuition, or even prejudice. Notwithstanding legal burdens to the contrary, juries already operate under something of a presumption of guilt, particularly when defendants "look like criminals" or come from known high-crime areas. The disempowered (and therefore potentially less vigilant) jury might exacerbate this problem. And, although Leipold's proposal would succeed in making appellate *rights* equivalent, appellate *abilities* would be asymmetrical: The fact remains that the government has greater resources to appeal cases than most defendants. The likeliest defendant to be convicted wrongfully by the incautious jury (the indigent defendant from a distressed community) would also be the likeliest to see prejudicial errors go uncorrected.

Likewise, the act of jury nullification itself might have accuracy-enhancing and crime-fighting value. Counterintuitively, jurors are likelier to respect a system and code that they have the power to disregard in exceptional cases. The nullifying jury makes the decision—notwithstanding strong evidence of guilt—that this particular defendant should not suffer the stigma of criminal conviction and the consequent loss of liberty or even life. If courts were permitted to negate a unanimous juror expression of communal dissent, it might promote disaffection and foster pernicious lay perceptions of an ever-more insider-dominated justice system. Conversely, systemic acceptance of nullification might serve to entrench crime-fighting norms: Nullifying jurors (whose decisions go untouched) may prove less likely to commit future crimes and more likely to cooperate with police and prosecutors when crimes are committed.

But does my legitimacy point prove too much? After all, courts already can (and do) review and reverse jury *convictions*. Admittedly, these reversals might already impact juror and communal perceptions of systemic validity—particularly in high-profile cases where reversals and their consequences are apparent. (Anti-*Miranda* backlash and calls to impeach Earl Warren come to mind.) But judicial oversight of convictions is required to preserve the constitutional rights of the accused; any legitimacy impact is a fair (or at least necessary) tradeoff. There is no corresponding necessity to correct presumed erroneous acquittals, and there is nothing terrifically novel about a lack of symmetry between the rights and obligations of prosecutors and defendants (e.g., nonreciprocal discovery).

Leipold fails to consider that accuracy could suffer in a world without jury nullification. In one sense, he paints with too narrow a brush when he posits that systemic acceptance of erroneous acquittals is merely an affirmation of the jury's power to nullify; in reality, it's an affirmation of the sanctity and power of the jury itself—an affirmation of the fact that the decision to sanction criminally is graver than, say, the decision to grant or withhold civil judgments. If jury power is circumscribed, then jurors may well grow disenchanted with their more anemic roles and quiet voices. Just as children tire of routinized tasks, jurors who are asked only to stick pegs in holes may choose not to take the time to determine what goes where.

REPLY

ANDREW D. LEIPOLD

Richard McAdams and Carol Steiker both forcefully argue that limits on jury nullification are out of step with the times. In a world where incarceration is the answer to all social problems, they say that practically *anything* that allows popular discontent to check this trend is worth nurturing. As McAdams puts it, "we need the threat of nullification *every day* to deter prosecutors from enforcing the intentionally overbroad parts of the law in cases where the public would not approve."[1]

A nice point, one with which I have great sympathy, but one that requires an important assumption—that most of the charges that prosecutors are deterred from bringing are ones that sensible people would agree should not be brought. This might be true, but I'm not so sure that "public" disapproval of charges is necessarily or routinely a valid consideration. A prosecutor might be restrained from bringing legitimate charges because she thinks the jury in this community will never convict the popular politician who took bribes; or the person who vandalized an abortion clinic; or the date rape defendant when the victim put herself in the dangerous situation; or the kids who beat up their gay classmate. McAdams and Steiker are surely right that prosecutors need to be restrained, but even if we make the leap that jury verdicts are good proxy for public sentiment (think how often have we heard complaints about "unrepresentative" juries) it is not obvious that this type of check does more good than mischief.

Agreeing that juries often lack enough information to nullify wisely, Steiker also offers straightforward, albeit incomplete, corrective steps—in particular, tell the jury the sentence the defendant faces if he is convicted. This might be a good idea, although it is easy to be distracted by the implementation problems—do we tell the jury the maximum statutory sentence? The maximum that this first-time offender is likely to get? That this defendant already has two strikes, i.e., two priors?—but we can leave those details for another day. The larger concern is

---

1. McAdams comment at 552.

that revamping trials to make more room for nullification might have the perverse effect of making legislators *more* willing to write harsh laws and prosecutors more likely to bring aggressive charges. Modest responses to uncomfortable difficulties run the risk of creating a "problem solved" mentality, where the answer to all future criticisms about overbroad laws is that nullification will catch the worst excesses.

Sherry Colb argues that nullification is not really a "right," and finds unpersuasive my claim that treating it as if it were a right explains the finality of acquittals. I agree with the first point and she might be right about the second. Nullification cannot be a right in any usual sense of the term, but I do think it is descriptively correct to say that the power of the jury has been protected against encroachment in part by making acquittals beyond review. I certainly agree, however, that this is not the only plausible argument for this strand of Double Jeopardy jurisprudence.

But when Colb says "[t]he sacred quality of an acquittal, in other words, appears to have much to do with protecting the process by which a jury properly reaches an acquittal—lay fact-finding by nongovernment officials,"[2] this proves too much. It would be logical to say as a matter of first principles that juries should get the last word, but that is not our system. Juries get the last word on acquittals but never for convictions: there we assuredly do not "trust a jury (and, absent waiver, only a jury) to review the evidence and decide that a conviction is proper."[3] This requires us to explain why acquittals are different, and indeed so different that we not only refuse to relook at the facts found by the jury (which are practically unreviewable), but also ignore obvious and significant legal errors that get made at trial.

Josh Bowers makes a similar point, and recognizes that the "sanctity of the verdict" argument only takes us so far. He correctly notes that this asymmetry in verdict treatment can be explained by the different interests at stake: Defendants have a huge interest in making sure their convictions are as accurate and error free as possible, while the state has a lower interest in making sure that acquittals are pristine.

This is true enough, and would be more persuasive if accuracy and lack of error in trials were a scarce resource, such that increasing accuracy in cases of acquittals meant there was less available in cases of conviction. But I'm not sure that this tradeoff exists.

Among the reasons Bowers thinks that the nullification power could make verdicts more accurate (and thus, why I'm wrong to speak of "error-correcting devices") is that juries may feel less ownership of a verdict if they knew judges might tinker with it later. But I doubt that juror seriousness and diligence would

---

2. Colb comment at 556.
3. *Id.*

be affected more than it is now, knowing as they do that a guilty verdict can be subject to multilayered review. If you really want to discourage a jury, reverse a *conviction* that took three weeks of deliberations to reach. We don't worry about the jury when judges do that, and we shouldn't. But if Bowers is right that "if juries come to believe that professional jurists are micromanaging their lay decisions, then these juries may treat their diminished roles as consisting of only rote exercises that are less meaningful and less deserving of considered deliberation. Error rates would increase,"[4] we should be darn worried about the many guilty verdicts that juries return now.

My bottom line is that jury nullification is not always bad. But it is not a necessary or even particularly useful tool for reforming the problem-plagued criminal system, and protecting this power, as I think we do now, brings with it significant and ultimately unnecessary costs.

---

4. Bowers comment at 557.

26. RACE-BASED JURY NULLIFICATION
Black Power in the Criminal Justice System

PAUL BUTLER*

I was a Special Assistant U.S. Attorney in the District of Columbia. I prosecuted people accused of misdemeanor crimes, mainly the drug and gun cases that overwhelm the local courts of most American cities. As a federal prosecutor, I represented the United States of America and used that power to put people, mainly African-American men, in prison. I am also an African-American man. During that time, I made two discoveries that profoundly changed the way I viewed my work as a prosecutor and my responsibilities as a Black person.

The first discovery occurred during a training session for new assistants conducted by experienced prosecutors. We rookies were informed that we would lose many of our cases, despite having persuaded a jury beyond a reasonable doubt that the defendant was guilty. We would lose because some Black jurors would refuse to convict Black defendants who they knew were guilty.

The second discovery was related to the first but was even more unsettling. It occurred during the trial of Marion Barry, then the second-term mayor of the District of Columbia. Barry was being prosecuted by my office for drug possession and perjury. I learned, to my surprise, that some of my fellow African-American prosecutors hoped that the mayor would be acquitted, despite the fact that he was obviously guilty of at least one of the charges—an FBI videotape plainly showed him smoking crack cocaine. These Black prosecutors wanted their office to lose its case because they believed that the prosecution of Barry was racist.

Federal prosecutors in the nation's capital hear many rumors about prominent officials engaging in illegal conduct, including drug use. Some African-American prosecutors wondered why, of all those people, the government chose to "set up" the most famous Black politician in D.C. They also asked themselves why, if crack is so dangerous, the FBI had allowed the mayor to smoke it. Some members of the predominantly Black jury must have had similar concerns: They convicted the mayor of only one count of a fourteen-count indictment, despite the trial judge's assessment that he had "never seen a stronger government case."[1] Some African-American prosecutors thought that the jury, in rendering

---

* Carville Dickenson Benson Research Professor of Law, George Washington University Law School. This core text is drawn from Paul Butler, *Racially Based Jury Nullification: Black Power in the Criminal Justice System*, 105 YALE L.J. 677 (1995).

1. Christopher B. Daly, *Barry Judge Castigates Four Jurors: Evidence of Guilt was "Overwhelming," Jackson Tells Forum*, WASH. POST., Oct. 31, 1990, at A1 (quoting U.S. District Judge Thomas Penfield Jackson).

its verdict, jabbed its black thumb in the face of a racist prosecution, and that idea made those prosecutors glad.

There is an increasing perception that some African-American jurors vote to acquit Black defendants for racial reasons, sometimes explained as the juror's desire not to send another Black man to jail. There is considerable disagreement over whether it is appropriate for a Black juror to do so. I argue that the race of a Black defendant is sometimes a legally and morally appropriate factor for jurors to consider in reaching a verdict of not guilty, or for an individual juror to consider in refusing to vote for conviction.

My thesis is that, for pragmatic and political reasons, the Black community is better off when some nonviolent lawbreakers remain in the community rather than go to prison. The decision as to what kind of conduct by African-Americans ought to be punished is better made by African-Americans, based on their understanding of the costs and benefits to their community, than by the traditional criminal justice process, which is controlled by White lawmakers and White law enforcers. Legally, the doctrine of jury nullification gives the power to make this decision to African-American jurors who sit in judgment of African-American defendants. Considering the costs of law enforcement to the Black community, and the failure of lawmakers to devise significant nonincarcerating responses to Black antisocial conduct, Black jurors have the moral responsibility to emancipate some guilty Black outlaws.

My goal is the subversion of American criminal justice, at least as it now exists. Through jury nullification, I want to dismantle the master's house with the master's tools. My intent, however, is not purely destructive; this project is also constructive, because I hope it will lead to the implementation of beneficial noncriminal ways of addressing antisocial conduct. Outlaw conduct among African-Americans is often a predictable reaction to oppression. Sometimes Black crime is a symptom of internalized White supremacy; other times it is a reasonable response to the racial and economic subordination African-Americans face every day. Punishing Black people for the fruits of racism is wrong if that punishment is premised on the idea that it is the Black criminal's "just deserts." Hence the new paradigm of justice that I suggest rejects punishment for the sake of retribution and endorses it, with qualifications, for the ends of deterrence and incapacitation.

I wish that Black people had the power to end racial oppression right now. African-Americans can prevent the application of one particularly destructive instrument of White supremacy—American criminal justice—to some African-American people, and this they can do immediately. I want to make the case for why and how they should.

I. RACIAL CRITIQUES OF AMERICAN CRIMINAL JUSTICE

Why would a Black juror vote to let a guilty person go free? Assuming the juror is a rational, self-interested actor, she must believe that she is better off with the defendant out of prison than in prison. But how could any rational person believe that about a criminal?

The Black community bears real costs by having so many African-Americans, particularly males, incarcerated or otherwise involved in the criminal justice system. These costs are both social and economic, and they include the large percentage of Black children who live in female-headed, single-parent households; a perceived dearth of men "eligible" for marriage; the lack of male role models for Black children, especially boys; the absence of wealth in the Black community; and the large unemployment rate among Black men.

Imagine a country in which a third of the young male citizens are under the supervision of the criminal justice system, either awaiting trial, in prison, or on probation or parole. Imagine a country in which two-thirds of the men can anticipate being arrested before they reach age thirty. Imagine a country in which there are more young men in prison than in college.

Such a country bears some resemblance to a police state. When we think of a police state, we think of a society whose fundamental problem lies not with the citizens of the state but rather with the form of government, and with the powerful elites in whose interest the state exists. Similarly, racial critics of American criminal justice locate the problem not with the Black prisoners but with the state and its actors and beneficiaries.

According to a 1995 USA Today/CNN/Gallup poll, 66 percent of Blacks believe that the criminal justice system is racist and only 32 percent believe it is not racist.[2] Interestingly, other polls suggest that Blacks also tend to be more worried about crime than Whites; this seems logical when one considers that Blacks are more likely to be victims of crime. This enhanced concern, however, does not appear to translate into Black support for tougher enforcement of criminal law. For example, substantially fewer Blacks than Whites support the death penalty, and many more Blacks than Whites were concerned with the potential racial consequences of the strict provisions of the Crime Bill of 1994. Along with significant evidence from popular culture, these polls suggest that a substantial portion of the African-American community sympathizes with racial critiques of the criminal justice system.

African-American jurors who endorse these critiques are in a unique position to act on their beliefs when they sit in judgment of a Black defendant. As jurors, they have the power to convict the accused person or to set him free. May the responsible exercise of that power include voting to free a Black defendant who the juror believes is guilty? The answer is "yes," based on the legal doctrine known as jury nullification.

---

2. Maria Puente, *Poll: Blacks' Confidence in Police Plummets*, USA TODAY, Mar. 21, 1995, at 3A.

II. JURY NULLIFICATION: A PRIMER

Jury nullification occurs when a jury acquits a defendant who it believes is guilty of the crime with which he is charged. In finding the defendant not guilty, the jury ignores the facts of the case and/or the judge's instructions regarding the law. Instead, the jury votes its conscience.

In the United States, the doctrine of jury nullification originally was based on the common-law idea that the function of a jury was, broadly, to do justice, which included judging the law as well as the facts. If the jurors believed that applying a law would lead to an unjust conviction, they were not compelled to convict someone who had broken that law. Although most American courts now disapprove of a jury's deciding anything other than the "facts," the Double Jeopardy Clause of the Fifth Amendment prohibits appellate reversal of a jury's decision to acquit, regardless of the reason. Thus, even when a trial judge thinks that the jury's acquittal directly contradicts the evidence, the jury's verdict must be accepted as final. The jurors, in judging the law, function as an important and necessary check on government power.

There are well-known cases of nullification throughout American history. In the Revolutionary War era American patriots were charged with political crimes by the British crown and acquitted by American juries. Later, people prosecuted for violating the Fugitive Slave law for helping Black slaves escape to the North were often freed by Northern juries with abolitionist sentiments. In the twentieth century, some Southern juries refused to punish White violence against African-Americans, especially when it was directed at Black men raping White women.

The Supreme Court has officially disapproved of jury nullification but has conceded that it has no power to prohibit jurors from engaging in it. In *Sparf v. United States*, the Court acknowledged that juries have the "physical power" to disregard the law, but stated that they have no "moral right" to do so.[3] The Court's concern was that "if the jury were at liberty to settle the law for themselves, the effect would be . . . that the law itself would be most uncertain, from the different views, which different juries might take of it."[4] *Sparf* created an anomaly that has been a feature of American criminal law since: Jurors have the power to nullify, but in most jurisdictions, they have no right to be informed of this power.

Some lower appellate courts have not been as critical of the concept of nullification as was the *Sparf* Court. The D.C. Circuit, in *United States v. Dougherty*, note that the ability of juries to nullify was widely recognized and even approved as a "necessary counter to case-hardened judges and arbitrary prosecutors."[5]

---

3. 156 U.S. 51, 74 (1895).

4. *Id.*

5. 473 F.2d 1113 (D.C. Cir. 1972).

Still the court was concerned that "[w]hat makes for health as an occasional medicine would be disastrous as a daily diet."[6]

III. THE MORAL CASE

Jury nullification is subversive of the rule of law. Nonetheless, the judgment of history seems to be that it was morally appropriate in the cases of the White American revolutionaries and the runaway slaves. The issue, then, is whether African-Americans today have the moral right to engage in this same subversion.

Most moral justifications of the obligation to obey the law are based on theories of "fair play." Citizens benefit from the rule of law; that is why it is just that they are burdened with the requirement to follow it. Yet most Blacks are aware of countless historical examples in which African-Americans were not afforded the benefit of the rule of law: Think, for example, of the existence of slavery in a republic purportedly dedicated to the proposition that all men are created equal, or the law's support of state-sponsored segregation even after the Fourteenth Amendment guaranteed Blacks equal protection. That the rule of law ultimately corrected some of the large holes in the American fabric is evidence more of its malleability than its goodness; the rule of law previously had justified the holes.

The Supreme Court's decisions in some of its major "race" cases underscore the continuing failure of the rule of law to protect African-Americans through consistent application. Dissenting in a school desegregation case, four Justices stated that "[t]he Court's process of orderly adjudication has broken down in this case."[7] In a voting rights case Justice Stevens described the majority opinion as a "law-changing decision."[8] In an affirmative action case, Stevens argued that "the majority's concept of stare decisis ignores the force of binding precedent."[9]

If the rule of law is a myth, or at least not valid for African-Americans, the argument that jury nullification undermines it loses force. The Black juror is simply another actor in the system, using her power to fashion a particular outcome. The juror's act of nullification—like that of the citizen who dials 911 to report Ricky but not Bob, or that of the police officer who arrests Lisa but not Mary, or the prosecutor who charges Kwame but not Brad, or that of the judge who finds that Nancy was illegally entrapped but Verna was not—exposes the indeterminacy of law but does not in itself create it.

A similar argument can be made regarding the criticism that jury nullification is antidemocratic. This is precisely why many African-Americans endorse it; it is perhaps the only legal power Black people have to escape the tyranny of the

---

6. *Id.*

7. *Missouri v. Jenkins*, 115 S. Ct. 2038, 2073 (1995).

8. *Miller v. Johnson*, 115 S. Ct. 2475, 2497 (1995).

9. *Adarand Constructors v. Pena*, 115 S. Ct. 2097, 2141 (1995).

majority. Black people have had to beg White decision-makers for most of the rights they have: the right not to be slaves, the right to vote, the right to attend an integrated school. Now Black people are begging White people to preserve programs that help Black children eat and Black businesses survive. Jury nullification affords African-Americans the power to determine justice for themselves, in individual cases, regardless of whether White people agree or even understand.

On several occasions the Supreme Court has referred to the usefulness of Black jurors to the concept of the rule in the United States. In essence, Black jurors symbolize the fairness and impartiality of the law. They serve a symbolic function, especially when they sit on cases involving African-American defendants. I refer to this role of Black jurors as the "legitimization function."

When Blacks are excluded from juries, the social injury of the exclusion is that it "undermine[s] . . . public confidence—as well [it] should."[10] Because the United States is both a democracy and a pluralist society, it is important that diverse groups appear to have a voice in the laws that govern them. Allowing Black people to serve on juries strengthens "public respect for our criminal justice system and the rule of law."[11]

The Supreme Court has found that the legitimization function is particularly valuable in cases involving "race-related" crimes.[12] According to the Court, in these cases, "emotions in the affected community [are] inevitably . . . heated and volatile."[13] The potential presence of Black people on the jury in a race-related case calms the natives, which is especially important in this type of case because "[p]ublic confidence in the integrity of the criminal justice system is essential for preserving community peace."[14] The very fact that a Black person can be on a jury is evidence that the criminal justice system is one in which Black people should have confidence, and one that they should respect.

But what of the Black juror who endorses racial critiques of American criminal justice? Such a person holds no "confidence in the integrity of the criminal justice system." If she is cognizant of the implicit message that the Supreme Court believes her presence sends, she might not want to be the vehicle for that message. Let us assume that there is a Black defendant who, the evidence suggests, is guilty of the crime with which he has been charged, and a Black juror who thinks that there are too many Black men in prison. The juror has two choices: She can vote for conviction, thus sending another Black man to prison and implicitly allowing her presence to support public confidence in the system that put him there, or she can vote "not guilty." In choosing the latter, the juror makes a decision not to be a passive symbol of support for a system for which

---

10. *Georgia v. McCollum*, 505 U.S. 42, 49 (1992).

11. *Batson v. Kentucky*, 476 U.S. 79, 99 (1986).

12. *See McCollum*, 505 U.S. at 49.

13. *Id.*

14. *Id.*

she has no respect. Rather than signaling her displeasure with the system by breaching "community peace," the Black juror invokes the political nature of her role in the criminal justice system and votes "no." In a sense, the Black juror engages in an act of civil disobedience, except that her choice is better than civil disobedience because it is lawful. Is the Black juror's race-conscious act moral? Absolutely. It would be farcical for her to be the sole color-blind actor in the criminal process, especially when it is her Blackness that advertises the system's fairness.

At this point, every African-American should ask herself whether the operation of the criminal law system in the United States advances the interests of Black people. If it does not, the doctrine of jury nullification affords African-American jurors the opportunity to exercise the authority of the law over some African-American criminal defendants. In essence, Black people can "opt out" of American criminal law.

IV. A PROPOSAL FOR RACE-BASED JURY NULLIFICATION

How far should they go—completely to anarchy, or is there someplace between here and there that is safer than both? To allow Black jurors to exercise their responsibility in a principled way, I propose the following: African-American jurors should approach their work cognizant of its political nature and of their prerogative to exercise their power in the best interests of the Black community. In every case, the juror should be guided by her view of what is "just." (I have more faith, I should add, in the average Black juror's idea of justice than I do in the idea embodied in the "rule of law.")

In cases involving violent malum in se (inherently bad) crimes, such as murder, rape, and assault, jurors should consider the case strictly on the evidence presented, and if they believe the accused person is guilty, they should so vote. In cases involving nonviolent, malum prohibitum (legally proscribed) offenses, including "victimless" crimes such as narcotics possession, there should be a presumption in favor of nullification. Finally, for nonviolent, malum in se crimes, such as theft or perjury, there need be no presumption in favor of nullification, but it ought to be an option the juror considers. A juror might vote for acquittal, for example, when a poor woman steals from Tiffany's but not when the same woman steals from her next-door neighbor.

If this model is faithfully executed, the result would be that fewer Black people go to prison; to that extent, the proposal ameliorates one of the most severe consequences of law enforcement in the African-American community. At the same time the proposal, by punishing violent offenses and certain others, preserves any protection against harmful conduct that the law may offer potential victims.

In the language of criminal law, the proposal adopts utilitarian justifications for punishment: deterrence and isolation. To that extent, it accepts the possibility that law can prevent crime. Still, I do not judge lawbreakers as harshly as some retributivists do. Rather, the proposal assumes that, regardless of the reasons for their antisocial conduct, people who are violent should be separated from the community, for the sake of the nonviolent. I am confident that balancing the social costs and benefits of incarceration would not lead Black jurors to release violent criminals simply because of race. Although I confess agnosticism about whether the law can deter antisocial conduct, I am unwilling to experiment by abandoning punishment premised on deterrence.

Of the remaining traditional justifications of punishment, the proposal eschews the retributive or just deserts theory for two reasons. First, I am persuaded by racial and other critiques of the unfairness of punishing people for "negative" reactions to oppressive conditions. In fact, I sympathize with people who react "negatively" to the countless manifestations of White supremacy that Black people experience daily. Although my proposal does not "excuse" all antisocial conduct, it will not punish such conduct on the premise that the intent to engage in it is "evil." The antisocial conduct is not more evil than the conditions that cause it, and accordingly, the "just deserts" of a Black offender are impossible to know.

Even if just deserts were susceptible to accurate measure, I would reject the idea of punishment for retribution's sake. My argument here is that the consequences are too severe: African-Americans cannot afford to lock up other African-Americans simply on account of anger. There is too little bang for the buck. Black people have a community that needs building, and children who need rescuing, and as long as a person will not hurt anyone, the community needs him there to help. Assuming that he actually will help is a gamble, but not a reckless one, for the "just" African-American community will not leave the law-breaker be. It will, for example, encourage his education and provide his health care and, if necessary, sue him for child support. In other words, the proposal demands of African-Americans responsible self-help outside of the criminal courtroom as well as inside it.

The final traditional justification for punishment, rehabilitation, can be dealt with summarily. If rehabilitation were a meaningful option in American criminal justice, I would not endorse nullification in any case. It would be counterproductive, for utilitarian reasons: The community is better off with the antisocial person cured than sick. Unfortunately, however, rehabilitation is no longer an objective of criminal law in the United States, and prison appears to have an antirehabilitative effect. For this reason, unless a juror is provided with a specific, compelling reason to believe that a conviction would result in some useful treatment for an offender, she should not use her vote to achieve this end, because it is not likely to occur.

How would a juror decide individual cases under my proposal? Simple cases would include a defendant who has possessed crack cocaine and an abusive husband who kills his wife. The former should be acquitted and the latter should go to prison.

Difficult scenarios would include the drug dealer who operates in the ghetto and the thief who burglarizes the home of a rich family. Under my proposal, nullification is presumed in the first case because drug distribution is a nonviolent malum prohibitum offense. Is nullification morally justifiable here? It depends. There is no question that encouraging people to engage in self-destructive behavior is evil; the question the juror should ask herself is whether the remedy is less evil. (The juror should also remember that the criminal law does not punish those ghetto drug dealers who cause the most injury: liquor store owners.)

As for the burglar who steals from the rich family, the case is troubling, first of all, because the conduct is so clearly "wrong." Since it is a nonviolent malum in se crime, there is no presumption in favor of nullification, but it is an option for consideration. Here again, the facts of the case are relevant. For example, if the offense was committed to support a drug habit, I think there is a moral case to be made for nullification, at least until such time as access to drug-rehabilitation services available to all.

Why would a juror be inclined to follow my proposal? There is no guarantee that she would. But when we perceive that Black jurors are already nullifying on the basis of racial critiques (i.e., refusing to send another Black man to jail), we recognize that these jurors are willing to use their power in a politically conscious manner. Further, it appears that some Black jurors now excuse some conduct—like murder—that they should not excuse. My proposal provides a principled structure for the exercise of the Black juror's vote. I am not encouraging anarchy; rather I am reminding Black jurors of their privilege to serve a calling higher than law: justice.

I concede that the justice my proposal achieves is rough. It is as susceptible to human foibles as the jury system. But I am sufficiently optimistic that my proposal will be only an intermediate plan, a stopping point between the status quo and real justice. To get criminal justice past the middle point, I hope that this proposal encourages African-Americans to use responsibly the power that they already have.

COMMENTS

CONFUSING CAUSE AND EFFECT

LAWRENCE ROSENTHAL*

Like Paul Butler, I did a stint in a U.S. Attorney's Office in a majority-minority city, in my case, Chicago. At that time, my primary exposure to the typical African-American residents of the high-crime neighborhoods of Chicago was by watching them in the jury box. Like Butler, I learned that African-American

---

* Professor of Law, Chapman University School of Law.

jurors—or at least some of them—were frequently skeptical of cases against African-American defendants.

But unlike Butler, after I left that job I remained in law enforcement, working in a far more politically accountable branch of government—Chicago's City Hall. There I dealt on a regular basis with African-American residents of Chicago's high-crime neighborhoods. I quickly learned that the residents of these communities were enormously dissatisfied with the criminal justice system. Yet, in some fifteen years in municipal government, not a single resident of one of these neighborhoods ever suggested that the Chicago Police Department stop enforcing the drug laws in their neighborhood. I did hear such proposals repeatedly, from ACLU lawyers, White liberals, and especially from law professors, but never once from anyone who lived in these high-crime neighborhoods. What they complained about, especially during the period discussed in Butler's article, was the failure of the criminal justice system to keep them safe.

In fact, the spike in violent crime in the late 1980s and early 1990s hit young African-American males particularly hard. From 1984 to 1993, the homicide victimization rate per hundred thousand for Whites aged eighteen to twenty-four rose from 11.9 to 17.1, while the homicide rates for African-American males in the same age range rose from 67.9 to 183.4.[1] Something of a consensus exists among criminologists as to the cause of this spike—the introduction of crack cocaine into urban markets[2]. Crack was unusually profitable, and street gangs engaged in violent competition to dominate this market. One respected study of a drug-dealing African-American gang found that over a four-year period, gang members had a 25 percent mortality rate.[3] I have always remembered what an African-American police officer who grew up in one of the most violent areas of Chicago told me about programs to improve education and job training programs: "You have to remember, when I was seventeen, I didn't expect to live to be twenty-one."

Butler will have no truck with jury nullification in cases involving violent crime, and properly so, but he ignores the difficulties in prosecuting drug and

---

1. James Alan Fox, *Demographics and U.S. Homicide, in* THE CRIME DROP IN AMERICA 288, 300 tbl.9.3 (Alfred Blumstein and Joel Wallman eds., 2d ed. 2006).

2. *See, e.g.,* Alfred Blumstein and Jacqueline Cohen, DIFFUSION PROCESSES IN HOMICIDE 6–9 (Nat'l Crim. Just. Ref. Serv. July 17, 1999); James Alan Fox, Jack Levin, and Kenna Quinet, THE WILL TO KILL: MAKING SENSE OF SENSELESS MURDER 87–88 (rev. 2008); Philip J. Cook and John H. Laub, *After the Epidemic: Recent Trends in Youth Violence in the United States, in* CRIME AND JUSTICE: A REVIEW OF RESEARCH 1, 21–31 (Michael Tonry ed., 2002); Alfred Blumstein and Richard Rosenfeld, *Explaining Recent Trends in U.S. Homicide Rates,* 88 J. CRIM. L. & CRIMINOLOGY 1175, 1209–10 (1998); Alfred Blumstein and Joel Wallman, *The Crime Drop and Beyond,* 2006 AM. REV. SOC. SCI. 125, 131.

3. *See* Sudhir Venkatesh, *The Financial Activity of a Modern American Street Gang, in* AMERICAN YOUTH STREET GANGS AT THE MILLENNIUM 239, 242 (Finn-Aage Esbensen, Stephen F. Tibbets, and Larry Gaines eds., 2004).

gang-related violent crime. In communities terrorized by gangs, witnesses to violent crimes remain silent. Urban drug crime is prosecuted with vigor because it has turned out to be a good proxy for the type of violent crime that destroys all too many inner-city communities, and it can be prosecuted without placing civilian witnesses in harm's way.

So why are so many inner-city residents angry at the criminal justice system? The studies reach a uniform conclusion—satisfaction with local law enforcement is not a function of race, but of perceived local rates of crime and disorder.[4] When the police seem helpless to stop the gangs and drug dealers, community residents naturally think the worst—the police must be inept or corrupt, and even racist, because they surely would not tolerate this state of affairs in White neighborhoods.

Rates of inner-city violent crime have declined considerably since the mid-1990s. Consider, for example, New York City. At the 1991 peak of New York's crime wave, the homicide victimization rate was 58 per 100,000 population for African-Americans, 44 for Hispanics, and 8 for Whites.[5] By 1998, the African-American homicide victimization rate had declined to 17 per 100,000 population, the Hispanic rate to 8, and the White rate was at 4.[6] A good deal of evidence suggests that New York City's aggressive stop-and-frisk policy is responsible for a substantial proportion of the decline.[7] More important for present purposes, we have no reason to believe that a regime of jury nullification could have achieved the same result; if anything, it would have only promoted violent gang and drug competition, as the cost/benefit ratio associated with gang membership and drug dealing concomitantly declined.

Butler's primary concern is with the morality of the criminal justice. I have no doubt that high rates of crime in impoverished African-American neighborhoods are a part of racism's legacy. Still, I think it more important to save African-American lives than encourage symbolic protests of that legacy. A regime of race-based jury nullification achieves only the latter.

---

4. See, e.g., Cheryl Maxson, Karen Hennigan, and David C. Sloane, U.S. DEP'T OF JUSTICE, FACTORS THAT INFLUENCE PUBLIC OPINION OF THE POLICE 8 (June 2006).

5. Andrew Karmen, NEW YORK MURDER MYSTERY: THE TRUE STORY BEHIND THE CRIME CRASH OF THE 1990s 54 fig.2.2 (2000).

6. Id.

7. For a valuable review of the evidence, see Franklin E. Zimring, THE GREAT AMERICAN CRIME DECLINE 135–68 (2006).

THE EFFECT OF RACE-BASED JURY NULLIFICATION ON *BATSON*

ROBIN CHARLOW*

Having worked as a Federal Defender, I find myself considering the likely effect of Paul Butler's proposal on the disproportionately African-American population of defendants to whom it would apply. Is it really in their interest to urge jurors to engage in race-based jury nullification? How exactly would the message of outrage—that the criminal justice system is considered biased by the African-American community—redound to their collective benefit? Even if the strategy were successful in acquitting a certain number of nonviolent Black defendants, are we really sure that its effect on Black defendants more generally, and on the larger African-American community, would start and end there? It seems to me that any such policy, publicly urged and carried out, would lead to a backlash. One form this backlash might take involves the use of race-based peremptory challenges.

Normally parties may strike prospective jurors who they surmise are not likely to be on their side. However, when African-American jurors are challenged because the party exercising a strike assumes that Blacks generally will not judge his case beneficially, the strike is "race-based" and illegal under *Batson*.[1] Race may not serve as a proxy for outlook, presumably because using it in this way lumps all Blacks together and treats them as members of a group rather than as individuals, even if a stereotype centering on race is accurate as to a majority of the group. Thus, *Batson* is premised, at least in part, on the idea that race-based stereotypes about jurors are unacceptable under the Equal Protection Clause, so that their use in the exercise of peremptory challenges is unconstitutional.

But *Batson* is in tension with itself, insofar as it permits peremptory strikes but condemns the group-based stereotyping that forms the basis for such strikes. Peremptory challenges allow for removal of those for whom a challenge for cause would not be valid- people you simply do not feel good about having on your jury. Such unfavorable intuitions boil down to unsubstantiated assumptions about unknown individuals. The only information on which they might be premised falls into two categories: that which is observed in court (body language, answers on voir dire), and objective facts that are revealed, such as occupation, religion, and race. The first category is largely individually determined, that is, it turns on whether a particular potential juror seemed hostile, ignorant, insecure, or possessed of some other undesirable trait or attitude toward one's case. But the second category is largely group-based, that is, it is determined by

---

* Professor of Law, Hofstra University School of Law.
1. *Baston v. Kentucky*, 476 U.S. 79 (1986).

whether people who fall within the same group as a potential juror (for example, blue-collar workers, or residents of a wealthy neighborhood) are likely to be positively or negatively disposed to one's cause.

As a result primarily of this second category, the logic of *Batson* and the logic of peremptory challenges are at odds with one another. Peremptories are the home for unsubstantiated group-based generalizations, while *Batson* forbids considering a subset of them. So far the two have lived in a tenuous, possibly unprincipled peace.

Butler's proposal might upset that delicate equilibrium. *Batson* might be even less vigorously enforced in Butler's world than it is today. Moreover, with guilty African-American defendants leaving the courthouse free, courts might even reconsider the wisdom of the *Batson* decision altogether. Maybe racial group-based decision-making in this context will suddenly seem less invidious or irrational, and less unconstitutional. Maybe the affront to the ordinary workings of the criminal justice system would be viewed as a countervailing compelling state interest, overriding any presumptive *Batson* violation and permitting race-based strikes.

Perhaps *Batson* is already so toothless that its total demise wouldn't matter. But it has at least symbolic value, to the extent that it confirms that racial prejudice in governmental functions like jury selection is impermissible. If it were eliminated, this message would be undermined. It seems a toss-up whether more African-American defendants would ultimately benefit from *Batson*-controlled juries or race-based jury nullification.

Backlash might take other forms as well. Angry courts might be more inclined to find cause to unseat Black jurors. Outraged White jurors might react by being more prone to convict Black defendants. Non-Black jurors might nullify for non-Black defendants who prey on African-American victims. Would Butler's entreaty to controlled, race-based lawlessness really stop at his personally preferred endpoint? I fear the potential fallout of a call for protest of this sort, one that removes social consequences from destructive or immoral activity, particularly that which burdens the very community the protest is intended to serve. A preferable solution might be to attack the sources of alienation of African-Americans from the criminal justice system that have resulted in Butler's proposal.

THE PERNICIOUS MYTH OF RACIAL JURY NULLIFICATION

LAJUANA DAVIS*

Paul Butler argues that Black jurors, in response to injustice in the criminal justice system, have a moral right and responsibility to acquit some guilty defendants. I fear, however, that some readers may disingenuously use Butler's call to arms as a justification for the exclusion of Blacks from criminal juries.

Jury nullification does not have much impact on the *results* of criminal cases. Jury nullification verdicts, when they occur, are necessarily a minuscule fragment of adjudicated criminal cases.[1] However, the *perception* of widespread Black juror nullification does have an impact on Black participation in the criminal justice system.

Butler's description of the socialization process when he was a new assistant U.S. attorney reflects a conventional prosecutorial wisdom. Butler recalls that new prosecutors were warned that they would lose many cases "because some Black jurors would refuse to convict Black defendants who they knew were guilty."[2] Thus, from the first day, those new prosecutors were indoctrinated with a mythology—to win cases, Blacks must be excluded from jury participation.

Once programmed to think of Black jurors as race-refuseniks, prosecutors can understandably get comfortable with the myth. The nullification myth conveniently explains less-than-desirable trial outcomes. Rather than conduct a self-referential, and quite possibly, painful post-mortem of how the prosecution failed to persuade twelve citizens to convict a defendant who commits a crime on video, the conclusion that Black jurors "let off" the defendant is much easier—*nothing to do with us.*

For prosecutors who believe the nullification myth, every aberrant verdict feeds a racial paranoia that Black jurors intentionally subvert the law. To correct Black jurors' presumed proclivity to excuse lawless behavior, some prosecutors resort to racial discrimination. The following are a few examples of reasons offered to exclude Blacks from criminal juries: affiliation with a historically Black university; preserving the presence of Whites on the jury; associating with

---

* Assistant Professor of Law, Cumberland School of Law, Samford University.

1. For example, of 83,391 criminal defendants whose cases were disposed of in a U.S. District Court in 2004, 490 (or 0.58 percent) cases ended with an acquittal or a mistrial at a jury trial. *See* BUREAU OF JUSTICE STATISTICS, U.S. DEP'T. OF JUSTICE, COMPENDIUM OF FEDERAL JUSTICE STATISTICS, 2004, at 2 (2006).

2. Butler core text at 561. This assessment of federal conviction rates is far too modest. In 2004, the federal prosecution conviction rate was about 90 percent of the cases adjudicated in federal court; about 96 percent of those convictions were guilty pleas. *Id.*

"members of the drug community"; and the perennial prosecutorial favorite, living in a "high-crime area."

Although the myth encourages sound-bite conclusions that attribute unexpected acquittals to racial nullification, these cases can be more complicated than that. For example, the O.J. Simpson jury verdict is classed as a tit-for-tat "payback" for the Rodney King verdict. However, the case defies such a simplistic conclusion. Simpson was a celebrity defendant who, unlike virtually every other criminal defendant, had the resources to employ an impressive team of defense lawyers and experts. Concluding that Black juror nullification fully explains cases like Simpson's is lazy analysis.

If prosecutors are correct in perceiving that Black jurors are more acquittal-prone, we may wish to examine why an entire segment of the community, across generational, economic, social, and geographical lines, thinks that the justice system cannot identify and deal with criminals fairly. Rather than figuring out ways that the criminal justice system can go about winning more trust from the African-American community, we only maintain the status quo by rationalizing the exclusion of Blacks from jury service because of race.

REJECTING RACIAL JURY NULLIFICATION

SHERRY F. COLB*

Although I sympathize with the motives behind Paul Butler's proposal for racially based jury nullification, I suspect that race-conscious nullification is a counterproductive strategy for achieving racial equality.

There is at least one serious practical drawback to encouraging African-Americans to use the acquittal of guilty people to effectuate justice. As it is, high-profile acquittals that appear to be the product of nullification engender anger and divisiveness. O.J. Simpson's acquittal, for example, gave rise to fury among many outside the African-American community who believed that the verdict contradicted the evidence, was a product of racial nullification, and demonstrated a deep-seated anti-White sentiment. After the verdict, White people apparently aggrieved by what was possibly an act of racial jury nullification might have lost their appetite for more lasting steps toward racial healing and reconciliation.

Butler could argue, of course, that the results might be better if more jurors actively engaged in nullification but confined such "civil disobedience" to malum prohibitum crimes, as he proposes they do. Yet if jurors, deliberating in secret and anonymously, can individually judge when to apply the law and when to ignore it, it is not clear that they would confine their nullification practices to malum prohibitum crimes. One lasting effect could therefore be to unleash

---

* Professor of Law and Charles Evans Hughes Scholar, Cornell Law School.

understandable outrage in the African-American community in the form of refusals to convict African-American defendants of crimes, however serious, especially perhaps when the perpetrator is African-American and the victim is White.

If the widespread adoption of the Butler proposal led to such practices, this would not go unnoticed by the larger society. Prosecutors might begin asking potential jurors during voir dire whether they share the view that jury nullification is appropriate in some instances. An affirmative response could lead to dismissals for cause. (A juror may be dismissed for cause if she is unwilling to apply the law to the facts as instructed by the judge.) If people were honest in their voir dire responses, Butler's proposal could mean the elimination from juries of the very people whom Butler would empower through the tool of jury nullification.

I would suggest that a more effective systematic means of protecting people from the injustice of unwarranted incarceration is a change in the law. Butler is undoubtedly right that African-Americans who violate the bloated and excessive criminal law could help the community much more on the outside than as prisoners. But this is also the case for non–African-Americans who commit malum prohibitum, "victimless" crimes. We should therefore reduce the size of the criminal law to make a dent in the shockingly high incarceration levels in the U.S., levels that differentially but by no means exclusively harm the African-American community.

Jury nullification might feel right on occasion, of course, but in large doses it will likely generate a backlash that impedes rather than ushers in true reform of the criminal law. Like the petty crimes that land so many people in jail, racially based jury nullification strikes me as a symptom of—rather than a solution to—the problem of inequality in the criminal justice system.

ON RACIALLY-BASED JURY NULLIFICATION

BENNETT CAPERS*

Although I am in broad agreement with Paul Butler's racial critique of our criminal justice system, I have two concerns regarding his proposal that African-Americans subvert our system by systemically exercising their right to jury nullification in criminal cases involving nonviolent minority offenders, based on their assessment of what is "just" and what is in the best interest of the community. The first concern is practical: Is such a proposal even feasible? The second involves policy: Are the costs worth the benefits?

* Visiting Associate Professor, Fordham Law School (2008–09); Associate Professor of Law, Hofstra University School of Law.

My concern about feasibility is serious. Other than in majority Black jurisdictions such as Washington, D.C., where Butler was a prosecutor, do African-Americans, who constitute roughly 13 percent of the general population, have the numbers to engage in systemic jury nullification? Of course not. Consider the racial disparity in the imposition of the death penalty. That disparity has more than one cause, but it's not because Blacks dominate juries.

My second concern ties in to the first and involves the collateral costs likely to result from Butler's proposal. Assuming, as I think we must, that African-Americans do not have the numbers needed to achieve nullification, then what we are really talking about is African-Americans systemically voting in a manner likely to result in deadlocked juries. However, the usual response to a deadlocked jury is not dismissal of the charges, but a retrial of the defendant with a different jury. Moreover, prosecutors will quickly learn from these deadlock juries to do what too many prosecutors do already: strike Black jurors, particularly Black male jurors, either using peremptory challenges or pretexts to challenge for cause. Given our current jurisprudence, this prosecutorial response may be impossible to counteract. *Batson* has been ineffective at eliminating racially motivated peremptory challenges.[1] The kind of racially based strikes that the Court recently found unconstitutional in *Miller-El v. Dretke*[2] continue to happen every day.

Let me be clear. I'm not opposed to the consideration of race in the determination of guilt or innocence. Such considerations are, as we know from social cognition research, already pervasive but under the radar, and too often result in racially biased outcomes. Indeed, I have proposed ways of bringing race to the fore so that jurors can see through and past their racial biases.[3] Nor do I have a problem with jurors considering the impact of their verdicts on the larger community. This is not that different from the victim impact considerations the Court sanctioned, at least in the death penalty context, in *Payne v. Tennessee.*[4] I'm even fine, in theory at least, with the concept of race-based nullification. For example, a jury engaging in nullification as a response to a racially based prosecution. My problem, again, is this: How does one keep racially based nullifications from backfiring, with minorities being struck from juries more often? How does one avoid a result in which minorities have less power, not more?

---

1. *Batson v. Kentucky*, 476 U.S. 79 (1986).
2. 545 U.S. 231 (2005).
3. I. Bennett Capers, *Cross Dressing and the Criminal*, 20 YALE J. L. & HUMAN. (1, 2008).
4. 501 U.S. 808 (1991).

GRAND-JURY NULLIFICATION: BLACK POWER IN THE CHARGING DECISION

JOSH BOWERS*

Paul Butler wants to "dismantle the master's house with the master's tools."[1] He faces a first-order problem: his wrecking ball is aimed at a largely deserted building. Vanishingly few criminal defendants take cases to trial. And, of those who do venture trial, many (particularly those from poor and minority communities) are detained pretrial and must spend months awaiting their slim chance at nullification. As a remedial measure, then, trial-jury nullification is too little, too late, for too few.

If Butler wishes to achieve more than symbolic revolution, *grand-jury* nullification is a better vehicle. Of course, the refrain that a grand jury "would indict a ham sandwich" has some truth, but this old saw is least true of juries in the very majority-minority communities that are the presumed focus of Butler's proposal. Grand juries from these marginalized communities can, and sometimes do, choose not to rubber-stamp prosecutors' felony charging decisions—even in instances where the evidence amply supports those charges. Significantly, these grand juries exercise nullification power at the time that matters most—before the case has even started. Moreover, defendants can use the grand jury to test public sentiment with less risk: the grand-jury decision is not an all-or-nothing proposition. If the grand jury decides to indict, the defendant lives on to fight (or plea) another day.

Butler raises an interesting point that nullification may counterintuitively entrench crime-fighting norms in marginalized communities by fostering greater respect for a justice system that historically has frozen them out of the decision-making process. But there's a potential cost that all-too-public instances of race-based trial jury nullification could engender backlash by reinforcing negative perceptions of minorities and by ultimately undermining the already-slender protections that exist against racial discrimination in jury selection. In this reading, systemic legitimacy is something of a zero-sum game: as perceptions of systemic legitimacy increase in majority-minority communities, Whiter, more affluent communities lose systemic confidence.

Grand-jury nullification provides a way out of this box. Minority communities get to shape the law's application, but the blowback from other sectors is minimized because nullification happens in the privacy of the grand-jury chamber. Of course, the grand jury's actions are not wholly invisible: prosecutors remain keenly aware of what grand juries do. But, significantly, prosecutors would

---

* Associate Professor of Law, University of Virginia.
1. Butler core text at 562.

respond in different fashions to more frequent race-based grand-jury nullification than to trial-jury nullification. As Butler's critics note, prosecutors would try to avoid race-based trial nullification by working to keep minorities off juries. But grand-jury prosecutors have no similar power to strike prospective minority jurors. Instead, they would try to minimize grand-jury nullification by keeping communally perceived borderline (typically drug) cases out of the grand jury in the first instance—either by reducing felony charges to misdemeanors, by initially charging only misdemeanors, or by offering pleas to misdemeanors.

Unlike the normatively problematic prosecutorial response of keeping minorities off of trial juries, these latter responses to grand-jury nullification are normatively desirable. In effect, a kind of dialogue would open up between prosecutors and majority-minority communities. The result would only be charge reduction, but minority communities might conclude that charge reduction is revolution enough. After all, minority communities want drugs criminalized and drug offenders punished.[2] Their principal (and proper) objection is to the *severity* of penalties and to the shared costs of these penalties.

As a public defender in the Bronx, I put many clients in front of grand juries. The majority of those who testified succeeded in "blowing out" drug charges. Many of those who testified did so because they had strong defenses, but some testified because they had little left to lose, and some of these clients could offer up nothing more than incredible testimony. Yet many grand juries were resistant to indict even these seemingly guilty clients. The grand juries were either sympathetic to my clients' circumstances (which I counseled them to inject at the beginning of their testimony), or the juries simply did not want to warehouse more community members. Butler would conclude that these juries were morally justified in rejecting felony drug charges, and I'm inclined to agree. If our drug laws are broken (and if the legislative path to reform is effectively blocked), then grassroots and judicial correctives are permissible next options—options that should be exercised or threatened (like the old saying goes about voting) "early and often." Grand-jury nullification provides an opportunity for such frequent and quick expression of community power; trial nullification does not.

---

2. *See, e.g.,* BUREAU OF JUSTICE STATISTICS, U.S. DEP'T OF JUSTICE, SOURCEBOOK OF CRIMINAL JUSTICE STATISTICS 130–35, 158–59 (2003) (finding greater crime fears and resistance to drug legalization in minority communities).

REPLY

PAUL BUTLER

Lawrence Rosenthal seems unaware that the African-American community has been victimized by punishment as well as crime. Even more startlingly, he suggests that Blacks themselves are ignorant of the collateral effects of the war on drugs, including racial profiling, voter disenfranchisement, and mass incarceration. Rosenthal's evidence? When he worked at Chicago's City Hall, "never once" did any inner city residents complain to him about selective enforcement of the drug laws in their community.[1]

If storytelling is going to be a basis for our epistemology (and as a postmodernist, I'm okay with that), let me tell a story as well. I was born and raised in Chicago, in an inner-city African-American neighborhood. The Black people I know have the gall, or perhaps the faith in government, to believe that the criminal justice system should keep them both safe and free. The kinds of trade-offs that Rosenthal suggests—the New York police department's "aggressive stop-and-frisk policy," for example, in exchange for lower crime—are false choices. Jury nullification addresses a different problem than Black-on-Black crime, and that's okay. African-Americans are allowed to petition their government about more than one grievance. Rosenthal doesn't explain why Black concerns about the mass incarceration of their young men, especially for nonviolent crime, are illegitimate; he pretends that African-Americans don't actually care about those kinds of issues, making his analysis incomplete and unpersuasive.

Robin Charlow, along with several other commentators, is concerned that race-based jury nullification will ignite backlash. I have argued elsewhere that if African-Americans adapted their political and self-help strategies in order to avert White backlash they would scarcely achieve any progress at all. The most vociferous backlash has been not in response to jury nullification but rather to Black desires for equal educational opportunities, from the massive resistance of the 1950s and 1960s to the violent anti-busing campaigns of the 1980s.

So warnings about backlash are the basis for an argument not just against race-based jury nullification, but against any effort to advance civil rights for people of color.

---

1. I contest the data Rosenthal cites, without rehearsing the worn debate about the actual cause of the crime drop in New York. Crime fell in most jurisdictions during the 1990s, not just in New York City, and including in jurisdictions where the police didn't act like storm troopers in minority communities. It's hard to think of a more reviled figure among African-Americans than Rudolph Giuliani, the city's mayor during this period; he's regarded as the urban Bull Connor precisely because of the ways in which his police ran roughshod over the human and constitutional rights of people of color.

Charlow's specific concern is that nullification will do something bad to the *Batson* doctrine, although she's unclear on the exact nature of the harm, since she concedes that "[p]erhaps *Batson* is already so toothless that its total demise wouldn't matter."[2] In the end she states that whether Blacks would benefit more from race-based nullification or "*Batson*-controlled juries" is a "toss-up."[3] If the case is that close, let's try another approach. More than twenty years after *Batson*, African-Americans are roughly half the people in prison. A Black man who is born in the 1990s can expect to do jail time. Black women are among the fastest rising segment of the prison population. And things are only getting worse. Nullification offers a way to keep people who aren't likely to victimize others out of jail.

LuJuana Davis makes empirical claims about the actual incidence of jury nullification, but she cites no evidence to support those claims. She can't, because no such evidence exists. When jurors render a verdict in criminal cases, they do not complete a form that says: "Our 'not guilty' verdict is based on [reasonable doubt] [jury nullification]. Please check one." So how Davis knows that nullification verdicts are "a minuscule fragment of adjudicated criminal cases"[4] is beyond me. For the record, two other commentators who have practiced criminal law seem to agree with me that the phenomenon of race-based nullification is far from rare: Rosenthal says that when he was a Chicago prosecutor some Black jurors were "frequently skeptical of cases against African-American defendants."[5] Josh Bowers, a former public defender in the Bronx, describes a majority of his clients as "blowing out" drug charges in front of the grand jury, including those of defendants who were "seemingly guilty."[6]

Davis describes the idea that Black jurors might intentionally subvert some criminal laws as "racial paranoia." She does not explain why it is paranoid for Blacks to challenge laws that are selectively enforced in their community. According to the National Institutes of Health, for example, Blacks are about 13 percent of drug users. The Justice Department states, however, that Blacks account for almost 75 percent of people who are imprisoned for drug offenses. Just because you are paranoid, the old joke goes, doesn't mean they're not out to get you.

Sherry Colb is afraid that race-based jury nullification engenders "anger and divisiveness."[7] She confuses the solution with the problem. It is actually the criminal justice system that has inspired anger among African-Americans, because it is so divisive. I didn't invent race-based jury nullification; I learned it

---

2. Charlow comment at 573.
3. *Id.*
4. Davis comment at 574.
5. Rosenthal comment at 570.
6. Bowers comment at 579.
7. Colb comment at 575.

from Black jurors in Washington, D.C. They had little power over the criminal law, other than when they sat as jurors, so when they got that power they used it the best way they could. Sometimes they performed a cost-benefit analysis based on the interests of their community. When they were better off with a defendant not locked up, they emancipated him, even if he was guilty. They were acutely aware of the costs of having so many nonviolent Black people in prison, because they lived in the communities from which those people were absent.

I do not share Colb's concern that Black jurors might acquit Blacks who have committed violent offenses because I know that Black jurors have good sense. It would not be in their interest to release murderers, rapists, and robbers back into the community, and one rarely hears them accused of this: the systematic nullification that Black jurors are sometimes described as practicing almost always involves drug crimes.

Colb admits sympathy to the reasons why Black jurors might nullify, and agrees that inequality is a problem in the criminal justice system. Her alternative to nullification? "We should therefore reduce the size of the criminal law to make a dent in the shockingly high incarceration levels in the U.S."[8] Yes, and then we should have a cure for cancer, and after that, world peace. Colb doesn't describe how "we" are supposed to achieve her utopian vision. In fact, African-Americans have been complaining about the selective incarceration of Blacks for as long as it has existed, but the problem is getting worse, not better. Nullification is partly intended as a political protest, to move legislators to create alternatives to incarceration. If Colb has a better way to achieve this goal I wish she had described it. Given the dysfunctional politics of crime, the traditional methods have not been effective.

Bennett Capers and Josh Bowers have more strategic than substantive difference with my proposal. Capers is worried that because Blacks are only 13 percent of the population, they could not implement a nullification strategy in every jurisdiction. I agree. My proposal does not present race-based nullification as The-Complete-Solution-To-Racism-In-The-Criminal-Justice-System. Rather, the proposal has two purposes: first, self-help, i.e., permitting the emancipation of some Blacks for whom prison will do no good, and second, political protest: sending a message to legislators and prosecutors that mass incarceration and selective prosecution are unacceptable. Even nullification in majority Black jurisdictions can achieve those goals.

Like Charlow, Capers is concerned that nullification will cause prosecutors to challenge Black jurors and, like Charlow, he concedes that they already do. Capers says that "*Batson* has been ineffective," that "too many prosecutors" exclude Black jurors, and that race-based challenges of Black jurors "happen

---

8. *Id.* at 576.

every day."[9] I doubt, then, that race-based nullification would make things worse than they already are. I am gratified that Capers agrees with me that it is appropriate for jurors to consider race and the impact of their verdicts on an entire community.

Josh Bowers recommends grand-jury nullification. His proposal works as a supplement to petit-jury nullification, but not as a replacement. Relying exclusively on grand jurors is insufficient for two reasons. First, as a former prosecutor who has practiced in front of grand juries many times, I have less confidence in them than does Bowers, a former defense attorney. They don't indict ham sandwiches just because the prosecutor asks, but rather because the sandwich's defense attorney isn't allowed to be there, illegally obtained evidence is permitted, and exculpatory evidence does not have to be presented. When the prosecutor acts as the legal advisor to a grand jury, she is in control, making nullification significantly less likely.

Second, if a prosecutor doesn't get an indictment from one grand jury, she can just go to another grand jury. Juror verdicts of acquittal, on the other hand, are final. In the end, petit jurors have more power.

---

9. Capers comment at 577.

27. IN SUPPORT OF RESTORATIVE JUSTICE

ERIK LUNA[*]

I. INTRODUCTION

The United States is a criminal justice leviathan without equal. Even a cursory statistical review bears out the uniquely American problem of crime and punishment: In 2006, more than 25 million persons (or households) were victimized and more than 14 million suspects were taken into custody, with crime and arrest rates actually *improving* in recent times. At the beginning of 2008, the United States had an adult inmate population of 2.3 million people, meaning that one out of every ninety-nine Americans was incarcerated. If you placed a prison wall around North Dakota, South Dakota, and Wyoming and counted every single person as an inmate, it would still not equal the nation's total prison and jail population (but the number gets close by adding, say, American Samoa, Guam, and the U.S. Virgin Islands as penal colonies).[1]

Whatever the benefits of mass incapacitation, the statistics show a disturbing rate of recidivism among released inmates; and in turn, the cost to support America's criminal justice system, from arrest to incarceration, seems pretty steep: $185.5 billion in 2003, or $638 for every single person in the United States. In terms of expenditures, our ostensibly future-oriented government, one committed to technological advancement, spends more than twice as much on all aspects of the justice system as on scientific research and development.

From a comparative perspective, America comprises less than 5 percent of the human population but incarcerates one out of every four inmates in the world, resulting in the highest prison population and incarceration rate on the planet. Indeed, the United States spends about the same amount on corrections alone as the gross domestic product of two-thirds of the world's nations. But the price of warehousing prisoners (about $25,000 per year for each inmate) and other quantifiable expenses do not include the incommensurable yet very real costs of children growing up in fatherless homes, for instance, or crime victims being paralyzed by the fear of further violence.

---

* Professor of Law, Washington and Lee University School of Law. This core text is based upon Erik Luna, *Introduction: The Utah Restorative Justice Conference*, 2003 UTAH L. REV. 1; Erik Luna, *Punishment Theory, Holism, and the Procedural Conception of Restorative Justice*, 2003 UTAH L. REV. 205; Erik Luna and Barton Poulson, *Restorative Justice in Federal Sentencing: An Unexpected Benefit of Booker?*, 37 McGEORGE L. REV. 787 (2006); and Erik Luna, *Traces of a Libertarian Theory of Punishment*, 90 MARQUETTE L. REV. 263 (2007).

1. *See* J.C. Oleson, *The Punitive Coma*, 90 CAL. L. REV. 829, 835 n.24 (2002).

This gloomy picture raises some important questions: *Can there be another approach to crime and punishment in the United States? Is there a theory that takes into consideration the interests of those directly affected by crime—the victims who are injured, the offenders who are punished, the families of both, and the relevant communities in which they reside? Do the practices of other countries and cultures offer an alternative to the dismal state of American criminal justice?* In search of answers, some practitioners and scholars have begun to explore the idea of "restorative justice," a relatively new and promising approach to the criminal sanction slowly emerging around the globe. Among other things, its advocates claim that restorative justice can be more cost effective, more likely to reduce crime rates and recidivism, and more humane and respectful than the current American scheme.

II. THE THEORY OF RESTORATIVE JUSTICE

Restorative justice can be described as an approach to punishment that includes all relevant parties to a crime in a group decision-making process to reach a mutually agreeable outcome. As a general rule, the participants are those who have been directly affected by the crime and/or have a cognizable stake in its resolution: victims, offenders, family members, law enforcement representatives, and others within a "community of interest."[2] Although it has been subject to various interpretations by scholars and practitioners, restorative justice can be separated into (at least) two distinct conceptions: one that takes the form of a substantive theory challenging retributivism, utilitarianism, and other philosophies of punishment; and another that sees restorative justice as merely a procedure that allows all legitimate sentencing theories, as represented by the participants, to have a say in the decision-making process and ultimate outcome.

A. The Substantive Conception of Restorative Justice

In seeking to justify restorative justice as a substantive theory of punishment, some advocates rely upon religious tenets or non-Western traditions. But many proponents view restorative justice as a set of secular practices oriented toward restitution, for instance, or having numerous psychological benefits for participants and a greater impact on consequential goals like deterrence.

Of special note is the work of John Braithwaite, who has developed both a positive account and normative justification for substantive restorative justice.[3]

---

2. Allison Morris and Warren Young, *Reforming Criminal Justice: The Potential of Restorative Justice, in* RESTORATIVE JUSTICE: PHILOSOPHY TO PRACTICE 11, 14 (Heather Strang and John Braithwaite eds., 2000).

3. *See, e.g.,* John Braithwaite, CRIME, SHAME, AND REINTEGRATION (1989); John Braithwaite and Philip Pettit, NOT JUST DESERTS: A REPUBLICAN THEORY OF CRIMINAL JUSTICE (1990).

The former is based on his analysis of "reintegrative shaming," with restorative justice reducing crime by effectively shaming offenders and then reintegrating them into law-abiding society. The latter is premised on a republican vision of criminal justice, which endorses an understanding of liberty as more than just freedom from state interference. This republican model is relational in the broadest sense: Liberty cannot exist if an individual is subjugated by any force or entity, nor can it be enjoyed outside of society and in isolation from other people.

Regardless of its exact underpinnings, however, substantive restorative justice is usually presented as an alternative to pure utilitarianism or retributivism. Unlike the traditional theories, restorative justice claims that a punishment should be both backward-looking—condemning the offense and uncovering its causes—and forward-looking—making amends to the victim and the general community while facilitating moral development and constructive behavior in the offender. Metaphorically, restorative justice views crime as a point in the middle of a motion picture, with action both before and after the criminal event. In contrast to the temporal bracketing of retributivism and utilitarianism—with the former interested only in past acts and mental states and the latter focusing solely on future consequences—restorative justice is concerned with the causes of crime and issues of personal responsibility *and* the effects of sentencing on individuals, families, and communities.

Advocates often speak of "healing rather than hurting," rejecting punishment as just deserts, for instance, or as a means of incapacitation. With this in mind, substantive restorative justice incorporates a few core principles, beginning with the notion that crime is not just an action against the state but against specific victims and the relevant community. Offending is reframed as a violation of social relationships that also violates the law, with the source of beneficial norms and crime control located in families, support networks, and communities, rather than penal codes and courts. Accordingly, restorative justice promotes the involvement of victims, families, community representatives, and other stakeholders to deal with the causes and consequences of wrongdoing. Moreover, the substantive conception views crime as creating affirmative duties that offenders must meet with active responses instead of passive submission to a penalty.

In particular, a central ambition is making amends for the offense—especially for the physical, emotional, and economic harm to the victim—not just imposing pain upon the offender. Accountability tends to be characterized as an offender acknowledging the wrongfulness of his behavior, communicating remorse for the damage he has caused, and taking actions to mend the breach in social relationships. Toward this end, substantive restorative justice envisions a collaborative sanctioning process that involves all stakeholders concerned with the offense and offender. The primary feature is largely uninhibited dialogue among the parties, allowing all present to express their emotions and ideas in an open forum. Through discussion and deliberation, this approach contemplates mutual agreement on the steps that must be taken to heal the victim and the community, resulting in the formation of a plan to confront the factors contributing to the offender's conduct and to facilitate his development as a law-abiding citizen.

Substantive restorative justice also offers a fairly straightforward challenge to the actual practice of punishment, questioning the very foundation of modern criminal justice systems. An offense is not merely a "breach of the King's peace," to use the historical phrase, but a direct violation of the victim's rights and interests, a grave concern to loved ones (both of the victim and of the offender), and a threat to the community. Although state intervention stems the brutality of a private settling of scores, contemporary criminal justice systems are premised not on public intercession but government domination, often drastically limiting the input of affected parties or wholly excluding them from the process. Restorative justice recognizes that the victim, families, and community members have, in Nils Christie's words, a type of "property" interest in the case as a matter of process and outcome.[4]

In addition, substantive restorative justice argues that crime cannot be isolated or reduced to a problem with the criminal. Offending has a context, a history surrounding the event, and thoughtful solutions to crime will not focus on the offender alone. Although the wrongdoing must be firmly denounced and the nature of the harm made clear to the perpetrator, the substantive conception insists that the needs of the victim must be addressed as well, including repairing any harm caused by the offense. In addition, the occasion should be an opportunity for the community to reflect: *Did the social environment contribute to the offending and, if so, how are the relevant criminogenic influences remedied? What must be done to regain a sense of security and reaffirm pro-social values? How can the community and its members facilitate the moral education and social integration of the offender?* These questions are not asked as a means to exonerate a defendant for his harmful wrongdoing, but instead to restore the community's sense of well-being and to take affirmative, prophylactic steps against future offending.

B. The Procedural Conception of Restorative Justice

Needless to say, the substantive conception of restorative justice draws strong contrasts between its normative values and those of retributivism, utilitarianism, and other justifications of punishment. As such, it joins a relentless scholarly fight, where punishment theories brutalize one another, stake out turf on principle, and refuse to budge from their respective positions. The various theoretical camps spend most of their time on three endeavors: demonstrating the superiority of their theory of punishment, subjecting all others to harsh criticism, and repairing the damage done to their own theory from equally severe attacks.

---

4. *See* Nils Christie, *Conflicts as Property*, 17 BRIT. J. CRIMINOLOGY 1 (1977).

The upshot is an unwinnable war of critiques within an ethos of mutual exclusivity: It is either one theory or another, but certainly not both.

Let's pause for a moment to think about the idea that there is a single correct justification of punishment. As a matter of experience, this claim has not worn well over time. The battle among punishment theorists is millennia old and shows no signs of resolution. It is hard not to conclude that people in good conscience can and will have different opinions about the purpose of the criminal sanction. Moreover, that is exactly what should be expected in a free society, one consistent with America's long-avowed dedication to pluralism of thought. This is not to say that there are no right answers to issues like the rationale for punishment. Maybe there are such answers, and an individual can believe that his own justification is superior to all others. But one need not take a metaphysical stance on these theories, given the epistemological difficulty (if not impossibility) of knowing whether any particular theory can be or is in fact correct.

The uncompromising style of argumentation in this area would still be tolerable, however, if it were just another scholastic exercise. Unfortunately, it has ramifications that extend far beyond academe. Punishment theories have informed contemporary sentencing, as codified in the penal law and administered by criminal justice actors. More importantly, the transition from theory to practice has produced some troublesome repercussions in the real world, with politicians and political movements co-opting theoretical arguments in support of otherwise irrational sentencing policies. The end results are often sanctioning schemes and practices that cannot be squared with any theory. Though the risk may be low that these troubling phenomena would occur with restorative justice, surely its advocates want to avoid both the distortion of sanctioning theory for political gain and the imposition of viewpoints on those whose own views should matter the most.

As it turns out, restorative justice need not be seen as just another substantive theory of punishment. Rather, it can be viewed as a procedural approach that includes all stakeholders in a specific offense in a process of group decision-making on how to handle the crime and its implications for the future. This conception would not embody a particular justification of punishment but instead would view restorative justice as providing a process that does not take a stand on the merits of utilitarianism, retributivism, communicative and compensatory models, and so forth. Each punishment rationale will have virtues for its sponsors and vices for its detractors, and as noted above, perfectly sensible people can and will adopt their own visions of justice in sentencing.

Procedural restorative justice tries to steer clear of the ongoing debate among philosophers of punishment. After all, real-world cases do need to be resolved regardless of enduring uncertainties about punishment theories, and what does seem feasible is that a dialogic process might lead affected individuals to agree on a sanction without necessarily agreeing on its justification. By bringing together victims, offenders, their supporters, and various other stakeholders, and then providing them an opportunity to express their opinions in an undominated forum, procedural restorative justice offers a broad framework for parties to find common ground on outcomes—an "overlapping consensus"[5] of sorts—while maintaining their personal interpretations of justice.

This does not mean that the victim may demand any sanction or none whatsoever, applying his chosen justification of punishment. The offender has rights, too, and he will have his own perspective on justice, something that would inform a punishment rationale. And although not as direct or compelling as those of the victim and offender, the rights of others may be at stake in the resolution of a criminal episode. The commission of a crime can place third parties in fear for their lives and property, impeding full enjoyment of their rights and fulfillment of their visions of the good life. Of course, government has an important job as well, protecting against an atavistic state of nature where crimes result in undue punishment or, conversely, no sanction at all.

Officials must establish a fair process by which conflicting rights and punishment rationales—those of victims, offenders, and affected third parties—can be mediated toward a reasonable outcome. If an agreement among all the stakeholders proves impossible—because the victim or offender refuses to participate, for instance, or their dialogue fails to reach a resolution—the traditional criminal justice system would need to be invoked to achieve an appropriate punishment in light of the views of the interested parties. But what the procedural conception does not foresee is a particular theory of punishment being foisted upon these parties in the first instance.

III. THE PRACTICE OF RESTORATIVE JUSTICE

Whether conceived as a substantive or procedural theory, restorative justice could be part of a layered system of punishment. Among the potential decision-makers, distant legislators usually lack contextual knowledge of specific crimes and are therefore poorly positioned to determine suitable case resolutions. But given its broad, diverse composition and popular charge to serve the best interests of an entire jurisdiction, a legislature may be the most suitable entity to set general boundaries for punishment against the background of widely shared values and constitutional constraints. Within these boundaries, the stakeholders can discuss the offense, relevant context, and potential consequences in attempting to reach a suitable outcome. In turn, judges represent an intermediate entity within the field of decision-makers, offering professional repeat players somewhat removed from a case, but who are capable of reviewing the parties' resolution against the background of other cases and the general values embraced by the larger polity.

---

5. *See generally* John Rawls, POLITICAL LIBERALISM (1993).

The first and third parts, those involving legislators and judges, would not require anything that was not already within the general purview of the relevant decision-makers. As for the second part, several restorative justice practices have slowly emerged in many Western nations, with programs such as victim-offender mediation, sentencing circles, and family group conferences being implemented or tested in Australia, Britain, Canada, New Zealand, and even the United States. And although the jury is still out on these programs, so to speak, the empirical studies to date have been very favorable.

A. Mediation, Circles, and Conferences

Victim-offender mediation programs have existed for more than two decades, typically employed for property crimes but also increasingly used for certain serious and violent offenses. In most jurisdictions, cases are referred for mediation as a form of diversion from prosecution or as a condition of probation after an accepted guilty plea. Both the offender and the victim must agree to participate in the program, with the mediator establishing contact with these parties, explaining the process, and setting an acceptable time and safe location for the meeting. Although procedures vary, the victim usually speaks first during a mediation, describing the crime's impact on his life, such as the physical and emotional harm and financial loss caused by the event.

The process provides the victim an opportunity to ask any lingering questions about the incident and its author. In turn, the offender is given a chance to tell his story, to explain the circumstances of the crime as well as his past and potential future, and to apologize and accept responsibility for the offense. Through facilitated dialogue, the victim and offender can discuss and possibly reach an appropriate outcome, such as an agreement that the offender will provide restitution for property damage and volunteer for community service. Depending on the jurisdiction and legal posture of the case, a mediator, probation officer, or program personnel may follow up to ensure that the offender is making progress and meeting his obligations under the agreement.

Family group conferencing also employs facilitated dialogue, but it expands the prospective participants and collective decision-making beyond the limited number of parties included in dyad-based mediation programs. Cases referred for conferences may come as a type of diversion, although New Zealand uses family group conferencing throughout its juvenile justice system, whether in lieu of formal charges or in response to admissions or verdicts of guilt in all but the most serious offenses (e.g., homicide). In general, the coordinator will consult with the victim, the offender, their families and supporters, social service providers, law enforcement officials, and other stakeholders to determine who should be invited to participate and when and where the conference should be held. The coordinator is also responsible for informing the invited parties about the relevant background of the offense, how the conference will likely proceed, and any other information necessary for voluntary, knowledgeable participation.

A conference typically begins with an introduction of the participants and a coordinator's description of the ensuing steps in the process. A law enforcement representative may summarize the offense, and the parties will have a chance to comment on the factual synopsis. The victim then has the opportunity to discuss his feelings about the crime, its aftermath, and possible outcomes of the conference, and to ask questions about the offense and other issues of importance, followed by similar opportunities for the offender and other participants to express their views. After open dialogue about the crime and general discussion of available options, the process seeks negotiation on and formulation of a mutually agreed-upon plan for the offender (e.g., providing restitution, engaging in community service, undergoing counseling, etc.). In the New Zealand model, the coordinator is responsible for following up on the offender's advancement and checking that the conditions of the conference plan are being met.

Circle sentencing expands the participants even further, adding various community members and possibly judges, prosecutors, defense attorneys, and relevant court personnel. The basic methodology uses a variation on the decision- and peace-making practices of indigenous cultures around the globe, including the First Nations people of Canada and Native American tribes such as the Navajo. A circle may be employed as an alternative to the traditional sentencing hearing after an offender has pled to or been found guilty of the underlying offense. Pursuant to one version of this model, the offender applies to participate in a circle, with the decision made by a community justice committee and affected parties. If the case is accepted, committee members will meet separately with the offender and victim, and help establish support groups for both individuals.

The participants will gather together at a convenient time and place and will literally sit in a circle facing one another. The facilitator is known as a "keeper," who begins the session with an introduction and description of the process to be followed. In particular, sentencing circles pass a "talking piece" (i.e., a small item of symbolic value) from one participant to another, signifying the item's holder as the person whose turn it is to speak and requiring all others to listen respectfully. Each speaker is thus provided an uninterrupted opportunity to express his feelings about the crime, the parties, and potential resolutions. As the talking piece moves around the circle, often multiple times, the process allows all participants to contribute meaningfully to the discussion, to understand better their fellow contributors and the incident in question, and to reach a consensus on an appropriate sentencing plan. It also invests the participants in a successful outcome, with members of the justice committee and support groups following up on the sentencing circle and assuring that the offender is abiding by the plan (possibly by convening additional circles).

B. Empirical Research

Although diverse in style and usage, as well as having distinct advantages and limitations, these programs have some key aspects in common. For instance, all are premised on an admission or finding of guilt on the part of the offender and the freely chosen, fully informed participation of the parties. Each utilizes non-adversarial, informal procedures and provides the participants with a degree of process control over time, place, and format. To varying degrees, the practices incorporate those individuals whose interests are most affected by the crime and punishment, and they all utilize a collaborative, consensus-based decision-making process to reach an appropriate resolution. As such, the programs could be tailored to fulfill either the substantive or procedural conception of restorative justice.

Nonetheless, the theoretical conceptions and practical applications are likely to be adopted only if they benefit the participants and society at large, given the status quo bias in favor of America's traditional theories and practices of punishment. Restorative justice can surmount this hurdle, however, with the studies to date showing numerous salutary effects. For instance, a review of the empirically veri-fied benefits of restorative justice found that, relative to parties in traditional court processes, those who participated in restorative programs were more likely:

(1) to believe that the criminal justice system was fair;
(2) to say that the mediator or judge had been fair;
(3) to rate the outcome of their proceedings as fair;
(4) to be satisfied with the way that their case was handled;
(5) to be satisfied with the outcome of the proceedings;
(6) to believe that they had been able to tell their stories during the proceedings;
(7) to believe that their opinions were adequately considered;
(8) to believe that the offender had been held accountable;
(9) to have better perceptions of the other party's behavior; and
(10) to apologize to the victim/to forgive the offender.

In addition, victims who participated in restorative programs tended:

(11) to be less upset about crime; and
(12) to be less afraid of revictimization.[6]

Not only are the data favorable to restorative justice, but the results were practically identical in each of the studies. The consistency of the data is remark-able in light of the substantial variability of the studies, with restorative justice displaying clear, dependable benefits for almost all participants.

In addition, restorative justice has at least two important behavioral advantages: increased reparations and decreased recidivism. Meta-analysis has shown that offenders who participate in restorative programs have substantially higher rates of completing their obligations (e.g., compensating victims for property damage)

---

6. Barton Poulson, *A Third Voice: A Review of Empirical Research on the Psychological Outcomes of Restorative Justice*, 2003 UTAH L. REV. 167, 177–98.

than do traditionally processed offenders. In one study, for instance, 81 percent of restorative justice participants completed their requirements, which was significantly more than the 57 percent of those not in the victim-offender mediation program. Another study compared average payments from the two groups and discovered that restorative justice offenders paid between 95 percent and 1,000 percent more than offenders in court. In general, completion of agreements is significantly more common, and more bountiful, through restorative processes.

Meta-analysis on the effects of restorative justice on recidivism was also supportive. One review found that after a year, 28 percent of participants in traditional sanctioning procedures had committed new crimes, compared to 19 percent of participants in restorative programs, a statistically significant reduction of 32 percent, while a second study found a smaller but still significant impact on recidivism. Interestingly, two other reviews discovered that restorative justice had the strongest effects on recidivism when the crimes were more severe. Moreover, research has shown that among offenders who do reoffend, those who participated in restorative programs tended to commit less-serious crimes. As an empirical matter, then, it can be said that restorative justice outperforms standard court processes in facilitating the completion of reparations for the present offense and reducing the chance of future crime.[7]

IV. CONCLUSION

Restorative justice cannot substitute for many of the core functions of modern legal systems. It is not an investigative tool for determining whether a crime has been committed and who is responsible, and it certainly lacks the fact-finding apparatus of the traditional court process. In other words, restorative justice can address neither the "whodunit" questions nor various aspects of culpability—whether an individual committed the crime at issue, whether an affirmative defense like mental illness or self-defense has any validity, whether the defendant is guilty of the highest charged crime or a lesser included offense, and so on. Likewise, restorative justice has no capacity to interpret penal codes or constitutional provisions, for example, a claim that the statute of limitations bars prosecution or that a government search violated the defendant's Fourth Amendment rights.

Nor is restorative justice a panacea for the problems mentioned at the outset, such as America's high rates of crime, victimization, and imprisonment.

---

7. Citations for the referenced studies can be found in Luna and Poulson, *supra* note *. In addition to restorative justice's verified contributions to desirable cognitive, affective, and behavioral outcomes, Barton Poulson and I have suggested that the programs may help reduce mental health disorders among participants. *See id.* at 801–07.

But studies have shown numerous cognitive, affective, and behavioral benefits from restorative justice, including a reduction in recidivism and the fear of revictimization. In addition, the substantive conception of restorative justice largely eschews incarceration, while the procedural conception empowers affected individuals to craft appropriate resolutions, with the process engendering feelings of fairness and satisfaction among the participants.

If nothing else, restorative justice cannot do any worse than the current approaches to punishment, and it may well check the opportunistic tendency of political demagogues to put forward ruthless sentencing policies. The theory and principles of restorative justice can be tremendously stimulating, forcing punishment philosophers and state actors alike to reevaluate their own intellectual commitments and the merits of their chosen sentencing methodologies. After all, the specific programs offer nonadversarial, context-sensitive means to integrate those most directly impacted by crime in a dialogic, consensus-based decision-making process on how to address an offense and its future consequences—quite a change from the status quo.

Many questions remain to be answered and many obstacles removed before the idea of American restorative justice can become a reality, and along the way, legitimate concerns about restorative justice must be aired and discussed in depth. As Braithwaite notes, a thoughtful critique "helps us to be systematic in accounting for the negatives," and the interaction between advocacy and critique "is the stuff of the most productive intellectual work." At the same time, it is important to be "careful not to kill fertile ideas in the womb,"[8] particularly those like restorative justice that challenge the status quo and may face a level of system inertia or even professional intransigence. Restorative justice cannot solve all dilemmas of criminal justice, of course, but it may be a good start. And given the sad state of crime and punishment in America today, there is little to lose and much to gain from at least taking restorative justice seriously.

---

8. John Braithwaite, *Holism, Justice, and Atonement*, 2003 UTAH L. REV. 389, 389.

COMMENTS

RESTORATION, BUT ALSO MORE JUSTICE

STEPHANOS BIBAS[*]

Erik Luna writes a strong and concise defense of restorative justice, a sprawling international movement against some of the impersonal, state-centered, punitive trends of our times. Although there is much to admire in it, restorative justice

---

* Professor of Law, University of Pennsylvania Law School.

sacrifices traditional notions of criminal justice. It has become a cover for left-wing hostility to punishment, just as victims' rights has become a cover for right-wing toughness on crime. Restoration nevertheless deserves to supplement but not supplant retribution, and its processes should indeed give ordinary victims and criminals much greater roles.

Luna ably catalogues the strengths of a movement that spans substantive and procedural goals. Substantively, criminal law is not just an impersonal effort to deter, incapacitate, or extract bloodless Kantian retribution. Victims and criminals are wounded, ill, scared, angry, defiant . . . the list goes on. They need to heal these wounds and vent these emotions, but abstract academic discourse ignores them. In the messy real world, as Luna recognizes, punishment must serve multiple goals, including these.

Procedurally, criminal justice too often is divorced from the substantive goals it supposedly serves. All it seems to do is to work as a speedy assembly line, efficiently dispensing incapacitation but doing so coldly and with little concern about human feeling or healing. Procedure does need to better serve the other substantive values it is supposed to implement.

Luna is also right that when they agree to take part in restorative justice, victims, criminals, and their families usually come away happier and better off. Face-to-face discussions, mediation, and circles let people tell their stories, vent, apologize, forgive, and heal. And these human interactions, by relatives and friends who often must go back to living with one another, matter immensely to them.

Modern justice has become too state-centered and impersonal. Crime is centrally about harm to victims. It makes them feel helpless, and criminal justice does too little to reempower them. Victims deserve to be heard, to influence processes, and to have the power to forgive some portion of punishment.

The problem, though, is restorative justice's megalomaniacal ambition to sweep away the traditional goals and processes of criminal justice instead of merely supplementing them. To restorative justice advocates, retribution for retribution's sake seems pointless. Their overoptimism about human nature leads them to slight deterrence and incapacitation as at best secondary, at worst needless. Prison seems like a pure waste of human life.

But punishment is supposed to hurt. The bite of punishment sends an unequivocal message condemning the wrongdoer and vindicating the victim. It pays the criminal's debt to society. It teaches criminals and others not to hurt others, humbling proud wrongdoers. Restitution and fines can supplement prison and perhaps reduce the need for it. But because they lack the bite of condemnation and pain, they send too soft a message, overlooking the wrong and trying to hurry by it too fast. Criminals need to atone, to be humbled, to suffer. If they do not, the criminal does not learn a lesson and victims and the public never see justice done, leaving them dissatisfied.

True, there are more minor offenses for which prison may not be necessary. Thus, it is no surprise that restorative justice is most prevalent for juvenile crime and minor adult crimes, not violent felonies. Shaming punishments are among the most promising alternatives to prison; they can do what fines and restitution cannot, precisely because they unequivocally blame and inflict pain. And until the public sees serious criminals suffer, it is reluctant to reintegrate and welcome them back.

Restorative justice deserves more of a role in American criminal justice. Already, several states have instituted restorative processes for victims and inmates to meet after conviction and sentence. Shorn of its political baggage and reflexive hostility to punishment, restorative justice has much to teach us. But to restore victims and criminals who commit serious crimes, the state must first punish before it and we can forgive. Cheap grace and promiscuous forgiveness demean the crime and the victim.

RESTORATIVE CAVEATS

DAVID DOLINKO*

There is no reason to dispute Erik Luna's picture of the United States as "a criminal justice leviathan without equal" practicing incarceration on an unparalleled scale.[1] One can, however, ask whether reforms less drastic, and thus possibly more attainable, than the adoption of the restorative justice approach might go a long way toward alleviating the problems Luna highlights. Luna's arguments also raise interesting theoretical issues.

It is intriguing that Luna describes restorative justice as "a relatively new and promising approach to the criminal sanction *slowly emerging* around the globe."[2] This suggests that other nations have been able to avoid the extraordinary harshness of American law enforcement methods without having implemented the conceptions and techniques of restorative justice.

Indeed, James Whitman's recent book *Harsh Justice* vividly depicts the startling mildness—by American standards—of the French and German criminal justice systems.[3] Those countries have not adopted restorative justice principles. Yet in both these countries prison sentences are much shorter than in the United States, with the overwhelming majority of nonviolent offenders not incarcerated at all.[4] In France, community service is given to most property offenders, whereas such offenders "make up roughly half of the total population"

---

* Professor of Law, UCLA School of Law.
1. Luna core text at 585.
2. *Id.* at 586 (emphasis added).
3. James Q. Whitman, HARSH JUSTICE (2003).
4. *Id.* at 71.

of American state prisons.[5] Prison conditions are significantly better than in America.[6] Perhaps the most striking divergence from American practice is that both France and Germany seek "to avoid any sort of punishment practice that would create any sense of status differentiation between prisoners and the general population. On the contrary, practices in both countries are supposed to dramatize the fact that inmates are *just like everybody else.*"[7] Of course, it may well be politically impossible, at present, for American jurisdictions to emulate these European practices. Yet might it not be even more difficult to induce Americans to make the radical reorientation of their approach to crime that advocates of restorative justice seek?

Moreover, it is not clear just what reorientation restorative justice would involve. Luna describes restorative justice as "an approach to punishment that includes all relevant parties to a crime in a group decision-making process to reach a mutually agreeable outcome."[8] *Who*, exactly, are the "relevant parties" that should take part in the "decision-making process"?

Recall, for example, the well-publicized 1998 murder of Matthew Shepard, a young gay man in Laramie, Wyoming, who was tied to a fence, pistol-whipped, and left to die in the frigid night. If restorative justice methodology were applied in this case, who would the "relevant parties" be? Obvious candidates include the two men who committed the crime, and Matthew Shepard's family members. But who else? Shepard's friends—both gay and straight? Other gay residents of Laramie, who were extremely frightened, angered, and concerned about the flagrant hate crime? Gay people in other parts of Wyoming—or in other states altogether? National leaders of gay-rights organizations? How about *all* the residents of Laramie, given the worldwide notoriety the Shepard murder gave to that city? And what of the leaders or members of the various groups *opposed* to the gay-rights movement? (For an extreme example, think of Fred Phelps, a Baptist pastor in Topeka, who has picketed military funerals, gay-pride events, and high-profile political gatherings around the nation carrying virulently anti-homosexual banners and placards.)

On a more theoretical note, Luna presents restorative justice as a potential way to circumvent the "relentless scholarly fight" over theories of punishment—"an unwinnable war" whose protagonists agree that "[it]t is either one theory or another, but certainly not both."[9] This ignores the numerous attempts that *have* been made at a compromise or mixed theory incorporating both retributive and

---

5. *Id.* at 72.
6. *Id.* at 74–80.
7. *Id.* at 85.
8. Luna core text at 586.
9. *Id.* at 588, 589.

consequentialist elements.[10] And other scholars have disputed the notion that there must be one right theoretical justification of punishment.

Besides, isn't restorative justice itself a consequentialist theory? It calls for treating offenders in ways designed to heal the wounds crimes create, reintegrate the offender into society, and make amends to the victims. Thus it calls for punishment to be shaped, and justified, by the desirable *consequences* it can achieve. (Classic utilitarians, contra Luna, did not focus *solely* on future consequences— these theorists obviously took account of what it was that the defendant had done in deciding how he should be treated.)

---

10. Luna has, however, dismissed attempts at mixed theories. *See* Erik Luna, *Punishment Theory, Holism, and the Procedural Conception of Restorative Justice*, 2003 UTAH L. REV. 205, 242.

RESTORING JUSTICE THROUGH INDIVIDUALIZED PROCESSES

MARGARETH ETIENNE*

Erik Luna's account of restorative justice promises to deliver something to everyone, including both procedural and substantive sentencing reform. In this sense, Luna overstates the virtues of restorative justice, a system that may be transformative procedurally but is substantively vacuous. This is not a flaw. On the contrary, the malleability of restorative justice when it comes to substantive criminal law is one of its strengths.

Still, its adaptability to a host of penological goals has rendered restorative justice vulnerable to strong criticism. Some critics worry that sentencing under restorative procedures risks being unduly harsh if hijacked by victims and their allies. Others gripe that sentencing will be insufficiently punitive if concerns regarding rehabilitation and forgiveness for offenders are given priority. Luna would like to deny these claims but can hardly do so persuasively. He might argue instead that restorative justice is no worse in this regard than existing criminal justice regimes.

Many critics of restorative justice raise concerns that are genuine, but that exist in all sentencing schemes where discretion plays a role. The criticism has little to do with restorative justice. Two aspects of modern day sentencing—the acceptance of a wide range of sentencing results and the acceptance of a wide range of sentencing goals—demonstrate at the very least that the reservations often associated with restorative justice are willingly endured in other sentencing areas.

---

* Professor of Law, University of Illinois at Urbana–Champaign College of Law.

True, restorative justice shares some of the flaws of other sentencing systems, but it also provides a benefit that other systems do not: sentencing based on the individualized needs of all the parties.

First, that a broad range of sanctions—some displeasing to victim advocates and some displeasing to defense advocates—might be imposed in any particular case is not unique to restorative justice. Imagine a sentencing system in which the sentencer is permitted, once guilt is established, to consider an unlimited array of factors in determining a sanction. The sentencer's discretion in devising a sentence is limited only by the legislature's ex ante assignment of statutory minima and maxima. This sounds a lot like indeterminate sentencing—the sentencing system in place in a significant number of states. But it is also consistent with Luna's description of restorative justice.

In Luna's rendition, the sentencing body can consist of a mediation panel, circle, or conference of offender, victim, and community representative rather than the solitary sentencing judge. And although a particular circle might—based on factors too many to name—punish a particular defendant too severely or not severely enough, this happens in hundreds of courtrooms every day throughout the nation. As Luna explains, the sentences derived from restorative practices have the added benefit of being reviewed by a traditional sentencing judge to prevent abuse and eliminate unwarranted disparity. How can these sentences be substantively inferior to those imposed under most indeterminate sentencing procedures?

Second, that differing sentencing goals—some displeasing to victim advocates and some displeasing to defense advocates—could be justified by different sentencing institutions is hardly a new problem in a federalized system of government. One sentencing circle might prioritize rehabilitation over reducing recidivism or retribution over reintegration. Another might do just the opposite. But the same variation does not worry us if California focuses on recidivism, Texas on retribution, Minnesota on rehabilitation, or Virginia on efficiency.

Restorative justice principles simply permit the goals of punishment to be determined even further down the chain and closer to the people most impacted by the offense and the imposition of sanction. Sentencing is truly individualized based not only on the offender and offense characteristics but on the needs and characteristics of all the stakeholders. In a sense, it is federalism taken to its logical extreme. It is federalism exponentialized—although not privatized. Here, too, the legislature's statutory limits and the judge's experience with like cases work together to establish safeguards against possible sentencing abuses.

In the end, Luna oversells restorative justice and its promise for reforming the substantive law of sentencing. Restorative justice improves upon our sentencing system not because it avoids all of the substantive pitfalls of current sentencing models. It doesn't. But to single it out for the failings it shares with most sentencing systems overlooks its potential as a procedural salve for victims, offenders, and communities who have long lost ownership and confidence in sentencing. Luna's core text reminds us of the direct and collateral benefits of truly individualizing sentencing penalties and goals—within acceptable limits, of course—by restoring it to those who have the greatest stake in its success.

RESTORE TO WHAT? SUPPLEMENTING RESTORATIVE JUSTICE

JOSEPH E. KENNEDY[*]

Erik Luna lays out a concise brief for restorative justice, no easy feat given the volumes that have been devoted to the subject. As Luna recognizes, restorative justice is understood as a theory as well as a range of particular practices. As practice, restorative justice works well under a limited set of circumstances. Luna and other proponents recognize this limitation and offer restorative justice as a supplement to existing practices, not as a replacement. As a theory, restorative justice is also limited, but in a way that has not been sufficiently acknowledged. Taking restoration in response to crime as its animating goal, restorative justice does not give a sufficient answer to the question, "restore to what?"

Restorative justice naturally accords the victim's interests and wishes very special consideration. The problem is that restorative justice doesn't tell us what a just restoration for the victim would consist in. What does it take to restore the victim? Simple property crimes or slight offenses amenable to sincere apologies aside, what constitutes restoration when a serious violent crime has been committed? For some, making the victim whole requires making the defendant suffer in a proportionate way. Terms of years are assigned to various degrees of suffering inflicted. The real-world result of such thinking has been very long prison sentences.

The problem is most acute in the case of homicides. How do you restore society when a life is lost? The prevailing mindset holds that the maximum punishment is owed for the loss of a life. If the death penalty is available, a life sentence is an insult to the victim's memory. If a life sentence is available, then anything less than life is an insult. And so it goes. Victims and their survivors are caught in an inflationary sensibility of punishment where only the highest possible punishment will do.

A philosophy of punishment that accords the interests of victims special status, as restorative justice does, must contain principles designed to limit the space within which the victim's vengeance can operate. Theories of punishment are sources of social meaning, and victims to some degree take their cue about what would be a just restoration from the collective understanding of what

---

[*] Associate Professor of Law, University of North Carolina School of Law.

punishment is supposed to accomplish. Ultimately, only some robust vision of the moral value of restraint in punishment for the community at large can serve as an effective counterweight to a vengeful victim's wishes. Articulating such principles is an important challenge for contemporary penal philosophy, and all the more so for restorative justice. The proponents of restorative justice, including Luna, have yet to meet that challenge.

DANGERS OF THE BIG TENT

MICHAEL M. O'HEAR*

In making the case for restorative justice, Erik Luna invokes the familiar narrative of a pathological American criminal justice system—political demagogues pushing ever tougher sentencing policies on an uninformed public, resulting in wildly escalating prisons populations and fiscal burdens—and asserts that restorative justice cannot possibly do any worse. Indeed, he suggests, restorative justice may bring about a change in heart among the demagogues: The theory and principles of restorative justice may force policy-makers "to reevaluate their own intellectual commitments and the merits of their chosen sentencing methodologies."[1]

The picture is attractive, and not entirely implausible, but I fear that Luna may underestimate the strength of the ideological commitments undergirding America's penal harshness and overestimate the extent to which restorative justice must necessarily rest on different and more humane premises. Or, to put the matter differently, Luna's "big-tent" take on restorative justice—it can be substantive, it can be procedural, it can coexist peacefully with a diverse set of other theories of punishment, and it can be integrated comfortably into existing criminal justice processes—may do more to reinforce than to challenge the suppositions of those who advocate ever-greater toughness.

I am quite sympathetic to the restorative justice project. What I find most attractive about restorative justice is its insistence that victims and offenders are real human beings, not just wooden marionettes to be brought upon the criminal justice stage as it serves the convenience of the lawyers; that the criminal justice system should address itself more directly to the needs of these human beings than to abstract ideals like retribution and deterrence; and that among the most compelling of these real human needs are opportunities to speak about the offense and its aftermath—to tell one's story—and to participate in developing a communal response to the offense. If these principles were consistently recognized as the essential core of restorative justice, then restorative justice would

---

* Professor of Law and Associate Dean for Research, Marquette Law School.
1. Luna core text at 595.

indeed represent a profound challenge to business as usual in American criminal justice.

But restorative justice can be presented and understood in quite different ways. Including victims may reinforce the basic, antidefendant narrative of the victims' rights movement: The court system has grown too attentive to defendants' rights, and victims must now be given greater rights in order to combat the system's domination by defense lawyers. The emphasis on "holding offenders accountable," so common in restorative-justice rhetoric, may reinforce common assumptions that crime is always a matter of free choice made by rational actors—missing the important crimogenic roles played by mental illness, substance abuse, peer pressure, poverty, racism, and the like—and may thereby implicitly deny the need to hold *communities* accountable, too. Similarly, the use of processes that have no capacity to adjudicate factual disputes and that are typically expected to culminate in an apology may reinforce beliefs that all defendants are legally and morally guilty. Finally, the use of shaming sanctions (as has been advocated by John Braithwaite and others associated with the restorative justice movement) may reinforce the perception that incarceration is too easy on defendants.

If restorative justice advocates wish to empower *both* victims and offenders, then they ought to be clear about that. If they wish to reduce American incarceration rates—and this must follow almost automatically from a genuine victim-offender empowerment agenda—then they must also be clear about that. Being coy about one's objectives or undiscriminating about one's alliances can be terribly counterproductive when it comes to criminal justice policy.

Marvin Frankel and others who laid the intellectual groundwork for the federal sentencing guidelines were concerned about a system that seemed too harsh to them in the 1970s—a proposition that seems almost laughable by today's standards—but they made uniformity, not penal restraint, their rallying cry, and eventually allied themselves with some of demagogues. The result was a set of guidelines that dramatically increased the harshness of the federal system. Drug treatment courts are another recent innovation that has been fueled by skepticism of mass incarceration, but that has not demonstrably improved—indeed, has arguably worsened—the lot of drug offenders. Without an appreciation that many of the practices and much of the rhetoric associated with restorative justice have the potential to reinforce the ideology of mass incarceration, the big-tent approach to restorative justice may prove similarly disappointing.

If the tent is to be made smaller, I would particularly urge the exclusion of general deterrence theories, that is, of the notion that punishment may appropriately be imposed to make an example of the offender. Although Luna seems reluctant to take any of the warring theories of punishment off the table, deterrence seems especially hard to square with the basic aim of so much restorative justice theory and practice to affirm the equal human dignity of all members of the community, including criminal offenders. Even in a process-based approach to restorative justice, deterrence's instrumental treatment of offenders can only corrupt the ideal of genuine, undominated dialogue between victims, offenders, and representatives of the community.

LUNA-INSPIRED SPECULATIONS ON RESTORATIVE JUSTICE

ROBERT WEISBERG*

Erik Luna suggests that restorative justice challenges the normal jurisprudential rhetoric by which lawmakers and commentators vie to assert one of the classic purposes of punishment as our guiding principle. Luna rightly asserts that any "substantive" restorative justice doctrine is incomplete unless it generates and rests on a restorative justice-specific criminal procedure, for which he lays out details. This approach of delineating restorative justice in parallel analogy to the conventional system leads me to two further speculations.

First, an abstract speculation that is also concrete in the sense of strategy. Luna suggests that restorative justice offers a different jurisprudence of criminal justice on both substance and procedure. Fair enough, but if we recharacterize the question not as one of comparing two theoretical systems but instead in terms of the rhetoric of jurisprudential advocacy for restorative justice, a different approach emerges—the ostensibly more conservative (though perhaps subliminally manipulative) one of casting restorative justice as essentially a refinement or subtle distillation of the conventional system.

In substance, Luna is surely right that restorative justice does not "punish" or look retrospectively the way the conventional system does—it is more relational, more concerned with coordinating the social roles of victim, neighborhood, offender, judge, etc., into a holistic set of overlapping interests. But these distinctions risk being too binary for capturing the conventional system. All the utilitarian rationales for punishment look forward as well as backward. And retributivism has flavors that are forward-looking as well, the ones associated not with the categorical need to attribute desert but with the benefits of affirming the values on which the retribution rests.

Similarly, on the procedural side, the focus on the victim and on restitutionary remedies is not entirely alien to the conventional system. Much of the success of the victims' rights movement has rested on its advocates' ability to cast victims' interests not as an alien intrusion on, but a modest refinement of, existing procedure, while appropriating for the victim the conventional system's s due

---

* Edwin E. Huddleson, Jr. Professor of Law, Stanford University.

process defendant-focused principles of notice, right to speak, etc. Thus, I merely pose the question—I am unsure of the answer—whether the best rhetorical strategy for restorative justice is to stress its unconventionality, or instead its familiarity.

My second comment is more concrete but follows the same theme of placing restorative justice within the conventional system. What may go undernoticed in Luna's rendering of restorative justice is that the process only kicks in after an admission or finding of guilt. Obviously, that premise raises concerns about what system, conventional or unconventional, precedes that moment. I finesse that question here, but I suggest that much of what Luna describes about restorative justice should become relevant during the period after another moment: parole release.

I write from California, un-proud home of the nation's most dysfunctional correctional system. In our overcrowded, unconstitutional, and crime regenerating conditions, Exhibit A is our parole scheme. We churn thousands of prisoners each year under our mandatory parole policy, whereby most parolees enter a formulaic but underfunded and underexamined supervision system, and whereby most recidivate. Some recidivism takes the form of new crimes and some the form of administrative violations of the parolee's "contract." Either way, the prisoner goes back to prison, where the so-called "reception center" serves as the figurative bus station of the state criminal justice system. But the bus station allusion is not so metaphoric when we examine what happens to the released inmate: He is usually left at a bus station near the prison, with just enough money to buy a ticket to some destination in a city where he is ostensibly required to check in with his parole officer and then seek reentry services.

Space does not begin to permit me to lay out the myriad ways that things go awry. But all commentators on our parole system say we lack mechanisms for enabling the parolee to reintegrate with that amorphous set of social and family networks we dangerously euphemize under the term "community." And communication, direct or brokered, with the victims may often be useful to reintegration, especially if it includes the parolee's extended family, which is both "victim" and "community" in some ways. We need a resilient but stable legal regime to make these good things happen at the local level. So I suggest that while the restorative justice movement seeks to establish a comprehensive alternative to the conventional system, it might also more modestly do great service at this more narrowly circumscribed but highly exigent point within the conventional system.

605

REPLY

ERIK LUNA

The commentators provide restorative justice advocates much to think about—like the notion of restorative justice as "federalism exponentialized"[1] and the suggestion that restorative justice could play an important part at parole.[2] As is true of virtually any academic debate, some minor protests can be lodged[3] and quibbles had—whether a utilitarian theory need "not focus solely on future consequences,"[4] for instance, or whether a forward-looking justification associated "with the benefits of affirming the values on which the retribution rests"[5] is really retributivism or instead consequentialism in drag.

Undoubtedly some of this would be a matter of semantics, and in the end, I might just defer to my learned colleagues anyway. Given the limited space here, it may be best for me to offer a few thoughts on what I see as the flawed nature of many restorative justice criticisms and, for that matter, debates over punishment theory in general. Sometimes scholars level attacks against restorative justice seemingly oblivious to the fact that nearly identical criticisms would apply to every justification of punishment. For example, one commentator asserts that restorative justice has been unclear about its objectives;[6] another maintains that it fails to delineate what is to be restored;[7] and yet another implies that the relevant parties are so ill-defined that a decision-making process concerning a horrific hate-crime against a young gay man might include an outspoken homophobe from another jurisdiction.[8]

To these points, I could simply cite previous works on restorative justice that, among other things, would reiterate the goals of its substantive conception, such as making amends for an offense and healing those who have been injured. Or I could just turn the tables on the commentators: Restorative justice is no less clear about its objectives or what is to be restored than, say, deontological retributivism is about the idea of an offender receiving his "just deserts," which appears to be determined, at least under some views, through a transcendental conversion chart of crime-to-punishment. As for any reductio ad absurdum regarding potential participants, I might point out that it is unlikely that the parties would extend beyond the family, close friends, and immediate community

---

1. Etienne comment at 600.
2. *See* Weisberg comment at 605.
3. For example, restorative justice programs *do* exist in Europe, *contra* Dolinko.
4. Dolinko comment at 599.
5. Weisberg comment at 604.
6. *See* O'Hear comment at 603.
7. *See* Kennedy comment at 601.
8. *See* Dolinko comment at 598.

directly affected by the offense. Or I could note that every justification must in practice incorporate limits that may undermine its theoretical elegance but ensure against a philosopher's parade-of-horribles—consider utilitarianism's tap dance around the scapegoat hypothetical, the innocent man whose punishment would avoid some social disutility. Or I could simply embrace the arguendo: Maybe participation in a restorative process and witnessing the pain suffered by family and friends would change a bigot's heart, thereby presenting an argument in favor of restorative justice rather than against it.

In a similar fashion, restorative justice has been the target of a variation on the so-called *Nirvana fallacy*, implicitly comparing restorative justice to a mythical alternative rather than what currently exists or might be achieved. For example, some suggest that restorative justice may ignore the "crimogenic roles played by mental illness, substance abuse, peer pressure, poverty, racism, and the like," and thus may fail "to hold communities accountable, too."[9] Yet current sentencing approaches often neglect these factors, and it seems to me that restorative justice would fare no worse (and may do much better) than the traditional system in considering issues such as racial discrimination, socio-economic deprivation, and so on. After all, restorative practices (unlike in-court sentencing colloquies) allow the participants to fully discuss the offense and offender, including any factors that may have lead to the crime (e.g., peer pressure) as well as any dysfunctions of the relevant community, and to take these into consideration in crafting an appropriate resolution. When compared to present practices, restorative justice is hardly "cheap grace and promiscuous forgiveness."[10]

For me, the most telling aspect of restorative justice criticisms is the extent to which different commentators make claims that, when taken together, appear irreconcilable. Some argue that restorative justice harbors a "reflexive hostility to punishment" and has become "a cover for left-wing" antipunishment aspirations.[11] Conversely, others allege that restorative justice lacks principles to limit "victim's vengeance"[12] and may "reinforce the basic, antidefendant narrative of the victim's rights movement," leading to even greater punishment. [13] At least one of the commentators recognizes the vacillating nature of these claims—that "[s]ome critics worry that sentencing under restorative procedures risks being unduly harsh if hijacked by victims and their allies," whereas "[o]thers gripe that sentencing will be insufficiently punitive if concerns regarding rehabilitation

---

9. O'Hear comment at 603. *See also* Richard Delgado, *Goodbye to Hammurabi: Analyzing the Atavistic Appeal of Restorative Justice*, 52 STAN. L. REV. 751, 763–71 (2000).
10. Bibas comment at 597.
11. *Id.* at 596–97.
12. Kennedy comment at 601.
13. O'Hear comment at 603.

and forgiveness for offenders are given priority"—only to conclude that "Luna would like to deny these claims but can hardly do so persuasively."[14]

Actually, I do not deny these allegations as much as I find them indicative of a relentless war of criticisms in punishment theorizing, a battle consistent with the traditional style of academic forensics. "The terminology of philosophical art is coercive," Robert Nozick once suggested, with the typical lecturer trying "to ram an opinion into [the audience members'] minds, so quite appropriately the audience resists, because even if it is something they want to believe anyway, they don't want to allow themselves to be *forced* to believe it."[15] As I mention in the core text, the combat among punishment theorists has been going on for quite some time now, with leading minds of each generation taking diametrically opposed positions. In the words of Herbert Morris, "[W]hat surfaces in discussions of punishment is the unsettling fact that among individuals apprised of all the relevant facts, apparently intractable differences arise over what can and cannot serve as a justification."[16] These "theoretical differences often are rooted in temperamental differences," and "it would be unduly optimistic to predict anything like theoretical consensus."[17]

When the contest occurs in faculty lounges, the penalty for disagreement is rather trifling: "[I]f the other person is willing to bear the label of 'irrational' or 'having the worse arguments,' he can skip away happily maintaining his previous belief."[18] But outside of the ivory tower, sanctioning rationales can be forced upon those who cannot "skip away happily" precisely because the process and outcome are not part of an academic exercise. Instead, victims and offenders, as well as their families and communities, must live with the aftermath of punishment theories in action. Forcing a given justification and its case-specific outcome on those most intimately affected by the crime and punishment is not a "nice way to behave toward someone,"[19] to put it mildly.

The procedural conception of restorative justice might offer a partial exit-strategy, providing a "big tent"[20] where distinct punishment theories can be integrated to resolve particular cases without requiring the adoption of one justification to the exclusion of all others. And rather than having punishment determined by distant lawmakers and sentencing commissions (or law professors), restorative justice allows the individuals most knowledgeable about and affected by the crime and its aftermath to help shape an appropriate response.

---

14. Etienne comment at 599.

15. Robert Nozick, PHILOSOPHICAL EXPLANATIONS 4–5 (1981).

16. Herbert Morris, *Concluding Remarks: The Future of Punishment*, 46 UCLA L. REV. 1927, 1930 (1999).

17. *Id.* at 1931.

18. Nozick, *supra* note 15, at 4.

19. *Id.* at 5, 13.

20. O'Hear comment at 602.

So conceived, restorative justice has no "megalomaniacal ambition to sweep away the traditional goals"[21] of the criminal sanction. To the contrary, it hopes to facilitate the harmonization of justifications to resolve real cases, not according to the paternalistic views of the state or the self-confident theories of punishment philosophers, but based on the perspectives of those whose very lives are in the balance. After centuries of theoretical warfare, maybe it's time for some practice at peace.

---

21. Bibas comment at 596.

28. THE VIRTUES OF OFFENSE/OFFENDER DISTINCTIONS

DOUGLAS A. BERMAN[*]

Many view the Supreme Court's modern Sixth Amendment rulings concerning the roles of judges and juries at sentencing as reflected in *Apprendi v. New Jersey*,[1] *Blakely v. Washington*,[2] and *United States v. Booker*,[3] to be jurisprudentially confusing at best, and conceptually incoherent at worst. But lurking within this muddled and dynamic jurisprudence, which itself emerges from muddled and dynamic evolutions in sentencing law and policy, are important concepts that can and should be recognized and embraced as a means to differentiate juries' and judges' roles in the criminal justice system, both in principle and in practice.

Specifically, the universe of criminal justice and sentencing considerations can and should be usefully divided between offense conduct and offender characteristics. Historically, offense conduct (e.g., harms to victims, whether a weapon was used, the amount of money stolen, or drugs trafficked) and offender characteristics (e.g., an offender's prior criminal history, employment record, family circumstances) have both played a significant role in much criminal justice decision-making, and both types of considerations remain central in modern sentencing systems. But the distinctive import and impact of offense conduct and offender characteristics at sentencing have not often been carefully and systematically examined.

I. SHIFTS IN SENTENCING THEORY AND OFFENSE/OFFENDER FOCUS

A. Background

The "rehabilitative ideal," which dominated sentencing theory and practice for nearly one hundred years before modern reforms, focused sentencing decision-making principally on offender considerations. Born of a deep belief in the possibility for personal change and improvement, the rehabilitative ideal was often conceived and discussed in medical terms with offenders described as "sick" and

---

* William B. Saxbe Designated Professor of Law, Moritz College of Law, Ohio State University. This core text is based on Douglas A. Berman, *Distinguishing Offense Conduct and Offender Characteristics*, 58 STAN. L. REV. 277 (2005).
1. 530 U.S. 466 (2000).
2. 542 U.S. 296 (2004).
3. 543 U.S. 220 (2005).

punishments aspiring to "cure the patient." Judges and parole officials were given broad and essentially unregulated sentencing discretion to consider offenders' personal history and characteristics to facilitate the individualized tailoring of sentences to the rehabilitative prospects and progress of each offender.

In 1949, the Supreme Court constitutionally endorsed this philosophical and procedural approach to sentencing in *Williams v. New York*.[4] The *Williams* Court explained that "[r]eformation and rehabilitation of offenders have become important goals of criminal jurisprudence" and spoke approvingly of the "prevalent modern philosophy of penology that the punishment should fit the offender and not merely the crime." Rejecting a claim that traditional trial procedures should be applicable at sentencing, the *Williams* Court stressed the importance of judges having "the fullest information possible concerning the defendant's life and characteristics." The value of "modern concepts individualizing punishments" meant that sentencing judges should "not be denied an opportunity to obtain pertinent information by a requirement of rigid adherence to restrictive rules of evidence properly applicable to the trial."[5]

Significantly, the *Williams* Court suggested that the rehabilitative model of sentencing, with its distinctive offender-focused approach and less formal procedures, had benefits for offenders as well as for society. The Court stressed that "modern changes" justified by the rehabilitative model of sentencing "have not resulted in making the lot of offenders harder." Rather, explained the Court, "a strong motivating force for the changes has been the belief that by careful study of the lives and personalities of convicted offenders many could be less severely punished and restored sooner to complete freedom and useful citizenship."[6]

But starting in the 1960s, the "modern philosophy of penology" began to change quite rapidly, and it has continued to evolve over the last four decades. Through the 1960s and 1970s, the rehabilitative model and highly discretionary sentencing systems were reexamined and became the target of significant criticism. Researchers and commentators contended that efforts to rehabilitate offenders had proved largely ineffective and that broad judicial sentencing discretion produced unjustifiable differences in the sentences meted out to similar defendants. Troubled by the apparent disparity resulting from highly discretionary sentencing practices—and fueled by concerns over increasing crime rates and powerful assertions about the ineffectiveness of the entire rehabilitative model of punishment and corrections—many criminal justice experts proposed reforms in order to bring greater certainty and consistency to the sentencing enterprise.

An integral component of the modern sentencing reform movement was a repudiation of rehabilitation as a dominant sentencing purpose and a far greater

---

4. 337 U.S. 241 (1949).
5. *Id.* at 247.
6. *Id.* at 249.

concern for increased sentencing uniformity. Enhanced concerns about more consistently imposing "just punishment" and deterring the most harmful crimes prompted structured sentencing reforms that focused sentencing determinations principally on offense conduct and limited judicial consideration of "the defendant's life and characteristics."

Consider, as but one example, the Pennsylvania Mandatory Minimum Sentencing Act of 1982, which was at issue in the Supreme Court case of *McMillan v. Pennsylvania*.[7] That Act provided for the imposition of a five-year mandatory minimum sentence if a judge found, by a preponderance of evidence, that an offender visibly possessed a firearm during the commission of certain offenses. The Act clearly was not enacted in service to the rehabilitative model of sentencing; rather, in the words of the Pennsylvania Supreme Court, the state legislature was seeking "to protect the public from armed criminals and to deter violent crime and the illegal use of firearms generally, as well as to vindicate its interest in punishing those who commit serious crimes with guns."[8] Tellingly, the Pennsylvania Mandatory Minimum Sentencing Act tied specific sentencing consequences to specific offense conduct (i.e., visible firearm possession triggered the mandatory minimum sentence), and the Act did not incorporate any consideration of offender characteristics (i.e., an offender's personal history was of no relevance to the mandatory minimum sentence).

B. Federal Sentencing Reforms

Modern federal reforms reflect these broad shifts in sentencing philosophy and goals. Prior to recent reforms, the federal sentencing system had been organized around the rehabilitative ideal for nearly a century. But the Sentencing Reform Act of 1984 (SRA) rejected rehabilitation as the central principle for sentencing and corrections: the SRA expressly called for judges to impose sentences that would provide just punishment, deter, and incapacitate. The goal of providing "the defendant with needed educational or vocational training, medical care, or other correctional treatment" was relegated to only one of a broader set of sentencing purposes.[9] The SRA also instructed judges to recognize that prisons were poorly suited to promote "correction and rehabilitation,"[10] and it instructed the U.S. Sentencing Commission to develop sentencing guidelines that would avoid "unwarranted sentencing disparities among defendants with similar records who have been found guilty of similar criminal conduct."[11] Congress has also purportedly been pursuing similar goals through its enactment of statutory mandatory sentences over the past two decades: advocates of mandatory

---

7. 477 U.S. 79 (1986).

8. *Commonwealth v. Wright*, 494 A.2d 354, 362 (Pa. 1985).

9. *See* 18 U.S.C. § 3553(a)(2).

10. *See* 18 U.S.C. § 3582(a).

11. *See* 28 U.S.C. § 991(b)(1)(B).

sentencing statutes have claimed that these laws deter, incapacitate, and punish offenders, as well as foster more uniform sentencing practices.

The new sentencing philosophies and goals reflected in the federal guidelines and mandatory sentencing statutes have emphasized offense conduct at sentencing and have limited judges' opportunity to consider offender characteristics. Most of the mandatory sentencing provisions that Congress has enacted over the last two decades are triggered by particular offense conduct—e.g., a five-year mandatory sentencing enhancement arises from use of a firearm in certain crimes and mandatory minimum penalties for drug trafficking are pegged to drug quantities. These statutory provisions entail that many federal sentencing outcomes will be driven by one aspect of offense conduct, and they thereby necessarily diminish the significance of offender characteristics in federal sentencing.

The relative roles of offense conduct and offender characteristics within the Federal Sentencing Guidelines (Guidelines) are a bit more nuanced, but similarly emphasize offense conduct relative to offender characteristics. The bulk of the Guidelines' intricate sentencing instructions to judges focuses on various aspects of offense conduct, and the Guidelines sentencing process revolves around the determination of which of forty-three possible "offense levels" should apply in a particular case. Moreover, for many federal offenses—particularly drug crimes and financial crimes—the seriousness of the offense within the Guidelines is based on quantitative measures: for drug crimes, the severity of the punishment is determined by the type and quantity of the drugs involved; for financial crimes, the severity of the punishment is determined by the amount of monetary loss. Larger quantities of drugs or larger financial losses mean a more severe sentence, and the extent of such "quantified harm" can have a dramatic impact on sentence length, often eclipsing the impact of all other sentencing factors.

Because "quantified harm" is so central to determining sentence lengths, the Guidelines rules on drug amounts and financial loss calculations have generated much litigation and numerous doctrinal splits within the federal circuits. Moreover, and more importantly, commentators and courts have long questioned whether the Guidelines' efforts to precisely quantify offense harms serve as an effective measure of offenders' true culpability. Especially in drug cases, couriers with a relatively small role in a drug conspiracy may receive a severe sentence based on drug quantity calculations that are an inappropriate proxy for the relative severity of their crimes.

Furthermore, the consideration of offense conduct within the Guidelines is not confined to offenses charged and proven at trial or to those resulting from a guilty plea. Because of the Guidelines rules for considering so-called "relevant conduct," judges are required to take into account certain offense conduct that was never formally charged or proven. Sometimes even evidence of offense conduct that related to a charge on which a defendant was acquitted at trial will, under the Guidelines' relevant conduct rules, require the enhancement of the defendant's sentence. Applicable offense levels within the Guidelines, and in turn applicable sentencing ranges, can often be increased dramatically by uncharged or even acquitted offense conduct that qualifies as relevant conduct.

Offender characteristics do play a role in Guidelines sentencing, but their most tangible impact is as an aggravating factor through the consideration of a defendant's criminal history. The Guidelines set forth intricate rules for converting prior criminal records into a criminal history score, and these calculations combine with offense-level determinations to establish defendants' applicable sentencing ranges. Judges can consider other offender characteristics when selecting a specific sentence within the Guidelines' ranges, but these ranges are relatively narrow, and the overall severity of Guidelines sentences may lead many judges to sentence at the bottom of applicable Guidelines ranges even before considering offender characteristics.

Furthermore, since the outset of the Federal Sentencing Guidelines era, the U.S. Sentencing Commission has declared through a series of policy statements that many potentially mitigating offender characteristics—such as a defendant's education and vocational skills, mental and emotional conditions, previous employment record, and family and community ties—are either "not ordinarily relevant" or entirely irrelevant to whether a defendant should receive a departure below the Guidelines sentencing range. Moreover, a number of early Sentencing Commission amendments declared off-limits certain offender factors that courts had started to rely upon for Guidelines departures; in this way, the Commission essentially overruled some initial judicial efforts to consider particular offender characteristics at sentencing.

In light of these realities, it is perhaps unsurprising that, since the very start of the Guidelines era, judges have assailed the Guidelines as "a mechanistic administrative formula," which made sentencing a task of "filling in the blanks."[12] The Guidelines' inordinate focus on determining and quantifying offense conduct led many judges—particularly those judges that had prior experiences with offender-oriented sentencing systems—to complain that the Guidelines converted them into "rubber-stamp bureaucrats" and "judicial accountants" in a sentencing process that had been drained of its humanity.[13] Moreover, these realities also make it unsurprising that many federal district judges have utilized

---

12. *United States v. Bogle*, 689 F. Supp. 1121, 1163 (S.D. Fla. 1988) (Aronovitz, J., concurring); *United States v. Russell*, 685 F. Supp. 1245, 1249 (N.D. Ga. 1988); *see also United States v. Justice*, 877 F.2d 664, 666 (8th Cir. 1989) (suggesting that, under the Guidelines, sentencing has been relegated to a "mechanical process"); *United States v. Swapp*, 719 F. Supp. 1015, 1026 (D. Utah 1989) (complaining that Guidelines sentencing is "[s]entencing by the numbers").

13. Jack B. Weinstein, *A Trial Judge's Second Impression of the Federal Sentencing Guidelines*, 66 S. Cal. L. Rev. 357, 364 (1992); *see also* John M. Walker, Jr., *Loosening the*

the new discretion they possess under the current advisory Guidelines system created by the Supreme Court in *United States v. Booker* to give greater attention to offender characteristics at sentencing.

II. THE SUPREME COURT'S RECENT SENTENCING JURISPRUDENCE AND THE OFFENSE/OFFENDER DISTINCTION

The greater focus on offense conduct in structured sentencing reforms has transformed modern sentencing decision-making into a more trial-like enterprise. Under the rehabilitative ideal, judges were to exercise judgment and discretion while exploring various offender characteristics in order to tailor punishments to individual offenders. Under modern structured sentencing provisions, judges are typically required to follow legislatively prescribed directives while adjudicating particular offense conduct in order to apply predetermined punishment levels for certain criminal conduct. In a recent commentary, U.S. District Judge Nancy Gertner has effectively spotlighted this modern transformation in sentencing decision-making:

> Under a sentencing system whose goal was rehabilitation, crime was seen as a "moral disease"; the system delegated its cure to "experts" like judges. Each offense carried a broad range of potential sentences; the judge had the discretion to pick any sentence within the range. In order to maximize the information available to the judge, and to minimize constraints on her discretion, sentencing procedures were less formal than trial procedures. No one challenged judges' sentencing procedures as somehow undermining the Sixth Amendment's right to a jury trial precisely because judge and jury had "specialized roles," the jury as fact finder, the judge as the sentencing expert. However flawed a judge's decision might be, it was not the case that he or she was usurping the jury's role.
>
> Twentieth century determinate sentencing regimes, however, changed the landscape and have appropriately raised Sixth Amendment concerns. In determinate regimes, facts found by the judge have fixed consequences—the judge finds x drug quantity, the result is y sentencing range. In this regard, the judge is "just" another fact finder, doing precisely what the jury does: finding facts with specific and often harsh sentencing consequences.[14]

Given this transformation of the sentencing enterprise, the Supreme Court's rulings in *Apprendi*, *Blakely*, and *Booker* can be seen and defended as a reasonable

---

Administrative Handcuffs: Discretion and Responsibility Under the Guidelines, 59 BROOK. L. REV. 551, 551–52 (1993).

14. Nancy Gertner, *What Has* Harris *Wrought?*, 15 FED. SENT'G REP. 83, 83–85 (2002) (footnotes omitted).

reaction to the new substance of modern sentencing decision-making. Responding to the reality that structured sentencing reforms have made sentencing determinations more offense-oriented and fact-driven, the Supreme Court in its *Apprendi* line of cases has now come to require traditional trial procedures for factual determinations that increase a defendant's potential punishment.

The offense/offender distinction not only provides insight into the development of the *Apprendi* line of cases, it also suggests an important conceptual limit for the principles articulated in *Apprendi*, *Blakely*, and *Booker*. The Constitution frames the jury trial right in terms of "crimes" that are the basis for a "prosecution" of "the accused";[15] this language connotes that the jury trial right should attach to all offense conduct for which the state seeks to impose criminal punishment, but it also suggests that the jury trial right should not attach to any offender characteristics that the state may deem relevant to criminal punishment. That is, one sensible understanding of the principles articulated in *Apprendi* and *Blakely* is that only those facts relating to offense conduct that the law makes the basis for criminal punishment should trigger the jury trial right.

As I have explained more fully elsewhere,[16] the jury trial right should be understood to concern only offense conduct and not offender characteristics: The jury trial right entitles a defendant to demand that a jury determine whether the defendant committed whatever alleged offense conduct the state believes merits a criminal sanction and seeks to punish. However, once this offense conduct has been properly established—either through a jury trial or a defendant's admission—a judge should be able to consider whether and to what extent offender characteristics may justify more or less punishment in response to that conduct. When the law ties punishment consequences to aspects of a person's past and character—such as a defendant's criminal history, his employment record, or his age—the state is not defining what conduct it believes merits criminal sanction, but rather is instructing judges how to view and assess an offender's personal history at sentencing. A state should be able to structure through statutes or guidelines precisely how a judge considers offender characteristics without implicating the jury trial right.

In short, the offense/offender distinction helps inform the jury trial right that the Supreme Court is applying in the *Apprendi* line of cases. Perhaps even more importantly for purposes of planning future criminal justice and sentencing reforms, the offense/offender distinction, in addition to being suggested by the text of the Constitution, resonates with and is buttressed by the distinctive institutional competencies of juries and judges and the distinctive ambit of trials and

---

15. Section 2 of Article III provides: "The Trial of all Crimes, except in Cases of Impeachment, shall be by Jury." U.S. CONST. art. III, § 2. The Sixth Amendment provides: "In all criminal prosecutions, the accused shall enjoy the right to a speedy and public trial, by an impartial jury. . . ." U.S. CONST. amend. VI.

16. *See* Douglas A. Berman, *Conceptualizing* Blakely, 17 FED. SENT'G REP. 89 (2004).

sentencings. Trials are about establishing the specific offense conduct that the state believes merits criminal punishment; sentencing is about assessing both the offense and the offender to impose a just and effective punishment. Juries can reasonably be expected to determine all offense conduct at a (pre-sentencing) trial, and the state can reasonably be required to prove to a jury at trial all the specific offense conduct for which the state seeks to impose punishment. But judges are better positioned to consider (potentially prejudicial) offender characteristics at a (post-trial) sentencing, and the state should be permitted to proffer information concerning an offender's life and circumstances directly to a judge to assist in punishment determinations.

To paraphrase Justice Scalia's opinion for the Supreme Court in *Blakely*, we can "give intelligible content to the right of jury trial" by providing that juries must find all the "facts of the crime the State *actually* seeks to punish."[17] Though jurisdictions are certainly permitted to provide for jury consideration of offender characteristics, the Constitution's jury trial right does not demand as much. (Of course, other constitutional provisions and concepts—some of which are raised, but not clearly discussed, in the *Apprendi* line of cases—may further impact the consideration of offense conduct and offender characteristics at sentencing. One could develop an argument, for example, that the Due Process Clause requires effective notice and a high burden of proof for all matters—whether based in offense conduct or offender characteristics—that can have significant punishment consequences for a defendant.)

The doctrinal specifics and future development of the Supreme Court's still-evolving sentencing jurisprudence must, of course, be a primary concern to all institutions and individuals involved in the development and application of the federal sentencing system. Only time will tell if the Supreme Court will come to articulate the reach of the jury trial right in offense/offender terms. But regardless of the future direction of constitutional jurisprudence, policy-makers can and should (1) reflect on how this jurisprudence arose in response to the modern transformation of sentencing decision-making and (2) examine more broadly and more systematically the distinct nature of offense conduct and offender characteristics at sentencing.

III. CHARTING FUTURE SENTENCING REFORMS IN OFFENSE/OFFENDER TERMS

In the continued evolution of modern sentencing systems, the distinction between, and distinctive nature of, offense conduct and offender characteristics can and should directly inform the consideration of sentencing purposes

---

17. *Blakely*, 542 U.S. at 305–07.

and procedures. In the federal system, Congress, the U.S. Sentencing Commission, judges, prosecutors, defense attorneys, and probation officers should be attentive to the offense/offender distinction in the development and application of federal sentencing doctrines and practices.

Ultimately, no matter what theories or goals are pursued within a sentencing system, both offense conduct and offender characteristics should play a significant role in sentencing decision-making. Different aspects of offenses and offenders may be of greater significance once a sentencing system has committed itself to pursuing particular goals, but every type of sentencing system is well served by incorporating both offense and offender considerations into the sentencing process. Proponents of backward-looking retributivist theories of punishment typically contend that both offense conduct and offender characteristics should play a central role in meting out punishment based on an offender's culpability; likewise, proponents of forward-looking utilitarian theories of punishment typically view both offense conduct and offender characteristics as central considerations when seeking to predict and prevent future criminal behavior.

Consequently, it is not surprising that a historical and a modern review of various sentencing systems reveals a broad consensus that punishment schemes and sentencing practices should generally be attentive to both the nature of the offense and the character of the offender. But, as indicated above, the relative balance of these considerations and their impact at sentencing has evolved considerably over time. This balance should continue to evolve as policy-makers define what theories and goals should come to dominate modern sentencing decision-making.

Though the federal sentencing system incorporates both offense conduct and offender characteristics in various ways, existing federal doctrines and practices have some distinctive and disconcerting qualities. First, offense conduct—and especially quantifiable harms such as the amount of drugs or money involved in an offense—has an extraordinary and arguably disproportionate impact on sentencing outcomes. Allegations at sentencing that an offense involves a large amount of drugs or monetary loss can often render functionally insignificant a host of seemingly important offender characteristics. Second, the Guidelines call for federal judges to enhance sentences based not only on offense conduct for which a defendant was convicted, but also on all related "relevant conduct." Third, only one aggravating offender characteristic—namely, the defendant's criminal history—plays a central and regularized role in federal sentencing decision-making. A broad array of potentially mitigating offender characteristics have been formally or functionally rendered "not ordinarily relevant" or largely inconsequential to federal sentencing determinations. Collectively, these distinctive features of federal law make for a particularly imbalanced sentencing decision-making process. Even after a defendant has been convicted or has pled guilty, prosecutors and defense attorneys must still dicker over the particulars of offense conduct, and they have little reason or opportunity to explore potentially mitigating personal attributes of offenders.

Interestingly, in *Koon v. United States*,[18] and more recently in *Gall v. United States*,[19] the Supreme Court spoke in grand terms that it "has been uniform and constant in the federal judicial tradition for the sentencing judge to consider every convicted person as an individual and every case as a unique study in the human failings that sometimes mitigate, sometimes magnify, the crime and the punishment to ensue."[20] However, before *Booker*, when the Guidelines operated as mandatory sentencing rules, and even after *Booker*, in cases involving mandatory minimum sentencing provisions, federal sentencing judges have had relatively little opportunity to "consider every convicted person as an individual." Though the *Koon* decision endorsed federal judges' authority to give effect to potentially mitigating offender characteristics, the structure and specifics of modern federal sentencing have often worked to severely undermine that authority.

Significantly, state sentencing guideline systems have typically achieved a much better overall balance in the consideration and application of a range of sentencing factors. In most state systems, only the offense for which conviction is obtained and not a broad range of "relevant conduct" determines the applicable offense level. In addition, state sentencing systems typically do not seek to intricately quantify all offense harms. Through the use of broader sentencing ranges, more liberal departure criteria, and other formal and informal mechanisms, state sentencing structures typically provide judges with far greater discretion to consider potentially mitigating offender characteristics at sentencing. Having said that, a number of state systems have mandatory minimum sentencing statutes that raise some of the offense/offender problems so prevalent in the federal sentencing system.

To some extent, a guideline sentencing system that is centered on number-driven calculations that map onto a number-driven sentencing grid will necessarily prompt the development of sentencing rules that (over)emphasize certain types of offense conduct. Offense harms in general, and drug and monetary loss amounts in particular, are more readily quantified and calibrated in a sentencing calculus. Offender characteristics, in contrast, are difficult to measure systematically and cannot be easily plotted on a sentencing chart. Nevertheless, the experiences of many state guideline systems, even those relying on detailed sentencing grids, demonstrate the possibility of achieving a better balance in the consideration and application of offense conduct and offender characteristics than currently exists in the federal system.

Even without a fundamental restructuring of the current federal sentencing system, a few relatively simple changes to the existing Federal Sentencing Guidelines would help achieve a better balance in the consideration of offense conduct and offender characteristics in federal sentencing: e.g., (1) moving away

---

18. 518 U.S. 81 (1996).
19. 128 S. Ct. 586 (2007).
20. 518 U.S. at 113.

from efforts to precisely quantify offense harms, (2) limiting the consideration of nonconviction conduct, (3) developing rules for the consideration of offender characteristics other than criminal history within the context of Guidelines calculations, and (4) expanding departure authority or applicable sentencing ranges so that judges have a greater opportunity to take into account hard-to-quantify offender circumstances.

IV. CONCLUSION

Many federal district judges have started to use the new discretion they possess in the wake of the Supreme Court's decision in *Booker* to consider and give effect to offender characteristics at sentencing. Congress and the U.S. Sentencing Commission should give particular attention to those offender characteristics (such as age and family circumstances) that are now being most frequently discussed by sentencing courts after *Booker*. As a result of the unique remedy developed by the Supreme Court in *Booker*, federal sentencing judges, guided by the sentencing mandates of § 3553(a) of the Sentencing Reform Act, are now able to develop a "common law of sentencing" through their fact-specific, case-by-case consideration of federal sentencing policy and practices. In keeping with both the original spirit and goals of the Sentencing Reform Act, Congress and the Sentencing Commission should seek to integrate the common-law wisdom being developed in the courts into all future federal sentencing reforms.

Though legislatures and sentencing commissions, considering crimes in the abstract, are inevitably likely to focus sentencing rule-making on the particulars of offense conduct, sentencing judges must necessarily consider and pass judgment on the individuals that have engaged in such conduct. Sentencing judges have a unique and uniquely important case-specific perspective on the real persons who actually commit offenses, and the significance of offender characteristics and of the human realities of sentencing are especially significant for district judges who interact with defendants first-hand. Because sentencing judges are uniquely well positioned, in the words of the Supreme Court in *Koon*, "to consider every convicted person as an individual and every case as a unique study in the human failings that sometimes mitigate, sometimes magnify, the crime and the punishment to ensue,"[21] their post-*Booker* discussion of offender characteristics should play an especially important role in future criminal justice debate and sentencing reforms.

---

21. *Id.*

COMMENTS

FROM EACH ACCORDING TO HIS ABILITY

RICHARD E. MYERS II*

Douglas Berman proposes that any system involving separated powers between a judge and a jury should be designed to take advantage of their relative strengths. His offense conduct/offender characteristics distinction accomplishes that goal in some ways. I propose a corollary: The jury should be responsible for judgments that compare the defendant against a standard we as a society wish to apply to all people, while the judge should be responsible for judgments that compare a particular defendant among defendants.

To understand what this division of labor entails, and why it makes sense, imagine the following case: A driver, Bill, has been charged by the prosecutor with negligent homicide because he was driving in a rainstorm at dusk and struck another vehicle from behind, killing its driver. He was driving at the posted speed limit, 65 miles per hour, and the car he struck was driving at 25 miles per hour, with its lights off.

There are at least two possible kinds of determinations we expect juries to make—facts and judgments. Whether Bill was driving at 65 miles per hour is a historical fact. Whether Bill was driving too fast for conditions is based on findings of fact, but contains embedded judgments about social expectations. Whether Bill was criminally negligent, because his driving under the conditions was such a gross deviation from the standard of care that it is worthy of criminal punishment, is a complex application of the law to the historical facts. Whether the other driver was also negligent and relieves Bill of responsibility also requires a complex determination. This kind of determination—whether, compared to all possible drivers, this defendant has failed to meet a standard we wish to apply to all of society—is a judgment, not a finding of historical fact. We expect juries to make such complex judgments all the time.

But judges are better suited to make other judgments: relative judgments among defendants. Whether Bill's decision to drive in this way, under these conditions, makes him one of the worst negligent killers or a relatively less culpable negligent killer is a judgment about where he fits on the scale of defendants. The judiciary, which collectively sees all such defendants, is institutionally competent to make determinations about which defendant is the worst, and where in a range of possible punishments a particular defendant should fall to maintain a fair allocation of punishment. This is in part an offense conduct determination, in Berman's parlance, but it compares offense conduct among offenders, something that we cannot expect a trial jury to do.

---

* Assistant Professor of Law, University of North Carolina School of Law.

Deciding who is best situated to make a particular choice is complicated. At sentencing, the system may seek to accomplish one or all of several widely understood goals: retribution, deterrence, rehabilitation, or incapacitation. Our institutional design might change depending on the emphasis one chooses. In a retributive system, based on the defendant righting the scales by repaying social harm he caused with harm to himself, a jury, as proxy for society, might be better positioned to decide how much harm the defendant did and how much he owes. This judgment is about the harm caused and does not require relative judgment among defendants. If, however, we are asking for relative punishment, not an-eye-for-an-eye repayment, then the judge will be better equipped to allocate punishment among defendants in a way that reflects their relative debts to society.

If the goal is deterrence, the jury might be better positioned to say what would deter otherwise law-abiding citizens, and a judge might be better positioned to say what would deter the defendants she sees. Rehabilitation calls for a defendant-focused and outcome-based determination about how and when a particular defendant can have his propensity for criminal behavior altered. This is partially predictive, so a judge and jury should participate at the guilt phase, but also requires a later determination of whether the defendant is in fact rehabilitated. Historically, we assigned this determination to experts in the form of a parole board, but we could easily see a design where this determination was made by a parole jury.

If Berman is right, and I think he is, we have once again fundamentally changed our underlying principles of punishment, without altering the Constitution's requirement that we use both judge and jury as central components of the decision-making structure. Unless we are able to decide precisely what we seek to accomplish with criminal punishment, it will be impossible to make definitive statements about the proper allocations of judgment between the judge and the jury.

CHARACTERISTICS RELATED TO PUNISHMENT EXPERIENCE

ADAM J. KOLBER*

Our prison sentencing policies have a duration fetish. We focus on the amount of time offenders spend incarcerated but ignore other important aspects of punishment severity. In particular, we generally ignore the dramatically different ways in which offenders *experience* incarceration, even when they are held in

---

* Associate Professor of Law, University of San Diego School of Law.

identical prison conditions. A person with borderline symptoms of claustrophobia will likely find prison much more difficult to bear than a person with ordinary sensitivities who has already been to prison several times before. If we accept Douglas Berman's invitation to examine a broader set of offender characteristics, we ought to consider characteristics of offenders that reveal how offenders are likely to experience punishment.[1]

According to prevailing versions of retributivism, the severity of a punishment should be proportional to an offender's blameworthiness. So if a borderline claustrophobe and an ordinary person commit crimes of equal blameworthiness, they are supposed to receive equal punishments. Nevertheless, the borderline claustrophobe will suffer more in prison, even though he is not at fault for having his particular sensitivity. From a retributive perspective, these offenders deserve equal punishments yet receive unequal ones.

True, offenders ought to take their sensitivities into account before they commit crimes. But even if advance notice makes the disproportionality of their punishments less troubling for retributivists, it does not eliminate the disproportionality. If we punish lefties who murder with one year in prison and righties who murder with life in prison, our punishments are still disproportional, even if every offender knows his punishment in advance. Similarly, even if borderline claustrophobes are aware of their sensitivities before they commit crimes, they are still punished disproportionally.

Consequentialists are also obligated to take subjective experience into account. In order to optimize punishment, consequentialists must consider many factors, including how a particular punishment is likely to deter. In addition to measuring *perceptions* of severity, consequentialists must also take into account the amount of distress offenders are actually likely to experience in prison. Such distress is one of the negative consequences of punishment. If consequentialists fail to take account of the distress that offenders experience, they will leave an important negative consequence of punishment out of their cost-benefit analysis. We seek a justification of punishment in the first place because we ought not knowingly or intentionally inflict substantial distress on people without good reasons for doing so. Consequentialists are incapable of justifying the distress of punishment—one of its most salient negative consequences—unless they take it into consideration.

Although both retributivists and consequentialists are obligated to take an offender's experience of punishment into account, they are not obligated to do so in the same manner. Given the retributivist interest in proportional punishment, retributivists ought to calibrate individual sentences in ways that take account of offender characteristics that affect likely punishment experience. While this is

---

1. *See* Adam J. Kolber, *The Subjective Experience of Punishment*, 109 COLUM. L. REV. 182 (2009) (providing more in-depth discussion of the issues raised in this comment).

no easy task, we do give defendants a constitutional right to an elaborate criminal trial to force the state to prove mens rea—a different kind of difficult-to-prove mental state. Also, many jurisdictions have parole boards that seek to determine an inmate's dangerousness, even though dangerousness is difficult to measure and inmates have incentives to hide the truth. Moreover, in the torts context, we frequently measure subjective experience when assessing personal injuries, even though plaintiffs have incentives to lie about the severity of their symptoms. Thus, it is surely possible to develop better individualized sentencing that takes account of an offender's anticipated punishment experience or monitors the severity of an inmate's ongoing punishment. To the extent that we resist the idea of experiential punishment calibration, it is not because subjective experience does not matter; rather, it is because we care about other things besides delivering proportional retributive punishment.

Consequentialists have no general commitment to punishing individuals proportionally. If individualized calibration is too expensive, consequentialists can seek out rough proxies. But unless they have some reasonable beliefs about the amount that prisoners suffer in the aggregate, they cannot confidently conclude that they are punishing in a manner in which the benefits exceed the costs. Even if individualized calibration is too expensive, consequentialists ought to at least take punishment experience into account when setting general punishment policies.

Berman argues that offender characteristics should once again occupy an important role in sentencing decisions and that courts have greater freedom to make it so in the wake of the *Blakely/Booker* line of cases. While Berman principally focuses on offender characteristics that augment or mitigate culpability, I note that offender characteristics that affect punishment severity are relevant as well. If, at sentencing, we are unwilling to take into account individual offender characteristics that affect punishment severity, then we should question whether we really are committed to the notion that punishment severity should be proportional to offender blameworthiness.

OFFENSE/OFFENDER DISTINCTION AND COMPETENCE

NANCY GERTNER[*]

Douglas Berman's approach—using the distinction between offense and offender conduct to differentiate the roles of judge and jury in sentencing—is an important first step in providing conceptual support for the lines suggested by the Supreme Court's decisions in *Apprendi, Blakely,* and *Booker.*

---

[*] Judge, United States District Court for the District of Massachusetts; Visiting Lecturer in Law, Yale Law School.

After *Apprendi*, it was not at all clear how the Court would articulate the line between judge and jury decision-making. There were at least three interpretations. The most narrow interpretation was that *Apprendi* only involved a legislative drafting problem. The legislature could satisfy the Court's concerns by setting a wide range of sentences per offense.

By the time of the Court's decisions in *Blakely* and *Booker*, it was clear the Court was reaching for an external standard by which legislative definitions of crimes would be judged. One approach was to require a jury trial with respect to certain substantive factors, but not for traditional sentencing factors. (*Almendarez-Torres v. United States*[1] seemed to fit this approach.) Another, with far reaching implications, was an impact test, suggesting that facts with a substantial impact on the outcome had to be heard by the jury. Neither approach was particularly coherent.

Berman's offense/offender standard melds the "traditional factor" approach and the "impact" test. The line between offense conduct and offender characteristics is, to some degree, a traditional one. Offense conduct is, at least in theory, what juries typically deal with—who did what, when, and where. Offender conduct is traditionally—at least predeterminate sentencing—what judges had dealt with. And in a sentencing regime that focuses so substantially on quantitative measures—the amount of drugs, the amount of loss—what the jury finds typically has a substantial impact on the outcome.

But the Berman offense/offender distinction obviously shares some of the problems of the other tests. Offenses have been defined to include offender characteristics, like a felon in possession of a firearm, and most of the recidivism statutes. Either Berman is suggesting that a legislature may not constitutionally muddy the waters as they have with these kinds of offenses, or he is suggesting that if they do, the court must divide the responsibility between judge and jury along offense/offender lines regardless of the legislative definitions. And looking at an impact test, offender characteristics determined by a judge with limited procedural protections could well be outcome determinative. (Sentencing of sex offenders comes to mind.)

Berman also argues appropriately that the offense/offender line reflects the competence of judges and juries. Indeed, one explanation of the *Booker-Blakely* jurisprudence is just that—in an era of determinate sentencing, what judges did was identical to what juries did, only in the classic "second-string fact-finding process," i.e., sentencing. With *Booker* and the advisory Guidelines remedy, judges were restored to making their unique contribution: not merely finding facts with foreordained consequences, but making judgments about the appropriate sentence.

---

1. *Almendarez-Torres v. United States*, 523 U.S. 224 (1998).

The offense/offender distinction fits with the competence of the respective players but again, it is an imperfect fit. Juries are supposed to focus on the case in front of them. Evidentiary rules eschew generalizations about the defendant's conduct—habit and custom are the exception—or generalizations about the offender—as in character evidence. Trials are not about situating the offense in the context of like offenses; jurors have no such context within which to place the case in front of them. In contrast, judges can reason laterally—situate a case in the context of the offender's life history, on the one hand, and against a backdrop of other offenders.

One can argue that offense conduct evaluation requires a bit of both—what happened and how does it compare to others. But offender characteristics surely involve more of the judicial function—generalizations about the individual, lateral comparisons to others. Again, Berman's categories are roughly coincident with the competence of judge and juries but need some tweaking.

Ultimately, Berman is arguing not just for an offense/offender distinction as a way of assigning constitutional sentencing and trial responsibilities. He is arguing for a system in which offender characteristics are critical to sentencing and critically left for judicial decision-making. He would reject a pure offense-based system in which juries are charged with determining offense elements, with no judicial role. He would also reject a mixed offense/offender system that gave all sentencing authority to the jury, as with a capital jury.

To the extent that the offense/offender categories necessarily overlap, Berman might reconsider the role of Due Process protections at sentencing. The distinction between the procedural protections offered at trial and sentencing is a function of the case law. Even if offender characteristics are reserved for judicial decision, we may do well to reconsider how those decisions are made and the procedural protections surrounding them.

SPLITTING THE BABY: THE DANGER OF DISTINGUISHING BETWEEN OFFENSE AND OFFENDER CHARACTERISTICS

LAURA I APPLEMAN*

Doug Berman's understanding of *Blakely* holds that juries need only determine offense conduct, not offender characteristics, since offender characteristics do not define a crime and thus fail to implicate the jury trial right. In other words, according to Berman, the Constitution's jury trial right does not stop a judge from alone making findings about offender characteristics relevant to sentencing

---

* Assistant Professor of Law, Willamette University.

determinations. This interpretation also helps clarify the *Almendarez-Torres* prior-conviction exception, because the fact of a prior conviction goes to the offender's personal history—an offender characteristic rather than an element of offense conduct.

The problem with this interpretation is the difficulty in distinguishing offense conduct from offender characteristics. Although certain categories easily sort themselves out into one or the other, such as age, former employment, or schooling, other areas, such as criminal history, rehabilitative promise, and determinations of "future dangerousness" are mixed, making it difficult to classify them as either conduct or characteristic. For better or for worse, lawmakers have a natural tendency to define and delineate punishment in complicated and interconnected ways, ways that often make it very difficult to distinguish offense conduct and offender characteristics. Accordingly, it is hard to imagine creating a post-*Blakely* regime that incorporates such a distinction.

Relying on this narrower interpretation of *Blakely*, Berman argues further that such mixed categories should be treated as offender characteristics rather than offense conduct because they are not really part of the defendant's crimes and thus are not essential jury issues. But this kind of analysis begs the question by reclassifying traditional jury issues—whether a defendant has obstructed justice, whether a defendant will be dangerous in the future, etc.—as factual issues for the court to decide, not the jury.

Stated differently, arguing that mixed categories should be treated as offender characteristics, and thus determined by the judge, is very similar to the argument that the Court specifically rejected in *Blakely* to the effect that "the jury need only find whatever facts the legislature chooses to label elements of the crime, and that those it labels sentencing factors—no matter how much they may increase the punishment—may be found by the judge."[1] A broader view of *Blakely* avoids this problem by assuming that only the most basic offender characteristics may be determined by nonjury actors.

Moreover, *Blakely*'s relatively expansive language seems to reject such line-drawing—whether between mixed offender/offense categories and offender characteristics, or indeed, even between offense conduct and offender characteristics. This is particularly true in light of *Cunningham v. California*, where at least six Justices seem to reject the offense/offender distinction entirely.[2]

A broad *Blakely* mandate stems from the importance the Court currently places on the role of the jury. The Sixth Amendment's "reservation of jury

---

1. *Blakely v. Washington*, 542 U.S. 296, 306 (2004).

2. 549 U.S. 270, 291 n.14 (2007) ("Justice Kennedy urges a distinction between facts concerning the offense, where *Apprendi* would apply, and facts concerning the offender, where it would not. . . . *Apprendi* itself, however, leaves no room for the bifurcated approach. . . .").

power"[3] and the constitutional requirement that all facts legally essential to the punishment be proved to a jury beyond a reasonable doubt combine in *Blakely* to form a new principle for sentencing. Ultimately, by stating that the jury trial right applies to all facts legally essential to the punishment,[4] the Court rejected a narrow understanding of the jury's role, including the offense/offender distinction. The job of determining both offense conduct and offender characteristic should be left to the jury.

---

3. *Blakely*, 542 U.S. at 308.

4. *See id.* at 313.

BLAKELY, BOOKER, ACCOUNTABILITY, AND INTELLIGIBILITY

JOSEPH E. KENNEDY*

Douglas Berman's offense/offender interpretation of *Blakely* and *Booker* serves two related values in the administration of criminal justice: increasing the intelligibility of the criminal law and making the legislative branch more accountable for the crimes it creates. On the other hand, it does not necessarily produce the sort of contextual decision-making at sentencing that Berman favors.

By intelligibility I mean something other than simple clarity. Indeed, the Federal Sentencing Guidelines provide many examples of laws that are clear yet unintelligible. Line by line, the Guidelines are drafted in relatively straightforward language. Yet what boggles the mind of the nonspecialist is that many provisions must often be combined to calculate the sentence for a single crime. An algorithmic form of reasoning takes the place of the more linear form of reasoning with which people interpreting laws are acquainted. It is often difficult if not impossible to keep in mind all the possible combinations of the variables involved. The Guidelines contain so many "if . . . then" statements that a coherent understanding of what the relevant provisions mean as a whole is exceptionally difficult. You can perform the necessary calculations and arrive at a result, but having arrived, you can't explain how you got there other than to repeat the calculations. As such, who can say what these provisions "mean"? In this sense, many provisions of the Guidelines are unintelligible to the nonspecialist.

Berman's reading of *Blakely* and *Booker* would discourage such unintelligible provisions. Because all of the offense elements must be proven to the jury, legislators would have a strong incentive to create more straightforward definitions of crimes. Jurors would have trouble returning convictions for offenses whose

---

* Associate Professor of Law, University of North Carolina.

meaning they could not comprehend. Algorithmic justice does not work for lay people.

Such a result would in turn make lawmakers more accountable for the crimes they create. Legislatures cannot easily be held accountable for algorithmic sentencing provisions because few can understand what has been done. The distinctions between graver and lesser harms that are so vital to penal drafting become obscure for those who can't foresee all the possible variations of the "legal math." When a legislature writes its offenses in more linear ways, the constituents of the legislature can more readily understand these distinctions and are in a better position to hold their elected officials responsible for their work.

But Berman's offense/offender distinction will not necessarily lead where he wants to go in all respects. Berman argues for less quantification of offense harms, less consideration of conduct not related to the conviction, more consideration of offender circumstances other than criminal history and generally more sentencing discretion for the judge. Intelligibility concerns would limit the degree to which legislatures could quantify harms in the definition of the offense and strict distinctions between offense and offender might greatly restrict the use of "other conduct" at sentencing. A more contextual consideration of the offender's circumstances and greater discretion for the sentencing judge generally does not necessarily follow from the offender/offense distinction, however. Intelligibility and legislative accountability can be achieved by simple offense definitions tied to mandatory draconian sentences that tie the hands of the judge. Can a legal principle be extracted from the *Blakely* and *Booker* decisions that would constrain legislatures from limiting the sentencing judge's consideration of the offender's circumstances? This might be the next big question that any interpretation of these cases must answer.

IN NEED OF A THEORY OF MITIGATION

MARGARETH ETIENNE*

Douglas Berman has nicely captured an important thread that runs through the Supreme Court's recent jurisprudence on sentencing: a reading of the Sixth Amendment that requires offense-related, but not offender-related, facts to be determined by a jury. This approach to the Sixth Amendment interprets "criminal prosecutions" not as trial adjudications versus sentencing adjudications but rather as offense-related adjudications versus offender-related adjudications without regard to the phase of the criminal process in which these determinations are made. Berman's offense/offender distinction is a credible reading of

---

* Professor of Law, University of Illinois at Urbana–Champaign College of Law.

the Court's *Apprendi* line of cases, and his conclusion that sentencing reform must be attentive to both offense and offender characteristics is wise.

Still, the assumption that the offense/offender distinction dictates a practical—not to mention a constitutionally mandated—division of roles between jurors and judges is questionable. Some legal concepts and principles connected to offense definition are notoriously difficult for juries to apply. The "beyond a reasonable doubt standard" is but one well-known example. Insanity, conspiracy, and reasonableness in self-defense, among others, also raise problems for jurors. Jurors, even with guidance from the bench, are not always better suited to assess offense conduct. On the other hand, judges are not uniquely (or even better) qualified to assess individualized characteristics such as temperament, remorsefulness, or family circumstances. Indeed, if jurors are to be left out of assessing individual offender characteristics, what ought we make of the old adage that defendants should be judged by a jury of their "peers?" Of course the Constitution guarantees no such thing. Yet the notion of a trial by peers suggests an expectation that part of a jury's role is to assess the defendant based on the individual jurors' similar experiences and life circumstances.

The offense/offender distinction is useful in part because it leads Berman to important reform principles such as evaluating harms in less quantifiable terms, limiting the use of relevant conduct, and taking greater account of offender characteristics through new rules and expanded judicial authority to depart. These measures, many of which exist in state sentencing systems, might well improve federal sentencing. But nothing about the offense/offender divide necessitates either jury or judicial decision-making.

In my view, who determines offense and offender characteristics is far less important than the measures by which they are determined. What is grossly missing from federal sentencing—and Berman alludes to this—is any sense of an accepted theory of mitigation. Is age a mitigating or aggravating factor? Does inebriation at the time of the offense mitigate or aggravate the crime? Should economic privilege or a rotten social background mitigate punishment or aggravate it? What emotions should mitigate punishment—fear, anger, hatred, indifference—and when are they offense characteristics versus offender characteristics?

Little consensus remains about many of these issues. Indeed, the hard questions go well beyond how to quantify these sentencing factors or who, as between jury and judge, is most competent in assessing them. For this reason, to leave these hard questions in the hands of any one institutional actor—the judge, jury (or commonly, the prosecutor)—is to leave that group susceptible to accusations of caprice and lawlessness. In the case of the federal judiciary, this concern has led to sustained efforts to cabin its power to mitigate punishment under almost any circumstances. The true answer to this perceived lawlessness is to develop a law or theory of mitigation. Only then will the offender characteristics side of the offense/offender divide possess the support it needs.

REPLY

DOUGLAS A. BERMAN

I am pleased and gratified that commentators recognize and extol some of the virtues I have identified in dividing the universe of criminal justice and sentencing considerations between offense conduct and offender characteristics. I am also pleased and gratified that commentators recognize and stress some of the limitations they see in dividing the universe of criminal justice and sentencing considerations between offense conduct and offender characteristics. I share the view that the offense/offender distinction has limitations. But these limitations do not undermine the fundamental value of the distinction as a conceptual tool for better describing past sentencing reform efforts and for prescribing future sentencing reform doctrines.

The nuanced and multifaceted dynamics that surround criminal justice policy and sentencing decision-making—both historically and in modern legal systems—defy a simple taxonomy or comprehensive synthesis through any single analytical framework. My core text does not seek to argue that the offense/offender distinction provides a silver bullet that can extinguish all conceptual confusion concerning past reforms or modern sentencing considerations. Rather, my primary goal is to ensure that theorists and policy-makers recognize the distinct and distinctly important roles that offense conduct and offender characteristics have played—both historically and in modern legal systems—in criminal justice policy and sentencing decision-making.

The commentators raise some common themes. Richard Myers and Adam Kolber both highlight that complete analysis and assessment of offense/offender distinctions may often depend on underlying theories of punishment. Nancy Gertner and Laura Appleman both highlight that the offense/offender distinction does not provide a perfect account of what constitutional rights now apply (or should apply) to judicial fact-finding authority at sentencing. Joseph Kennedy and Margareth Etienne both highlight that the offense/offender distinction does not fully address all conceptual or practical questions concerning the structural allocation of power in criminal justice systems.

Though I might squabble with some smaller points made in response to my core text, I largely agree with the commentators' accounting of the limitations of the offense/offender distinction. But their astute insights do not undermine the offense/offender distinction's core virtue: The distinction still provides a useful and arguably essential conceptual tool for understanding and examining many hotly debated issues surrounding criminal justice policy and sentencing decision-making—whether the issues concern punishment theory or constitutional doctrine or the structural allocation of institutional roles in criminal justice systems.

Indeed, I view all the comments as highlighting the virtue of offense/offender distinctions to foster an effective dialogue concerning the form and function of modern issues and enduring debates. Various limitations notwithstanding, the distinction provides a conceptual lens for examining the sentencing work already being done, and the sentencing work that still needs to be done, by courts, commissions, and legislatures in order to improve modern sentencing policy and practices. If these commentators and others will now regularly view sentencing debates with offense/offender distinctions in mind, my work here is done.

29. THE HEART HAS ITS REASONS
Examining the Strange Persistence of the American Death Penalty

SUSAN A. BANDES*

The standard arguments for capital punishment, familiar to any first-year law student, are that it will deter others from committing similar crimes, that it is retributive in nature (the "just desert" for the crime committed), and that it will permanently incapacitate the defendant so he cannot commit further crimes. More recently, these arguments have been supplemented by the notion that capital punishment serves expressive or symbolic goals. The legal and philosophical debate has tended to proceed along a predictable path: focusing on whether the death penalty serves a standard goal like deterrence or retribution, or an expressive goal. The public debate about the death penalty generally follows the same path, since that debate is often framed and summarized by social scientists and pollsters whose questions track the traditional discourse.

What is noteworthy about the traditional debate is that it is oddly devoid of reference to emotion. This attitude is problematic for two interrelated reasons. First, the "legally grounded" discussion, with its reference to time-honored but affectless concepts like "deterrence" and "incapacitation," fails to describe with any accuracy the way people actually arrive at decisions about the death penalty. Second, the official discourse perpetuates a misleading normative assumption: that to be legally acceptable, reasons ought to be devoid of emotion.

I argue that we need a more explicit account of the emotional sources of support for and opposition to the death penalty. The decision whether to maintain and implement our system of capital punishment is inescapably emotional. The official discourse ignores or denigrates much of this emotional content. The result is not to banish emotion from the system, but to drive discussion of it underground and to perpetuate a system that depends on moral and emotional distance and even disengagement.

* Distinguished Research Professor, DePaul University College of Law. This core text is adapted from Susan A. Bandes, *The Heart has its Reasons: Examining the Strange Persistence of the American Death Penalty*, 42 STUD. IN L., POL., & SOC'Y, 21 (Austin Sarat ed., 2008).

I. THE TRADITIONAL RATIONALES REVISITED

A. Retribution

The omission of emotion is easiest to discern in the discourse on retributive theory. Retributivists "seek to punish an offender because she deserves to be punished in a manner commensurate to her legal wrongdoing and responsibility. . . . Not more, not less."[1] What is interesting about standard retributivist arguments is that they present the need to punish the offender, as well as the ability to determine what punishment the offender "deserves," as bloodless and abstract philosophical questions. Retributivism is often portrayed as a way to avoid or civilize emotional reactions to crime; a means of determining the fair and just punishment from the community's point of view, rather than acquiescing to the punishment that the victim or the community might desire out of anger and vengeful feeling.

To what extent can retributivism, without reference to emotional affect, explain how societal or individual notions of fair and just punishment are shaped, particularly when the death penalty is at issue? What motivates a polity, or a community, to determine that the death penalty is the just desert for certain crimes? My contention is not that the institution is fueled solely by the thirst for vengeance, or that jurors who vote for death are motivated solely by vengeful impulses. The emotional landscape is far more complex than that. Rather, the traditional debate suffers for its insufficient attention to the emotional landscape in all its complexity. Without attention to emotion, retributive theory becomes circular, empty, and unhelpful—we punish because it is the right thing to do, and we mete out the punishment that is right.

There are two separate but overlapping questions. First, why does the United States (but no other Western country), and why do thirty-six of the states (but not the other fourteen), consider the death penalty the "just desert" for certain categories of murder? Retributive theory has no good answer to this question. Second, why do some jurors, in some cases, determine that a particular capital defendant deserves to die? Capital punishment in its "idealized" form has always assumed the existence of a group of heinous offenders, the worst of the worst, for whom there should be consensus that death is a just desert. This idealized form bears little resemblance to the actual decision-making process engaged in by those faced with life-or-death decisions. In practice, the decision is—and always has been—heavily influenced by emotional factors unrelated to the nature and circumstances of the crime.

Both the retributive philosophy and the retributive impulse are better understood with reference to the emotional dynamics that help shape our intuitions of justice. These intuitions are affected by social and political context; for example

---

1. Dan Markel, *Against Mercy*, 88 MINN. L. REV. 1421, 1439 (2004).

by societal views of crime and what needs to be done to keep us safe. They are also highly influenced by portrayals (for example, media coverage or official pronouncements) that evoke strong emotions, including outrage, fear, and the urge to blame. We would better understand the attitudes of individual capital jurors in particular if we examined all these same factors, as well as the anger, fear, compassion, empathy, or prejudice a capital case may elicit.

B. Deterrence

The lack of attention to emotion's role in the debate about deterrence poses a different problem—how to account for the fact that those who rely on this rationale do not change positions when confronted with evidence that deterrence fails to work as advertised. Deterrence theory posits that capital punishment will dissuade others from committing similar crimes in the future and that it will do so more effectively than alternative sentences like life imprisonment. It is the most explicitly instrumental rationale for capital punishment, and the only one that makes what seems to be a testable empirical claim. Since capital punishment was held constitutional in the early 1970s, the deterrence rationale has been—until quite recently—the primary justification for the death penalty. During the more than three decades of the modern death penalty era, as in earlier eras, we have remained in what can most charitably be described as an empirical standoff on the question of whether the death penalty deters crime.[2] By the late 1990s, the public was becoming disenchanted with the notion of deterrence: It saw rising rates of execution but did not perceive a decrease in crime. Yet instead of withdrawing support for the death penalty, the populace simply shifted rationales—to retribution.

Put simply, in the capital context, the reasons people give for their positions on the death penalty seem to have little connection to their actual reasons. If we want to learn why people support capital punishment, and why they do not change their position in the face of information refuting the rationale for their support, we will have to look beyond the standard rationales. Such an understanding requires reckoning with the role of emotion.

C. Incapacitation

The incapacitation argument, when applied to the death penalty, is that we need to execute the most heinous killers in order to prevent them from killing again. The label "incapacitation" has an almost scientific, clinical ring to it—it doesn't sound angry or uncivilized, the way the term "retribution" might. The emotional content of this justification operates below the radar.

---

2. John Donahue and Justin Wolfers, *Uses and Abuses of Statistical Evidence in the Death Penalty Debate*, 58 STAN. L. REV. 791 (2005).

But no matter how it's dressed up, the question is how to take the worth of a life. How do we decide if a person is so irredeemable, and so threatening to our future safety, that he should be permanently cast from the human community? This question draws on deeply held attitudes, including perceptions and fears about crime, beliefs about character (for example, about the ability of people to change, or about personal and societal responsibility), and attitudes toward mercy, forgiveness, and retribution. Fear, in particular, is one of the most prominent factors influencing jury decisions to impose capital sentences. Juries are fearful that even if they impose a sentence of life without parole, the defendant will be released and perhaps cause more harm. This fear is based on an erroneous assumption that could be addressed by a change in judicial practice. Studies show that people assume life without parole really means something like "ten years in prison." When capital jurors try to clarify what the phrase means, the general judicial practice is to refuse to answer, and when jurors remain uncertain, they are more likely to sentence a defendant to death.

II. THE EXPRESSIVE RATIONALES COMPARED

The question of why the death penalty persists cannot be answered without reference to the expressive dimension of capital punishment. Capital punishment might express a range of messages, among them a societal commitment to living by moral rules, the strongest condemnation of those who break the rules, recognition of the moral worth of the victim, the community's anger and grief at the loss of a valued member, the desire to purge evil from the community, and reassurance that the world is an orderly rather than a chaotic, unsafe place.

Although the expressive rationale is usually viewed as a supplement to the traditional reasons for punishment, all rationales for capital punishment have an expressive dimension. Retribution is explicitly expressive; all its benefits flow from the communication of the existence and implementation of punishment. Deterrence, though not often classified as such, is explicitly expressive as well. It is premised on the belief that would-be murderers will desist based on the advertised consequences to previous murderers. Punishment—and certainly capital punishment—is always a "deeply symbolic event,"[3] and we—as individuals and members of the polity—construct and understand that symbolism in a way that is not purely cognitive. Attitudes about whether the social order "requires" capital punishment, or about whether certain people "deserve" to die, or about which sorts of victims might be "owed" this punishment, are imbued with symbolic value. Moreover, they are premised on assumptions about how the world works,

---

3. David Garland, *Frameworks of Inquiry in the Sociology of Punishment*, 41 BRIT. J. SOC. 1, 10 (1990).

and how it ought to work. There are no purely instrumental rationales or purely legal justifications that float free of emotional and political influence, or of communicative content. And just as our American death penalty is an expression of culture, politics, religion, and other values, these values are themselves intricately tied to, and in many respects a product of, our emotional commitments.

III. THE ESSENTIAL ROLE OF EMOTION

The longstanding debate about the death penalty is intense, even polarized, despite (or perhaps in part because of) the fact that the death penalty has little direct impact on most people. To understand why our society continues to support the death penalty, and whether we are likely to abandon that support any time soon, we must first consider how people arrive at moral judgments and under what conditions they will reconsider these judgments. The standard assumption is that people encountering a moral dilemma engage in moral reasoning, that this reasoning leads to a judgment, and that "emotion may emerge from the judgment, but is not causally related to it."[4] Although there is no unanimity about how moral reasoning works, this standard model is under serious attack, particularly in light of recent findings in cognitive and social psychology calling its descriptive accuracy into question.

The phenomenon that perplexes those who study capital punishment, the stickiness of support for the death penalty even when the grounds for that support are shown to be spurious, is a nice illustration of what cognitive psychologist Jonathan Haidt calls "moral dumbfounding." He noted that groups interviewed about their attitudes toward hot button issues "were often 'morally dumbfounded,' that is, they would stutter, laugh, and express surprise at their inability to find supporting reasons, yet they would not change their initial judgments."[5]

This effect has been observed in numerous studies, many using neuro-imaging techniques like fMRI and PET scans, whose results challenge the notion that moral reasoning is the cause, rather than the consequence, of moral judgment. Cognitive scientists have generated alternative models of moral reasoning consistent with these findings. For example Haidt's social intuitionist model posits that emotion triggers judgment, and that reasoning occurs after judgment, offering a "post-hoc rationalization" for a judgment already intuitively reached. Studies by Joshua Greene and others suggest that emotion is triggered

---

4. Mark Hauser et al., *Reviving Rawls' Linguistic Analogy: Operative Principles and the Causal Structure of Moral Action, in* MORAL PSYCHOLOGY AND BIOLOGY 6 (Walter Sinnott-Armstrong ed., forthcoming).

5. Jonathan Haidt, *The Emotional Dog and Its Rational Tail: A Social Intuitionist Approach to Moral Judgment*, 108 PSYCH. REV. 814, 817 (2001).

in moral dilemmas of a personal nature, whereas reason prevails in situations of a more impersonal nature.[6] Although there is no definitive answer to exactly *how* emotion and cognition interact, it is no longer controversial among those studying the role of emotion that moral judgment is the product of both emotion and cognition.

Emotion affects our evaluation of capital punishment at the most basic level. Our preexisting attitudes about how the world works affect our beliefs about particular issues. Indeed, particularly when the attitudes are deeply held, they *protect* our beliefs from contradictory or threatening information. They affect the way we process and evaluate information. They affect *whether* we even consider new information, what category we assign it to, how much importance we give it, and how much we care about it. When people are strongly attached to a particular belief, they attempt to construct a persuasive rationale for their desired conclusion, so that it looks, even to them, as if they are engaging in an open-minded process of reasoning. Hence Haidt's "moral dumfoundedness" effect: "[P]eople are resistant to information that contradicts their pre-existing attitudes and often turn away such information at an early stage, but they are not conscious that they are doing this."[7]

As an illustration of the importance of preexisting attitudes, consider the question of whether the death penalty is an effective deterrent. To answer this question requires some notion of how people will behave when faced with the threat of harsh (and in most cases uncertain) consequences. It also requires a sense of whether the draconian consequence of taking a life is called for. In order to answer these questions, people draw—intuitively or consciously—on their attitudes about how the world works. The way we view the world will affect both our notions of whether a punishment is effective and our sense of what punishment ought to express. In other words, those who support the death penalty will both think it works and agree with its symbolic message. Those who oppose it will consider it both ineffective and morally wrong. The death penalty serves as both a concrete policy and an abstract symbol—a symbol of toughness, control, and certainty, or of inequality, vengeance, and irreversible error.

IV. THE FEEDBACK LOOP

Emotion exists in a complex feedback loop with institutions like the criminal justice system. It plays a role in shaping our institutions, and the institutions in turn play a role in shaping emotions—their expression, their display, and even

---

6. Joshua Greene et al., *An fMRI Investigation of Emotional Engagement in Moral Judgment,* 293 SCIENCE 2105 (2001).

7. Ziva Kunda, *The Case for Motivated Reasoning,* 108 PSYCHOL. BULL. 480, 490 (1990).

the way we experience them internally. As Martha Nussbaum argues, we construct institutions that embody what we value, and these institutions can "either promote or discourage" emotions, and "can even shape [emotions] in various ways."[8] The capital punishment system embodies certain emotional commitments. Its continued existence is a societal declaration that death is the appropriate punishment for the most terrible crimes. This declaration rests on shifting judgments about what we require in order to restore the sense of order and justice that is disturbed by a heinous crime. Those judgments draw on many sources, including politics, law, religion, morality and emotion.

Over the years, it has been possible to chart shifts, not only in public attitudes toward capital punishment, but in the emotional content and the emotional rhetoric of those attitudes. For example, where once it was considered harsh and unenlightened to rely on retributive theory in support of the death penalty, in recent years it has become acceptable and common. At the same time, the retributive rhetoric has been softened, as the imposition of capital punishment has become viewed as a way to acknowledge the worth of victims and provide a forum for "closure" and healing to their families. The trial court has been drafted into a therapeutic role, without much thought to whether it can or should serve that purpose. Survivors have been assured that only a death sentence can heal their wounds. Victim impact statements, efforts to truncate the appellate process, and other initiatives have been premised on the survivors' need to attain closure. This is an example of how the feedback loop works. The capital system has come to be seen as a means of providing closure to survivors. Changes in the system have been made based on the need for closure. Survivors have come to expect that the system will provide them closure, and now the system must be perpetuated to fulfill this promise.

V. SALIENCE

A unique aspect of the death penalty debate is the strange confluence between the broad, intense, public debate on the topic and the lack of personal exposure to the capital system. The intensity (or salience) of public opinion on the topic is significant for a number of reasons. People often engage in motivated reasoning that leads them to ward off any information threatening to their beliefs. The intensity of belief contributes not only to the solidifying of individual opinion, but to the polarization of group opinion. The mix of intense emotional investment in the issue, polarization, and lack of exposure to the facts on the ground is lethal to informed debate. The conversation might begin couched in terms of

---

8. Martha C. Nussbaum, UPHEAVALS OF THOUGHT: THE INTELLIGENCE OF EMOTIONS 405 (2001).

deterrence or retribution; it might move to broader claims about federalism, vigilantism, and crime control; but it does not take long to get to the ultimate polarized place, in which one side is arguing for purging the society of evil and the other side is calling the first side evil for advocating murder.

To communicate across this divide, we would do well to acknowledge the intensity of belief and craft arguments that take it into account. At one level, the highly abstract conversation is peculiarly sensitive to high-profile events and trends. It has long been shaped by perceptions of violent crime, such as those driven by constant, sensationalized images of random, racialized violence. It has been fueled by certain high-visibility crimes, such as the Oklahoma City bombings, which provided Timothy McVeigh, the poster boy for capital punishment. But it has also worked the other way, responding to the occasional high-profile execution of a sympathetic person—for example, Karla Faye Tucker—and to high-profile exonerations like that of Rolando Cruz. These cases have elicited strong moral reactions of a different sort. The DNA exoneration cases in particular have been effective in part because they provide vivid, easy-to-grasp illustrations of the unfairness and immorality of executing someone who has been scientifically shown to be innocent.

But the exoneration cases also illustrate a different, more nuanced point about salience and persuasion. People are often able to pierce or move beyond abstractions when confronted with actual human lives in all their complex, messy concreteness. One of the most important characteristics of the capital trial is the insistent message that the issue of whether the defendant should live or die is not an emotional issue. The very appearance of dispassionate process is an important part of the system's emotional landscape; a powerful implicit message to the jury as well as the other legal actors. When people are confronted with concrete information about actual defendants, the mechanics of lethal injection or other execution methods, or alternatives like life without parole, support for the death penalty lessens considerably.

VI. CONCLUDING THOUGHTS

The reluctance to confront the emotions pervading the legal system is deeply problematic. Ignoring these emotions doesn't diminish their power. On the contrary, it increases the chance that law will regulate human behavior without understanding how it works. It also insulates the current emotional dynamics of the legal system from scrutiny and debate.

Opposition to capital punishment is often denigrated as emotional, and therefore lacking in the rationality and tough-mindedness the law requires. Yet both supporters and opponents of the death penalty are driven by passions. It's just that the passions of those who support capital punishment are so ingrained in the legal landscape that their emotional nature has become invisible. For example, the capital system raises a host of wrenching questions about empathy. We might debate whether the system should encourage empathy for the suffering of the victim and discourage empathy for the defendant. We might debate what role empathy for the victims' families ought to play in the capital system, or whether empathy for the families of capital defendants ought to play a role. What we should not do is classify empathy for the victim or his family as "just following the law" and empathy for the defendant or his family as soft-minded and legally irrelevant.

The death penalty thrives under a set of rules, spoken and unspoken, about what sorts of emotions can be displayed and even experienced in the legal arena. These rules encourage moral disengagement and discourage empathy for the defendant. They keep the concrete reality of the death penalty at a safe remove. Support for the death penalty is often strongest in the abstract. Support wanes when people become viscerally aware of the fact that capital punishment involves the killing of human beings. Certain realities need to be made salient: the humanity and individuality of each capital defendant, the horror of the execution itself, and the fact that each of us is implicated in and responsible for each execution and for the system that facilitates state-sponsored killing. These realities are at the moral and emotional center of the American system of capital punishment, and they should be at the center of the debate about its fate. They should incite passion and commitment. When that happens on a broad scale, the death penalty will die a well-deserved death.

COMMENTS

THE HEART HAS ITS VALUE: THE DEATH PENALTY'S JUSTIFIABLE PERSISTENCE

DOUGLAS A. BERMAN* AND STEPHANOS BIBAS**

Susan Bandes is right that emotional currents drive death-penalty debates and deserve more respect. But putting emotions "at the center of the debate about its fate" will not lead the death penalty to "die a well-deserved death."[1] On the contrary, reengaging with emotion will reinvigorate capital punishment.

Historically, societies that emphasize emotions are *more* likely to embrace capital punishment. Well into the twentieth century, Americans could hardly be

---

* William B. Saxbe Designated Professor of Law, Moritz College of Law, Ohio State University.

** Professor of Law, University of Pennsylvania Law School.

    1. Bandes core text at 643.

accused of "moral and emotional distance and even disengagement"[2] from the death penalty. At the last public execution in 1936, more than 20,000 people flooded into Owensboro, Kentucky, to see Rainey Bethea hanged for raping and murdering a 70-year-old woman. Thwarting public desires for extreme punishment of the worst offenders may simply deflect punitive emotions elsewhere, leading them to warp other areas of criminal justice. Perhaps hiding punishment behind prison walls has frustrated these emotions and created upward hydraulic pressure on prison sentences, such as life without parole even for some nonviolent and juvenile offenders.

Turning from history to human nature, emotions keep the death penalty on the books in almost three-quarters of American states. Legislatures still champion this ultimate sanction because the public values its unique symbolism. Juries, in deciding whether to execute particular killers, serve as a legitimate outlet for emotions. Judges exemplify dispassionate reason; juries, communal emotional judgment.

Bandes suggests that vengefulness and punitive emotions are inflamed in the abstract and that focusing more on individual cases will lead her preferred emotion, empathy, to predominate. Indeed, she brings forth promising candidates for empathy, such as repentant Karla Faye Tucker and innocent Rolando Cruz. But these examples, who are well known because they are emotional outliers, hardly undercut capital punishment as an institution. On the contrary, they confirm that even death-penalty supporters distinguish murderers based on desert and empathy, rather than angrily calling for every killer's head. Other renowned capital defendants elicit very different, contextualized emotional responses. Think of Oklahoma City bomber Timothy McVeigh or serial killer Ted Bundy. Such examples of pure hatred and evil justifiably evoke little empathy and enormous righteous indignation. These men deserve emotional condemnation and a punishment different in kind from the ones we give to common thieves and drug dealers.

Likewise, Bandes rightly suggests that jury instructions should not preclude empathy. But in fairness, both sides should be equally able to bring emotional arguments to bear and seek catharsis and healing. If defendants can emphasize their humanity and plead for leniency, then prosecutors and victims' families should be equally free to make the emotional case for retribution. From an emotional point of view, the return of victim-impact evidence is cause for celebration, not Bandes's dismay. How else can juries make emotionally well-rounded judgments?

Finally, we must respect punitive emotions as a central part of what makes us human. We are angry at moral agents because they were free to choose but chose wrongly. We are angry because we care about the victim as a fellow man and are outraged at the criminal who abused his freedom. Crimes tear the social fabric

---

2. *Id.* at 635.

and demand payback to vindicate victims, condemn crimes, and denounce wrongdoers. Without anger, there is neither justice nor sense of community. We must express our indignation and respond to grave moral wrongs. Though there was no need to deter or incapacitate Adolf Eichmann, executing him appropriately condemned the Holocaust and vindicated its victims.

Bandes prefers the warm-and-fuzzy emotion of empathy, but offers little justification for squelching the visceral capital emotions. Certainly we can take them too far and can critique and restrain their excesses. But properly limited, these emotions rightfully demand a place at the table. Perhaps Vulcan criminal justice would not need to vent outrage at the worst killers, but human criminal justice must and inevitably will. At least for these epitomes of evil, the only emotionally effective punishment may be the ultimate one, death.

In sum, the heart has its reasons, but also its value. The heart not only explains the death penalty's persistence, but also justifies it. A humane and human criminal justice system needs both head and heart. Such a system may well praise the death penalty, rather than burying it. We should certainly educate and critique emotions and their excesses, such as lynchings. Momentary eruptions of anger may cloud reflective emotional judgments. The job of the justice system is not to stifle or skew emotions, however, but to promote reflective emotional deliberation. We can neither ignore punitive emotions nor assume that enlightened emotional progress will make the death penalty fade into the obscure mists of the past.

EMOTIONS, RETRIBUTIVISM, AND THE DEATH PENALTY

MARY SIGLER*

Susan Bandes reminds us that it is a mistake to draw a sharp distinction between reason and emotion in legal and moral decision-making. Despite her call for a careful assessment of the emotions involved in capital punishment, however, she does not seem fully committed to the enterprise. Although Bandes laments the denigrating clichés about emotion aimed at opponents of capital punishment, she seems unconcerned about the familiar caricature of the blood-thirsty, vengeful supporters of capital punishment. Thus she fails to come (sympathetically) to grips with their emotional perspective.

Instead, she assumes that a greater focus on the emotions in the context of capital punishment will result in the practice's "well-deserved death."[1] Additionally, despite Bandes's commitment to evaluating punishment realistically rather than

---

* Professor of Law, Sandra Day O'Connor College of Law, Arizona State University.
1. Bandes core text at 643.

relying on the cold abstractions of moral philosophers, she neglects to consider the reality of the alternative to capital punishment—a lengthy prison sentence. Before we celebrate the impending demise of the death penalty, we should acknowledge the fate to which we are thus consigning serious criminal offenders. Although a life sentence lacks the emotional salience of a death sentence, it is no less effective a means of "permanently cast[ing offenders] from the human community."[2] And regardless of whether it tugs at our emotions, it is no less deserving of our thoughtful attention.

Bandes contends that the inattention to emotions in the capital punishment debate is most obvious in the discourse on retributive theory. Thus, "[r]etributivism is often portrayed as a way to avoid or civilize emotional reactions to crime; a means of determining the fair and just punishment from the community's point of view, rather than acquiescing to the punishment that the victim or the community might desire out of anger and vengeful feeling."[3] This observation seems essentially accurate—but lifted out of the very discursive context Bandes means to illuminate. A recurring theme in the capital punishment debate is that retributivism is just a thin veneer for vengeance. This view figures prominently in Supreme Court rhetoric about punishment and is an explicit charge in much of the academic literature.

It is probably true that the retributive emotions and the vengeful emotions spring from a common source. But that is just the point: Retributivism rejects the *unchecked* emotionalism of the impulse for revenge. Retributivism's virtue is precisely to distance us from the intense emotional reaction of victims and their families; this is why we do not let them serve on juries or otherwise stand in judgment of those who have wronged them. At the same time, a powerful sense of justice animates even those whose lives are not directly affected by the offender's actions. Because retributivists have devoted so much energy to repudiating the association with vengeance, perhaps they have neglected the emotional dimension of retributivism.

Unfortunately, Bandes's attempt to highlight this aspect of retributivism is rather unconvincing. Her brief for the retributive emotions is limited to observing that retributivism is animated by our intuitions about justice. But these, she suggests, are little more than the product of media manipulation—provoking outrage, fear, and blame. This hardly does justice to the *commitment* to justice that is the distinctive hallmark of retributivism. Surely one of the most affecting attributes of the human animal is the capacity to experience profound outrage at the harms and indignities perpetrated against strangers—*and* to stop short of indiscriminately annihilating anyone perceived to be a threat. Although Bandes worries—as I do—about the limited empathy we sometimes muster for the fate

---

2. *Id.* at 638.

3. *Id.* at 636.

of wrongdoers, she seems positively indifferent to our singular capacity for a sense of justice.

Meanwhile, the scholarly and media preoccupation with the death penalty draws attention away from other aspects of criminal punishment, including the length and harshness of prison terms. Although the death penalty affects only a fraction of criminal offenders in the United States, capital punishment looms large in our discourse, veritably sucking all of the emotional oxygen out of the discussion of our punitive institutions and practices. Without discounting the importance of resolving the capital punishment controversy, I fear that the powerful emotions that dominate that debate may disproportionately absorb our attention, causing us to neglect more mundane sources of concern.

Although Bandes recognizes that our emotions may misdirect us, she offers unqualified approval of those emotions—but only those emotions—likely to discourage people from sentencing an offender to death. As a result, what purports to be a scholar's call for a careful assessment of the emotions in the capital punishment debate reads more like an advocate's call for the death of the death penalty.

WHEN CLEARLY UNDERSTOOD, RETRIBUTIVE THEORY HAS MUCH TO OFFER

JEFFRIE G. MURPHY*

There is much wisdom in Susan Bandes's essay. I think that she does, however, sometimes confuse two things that, in the interest of conceptual clarity, should not be confused: questions of empirical explanation and questions of philosophical justification. She notes that "the United States (but no other Western country), and thirty-six of the states (but not the other fourteen), consider the death penalty the 'just desert' for certain categories of murder"[1] and that the unpredictable way in which jurors determine who deserves to die reveals a lack of consensus on such matters. She raises the question of why this is the case, and says that "retributive theory has no good answer to this question."[2]

But, of course, it would not. Surely philosophical retributive theory (Immanuel Kant's for example) is an attempt to articulate an ideal model of how punishment should be determined in a just society—a model that can be used to evaluate actual punitive practices to determine the degree to which they fall short of justice. And such a theory is not, contrary to Bandes's claim, "bloodless and

---

* Regents' Professor of Law, Philosophy, and Religious Studies, Arizona State University.

1. Bandes core text at 636.

2. *Id.*

abstract"³—unless a passionate commitment to justice and what justice requires is bloodless and abstract. It is the job of the empirical social scientist, not the philosopher, to ask why in application the idea of just deserts may point in a variety of conflicting directions. Maybe jurors are stupid or ignorant or corrupt, or perhaps the concept of just deserts is not properly explained to them (because judges are stupid or ignorant or corrupt)—who knows? Certainly not the philosopher, since this is an empirical matter. And surely the philosophical retributivist will not place too much weight on the presence or absence of social consensus (another empirical matter) because such a theorist will not use social agreement as a test for moral justification. For all I know, there may be an emerging social consensus in America in favor of torture (even if not in favor of calling it "torture") and, if so, the retributivist—like any other morally decent person—will hardly regard that as easing moral doubts about the practice. It will instead raise doubts about the virtue of our citizens and the degree to which their opinions should matter to a rational and moral person.

If the actual process we have in America of determining who gets executed and who does not is arbitrary, random, and unpredictable, this is of course deplorable. But who will be first in line to condemn this? The philosophical retributivist. And why will such a philosopher condemn it? Because it is grossly unjust to support a practice that regularly punishes people *more (or less) than they deserve.*

It might be true, as a conceptual matter, that the concept of retributive just deserts is inherently incoherent (a confused product of confused philosophy) or that it is simply, like much philosophy, too complex and too likely to be misunderstood to be used in providing useful counsel to those who must determine the sentencing of criminals. The first problem is a philosophical problem and requires philosophical examination. The second problem is empirical and awaits controlled empirical investigation.

It is also possible, as Friedrich Nietzsche warned, that the language of retributive just deserts subconsciously draws on corrupt aspects of the human character—human *ressentiment,* to use Nietzsche's term. If this is true—and establishing it would take some hard psychological work—then this is a powerful reason for avoiding this language in the practice of sentencing—capital or otherwise. This is not a critique of philosophical retributivism, however, since such a theorist would be the first to abandon the practical use of his own language if it had a tendency to lead people to sentence based on malice, envy, cruelty, and spite (the essence of *ressentiment*) instead of just deserts.

In summary: There may, for all I know, be good empirical reasons for avoiding the use of retributive language in the actual practice of criminal sentencing. It is hardly a valid criticism of retributive theory, however, that it is not in a position to

---

3. *Id.*

assess such empirical claims. Even if the claims are true, indeed, this should not upset the philosophical retributive theorist since he can still take pride in having the very best theory to bring to bear in deploring these very empirical outcomes.

REASON AND EMOTION IN CAPITAL SENTENCING

ROBERT F. SCHOPP*

Susan Bandes states that "[o]ne of the most important characteristics of the capital trial is the insistent message that the issue of whether the defendant should live or die is not an emotional issue."[1] Capital punishment is our most severe form of criminal punishment, a legal institution that expresses condemnation, including judgments of reprobation and expressions of vindictive resentment. It is difficult to understand how an institution that expresses vindictive resentment can avoid emotion. That emotional component of criminal punishment as an expression of vindictive resentment might, however, justify a rigorous attempt to impose an institutional structure that disciplines the manner in which we apply criminal punishment through the application of reason in the form of rules and statutory sentencing factors.

Many capital sentencing statutes list statutory aggravating and mitigating factors intended to guide judicial decisions regarding the admission of proffered aggravating and mitigating evidence as well as sentencing decisions regarding a specific offender and offense. Convicted offenders must be allowed to present relevant mitigating evidence that provides a basis for the compassionate exercise of mercy in sentencing. Mercy involves treatment better than the individual merits in justice motivated by compassion. Thus, the Court's Eighth Amendment doctrine explicitly recognizes the emotional response of compassion as a legitimate component of the sentencing process.

The Court's decision to allow victim impact statements in the capital sentencing process recognized the relevance of evidence that elicits emotional responsiveness to the plight of the victim and survivors by explicitly presenting the harm done to those individuals. Part of the Court's rationale for allowing that evidence was based on its role in balancing the broad range of mitigating evidence that elicits emotional responsiveness involving sympathy for the offender and the offender's family.[2]

Thus, it is difficult to sustain the proposition that the capital sentencing process is designed to preclude the influence of emotion. Rather, the process

---

* Robert J. Kutak Professor of Law, Professor of Psychology and Philosophy, University of Nebraska.

1. Bandes core text at 642.
2. *See Payne v. Tennessee,* 501 U.S. 808, 825–27 (1991).

attempts to guide sentencers in making sentencing decisions on the basis of a complex interaction of reason and emotion. The instructions, rules of evidence, and appeal to reason are intended to discipline the emotional responsiveness to the offense, the offender, and the victims in a manner that promotes relative consistency in the interpretation and application of sentencing standards to highly emotional decisions.

If this interpretation is roughly accurate, concern for comparative and non-comparative justice in the capital sentencing process should lead us to rigorously pursue two lines of inquiry. The first is a justificatory inquiry regarding the legitimate roles of legal sentencing factors, findings of fact, and emotional responses in the application of capital sentences that express our most severe condemnation. In what manner and to what degree, for example, should anger at the offender or empathy with the families of the victims or of the offenders be considered a legitimate sentencing factor or a distortion of the sentencing process? What justification of criminal punishment would accommodate these factors as relevant or reject them as distortions of the sentencing process?

The second is the empirical inquiry regarding the sentencing procedures and instructions that most closely approximate attainment of just capital sentencing by accommodating legitimate sentencing considerations and minimizing the influence of illegitimate factors. Clearly identifying, pursuing, and applying these distinct but related inquires might enhance our ability to develop sentencing rules and procedures that conform to the underlying justification of punishment.

In short, the most defensible approach to the role of emotion in capital sentencing is not to attempt to purge the process of emotional responsiveness. Rather, it is to discipline the manner in which emotional responses are elicited and applied. Ideally, the sentencing process would promote disciplined application of emotional responses that were consistent with the justification in principle of capital punishment, and it would minimize the effect of emotional responses that were not consistent with that justification. As with other aspects of the capital sentencing process, satisfactory resolution of the legitimate role of emotional responses requires integration of this inquiry with the more fundamental inquiry regarding the justification in principle, or the lack thereof, for capital punishment. Regardless of the most defensible answer to that underlying question, however, a similar pattern of analysis regarding the legitimate role of emotions and the justification of punishment in principle and in practice applies to criminal punishment more generally.

OUTRAGE VERSUS ANGER AND HATRED

JOSEPH E. KENNEDY*

The single greatest obstacle to abolition of the death penalty is what I think of as "front page moments." An otherwise not particularly punitive person reads of a terrible murder on the newspaper's front page. The murder might involve the death of a child, or the death of many, or a particularly sadistic manner of killing. Think of Timothy McVeigh, who blew up a large government building that contained a day care center for children, or of the serial killer Charles Ng, who videotaped himself taunting a mother about whether he had killed her baby boy (he had) before Ng tortured, raped, and killed her. At this moment our otherwise peaceable reader becomes consumed with rage, puts down the newspaper and thinks, "I would kill that person myself right now if I could."

These front-page moments crystallize the simplest and most powerful way that emotion operates in high-profile capital cases. The American public cannot abide the abolition of the death penalty in part because of the punitive emotions unleashed by "the worst of the worst."

Susan Bandes has done us a great service by focusing our attention on the role the "heart's reasons" play in support of the death penalty. Distinctions need to be made between the different types of emotions generated by horrible crimes, however. The deeds of McVeigh and Ng trigger strong visceral reactions: horror, shock, and disgust. Following fast upon the heels of these immediate responses come anger and hatred as one thinks about the perpetrator. These emotions have a more purposive quality because they cannot exist without a person as a target. One can feel horror at something, but one can only feel anger or hatred toward someone.

The last stage in the emotional response to a terrible crime should involve outrage. Outrage goes beyond one's individual, immediate moral reaction. Outrage involves an offense against shared standards of decency or morality. It is an intrinsically social emotion. One can wish that a transgressor suffer for something he has done without feeling obliged or entitled to act on that wish. That would be anger or hatred. Outrage, however, implicates us all in the response because it involves some norm by which we purport to live. What sort of community or society would we be if we failed to respond adequately to this sort of savage murder? In this sense, we have literally moved outside our own personal rage at the act committed to a more communal rage. To feel outrage is to feel in a social way.

Making these distinctions between emotions is important because some can be more successfully managed or channeled than others, an important point in

---

* Associate Professor of Law, University of North Carolina School of Law.

the larger debate about the proper role of the emotions in punishment. Because it is an intrinsically social emotion, outrage is more susceptible to restraint than anger or hatred.

Let me return to my American newspaper reader. At the moment he reads the article described, my reader feels he would be willing to kill the offender. But he won't get to. He would have to kill the offender after a trial in which all the facts were established, long after the initial passions have cooled. What would it cost my reader to look into the eyes of this other human being and take his life if the offender would otherwise face life-long incapacitation in prison? I think it would cost him a lot psychologically and emotionally because most human beings have a deeply felt sense of revulsion against taking life.

This emotion of revulsion against killing is itself a communal emotion. Our imagined reader would assume a very distinctive identity in the eyes of his community after carrying out the execution: he would have become a killer. Capital punishment is, of course, replete with rituals and mechanisms designed to absolve any one person from ultimate responsibility for the execution. That is the point. Becoming a killer is no small thing, for a person or for a community.

What remains to be understood is how and why the collective emotion of anger that terrible crimes inspire in the United States fails to mature into the more restrained emotion of outrage. More to the point, how does Bandes propose that we get our society to experience the natural revulsion against killing that capital punishment should, but currently does not, inspire? Calling for debate about the proper role emotions play in capital punishment is a useful first step, but how do we convince a society to feel that which it does not? The heart may have its reasons, but can reason change the heart's mind?

WILL EMPATHY KILL THE DEATH PENALTY, OR VICE VERSA?

CAROL S. STEIKER*

Susan Bandes offers a wise plea not to ignore or marginalize the role of emotion in the administration of capital punishment and in the wider moral and political debates about its future. In particular, Bandes depicts the capacity for empathy with, and the emotion of compassion for, capital defendants—as well as the victims of potentially capital crimes—as a crucial ingredient in the litigation of individual cases and the broader abolitionist struggle. In fact, empathy and compassion are even more deeply implicated in the debate about capital punishment than Bandes suggests. Indeed, fears about the effect of the death penalty on

---

* Howard and Kathy Aibel Professor of Law, Harvard Law School.

empathy and compassion (rather than hopes for a reverse effect) lie at the heart of some versions of abolitionism.

Bandes categorizes empathy as an emotion, when in fact it is more of a human *capacity*, an ability to feel certain kinds of emotions. Empathy allows us to imaginatively enter into the emotions of others whose experiences we have not shared. It may allow us to feel emotions as diverse as joy and despair, hope and fear, satisfaction and indignation.

The capacity for empathy plays a role in many of the standard arguments against the death penalty. In retributive terms, once we empathetically enter into the circumstances of a capital defendant's life and crime, we can often then reject the ultimate sanction as "undeserved." Karla Faye Tucker's redemption on death row offers one example of an empathetic challenge to the "fit" of punishment to crime. Concern about the imposition of the death penalty on less than fully culpable offenders (such as the young, mentally impaired, or mentally ill) is another. In utilitarian terms, our ability to empathize not only with the families of victims but also with the families of capital defendants, and to project the myriad effects of a robust use of the death penalty on communities, may make us better able to perform the complex interest balancing that the utilitarian calculus demands.

But empathy can be implicated in debates about capital punishment in a different way. Instead of asking us to empathize with the plight of the capital defendant or his/her family, abolitionists sometimes appeal to the effects of capital punishment on *executioners*, and through their experience, on ourselves and our society. To be able to put someone to death requires a suppression of empathy and compassion, a resistance to the anguish, fear, and physical pain of another. It is this experience that leads many to draw a parallel between capital punishment and torture. To be sure, many valuable jobs—military service, criminal prosecution, and dentistry among them—require individuals to inure themselves to the pain that they must inflict for what society accepts is a justified cause.

Two things distinguish capital punishment from these other sorts of jobs. First, the suppression of empathy in the capital context is much more thoroughgoing than it is in many of these other contexts (actual military combat excluded), because it involves the personal infliction of the most serious kind of harm. Moreover, the suppression of empathy is conjoined with rituals that suggest that the infliction of harm is not merely necessary and regrettable, but righteous and even a cause for celebration. These latter emotions create a risk that executioners—and through them the wider society—will come both to perceive and to portray those subject to capital sanctions as less than human. In doing so, we will build a more impervious shell against the emotion of compassion and will thereby damage, perhaps irretrievably, our capacity for empathy.

As Bandes so eloquently maintains, the human capacity for empathy and the emotion of compassion lie at the heart of the limits on punishment imposed by widely different justificatory theories. Thus, the fear that the robust practice of capital punishment may suppress or permanently impair our capacity for empathy (on an individual *and* social basis) should be central arguments against the practice. Indeed, one of the arguments against public executions—which were eventually moved to their current venue behind prison walls—had to do with the "coarsening" effect that witnessing such events might have on the public. These early concerns are echoed in different terms today, but it is concern about "the death of empathy"—a capacity that Bandes rightly brings to center stage—that underlies arguments about capital punishment based on its irreparable effects on ourselves, the punishers. It is thus perhaps more important to ask what the death penalty can do to empathy than it is to ask what empathy can do for the death penalty.

OVERRIDING EMOTION

LAJUANA DAVIS*

Susan Bandes's account of the role of emotion in capital cases should also include those actors that influence the jury: prosecutors and judges. First, to bring decision-makers in death penalty cases to the discussion table, retribution must be discussed in terms other than thinly disguised bloodlust or a clumsy attempt at therapeutic justice. Prosecutors' closing arguments across America's courtrooms justify the death penalty in other ways—for example, as an expression of the community's moral standards about acceptable conduct and as a restoration of societal dignity against those who offend it. Bandes might argue that notions of societal respect are illegitimate concerns in capital case decision-making. But the law permits prosecutors to make these arguments, and state's attorneys insist that these arguments are more than cries for vengeance. Exploring and responding to these justifications must be part of the nuanced conversation that Bandes encourages.

Second, an open conversation about emotion's role in capital punishment should also examine the legal system's reaction to emotion. A recent Alabama case presents an example of the law's continuing abhorrence of emotional responses. In that case, some jurors cried while the verdict was read at a capital trial. Because of that emotional display, the court concluded, those jurors' verdict of life imprisonment without parole could be properly accorded "very little weight."[1] The life sentence verdict was overridden, because the "jurors' outbursts of emotion after they found the defendant guilty of capital murder indicated that they were overwhelmed by their impending duty to consider the death penalty as

---

* Assistant Professor of Law, Cumberland School of Law, Samford University.
1. Ex parte *Taylor*, 808 So. 2d 1215, 1219 (Ala. 2001).

required by law."[2] In other words, in Alabama, where the judge has the power to override the jury's verdict of life imprisonment and impose death, an emotional outburst by the jury is sufficient grounds for so doing. Bandes notes that the law often ignores emotion, but far from ignoring it, jurors' emotional displays in this case resulted in the death penalty.

Bandes rightly argues that emotion is deeply involved in legal and moral judgment. Jurors' moral accounting, therefore, naturally incorporates emotion regardless of jury instructions discouraging emotional responses to the evidence. But juries, as seen in the example above, may not be the only actors to include in the discussion. What may ultimately influence the outcome of capital cases is convincing other legal actors, such as lawyers and judges, that emotion affects their decision-making in capital cases as well.

Some judges and prosecutors are reluctant to acknowledge that emotions, other than moral outrage or condemnation, guide their attitudes and decisions in criminal cases. One reason for this reluctance may be the scornful societal attitudes that Bandes identifies about expressions of "soft" emotions like empathy. In capital cases, some decision-makers feel that they must go to the extremes of condemnatory rhetoric to demonstrate their commitment to justice, which creates further polarization on the capital punishment issue. (One response to this polarizing behavior would be, as many have suggested, to discourage judicial candidates from promising to impose the death penalty in every case presented to them—or from condemning candidates who have not imposed death in a particular capital case.)

When our legal system discounts or excludes empathetic responses, our decision-makers may seem uncaring and indifferent. To address this, society and the legal community should eliminate disincentives for prosecutors and judges to respond empathetically to crime.

---

2. *Id.* (quoting trial judge).

CAN THE THEORY AND PRACTICE OF CAPITAL PUNISHMENT BE MORE EMOTIONALLY INTELLIGENT?

TERRY A. MARONEY*

Susan Bandes surely is correct that the death penalty can be fully understood only by engaging with the pervasive role of emotion. Its emotional landscape is enormously complex, as she argues, and our failure to thoughtfully mine it has done a great disservice to both theory and practice.

What is not clear is that the emotions at play are ever, as Bandes asserts they could be, "unrelated to the nature and circumstances of the crime."[1] Those words call to mind so-called "antisympathy instructions," in which capital sentencing jurors are admonished to set aside "sentiment, conjecture, sympathy, passion, prejudice, public opinion or public feeling."[2] The Supreme Court has approved such instructions—and, indeed, has strongly suggested they are constitutionally required—because of its view that emotions, likened to "whim" and "caprice," are likely to be "untethered"[3] from the "actual evidence regarding the crime and the defendant."[4]

But this view is not correct, and I do not believe Bandes actually endorses it. Emotions are a primary mechanism for understanding and responding to our environment and reflect cognitive assessments of the world. A capital juror's emotions will reflect her judgments about the nature and circumstances of the crime, based on the evidence, as filtered through her worldview—including her prior emotional commitments. To the extent that Bandes is concerned about untethered juror emotion, then, perhaps that filter is the object of her concern.

We may worry, for example, about a juror's racial biases. This worry is directed not to the emotional nature of the precommitment, but to its content. Or perhaps we worry about prejudgment because of emotional commitment to death for crimes involving certain victims (like children) or acts (like rape); but then the concern is that a category judgment will prevent an individual one. In both examples the juror's emotions are related to the nature and circumstances of the

---

* Assistant Professor, Vanderbilt University Law School.

1. Bandes core text at 636.

2. *California v. Brown*, 479 U.S. 538, 542–43 (1987). Although the quoted language in *Brown* was preceded by the word "mere," the Court in *Saffle v. Parks*, 494 U.S. 484 (1990), approved a similar instruction without that qualifier.

3. *Brown*, 479 U.S. at 542–43.

4. *Saffle*, 494 U.S. at 493 (juror's decision must be a "reasoned *moral* response . . . rather than an emotional one").

crime. The criticism—a good one—is that her emotions reflect judgments that demonstrate bad values or an inadequate appreciation of her task's parameters.

Similarly, legislators' choices whether and for what to authorize the imposition of the death penalty are related to the nature and circumstances of the crime, though in a more general sense; it's precisely those factors that will render a crime death-eligible. As Bandes acknowledges, even such abstracted moral judgments are emotional. Further, it's not always so abstract; proposals to expand the death penalty—for example, to crimes involving discrete classes of victims— often are justified by reference to individuals and even given their names. It is not clear why these debates might encourage "moral disengagement": this process surely is a form of moral engagement. It's just one with whose premises, processes, and conclusions one can (for good reasons) disagree.

The clearest point is that in the death penalty context we systematically privilege certain emotional commitments over others. Moral outrage at bad acts, revulsion for bad actors, and sympathy for victims and families are regarded as so obviously appropriate that they simply are not noticed. This privileging operates within a bizarre (yet robust) narrative in which emotion opposes legal reasoning, including morally infused legal reasoning. Privileged emotional commitments therefore are regarded as not emotional at all, and disfavored ones are stuck with the tag and disavowed.

This adherence to a demonstrably false narrative is hugely distorting. Jurors are bombarded with emotionally saturated facts and arguments and then promptly admonished to ignore emotion. Rather than distinguish between permissible and impermissible emotions (did the Supreme Court really mean to banish "passion," including passion for justice or fairness, along with "prejudice"?), current practice bundles them together and then tosses them all out. Jurors may then become morally disengaged and treat sentencing as if it were an amoral accounting task; they may continue to draw on emotions, but only ones so normalized as to evade the negative branding. Who knows?

Bandes's final comments reveal her opposition to the death penalty. I, too, am opposed. But I am not so sure that a finer understanding of its emotional aspects will lead to its demise. Because law historically has done such a miserable job reckoning with emotion, and because the landscape *is* so complex, I am not sure *what* the more emotionally intelligent world will look like. Perhaps in this world the death penalty dies; perhaps it survives but with fewer glaring contradictions and flaws. We'll certainly be better off than we are now, but precisely where we'll be is an open question.

REPLY

SUSAN A. BANDES

Sometimes, as Robert Schopp and LaJuana Davis point out, the capital system explicitly regulates emotion. But too often its regulatory choices occur below the radar. The antisympathy instructions Schopp mentions illustrate the problem. Capital cases evoke anger toward the defendant, grief for the victim, and empathy for the survivors. As Terry Maroney articulately explains, these reactions are considered so natural they are not even classified as emotional. That term is reserved for reactions that deviate from the norm. When jurors are instructed to avoid sympathy, but given no instruction on how to handle anger or grief, they may well assume that sympathy is off-limits *because* it is emotional, and that their other reactions are appropriate because they are purely rational. Choices about which emotions the law should encourage or discourage go unacknowledged.

Thus in the case Davis describes, the problem is not that the law abhors emotional responses, or that it scorns empathic responses, but that it uses the category "emotional" to dismiss disfavored attitudes without analysis. Jurors who cry when deciding whether to put a defendant to death are branded emotional and unreliable. Jurors who show no ambivalence about sentencing a defendant to death, including those whose empathy for the victim or his family seems to overwhelm their ability to evaluate the defendant's mitigation evidence at sentencing, are regarded as rational and tough-minded. We need to recognize all these reactions as emotional. Then, as Schopp recommends, we can debate which emotions advance the appropriate goals of the system and learn how channel those that do not.

Douglas Berman and Stephanos Bibas argue in support of victim impact statements that "in fairness, both sides should be equally able to bring emotional arguments to bear and seek catharsis and healing,"[1] but they offer no support for their assertion that fairness in capital cases means "equal treatment" for both sides. Nor is it clear what "both sides" means in this context. The defendant and his family are not seeking catharsis or healing; they are seeking to keep the defendant alive. The state may argue that its role is to help the victim's family heal, but at bottom it is the survivors, not the parties, whose healing is implicated. Bibas and Berman blur the distinction between the state's goals and the needs of victims and survivors.

There is no empirical evidence that capital punishment promotes healing. In fact, there is no agreement on what healing means in the capital context—or what it would require. A chance for the survivor to address the court or confront the defendant? A death sentence? An execution? We need a careful discussion

---

1. Berman and Bibas comment at 644.

about whether capital punishment should serve therapeutic ends. The more nuanced our discussion about the goals of punishment—including the emotional goals—the better we can determine what sorts of punishment will advance them.

Moreover, any evaluation of victim impact statements must be part of a larger discussion about the emotional dynamics of the capital trial as a whole. There is evidence that by the time many capital jurors reach the penalty phase, they tend to be so angry at the defendant and so sympathetic toward the victim and his family that they cannot consider the defendant's mitigation evidence.[2] Whether it is fair to introduce additional emotionally charged evidence about the victim at this point depends on the effect the evidence has on the jury's ability to deliberate in accord with constitutional requirements.

I do not argue, as Jeffrie Murphy suggests, that the desire for retribution is illegitimate or corrupt, or that, as Davis suggests, it is "thinly disguised bloodlust."[3] I argue that retribution draws on a complex blend of emotions and that we can't identify the emotions retribution draws upon unless we let the language of emotion into the conversation. Likewise I do not argue, as Mary Sigler claims, that intuitions of justice are "little more than the product of media manipulation."[4] I argue that traditional retributivist discourse relies on a simplistic and sanitized model of how attitudes about punishment are formed and communicated.

I agree that a core purpose of the criminal justice system is to give voice to shared moral outrage at heinous crimes. But to what punishments ought that moral outrage lead? That question is key. The history of capital punishment in the United States has veered between enthusiasm for the death penalty and revulsion at its excesses. It has been animated by moral outrage but also by racism and other ugly emotions. If we want to give voice to moral outrage, but not to the impulse for revenge that Sigler addresses, the immediate visceral hatred that Joseph Kennedy talks about, or the racism that has long infected our criminal justice system, we need to distinguish these emotions and debate what governmental actions should follow from them.

Berman and Bibas speculate that if we don't execute people, the unsatisfied punitive emotions of the populace may be expressed in harmful ways. But this prediction assumes shared moral intuitions not just about which crimes deserve the most serious punishment, but about what that punishment should be. Paul Robinson's studies of empirical desert reveal widely shared intuitions about what crimes are most serious, but no similar shared intuitions about how to punish those crimes.[5] Moreover, the justice system does not merely reflect moral

---

2. *See, e.g.*, William J. Bowers, *The Capital Jury Project: Rationale, Design, and Preview of Early Findings*, 70 IND. L.J. 1043, 1100–01 (1995).

3. Davis comment at 654.

4. Sigler comment at 646.

5. *See* Paul H. Robinson and Robert Kurzban, *Concordance and Conflict in Intuitions of Justice*, 91 MINN. L. REV. 1829 (2007).

outrage. It helps shape emotional expectations about what punishments ought to satisfy punitive emotions.

Murphy says the question of whether traditional retributive theory provides useful counsel to those who determine sentencing "awaits . . . investigation."[6] The Supreme Court's recent decision in *Kennedy v. Louisiana*[7] illustrates my point that retributive theory cannot provide sufficient guidance without reference to emotion. When the Court turned to traditional retributive theory to help determine whether the death penalty is a just punishment for child rape, it found little guidance. Both the majority and the dissent analyses of retribution quickly evolved into discussions of the emotional aspects of retribution: the depraved heart of the perpetrator; the anguish, fear, and betrayal felt by victims and their families; the psychological impact of a capital trial. These discussions revealed a profound confusion about the role of emotion in death penalty jurisprudence. A robust scholarly discussion about emotion would bring needed clarity to the retributive debate.

Murphy objects that I am demanding empirical answers from moral philosophers. He argues that the philosophical pursuit of "an ideal model of how punishment should be determined in a just society"[8] is separate from the empirical task of determining how punishment is implemented in *our* society. This sharp distinction troubles me. Capital punishment has long been defended based on the notion that an ideal model exists—if only human beings would behave differently and implement it correctly. Murphy promises that retributivists "will be the first in line to condemn" the capital punishment system if it is "arbitrary, random, and unpredictable."[9] It is.

As several commentators note, and as I have long argued, empathy provides no normative answer to the hard questions about whose emotions ought to be heard or privileged in the capital system. Carol Steiker has it exactly right—empathy is not an emotion.[10] It is an essential human capacity; one that allows us to consider the concerns and feelings of others. As Kennedy and Steiker both observe, the current system promotes distance from the consequences of execution. To fairly judge the death penalty, we need to make every effort to "imaginatively enter the emotions"[11] of victims and their families, defendants and their families, prosecutors, defense attorneys, judges, chaplains, wardens, and executioners.[12]

---

6. Murphy comment at 648.

7. 128 S. Ct. 2641 (2008).

8. Murphy comment at 647.

9. *Id.* at 648.

10. *See* Steiker comment at 653.

11. *Id.*

12. Davis suggests I consider actors other than the jury. This has been my project since 1996. *See, e.g.*, Susan Bandes, *Empathy, Narrative, and Victim Impact Statements*, 63 U. CHI. L. REV. 361 (1996) (judges); Susan Bandes, *Repression and Denial in Criminal*

Doing so will give us a fuller and more visceral understanding of what is at stake, not just in the front-page cases[13] but across the board. There is no guarantee that this understanding will result in abolition of the death penalty. My hope that it will is based, in part, on the regularity with which wardens, executioners, judges, and others who have seen the death penalty at close range have repudiated it.

Sigler charges that I approve mainly of the emotions that lead away from execution. If her point is simply that those of us who study the death penalty must make every effort to understand the emotions of all concerned, I agree. But if she is arguing that the job of the scholar is to avoid making normative distinctions among those emotions, she is arguing for something both impossible and undesirable. As Maroney rightly points out, the capital system unavoidably privileges some emotions and marginalizes others. Not every emotion can or should be given free rein in the capital system—there are choices to be made. If Sigler is arguing that scholars ought to have no stake in how the death penalty debate turns out, I strongly disagree. As the work of Antonio Damasio and others has taught us,[14] emotion is the essential property that makes us care not just about amassing information, but about getting things right—the essential ingredient in what Murphy eloquently calls "a passionate commitment to justice and what justice requires."[15]

Lawyering, 9 BUFF. CRIM. L. REV. 339 (2006) (defense attorneys); Susan Bandes, *Loyalty to One's Convictions: The Prosecutor and Tunnel Vision*, 49 HOW. L.J. 475 (2006) (prosecutors). However, my central argument is that others ought to join the conversation.

13. *See* Kennedy comment at 651.

14. *See, e.g.*, Antonio Damasio, DESCARTES' ERROR: EMOTION, REASON, AND THE HUMAN BRAIN 193 (1994).

15. Murphy comment at 648.

30. MERCY'S DECLINE AND ADMINISTRATIVE LAW'S ASCENDANCE

RACHEL E. BARKOW*

Americans are living in punitive and unforgiving times. A great deal of scholarship has sought to explain the punitiveness, particularly our skyrocketing rate of incarceration and the push for longer and mandatory sentences. But scholars have spent less time considering our growing reluctance to forgive, specifically the increasing resistance to executive clemency and jury nullification. These unreviewable acts of mercy are viewed with derision and suspicion, not applause.

Why is mercy on the decline? The political economy of punishment provides one answer, as does American culture and sociology. But there is an additional contributing cause for the decline of mercy: the rise of the administrative state and the concepts of law that have emerged alongside it.

The rise of the administrative state has made unreviewable discretion an anomaly in the law and a phenomenon to be viewed with suspicion. Indeed, the central concern of administrative law is the unchecked exercise of discretion. Courts therefore insist that agencies operate within legally defined boundaries and give explanations for their actions. With the rise of the administrative state and the dominance of administrative law, our legal culture has come to view this oversight as critical. Exercises of mercy such as jury nullification and an unqualified executive power to grant clemency sit uneasily beside an administrative state that faces such scrutiny, for these exercises of mercy are precisely the type of unreviewable exercises of discretion that administrative law seeks to control.[1]

---

* Professor of Law, New York University School of Law. A longer version of this core text appeared in Rachel E. Barkow, *The Ascent of the Administrative State and the Demise of Mercy*, 121 Harv. L. Rev. 1332 (2008).

1. There are other actors who have the power to deliver mercy in the criminal justice system. Parole boards, where they exist, can release offenders, and judges can exercise discretion in some cases to lessen sentences. These exercises of mercy have also faced criticism with strong links to administrative law concerns. Because of space limitations, my focus is exclusively on nullification and pardons because reforms to parole and sentencing have made nullification and pardons the last remaining forms of unreviewable mercy in some places. Moreover, the link between the administrative state and the diminished status of jury nullification and executive clemency is less obvious than the link between the administrative state and reforms in parole and judicial sentencing. The use of commissions and boards to regulate sentencing and parole through guidelines is directly tied to administrative law, so less explanatory work is necessary. But to the extent that the link is clear in the case of parole and judicial sentencing, it further supports the claim made here that administrative law is a pervasive force in criminal law today.

The development of the administrative state is also a significant part of the reason that our legal culture focuses on the courts—and courts alone—to prevent unfair applications of the law. The dominance of agencies has necessarily been accompanied by an increase in statutes that govern those agencies; concomitantly, courts have faced an ever-growing number of regulatory cases involving statutory interpretation. Through their power to ensure that agency actions are consistent with these laws, judges use a variety of interpretive tools to ensure that individual exercises of agency decision-making are consistent with legislative intent. In this legal culture, it is viewed as the role of courts, through statutory interpretation, to fix unfair applications of the law. A layperson juror or an elected executive has no obvious expertise in this world of statutes, so it is hard to understand why these actors should be permitted to operate unchecked.

This core text expands on these points and concludes with a normative critique, based on key differences between criminal law and administrative law, that challenges the application of an administrative law framework to the exercise of mercy in criminal cases.

I. THE OBSESSION WITH DISCRETION

The rise of the administrative state brought with it a new emphasis on the importance of predictable processes, reasoned decision-making, and judicial review. As these cornerstones of administrative law have become embedded in our legal culture, actions in tension with this model have fallen out of favor unless they are similar to the rare exceptions to these principles that exist within administrative law itself. The rise of administrative law therefore offers a key window to understanding both the decline of nullification and clemency, on the one hand, and the relative acceptance of prosecutorial discretion, on the other.

A. The Development of Administrative Law and the Importance of Judicial Review

The birth of administrative agencies posed a dilemma for traditional constitutional and legal analysis. Agencies challenged the nation's commitment to separation of powers by combining executive, legislative, and judicial power. Moreover, agencies have vast authority; their decisions have profound consequences for the nation's economy and for individual rights and liberties. If the officials at these agencies could exercise their authority without oversight, citizens would become subjects to unelected bureaucrats and democracy would be compromised. The central purpose of administrative law has been to control agency discretion to keep this leviathan in check.

Administrative law therefore requires that agencies provide reasons for their decisions, follow a regular process, and face judicial review. The Administrative Procedure Act (APA) dictates agency procedures and generally provides for judicial review to check against arbitrary and capricious decision-making. This means that agencies must provide the reasons behind their decisions, support in the administrative record for their conclusions, and an explanation if the agency departs from a prior practice. Additional open government laws make agencies further accountable.

As the administrative state has grown, so have these central concepts. Judicial review, reasoned decisions, and regularized processes have become the hallmarks of acceptable legal action. The importance of these concepts to modern legal culture can be seen time and again in judicial decisions covering a wide range of legal doctrines and in scholarship encompassing the sweep of law. It is the increasingly rare legal issue that falls outside the scope of judicial review.

B. The Threat of Unreviewable Discretion

Three central means by which mercy is exercised in criminal matters—jury nullification, executive clemency, and prosecutorial discretion not to charge— are not subject to the basic framework of reasoned decision-making, regularized process, and judicial review. Nullification and clemency have faced significant criticism for that reason; prosecutorial discretion to be lenient has not. The common thread that accounts for this difference is administrative law itself.

1. **Jury Nullification** Jury nullification occurs when a jury votes to acquit a defendant despite the fact that the defendant is guilty under the letter of the law. A jury may nullify because it believes the law is generally unjust, because applying the law in the particular case would be unfair, or because it believes the punishment is too harsh.

The contrast between jury nullification and the core principles of administrative law is stark. No two juries are the same, they need not provide reasons for their decisions, and there is no particular process that they must follow when conducting their deliberations. When juries acquit, their decision is unreviewable.

It should therefore come as no surprise that this broad power has faced criticism as the principles of administrative law have become entrenched in our legal culture. For example, Andrew Leipold has said of jury nullification that:

> [It] is startling . . . that the decisions are not subject to any review, that no explanations are ever required from the decision-makers, and that the aggrieved party—the community that is unable to punish a lawbreaker—has no recourse. In virtually no other context is a government-sanctioned decision given such deference, and in no other area would such unfettered decision-making be tolerated.[2]

---

2. Andrew D. Leipold, *Rethinking Jury Nullification*, 82 VA. L. REV. 253, 307 (1996) (emphasis omitted) (footnote omitted).

Other critics have similarly argued that to allow nullification is to endorse "a system of justice where the fate of both society and a defendant is left to the arbitrary and capricious notions of at most twelve individuals."[3]

It is not just legal scholars who have expressed worries about jury nullification because of concerns grounded in administrative law principles. Courts have sought limits on the jury's power that roughly track the emergence of the administrative state and the growing prevalence and influence of administrative law.

The most significant limitation on the jury's power to nullify came just as the administrative state was forming. In 1895, shortly after the birth of the first major federal agency in 1887, the Supreme Court held in *Sparf v. United States* that juries do not have a right to ignore a court's instructions on the law.[4] It was an era characterized by a widespread belief in the administrative sphere that there were right answers to be found by professionals with training and expertise. According to the Court in *Sparf*, the relevant professionals on questions of law, including criminal law, were judges, not untrained jurors.

The link between administrative law and judicial doubts about jury nullification can also be seen in court decisions rejecting defendants' requests to have jurors instructed about their power (as opposed to their right) to nullify the law. Courts refused to instruct juries about this power to "avoid[] . . . intolerable caprice."[5] These same courts, at the same time, were creating "hard-look" review of agency decision-making to avoid caprice.[6]

And once hard-look review of agencies was entrenched, courts began employing more aggressive mechanisms to limit jury nullification. This included removal or contempt proceedings against jurors who failed to follow the judge's instructions, as well as contempt, obstruction, or tampering charges against individuals who attempted to inform prospective jurors of their power to nullify. Courts also rejected attempts to inform juries about the sentencing consequences of their decisions for fear that jurors might use that information to nullify the law.

The public seems to have accepted these limits on nullification. For example, voters have rejected ballot initiatives that would allow defendants to make nullification arguments to jurors. Accounts in the media account also reflect skepticism about nullification.

It is not possible, of course, to prove definitively that the entrenchment of administrative law principles is a cause of greater distrust and discomfort with jury nullification among legal scholars, jurists, or the general public. The link could be attributed instead to the greater hostility toward criminals that has permeated society in recent decades. But the inference that administrative law

---

3. Rebecca Love Kourlis, *Not Jury Nullification; Not a Call for Ethical Reform; But Rather a Case for Judicial Control*, 67 U. Colo. L. Rev. 1109, 1111–12 (1996).

4. 156 U.S. 51, 101 (1895).

5. *United States v. Dougherty*, 473 F.2d 1113, 1134 (D.C. Cir. 1972).

6. *Greater Boston Television Corp. v. FCC*, 444 F.2d 841, 851 (D.C. Cir. 1970).

concepts are also playing a role in the greater distrust of jury nullification seems warranted for three reasons. First, there is a substantive inconsistency between the two frameworks. Second, the greatest limits on jury nullification have come alongside the birth of the administrative state and the most significant developments in administrative law. Third, those in the best position to feel the tension—scholars and jurists—have expressed skepticism about jury nullification in terms that resonate with administrative law principles. At the very least, then, administrative law is providing a framework for these criticisms. Because these legal elites are often in the position to protect or hinder exercises of mercy by shaping legal rules, their use of administrative law to support limits on nullification cannot be ignored as irrelevant.

2. Executive Clemency The jury is not the only actor vested by the Constitution with unreviewable power to dispense mercy. The Constitution gives the President the power to "grant Reprieves and Pardons for Offences against the United States, except in Cases of Impeachment."[7] The President can use this power, which cannot be limited by Congress, to issue a conditional or full pardon or to commute a sentence, and relief can be granted either before or after conviction. The President need not follow any particular process or provide reasons for his decision, and the decision is largely immune from judicial review. Clemency decisions at the state level likewise "have not traditionally been the business of courts."[8] Clemency is therefore a means of checking overbroad laws or overly harsh sentences and is similarly at odds with the traditional administrative law model.

Because of its tension with administrative law, the clemency power has faced increasing criticism. For example, five Justices of the Supreme Court recently indicated that they may be willing to review clemency procedures for some minimum level of process under the Due Process Clause.[9] This is a stark departure from the Court's prior approach to clemency, and the motivating rationale for the switch is grounded in concerns about arbitrary and capricious decision-making. Four of the Justices, for example, were concerned about not having a review mechanism in place to check a situation where "a state official flipped a coin to determine whether to grant clemency, or in a case where the State arbitrarily denied a prisoner any access to its clemency process."[10]

Legal scholars, elected officials, and the media have also criticized clemency and have emphasized concerns about process and the need for more administrative law checks. Scholars worry that the "absence of procedural and substantive constraints on the clemency power . . . permits arbitrary decisionmaking by the

---

7. U.S. CONST. art. II, § 2, cl. 1.

8. *Conn. Bd. of Pardons v. Dumschat*, 452 U.S. 458, 464 (1981).

9. *See Ohio Adult Parole Auth. v. Woodard*, 523 U.S. 272, 289, 292 (1998).

10. *Id.*

Executive that is, for most intents and purposes, unreviewable."[11] Members of Congress and the media have echoed these concerns.

Although politics is likely the central motivator of these critiques, it is important not to overlook administrative law's contribution. Although the decline in clemency correlates with tough-on-crime politics, this era is also the one in which hard-look review of agencies emerged. What is being said about clemency is also telling. The discourse on clemency is not simply dominated by get-tough rhetoric. On the contrary, much of the criticism of clemency focuses on the process and not on the substantive merits of particular cases. When President Bill Clinton granted a number of controversial pardons on his last day in office, for example, the criticism largely focused on the fact that the President bypassed the review process of the Office of the Pardon Attorney. The Justices who recognized a role for due process in clemency similarly used administrative law concepts to justify their position. Even if this rhetoric masks a real motivation to be tough on crime, the fact that administrative law concepts are employed shows that these principles are thought to have resonance.

Administrative law also provides a better explanation than raw politics for the existence and perceived importance of the administrative procedures, regulations, and institutions many jurisdictions employ for clemency decisions. Roughly two-thirds of the states use administrative boards that either provide the governor with nonbinding advice about pardons or share power with the governor in making pardon decisions. Five states vest the ultimate pardon decision in a board instead of the governor. These pardon boards were set up to check "arbitrary and capricious" pardon decisions. Indeed, most state pardon advisory boards were created contemporaneously with the birth of the administrative state, and after the New Deal some states modeled their boards along the lines of independent regulatory agencies. Federal regulations governing the issuance of pardons were similarly established around the time of the creation of the first major federal administrative agency. The link with administrative law and control of pardons is therefore a strong one.

Finally, and perhaps most importantly, it is not just tough-on-crime politicians, interest groups, and voters who have targeted pardons for criticism. As noted, legal elites—scholars and jurists—have challenged clemency, and they have done so in the language of administrative law. These individuals are critical in shaping the legal response to clemency, so their resistance based on administrative law concerns is important in its own right.

3. Prosecutorial Discretion Prosecutors possess a similar unreviewable power to be merciful because of their broad control over charging decisions. They need

---

11. Brian M. Hoffstadt, *Normalizing the Federal Clemency Power*, 79 Tex. L. Rev. 561, 597 (2001).

not follow any particular protocols or provide reasons before reaching a decision not to bring charges.

Despite its similarity to nullification and clemency, prosecutorial discretion has not faced the same intensity of attack or criticism that pardons and nullification have. To be sure, legal scholars have expressed concern about prosecutorial discretion, but most worry about the coercive power of prosecutors, not their power to be lenient. More importantly, courts have refused to police prosecutorial charging decisions, and prosecutorial power is rarely highlighted in the press as a cause for concern. As William Stuntz has noted, prosecutors' power to be lenient is "widely seen as necessary, and frequently as a good thing: It permits mercy, and it avoids flooding the system with low-level crimes."[12]

Why are the jury's power to nullify and the executive's power to grant clemency viewed with suspicion whereas prosecutorial power to be lenient is seen "as a good thing"? One possibility might be that prosecutors are seen as more accountable for their actions. Most local prosecutors are elected, so voters ultimately police the decisions of most prosecutors. Juries, in contrast, answer to no one. And even though the executive is also elected, clemency decisions are such a small part of the executive's decision-making portfolio that it might not be realistic to say that voters can hold the executive accountable for clemency decisions when other types of decisions are more important to voters. Clemency decisions are also often made in the waning days of an administration that is not facing reelection.

But although accountability might explain part of the varying treatment of different actors exercising mercy, it does not offer a full explanation. As an initial matter, not all prosecutors are directly accountable. Federal prosecutors are not elected, yet they have received the same deferential treatment as prosecutors who are elected. Moreover, even if prosecutors are accountable in an election, for what are they are accountable? They are likely judged on their affirmative charging decisions, not their declinations, because a prosecutor's decision not to charge is sequestered from *any* kind of review, not just judicial review. Decisions not to charge are generally unknown to any actor other than the defendant or, if relevant, the victim. Unless the crime received media attention, the public and elected officials will have no knowledge of the facts that support bringing charges. Juries, in contrast, sit in public trials, so the evidence in favor of a conviction is there for all to see. Pardon decisions also typically take place after a conviction, so the case against the defendant is similarly accessible. This openness makes it much easier to identify cases where the jury or an executive has abused its discretion, which in turn can cast doubt on why discretion rests with that actor in the first place.

---

12. William J. Stuntz, *Self-Defeating Crimes*, 86 VA. L. REV. 1871, 1892 (2000).

Administrative law also provides an answer for why prosecutorial discretion is viewed with less suspicion than the other mechanisms of mercy. In contrast to juries and executives, prosecutors are seen as making an "expert" determination about priority-setting when they choose not to bring charges. Just as agencies escape oversight when they refuse to act—because they are balancing resource constraints and other considerations—prosecutors avoid scrutiny because they are viewed as making a professional determination based on their expertise in prioritizing cases. Indeed, the Supreme Court cited the parallels between prosecutorial decisions not to indict and agency decisions not to bring enforcement actions when it determined that the latter are not subject to judicial review.[13] Thus, one of the rare pockets of administrative decision-making that lies beyond court oversight can be understood to justify a similarly discretionary feature of criminal decision-making. It is therefore not surprising that prosecutorial power to be lenient has not been subject to the same level of scrutiny as the other pockets of mercy, for it is the only one that is consistent with current administrative law doctrine.

II. THE CENTRALITY OF JUDGES

Judges are critical to administrative law, and their key role as overseer has permeated our legal culture. Because agencies are creatures of statutes, and because statutory interpretation is a question of law, judges have gained new powers as interpreters of statutes. Judges have used their interpretation powers to correct perceived deficiencies with a law's application in a particular case, to reject agency actions as inconsistent with even the broadest statutory mandates, and to reach outcomes consistent with the judge's policy preferences.

Judges have also given themselves broad authority over agencies by interpreting the APA to allow judges to take a hard look at an agency's justifications for its policies. Courts look to see whether the agency "examine[d] the relevant data and articulate[d] a satisfactory explanation for its action including a 'rational connection between the facts found and the choice made.'"[14] This, too, allows judges to reject outcomes they view as unfair or unwise.

As a result of judges' broad powers over the statutes that govern the administrative state and their willingness to interpret such statutes to ensure justice in particular cases—not to mention the judiciary's similar approach to interpreting the Constitution—our legal culture looks to judges as uniquely qualified to solve inequities in a law's application.

---

13. *See Heckler v. Chaney*, 470 U.S. 821, 832 (1985).

14. *Motor Vehicle Mfrs. Ass'n v. State Farm Mut. Auto. Ins. Co.*, 463 U.S. 29, 43 (1983) (quoting *Burlington Truck Lines, Inc. v. United States*, 371 U.S. 156, 168 (1962)).

Because judges stand ready to police failings in the legal system and seemingly have the power to correct what might be wrong with a law in the administrative context, it is difficult for lawyers and the public to see why there might be a need for someone without expertise in the law—for example, a lay jury, a governor, or the President—to have the same power in criminal cases. Indeed, if even the experts who work at agencies in highly technical fields are subject to oversight by the courts, why should a group of laypersons or the President escape judicial oversight for their decisions? This impulse explains why legal scholars who identify problems with the administration of criminal justice tend to look to judges to provide the answers—and why decisions by other actors are disfavored.

III. THE PLACE FOR MERCY

Administrative law has valuable insights for criminal law, but there are also key differences between the two fields that should not be overlooked. The administrative state rests on the notion that agencies must be held to the laws that govern them. Those laws are, in turn, assumed to represent a balancing of the relevant interests, and to the extent provisions of these laws are not drafted perfectly or do not seem to fulfill the larger purpose of the legislation, judges are relied upon to correct these failings.

Critically, neither of these assumptions holds true for criminal law. The process that produces criminal laws is far less balanced than the one that produces administrative laws, because in criminal law, the powerful groups uniformly line up in favor of greater government power and harsher penalties. Criminal laws will therefore be more likely to yield unjust results in particular cases unless there is a check that can operate outside the laws themselves.

While judges might be the appropriate check in the context of administrative law, they have little freedom to provide individual justice in criminal cases. Modern criminal laws are written in broad terms that give prosecutors broad charging discretion. Most cases never go to trial. Once a defendant admits guilt, laws often dictate a particular sentence—and a particularly harsh sentence—regardless of individual facts or circumstances.

Nullification and clemency can provide the individualization otherwise lacking in criminal law. With judges out of the picture as a viable option, the only other actor that can check overbroad or overly punitive criminal laws is the prosecutor. But prosecutors do not have the same incentives to exercise this power. Prosecutors are unlikely to advocate for systemic reform, because current laws are used as bargaining chips to make obtaining convictions easier. Nor can prosecutors be relied upon to act as a sufficient check in individual cases, because their success is often judged by the number of convictions they obtain, not the cases they dismiss. And after investing time and energy in investigating a case, they are far less likely to decide to exercise mercy than is a jury or executive that has not expended the same effort. Thus, even though prosecutors possess the same discretion as jurors and executives to show leniency, they face institutional pressures that push against its exercise.

Moreover, although prosecutors have more expertise in criminal law than do jurors or the executive, the question of what constitutes justice in a particular case is one on which the entire polity has the relevant expertise. Jurors and the executive bring particularly useful perspectives. Jurors are the best representatives of that community's sense of what justice would require in a particular case. The executive's perspective on mercy is also valuable because he or she must balance law enforcement interests against other values of his or her constituents.

Requiring juries or executives to give reasons for their decisions and subjecting those reasons to judicial review would depress mercy and individualized justice. The jury is valuable precisely because it acts as a nongovernmental check that functions outside the law. Any scrutiny of the reasons for a jury's decision by a governmental body (either an agency or a court) would compromise the jury's ability to provide individualized justice based on the community's values. As for clemency, in the current political climate, executives already face disincentives to exercise it. If an executive had to provide reasons and face a review process, it is likely that the already depressed numbers of pardons and commutations would fall still further. More fundamentally, review requires that there be some specified standard to allow good reasons for leniency to be sifted from bad ones. But ex ante specification of when mercy is appropriate contradicts the reason for having mercy in the first place: It is because not all factors can be anticipated in advance that the discretionary check is important.

So although unreviewable discretion is not without costs—there is always the risk of inappropriate discrimination—that risk is outweighed by the need for individualized justice in criminal cases. In today's political climate, in which legislators succumb to get-tough politics, write harsh laws, and tie the hands of judges, juries and executives are often the last hope for individualized justice. And justice should be the aim of all law, administrative or criminal.

COMMENTS

SUBJECTIVE AND OBJECTIVE DISCRETION OF PROSECUTORS

RONALD F. WRIGHT* AND MARC L. MILLER**

The administrative state generates its own body of procedural law—administrative law—and its own legal mindset. It also generates its own distinctive brand of criminal justice. Rachel Barkow notes the effects of the administrative state mindset on the "mercy" institutions of criminal justice, especially jury nullification, executive clemency, and prosecutorial discretion. Our comment lays out the distinction between "subjective" and "objective" discretion. Once we attend to this distinction, the answer to one of the puzzles Barkow identifies—why we tolerate prosecutorial mercy, but not jury or executive mercy—comes into sharper focus.[1]

The objective (or external) account of discretion is a staple of administrative law, grounded in various positivist theories of law. The law sets outer boundaries, but any administrative choice that falls within those boundaries is something distinct from law—call it discretion—because there is no law to apply. From the objective perspective, only the boundaries amount to "legal" rules, because only at that point can one government institution (typically a court) impose those limits on another unwilling government actor. Under this objective account of discretion, prosecutors encounter few *legal* limits—limits imposed from outside the prosecutor's office. They have plentiful charging options within generous (or overlapping) criminal codes in the United States, and act without fear that some other institutional actor will enforce a boundary.

The subjective (or internal) perspective on discretion offers a very different portrait of prosecutors at work.[2] Public actors, viewing their work from inside an administrative organization, tell outsiders that they actually hold little discretion. The choices that the law theoretically leaves open are misleading; they significantly overstate what is realistically available. Executive branch actors—whether lawyers or not—feel obliged to justify their choices based on public-regarding reasons. Officials with legal training take formative educational experiences with them: They feel bound to remain consistent and to offer equal treatment to all members of the public. Actors also assert that they see the risks of bias and work

---

* Professor of Law and Associate Dean for Academic Affairs, Wake Forest University School of Law.

** Ralph W. Bilby Professor of Law, James E. Rogers College of Law, University of Arizona.

1. *See* Marc L. Miller and Ronald F. Wright, *The Black Box*, 94 IOWA L. REV. 125 (2008).

2. *Cf.* H.L.A. Hart, THE CONCEPT OF LAW 90–91 (2d ed. 1994).

consciously to eliminate it. Such obligations mark the weakness of discretion as public officials experience it from the inside.

An objective perspective on discretion makes it hard to listen with open ears when executive agents explain their decisions. Such listeners might say that executive explanations are "self-justifying." From this vantage point, explanations of an official decision that appear in the absence of external enforcement merely amount to the statement, "trust me."

But executive agents explain the constraints on their choices in consistent and heartfelt terms, suggesting that they reflect a psychological reality and not mere rationalization. How often have you heard a prosecutor say something like "we rarely deviate from the sentencing guidelines," or "we carefully control any decision not to charge domestic violence cases"? How sincere does the prosecutor seem to you when asserting that any apparent departures from general rules are "consistent" and "reasonable"?

Subjective discretion helps explain one of the mysteries of the mercy institutions that Barkow explores: Why does the legal community accept mercy from a prosecutor's office, but not from jury nullification or executive clemency? One distinction among the mercy institutions of the criminal justices system is how long they remain intact. It takes time to develop the social norms that supplement legal constraints to form a sense of accountability and restraint. Prosecutors' offices have the time to develop this culture of limits; juries that decide a single case do not. Executives who grant clemency do not repeat the task often enough to develop a real culture of consistency.

This culture of consistency and principle is related to expertise, but also distinct; it is related to electoral accountability, but also distinct. The legal community senses that prosecutors respect something more than legally enforced rules as they stay within their boundaries: They respect the norms that show them how to do their jobs well.

Most prosecutors experience discretion in light of norms—and not just external legal limits—because they work in groups. Prosecutors' offices collect data and train new attorneys; supervisors review personnel and announce policies. The subjective perspective on discretion derives from the prosecutors' office that creates incentives to act and to explain cases in consistent terms. Prosecutors learn from other prosecutors how to do the job well; these social norms add a layer onto the legal rules that prosecutors must apply. This sense of consistency and constraint, developed from within, best explains the wide acceptance of prosecutors as dispensers of mercy. It explains more, we believe, than the arguments based on expertise and lack of visibility that Barkow emphasizes.

MERCY'S DISGUISE, PROSECUTORIAL POWER, AND EQUALITY'S MODERN CONSTRUCTION

DOUGLAS A. BERMAN*

Rachel Barkow astutely examines the decline of two historically important criminal justice safety valves: jury nullification and executive clemency. But I doubt the ascendance of administrative law truly explains the demise of these mechanisms of mercy; rather, I attribute their decline to the modern tendency of equality concerns to foster criminal-justice punitiveness. Any act of jury nullification or executive clemency provides disparate leniency for certain defendants and thus can offend a norm of equal justice in the criminal justice system. And this equality norm is now promoted principally by prosecutors, who can construct it to foster their power and discretion to be merciful or punitive with little oversight.

To begin, I must take issue with Barkow's claim that mercy is in decline. Modern legislatures have greatly expanded criminal codes and enacted tougher sentencing rules. But modern prosecutors rarely pursue all possible criminal charges and seek to max out all possible punishments. Rather, armed with lots of punitive bargaining chips, modern prosecutors practice mercy in virtually every case through their declination, charging, and plea bargaining choices. Mercy is still being exercised on a regular basis, but it is now largely hidden inside the offices (and minds) of prosecutors.

Prosecutors might resist the suggestion that declination, charging, and plea bargaining choices involve mercy. But it seems accurate and fair to describe a prosecutor's decision to keep a lawbreaker from facing the full wrath of the criminal justice system as an act of mercy. Indeed, though prosecutors may assert that office priorities and limited resources explain discretionary choices, the setting of prosecutorial priorities is surely influenced by assessments of which classes of offenders should and should not be spared from the unforgiving realities of our modern criminal justice system. In sum, despite the modern demise of jury nullification and executive clemency, I submit that mercy is not in decline: mercy abounds, but is disguised within the enormous black box of prosecutorial discretion.

To her credit, Barkow properly acknowledges that prosecutors possess "unreviewable power to be merciful,"[1] and she recognizes that prosecutorial discretion has escaped the kind of judicial supervision characteristic of the rise of administrative law. But she claims this is "consistent with current administrative law

---

* William B. Saxbe Designated Professor of Law, Moritz College of Law, Ohio State University.
1. Barkow core text at 668.

doctrine"[2] because "prosecutors are seen as making an 'expert' determination about priority-setting when they choose not to bring charges."[3] I am not convinced.

With the rise of administrative law, generalist judges wholly lacking in scientific or economic training now vigorously review the "expert" work of the EPA, the FCC, the FDA, the SEC, and other alphabet agencies. I find peculiar the notion that these same judges—many of whom come to the bench with experiences as prosecutors—feel unqualified to second-guess "expert" prosecutorial decisions. Moreover, many recent prosecutorial mistakes and scandals—ranging from wrongful convictions, to the notorious Duke lacrosse case, to recent U.S. Attorney firings—should undermine any claim that expertise drives all prosecutorial choices and that their discretion must be free from any judicial scrutiny. Yet despite obvious prosecutorial problems, few state or federal judges have started to scrutinize carefully or even question seriously the consequential declination, charging, and plea bargaining choices made by prosecutors.

These realities prompt my assertion that Barkow puts too much stock in administrative law and gives too little attention to prosecutors' use of equal justice norms to serve their parochial interests. Given prosecutors' awesome power over individuals, the exercise of prosecutorial discretion could and should be a central concern for modern administrative law. And few prosecutors likely have read (or even have heard of) the cases and doctrines Barkow discusses. What prosecutors do know is how to take advantage of equal justice concerns: They will contest acts of mercy by others—not just juries and governors, but also sentencing judges—by lamenting the prospect of unwarranted and unjust disparities. But if pressed about their own charging and bargaining choices, prosecutors will often just baldly assert that their own discretionary decisions were actually intended to serve equal justice principles.

The most tangible and troublesome example of these realities appears in the modern federal sentencing system. Federal prosecutors have aggressively and repeatedly assailed judicial decisions to sentence below ranges suggested by the federal guidelines by bemoaning transgressions of the norm of equal justice. But federal sentencing data and expert analysis regularly reveal (1) that prosecutorial charging and bargaining practices are far more consequential in determining federal sentencing outcomes than judicial discretion, and (2) that discriminatory and otherwise unjustified factors seem to influence the exercise of sentencing discretion by federal prosecutors. But even while the evidence mounts of federal prosecutors exercising discretionary mercy in unjust and unequal ways, observers and defendants are all still waiting for administrative law to start taking note of these realities.

---

2. *Id.* at 670.
3. *Id.*

POLITICAL VERSUS ADMINISTRATIVE JUSTICE

STEPHANOS BIBAS*

Rachel Barkow's core text captures an important and overlooked dimension of the decline of mercy: the administrative ideal of justice as rules and discretion as danger. Though most commentators applaud this trend to equate law with specified, judicially enforceable rules, Barkow rightly finds it worrisome and regrettable.

The problem, as Barkow explains, is that equating justice with rules makes the law judiciocentric. Emphasizing rules does reduce dangers of discrimination and idiosyncratic preferences. But it hardly eliminates them, as shown by prosecutors' manipulation of sentencing guidelines and mandatory minimum penalties. Although actors may comply with moderately binding rules, rigid rules simply drive discretion underground. A mandatory death penalty for all thefts of forty shillings, for example, drove colonial jurors to "pious perjury" by downvaluing thefts to thirty-nine shillings.[1]

Deferring to government officials makes sense when they possess technocratic expertise. But as Barkow notes, criminal justice policy is much more about lay moral intuitions than about apolitical expertise. That is the message of *Apprendi* and its progeny: Criminal justice policy belongs at least in part in the hands of populist juries because they enjoy democratic legitimacy.

One could imagine a criminal justice system that depended more on political than on doctrinal legal checks and balances. Prosecutors' decisions would be publicized and more open to scrutiny, so that their statistics would become live issues in district attorneys' electoral campaigns. Victims and community members would have greater information and participation in the prosecution of crimes, to check prosecutors' agency costs. Media coverage would give voters bigger-picture statistics as well as finer evaluations of police and prosecutorial misconduct. Better data collection and dissemination would promote this media coverage. Trials and clemency proceedings would be thoroughly public, allowing voters to reach their own conclusions about which defendants deserve acquittal, pardon, or mercy. Indeed, that vision harkens back to colonial American criminal justice: victims prosecuted pro se, the public sat in judgment in the jury box, and gossip about trials and punishment spread throughout small communities.[2]

Moving away from this administrative ideal would weaken the judiciary's strong commitment to policing equal treatment. But judicial regulation has not stamped out racial profiling or race disparities in capital sentencing, whereas

---

* Professor of Law, University of Pennsylvania Law School.

1. *See* John H. Langbein, *Shaping the Eighteenth-Century Criminal Trial: A View from the Ryder Sources*, 50 U. CHI. L. REV. 22, 53–55 (1983).

2. I have developed these arguments at greater length elsewhere. *See* Stephanos Bibas, *Transparency and Participation in Criminal Procedure*, 81 N.Y.U. L. REV. 911 (2006).

state executive branches have recently attacked both problems head-on.[3] Judges need not view criminal justice as their exclusive countermajoritarian province, but can trust political branches more.

Barkow is right, then, to question our reverence for administrative models. Procedural reform, expertise, and formality do not always translate into substantive legal and moral justice. On the contrary, popular morality has room for mercy as well as justice, discretion as well as rules.

But how far is Barkow willing to go? She is nostalgic for jury discretion, but in an era of plea bargaining, political justice must rely on other actors. Would she trust prosecutorial elections and legislative oversight hearings to regulate mercy, in the absence of active judicial oversight? Does she trust these majoritarian processes to prevent discrimination? Would she allow victims and community members much larger roles, even at the expense of equal treatment? And can we still trust executive clemency despite the Clinton pardon scandal and the political pressure to act tough so long as one faces reelection?

Although Barkow still has to work out these details, her overall message is sound. Lawyers have tried too hard to squelch discretion, as the rule of law ideal has hypertrophied. Discretion is necessary, and it should be more transparent and democratically accountable. Politics, reasoned judgment, and empathy deserve overt roles. Legislators and judges must be more humble about the power of rules and trust other actors more. Judges, Barkow rightly suggests, should stop trying to stamp out the political and moral judgments inherent in criminal-justice discretion.

---

3. *Compare McCleskey v. Kemp*, 481 U.S. 279 (1987) (finding no constitutional infirmity in Georgia's capital sentencing system despite overwhelming statistical race-of victim disparities), *and Chavez v. Illinois State Police*, 251 F.3d. 612 (7th Cir. 2001) (finding statistical racial disparity in police traffic stops inadequate to prove requisite discriminatory intent), *with* Francis X. Clines, *Death Penalty Is Suspended in Maryland*, N.Y. TIMES, May 10, 2002, at A20 (reporting Maryland's governor's moratorium on executions pending study of racial disparities in capital punishment), *and* David Kocieniewski, *Whitman and State Police: One Answer, Many Questions*, N.Y. TIMES Mar. 7, 1999, § 14 N.J, at 2 (reporting that political furor that erupted in New Jersey over racial profiling led governor to fire state police superintendent).

THE DECLINE OF CRIMINAL LAW REPRESENTATIVE POPULISM

ANDREW E. TASLITZ*

Rachel Barkow argues that the decline of the exercise of mercy in our criminal justice system stems from a fear of unreviewable discretion connected to the rise of the administrative state. But, I argue here, the *primary* fear is not simply of unreviewable discretion but rather of a subset of that category. Implicit in Barkow's position is the idea that the criminal justice system increasingly favors elite judgments (expertise akin to that of administrative agencies) over lay ones, albeit combined with transparency and external review of discretion to render democracy consistent with elite rule. It is this *implicit* position, or at least a variant of it, that I believe best explains when our system is most resistant to unreviewable discretion. The variant is this: The decline of populist representative institutions reflects and amplifies a fear of too direct exercise of discretionary power by the People rather than their elite rulers.

Pairing the words "populist" and "representative" seems oxymoronic, the first arguably connoting relatively direct rule by the people, the second rule by elected representatives. But the political reality of American institutions reveals a spectrum of relatively greater or lesser degrees of direct rule. The jury is one example. Jurors are not elected, and they vote on the resolution of a specific matter rather than on broad social policy. Yet jurors have often been viewed as being representatives of the People, bringing the People's voice into the daily administration of justice. Akhil Amar has even described the jury as a more populist level of the judicial branch, akin to the House of Representatives in Congress.[1] Although some thinkers view juries as nothing but bodies where group biases play out, another tradition views them as a deliberative body, creating truth from the interaction of individuals.

Jurors also do not simply apply clear rules to a set of facts. As Darryl Brown has pointed out, they necessarily interpret vague statutory terms, and this gives

---

* Welsh S. White Distinguished Visiting Professor of Law, University of Pittsburgh School of Law, 2008–09; Professor of Law, Howard University School of Law. The ideas in this comment draw on Andrew E. Taslitz, *The Jury and the Common Good: Synthesizing the Insights of Modern and Postmodern Legal Theories, in* FOR THE COMMON GOOD: A CRITICAL EXAMINATION OF LAW AND SOCIAL CONTROL (Robin Miller and Sandra Lee Browning eds., 2004); Andrew E. Taslitz, *Prosecutorial Pre-conditions to Plea Bargaining,* 23 CRIM. JUST. 14 (2008).

1. *See* Akhil Reed Amar and Ian Hirsch, FOR THE PEOPLE: WHAT THE CONSTITUTION REALLY SAYS ABOUT YOUR RIGHTS 52 (1998).

them a law-creating role as much as a law-applying role.[2] By design or not, this law-creating role has been especially important with respect to criminal statutes, which call upon jurors to decide, for example, whether provocation was "reasonable" or a killer's heart "depraved." But "reasonableness" and "depravity" require making moral judgments and political ones about proper behavior, not simply judgments about the raw "facts" of what happened.

There is, however, a very fine line between recognizing that jurors can "make law" by statutory interpretation and permitting "jury nullification." Both indeed involve law-creation, the latter occurring simply when the jurors are self-aware and candid about what they are doing. Perhaps nullification is a more extreme act, for jurors may see themselves as disobeying the law as they understand it. But this too has a populist justification, for it permits the People to have a say in what rules should govern what classes of cases and creates another tool for the People to check governmental or private tyranny. Yet this is no simple populism, for at its best, the jury is seen to speak only after deliberation and on behalf of all the People rather than to replace elite oppression with that by a majority.

The jury may be contrasted with the local prosecutor. Some populist elements characterize the prosecutor, for often he is highly responsive to local values and spends much time with constituents in the local community. Yet the prosecutor is elected, a traditional representative political role. He is supposedly elected to enforce the laws, but of course his vast discretion means that he creates them, too. Barkow says that prosecutors escape judicial review because they are thought to have especially strong expertise. But I think the perception among local majorities that prosecutors truly serve the People through a traditional representative role may be an even more important cause of this deference as well.

The problem is that lack of transparency and unequal distribution of political resources among the electorate sometimes give the lie to this perception. The more populist jury's power thus declines while the prosecutor's, despite much criticism, remains strong. To ignore decisions about the proper degree of populism we ask of our criminal justice institutions is to give sway to the rule of an elite in precisely the area where an informed, deliberative People most need to monitor a potentially overweening state.

---

2. *See* Darryl K. Brown, *Plain Meaning, Practical Reason, and Culpability: Toward a Theory of Jury Interpretation of Criminal Statutes*, 96 MICH. L. REV. 1199 (1998).

REPLY

RACHEL E. BARKOW

My core text argued that administrative law's rise helps explain why jury nullification and executive clemency are now so disfavored and why prosecutorial discretion has faced comparatively less criticism. I never claimed that administrative law is the only factor or even the most important one leading to the current state of affairs.

Nevertheless, some of the comments seek to offer competing theories that they think better explain the current administration of mercy, and particularly, the persistent deference to prosecutors. Ronald Wright and Marc Miller argue that prosecutors receive deference, not because of their perceived expertise, but because they adhere to norms of "consistency and constraint."[1] Doug Berman similarly argues that prosecutors are receiving deference because they have promoted themselves as adhering to a norm of equal justice. Whereas Wright and Miller believe prosecutors are in fact complying with these norms, Berman disagrees.

Wright and Miller claim that internal office structures and norms, such as training and supervision, create incentives for prosecutors to explain cases in consistent terms. But in many offices, training and supervision are negligible or nonexistent. With high turnover in many offices, and crushing case loads in most, senior attorneys may have little time to pass along guidance in any principled way. Wright and Miller can claim these norms exist, but we really have no way of knowing. As Andrew Taslitz and Stephanos Bibas point out, transparency is hardly the hallmark of a prosecutor's office today. And some of what we do know cuts against Wright and Miller's argument. Berman, for example, points to the federal system—a prosecutorial system with some of the best training and supervision—and notes that discriminatory factors are influencing the decisions of prosecutors. Without empirical support that prosecutors have internalized norms of consistency or more transparency so that this claim could be verified, this is a thin reed to explain prosecutors' unchecked discretion to treat some cases more leniently than others.

Although administrative law principles may not be the only explanation for why prosecutors receive deference, or even the strongest one, they offer stronger support than the norms theory. Indeed, one of the leading cases explaining why prosecutors receive deference not to charge explicitly echoes administrative law concerns. In *Inmates of Attica Correctional Facility v. Rockefeller*,[2] the court refused to second-guess a prosecutorial decision not to charge because it believed judges

---

1. Wright and Miller comment at 674.
2. 477 F.2d 375 (2d Cir. 1973).

were not well positioned to review the policy calls made by prosecutors. The court expressly doubted the "judiciary's capacity"[3] to determine how limited resources should be allocated or to decide when a prosecutor's decision to call for further investigation should be halted. Although a prosecutor's decision may not involve complex scientific or economic issues, Berman is wrong to think that administrative law deference results only when technical questions are at issue. On the contrary, the policy decisions that must be made in deciding how to expend limited government enforcement resources receive more deference than any other administrative law issue. They are not subject to judicial review precisely because they are seen as the kind of decisions that must be made by the officials who have the greatest expertise in the subject matter—whatever the subject matter happens to be.

But Berman's more fundamental point is correct: Prosecutorial discretion requires more scrutiny than it receives. Indeed, if any of the three actors I discuss should be subject to administrative law checks, it is the prosecutor. The executive possesses only the power to pardon or forgive; he or she cannot increase a defendant's sentence. And although juries can convict as well as acquit, their decisions to convict are reviewable to make sure that the evidence supports their verdict. Prosecutors, in contrast, possess both the unreviewable power to be merciful *and* the unreviewable power to impose punishment. And it is this combination of powers that has proven to be so dangerous and most in need of an effective check.

In our current system of plea bargaining with no effective judicial oversight, prosecutors are the final adjudicators in most cases. Prosecutors frequently ask legislators to enact harsh punitive laws not because prosecutors believe the sentences on the books are the appropriate ones—indeed, often no one believes those sentences are justified in most cases. Rather, prosecutors make these requests for mandatory minimums and other harsh sentencing laws so that they can use them as bargaining chips to extract pleas and cooperation. It is hard to characterize this prosecutorial tactic as the dispensation of mercy. It is the discretion to impose punishment, and it should receive greater scrutiny than it does.

Indeed, this political dynamic is why real mercy is needed and why I would reject Bibas's suggestion for political justice from prosecutors or legislators. We need checks from outside this system. Juries and executives could provide it—but only if we rethink what our administrative system of criminal justice should look like.

---

3. *Id.* at 380 (raising a series of difficult questions that "engender serious doubts as to the judiciary's capacity to review" prosecutorial decisions).

31. CRIMINAL LAW COMES HOME

JEANNIE SUK[*]

The traditional reluctance of criminal law to enter the intimate space of the home is now seen as having long enabled state acquiescence in violence against women. During the decades in which the criminalization of domestic violence has been in the making, feminists have sought to recast as "public" matters previously considered "private." The recognition of domestic violence (DV) as a public issue is manifest in law reform aimed at reshaping law enforcement response to treat DV as crime. DV remains a serious problem, with estimates of women in the United States who experience assault by intimate partners each year numbering in the millions. But it is no longer marginal to prevailing notions of what crime is. As law enforcement continues to embrace and amplify that development, the relation between the home and the criminal law is being remade in surprising ways that have gone largely unnoticed.

Here I describe the legal regime that has grown up around misdemeanor offenses associated with DV, emerging under the aegis of correcting the criminal justice system's shameful past inaction, that seeks to do something meaningfully different from punishing violence. The home is becoming a space in which criminal law deliberately and coercively reorders and controls property and intimate relationships. I discuss two means by which the criminal law accomplishes this goal: protection-order criminalization and what I call "state-imposed de facto divorce."

If a rhetoric of privacy has worked in our history to justify nonintervention in the home, the new regime relies on a rhetoric of publicness to envision the home as in need of public control, like the streets. The home, the archetype of private space, becomes a site of intense public investment, suitable for criminal law control.

Perhaps because of the urgency and magnitude of the problem of DV, much-needed law reform has been rapid and has resulted in novelties we do not yet fully understand. Here I try to make intelligible some important conceptual, practical, and normative consequences of that law reform. Realistic consideration of surprising aspects of the current landscape, including practices that may fly under the radar in prosecutors' offices and criminal courts, can enable us to see how the characteristic logic, ideology, rhetoric, and momentum of a law-reform project can become conventional wisdom and be extended without reflection on their meaning. The stakes are particularly sensitive because of the unique and complex vulnerabilities, interests, rights, and freedoms that inhabit the home.

---

* Assistant Professor of Law, Harvard Law School. This core text is drawn from Jeannie Suk, *Criminal Law Comes Home*, 116 YALE L.J. 2 (2006).

I. PROTECTION ORDER CRIMINALIZATION: PRESENCE AT HOME AS PROXY CRIME

In most jurisdictions today, criminal courts, which always had the power to set conditions of pretrial release, issue protection orders at the prosecutor's request as a condition of pretrial release after a DV arrest. Many states have statutorily authorized or mandated issuance of the criminal protection order as a condition of bail or pretrial release. Criminal protection orders remain in effect while prosecution is pending and can become more permanent as part of a criminal sentence.

Whereas the civil protection order is sought voluntarily by the victim, the criminal protection order is sought and issued by the state in the public interest. The practice of criminal courts issuing protection orders—initiated, requested, and enforced by the state—shifts the decision to exclude an alleged abuser away from the victim and to the state. Moreover, the DV protection order criminalizes conduct that is not generally criminal—namely presence at home—in order to punish or prevent the target criminal conduct. Violating the order is a crime even if the conduct the order prohibits ordinarily is not. To prosecutors and courts, an abuser's presence in the home comes to seem interchangeable with DV. Presence at home is a proxy for DV.

The advantages of using presence at home as a proxy are evidentiary and preventive. The evidentiary problems with prosecuting DV are well known. Victims are typically unwilling, sometimes out of fear, to cooperate with the prosecution. Thus criminal cases are often weak and proof of guilt beyond a reasonable doubt elusive. Prosecutions for protection-order violations can enable circumvention of the burden of proof—a more efficient and effective means of convicting domestic abusers. A protection-order violation is far easier to prove than the target crime of DV. Victim testimony is less important. No physical injury need be shown. The existence of the protection order and the defendant's presence in the home, to which the arresting officer can usually testify, are sufficient. All that may need to be shown is that the defendant telephoned the protected party. Furthermore, using presence at home as a proxy is designed to prevent conduct that, though innocent itself, can lead to the target crime. Prohibiting a person's presence at home via the protection order may reduce his opportunity to engage in DV.

The protection order thus enables the creation of a crime out of the ordinarily innocent behavior of being at home. Through this tool, the criminal law gains a foothold for its supervisory presence in the home. Once the protection order is in effect, police presence is required in that space. That monitoring opens up a range of conduct in the home to criminal law control.

II. DE FACTO DIVORCE

When the state is in the home, how does it control intimate relationships through the criminal law? I turn to a leading jurisdiction, New York County (i.e., Manhattan), that is considered to be "in the forefront of efforts to combat domestic violence,"[1] and that has seen significant changes in its enforcement approach in the last fifteen years.[2] A routine practice there in the prosecution of misdemeanor DV exemplifies the expanding criminal law control of the home: The prosecutorial use of criminal court protection orders to seek to end an intimate relationship. The use of such protection orders in the normal course of misdemeanor DV prosecution amounts in practice to state-imposed de facto divorce.

A. Temporary Orders of Protection

The Manhattan District Attorney's Office (DA's Office) defines DV as "*any* crime or violation committed . . . against . . . a member of [the defendant's] family or household."[3] The vast majority of DV cases involve charges of misdemeanor or lesser severity, which by definition do not allege serious physical injury. Many DV misdemeanor cases charged do not allege any physical harm.[4] Accordingly, my discussion here primarily concerns the enforcement of misdemeanor DV, for which serious physical injury is not at issue.

The DA's Office considers DV to be a very serious and distinctive category of crime. Cases deemed to fall in the category of DV trigger a "mandatory domestic violence protocol" not applicable to other (even violent) crimes. Even as the "violence" of DV has been defined down to include cases with no physical violence, the mandatory protocol applies in all cases falling in the category, regardless of the seriousness or injuries in the particular case.

The use of a uniform mandatory protocol in every case represents the prosecutorial response to a paradigm story in which DV is a prelude to murder. In the oral culture of a prosecutor's office, a misdemeanor DV defendant has the potential to turn out to be an O.J. Simpson. Rookie prosecutors are warned that their DV misdemeanor cases could get them negative media attention for failure to prevent something more serious. Thus prosecutors make decisions in the shadow of public oversight and have an enhanced incentive to use every means available to protect DV victims.

---

1. Richard R. Peterson, N.Y. City Criminal Justice Agency, The Impact of Manhattan's Specialized Domestic Violence Court 1 (2004).

2. For overviews and details of misdemeanor DV enforcement practice in New York City, see Chandra Gavin and Nora K. Puffett, Ctr. for Court Innovation, Criminal Domestic Violence Case Processing: A Case Study of the Five Boroughs of New York City (2005); Richard R. Peterson, N.Y. City Criminal Justice Agency, Combating Domestic Violence in New York City: A Study of DV Cases in the Criminal Courts (2003); Richard R. Peterson, N.Y. City Criminal Justice Agency, Comparing the Processing of Domestic Violence Cases to Non-Domestic Violence Cases in New York City Criminal Courts (2001) [hereinafter Peterson, Comparing]; Peterson, *supra* note 1.

3. 2004 Criminal Court Crimes Manual 18 (2004).

4. *See* Peterson, Comparing, *supra* note 2, at 30; Gavin and Puffett, *supra* note 2, at 35.

The enforcement protocol consists of the following practices. Police officers must arrest if there is reasonable cause to believe that a DV crime, including violation of a protection order, has been committed. Once a DV arrest is made, the DA's Office has a no-drop prosecution policy, wherein the decision to charge and prosecute does not hinge on the victim's willingness to cooperate. Prosecutors pursue cases in the face of victims' opposition and routinely inform them that the choice to prosecute belongs solely to the state. The mandatory practice in this area includes rules that do not generally apply in non-DV cases. One of them is that at the defendant's arraignment, prosecutors must request from the criminal court a temporary order of protection (TOP) that prohibits the defendant from contacting the victim and from going to her home, even if the defendant lives there.

At the arraignment of any defendant charged with a DV crime, the DA's Office's mandatory practice involves asking the criminal court to issue a TOP as a condition of bail or pretrial release. The TOP normally prohibits any contact whatsoever with the victim, including phone, e-mail, voice-mail, or third-party contact. Contact with children is also banned. The order excludes the defendant from the victim's home, even if it is the defendant's home. Ascertaining that the victim wants the order is not part of the mandatory protocol. The prosecutor generally requests a full stay-away order even if the victim does not want it.

The criminal court routinely issues the TOP at arraignment, the defendant's first court appearance. The brief, formulaic, and compressed nature of arraignments in criminal court, which run around the clock to ensure that all defendants are arraigned within twenty-four hours of arrest, means that courts often issue orders with little detailed consideration of the particular facts. DV orders are generally requested and issued as a matter of course. When the TOP goes into effect, the defendant cannot go home or have any contact with the victim (usually his wife) and his children. If the defendant does go home or contact the protected parties, he could be arrested, prosecuted, and punished for violating the order—even if the victim initiates contact or invites the defendant to come home. Police officers then make routine unannounced visits to homes with a history of domestic violence. If a defendant subject to a protection order is present, he is arrested.

Thus even when a DV case is destined ultimately to end in dismissal because the victim is uncooperative and there is insufficient evidence for conviction, keeping the case active for as long as possible enables the prosecutor and the court to monitor the defendant for months prior to dismissal. A violation of the order can lead to arrest and punishment for the more easily proven criminal charge. But in addition to the prospect of punishment for the proxy conduct of being present at home, the protection order shifts the very goal of pursuing criminal charges away from punishment toward control over the intimate relationship in the home.

The common wisdom is that the criminal court protection order practice is meant to safeguard the integrity of criminal proceedings by protecting the victim from violence and intimidation. But the practice of separating couples in DV cases by way of criminal protection orders extends beyond the needs of the judicial process. Court-ordered separation becomes a goal of prosecutors in bringing criminal charges—a substitute for, rather than a means of, increasing the likelihood of punishment. Punishment as a goal can be put on the backburner because separation is a more direct and achievable way to address or prevent violence. The practice that results amounts to what I term state-imposed de facto divorce, a phenomenon that is so routine in criminal court that it disappears in plain sight.

B. Final Orders of Protection

The full and final order of protection formally transforms the TOP, issued at the defendant's arraignment and continually renewed while the case is pending, into a final order of lengthy duration. Of course prosecutors prefer to see criminal defendants tried, convicted, and punished with imprisonment. But the difficulty of trying DV cases because of the reluctance of victims to cooperate leads prosecutors to look to plea bargains imposing alternatives to imprisonment. The protection order is the most significant among these alternatives. Even if the defendant does not get jail time as part of the plea, at the very least, the protection order can provide the basis for new criminal liability on the more easily proven crime of violating the order.

Already in effect on a temporary basis since the defendant's arraignment, the protection order is deployed as follows: The prosecutor offers the defendant a plea bargain consisting of little or no jail time (or time served) and a reduction of the charge, or even an adjournment in contemplation of dismissal, in exchange for the defendant's acceptance of a final order of protection prohibiting his presence at home and contact with the victim. This offer presents the opportunity to dispose of the criminal case immediately with little or no jail time, and in some cases, no criminal conviction or record. The offer is particularly attractive for a defendant who has remained in jail since arraignment pending disposition of his case: If he agrees he will be released.

Depending on the terms of the plea bargain, the court issues the final protection order as part of the defendant's sentence pursuant to a guilty plea, or as a condition of an adjournment in contemplation of dismissal. In light of the evidentiary difficulties of obtaining a DV conviction at trial, especially when victims are uncooperative, many defendants do not take pleas, in anticipation of eventual acquittal or dismissal. But many do.

As the literature on plea bargaining increasingly recognizes, plea bargains are not struck narrowly in the shadow of the strength of the evidence and the likely results of trials. In the context of the final protection order, motives for defendants' acceptance of plea bargains may include defendants' desire to resolve cases quickly without much or any jail time, and defense attorneys' need to manage large case loads as repeat players in the criminal court. A defendant may also be unwilling to wait the time leading to trial, and fear losing his job because of the days he must take off to make repeated court appearances. A plea bargain that ends the case, takes jail off the table, often reduces the charge down to a violation, and leaves no criminal record is similar enough to dismissal that defendants may readily accept. The idea that "law's shadow may disappear altogether"[5] has particular resonance for misdemeanor DV, in which the final order of protection is so common that it is plausible to consider it a standard disposition sought by prosecutors.

C. Consequences of De Facto Divorce

Protection orders enable the state to seek de facto divorce between DV defendants and their intimate partners. But de facto divorce is not de jure divorce. The order of protection does not have the effect of ending formal marriage. And many intimate partners affected by orders are not married. Spouses can surely remain legally married even as they obey all the prohibitions of the order, but cannot live or act in substance as if they are in an intimate relationship. Furthermore, the imposed separation is not accompanied by the family law divorce regime of property division, alimony, child custody, and child support, of which the order ordinarily makes no mention. A de facto divorce does not trigger the family law apparatus that surrounds de jure divorce. Apart from the fact that the criminal court does not have jurisdiction to enter new orders regarding child custody, visitation, or support, prosecutors have neither interest nor experience in dealing with family law.

But de facto divorce does entail de facto family arrangements—no custody, no visitation, and no support. Thus in the imposition of de facto divorce, criminal law becomes a new family law regime. But because it is criminal law regulation, the parties cannot contract around the result except by risking the arrest and punishment of one of them.

Indeed, the order goes much further than would ordinary divorce, prohibiting any contact, even by express permission of the protected party. It is super-divorce. Criminal law does not purport to give effect to private ordering, nor does it tolerate parties' contracting around default rules; rather, it regulates individuals' conduct through the threat of punishment to serve the public interest. Moreover, state-imposed de facto divorce is so class-contingent that it could be called poor man's divorce. The initial arrest that sets the wheels in motion is much more likely to occur if people live in close quarters in buildings with thin walls, and neighbors can hear a disturbance and call the police. Those arraigned in New York County criminal court for DV crimes are by and large minorities who live in the poorest part of Manhattan.

---

5. William J. Stuntz, *Plea Bargaining and Criminal Law's Disappearing Shadow*, 117 HARV. L. REV. 2548, 2549 (2004).

In practice, some, perhaps many, couples do remain together in disobedience of the criminal protection order. They are in marriages or intimate relationships whose continuation is criminal—in the shadow of the potential arrest and criminal prosecution of the person subject to the order. The enforcement of the order does not depend solely on the victim's wishes, as the police do make surprise home visits and arrest people who are present in homes from which they are banned. This means that the victim is not simply the recipient of a strategic tool that shifts power to her. Many protected by protection orders lack sophistication about the operation of the enforcement protocol. They may not speak English well. They may be illegal immigrants for whom contact with government authorities is highly undesirable, frightening, and risky. Indeed some may believe that they themselves are subject to criminal sanction should they allow their partner to contact them. Under these conditions, the overall effect of the protection order is not to confer power on victims, but rather to impose an end to the intimate relationship without their consent.

III. TENSIONS

A distinctive feature of the criminal law expansion described here is the invocation of the public interest to justify the control of home space and intimate relationships. This expansion, often on the basis of an alleged misdemeanor, takes place in a world in which "violence" is defined down to include incidents not causing physical injury. Through it, the state excludes people from their homes, reallocates property interests, reorders intimate relationships, and imposes de facto divorce.

The expanding criminal law control of the home described above is in tension with the most powerful legal trend in the relationship between criminal law and the home over the last fifty years. Beginning with the fundamental right to marry and the right to privacy in personal sexual matters, the notion that the Constitution disfavors the criminalization of intimate relationships between consenting adults has gained ground. In the words of Justice Douglas in *Griswold v. Connecticut*, "Would we allow the police to search the sacred precincts of marital bedrooms for telltale signs of the use of contraceptives? The very idea is repulsive to the notions of privacy surrounding the marriage relationship."[6] As Laurence Tribe famously stated, discussing *Bowers v. Hardwick*,[7] the question was not what Hardwick "was doing in the privacy of his bedroom, but what the State of Georgia was doing there."[8] This logic has progressed to the holding in

---

6. 381 U.S. 479, 485–86 (1965).
7. 478 U.S. 186 (1986).
8. Pet. for Reh'g of Resp. at 10, *Bowers v. Hardwick*, 478 U.S. 186 (1986) (No. 85-140).

Lawrence v. Texas[9] that the criminal law may not prohibit private consensual sexual conduct between adults. This trend connects home privacy with individual autonomy in intimate relationships.

In *Lawrence*, Justice Kennedy relied on the concept of the home to mark off a private space of autonomy for intimate relationships. He spoke of the protected right as the right to engage in "intimate conduct with another person" that "can be but one element in a personal bond that is more enduring."[10] The effect of this much-noticed move was to suggest that the state ought not prohibit the exercise of private choice of intimate partner—quite apart from state recognition of that choice in the form of marriage.

In the context of constitutional due process, the rising legal sensibility disfavors the idea of the state as an omnipresence regulating intimate choices in the home. Meanwhile, under the DV rubric, the criminal law actively prohibits some individuals' choices to live as intimates, criminalizing most if not all practical aspects of sharing a life in common. To make good on the prohibition, the state must become a dominant presence in the home, with the police on the lookout for telltale signs of husbands. These two trends stand in tension at the intersection of criminal law and family law.

The simultaneous expansion and contraction of the criminal law in the home could of course be rationalized: consensual sex between adults in private space does not cause harm, whereas DV, a nonconsensual phenomenon, does. But it would be too simple to pigeonhole the competing developments as joint manifestations of the principles of harm and consent. State-imposed de facto divorce goes meaningfully beyond the prohibition and punishment of violence per se. It seeks to criminalize intimate relationships that adults have chosen for themselves and have not chosen to end. One would need to take a strong view of gendered coercion in intimate relationships generally to rationalize a world in which this kind of state control is regularly triggered by misdemeanor arrests not involving serious physical injury, particularly as the category of nonviolent conduct that constitutes DV expands.

The tension between protecting women from intimate violence and promoting their self-determination reflects underlying questions about women's capacity generally to make autonomous judgments and decisions about their intimate relationships. While the academic debate continues, prosecutors, police, and courts operate in a world primarily motivated by the distinctive interests of the criminal law. In the language of the cases, the culture of police and prosecutors, and the structuring ideology of the criminal justice system, a powerful rhetoric of public interest informs reluctance to allow the particular desires of individual women to control. We can see a distinctive nexus between the objective of

---

9. 539 U.S. 558 (2003).
10. *Id.* at 567.

state control backed by the public interest and the derogation of individual autonomy.

IV. CONCLUSION

My goal has been to interpret the moves of a still developing legal regime that has largely not been recognized. Prosecutors, police, and judges in many jurisdictions have at long last adopted a feminist theory of DV as a manifestation of gendered power inequality in the marital relationship. But the literalization of this theory has resulted in the practice of state-imposed de facto divorce: if the root of DV is marriage, end marriages that have signs of DV.

This solution to the DV problem need not inevitably follow from strong, consistent, even mandatory, enforcement of DV crimes. Of course, alternative approaches may create costs, namely that violent crime might go unprevented. I have not meant to offer a law reform proposal, but rather to give shape and texture to surprising novelties of the law reform we have had, in order to make visible the meanings and costs of a developing legal regime. We might well ultimately conclude that this regime is worth its costs. But my goal here, antecedent to that conclusion, has been to show the dramatic changes in how the criminal law is giving effect to a well-accepted antiviolence policy.

State-imposed de facto divorce may well be appropriate for truly violent and dangerous abusive relationships; in these cases, the state may more readily conclude that victims' autonomy and consent are already worn so thin that paternalism will best enhance them. But the extraordinary legal innovation wherein de facto divorce becomes a standard prosecutorial tool needs close interrogation before it becomes a uniform, mechanical solution for the large number of cases now coming into the criminal system under the rubric of DV that do not involve serious physical injury.

The expanding definition of violence, mandatory arrest, and no-drop policies, the prosecution of many more cases than can ultimately be proven, and the decreasing emphasis on punishment are all developments that contribute to making de facto divorce a de facto solution to DV. As de facto divorce becomes a more prevalent alternative to traditional punishment, it is likely to reinforce the expansion of the definition of DV crime and an increase in DV arrests and prosecutions for nonviolent conduct, as law enforcement personnel increasingly imagine the consequences of bringing such domestic incidents into the criminal system to be less draconian than incarceration. A wide range of nonviolent conduct in the domestic space then becomes subject to criminal law regulation, down to the existence of an intimate relationship itself.

The result would be a shift in emphasis from the goal of punishing violence to state control of intimate relationships in the home. This shift has not been completely accomplished, but it is underway. Of course, we must continue to pursue remediation of the flawed criminal justice models of the past that simply accepted the distinction between private and public as unproblematic. But the ongoing change explored here creates an opportunity for critical reflection on the increasing subordination of individual autonomy in domestic space to state control in the public interest.

COMMENTS

THE PRIVATE LIFE OF CRIMINAL LAW

MELISSA MURRAY*

Jeannie Suk makes an important contribution to our understanding of criminal law and the regulation of private life. By arguing that the use of criminal protective orders in domestic violence enforcement "deliberately and coercively reorders and controls"[1] private relationships, Suk builds on the work of others who have identified criminal law's increasing role in shaping and controlling behavior in the public sphere. Of course, Suk's claim is that criminal law's tentacles not only have reached out to regulate more *public* terrain, they have turned inward to regulate the *private* sphere as well. This move, Suk makes clear, is wholly at odds with an inherited legal narrative that denotes marriage, family, and the home as "private," and therefore insulated from criminal regulation.

I would argue, however, that criminal law's regulation of private relationships is not a new development. Certainly, criminal law has resisted intervening in the home, as the history of domestic violence enforcement makes evident. However, despite this resistance, criminal law has been an important force in defining and regulating the content of private life. As I describe below, criminal law has worked in tandem with family law to police the normative contours of marriage and intimate life. With this history in mind, the developments that Suk identifies are even more troubling because they suggest that criminal law is moving beyond its already quite significant role in structuring the parameters of lawful intimacy to directly regulate within the private sphere.

It goes without saying that family law regulates the formation of families, in large part through the regulation of entry into and exit from marriage. Each jurisdiction sets forth a series of procedural and substantive requirements for entering into a valid union. Procedurally, lawful marriage requires compliance with the state's licensing apparatus, through which the couple confirms to each other, and the overseeing state, their consent to marriage.

---

* Assistant Professor of Law, University of California, Berkeley, School of Law.
1. Suk core text at 683.

Substantively, the state regulates who may and may not marry. Presently, all jurisdictions prohibit marriages between more than two people, between consanguineous relatives, and between parties either of whom is below the jurisdiction's age of consent. Historically, this litany of substantive restrictions was even more comprehensive. Until 1967, many Southern states prohibited interracial marriages, and until very recently, same-sex marriages were universally prohibited as well.

Together, these procedural requirements and substantive restrictions enunciate a normative ideal of what marriage should be. Until the twentieth century, this normative ideal specified that marriage was an intraracial, monogamous, exogamous, and heterosexual union between consenting adults. Today, marriage may be interracial or (more limitedly) between persons of the same sex, but it is still understood to be an exogamous, monogamous enterprise between consenting adults. However, because family law regulates only entry to and exit from marriage, its opportunities to police this normative vision of intimate life are limited. In order to advance its normative project, family law, historically and presently, has relied on criminal law's assistance.

In most—if not all—jurisdictions, family law's substantive marriage restrictions are reinforced by criminal bars on the same behavior. For example, not only was interracial marriage once prohibited as a civil matter, it also was subject to criminal penalties. Similarly, while marriage between consanguineous relatives is prohibited as a civil matter, sex (an essential incident of marriage) between such persons also is criminalized as incest. Through its substantive restrictions, family law says what marriage is and should be, and criminal law reinforces these norms by criminalizing behavior ineligible for marriage.

Criminal law goes even further in defining the normative content of intimate life. Although family law regulates entry into and exit from marriage, it does not regulate *inside* of intact marriages, and historically it did not regulate outside of marriage. Instead, criminal law—affirmatively and by omission—elaborates family law's normative vision of intimate life in critical ways. With respect to the regulation of sex outside of marriage, criminal law, through fornication laws and other morals legislation, prohibited out-of-wedlock sex, thereby underscoring marriage's position as the lawful site for sexual expression. Likewise, behavior deemed incompatible with marriage and its procreative purpose also was criminalized through laws prohibiting prostitution, adultery, contraception, and sodomy.

With respect to intact marriages, criminal law has further entrenched family law's normative understanding of marriage as a private enterprise by *refusing* to intervene in the interior of marital life. Until very recently, marriage was a defense to criminal liability for rape—an omission that expressly served family law's interest in promoting and maintaining family privacy in the face of state intrusion. And as Suk notes, criminal law rarely intervened to police domestic violence, reflecting the understanding of the marital home as a quintessentially private space.

Suk rightly observes that today, criminal law's reluctance to intercede in the home has eroded as new approaches to domestic violence enforcement permit criminal law to renegotiate property rights and personal relationships. But attention to these important developments should not obscure the fact that criminal law long has been a regulatory force in the legal construction of private life. Through its regulation of sexuality and its historic refusal to intervene inside the marital home, criminal law has played an important role in the regulation of marriage, family, and sexuality. It has been family law's "muscle," reinforcing and refining intimate norms. In this way, criminal law *always* has been at home—or at least on the porch with shotgun in hand—policing and protecting the boundaries of private life.

WHOSE PRIVACY?

LAURA A. ROSENBURY*

The state has long decided what conduct is sufficiently intimate to be protected by both common law and constitutional notions of family privacy. The state has consistently regulated who may marry, often with the assistance of criminal law. The state has also criminalized certain forms of sexual activity outside of marriage, as illustrated by the anti-sodomy statute at issue in *Lawrence v. Texas*.[1] Although the Supreme Court held that statute unconstitutional, the state continues to regulate sexual activity in various forms. In fact, some lower courts have refused to extend *Lawrence* to forms of sex perceived to be lacking the type of emotional intimacy celebrated by Justice Kennedy in *Lawrence*.[2] Private sexual and emotional conduct therefore remains a state concern, despite popular misconceptions about the state's grant of privacy to such relationships.

Why, then, might we view the criminal law's reach into the realm of domestic violence as new and uniquely problematic? I suspect that the alarm bells ring because the state is entering not just any home, but instead is often entering the marital home. The marital home has long been the organizing principle of family law, from the days when the field was called "domestic relations" and encompassed all the internal relationships found in a husband's household, to recent proposals to extend state recognition and benefits to any interdependent group of individuals sharing a home, regardless of conjugality. A home occupied by spouses (or, more recently, individuals in marriage-like relationships) is thus a crucial component of the state's very definition of family. And once that

---

* Professor of Law, Washington University Law School.

1. 539 U.S. 558 (2003).

2. *See* Laura A. Rosenbury and Jennifer E. Rothman, *Beyond Intimacy* (work in progress, on file with author).

definition is met, the state generally accords privacy to the family, meaning that the state typically will not intervene in the home.

Accordingly, when the state intervenes in the marital home, it seems to be reneging on a core aspect, and some would even say benefit, of being in a marriage or marriage-like relationship: being left alone by the state. Jeannie Suk therefore insightfully identifies the dissonance that can be created by aggressive domestic violence prosecution policies like those of New York County. However, this dissonance is solely the result of a putative privilege granted by the state in the first place, the privilege of family privacy that attaches to certain forms of intimacy but not others. We might want to be weary of the erosion of that privacy, as Suk urges, but we also might want to examine the interests served when the state limits that privacy in circumstances like those Suk describes.

Other scholars have written at length about the ways family privacy often reinforces the power of certain family members over others, particularly husbands over wives and parents over children.[3] That focus on private power, rather than state power, reveals the ways that privacy is not a monolithic good but instead can be experienced differently by different members of the same family. For example, family privacy may mean very little to children, who often find their lives controlled by parental directives. Similarly, women experiencing forms of intimidation and abuse by their partners often find their "individual autonomy in domestic space" subordinated by their partners' desires, making the "increasing subordination" of the state described by Suk anything but subordinating.

So whose privacy should the state respect? Although I welcome Suk's critical project, I fear that she reinforces the public/private distinction when she posits criminal law as the principle object of her concern, instead of also examining the ways that the state's grant of privacy can also limit autonomy within the family. Criminal law may be oppressive for some family members, but for others it may serve as a potential route to increased autonomy, and even privacy, within the family home. Such intervention may very well transform intimacy, but no more so than when the state privileges marriage over other forms of relationship and permits private power to flourish under the rubric of family privacy.

---

3. See, e.g., Lee E. Teitelbaum, *Family History and Family Law*, 1985 Wis. L. Rev. 1135, 1174–80; Barbara Bennett Woodhouse, *The Dark Side of Family Privacy*, 67 Geo. Wash. L. Rev. 1247, 1255 (1999).

FROM NEOLIBERALISM TO LIBERTARIANISM: WHY NEITHER CRIMINALIZATION NOR PRIVACY IS THE ANSWER FOR BATTERED WOMEN

AYA GRUBER*

Jeannie Suk's thoughtful, somewhat "Lockean" (rights-based) criticism of domestic violence criminalization and forced separation is an important, timely contribution to feminist literature. Suk insightfully observes that state power, once invited into the home, easily becomes an unwanted long-term guest, resistant to giving up its supervisory authority over what it considers "disordered" homes and "damaged" women. Suk encourages feminists to reexamine where the movement has been, where it is going, and the benefits and drawbacks of continued investments in the criminal law.

Where I part ways with Suk is her singular focus on the importance of "privacy," denoted as the "negative" right to be free from police intervention. By locating marital privacy as the center of her critique, Suk adopts liberalism, a philosophy arguably consonant with gender hierarchy, as her normative position and fails to see domestic violence as a distributive phenomenon. Suk's privacy-based critique of domestic violence criminalization reinforces the false consciousness that there exists a neutral "private" sphere, unconstructed by law, whose maintenance has intrinsic value.

I agree that the overwhelming feminist effort to strengthen existing criminal laws and to create new ones is problematic, but not on the ground that state nonintervention is an end in itself. Critical scholars have long rejected the public/private distinction and the notion of an intimate realm untouched by law. The home is deeply ordered by existing legal arrangements. Moreover, a myriad of socio-economic conditions—some explicitly created by law, like immigration status, and others tolerated by the state, such as gender discrimination—enable abusive men and prevent victims from leaving. Thus, feminists were right to criticize the public/private distinction and object to the widespread mindset that "domestic violence is not my problem." It was important to highlight the ways in which privacy rhetoric was employed to cover the government and society's complicity in abused women's continued subordination.

Unfortunately, instead of focusing on state distributive remedies as the counter to abuse-enabling privacy, feminist domestic violence reformers made the misguided choice to juxtapose privacy solely with state police power. In doing so, they became unwittingly complicit in a neoliberal program whose philosophy runs directly counter to feminist ideology. The "that's-not-our-problem" attitude

---

* Associate Professor of Law, Florida International University College of Law; Visiting Professor of Law, University of Iowa College of Law.

toward social injustice is a product of a distinct neoliberal economic and social agenda that reached its pinnacle during the Reagan'80s. According to this philosophy, society was not responsible for social ills, which were due only to individual failings. Poor women were, at best, too lazy to get real jobs, and at worst, welfare queens leeching off of hard-working folk. The one area of government intervention permissible was criminalization, precisely because it entrenched the position that crimes, like battering, were problems of individually deviant "bad guys," who had "no excuse" for what they did. The genius of this neoliberal move is that recognizing battering as "our problem" entailed no more than putting men, mostly Black and poor men, in jail because of individual fault.

Feminist reformers fell in line by advocating incarceration as the response to social indifference to battering. Conservatives were more than willing to "throw the book" at batterers and dismantle "worthless" relationships, rather than focusing on the inequities giving rise to battering. Concentrating on separating dangerous batterers and "threatened, irrational" women who stayed with them obscured the racial, socio-economic, and other conditions underlying battering. In addition, the criminalization and separation models caused numerous harms to individual women, as Suk duly notes.

Although Suk's general stance against police intervention has great appeal to those who, like me, characterize the criminal justice system as a deeply flawed consequentialist failure, her effort to revitalize the public/private distinction and forge a stand-alone objection to state intercession is troubling. Suk moves away from the neoliberal criminal paradigm toward a libertarian model equally at odds with feminism's antisubordination agenda. The problem with domestic violence criminalization is not that it gives the government a role in combating battering, but that the myopic focus on criminal law solutions is part of a larger program of denying the state's obligation to provide "positive" rights to poor, abused, and immigrant women, or otherwise remedy the socio-economic conditions precedent to battering. In fact, casting domestic violence as a public problem is one of the few positive aspects of criminalization. Suk's emphasis on privacy suggests that the state ought to be less involved in domestic violence, when what is really needed is more involvement, albeit the right kind of involvement. Turning the focus away from criminalization does not mean that the state should once again put on privacy blinders and ignore its role in the maintenance of abuse.

CRIMINAL LAW COMES HOME TO A FAMILY

JENNIFER COLLINS*

Jeannie Suk raises provocative questions about the new ways in which the criminal law "deliberately and coercively reorders and controls property and intimate relationships."[1] Drawing on New York City's treatment of domestic violence cases, she suggests that the willingness of criminal courts to impose protection or "stay-away" orders, even against a victim's wishes, amounts to state imposition of "de facto divorce" upon parties in abusive relationships. Suk ultimately refrains from offering normative proposals; she is instead identifying some previously hidden consequences of a law reform movement in the domestic violence arena.

My concerns with Suk's arguments are two-fold: First, it is critically important to recognize that New York City's aggressive approach to domestic violence cases is simply not representative of many—if not most—jurisdictions in this country. For example, in another major metropolitan area, prosecutors typically do not ask for, and judges do not impose, stay-away or no-contact orders at the time of sentencing if the victim objects.[2] The defendant probably will be subject to an order directing him not to assault or harass the victim, but surely that kind of order does not result in the imposition of a "de facto divorce." In addition, even if a more aggressive stay-away order were to be imposed, it would not be enforced absent the cooperation of the victim, because the police simply do not have the time, resources, or inclination to make the kind of random, unannounced visits to the home that Suk describes. As a result, contempt charges would only be filed if the victim herself contacted the police to complain that the defendant violated the terms of a protection order.

Suk also suggests that these protection orders are especially troublesome because they are issued even in misdemeanor cases, "which by definition do not allege serious physical injury."[3] However, we must recognize that serious physical injury is often involved even in cases that a prosecutor charges as a misdemeanor rather than as a felony. The reason prosecutors elect to proceed with a misdemeanor charge even when faced with brutal injuries is plain: misdemeanor defendants facing a sentence of six months or less are not entitled to a jury trial. If the state must try a domestic violence case without the cooperation of the victim, as often happens, many prosecutors believe that it is easier to explain the

---

* Associate Professor of Law, Wake Forest School of Law.

1. Suk core text at 683.

2. This description is based on conversations with both a judge who sat on a domestic violence calendar and a prosecutor in charge of her office's domestic violence unit in a major metropolitan area.

3. Suk core text at 685.

victim's absence, and the dynamics of abusive relationships, to a judge rather than to a jury. It is important to understand that the nature of the charge may not necessarily correspond with the seriousness of the particular offense being tried or the pattern and history of abuse in the relationship generally; use of protection orders in misdemeanor cases does not therefore by itself raise a normative red flag.

My second major concern is that we must recognize that domestic violence is often a *family* problem, and not just a problem between intimate partners. Domestic violence directly impacts any children of the couple, who, through no choice of their own, live in a home filled with violence. The potential impact upon children is two-fold: Children may themselves be the victims of abuse and, even if they are not direct targets of violence, they are unquestionably harmed by witnessing the violence inflicted upon their mother. It is important to recognize that the state retains a special obligation to protect children from harm in situations where their parents cannot. Stay-away orders may be imposed in part to protect the children of the relationship, and we cannot assess the validity of a legal regime that relies upon them without considering the needs and interests of both a mother and her children.

Indeed, the real threat to women's autonomy in domestic violence cases is not state-imposed protection orders; it is instead the problem that mothers often face impossible choices when deciding whether to leave abusive relationships. For example, should she stay in her home with her abuser, or flee and risk rendering her children homeless? Thus, more aggressive use of the criminal justice system cannot happen in a vacuum. We cannot truly ensure women's autonomy to make decisions about their intimate relationships until we provide them with workable alternatives to staying in abusive ones. Women need meaningful access to housing, jobs, child care, transportation, and the like before they can decide whether their interests are better served by continuing their relationship with their abuser, and trying to improve it, or by leaving the relationship altogether and requesting the assistance of a protection order, enforceable through the use of criminal contempt charges, to help effectuate that decision. Criminal law can be a powerful weapon in the fight against domestic violence, but it cannot be the only one.

BECAUSE BREAKING UP IS HARD TO DO

CHERYL HANNA*

Just about everyone has been in a romantic relationship that, in hindsight, should have ended sooner than it did. Why do people stay? Hope, or commitment, or because they share a lease or she owns the car. Life and love are complicated, and as Neil Sedaka sang, "Breaking up is hard to do." That's true even for those who are abused by their partners.

It's within this context that we ask the criminal law to respond aggressively to domestic violence while respecting the victim's unique situation. As Jeannie Suk describes, prosecutors in a few jurisdictions have begun to pursue these sometimes conflicting goals by routinely requesting that the court grant a protective order before releasing defendants charged with a domestic offense. Protective orders can forbid the defendant from contacting the victim and can include an order to vacate the home. This practice is part of a larger strategy to treat intimate violence as a public crime rather than a private family matter.

What apparently troubles Suk is that defendants can face criminal misdemeanor charges for nothing more than going home. In her view, the state is exerting too much control of the home and undermining people's decisions to live as intimate partners.

Enabling autonomy is indeed a paramount objective, but what troubles me about this argument is its near obsession with basing law and policy on what victims want. Most folks, at some point in our lives, will experience a less-than-perfect relationship and will struggle with whether or not to end it. To ask someone who has recently experienced trauma to be clear and decisive about the future of their relationship is to ask more of the victim than we can often ask of ourselves. Who among us could possibly comprehend or embrace the difficult choices we face while in a courthouse, just hours after a violent incident, talking to a DA we've never met? To base any legal doctrine or policy on autonomy compromised by violence is misguided and will likely undermine the progress that has been made in protecting intimate partners from abuse.

Rather than ask what a victim wants, let's ask what she or he doesn't want. None of us want violence, or the threat of violence, to dictate how we live our lives. Criminal protection orders achieve this simply by providing some breathing room to make decisions about one's future uninhibited by the constant threat of violence. The fact that criminal law comes home today to promote autonomy, rather than to affirm a husband's right to punish his wife as it did in centuries past, should be a welcome development.

---

* Professor of Law, Vermont Law School. This comment draws from *Because Breaking Up Is Hard To Do*, 116 YALE L.J. POCKET PART 92 (2006), *available at* http://www.thepocketpart.org/2006/10/12/hanna.html.

Furthermore, domestic violence prosecutors understand that victims and defendants often reunite after cases end, if not before. So when they obtain criminal protection orders, their goal is not to separate couples permanently. Misdemeanor domestic cases rarely result in much, if any, jail time. Even in New York City, one of the country's most aggressive jurisdictions, only one-third of those arrested for domestic violence are convicted, and of those, fewer than 20 percent are sentenced to prison. Seventy-two percent receive a conditional discharge, which can include participation in a batterer treatment program or drug and alcohol counseling—interventions intended to help abusers and their partners have nonviolent relationships.[1]

Based on this data, I am more concerned about the underenforcement of domestic violence laws throughout the country than the overenforcement that troubles Suk. The number of domestic homicides in the United States has decreased significantly since the 1970s, and one reason for that decline is our decision to treat domestic violence as a crime against the community.[2] Underenforcement nonetheless remains prevalent across the country. It can be incredibly difficult to get the criminal law to respond—even when a victim is clear and consistent about what she wants. I fear that contrary arguments like Suk's will undo the progress we've made.

That's not to say that the law can't do better. We should always rethink our strategies and avoid one-size-fits-all approaches. The criminalization of domestic violence is still in its infancy, and we have much to learn about what works best and for whom. As Suk notes, we need to be especially concerned about the impact of our policies on poor and minority communities, for whom the criminal law has often been an adversary rather than an ally. The goal, then, is to refine our practices, but not to return to a time when the law and its officers were unable or unwilling to intervene when abuse happened behind closed doors.

1. Ryan R. Peterson, N.Y. City Criminal Justice Agency, Combating Domestic Violence in New York City: A Study of D.V. Cases in Criminal Court (2003).

2. Bureau of Justice Statistics, U.S. Dep't of Justice, Homicide Trends in the United States: Intimate Homicides (June 29, 2006).

THE CRIME OF DOMESTIC VIOLENCE

EMILY J. SACK*

Battered women's advocates have long debated whether criminal justice responses to domestic violence offer the most effective path to safety and autonomy for survivors. Jeannie Suk makes an important contribution to this debate, arguing that criminalization has had unintended negative consequences on privacy. I would argue that in practice, her concerns are overstated, and in theory, alternative policies present greater risks to battered women.

The widespread use of criminal protection orders is relatively rare outside of New York, in which criminal orders are used largely because of the limited jurisdiction of its Family Court, in which only a petitioner related by blood, marriage, or with a child by the respondent can obtain a civil order. In most states, civil orders are available more broadly and are more widely used, even when criminal charges are pending.

But even assuming their widespread use, criminal orders do not constitute any novel incursion into individual privacy. These orders serve as nothing more than bail or pretrial release conditions. In criminal cases generally, conditions such as geographic restrictions frequently control the defendant's conduct. The court is able to make otherwise legal actions illegal because the defendant has been criminally charged. Moreover, bail conditions often prohibit victim contact. In a domestic violence case, when the defendant lives with the victim, this condition is designed not to punish the defendant by banning him from the home, but to prevent victim contact.

Suk is concerned that the use of criminal orders conflicts with the respect for privacy reflected in the line of cases from *Griswold v. Connecticut*[1] to *Lawrence v. Texas*.[2] However, it is not domestic violence criminalization, but the concept of privacy in constitutional law, that can be problematic. Grounding substantive due process rights in privacy has ignored the way in which it served historically as the legal concept that shielded domestic violence from public view. This is one reason, for example, that many feminist scholars have argued that equality, not privacy, should provide the foundation for protection of reproductive rights.

Suk also underestimates the seriousness of domestic violence offenses. The typical misdemeanor domestic violence charge in New York is third-degree assault, which requires physical injury. Such cases often plead out to attempted assault or harassment, which can involve stalking or other acts causing fear of injury. These are crimes of violence. Domestic violence's repetitive nature and targeting of a specific victim makes the likelihood of further violence high. The defendant's

---

* Professor of Law, Roger Williams University School of Law.

1. 381 U.S. 479 (1965).

2. 539 U.S. 558 (2003).

presence in the home is not a "proxy" for violence; contact with the victim itself is dangerous and promotes violence. Sometimes a defendant poses such danger that the state must argue for a stay-away order, even when the complainant objects.

In addition, the distinction between civil and criminal orders is less significant than Suk suggests. Rather than blanket imposition of final stay-away orders, judges frequently consider each victim individually, often in consultation with an advocate, to ascertain her true wishes. If reassured that she is not being coerced, and the situation does not pose great danger, the judge often will grant a victim's request for a "limited" order, permitting contact. Conversely, judges often will not routinely dismiss a civil order upon the petitioner's request, but will undertake a similar process. More generally, the criminal justice system's response to domestic violence has become more nuanced in recent years. Revised policies and trainings have addressed flaws in initial efforts, and the development of Family Justice Centers and other programs linking victims to civil legal assistance and additional services demonstrate that a criminal case can provide survivors with access to an array of resources.

Finally, Suk argues that criminal orders permit de facto divorces without providing the rights women would obtain in a formal divorce. But it is not a protection order that permits a batterer to walk away without paying child support or other obligations. On the contrary, bringing a domestic violence prosecution increases the chances that survivors will access resources to hold the abuser financially responsible and ensure a safe custody plan. Moreover, in many jurisdictions, child support and custody terms can be incorporated directly into a criminal protection order.

Suk certainly would not support policies condoning or ignoring domestic violence. But if we believe in state intervention at all, we must confront the real conflicts between this intervention and survivors' autonomy. The solution is neither to abandon state involvement nor to ignore survivors' legitimate concerns, but rather to continue refining criminal justice approaches, while expanding the resources available to battered women and their children. It is underenforcement— failure to arrest and prosecute aggressively, reluctance to issue protection orders and enforce them consistently—that remains the most serious concern in domestic violence criminalization. With over a thousand women killed by intimate partners annually and millions more injured, the real question is why we are permitting violence against women to continue with impunity.

DOMESTICATING CRIMINAL LAW:
A NORMATIVE DEFENSE

DEBORAH TUERKHEIMER*

Without purporting to advocate a normative position, Jeannie Suk describes what she views as stark and surprising features of the legal landscape of misdemeanor domestic violence prosecution. In this recounting, the status quo represents a dramatic departure from an established criminal law regime, implicitly calling for justification. Yet each practice Suk discusses can be understood not as a move away from traditional legal tenets but rather as an imperfect adaptation of these tenets to a context characterized by an abuser's power and control over his victim. So conceptualized, the changes Suk describes are less surprising, less dramatic, and certainly less threatening to meaningful notions of autonomy than what might first appear to be the case.

What justifies a criminal contempt charge when a defendant violates an order of protection (OP) requiring him to stay away from the victim and her home? Although the evidentiary and preventative advantages that Suk points to are certainly real, the more fundamental reason for keeping an abuser away from his victim is that the abuser's mere presence is itself harmful. Even in the absence of overt violence, his presence has meaning that can only be appreciated if the culture of battering is taken into account. Many of the cases that I handled as a domestic violence prosecutor in Manhattan reflected this reality. In one, the victim, whom I'll call Ana, had endured years of abuse involving ongoing, patterned conduct. When Ana finally called the police for the first time after a typical beating, the defendant was arrested, arraigned, and charged with a misdemeanor. He was released and a full OP issued. Ana came home that evening to find that he had left her flowers. Fully grasping the significance of this gesture, she was as terrified as any witness I have encountered. This harm was worthy of separate redress, as the law finally recognizes.

Temporary orders of protection (TOPs) are issued as a matter of course at arraignments and typically remain in effect until the case is resolved. The obvious rationale for the practice—protecting the integrity of the proceedings—is compelling. No other category of crime raises the prospect of prolonged contact of an intimate nature between the accused and the key witness for the prosecution. The victim must decide whether to cooperate with prosecutors and, if so, to what extent. Moreover, she has the option of expressing her preferences regarding case disposition—preferences which, even in a "no drop" office like Manhattan's, are always taken into account and frequently honored. Whether, in a context of abuse, the victim's wishes can be made "freely" is a question that can be (and has

---

* Professor of Law, University of Maine School of Law; Professor of Law, DePaul University College of Law (effective July 1, 2009).

been) debated. But what should be evident is that contact with the defendant while a criminal case is pending inevitably impacts a complainant's ability to exercise choices that are in her best interest. When defendants violate TOPs, their conduct almost always functions to (re)align the victim with the defendant, thus undermining the state's interest in prosecution. The practice of issuing TOPs is thus justified by accepted criminal justice norms.

Final orders of protection (FOPs), issued when a case is resolved, are a standard disposition in domestic violence cases. However, in my experience prosecuting and supervising these cases, the final order of protection is often "limited" (FLOP), rather than "full" (FFOP). A FLOP, unlike a FFOP, does not require the defendant to stay away from the victim. It only prohibits the defendant from engaging in conduct that is itself criminal. FLOPs are typically requested when a victim has indicated her desire to pursue a relationship with the defendant.

So, in the vast majority of cases in which a FFOP is entered, the victim wants the order because the defendant has subjected her to a course of conduct (involving at least one criminal act) resulting in an extreme power imbalance that has made it difficult for her to extricate herself from the relationship.[1] FFOPs are routinely marked "subject to modification by family court order," evidencing full awareness that criminal court is not the place to resolve questions of custody, visitation, or support. As for a defendant's "right" to choose to continue the relationship, any such right is properly subordinated to the victim's right to escape it. In some intimate relationships, violence is endemic. It cannot end without the relationship ending.

To the extent that the world of misdemeanor domestic violence prosecution looks different from what came before, then, what we see is progress.

---

1. In Manhattan, as in many jurisdictions, domestic violence victims are most often women of color who are poor and, along a number of dimensions, socially oppressed. The subordination resulting from battering exacerbates and is exacerbated by the many obstacles that these women must confront.

DOMESTIC VIOLENCE MISDEMEANOR PROSECUTIONS AND THE NEW POLICING

ALAFAIR BURKE*

Jeannie Suk's descriptive project raises interesting normative questions (which Suk herself cautiously eschews). But she could have raised still more—and more troubling—questions had she contrasted contemporary domestic violence (DV) prosecutions not only with traditional criminal punishment but also with the

---

* Professor of Law, Hofstra Law School.

increasingly common approach of "new" policing.[1] Criminal law's willingness to dispense with traditional punishment in favor of nontraditional prevention mechanisms is not limited to DV misdemeanor cases. As a prosecutor ten years ago, I was transferred from DV misdemeanors into our office's community-based prosecution unit. My new supervisor warned that my job would focus not on convictions and sentences, but on solving problems. As I became indoctrinated into this new style of law enforcement, I learned to retell a favorite tale: After drug unit officers struggled for months to disrupt chronic drug dealing in a local park, a Neighborhood DA solved the problem by asking the Parks Department to run the sprinklers during prime dealing hours.

DV would appear to have little in common with the crimes that new policing is intended to address. Whereas new policing uses an expanded harm principle to justify enforcement of victimless, low-level nuisance crimes in the name of affected communities, DV cases involve actual or threatened violence and have identifiable and immediate victims. Nevertheless, the trends in DV remediation that concern Suk reflect trends in new policing: Sprinklers serve to separate dealer and buyer and thereby prevent future drug transactions; trespass laws serve to separate prostitute and john and thereby prevent future vice offenses; and no-contact orders separate batterer and victim (and husband and wife) and thereby prevent future domestic violence offenses. Had Suk compared DV prosecutions to other forms of new policing, she may have unearthed two troubling sets of questions, the first asking why law enforcement resorts to new policing in DV cases but not other crimes of violence, the second asking why law enforcement does not fully respect common tenets of new policing in the DV context.

In non-DV crimes of violence, the victims' rights movement calls for victim participation in the prosecution, while sentencing reforms require harsh mandatory minimum sentences. So why in DV cases do we ignore the agency of victims and readily waive away jail sentences in favor of no-contact orders? Perhaps DV misdemeanors reflect a philosophy designed for victimless nuisance offenses because law enforcement has come to see DV as precisely that. Mandatory arrest laws force officers to arrest over the victim's objections and when they know the case cannot be proven. Internal charging policies require prosecutors to pursue cases that cannot be won. Perhaps cops and prosecutors come to see the marriage itself as the source of these nuisances, and as with a bad neighborhood bar with more than its fair share of call-outs, they shut it down. The choice to disrupt

---

1. Several schools of policing fall under the "new" policing umbrella. For a general overview of the new policing models, see Tracey L. Meares and Dan M. Kahan, URGENT TIMES: POLICING AND RIGHTS IN INNER-CITY COMMUNITIES (1999); Philip B. Heymann, *The New Policing*, 28 FORDHAM URB. L.J. 407, 420 (2000); Debra Livingston, *Police Discretion and the Quality of Life in Public Places: Courts, Communities, and the New Policing*, 97 COLUM. L. REV. 551, 565–73 (1997); Richard C. Schragger, *The Limits of Localism*, 100 MICH. L. REV. 371, 377 (2001).

the relationship places blame not only on the offender, but also silently on the victim and the relationship itself. It treats the offender's violence as situational, triggered by this particular woman. It treats both victim and offender as part of the problem, guilty parties to be separated from transacting—like drug dealer and seller, prostitute and john.

Moreover, although contemporary DV policing unleashes the new policing in troubling ways, it does not fully respect aspects of new policing that would otherwise result in increased empowerment of DV victims. The new policing purports to be primarily utilitarian, seeking to prevent future offenses and dispensing with retributive punishment. A utilitarian evaluation of criminal law's intervention into the home would value not only the decreased violence within the relationship, but also the costs of the intervention, such as the victim's loss of financial and parenting support, the separation of joint children from their father, and the interference into a marriage that existed apart from the violence. The new policing also professes to be community-oriented as it looks to affected constituencies both to identify the problems that need to be solved and to evaluate the success of the solutions. But in DV cases, the constituencies most affected by criminal law's intervention have little voice.

REPLY

JEANNIE SUK

The purpose of my core text was to draw attention to the home as a space in which criminal law *controls* intimate relationships by effectively prohibiting their continuation. This is distinct from the *punishment* of violence between intimates. The distinction between punishment and control is the reason I focus on prosecutorial mechanisms for coercing an end to a relationship through the law of misdemeanor DV. Assuming that we all favor the criminal punishment of DV, I urge reflection on the distinctive consequences for women's autonomy of rising techniques of control in the home—*before* they become standard practices taken for granted in many more jurisdictions. The reflection required is simply not identical to that provoked by the (now largely uncontroversial) criminal punishment of DV.

The comments cluster around two broad reactions. One points to the shaping role that criminal law as family law has traditionally played in the "private" sphere of the family. The other argues that the primary problem in DV is still underenforcement.

Emphasizing the historical role of criminal law in private life, Melissa Murray notes that state regulation of who may marry or have sex, in what manner, and with whom has been reinforced by criminal prohibitions. As Murray would agree, these traditional criminal prohibitions have limited the autonomy of individuals to make intimate choices. In this way, the mechanism of state-imposed de facto divorce without consent of either party could be understood to be continuous with traditional criminal regulation of intimate sexual conduct. The comparison thus puts into relief tensions between derogation of autonomy in the DV regime I describe and the increasing legal recognition of the value of autonomy in intimate choices.

Laura Rosenbury seems to think that I object broadly to criminal law being in the home, when in fact I am concerned with what specifically criminal law is doing in the emerging regime. Surely one may generally favor criminal punishment of DV—as I do—and also criticize various modes of criminal-law intervention in the home that may occur under the DV rubric. But she hints that one who is troubled about the regime I describe might be motivated by an unspoken commitment to traditional notions of marital privacy that would justify keeping criminal law out.

Precisely because, as Rosenbury notes, marriage is the paradigm of intimacy in our law, and because the idea of husbands' power over wives has become so familiar to legal actors, the DV regime seems to have difficulty perceiving an intimate relationship that enters its radar as anything other than violent subordination of one partner by another. Thus, much conduct between intimates is forced to fit the paradigm of abusive marriage. That sweep includes people who are unmarried, homosexual, or in relationships that are not marriage-like or abusive. The DV regime I describe is equalizing insofar as it treats intimate relationships in its purview as ones the state may aim to end even against the wishes of the parties. The dissonance between state control of intimate relationships and individual autonomy is not "solely the result of a putative privilege granted by the state"[1] to marriage-like intimacy. It is also the result of the critique of the marriage paradigm—one that would value women's intimate choices to partake in relationships that they deem suitable.

Aya Gruber writes that I "fail[] to see domestic violence as a distributive phenomenon" and that I reinforce the notion "that there exists a neutral 'private' sphere unconstructed by law."[2] If so, this is unfortunate because my purpose was to show the distributive effects of the DV regime, which transfers authority to end relationships away from participants in those relationships—often poor minorities—to the state. Undoubtedly, social, economic, and legal forces play a role in why people begin, end, or continue relationships. It requires no commitment to some mythical neutral private sphere to observe that the DV regime alters the distribution of control over intimate choices in the direction of the state and away from the victim whom it is supposed to empower.

---

1. Rosenbury comment at 695.
2. Gruber comment at 696.

The point I wish to make in light of this first set of comments, then, is that a concern for autonomy is not a celebration of a traditional notion of privacy. State control through the regime I describe substantially curtails women's autonomy, even as DV reform has aimed to increase their autonomy. This is true even if we agree that law already constructs the private sphere, that intimate choices are never made in a vacuum, or that the autonomy of women who are abused and poor is more constrained than that of women who are not. The critical perspective should sharpen our conceptions of freedom, not make them slip away.

The second group of responses worries that it is underenforcement that remains the problem in the DV context. In this vein, Jennifer Collins points out that not all the practices I describe are common in all jurisdictions. Examination of a leading jurisdiction that has extended DV reform further than others puts into relief the gravitational pull exerted by the potent combination of prosecutorial imperatives and the push to reform. The unevenness of reform makes the contours of a set of practices more visible for examination.

Collins notes, for example, that prosecutors sometimes charge misdemeanors even in cases of serious physical injury to avoid a jury trial without victim cooperation. I have no doubt that is true at the very same time that in some places rigid and routine mandatory protocols for DV crime are invoked in the absence of serious physical injury. Collins is right that "the use of protection orders in misdemeanor cases does not . . . by itself raise a normative red flag."[3] My critique is based not on their use per se but on their use by the state to criminalize relationships without victim consent, as "domestic violence" is increasingly defined down to encompass conduct that may not involve serious or any physical injury, or even physical contact. This means that more conduct and more people can come to be treated as having relationships that the state ought to end. The juxtaposition of this state of affairs with the one Collins describes, in which serious crimes that should be felonies are charged as misdemeanors, underscores the difficulties endemic to this area of criminal regulation.

Cheryl Hanna criticizes my focus on women's autonomy rather than their protection. Indeed, she describes my concern about the state ending intimate relationships through misdemeanor criminal law as "near obsession with basing law and policy on what victims want."[4] Her criticism must draw on the classic trope of false consciousness, according to which certain adults—perhaps in part because of material disadvantages—cannot be deemed to know what is in their interests even when they seem to think they do. Rather, Hanna thinks we should systematically trust a prosecutor who has just met the victim, and may be subject to an invariant policy, to make the decision to end a relationship about which he or she knows little.

---

3. Collins comment at 699.
4. Hanna comment at 700.

The reason we punish violence is that violence derogates the autonomy of its victims. Autonomy is the value behind protection. Even when a relationship has led to a DV arrest, a woman's consideration of whether to continue a relationship is a better measure of autonomy than what advocates believe women ought to want. From the concern that violence is not sufficiently deterred in general it does not necessarily follow that the state should override what particular women want in the name of what they are supposed to want in theory but may inconveniently deny in practice. When typically the women in question are poor minorities, and DV advocates and prosecutors are middle class and White, state imposition of de facto divorce without regard to what victims want is troubling.

A further version of the concern about underenforcement is that "privacy" is a dirty word. The idea is that because the concept of privacy has traditionally worked to justify shielding DV from public intervention, the valuing of privacy must be code for allowing certain members of the family to subordinate the less powerful. Emily Sack suggests that my emphasis on autonomy has this effect. She says that underenforcement remains the most serious concern, and implies that concern about simultaneous overenforcement would work against the goal of addressing such underenforcement. Similarly, Hanna fears that arguments like mine "will undo the progress we've made."[5]

To this second group of comments, I respond that unevenness of reform poses a major challenge in critically evaluating the reform we have had. Persistent underenforcement in some areas is not itself reason to dismiss the costs of overenforcement where they exist. We need to be able to evaluate critically the effects of criminal law reforms that have been successfully introduced. The alternative would be adherence to DV reform, wherever it may take us.

This alternative, perhaps embodied in Deborah Tuerkheimer's comment, is the worldview of which my core text is critical. She first says the purpose of the protection-order practice is to protect the integrity of the proceedings. But that is difficult to maintain if the orders are routinely in place after proceedings have ended. Next she states that the violation of an order "almost always functions to (re)align the victim with the defendant,"[6] which is at odds with her claim that in the vast majority of cases, the victim wants an order.

Most poignantly, Tuerkheimer tells the story of the victim who discovers that her abusive partner has left her flowers. In Tuerkheimer's telling, the flowers are like chilling a scene from a horror movie. The possibility that the flowers might have a nonviolent meaning that is common in our culture—a pathetically inadequate apology—is not exactly a live one within the DV culture we have. The story is exemplary because it captures the world in which legal actors' interpretations flow from ideological commitment, anecdote governs analysis, and assumptions

---

5. Hanna comment at 701.
6. Tuekheimer comment at 705.

stand in for argument. The tendency in DV prosecution to proceed in this manner in, say, arresting people for sending flowers, is part of what I was attempting to reveal. Tuerkheimer captures this ethos better than I could.

Alafair Burke's comment deepens my analysis by juxtaposing DV enforcement and "new policing." Her suggestion that the DV regime I describe reflects the trend and philosophy of the enforcement of victimless nuisance offenses is intriguing, as is her observation that state imposed de facto divorce blames the victim and the relationship sub silentio. It is no coincidence that the effects of both new policing techniques and aggressive DV enforcement policies are predominantly on poor minority communities. The point I would add to Burke's contribution is that, while partaking of technologies of state control, DV discourse speaks a full-throated language of moral blame and victimhood that can clearly be seen in several of the comments. The emerging DV regime so powerfully combines an ideology that divides the world morally, into perpetrator and victim, with techniques of control that have become increasingly common in criminal justice. This formidable combination raises autonomy consequences that we need to take seriously.

INDEX

erroneous convictions (Type I), 557
excuse
  necessity, 366
  self-defense, 366–367
  See also justification
excused-based decision rules, 21, 27
executive clemency
  described, 667–668
  mercy, role of, 671–672
  as safety valve, 675
  vs. administrative law, 663
  on the wane, 553
  when made, 669
expressive rationales, 638–639

F

false consciousness, defined, 709
false positives
  and predictive technology, 81
  and preventative detention, 82
  and risk assessment, 79
family law. *See* Domestic violence (DV)
fatal circularity, and negligence, 278,
  286–288, 292–293
fear, and act reasonableness, 431–432
federal sentencing
  guidelines, and restorative justice, 603
  reform, history of, 613–616
Federal Sentencing Guidelines
  (Guidelines), 614–616, 620–621, 626,
  629
Federalist 51 (Madison), 538
Feinberg, Joel, 143
"felicity conditions," 192
feminists
  and domestic violence law, 696–697
  provocation defense, objections to,
    324–326, 329–331, 339
Ferzan, Kimberly Kessler, 409–410
Fifth Amendment, 555, 564
fines
  criticism of, 90–91
  deterrent effect of, 119
  vs. incarceration, 90, 121–122
Finland, 91
Finnis, John, 423
First Amendment, 528, 539
First Nations, circle sentencing and, 592
Fletcher, George, 362, 407, 410
fMRI, 639

Fodor, Jerry, 470
folk psychology
  behavior and, 461–463
  defined, 451, 465–466, 469–470
  defining a control problem, 450,
    451–455
  self-control and, 460–461
force
  and Public Authority restriction, 410
  See also duress
foreseeability, and risk of harm, 398, 399
forgiveness, defined, 340
fortitude, role in conduct rules, 12–13
Foster, Jody, 474
Foucault, Michel, 164, 167
Fourteenth Amendment, 565
Fourth Amendment, 175, 498, 501, 548
France, 597–598
Frankel, Marvin, 603
Frankfurt School, 164
fraud
  and acoustic separation, 14–15, 24–25
  and conduct rules, 13–14
  and decision rules, 14
  mail fraud, 517–518
  and overcriminalization, 519
freewill
  causation *vs.* choice, 147, 152–153,
    157–158, 159–160
  and control tests, 450
  and interpretive construction,
    218–220, 226
  and negligence, 274
"front-page moments," 651
Fugitive Slave law, 564
future dangerousness. *See* Dangerousness

G

Gacy, John Wayne, 479, 487
Gall v. United States, 620
Gallup poll, 563
Garrison, Jessie, 431
Garrison, State v., 431, 438, 439
Garvey, Stephen, 276–278
gender
  jury instructions regarding, 444
  and negligence liability, 289, 293
genetic predispositions and crime, 103
Gentili, Alberico, 411, 424
George III, King, 380n